# Inside the Norton Utilities 6.0, Third Edition

**Rob Krumm**

**Brady Publishing**

**New York    London    Toronto    Sydney    Tokyo    Singapore**

**Brady Publishing**

A Division of Simon & Schuster, Inc.
15 Columbus Circle
New York, NY 10023


Manufactured in the United States of America

10 9 8 7 6 5 4 3 2

**Library of Congress Cataloging-in-Publication Data**

Krumm, Rob, 1951-
    Inside the Norton utilities 6.0 / Rob Krumm. — 3rd ed.
       p.   cm.
    Includes index.
    1. Utilities (Computer programs)    2. Norton Utilities (Computer
programs)    I. Title.
QA76.76.U84K78  1991
005.4'3—dc20                                    91-27109
                                                       CIP


ISBN 0-13-465980-5

# Dedication

To Carolyn,
They say the first decade is the hardest.

## Limits of Liability and Disclaimer of Warranty

## Trademarks

# Contents

# Introduction

The goal of this book is to provide an *educational* resource for people working with MS-DOS computers and Versions 5.0 through 6.0 of the Norton Utilities programs. The use of the word educational is important because it indicates that this book is meant to be more than just a reference guide to the Norton Utilities, simply restating the information provided in the program manuals. An educational guide must do the following:

**Background.** Unlike standard applications such as word processing, programs like the Norton Utilities are directly linked to the basic structure of your computer system. While it may be possible to use the programs without understanding how DOS works or how a hard disk is organized, it is unlikely that you will get the full benefit of the programs. Chapters 1 through 4 are designed to explain to the average computer user the basic concepts upon which all MS-DOS computers operate. The concepts explained in these chapters will provide a solid basis from which you can learn to master the Norton Utilities and, in so doing, gain a degree of comfort and control over your system that will make using MS-DOS a pleasure instead of a horror.

**Learning Sequences.** The information in this book is organized according to the way an average user would learn and use various programs. This is in contrast to program manuals or reference books that use alphabetical order or menu order to organize topics. Each chapter is organized around an idea or concept. The Norton Utilities programs, or in some cases the specific features within a given program, that relate to the topic are discussed in that chapter. The goal is to include all the information necessary to understand and apply a concept in one learning unit, even if the procedures use a variety of programs and features.

**Examples and Procedures.** All the concepts raised in this book are supported by concrete examples, usually more than one for each important idea, and step-by-step procedures. Step-by-step procedures are important because many tasks involve specific combinations of a variety of MD-DOS and Norton Utilities commands and programs. The examples are designed so that you can reproduce them on your own system to learn how the features work.

**Batch Files and NDOS.** Batch file programming is one of the best ways to customize and simplify using MS-DOS computers. While MS-DOS computers have a reputation as being difficult to use, what is not as well know is that, using tools like the Batch Enhancer and NDOS programs provided with the Norton Utilities, you can quickly turn the MS-DOS environment into one that is at least as simple to operate as highly praised graphical systems, such as Windows or the MacIntosh. This book dedicates Chapters 15 through 17 to teaching users with little or no MS-DOS background how to customize and simplify their systems. The concepts cover batch operations for Version 4.5, 5.0, and 6.0 and include the new NDOS command processor.

It is this author's hope that the time and work spent on researching, testing, and writing has created a book that can provide a meaningful educational experience for its readers. The philosophy behind this book is that any user who understands the abilities and limitations of his or her computer will be able to achieve more, with less frustration and fewer catastrophes, than someone who has never been exposed to the concepts underlying computer use. If this book succeeds, the reader will not only be able to master the Norton Utilities, and to a great degree MS-DOS, but will be ready to absorb all sorts of new applications, programs, and challenges leading to an enriched computing experience.

Readers who would like to obtain a disk that contains the batch file programs discussed in Chapters 15 and 16, as well as a utility program that generates menu batch files compatible with the Norton Utilities 6.0 Batch Enhancer, can write to:

Rob Krumm Publications
Norton Batch
4830 Milano Way
Martinez, CA 94553

Please enclose a $10 handling fee.

Rob Krumm
Martinez, CA

# 1 Installing and Upgrading

Versions 6.0 and 5.0 of the Norton Utilities programs contain some significant changes from the previous versions. While this book explains the newest version of the Norton Utilities, it also seeks to serve users who have not acquired the latest version. The majority of the items discussed in this book apply to Versions 6.0 and 5.0, and all exceptions are noted. This chapter will discuss installation of the new program and the changes and enhancements made to the Utilities. Also, because some commands that existed in Version 4.5 have been eliminated in 6.0 and 5.0, this chapter will explain how you can duplicate those functions with features included in the new versions.

Of necessity, this chapter, and the Norton Utilities Install program, makes references to DOS concepts such as disks, directories, paths, AUTOEXEC.BAT files, and CONFIG.SYS files. If you would like more information about these DOS concepts, see Chapter 3. Keep in mind that you don't need to know all about these concepts to install the Norton Utilities. The information in Chapter 3 is provided as background information to deepen your understanding of how the Norton Utilities work and what they accomplish in your computer system.

## The Programs

The Norton Utilities is not a single program, but rather a collection of individual programs, each of which provides a specific set of features and functions.

A *utility* program is distinguished from an *application* program by the fact that a utility is used to manage your computer system, while an application carries out a task, such as word processing or spreadsheet math that you would need to accomplish, by one means or another, even if you didn't have a computer system. Because utility programs are designed to improve the management, maintenance, and performance of computer systems, they are by nature more technical than most applications, e.g., word processing. This book will attempt to fill in as much background information

1

as possible so you can learn to get the most out of the Norton Utilities programs.

Version 6.0 and 5.0 are the latest releases of the Utilities that first appeared back in 1982. Since that first release, the Norton Utilities have changed in two ways:

**Features.** The Norton Utilities programs have grown to include more features and operations so that you can enjoy expanded control over various aspects of your computer system. The features added respond to the changing needs of users and the PC hardware they work with. Version 5.0 adds some new functions to the Norton Utilities, as well as expanding and changing older operations.

**Program Interface.** The term *program interface* is used to refer to the basic organization of commands and options displayed by a program. The style and structure of the Norton Utilities has changed over the years as PC software has evolved. In previous versions, older utilities often maintained one type of interface, while newer utilities showed off more contemporary display styles. In Version 5.0, the Norton Utilities has added a *consistent* user interface, including pull-down menus and mouse support, that is the same for all the programs in the package.

## The Programs

The Norton Utilities is a collection of programs that can be used together or individually. The total amount of disk space needed to install the programs is about 2.5 megabytes. Note that if you have Version 5.0 installed on your hard disk you have plenty of room for the 6.0 upgrade, since 6.0 uses *less* space than 5.0 due to a special compressed format. The programs included in Version 6.0 are:

BE.EXE
(17K)
Chapters 15, 16, 17

**Batch Enhancer.** This program contains a number of commands that can be executed as part of DOS batch files. The Batch Enhancer program adds screen display and interactive commands that the DOS batch language does not include. These commands make it possible to write useful, easy-to-use programs that automate all types of operations.

CALIBRAT.EXE
(78K)
Chapter 8

**Calibrate.** This program is a disk utility that seeks to correct minor variations in hard disk data alignment that can lead to hard disk problems. The program performs a low-level format of a hard disk without erasing any of the data.

DISKEDIT.EXE
(131K)
Chapters 12, 14

**Disk Editor.** This program takes the place of the main Norton Utilities program in previous versions. The program allows you to make direct changes to the information stored on a disk. This is a powerful program that allows you to manipulate anything stored on a hard or floppy disk.

DISKMON.EXE
(48K)
Chapter 13

**Disk Monitor.** This program allows you to protect files or entire disks from accidental changes. The program also shows you when disk reads and writes take place, a feature that is useful on networks when the disk lights or noise cannot be heard while disks are in operation.

DISKREET.EXE
(144K)
Chapter 13

**Disk Encryption.** This program provides password security for files stored on your system. Files protected by Diskreet cannot be accessed without the proper password.

DISKTOOL.EXE
(79K)
Chapter 14

**Disk Tools.** This program provides special techniques for recovering data from damaged or misused disks.

DS.EXE
(55K)
Chapter 18

**Directory Sort.** Sorts the file names listed in a directory. Program restored from Version 4.5, but not included in Version 5.0.

EP.EXE
(62K)
Chapter 12

**Erase Protection.** This program alters the way in which files are erased so that you have the best chance of recovering erased files. The program maintains erased files in unused portions of the disk as long as possible. This program was called File Save in Version 5.0.

FA.EXE
(9K)
Chapter 18

**File Attribute.**  Lists and modifies file attributes. Program restored from Version 4.5, but not included in Version 5.0.

FD.EXE
(10K)
Chapter 18

**File Date.**  Changes the time and date of a file or group of files. Program restored form Version 4.5, but not included in Version 5.0.

FILEFIND.EXE
(74K)
Chapter 11

**File Find.**  This program provides a search tool for locating files. In Version 6.0, several new features are added to this program, including the ability to generate batch files using the files located during the search.

FILEFIX.EXE
(89K)
Chapter 12

**File Fix.**  This program is used to restore corrupted Lotus 1-2-3, Symphony, and dBASE files.

FL.EXE
(9K)
Chapter 18

**File Locate.**  Locates the specified file or group of files. This is a simpler version of File Find. Program restored from Version 4.5, but not included in Version 5.0.

FS.EXE
(9K)
Chapter 18

**File Size.**  This program calculates the total amount of space used by group of files. Program restored from Version 4.5, but not included in Version 5.0.

IMAGE.EXE
(11K)
Chapter 12

**Image.**  This program protects your hard disk from accidental formatting by making a duplicate of the key disk information. The Image program works in conjunction with Unformat to restore the formatted disk.

LP.EXE
(13K)
Chapter 18

**Line Print.**  Outputs text files to the printer and adds page formatting. Program restored from Version 4.5, but not included in Version 5.0.

NCACHE.EXE
(59K)
Chapter 10

**Norton Cache.**  Cache programs use RAM memory to improve the performance of hard and floppy disks.

NCC.EXE
(65K)
Chapter 9

**Norton Control Center.**  This program provides a way to control various aspects of your hardware, such as the cursor size and shape, screen colors, and video modes.

| | |
|---|---|
| NCD.EXE<br>(80K)<br>Chapter 11 | **Norton Change Directory.** This program is an alternative to the DOS CD command. The program uses a graphic tree display and searches to locate directories. |
| NDD.EXE<br>(114K)<br>Chapter 14 | **Norton Disk Doctor II.** This program is designed to locate and correct errors that occur on hard or floppy disks. The program can also be used to test new disks for errors or defects before you place data on them. |
| NDOS.COM<br>(12K)<br>Chapter 17 | **Norton DOS Command Interpreter.** This program is used to replace the DOS COMMAND.COM program in order to provide expanded operating system power and flexibility. |
| NDOS2E.COM<br>(2K)<br>Chapter 17 | **Norton DOS Command Interrupts.** This program provides programs that use undocumented DOS interrupts (e.g., INT 2E,) to run under NDOS. |
| NHELP.EXE<br>(40K)<br>Chapter 17 | **Norton Help.**   NDOS full-screen help program. |
| NORTON.EXE<br>(5K)<br>Chapter 5 | **Norton Utilities.**  The main Norton Utilities program is used to coordinate the other utilities, similar to the way the Norton Integrator program was used in Version 4.5 by listing all of the Norton Utilities in a single menu. The program also contains extensive help files about DOS under the Advise option. |
| NUCONFIG.EXE<br>(73K)<br>Chapter 1 | **Norton Utilities Configuration.**  This program is used to set up various features. |
| SFORMAT.EXE<br>(63K)<br>Chapter 12 | **Safe Format.**  This program, which is an alternative to the DOS FORMAT command, adds a number of safeguards to the formatting process that are not present in the DOS FORMAT command. |
| SPEEDISK.EXE<br>(80K)<br>Chapter 10 | **Speed Disk.**  This program reorganizes the information on your disk to maximize performance. The program sorts directories, unfragments files, and arranges data for the fastest possible access. |

| | |
|---|---|
| SYSINFO.EXE (90K) Chapter 8 | **System Information.** This program provides information about your computer, its memory, disks, and current status. It also performs benchmark tests to evaluate the performance of your system. |
| TS.EXE (19K) Chapter 18 | **Text Search.** Searches files for a specific word or phrase. Program restored from Version 4.5, but not included in Version 5.0. |
| UNERASE.EXE (111K) Chapter 12 | **Unerase.** This program provides tools for both automatic and manual recovery of erased files. This program combines the Quick Unerase and Unerase functions from the main Norton Utilities program in Version 4.5, placing all Unerase features in a single program. |
| UNFORMAT.EXE (58K) Chapter 12 | **Unformat.** This program recovers data on hard disks that have been accidentally formatted. |
| WIPEINFO.EXE (55K) Chapter 13 | **Wipe Information.** This program can wipe clear the spaces occupied by files or an entire disk. Wiping removes all vestiges of a file from a disk, unlike ERASE, which only removes the name of the file from the directory. This program is useful when security is important. |

# The Install Program

The Install program is supplied with the Norton Utilities to automatically copy and unpack the files supplied on the disks and place them onto your hard disk. The Install program also has a number of custom options that can be selected at the time of installation.

To start installation of Norton Utilities 5.0 place the disk labeled *Installation Disk* into the floppy disk drive on your system, e.g., drive A.

Start the Norton Utilities installation program by entering

```
A:install↵
```

The Install program begins by displaying a screen that asks you to select the type of video display, black and white or color, you will be using on your computer. You can make your selection in three different ways:

**Move Highlight.**  Use the ↑ or ↓ keys to move the highlight to the desired option and then press ↵.

**Type Letter.**  You can select an option by typing the first letter of the item, e.g., **B** for Black & White.

**Mouse.**  Click the left mouse button on the option you want to select.

Once you have made a screen type selection, the Install program will search the disk for any existing versions of the Norton Utilities programs.

## Recovering Formatted Disks or Erased Files

Next, the program displays a screen that warns you *not* to install the Norton Utilities if you have a disk that must be recovered from an accidental format or that contains erased files you want to restore with the Norton Utilities, as seen in Figure 1–1. This may seem like an odd warning since one of the reasons for purchasing the Norton Utilities is to recover formatted disks or erased files.

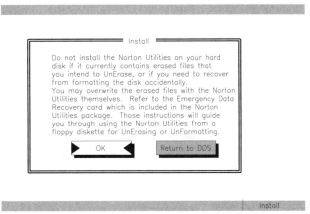

**Figure 1–1. Warning about installation on formatted hard disk.**

The reason for this warning is that installing a copy of the Norton Utilities, or for that matter any program, on a hard disk can cause some of the information that you want to recover to be physically overwritten and therefore unrecoverable by any means. The best time to install the Norton Utilities is *before* you accidentally erase important files or suffer an accidental format. The Utilities Image and Filesave programs create special hidden files that make accurate recovery of formatted hard disks or erased files more likely.

However, should you find that you have created one of these problems prior to placing the Norton Utilities on the hard disk, you should cancel the installation by selecting **Return to DOS**. You can attempt to recover the formatted hard disk or erased files by using the files on the Norton Utilities floppy disks (see Chapter 12).

Keep in mind that as soon as you realize you have formatted a hard disk or that you have erased valuable files by accident, you should *avoid adding* any new information to your hard disk until you have recovered the desired data, or determined, with the help of the Norton Utilities, that recovery is not possible.

For example, suppose you have accidentally erased an important file. You have a backup copy of the file on a floppy disk but that copy is a week old. This means the erased file contains some information not included in the backup. Your instinct would be to immediately copy the backup onto the hard disk in order to see how much information is missing from the backup. Then, if the loss appears significant, you might get the Norton Utilities to recover the lost file. However, by placing a copy of the backup file onto the hard disk, you have decreased the likelihood that the Norton Utilities can correct your mistake, since copying the backup file could overwrite some or all of the data that was part of the erased file.

If you are not concerned with recovering data on the current hard disk, continue by selecting the **Continue** option.

The next screen explains some of the operations that will take place during the installation process.

**Copy and Unpack Files**    This operation copies the Norton Utilities programs from the floppy disks onto the hard disk directory that you select. In the process, files stored in the compressed format are exploded to their true size.

**DOS 5.0 Help Extension**    If you have DOS Version 5.0 installed on your computer, you can have the install program add Norton Utilities command information to the standard DOS 5.0 help file. This means that when you use the DOS 5.0 HELP command, the list of commands displayed will contain the Norton Utilities commands along with the standard DOS commands.

**Modify System Files**    The CONFIG.SYS and AUTOEXEC.BAT files stored in the root directory of the disk from which your computer system boots, typically drive C, must contain certain commands in order for the Norton Utilities to function properly. The Install program will make the required changes to these file automatically. You can later modify the changes should you find it necessary.

**Configuration**    You will have the opportunity to select optional features of the Norton Utilities 6.0 programs. You have the option of installing special features if you select the *advanced* method of configuration.

At each stage in the installation process you will have the option to skip an optional feature or stop the installation by returning to DOS. If you skip a feature you can run Install again and choose **Reconfigure** to implement selected features without copying all of the files again. To continue to the next screen, enter ↵.

## Selecting a Directory

By default, the program suggests C:\NU, that is, drive C in a directory called NU. If you have a previous version of the Norton Utilities, e.g., 5.0, the default will show that directory (e.g., C:\NORTON), since Version 5.0 used \NORTON rather than \NU. The advantage of \NU is that it is easier to type than \NORTON. The directory in which the Norton Utilities are installed is referred to as the *home* directory since the programs will read and write special files stored in this directory during their operation. If you want to use a different drive and/or directory you can enter the desired location at this time.

Should you accept the default? There are some considerations. First, the Install program assumes that you want to place the Norton Utilities files in a directory that separates it from other programs on your hard disk. This has the advantage of making it very clear where the Norton Utilities are stored. However, as you will see shortly, in order to access the Norton Utilities from any location in your system, a new directory must be added to your PATH statement. An alternative would be to place the Norton Utilities in a directory that is probably already in your path list. For example, most users (or sellers of computers) set up a directory on the hard disk to contain DOS files (e.g., \DOS or \DOS401) and include that directory in the PATH statement for the hard disk. This enables you to use DOS utilities, such as FORMAT or CHKDSK, from any location in the system. If this is the case, you may want to place the Norton Utilities in the DOS directory along with the utilities supplied with DOS.[1]

Another instance where you may use a different location is on drives that are partitioned in several logical drives.[2] You may want to place the Norton Utilities on a drive other than C. If you want to change the *drive letter* only, e.g., from C to D, there is a little shortcut technique you can apply. If you type a character, e.g., D, the Install program will clear the entry line and begin a new entry with that letter. However, if you want to keep the directory name, \NU, you can *edit* the text using the [Del] key. For example, to change the C to a D, enter

```
[Del]
d
```

The path name now reads D:\NU.

### Configuration Method

The main choice that you are required to make during installation is between the *easy* and *advanced* configuration. The *easy* method allows the Norton Utilities to automatically make the required changes necessary to install its basic features. The *advanced* method allows you manual control over the specific options you want installed. In most cases the easy configuration is best if you are not sure. Keep in mind that you can always change the configuration after you have installed the program.

## Configuration Options

This section contains a summary of the configuration options available with the Norton Utilities 6.0. These features can be installed in two ways:

---

1. This is the way I usually set up my own computers. As a rule, I place all utility programs in the DOS directory. This simplifies the PATH statement. So long as a path is open to the \DOS directory, you can perform any of the utility programs (DOS, Norton, or other).

2. If you have a 40-megabyte or larger hard disk and are running under DOS 3.x, you will have a drive that has more than one DOS partition.

**Install.** Some or all of these options may be installed if you select the *advanced* method of configuration during the install process.

**Norton Configuration Program.** New in Version 6.0 is the NUCONFIG program. This program allows you to set up many of the advanced features of the Norton Utilities by making menu selections. This program can be run at any time by entering NUCONFIG ↵ in the Norton Utilities home directory, e.g. \NU.

When you select advanced configuration or run the NUCONFIG program (Figure 1–2) you will be presented with a menu of eight options. The following is a summary of what those options are and how they are implemented.

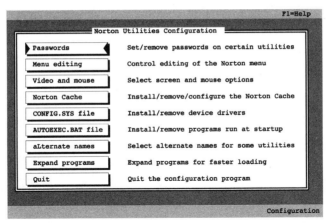

**Figure 1–2. NUCONFIG program menu.**

## Passwords

You can create password protection that will restrict access to the following Norton Utilities program to only those persons who can furnish the proper password. The programs that can be protected are Calibrate, Configuration, Disk Doctor, Disk Editor, Disk Tools, Filefix, Safe Format, Speed Disk, Unerase, Unformat, and Wipeinfo.

You can select one or more of these programs to receive password protection, but note that all of the protected files will use the *same* password.

If you place password protection on any one of the 11 programs, the password you use to protect the program becomes the password for the password feature. For example, suppose you select the password **MAKESAFE** for the Calibrate and Disk Editor programs. The next time you select the passwords option from the configuration menu you will be asked to enter the password, e.g., **MAKESAFE**.

You can use this option to remove passwords as well as add them to the listed programs.

## Menu Editing

The menu of commands that appears in the main Norton Utilities program can be modified by users. This procedure is discussed in detail in Chapter 5. In some circumstances you may want to prevent users from making changes in the Norton Utilities menu. The menu editing option allows you to disable or enable this feature.

## Video and Mouse Options

This menu selection allows you to fine-tune the video screen and mouse operation within the entire group of Norton Utilities programs. Use this only if you want to vary the current appearance of the screen or behavior of the mouse.

**Screen Colors**    This option allows you to select the screen colors used by all the Norton Utilities programs. The **Laptop** option provides maximum contrast for LCD screens used with laptop and notebook computers. You can select preset color combinations 1 or 2, or use the Custom colors button with the Customize Colors control button to create your own customized set of colors.

**Graphic Options**    The Norton Utilities programs run primarily in text mode. However, they can enhance the screen displays by using graphic elements. *Standard* displays use only standard text characters. The items labeled *graphics* add graphic elements to the Norton Utilities screens. Note that the dialog box options require an EGA or VGA screen adaptor.

**Screen Options**    These options control the use of zooming boxes, solid color backgrounds, and arrows marking the default control buttons. The **Ctrl-Enter** option changes the way that the cursor travels through a dialog box. If selected, ↵ moves the cursor from item to item within a dialog box, like the [Tab] key. To activate your selections you would then have to press [Ctrl-↵]. Without this option ↵ is sufficient to execute the selected control button.

**Mouse Options**    Use this to select Left-handed mouse operation or Fast mouse reset. This option is used to improve performance for serial mice or mice attached to the mouse port on IBM PS/1 and PS/2, and Compaq computers.

## Norton Cache

The cache program is used to improve hard disk performance. The program is discussed in detail in Chapter 10. If you want to install the cache program as part of your normal system startup you can install it from this menu, Figure 1–3. The cache menu can be used to install a command in either the CONFIG.SYS or AUTOEXEC.BAT files that will load the cache each time the computer is turned on or rebooted. If you use the CONFIG.SYS method you cannot uninstall the cache. If you use AUTOEXEC.BAT you can uninstall the cache program once it has been loaded assuming it is the last memory resident program installed in the computer.

If you have a computer running under a memory manager, such as HIMEM.SYS supplied with DOS 5.0, you can use the *High Memory* to

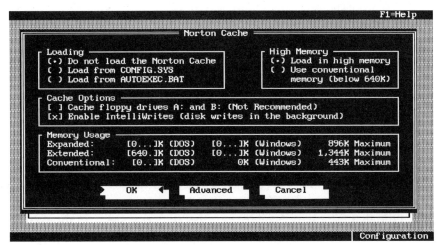

Figure 1–3. Norton Cache configuration menu.

conserve conventional memory. You can select the amount of conventional, expanded, or extended memory. Advanced optional can also be set. If you are not sure about these options see Chapter 10 for a full discussion of the Ncache program.

The NUCONFIG method of installing the cache program uses a initialization file, NCACHE.INI, rather than actually writing a detailed command line in the CONFIG.SYS or AUTOEXEC.BAT. The options listed on this screen are:

**Loading.**   This setting allows you to choose if you want to load the cache program from the CONFIG.SYS, AUTOEXEC.BAT, or manually from DOS.

**High Memory.**   Used if high memory is available in the form of XMS extended memory or mappable memory above 640, such as that created by QEMM386.SYS or the DOS 5.0 EMM386.EXE. If you want to force the cache program to ignore existing high memory you can select **Use conventional memory**.

**Cache Options.**   The primary advantages of the cache program are derived from the **IntelliWrites** and **SmartReads** features, which are selected by default. If you deselect this option the cache program uses less conventional memory, but it is also less effective at speeding up your access to disk information. In addition, the program will not normally cache information on floppy disks because the **IntelliWrites** and **SmartReads** features can be problematic if the disk is removed from the drive before all operations have been completed.

**Memory Usage.**   The cache program normally uses all available extended and/or expanded memory with the exception of a 64K block that is automatically reserved. By default, the amount of cache buffer memory reserved when Windows 3.0 has been run is about 25 percent less than the buffer allocated during DOS operations. You can manually override the default values if desired.

**Advanced.**   Advanced options are used to fine-tune the performance of the cache program. You can set specific values for the read and write ahead buffers that reside in conventional memory and other options that directly affect the way Ncache handles data transfers. In most cases you would need to experiment with your system to determine if the default values should be adjusted. This is discussed in Chapter 10.

## CONFIG.SYS

The CONFIG.SYS file is used to configure the DOS operating system. The DISKREET, password protection, and NDOS (the substitute command processor) use device drivers loaded by the CONFIG.SYS to implement their features. You can select to load the DISKREET.SYS, PCSHADOW.SYS, NDOS.COM, or KEYSTACK.SYS drivers. If you are not sure about loading these drivers read Chapter 13 for DISKREET or Chapter 17 for NDOS.

## AUTOEXEC.BAT

Several Norton Utilities programs can be automatically loaded each time you boot the computer. Keep in mind that the AUTOEXEC.BAT is a convenience. Unlike commands loaded in CONFIG.SYS, any commands executed as part of the AUTOEXEC.BAT can also be manually entered at the DOS prompt. The options available are:

**Environmental Variable.** You can use these options to add the home directory of the Norton Utilities programs to the PATH statement in the AUTOEXEC.BAT, and also to create an environmental variable called NU that sets the home directory of the Norton Utilities program. All initialization files (INI extensions) are written to the home directory.

**Load TSR Utilities.** The DISKMON and EP programs must be loaded into memory before their features can be used. See Chapter 12 for the EP program and Chapter 13 for the DISKMON program.

**Execute Disk Maintenance.** The IMAGE and NDD (Norton Disk Doctor) programs perform tests to catch and correct minor problems that occur on disk before they become major problems and protect you against accidental loss of data. For details of their operation see Chapter 12 for Image and Chapter 14 for Norton Disk Doctor.

## Alternate Names

Each of the Norton Utilities programs consists of a program file stored in the home directory. You may find it helpful to change the names of some of the programs that have full eight-character file names to two-character names. This can be done for DISKEDIT, SPEEDISK, SYSINFO, and FILEFIND. The SFORMAT program can also be renamed to FORMAT in order to prevent accidental use of the destructive DOS FORMAT command. Name changes have no effect on the operation of programs.

### Expand Programs

In order to save disk space the Norton Utilities program files are stored in a *compressed* format. The programs are automatically expanded each time they are executed. If you have a slow system that experiences significant delays when executing a Norton Utilities program, you may want to use some additional disk space in order to store the programs in their full disk size. This will speed up loading at the cost of about 1.5 megabytes of hard disk space. Note that this process is not reversible except by erasing the Norton Utilities programs and then reinstalling them from the original floppy disks.

# Moving from 4.5 to 5.0

If you have worked with Version 4.5 of the Norton Utilities you will find that there are some programs that existed in 4.5 that do not exist in Version 5.0. In most cases the functions performed by the individual programs in 4.5 has been integrated into one of the 5.0 programs. Below is a summary of where the functions provided by the missing programs can be found. Note that in Version 6.0 many of the 4.5 programs eliminated in 5.0 have been restored.

Directory Sort (DS)
Use SPEEDISK

Directory sorting is now performed as part of the Speed Disk program. Directory sorting can be done as part of the general Speed Disk optimization process. You can select the type of sort order you want to the directories using the *File Sort* dialog box, which is accessed from the *Configure* menu—[Alt-c] f. Once selected, you can have the sort performed as part of the overall optimization process, or select the **File Sort** only option from the *Optimization Method* dialog box on the *Optimize* menu—[Alt-o] o. However, you no longer have the ability to manually position file names in a directory listing as was possible in Version 4.5.

Program was restored in Version 6.0, but not included in Version 5.0.

Disk Information (DI)
Use SPEEDISK or
SYSINFO

Information about disk capacity and structure can be obtained with either the Speed Disk or System Information programs. The *Information* menu in the Speed Disk program contains displays, including Disk Statistics. System Information provides a *Disk* menu that contains a summary of disk data, an analysis of disk statistics, and disk partitions. Note that Speed Disk is a bit slower than System Information since it actually performs tests on the disk before it provides statistics.

Disk Test (DT)
Use NDD

The functions performed by Disk Test are carried out through the Norton Disk Doctor, making Disk Test unnecessary. Note that this was also true in Version 4.5, but Disk Test was included for compatibility with previous versions. Program was restored in Version 6.0, but not included in Version 5.0.

File Attributes (FA)
Use FILEFIND

The File Find program in Version 5.0 has been expanded from previous versions. The most significant change is that it runs as an interactive program with menus and dialog boxes, in addition to command line operations. Instead of simply displaying a list of files on the screen, File Find keeps the list in memory so you can perform a variety of actions on the selected files once you have found them. The **Set Attributes** option found on the *Commands* menu allows you to change file attributes for a selected file, or the entire group. Program was restored in Version 6.0, but not included in Version 5.0.

File Date (FD)
Use FILEFIND

The **Set Date/Time** option on the *Commands* menu can be used to set the directory date/time stamp for any of the files in the current list. Note that in Version 5.0, File Find must be used first to locate a list of files before you can execute the **Set Date/Time** option. Program was restored in Version 6.0, but not included in Version 5.0.

File Information (FI)
Use Describe

The File Information program that was used to create and display annotated directories is no longer supported in Version 5.0. Under the NDOS program in Version 6.0 you can use the DESCRIBE command to perform essentially the same function as File Information (see Chapter 17).

Format Recover (FR)
Use Unformat

Use Unformat to recover formatted disks.

File Size (FS)
Use Filefind

Version 5.0 does not provide a direct equivalent to the File Size program supplied with 4.5. Instead, you must use File Find to create a report that is sent to either the printer or a disk file, in order to obtain a total of the space used by the files or directories. The output cannot be directly displayed on the screen as was the case with File Size in 4.5. Also, the 5.0 report does not distinguish between actual file size and slack space as did the File Size in 4.5. If you use File Size on a regular basis, you should continue to use it since the size capabilities of File Find in 5.0 are limited. Program was restored in Version 6.0, but not included in Version 5.0.

List Directory (LD)
Use NCD

The directory features of the Norton Change Directory program (NCD) eliminates the need for the List Directory program. Note that one NCD will automatically attempt to create a directory listing file on the scanned disk each time it is run. If you want to eliminate the writing of this file, use the /N switch with the command.[3] Printing of the directory tree can only be done from the program menus. You cannot generate a printed directory tree from a DOS line command or batch file.

Line Print (LP)

Program was restored in Version 6.0, but not included in Version 5.0.

---

3. The /N switch is useful when you want to get a listing of a disk's directory tree but are concerned about overwriting an erased file. Since NCD normally creates a file called TREEINFO.NCD in the root directory of the active disk, you run the risk of overwriting erased disk areas that might be needed in an unerase procedure.

Norton Integrator (NI) Use Norton

The Integrator is now replaced with the Norton shell program, which has additional features and capabilities.

Norton Utilities (NU) Use SPEEDISK, DISKEDIT, UNERASE, and DISKTOOL

The main Norton Utilities program, NU, has been eliminated. The operations conducted with the main Norton Utilities program in Version 4.5 have been distributed to several programs in Version 5.0. The main Norton Utilities unerase feature is combined with Quick Unerase into a single program in 5.0 called UNERASE. Direct display and modification of disk information can be conducted with DISKEDIT. The technical information and disk map displays are found in the SPEEDISK program.

Quick UnErase (QU) Use UnErase

The functions of the Quick Unerase program have been placed into the UNERASE program.

System Information (SI) Use Sysinfo

The System Information program has been expanded and given the name SYSINFO. You can duplicate the screen output generated by Version 4.5 System Information by using the /STATUS switch with SYSINFO, e.g., **SYSINFO/STATUS.**

Time Mark (TM) Use NCC

The Time Mark program has been integrated into the Norton Control Center (NCC) program as command line switches. For example, to duplicate the effect of the Version 4.5 TM command **TM START/C1** in Version 5.0 you would use **NCC/START:1.**

Text Search (TS) Use FileFind

The Text Search program has been integrated with the File Find program in 5.0, making it possible to perform text as well as file searches across nested directories or entire disks. In Version 4.5 Text Search was limited to one directory at a time. For example, to duplicate the operation of the 4.5 command, **TS *.*norton**, you would use the command **FILEFIND.\*.*norton**, in 5.0. Note that FILEFIND in Version 5.0 always operates in a full screen, interactive mode and not in a direct DOS screen display mode, as does Version 4.5's Text

| | Search. Program was restored in Version 6.0, but not included in Version 5.0. |
|---|---|
| UnRemove Directory (UD) Use Unerase | The Unremove Directory command from 4.5 is integrated into the UNERASE program. |
| Volume Label (VL) Use NCD | The Volume Label program is now implemented as the **Volume Label** option on the *Disk* menu in the Norton Change Directory program. |
| Wipefile & Wipedisk Use WipeInfo | The functions of the WIPEDISK and WIPEFILE programs from Version 4.5 have been combined into the WIPEINFO program. |

In general, Version 5.0 has eliminated the use of separate programs in Version 4.5 that did not have a full-screen user interface, such as Text Search (TS), File Attribute (FA), File Date (FD), etc., and combined them with programs that can be used either in a full-screen menu mode, or executed from DOS or a batch file as command line programs. The elimination of the main Norton Utilities program is a much needed improvement since, through Version 2, 3, and 4, many features have been added to the main Norton Utilities program (NU), not all of which were very closely related in terms of functions. For example, in Version 4.5 the basic unerase feature was implemented with the Quick Unerase (QU) program, but the more complicated and powerful unerase feature was part of the NU program. In Version 5.0 all the various forms of unerasing have been consolidated into a single program, UNERASE. This enables you to have all the tools available for unerasing at your fingertips when you are trying to recover an erased file, instead of having to switch between two different programs, as was the case in Version 4.5.

# Installing Windows Icons

Because of the nature of Windows 3.0 (multitasking), not all of the Norton Utilities programs can be executed from Windows. The following program can be executed from Windows and are supplied with Windows 3.0 icons:

DISKEDIT, Disk Editor
DISKREET
FILEFIND, File Find

FILEFIX, File Fix
NCD, Norton Change Directory
NDD, Norton Disk Doctor
NDOS, Norton DOS
NORTON, Norton menu program
SFORMAT, Safe Format
SYSINFO, System Information

The Norton Utilities package supplies 11 icon files: one for each program that runs under Windows, plus PETER, which is a picture of Peter Norton. All of these icon files have the file extension ICO.

To install a Norton Utilities program in Windows using the Norton Utilities icons, load the Windows Program Manager as usual. Select the Windows group window into which you want to place the Norton Utilities program. Use the **File New** command to add a new program to the window. Enter: [Alt-f] n ↵.

Enter a description for the program, e.g., to install the NORTON program enter: Norton Utilities [Tab].

Next, enter the full path name of the program (e.g., C:\NU\NORTON.EXE), or use the **Browse** command to select the file from the selection box. With the program name entered, select the **Change icon** command by entering [Alt-i].

By default, Windows uses the PROGMAN.EXE program as the source for program icons. In this case you want to use one of the supplied Norton Utilities icons by entering the name of the icon file into the File name box. (Example: c:\nu\norton.ico ↵.-↵.)

The program using the supplied icon appears in the group window. Keep in mind that you do not have to use the icons that match the programs (e.g., FILEFIND.ICO with FILEFIND.EXE). You might want to use the PETER icon and differentiate the programs by their descriptions only.

# Summary

This chapter covered installation of the Norton Utilities 5.0 and the options you can select during the installation Process.

**Version 5.0**    Version 5.0 of the Norton Utilities programs uses more than twice the disk space of Version 4.5. If installed on a computer with an existing copy of 4.5 or older, the majority of the old files will be erased (or placed in a backup directory) when the new version is installed.

**System Files**    The Install program provides options that automatically modify the system files (AUTOEXEC.BAT and CONFIG.SYS) so that selected operations and features are automatically implemented each time you turn on the computer.

# 2 How Personal Computers Work

The Norton Utilities program was created to take the mystery out of using a computer. While personal computers are more complex than other electronic devices, such as televisions or radios, they are no more mysterious. Everything the computer does or does not do has a logical explanation. The difficulty with computers is that in order to understand a problem or find a solution, the information you need is often hidden by the system itself. The Norton Utilities programs provide tools that allow you to discover in detail what is going on in your computer. Other tools allow you to directly manipulate parts of the system in order to correct problems, improve organization or performance, or simply to fit your own personal preferences.

The purpose of this chapter is to explain the basic structure of personal computers and to describe their history. This information, while not absolutely necessary for using a personal computer, will help you better understand the features and functions of the Norton Utilities programs.

## Parts of a Personal Computer

Like many technical devices, a personal computer is not a single machine but a system composed of a number of individual devices put together to form a working computer *system*. In fact, some of the contents of a computer system employ devices used with machines other than personal computers. For example, keyboards were originally created for typewriters, and screens use the same basic technology as television sets. This is not unusual since most new technologies evolve from machines that have been previously developed. No device is ever 100 percent new. The parts of a computer system fall into three basic areas:

- **Micropocessor.** This is the heart of the computer. No matter how large or complicated the personal computer appears to be, a single microprocessor is responsible for executing all the instructions that carry out the work of the computer. The microprocessor contains a set of commands, called the *decoder set*, that translates numeric values into specific actions. All computer operations result from a process by which one or more numeric values are used to issue an instruction to the microprocessor.

- **Memory/Storage.** Memory and storage refer to the parts of the computer system that store the numeric information by which the microprocessor is controlled. A computer *program* is a list of microprocessor instructions stored in memory so that the microprocessor can access the instructions and carry out the program.

- **Input/Output.** In order for a computer system to interact with a human being it must be connected to devices that allow for input and output of information. The most common type of input devices are keyboards and mouse-type pointing devices. The most common form of output device is a computer monitor screen or a printer. These devices are usually the largest parts of the computer system because they must be scaled to the dimensions of a human being. Memory and microprocessors can be miniaturized, as is the case with notebook-size computers, but the screen and keyboard must still be large enough to be easily used by a person.

## Microprocessors

The Norton Utilities programs were first designed for users of the original IBM PC (Personal Computer) released in 1981. The latest version of the Norton Utilities, Version 6.0, can still be used on that computer, as well as all subsequent IBM and compatible models. The reason is that all these computers, despite a wide variety of differences, have in common a family of related microprocessors produced by the Intel Corporation. IBM has used these processors in all their personal computers. However, because they are manufactured by Intel, other companies use these same microprocessors in their computers as well. The Intel family of microprocessors differ in features and speed. However, all the microprocessors retain compatibility with the 8088 chip. This allows software written for the 8088 to run on the latest processors, such as the 80386 or 80486.

## Microprocessor Speed

One of the most important characteristics of a microprocessor is the speed at which it can process instructions. The speed is called the *clock rate* or *cycle rate*. This rate tells you the number of cycles per second that can be processed by the microprocessor. For example, the 8088 microprocessor can perform 4,772,727 cycles per second. The simplest operation carried out by the microprocessor takes two cycles. More complicated operations take more cycles to complete.

Processor speed is usually expressed in *megahertz*, MHZ (millions of cycles per second). The 8088 microprocessor is rated at 4.77 MHZ.[1]

**Table 2–1. Microprocessor speed.**

| Intel Microprocessor | Speed in MHZ |
| --- | --- |
| 8088 | 4.77 |
| 80286 | 8 |
| 80386 | 16–33 |
| 80386SX | 16–20 |
| 80486 | 25 |

# Memory and Storage

It is common for people to become disoriented by the technical language they encounter when beginning to work with computers. Language is not necessarily technical because it contains strange new words. However, there are some terms specific to certain disciplines, such as computer usage. The majority of problems with computer terminology arise from the use of some ordinary words. The difference is that in a technical field, these words have a specific, narrow meaning, as opposed to their broader, more general usage.

The most important terms in a computer-oriented vocabulary consist of common words borrowed from the general lexicon, or from other fields related to information management. The most important term involved

---

1.  The unit of measurement Hertz, which stands for cycles per second, was named after the 19th century German physicist Heinrich Rudolph Hertz, who first demonstrated the existence of radio waves.

with computers is *memory*. In its most general sense, memory is the ability to retain information over a period of time. Thus, there are two factors to consider when discussing memory:

- **Capacity.** How much information can be stored in a particular type of memory? Can it be erased, revised, updated, or expanded?

- **Duration.** How long will the information be retained? Is the memory permanent or temporary?

It is memory that distinguishes computers from other electronic devices, such as calculators. By using memory of various types, computers can retain long lists of instructions called *programs*, and large amounts of data called *databases*.

## Types of Memory

Computer systems contain several different types of memory. Each type of memory has a different set of characteristics that suit it for one type of task or another. Computer memory is divided into two fundamental types:

- **Internal Memory.** *Internal* memory can be directly accessed by the computer's microprocessor, and is highly structured. Each item of information is given a unique numeric address. This allows the microprocessor to access or modify any individual item of information directly. The primary weakness of the most flexible type of internal memory is that it cannot retain information permanently. When the computer is turned off, all the information is lost.

- **Mass Storage.** Mass storage refers to information that is stored in large blocks. These blocks are not as highly structured as internal memory and cannot be directly accessed by the microprocessor. In order to use this memory, the information must be transferred from the mass storage device to the internal memory where the microprocessor can then use it. Mass storage does have a quality that internal memory lacks. It can retain the information for an indefinite period of time, even when the computer is turned off or disassembled.

The two types of memory complement each other. No computer system can be of much practical use if it does not have both types of memory.

## Internal Memory

Internal memory is memory that the microprocessor can directly access and manipulate. Direct access by the microprocessor is achieved by giving a unique numeric address to each item of information stored in the internal memory. Each address is connected to the microprocessor by a wiring system called the *system bus*. The *bus* carries information from the internal memory to the microprocessor, or from the microprocessor to the internal memory.

The width of the system bus determines how much information can be transported at one time. A computer with a 16-bit bus width can transport roughly twice the amount of information to or from the microprocessor as can an 8-bit bus system, in the same amount of time. Today's most powerful personal computers have 32-bit data bus widths.

It is important to understand that in order for internal memory to actually be used by the computer it must fit into the addressing scheme of the computer. You will see in Chapter 2 that DOS imposes specific limits on the way memory is addressed, which limits the amount of memory that can be used in a computer.

- **RAM.** RAM stands for *random access memory*. This is the most common form of internal memory found in computers. RAM memory can be used to store any type of information. The memory can be updated, modified, erased, and used again and again. The primary drawback to RAM memory is that it can only retain information as long as it is supplied with a constant flow of electricity. When the electricity is cut off, even for a fraction of a second, all the information in RAM is lost and the memory returns to a blank state. Each time you turn your computer on, all the RAM in the system begins as blank memory. The RAM memory must be filled with data stored in a more permanent form of memory once the computer has been started.

- **ROM.** ROM stands for *read-only memory*. This type of memory has the exact opposite characteristics of RAM. Information stored in ROM memory is permanent and cannot be updated, changed, or reused for another purpose. However, unlike RAM, ROM memory does not depend on a constant flow of electricity in order to retain its information. Information stored in ROM memory is immediately available to the microprocessor when the computer is turned on.

RAM is by far the most flexible type of memory you can use. The RAM memory is used for loading programs and data. All new information or modifications made to existing information is made in RAM memory. The amount of RAM memory is expressed as the number of *bytes*. The letter **K** (kilobyte) is used to represent 1,024 bytes. **M** (megabyte) represents 1,048,576 bytes. When you purchase a computer, the amount of memory in the system will be expressed in terms such as 640K (640 x 1,024 = 655,360 bytes) or 4M (4 x 1,048,576 = 4,194,340 bytes).

ROM memory, while usually part of any computer system, is not typically included as part of the computer's memory because the information stored in ROM is fixed at the factory and cannot be changed. The information stored in ROM contains fundamental programming code needed for the basic operation of the system. Programs loaded into RAM can make use of the fixed routines stored in the system's ROM memory. ROM memory is often said to provide *services* for programs. These services eliminate the need for programs to contain basic routines, making it easier to write programs. It also creates consistency among programs because the same ROM routines are utilized by many different applications. In general, ROM memory is the easiest and least expensive way to store information in a computer system. The problem is that even the best programmers and engineers can make mistakes or fail to anticipate users' needs. If an error is included in ROM memory, the only way to correct it is to replace that ROM with a new one containing the correct or desired information.[2] This did occur with early versions of the IBM PC. The original ROM did not include routines that allowed for the use of hard disk drives. IBM issued a replacement ROM that corrected this problem. The chip was only available from IBM-authorized dealers and they required you to exchange your old ROM for the new one, fearful that users might place IBM ROM chips in non-IBM computers. The entire process was something less than convenient.

All computers contain both ROM and RAM in differing amounts. From the point of view of the microprocessor, both RAM and ROM operate in the same way—that is, every item of information stored in RAM or ROM has a unique location address. You will see in this chapter that the need for

---

2. Correcting problems in ROM memory can be quite a problem since it requires taking chips off the main board of the computer and replacing them with new chips. One solution that is often used to eliminate the need to replace the actual ROM chip is a *software patch*. A *patch* is a small computer program that is loaded into RAM memory. Once the system is turned on, it replaces the erroneous routine stored in ROM memory. This solution uses up some RAM space that otherwise would be free for programs or data.

unique addresses comes into conflict with the limits of the operating system program—DOS—used in IBM and compatible computers.

## Start-up Settings

One of the most versatile aspects of PC systems is that they can contain a number of different options for storage, screen display, and other devices. However, in order to get the system up and running you need to be able to store information about these options in the system so the microprocessor can access them when you turn on the computer.

The two basic types of memory, ROM and RAM, cannot be used effectively for this purpose. RAM cannot be used because it cannot retain the settings once the computer has been turned off. ROM memory cannot be used because it cannot adjust to changes made to the installed equipment. In order to solve this specific problem, two additional types of memory have been used along with the standard RAM and ROM:

- **Dip Switches and Jumpers.** Switches and jumpers are used to set options on computers and add-on boards. A dip switch is a small plastic box containing several small levers that can be moved up or down, using a pencil point. Jumpers are pins that stick out from the circuit board. If the pins are connected by a small block that fits over both pins, the jumper is turned *on*. If the block is removed, the circuit is broken and the jumper is *off*. When the computer is turned on, the switch and jumper settings are read information about the computer's installed equipment.

- **CMOS RAM.** An alternative to dip switches and circuit board jumpers is to use CMOS RAM memory to hold information about the computer's installed equipment. This type of memory functions exactly like normal RAM. This type of RAM will lose all its information if the electricity is turned off. The advantage of CMOS RAM over conventional RAM is that it requires far less electricity. It is possible to power a small amount of CMOS RAM with a battery for several years, in contrast to standard (called *dynamic*) RAM, which would drain even a large battery in hours or days. By combining battery power with CMOS RAM, computers can retain set-up information without the need for dip switches. CMOS RAM was introduced with the IBM AT, replacing the dip switches found on PC and XT circuit boards.

CMOS RAM is much easier and more efficient to use than dip switches. A ROM-based program can be included for the user to run, that allows him or her to enter start-up settings from menus of options. Many computers use special key combinations (e.g., [Ctrl-Alt-Esc]), to activate the built-in set-up program that accesses the current CMOS information, allowing users to make modifications.

Keep in mind that should your battery power fail, the CMOS data will be lost. The SYSINFO program, discussed in Chapter 6, will demonstrate how to access and print out the current CMOS information so you can re-enter the data in case of battery failure.

## Mass Storage

Since RAM memory loses all data when the computer is turned off, a computer system needs a method of storing that data in a form that can maintain the information for indefinite periods of time, with or without electricity.

There are primarily two types of disks used in computers today, *hard disks* and *floppy disks*. The names, hard and floppy, may be misleading. The usual distinction between the hard and floppy disk is that the hard disk contains *nonremovable* media, while a floppy disk system has two parts, a disk drive and a *removable* disk. The floppy disk got its name because it is made of a soft plastic called mylar. The disk is flexible enough to "flop," once it is removed from the drive.

Hard disks are constructed of rigid aluminum disks enclosed in a sealed metal case. The important distinction between a floppy and a hard disk is that hard disks are fixed in the disk drive and cannot be removed. In fact, hard disks are factory-sealed units, whose capacity is fixed when manufactured. Today, the average hard disk has a capacity of more than 40,000,000 characters and some disks boast capacities in the area of 100, 200, 600 or more million characters.

The floppy disk is characterized by its ability to be removed from the drive and replaced with another disk. The capacity of each disk, which average 360,000 to 1,400,000 characters, is much smaller than that of a hard disk. However, the advantage is that the disk can be removed and replaced with another. Today, 3.5-inch hard plastic disks have become popular. These disks are not "floppy," but are classified as floppy disks because they are removable.

On the other hand, special drives, such as Bernoulli drives, allow you to insert and remove cartridges with capacities of 40,000,000 characters. These are called removable hard disks because they have so large a capacity. Such drives combine the advantages of floppy and hard disks in a single drive. It may be better to classify disks as fixed or removable, but the traditional names are hard to shake. The key to remember is that all disks, regardless of their type, serve the same purpose—to store information in a form that will not be erased when the computer is turned off.

Another difference between hard and floppy disks is the speed at which data are accessed. Hard disks characteristically have a much higher rate of data transfer between internal RAM memory and the disk. Hard disks operate 10 or more times faster than floppy disks. As with most technical specifications, you can measure the speed of a device in many ways. Disks can be timed for transfer rate, latency, seek time, and access time. Each measures one part of the operation necessary to move information between the memory and the disk. When you purchase a hard disk, the most common speed rating is the *average seek* time measured in milliseconds (1/1,000 of a second), e.g., 28ms, meaning that the average seek time is 28/1,000 of a second. The faster the seek time the better overall performance you should expect from the drive. One key number that helps you picture the difference in performance between hard and floppy disks is the number of rotations per minute (RPM). A record player spins an LP at 33.3 RPM. A floppy disk drive spins a disk at 300 RPM. When your car idles, it turns the crankshaft at about 1,000 RPM. A hard disk rotates at about 3,600 RPM. It is that faster rotation speed that gives the hard disk much of its improved performance.

# A Primer on Disk Structure

Information stored on disks provides inexpensive, long-term storage for data and programs. Unlike RAM or ROM memory, data stored on disks are stored in large blocks rather than individual bytes.

Disks, both hard and floppy, are organized in roughly the same way. Disks differ mainly in the total capacity for storage and, to some degree, in the size of the individual storage blocks. All disks are divided into basic data blocks called *sectors*. The amount of information stored on a disk is determined by the number of sectors that a disk contains. In theory, the size of the sector can vary quite a bit. In practice, however, there is a remarkable conformity among PC manufacturers for using a sector that contains exactly 512 bytes of information.

Disk sectors are created by dividing the disk into a series of concentric circles called *tracks,* as seen in Figure 2–1. The number of tracks on a typical floppy disk is 40, while a 20-megabyte hard disk will usually have over 600.

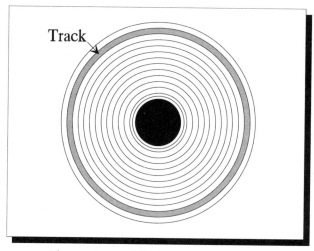

**Figure 2–1. Disk divided into tracks.**

To create the sectors, a disk is divided a second time, this time radially, by cutting the tracks into sections. A floppy disk will usually have nine sectors on each track, while a hard disk will have 17 or 34 sectors on each track, as seen in Figure 2–2.

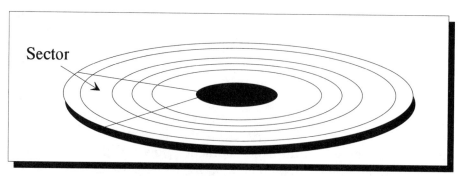

**Figure 2–2. Track divided into sectors.**

Note that disk information is not limited to just the top of the disk platter. Most floppy disks are *double-sided* disks; that is, a disk will have data on two sides, top and bottom, referred to as sides 0 and 1.[3]

Hard disks usually consist of several disks called *plates*, stacked on top of one another, with space left between for the read/write heads to reach each surface of the disk. A typical 20-megabyte disk drive contains two disk plates, sides 0 through 3, as seen in Figure 2–3.

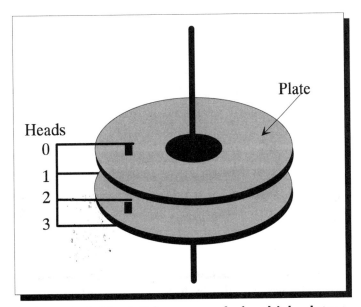

**Figure 2–3. Hard disk composed of multiple plates.**

When a disk uses both sides and/or one or more plates, DOS uses the term *cylinder* to represent all the tracks that fall in the same vertical plane. For example, suppose you have a floppy disk with 40 tracks on the top and 40 on the bottom, a total of 80 tracks. Because the tracks are on

---

3.  Note that the numbering begins with 0, not 1, as the first side. You will find this practice of numbering the first item as zero rather than 1 may be a cause for some confusion. For example, in a 512 byte disk sector the first byte is byte 0 while the last is byte 511.

opposite sides of the same disk, DOS views the disk as having 40 pairs (top and bottom) of matched tracks. Each pair, in this case, is a *cylinder*. Hard disks often use 4 or more surfaces to store data. A cylinder consists of all the tracks that align vertically, as seen in Figure 2–4. A cylinder is an important concept in hard disk operation because it represents an exact physical location on the disk. Once positioned to a given cylinder, the disk can read all the data on any of the surfaces, at a high rate of speed. Moving to a different cylinder causes a delay in the transfer of data. The number of cylinders is usually equal to the total number of tracks on each disk surface.

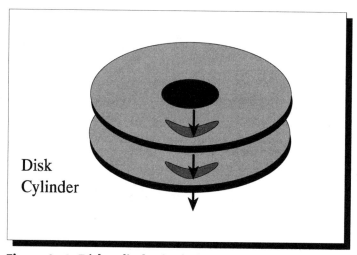

**Figure 2–4. Disk cylinder includes corresponding sectors on all surfaces.**

You can calculate the total amount of space on a disk by multiplying the following:

sectors × tracks × sides × 512

For example, a floppy disk with 9 sectors per track, 40 tracks, and 2 sides would be:

$9 \times 40 \times 2 \times 512 = 368,640$

The capacity is referred to as 360K (kilobyte) per disk. A hard disk with 17 sectors per track, 614 tracks, and 4 sides would have a capacity of:

$$17 \times 614 \times 4 \times 512 = 21,377,024$$

This would be referred to as a 20-megabyte disk.

In order to keep track of the information on the hard disk, each sector is given a unique number. The first sector is 0, the second 1, and so on. A 360K disk will have 720 sectors, numbers 0–719. A 20-megabyte hard disk will have over 41,000 sectors.

The tracks and sectors are created by a process called formatting, which makes use of a special computer program called *FORMAT*. You cannot use a disk, hard or floppy, before it has been formatted.

When the FORMAT command is run, a disk will be divided into the proper number of tracks and sectors. In addition, those sectors must be numbered for identification purposes. Also, the FORMAT program checks the integrity of the disk to make sure that all the sectors will correctly accept data. If a defect is found, the sector is marked as unusable.

The formatting process is a complicated one. It actually consists of two separate operations called *low-level* and *high-level* formatting. Low-level (physical) formatting consists of placing electronic marks in the disk to imprint the physical locations of the tracks and sectors. Once the marking has taken place, the high-level formatting organizes the sectors, which are all alike, into separate and distinct functions. This second type of formatting is called high-level or logical formatting.

In MS-DOS computers, the two stage formatting of floppy disks is implemented with a single command, FORMAT. The same command, when applied to a hard disk, will perform only the high-level formatting. The assumption is that the low-level or physical formatting of the hard disk has already been done.

Usually, low-level formatting of hard disks is something the average user is never faced with. Suppose you wanted to perform a low-level format on your hard disk. How would you do it? The supplier of the hard disk will usually provide a program that performs the low-level format. IBM includes the program as part of the diagnostic disk. If you are using a compatible computer you may find that the program for formatting is not on a disk but built into the ROM on the hard disk controller card. To run this program you will have to use the DEBUG program to access the location in the memory where the program is stored. The typical address of a hard disk device is C800, such as with the popular Western Digital controller supplied with many hard disks.

## Partitions

In some cases you may need, or be required, to divide a hard disk into two or more *logical* disks. This process is called *partitioning* the disk. The most common reason for creating disk partitions is a limitation in DOS versions prior to DOS 4.01, which limited the size of a hard disk to 32 megabytes or less. If you wanted to use a larger drive (e.g., 40 or 80 megabytes) you would need to partition the drive into two or more segments so that the DOS operating system would act as if you had two or more smaller drives instead of one large drive. Thus a single hard disk might appear to operate as several different *logical* disks.

# Summary

This chapter handled the basic concepts that underlie the details of PCs.

**Microprocessors**   The heart of any personal computer is the microprocessor. The microprocessor is the part of the computer that executes commands and performs operations. All the rest of the computer is designed to send information to, or receive information from, the microprocessor. PCs use the Intel family of microprocessors, starting with the 8086 and 8088 developed for the original IBM PC.

**Memory**   The information that is accessed directly by the microprocessor is stored in the computer's memory. Computers use several different types of memory such as RAM, ROM, and CMOS RAM.

**RAM**   RAM stands for Random Access Memory. This type of memory can store information so that the microprocessor can address individual bytes of data. However, the RAM memory cannot retain the information after the computer has been turned off.

**Disk Storage**   Disk storage is used to preserve information that is stored in RAM memory. Disks store information in large blocks that cannot be directly accessed by the microprocessor. However, the disk will maintain the information permanently, even when the computer is not turned on. Disks comes in many different forms and sizes. Hard disks are sealed units that work at very high speeds. Floppy (removable) disks are slower but allow for the disk to be removed from the disk drive and replaced with a different disk.

**Disk Sectors**     Data are stored on disks in blocks called sectors. The sector is the basic unit of disk storage.

**Disks Tracks**     Disks are divided into circular tracks that contain the data sectors.

**Bits**     A bit is the smallest piece of information that a computer can record. It is literally the state of an electronic switch: either on or off. Bits represent data in a binary system in which a zero represents an open switch and a 1 a closed or on switch.

**Bytes**     A sequence of eight bits is called a byte. The capacity of a computer is usually expressed in bytes, kilobytes (1,024), or megabytes (1,048,576). Coding systems relate specific bytes to characters such as letters in the alphabet.

**Hexadecimal Numbers**     The binary sequences that directly represent the data stored in the computer are difficult for humans to read and write. In order to speed up and compress the notation needed to describe computer data, binary (base 2) numbers are usually converted into hexadecimal (base 16) numbers.

# 3 | The Role of DOS

One of the most important but frequently misunderstood parts of the computer system is DOS. DOS, *disk operating system*, is often referred to as MS-DOS, where MS stands for *Microsoft Corporation*, the company that created the operating system.

DOS is important because it is the link that combines the computer hardware, discussed in Chapter 2, with software applications, such as word processing, spreadsheets, databases, or graphics.

Technically, DOS is a software program, although most people would not put it in the same classification as WordPerfect, Lotus 1-2-3, or dBASE IV. The reason is that unlike an application or utility program, which can be added or removed from the computer system at any time, DOS *must* be present in order for the computer to work at all.

Why is DOS so important? How is it different from applications like word processing, or utilities like the Norton Utilities? How can or should you use DOS? This chapter will attempt to answer these questions and supply you with the background in DOS needed to tap the full power of the Norton Utilities.

## What DOS Does in Your Computer

Most computer users take for granted that DOS is an important part of their computer, without having a very concrete idea of what DOS does, how it does it, and how they can control and manipulate their computer using DOS. You might also wonder why a book about the Norton Utilities spends so much time discussing DOS.

To begin with the second question first, the very nature of the Norton Utilities, or any utility program, is to extend, alter, or enhance the operating system of the computer. The Norton Utilities are intimately linked with the operating system and any understanding of the Norton Utilities requires some basic understanding of DOS. It is impossible to talk about the Norton Utilities without frequently referring to DOS concepts, features, and problems.

This now leaves the question of why DOS is so important and exactly what it does. The answer begins with the idea of *specialization*. In theory there is no requirement that a computer have a separate operating system like DOS. But programs that supply their own operating system are rare. The vast majority of the programs that exist for PCs require the presence of DOS. These programs use DOS to carry out the basic operations common to all computer programs. This means that the applications can provide only the features needed to carry out their specific function.

For example, when you use a word processing program such as WordPerfect, you can create documents on the screen that can be stored on computer disks. Since WordPerfect contains a command called **SAVE**, you tend to think that it is the WordPerfect program performing this task. In reality, WordPerfect is working in combination with DOS to accomplish the task. The WordPerfect program carries out the commands and features needed to edit the document on the screen. However, when you issue a **SAVE** command, WordPerfect taps into the facilities provided by DOS to actually create the disk file. As a user of WordPerfect you are unaware of this integration because it takes place in the background. This type of integration has some very important benefits:

**Reduces Program Size and Complexity.** Since DOS contains most of the routines needed to carry out basic tasks such as writing information to a disk, the application does not need to include these instructions, making it faster and easier to create programs.

**Uniform Procedures.** When all programs use the same DOS routines, operations are carried out in a standard manner by all the programs. Thus, applications as different as word processing, spreadsheets, graphics, or databases, all work with a common system of storing and retrieving disk information, connecting to printers, or network operations.

For these reasons and more, DOS is the essential foundation upon which all other programs are built. The more complicated the computer system (e.g., computers running on a network or a single computer performing multitasking) the more there is a need for standard methods of operations to which all programs comply.[1] DOS is responsible for six different areas of computer operations:

**Start-up Loader (booting).**   Recall from Chapter 2 that when a computer is turned off all the information contained in the RAM memory is erased. The start-up loader process, commonly called *booting*, is the process by which the operating system is loaded from the disk into the memory so that standard operations can begin. You will learn more about this process later in this chapter.

**Input/Output Management.**   The operating system can be used to manage the flow of information to and from standard devices, such as keyboards, monitors, and printers.[2]

**Memory Management.**   DOS is responsible for allocating memory for programs that are running on the computer. Memory management is most critical when there is more than one program resident in memory at a time.

**Storage Management.**   DOS is responsible for the filing system by which disk files are created, modified, or erased. DOS must maintain an accurate record of what information is stored on what part of the disk, and how that information should be combined to form program and data files.

**Network Management.**   If the computer is running on a local area network DOS provides routines that handle potential network conflicts by locking files when they are in use.

**User-interface Shell.**   The operating system *shell* is a program that enables the user to directly enter commands for DOS to carry out. In all versions of DOS prior to 4.xx, the user-interface was a command-driven environment characterized by the DOS prompt. In 4.xx the DOS shell

---

1.   Many programs written for the early IBM PC took advantage of quirks within the IBM PC, in order to improve features and performance. However, when you add complicated system features such as networks or multitasking with Windows 3, programs that use such shortcuts will play havoc with your system. If programs are to operate well in complex environments, they need to be *well behaved*; i.e., they must carry out tasks in ways that conform to standard DOS methods and avoid shortcuts.

2.   When a nonstandard device, e.g., a CD-ROM drive, is installed in the computer a special file called a *device driver* can be added to the DOS program in memory so that the operating system will know how to handle the new device. Device drivers are installed using the CONFIG.SYS file. They enable DOS to work with a wide variety of devices that would not normally be supported by the basic set of devices included with DOS.

was expanded to include a menu system from which commands and options could be chosen.

In computer terminology, the memory, storage, and network management features, used to directly support applications such as word processing or databases, are referred to as the operating system *kernel*.

It is important to note that most of the operations for which DOS is responsible are actions that take place in the background, invisible to the user, while an application is running. It is only in the last area, the DOS shell, the user comes into direct contact with DOS and its operations.

In order to work effectively with an MS-DOS system, there are two basic areas of skill that a user should acquire:

**File and Set-up Options.** Because all applications depend upon DOS to handle basic operations, such as storage of data in disk files and output of data to printers, it is necessary for a DOS user to understand the DOS filing system and how DOS refers to output options, such as printers and modem connections. This knowledge is handy since almost all programs will ask the user to fill in options based on standard DOS files and output port names.

**Direct Commands and Utility Programs.** The DOS shell allows the user to directly command the operating system. These commands can be used to perform everyday tasks, such as copying files from one location to another or creating new disk directories. A utility program is one that enhances the user's control over the operating system, beyond the basic set of commands included in the DOS shell. MS-DOS includes a number of utility programs. The Norton Utilities go beyond the DOS utilities by adding new features, superior performance, and a more comfortable user-interface than is supplied with the standard MS-DOS utilities.

## The DOS Files

In the previous sections *DOS* was referred to in a general, abstract sense. However, like all computer concepts, there must be a concrete implementation of the concept. MS-DOS is supplied to the user in the form of three disk files. Note that the IBM versions of DOS use different file names from the generic MS-DOS version supplied with non-IBM computers. Note that only the COMMAND.COM file will appear as part of the normal file listings. The other two files are marked as *hidden*, meaning that DOS will omit their names from any file lists generated by DOS commands. This is done to protect the basic operating system from accidental erasure or modification, which could damage the operating system, rendering the computer useless.

There are two parts of DOS that are not included in these files. The *Start-up Loader* portion of the operating system is a special case in which disk information is not classified as an actual file; this is discussed in the next section. Also, utility programs included with DOS, such as FORMAT, DISKCOPY, or CHKDSK, are each stored in separate disk files and not actually included in the basic DOS files.

# The Booting Process

Although it is not obvious to the user, the process that takes place when turning on the computer is one of the most complex, intricate, and obscure operations that a computer performs. This is because the start-up procedure must address a basic contradiction in the structure of the computer. The RAM memory, which is used to perform most of the tasks in the computer system, begins as a completely blank slate when the computer is first turned on. As discussed in the previous section, all the information making up the DOS operating system, the basis of all the computer's operations, is contained in three files stored on one of the computer's disks. If you think about this situation you will encounter a logical contradiction. The information that controls the use of disks, i.e., the operating system, is stored in *disk* files.

Thus, the system finds itself in a chicken and egg dilemma. The system can function only when the DOS files have been placed in RAM memory. But since RAM is empty when the computer is turned on, the computer does not have the information that will enable it to read the DOS files on the disk.

In order to overcome this contradiction, microcomputers employ a complicated technique called *bootstrapping*, or *booting*.[3] Put simply, the booting process involves the use of a built-in, hard-wired, ROM program that is immediately executed when you turn on the computer. The purpose of this program is to seek a special block of information stored at the very beginning of the disk called the *boot record*. This information, when loaded into the computer, provides sufficient information to enable the three crucial DOS files to be loaded into memory, thus getting the system up and running.

---

3.   From the cliché *to pull yourself up by your own bootstraps*.

When you say that a computer has been *booted*, you are saying that DOS has been loaded and is ready to accept an instruction. Note that until the *booting* process has been successfully completed, the user has no control over what is happening in the system because keyboard input requires the presence of DOS in order to function. If you have ever experienced problems with your computer during the boot process you will have found that just about the only thing you can accomplish with the keyboard is to *reboot* the computer using the [Ctrl-Alt-Del] combination. The booting process is composed of a number of individual stages:

**Testing.**  Most MS-DOS computers perform a series of self-tests when first turned on. The most common test is a memory test in which the system displays the amount of installed memory on the screen as it tests the reliability of that memory. Some systems display other information about installed boards, video monitors, and input/output devices. At the end of the testing the system will sound a beep.[4]

**Seek Boot Sector.**  Once the tests have been successfully concluded, the ROM program attempts to locate the boot sector on either the first floppy disk, drive A, or the first hard disk, drive C. In order for the boot process to continue, the boot sector must contain the *loader* instructions, which are read into the computer and executed. Keep in mind that not all disks have the loader program stored in the boot sector. The loader program is placed into the boot sector during the *formatting* process if you select the *system* option during formatting. If the disk that is read does not contain the loader program in the boot sector, the message "Non-system disk" will appear on the screen, indicating that the system cannot continue the boot process because the loader program is absent.[5]

---

4.  The beep that is issued is actually part of a collection of audio messages from the system. The pattern of the beeps can be used to determine problems in the computer's hardware. Beeps are used instead of visual messages because many hardware problems prevent the use of the display adapter and monitor. Audio prompts, such as the beeping, provide a nonvisual form of communication. The meaning of the beeps is usually documented in technical reference manuals for the system. These manuals are not generally provided to end users, but are sold to dealers who repair machines.

5.  In most MS-DOS systems the ROM program always attempts to search the floppy drive first, before it searches for a boot sector on the hard disk. If you leave a *non-system* floppy disk in drive A when you turn off your computer, you will probably encounter a *Non-system disk* error message when the system attempts to boot. You can solve the problem by opening the disk drive door and rebooting the system, allowing the boot sector from the hard disk to be read, instead of the one from the floppy disk.

**Load Input/Output and Kernel.** The loader program directs the computer to find, load, and execute the IO.SYS and MSDOS.SYS files (or their PC-DOS equivalents).

**CONFIG.SYS.** After the first two DOS files have been read, the disk is searched for a file called CONFIG.SYS. This file is used to modify the DOS system. CONFIG.SYS is used to change standard DOS parameters, such as the BUFFERS or FILES settings, and to load device drivers for hard disks, mice, or other nonstandard devices. The commands issued by CONFIG.SYS will change the amount of memory allocated to the operating system. For example, if your CONFIG.SYS file loads several device drivers, the amount of memory used by DOS will increase, leaving less memory for applications. Note that CONFIG.SYS is an optional file. If no CONFIG.SYS is found, DOS loads using the built-in default values. Devices that depend on device drivers, e.g., a mouse, will not be recognized if the CONFIG.SYS does not load the corresponding drivers into memory during the boot process.

**COMMAND.COM Shell.** When the CONFIG.SYS file has been read and executed, the next step is to load the COMMAND.COM shell program. It is through COMMAND.COM that you can directly enter commands to DOS at the *DOS prompt*. If the COMMAND.COM file is missing, the message "Missing command interpreter" will be displayed, indicating an error in the booting process.

**AUTOEXEC.BAT.** The AUTOEXEC.BAT file is an optional file that contains a set of DOS instructions to be carried out each time the computer is booted. If no AUTOEXEC.BAT file is found the system prompts you to enter the date and time. Note that the AUTOEXEC.BAT file does not accomplish anything that the user could not accomplish by manually typing in the same commands, one at a time. AUTOEXEC.BAT simply saves you the trouble of repeating the same set of commands each time the computer is booted.

Diagnosing and solving a problem that occurs during the booting process requires that you identify what part of the booting process is affected by the problem. Much of the booting process is automatic, and as such is beyond the control of the user. It is in the use of the AUTOEXEC.BAT and CONFIG.SYS files that the user can exert control over the way his or her system operates. Recall from Chapter 1 that the Norton Utilities install program will perform optional modifications to these two files in order to integrate Norton Utilities features into the operating system of the computer.

# How DOS Operates

DOS operates in three separate sections. As discussed previously, the main DOS files are loaded into the computer's memory during the boot process. The *kernel* files operate in the background to provide applications with basic operations, such as reading and writing disk files. The details of the kernel operations and commands are of interest to programmers who develop DOS applications. Users have no direct contact with the kernel. The two other sections of DOS are the commands that users can issue at the DOS prompt. These commands fall into two categories:

**Internal Commands.** Internal commands are DOS routines that are contained in the COMMAND.COM (DOS shell) program. The advantage of internal commands is that they can be executed at any time from the DOS prompt. These commands do not need any additional support files in order to operate. The most common internal commands are DIR, DEL, and COPY.

**External Commands.** External commands are actually utility programs stored in individual program files. When an external command is used you are actually running a small program. This means that the program file *must* be present in order to carry out the operation. For example, in order to format a disk, the FORMAT.COM or FORMAT.EXE file *must* be available. If DOS cannot find the file that corresponds to the external command the message "Bad command or filename" will be displayed.

Why two types of DOS commands? Internal commands are handy because they are loaded as a group when the COMMAND.COM file is loaded. However, as you increase the number of functions built into COMMAND.COM, you increase the amount of memory used by COMMAND.COM. External commands, since they are loaded like programs, occupy memory only when they are actually being used. The idea is that the internal commands should consist only of those basic commands that will probably be used most often. All other DOS operations can be placed into individual utility programs and stored in disk files until they are needed.

# The File System

The most important aspect of DOS for users to understand is the *hierarchical file* system first introduced into DOS with Version 2.0 in 1982. The structure of this file system bridged the gap between the floppy disk file system used in Version 1.0 and the sophisticated systems used in large computer systems such as the UNIX operating system developed by AT&T.

What is the purpose of the *hierarchical file* system and why is it so important to the average user?

Taking the second question first, the file system is the point at which most users will come in contact with the operating system and its conventions. No matter what types of applications you use you will have to create and use file names to designate the data you want to save, retrieve, or even erase.

The structure of the file system determines what those file names are like and how you can locate individual files.

## Drives

The largest unit of storage in a PC system is a *drive*, also referred to as a *volume*. The drive or volume represents all the data stored on a single storage device, such as a hard or floppy disk drive. DOS *assigns* a single letter identifier to each drive in the system. Letters A and B are reserved for the first two floppy drives in the system. The first hard drive is letter C. To distinguish the drive letter from other names a colon is placed after the letter. In DOS **A:** is a reference to the A drive.

You can select any drive in the system by entering the letter followed by a colon at the DOS prompt. The command below selects the C drive:

```
C:↵
```

In addition to physical drives, computers often have *logical* drives. Logical drives are created when a single hard disk is partitioned into several sections. Each section can be assigned a different drive letter, as shown in Figure 3–1. Disk partitions are the least flexible way of organizing a hard disk:

**Fixed Size and Location.** When a disk partition is created, you must select the area of the disk that will be included in that partition. Partitions

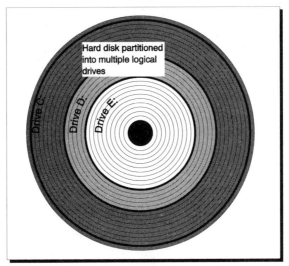

**Figure 3–1. Hard drive partitioned into several logical drives.**

are defined by the number of disk-consecutive *cylinders*[6] allocated to each partition. For example, the first partition would begin at cylinder 0 and stop at 100. The next would begin at 101 and so on, until all the cylinders were allocated to one partition or another.

**Inflexible.**  Since partitions occupy a specific area of the hard disk, you cannot expand the storage space allocated to one partition without affecting any data stored in the other partitions. This means that if you have incorrectly allocated disk space when you set up the partitions, you will probably have to erase the entire hard disk in order to change the partition set up.

Disk partitions should only be created when you are certain that you need to divide the hard disk permanently. The most common reason for creating hard disk partitions is related to a limitation in DOS 3.3, which limited the size of any one disk partition to 32 megabytes. If you were using a hard disk with a capacity greater than 32 megabytes, you would need to divide the disk into multiple 32-megabyte partitions or less, each of which

---

6.  See Chapter 2, "A Primer on Disk Structure," for the definition of cylinders.

would be a logical drive.[7] Disk partitions are also used to allow non DOS-based operating systems, such as various forms of UNIX, to reside on the same hard disk as DOS.

## Directories

The next level of organization in the DOS file system is the *directory*. Directories allow you to divide a disk into a tree-like structure of directories. Directories are needed to organize disks that can hold a large number of files, such as hard disk drives.

Because directories are logical, not physical structures, they possess several advantages over fixed-disk partitions:

**Flexible Size.** Unlike partitions, directories have no predefined size limits. The amount of information stored and the number of files used to contain that information is limited to only the total amount of space available on the drive.

**Add and Remove Easily.** Since directories have no fixed size you can add or remove directories without affecting the data in other directories.

**Nesting.** Directories are organized in a tree type structure. You can create directories *within* directories so that a single directory can be subdivided into two or more smaller directories. This *nesting* structure allows your directories to be organized like an outline with levels of major and minor subheadings.

All disks begin with a single directory called the *root* directory. The figure then shows that three user-defined directories called LOTUS, DBASE, and WP are created. In this example the directories correspond to three major applications (Lotus 1-2-3, dBASE IV, and WordPerfect) that are being run on the system. The purpose of the directories is to store program and data files related to those applications. Separating files into different directories

---

7.  In Version 4.xx, support for individual partitions larger than 32 megabytes was added to DOS, allowing an entire hard disk, such as a 40- or 80-megabyte drive, to operate as a single logical drive, e.g., C:. If you are using DOS 3.3 with a hard disk greater than 32 megabytes, you may find that you have a logical drive, usually drive D, that exceeds the 32-megabyte limit. This is usually the result of special hard disk partitioning software such as On Track or SpeedStor, which use device drivers (DRDVDM.BIN or HARDR-IVE.SYS, respectively) to implement larger partitions than are supported by DOS 3.xx.

makes it easier to locate individual files because all the files in any given directory have something in common.

You can further enhance the organization of the files by creating directories within the major directories. The LOTUS directory contains two additional directories called BUDGET and ACCOUNTS. Likewise, the DBASE directory contains CLIENTS and SALES, while WP contains LETTERS.

The number of directories and the number of levels (directories within directories) you create depends upon your organizational needs. Most major applications will create directories for their files during their installation process. The Norton Utilities Install program creates a directory called NORTON in which the programs are stored.

## File Names

The final level of disk organization is the *file*. The file is the smallest unit of organization in the filing system. For example, if you wanted to store a document with a single character, e.g., the letter A, you would have to create a file.

Every file on the disk *must* have a file name. The file name can be from 1 to 8 characters with an optional 1–3 character extension that is separated from the file name by a period. Examples of file names are COMMAND.COM, FORMAT.EXE, AUTOEXEC.BAT, or README.DOC. File names *must* be unique with any given directory. This means there cannot be more than one file with the same name in a single disk directory. You can, however, have files with the same name if they are stored in different directories. If you attempt to create a new file with the same name as an existing file, the operating system will react in one of two ways:

**Cancel.** The operating system will cancel the command because the new file name conflicts with an existing name. For example, the RE-NAME command will automatically be canceled if the new name selected for the file is already in use by another file. Commands that cancel when a name conflict is encountered are *nondestructive* commands because they will not erase any existing data.

**Overwrite.** In other cases DOS will replace the existing file with a new file with the same name. The COPY command will overwrite an old file when making copies. Such commands are *destructive* because they can erase old data as part of their operations.

Which DOS commands are destructive and which are nondestructive? The answer is that only a detailed knowledge of DOS will reveal that information. The Norton Utilities improve on DOS operations in many cases because they provide levels of protection from destructive operations not provided by DOS. For example, the FILESAVE program provides a safety net for recovery of accidentally erased data.

## File Types

There are two basic types of files stored on computer disks:

**Binary Files.**  Binary files are long sequences of numbers that contain coded information to be read directly by the computer. The microprocessor in your computer contains enough information to break the number sequence codes and interpret them as commands and/or data. Most programs are provided in the binary form. By convention, files that are program files carry either a **COM** or **EXE** extension. Binary program files are microprocessor-specific. This means that a program written for an IBM PC will run only on a computer that has the same decoder set as the IBM. If data are stored in a binary file it is likely that only the program and the computer it was designed to operate with can understand the data.

**Text (ASCII) Files.**  ASCII stands for the *American Standard Code for Information Interchange*. This code can be used to translate the values stored in a computer file into ordinary text by assigning one character to each of the 256 different numbers that can be represented by one byte. Storage in ASCII format is usually less compact than binary storage. However, the advantage is that ASCII provides a common basis for the interchange of information. As a computer user you will want to be aware of which programs work with ASCII files. Programs that can read and write ASCII files can exchange information with other programs that do the same. Programs that use only their own specially coded binary files are much more limited in terms of sharing information. A file that is standard ASCII format means that any program reading standard files can read and understand the information contained in that file. Therefore, the terms ASCII file, DOS text file, text file, and ASCII standard file refer to the same thing.

# DOS Commands

DOS provides the user with the ability to directly manipulate various parts of the computer system. In order to perform operations, you must enter DOS commands. While it is beyond the scope of this book to discuss in detail the full range of DOS commands, most of the commands have basically the same structure, grammar, and syntax. An understanding of those characteristics is also useful with the Norton Utilities program since all of the programs can be executed directly from DOS, or as part of DOS batch files.

# The DOS Prompt

A *prompt* is text that the computer displays on the screen when it is waiting for you to enter an instruction. At the end of the booting process, DOS will display its prompt and wait for you to enter an instruction. The DOS prompt is a very simple display such as **C:>** or **C:>**, followed by the blinking cursor. The computer is now waiting for you to enter an instruction. The difficult part of DOS is that there is no information, such as a menu or a help screen, which explains what command you can or should enter. The assumption is that you know in advance exactly what you want to enter and how it should be entered.[8]

## The DOS Command Language

The most important concept to understand about giving commands to DOS is that DOS is more like a language than a set of fixed commands. Each command has a number of specific parts, just like a sentence is composed of different parts of speech. The best way to use DOS commands (or direct DOS-type commands to the Norton Utilities) is to try to *compose* command sentences, rather than simply *memorize* commands. It is also important to be able to look at a DOS command, as found in a manual, book, or magazine, and be able to break down the command so that you can grasp its meaning. DOS commands are composed of six basic elements:

---

8. One difference between the Norton Utilities and the standard DOS utilities is that the Norton Utilities can be executed directly in the DOS command mode or, more typically, executed through an interactive, menu-driven mode with on-line help available.

**Commands.** The command is *always* the first part of any DOS command. The simplest commands consist of only the command word itself. More complicated commands require additional elements following the command. In all cases but one, the command corresponds to a utility file stored on the disk, e.g., the **FORMAT** command corresponds to a file called FORMAT.COM or FORMAT.EXE. The exceptions are the *internal* DOS commands directly supported by the COMMAND.COM shell program. Example: The command DIR[9] tells DOS to display a list of the files in the current directory.

**Parameters.** A *parameter* is a piece of information that specifies what item should be affected by or used by the command. In most cases the parameter is a disk item such as a file, a directory, or a drive. In some cases the parameter is the name of a device such as PRN, which stands for the printer. Commands can have one or more parameters. Commands can have required parameters that must be entered in order for the command to operate, or optional parameters. Example: The command below copies the file AUTOEXEC.BAT to drive A:

```
COPY AUTOEXEC.BAT A:
```

**Delimiters.** A *delimiter* is a character used to separate one item from another. In most cases DOS uses a space character to separate parts of a command. A command must be properly delimited in order to execute. This means that leaving out a *required* space can create an error. Example: The command below executes the EDLIN (line editor) program. Edlin *requires* a file name as a parameter in order to run. Note that a space is used to separate the command from its parameter:

```
EDLIN CONFIG.SYS
```

**Options Switches.** A switch is a letter or word that affects *how* the command will operate. Switches provide a means by which command options can be selected without the use of menus. DOS and Norton Utilities programs make extensive use of command switches. A switch is always preceded by a /(slash) character (not a \(backslash). Example: The /W switch changes the directory listing to the *wide* format:

```
DIR /W
```

---

9. DOS is not sensitive to the difference between upper- and lowercase letters. Commands can be entered in any combination of upper- or lowercase without affecting the meaning of the command.

**Redirection.**  Most commands output messages or reports to the screen. Redirection is used to send the output to another device. The most common use of redirection is to send information that would normally appear on the screen to the printer. Redirection can be used with DOS and Norton Utilities commands to obtain printed, rather than screen-displayed results. The > character is used to redirect output to a different device. Example: The command below sends the directory display to the printer instead of to the screen:

DIR>PRN[10]

**Wildcards.**  A *wildcard* is a special symbol that represents a group of files. Wildcards can be used in most instances where file name parameters are used in order to broaden the effect of a command from a single file to a group of files. The * character is a wildcard for a group of characters, while the ? character is a wildcard for a single character. One common wildcard is *.*, which is used to select all the files in a directory. For example, the command below prints a directory that includes only files ending with an EXE extension:

DIR *.EXE

## File Specification and Wildcards

There are times when it is advantageous to refer to files in a more general way. When you issue a command you may want to refer to more than one file at a time, so that the command can act upon more than one file.

For example, suppose there were 50 files on a disk that needed erasing. You might enter 50 commands, one to erase each file. However, the most convenient way would be to use a wildcard. The purpose of DOS wildcards is to refer to a group of files with a single command. DOS recognizes two special characters as wildcards: ? and *.

The * is even more general than the ?. An * used in a file name indicates that any character beginning at that position and continuing to the end of

---

10. Output sent to the printer with >PRN consists of the exact information that would have been sent to the screen. This means that the output will not include page formatting codes, such as a form feed, which will feed the rest of the page at the end of the printing. You can send a form feed to the printer from DOS by using the ECHO command. Example: **ECHO ^L >PRN**. Note that the ^L character is entered by holding down the [Ctrl] key and pressing the letter L.

the file name or extension are acceptable. For example, entering **\*.PAY** would refer to all files with the PAY extension.

## The Active Directory

Another important concept that affects a great number of DOS and Norton Utilities commands is the concept of the *active directory*. The active directory is the one that is used by DOS for all operations, unless otherwise specified.

**Programs.**  DOS will only execute the programs contained within the active directory. For example, if the NORTON directory is active, then you can execute any of the Norton Utilities programs contained within that directory. However, programs stored in other directories (e.g., DOS) will not execute while the NORTON directory is active.

**Files.**  Commands that use file names as parameters can affect only those files that are contained in the active directory. For example, if you entered the command **DEL\*.\***, DOS would delete all the files in the *active directory only*. Files stored in other directories will not be affected.

When you first boot the computer, the active directory is always set as the *root* directory of the disk from which the system was booted.[11]

The **CD** (change directory) command is used to activate a different directory. In order to indicate that a name refers to a directory and not a file, the \ character is used as punctuation. For example, to activate the dBASE directory you would enter

```
CD\DBASE ↵
```

Once activated, DOS will only execute the programs found in that directory or use the files located in that directory. Note that DOS does not include any programs or files stored in directories created within the current directory, e.g., CHECKS or SALES. If a directory is contained within another directory it is activated by using the names of higher-level directories written in sequence. For example, to activate the CHECKS directory

---

11. This assumes that the AUTOEXEC.BAT file is not used to select a different directory.

contained within the dBASE directory you would use the name **\DBASE\CHECKS**. Example:

```
CD\DBASE\CHECKS ↵
```

It is important to keep in mind that one and only one directory can be the active directory, no matter how many directories or disks are included in the system.

## Path Names

The active directory system is designed to limit operations to one area of the disk at a time. However, there may be times when you want to refer to a program or a file stored in a different drive or directory without changing the current directory.

DOS will execute a program or use a file in a different directory or drive if you enter its exact location as part of the command or parameter. This specific location is called the *path name*. A path name is similar to the file name, except that it includes a prefix that names the drive and/or directory where the file or program is located.

For example, when the directory \DBASE\CHECKS is activated, you have access to the files stored in this directory, e.g., database files related to your checking account. However, the dBASE IV program used to manipulate that data is stored in the \DBASE directory. If you were to enter the command **DBASE**, DOS would display the message "Bad command or filename," because it would not be able to find the dBASE IV program in the current directory \DBASE\CHECKS.

You can overcome this problem by specifying the location of the program in your command. Example:

```
\DBASE\DBASE ↵
```

The same basic approach works for programs on drives different from the active drive. Recall from Chapter 1 that when you run the Norton Utilities Install program, you leave the hard disk active but execute the Install program from the floppy disk. Example:

```
A:INSTALL ↵
```

You can use **path names** as part of the file specification parameters with DOS and Norton Utilities commands. For example, the command below deletes the README.DOC file from the NORTON directory, even if NOR-TON is *not* the active directory:

```
DEL \NU\README.DOC ↵
```

If you have several logical drives you can perform an operation on any directory, on any drive, by adding the drive letter to the file designation. The command below deletes the README.DOC file from the NORTON directory on drive D:

```
DEL D:\NU\README.DOC ↵
```

## Search Paths

The ability to execute programs located in other drives and directories is very handy. It allows you to take advantage of directories to store files in related groups and still be able to execute a program without having to activate the directory in which that program is stored. Remote execution of programs is particularly handy for utility programs such as DOS or Norton Utilities, since you may want to apply these programs to any number of different directories.

In order to make remote execution simpler DOS allows you to insert into memory a list of one or more directories that should automatically be searched if the requested program is not found in the active directory. For example, if the dBASE directory were added to the search path list, each time you entered the command **DBASE** ↵, DOS would search the current directory for the program. If the dBASE program was not found, it would then search the first directory in the search path list to see if the program was stored there. The path list can contain a list of directories. Note that directories in a list are delimited with semicolons (;), not spaces.

The PATH command is used to place a path list into memory. The following command would create a search path to the LOTUS, DBASE, and WP directories:

```
PATH \LOTUS;\DBASE;\WP; ↵
```

When you enter a command to execute a program, e.g., DBASE ↵, DOS begins by searching the current directory for that program. If that search fails, DOS searches the first directory in the path list. If that also fails, it searches the second directory listed in the path list, if any. The process continues until either the program is found and executed, or the path list is exhausted, as shown in Figure 3–2. This means that the order in which you enter the directories in the path list is the order in which the search is performed.

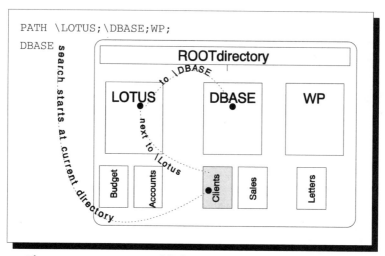

**Figure 3–2. PATH establishes search path for program.**

If your system contains more than one hard disk, you can include the drive location of the directory as well. If no drive is used with the directory, DOS assumes that the directory is located on the active drive. The path **C:\** refers to the root directory of drive C:

```
PATH C:\;C:\LOTUS;D:\DBASE;C:\WP;  ↵
```

As discussed in Chapter 1, the Norton Utilities programs are most valuable when they can be executed from any part of the system. That is why the Install program will ask you if you want the NORTON directory added to the PATH command in your AUTOEXEC.BAT file. Note that the path list is stored in RAM memory, which means it is lost each time you reboot or turn on the computer. By placing a PATH command in your AUTOEXEC.BAT file you ensure that the path is reset each time the system is booted.

Also note that each PATH command *overwrites* the previous path list. For example, suppose you entered the following two commands:

```
PATH \DOS;\LOTUS; ↵
PATH \NU ↵
```

The result is a path list that contains *only* the NORTON directory since
the second command wipes out the previous list. To create a path list with
all three directories you must issue a single command that lists all three,
e.g., PATH \DOS;\LOTUS;\NU;. If the path list contains a nonexistent
path name, DOS does *not* generate an error. This means that if you make a
typographical error, e.g., **PATH C:\NORTOM,** you will not be warned that
you have attempted to access a nonexistent directory. If you think you have
opened a path to a directory but cannot get DOS to execute the programs in
that directory, you may have simply spelled the directory name incorrectly
in the PATH command.

# Summary

This chapter introduced the basic concepts and procedures associated
with DOS. These concepts are essential because they define the environment in which the Norton Utilities operates.

**Disk Operating System**    Known as DOS, this program is used to control the basic operations of the computer system: start-up loader,
input/output management, memory management, storage management,
network management, user shell, and utilities. Many of the operations
performed by DOS take place in the background when applications such as
word processing or spreadsheets interact with DOS, in order to perform
basic tasks such as file storage and retrieval or printing. Users come into
direct contact with DOS when they issue commands to the DOS shell
program, COMMAND.COM, to perform tasks such as listing directories or
copying files. DOS also provides a set of utility programs that perform
tasks such as formatting disks.

**Booting**    DOS, like all programs, is erased from RAM memory when
the computer is turned off. When the computer system is turned on, a
special procedure called *start-up*, or commonly, *booting*, is initiated. This
process uses ROM, RAM, and disk files to bring the computer to the point
where DOS is in control of the computer's operations. Once the computer
is booted, the user can control the system by issuing commands through the
DOS shell to the operating system to run applications or utility programs.

**CONFIG.SYS**    As part of the booting process the computer will search the root directory of the boot disk for the optional CONFIG.SYS file. If found, the instructions contained in this file are used to configure DOS settings and load any additional device driver software needed to operate nonstandard devices, such as a mouse.

**AUTOEXEC.BAT**    This optional file is the last step in the booting process used to automatically execute a list of one or more DOS commands each time the system is booted. The system searches the root directory of the file and, if found, executes the DOS commands contained within it.

**Drives**    A drive is the largest unit of disk storage that refers to a single floppy or hard disk drive. Drives are assigned single letter designations, A–Z, starting with A and B as the first two floppy drives and C as the first hard disk in the system.

**Partitions**    Partitions are used to divide the storage space on a single physical hard disk into two or more logical drives, each with its own letter designation. Logical drives function as if they were individual disks. Partitions are used for organizational purposes and to overcome hard disk size limits that occur in DOS versions below 4.xx.

**Directories**    A directory is a logical unit of storage used to store groups of related files on a disk. Unlike partitions, directories have no fixed size or limits. Directories can also contain other directories, allowing you to create subsections within a given directory. Directories allow you to limit the number of files you have to deal with at any one time. Since hard disks can hold thousands of files, directories enable you to scale down file operations more to manageably sized groups.

**Files**    A file is the basic unit of storage in DOS. All data that are stored on a disk are stored in a disk *file*. Each file must have a unique name within the directory where it is stored.

**Path Name**    A path name is an extended form of the file name in which you can include the drive and directory location of the file. Path names allow you to access programs and files stored in different directories on the hard disk.

**Path**    The PATH command allows you to store in the computer's memory a list of directories that should be searched when a command is entered to run a program. DOS normally limits its search for programs to those that are located in the current disk directory. Search paths are very important for DOS and Norton Utilities program, since they are designed for use with many different directories.

# 4 Disk Organization: A Hands-on Exploration

The Norton Utilities programs provide a unique method of inspecting and analyzing the operations of your computer, when it comes to storing information on the disk. This means you can actually *see*—not just read about—how a disk is organized. Instead of discussing ideas of how a disk is used to store data, this section presents those ideas, using hands-on exploration. The purpose of this chapter is to learn the method by which information is stored on disk, under the DOS operating system. The structure used by DOS to accomplish this very important task lies at the heart of most of the functions of the Norton Utilities programs, in particular those that are concerned with recovery of lost, formatted, damaged, or erased data. While it is not absolutely necessary to understand the disk structure used by DOS in order to use the Norton Utilities, the information will make the Norton Utilities even more valuable since you will have a firm basis upon which to understand the features included in the programs.

## Formatting a Sample Disk

In order to learn about the DOS disk storage system, you will need to begin with a floppy disk. While most users are more concerned with their hard disks than with their floppies, floppy disks will exhibit all of the features of hard disks on a smaller scale. Using a floppy disk allows you to explore without running the risk of losing real data.

You will begin by formatting a disk and performing simple operations, such as copying files, deleting files, and using directories. However, in order to obtain a more concrete understanding of how DOS performs such tasks, you will use the Norton Utilities programs at each stage in the process, to examine in detail how the disk is changed. The Norton Utilities programs have unique features that enable you to analyze disks in great detail.

Most of the screens in this chapter will reflect the use of a 3.5" 720K diskette. For those users with a 1.2 megabyte 5.25" floppy disk, significant differences will be noted when necessary. The principles and concepts will apply to all disks, including those of hard disk drives.

## What Is Formatting?

If you have worked with computers for any length of time, you have probably learned how to *format* a disk. Formatting is required before a new disk, either hard or floppy, can be used to store data.

What actually takes place when you format a disk? The answer lies in the fact that formatting consists of two distinct operations:

**Low-level (Physical) Formatting.** The *low-level* or *physical* format is a process that establishes the basic structure used to store data on the disk. All disk storage is based on the use of small blocks of information called *sectors*. Most MS-DOS disks are structured so that bytes (characters) can be stored in each sector on the disk. The information placed on the disk as part of the low-level format is designed to be read and used by the hardware device that controls the disk drive, which is called the *disk controller*. Floppy drives and hard drives require different types of controllers although today it is common to find a single controller that contains the electronics needed to control several different types of hard and floppy disks. They allow the user more flexibility in installing different types of equipment.

Before any data can be placed on a disk, the disk must be organized by dividing the surface into a pattern of tracks and sectors, as seen in Figure 4–1. A *track* is a circle drawn on the disk. A floppy disk typically contains 40 (double density) or 80 (high density) tracks. Hard disks can have hundreds, sometimes over a thousand, tracks. The tracks are then divided into wedge-shaped areas called *sectors*. A floppy disk will typically have 9 sectors on each track. Hard disks typically have 17 sectors on each track.

The result of the low-level format is that the entire surface of the disk[1] is organized so that you can refer to any location on the disk by a unique

---

1.   A disk drive may use more than one disk surface to write data. Most floppy disk drives operate on both sides of the floppy disk, while hard disk drives may have several disk plates enclosed within the hard drive. Formatting creates the track and sector pattern on all usable disk surfaces.

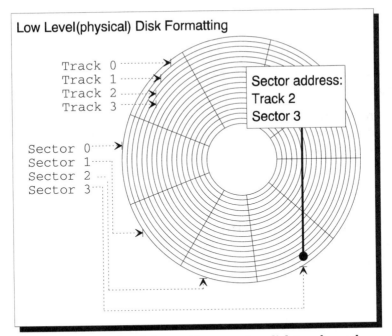

Low Level(physical) Disk Formatting

Track 0
Track 1
Track 2
Track 3

Sector address:
Track 2
Sector 3

Sector 0
Sector 1
Sector 2
Sector 3

**Figure 4–1. Low-level formatting creates disk tracks and sectors.**

track and sector *address*. For example, track 2 sector 3 refers to one specific area of the disk.[2] Sector addresses provide a means by which the computer can refer randomly to any block of data on the disk. This ability is crucial to making effective use of the disk storage space on the disk. The low-level format creates a *header* or *preamble* for each sector that store data needed by the hard disk controller. The header includes the sector address and the sync and gap bytes, which are used to position the disk drive heads correctly. It is important to note that low-level formatting is a destructive process. This means if you format a disk that already contains data, all that information will be erased as part of the formatting process.

**High-level** (Logical) **Formatting.** The second part of the format process is called the *logical* format. The purpose of the logical format is to

---

2.  If the drive contains more than one disk surface, each surface is also numbered. For example, a double-sided floppy disk would have sides 0 and 1. You would then have a sector address such as side 0 track 2 sector 3.

organize the disk sectors to work with the MS-DOS file system. In DOS, when information is saved as a file, the operating system records the name of the file, the date it was created, its size, any special attributes associated with that directory, and a list of data sector addresses used to store the file's contents.

In order to record this information, the logical formatting process creates a root directory for the disk and a file allocation table (FAT). The remainder of the disk space is organized as data clusters,[3] as shown in Figure 4–2.

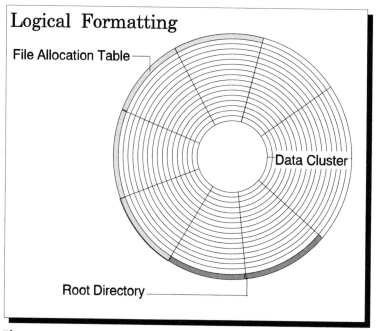

**Figure 4–2. Logical formatting establishes the root directory, the FAT, and data area.**

When the formatting process is complete, you have a disk that has all the structures needed to function as a DOS storage medium.

---

3. A data cluster consists of one or more disk sectors. The number of sectors per cluster differs with the DOS version and the type of disk.

## Safe Format

The first step is to create a blank, formatted disk. You should still be able to follow the steps if you make common sense adjustments, based on your system's configuration. Place a disk to be formatted in drive A. The disk should be a new disk, or one that contains data you no longer want to maintain. Instead of using the DOS Format program, you will use Norton Utilities *Safe Format*. Safe Format will perform the same basic task as the DOS Format program, but it includes a number of features and options that DOS does not. Start the Safe Format program by entering

```
sformat ↵
```

When the program loads, it will display the Safe Format dialog box in the center of the screen:

**Drive.**  This box lists the floppy drives available in the system.[4]

**Size.** This box lists the disk media sizes that can be used in the selected drive. For example, 1.2 megabyte disk drives can use 180K, 320K, 360K, and 1.2M capacity disks.

**System Files.**  This box allows you to select whether or not you want to have the DOS system files transferred to the disk. This option is used when you want to create a *bootable* floppy disk. A bootable disk is one that can be used to start up the computer once it has been turned off. System disks will be discussed in more detail later in this chapter.

**Format Mode.**  Unlike the DOS format command, the Safe Format program can perform disk formatting using several different methods, including the method used by DOS. This option allows you to select the method to use for the current disk.

**Volume Label.**  DOS allows you to add a descriptive label to each disk. This label has no function and is optional.

**Save IMAGE Info (5.0) /Save Unformat Info (6.0).**  When active, this option causes the program to save a disk *image*. The image can be used in conjunction with the Safe method of formatting to allow for the recovery

---

4.  By default the Safe Format program lists only the floppy drives. The Configure menu allows you to add hard drives to the drive list, if desired.

of data on disks that have been mistakenly formatted by means of the Unformat program. Note that the text of the prompt differs from Version 5.0 to 6.0, but the function is exactly the same.

Select the disk drive letter and size that is appropriate for your system. Move the highlight to the *Format Mode* option box by pressing the [Tab] key. In this dialog box select the **DOS** method for formatting the disk. The DOS method will automatically perform both a physical and logical format on the selected disk. By default, the Safe Format program uses the **Safe** method. Change the Format Mode to DOS by entering d.

In addition, turn off the **Save IMAGE Info** option by entering [Tab] [Tab] [space]. Begin the formatting process by entering ↵.

Because you have selected the DOS format method and turned off the IMAGE information function, the program displays a dialog box that warns you that the format process will destroy any existing data, beyond recovery even by the Norton Utilities. Continue to format the disk by entering ↵.

The formatting process now begins as the program displays a dialog box that contains information about the formatting process. This display also includes a bar that shows the percentage of the disk actually being formatted from moment to moment.[5] The box also shows the elapsed and estimated times for the formatting process.

On the right side of the box, information about the amount of disk space available is displayed. Space will be subtracted from the total if it is used for DOS system files (created when making a *bootable* disk) or bad space. *Bad space* results from flaws in the disk surface that prevent the program from accurately formatting that area of the disk. DOS works around bad space by marking those areas as unusable, allowing the rest of the good disk space to be used. At the end of the process a box with the message "Drive A: has been successfully Formatted" appears. Exit the format program by entering ↵ q.

---

5.  The display notes the number of *cylinders* and *heads* being formatted. A cylinder is a single track, e.g., track 0, on all the usable surfaces. Double-sided disks have two surfaces that the Norton Utilities refer to as *heads*. For example, to format cylinder 0, the program formats track 0 on side 0, then track 0 on side 1. Once complete, the program goes on to the next cylinder, e.g., cylinder 1, until the entire disk has been formatted.

# Disk Information

The floppy disk is now ready to be used. List a DOS directory of the disk. Enter dir a: ↵.

The information displayed by DOS, shown below, is quite sparse. There is very little useful information about the disk, its capacity, or its structure. Fortunately, the Norton Utilities provides a number of different ways to get information about disk:

**SYSINFO (System Information).**  As part of this program's abilities it provides detailed information about the structure and capacity of disks in the system.

**SPEEDISK (Speed Disk).**  The primary purpose of this program is to *fine-tune* the performance of the disk. As part of this process, the program displays information about the usage of space on the specified disk.

**DISKEDIT (Disk Editor).**  This program is a very powerful tool that allows you to display or change virtually any item of information stored on the disk.

Together, these three programs greatly expand what you can learn about a disk, its structure, and its usage.

## Disk Characteristics (SYSINFO)

The SYSINFO program provides detailed information about many different parts of your system. Here, you are interested in what SYSINFO can tell you about the disk you have just formatted. Execute the SYSINFO program by entering sysinfo ↵.

The SYSINFO program displays its initial display screen called *System Summary*. In this case you are interested in information about the disk in drive A. You can obtain that information from the **Disk Characteristics** option listed on the *Disks* menu. Enter [Alt-d] c. The display changes to reveal the **Disk Characteristics** screen. On the right side of the display is a box that lists all the drives in the system. Move the highlight to drive A, the drive that contains the disk you have just formatted, by entering [Home]. The screen shows information about the floppy disk in drive A; divided into three major areas:

**Size.** This box displays the capacity of the disk in K (kilobytes) or M (megabytes).

**Logical Characteristics.** This box displays a description of the *logical* structure of the disk. The logical structure was created during the high-level portion of the format process. This is the most complicated part of the display because it deals with a number of special structures that DOS maintains on the disk.

**Physical Characteristics.** This box displays information about the *physical* structure of the disk that describes the disk in terms of its basic, physical elements: sides, tracks, and sectors.

## Physical Characteristics

The **Physical Characteristics** portion of the **Disk Characteristics** lists three items that describe the effect of formatting on the disk, as in Figure 4–3. Recall that formatting creates the basic structure, a type of grid, that divides the disk surface into areas in which blocks of data can be stored:

**Sides.** This value reflects the number of disk surfaces that were format-ted. On floppy disks this number is either 1 or 2, corresponding to the top and bottom sides of the disk. On hard disks the number of sides will increase, since hard disk drives usually contain more than one actual disk platter in order to increase the total amount of disk space available.

**Tracks.** This value shows the total number of tracks drawn on each disk surface.[6]

**Sectors.** This value is the number of sectors each track is divided into.

If you multiply these values you can arrive at the total number of sectors on the disk. For example, a 720K capacity 3.5" floppy disk contains 9 sectors per track, 80 tracks, and 2 sides:

$9 \times 80 \times 2 = 1,440$

---

6.  In this case, the total number of tracks is also the total number of *cylinders*, since all the disk surfaces will have the same number of tracks. Recall that a cylinder refers to all the same tracks, e.g., track 0, on all disk surfaces. If a drive has 6 sides, then cylinder 0 is composed of track 0 on sides 0 through 5.

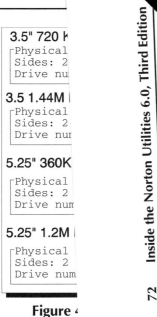

**3.5" 720 K**

⌐Physical
Sides: 2
Drive nu

**3.5 1.44M**

⌐Physical
Sides: 2
Drive nur

**5.25" 360K**

⌐Physical
Sides: 2
Drive num

**5.25" 1.2M**

⌐Physical
Sides: 2
Drive num

**Figure**

The *sector* is the basic unit of stora
sector is determined when the di
512 bytes, although DOS can s
is the smallest unit of stora
tures are composed of o
The last item in th
drive number is a b
number is used
vices. Knowi
are writin
to the N

If you look at _____ ___ ___, you will see that each sector contains 512 bytes. If you multiply the number of sectors by the number of bytes in each sector, you will arrive at the total capacity of the disk.

$$1{,}440 \times 512 = 737{,}280$$

The value you produce with this calculation, 737,280, may seem at odds with the designation of 720K as the capacity of the disk. However, you can resolve this apparent anomaly if you recall that K stands for 1,024 bytes—not an even 1,000—even though the metric system defines *kilo* as 1,000. Divide the total bytes by the K (kilobyte) unit, 1,024, to arrive at the total capacity in K.

$$737{,}280 / 1{,}024 = 720$$

Your analysis of the physical structure of the disk confirms the total capacity. Note that a 1.44M floppy disk differs from the 720K disk in that it can hold twice as many sectors (18) on each track. Doubling the number of sectors doubles the capacity of the disk, given that the sides and tracks remain the same.

...ge on a disk. In MS-DOS, the size of the
...sk is formatted. In most cases, that size is
...upport other sector sizes, as well.[7] The sector
...ge on the disk. This means all other disk struc-
...e or more disk sectors.

...e **Physical Characteristic** box is *Drive number.* The
...exidecimal value assigned to each physical device. This
... by programs to make references to specific physical de-
...g this number is usually not important to users unless they
... programs that perform very low-level disk operations (similar
...orton Utilities).

## Logical Characteristics

The *logical* characteristics provide information about the structures created by the *high-level* format. The high-level format takes the basic side,
track, and sector layout of a formatted disk, and builds the logical structures needed for the DOS filing system. Figure 4–4 shows typical displays
for both a 3.5" 720K and a 5.25" 1.2M floppy disk.

---

7. Large capacity hard disks, over 100 megabytes, may use larger sector sizes, e.g., 4,096
   bytes per sector, to increase storage capacity while increasing the number of sectors on
   the disk.

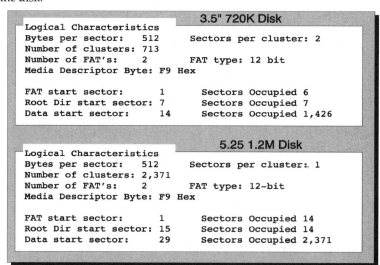

Figure 4–4. Logical characteristics for 3.5" and 5.25" disks.

The information on this screen looks very technical and forbidding. However, with a little effort you can decipher this data and begin to get an idea of how DOS goes about organizing a disk.

## Logical versus Physical Disk Organization

The physical organization of disks is a three-dimensional system. You can indicate the location of any sector by using the head, side, and sector number. For example, head 0, side 1, sector 5 would be the 5th sector on the bottom side(1) of the first disk platter(0). However, handling a three-dimensional system can be complicated. In order to simplify disk operations, DOS uses a one-dimensional system in which all of the sectors on all of the disk sides are simply numbered consecutively starting with sector 0, which is the first sector on the first side of the first disk.

This approach makes it much simpler to refer to any sector because each disk sector is assigned a unique number. The disadvantage is that the larger the number of sectors on a disk, the more digits will be needed to number all of the sector. DOS uses sector numbers that are limited to 16 bits. The largest value that can be represented by a 16 bit binary number is 65,536; i.e., 2 to the 16th power.

In practical terms this means that DOS cannot keep track of more than 65,536 disk sectors. If each sector contains 512 bytes, this places the upper limit on disk size at 65,536 times 512 = 33,554,432 bytes or 32 megabytes. Thus, DOS through Version 3.xx limits any single logical drive to 32 megabytes. DOS 4.xx solves this problem by allowing 32 bit sector addresses.

## The System Area

The best way to approach the information contained in the **Disk Characteristics** box is to skip over the first section and start with the bottom three lines of information, beginning with the *FAT start sector* item. These lines describe the effect that the high-level format had on the disk. The high-level portion of the format process allocated a small number of disk sectors to serve as the *system area* of the disk. This **system area** consists of three parts:

**Boot Sector.**  The first sector on every disk is reserved for the storage of information that will identify the disk to the operating system. Coded into the boot sector is information that tells the operating system such basic information as the disk type and number of bytes per sector. The boot sector is *always* stored in the first sector on the disk.

**Root Directory.**   The root directory is used to store the names of the files and any user directories stored on the disk.

**File Allocation Table (FAT).**   The *File Allocation Table* is used to connect the file names stored in the root directory with the data storage area. The table keeps track of which sectors in the data area belong to which files listed in the directory.

These three items are called the *system area* because the sectors they occupy cannot be used to store data or program files. The system area uses about 1 percent of the sectors on a floppy disk, and slightly less than 1 percent on a hard disk.

Even though the system area is but a small part of the disk as compared to the data storage space, it is critical to the operation of the disk as an effective data storage medium for the computer. It is only with the use of these system areas, in particular the directory and the FAT, that DOS can keep track of the actual locations on the disk where data related to specific program or data files are stored.

When a command requires DOS to retrieve data from a file stored on the disk, a three-step process takes place. For example, suppose you enter the DOS command **TYPE READ.ME**. The **TYPE** command displays the contents of text files on the screen. DOS goes through the following steps:

1.   **Search Directory.**   In order to carry out the **TYPE** command, DOS must first locate the file name that is specified, in this case READ.ME, in the disk directory. If the name cannot be found, the command is terminated with an error message.

2.   **Find Data Locations in FAT.**   If the file name is found, the directory entry tells DOS the place in the File Allocation Table (FAT) where further details about the file's data are stored.

3.   **Read Data.**   The FAT contains the exact locations of the disk where DOS can find the data that belong to the specified file. Note that the FAT is designed to accommodate files of any size. This means a file can be stored in one or more places in the data area of the disk.

The last three lines of the **Disk Characteristics** box show the actual number of sectors on the disk allocated for FAT, the root directory, and the data area. Note that as the total amount of disk space increases, the size of the FAT and root directories also increases. In order to utilize larger disk capacity, DOS must have sufficient space in the directory and FAT to account for all the sectors on the disk. Later in this chapter you will use the Disk Editor program to examine the actual directory and FAT on the disk, as files are added and erased.

If you look at the first four lines of the **Logical Characteristics** you will see the information DOS obtains by reading the data stored in the boot sector of the disk. The boot sector information is stored during the formatting process. It allows DOS to identify the structure of the disk. The type of disk is identified by the *Media Descriptor Byte*. This byte is a single hexidecimal value stored in the boot sector of the disk. One benefit of this approach is that DOS can use different types of disks in the same drive. For example, a high-density 5.25" drive can use 160K, 180K, 320K, 360K, or 1.2M floppy disks. This byte identifies the type of disk and shows the hex values used to indicate the disk type.

## Clusters

The **Logical Characteristics** box introduces a new and very important term to the discussion of disk structure, *clusters*. Recall that the high-level formatting divides the disk into two basic areas: system and data. The system area is composed of the boot sector, the FAT, and the root directory. The data area is organized into units called clusters. Why is it necessary to have another unit called a cluster when the data area is already divided into *sectors*?

The answer reveals an inherent weakness in the way disks are structured, and the sort of trade-offs involved in solving the problem. In order for DOS to locate information stored on the disk, a log must be maintained on the disk showing the usage of each sector. This is true even of empty sectors, since DOS needs to know where to put new information added to the disk, without overwriting existing data. If disk sectors alone were used as the basic unit of storage, DOS would have to account for each individual sector on the disk, e.g., 1,426 sectors on a 720K would require 1,426 entries. The task becomes even more formidable when you apply the system to hard disk drives with capacities in the tens or hundreds of millions of bytes. For example, a small hard disk, 20 megabytes, would have 41,620 data sectors.

The benefit of large disks with huge numbers of sectors is that you can store huge amounts of data. However, increasing the number of disk sectors has a negative side. The more individual units for which DOS must account can slow down the performance of the system. In order to provide DOS with some flexibility, the system relies not on individual sectors but on an intermediate unit called a *cluster*. A cluster is simply a unit formed by one or more adjacent sectors. For example, if each data cluster contained two sectors, you would cut in half the number of units for which DOS had to keep track. Using four or eight sectors per cluster would reduce that number even further.

It is important to realize that increasing the cluster size also has a negative effect. This effect is called *slack* space. Note that disk space, whether it is organized in sectors or clusters, uses a fixed number of bytes in each unit. However, it is unlikely that when you create a program or data file, it contains the exact number of bytes matching the size of the data clusters. In most cases, a file will end in the middle of a data cluster leaving some space at the end of the cluster empty. In Figure 4–5, a diagram shows how slack space occurs. The file being stored fills up the first two clusters completely, but the end of the file falls in the middle of the third cluster. The slack space is the remainder of the third cluster.

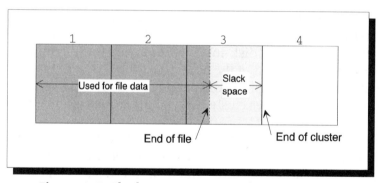

**Figure 4–5. Slack space occurs at the end of a file.**

Slack space is significant because data clusters are allocated on an all-or-nothing basis. Even if the file requires only a single byte of space in a given cluster, the entire cluster is allocated to that file. In other words, the cluster size determines the minimum allocation unit of data storage on the disk. Slack space is space that is not actually used by a file but is allocated to it because allocations for data are made on a cluster-by-cluster basis. Slack space is wasted space because it cannot be allocated to a different file, since DOS does not permit the allocation of partial data clusters.

The fixed length sector and cluster system make some slack space inevitable; however, the larger the cluster size, the more slack space you are likely to create. A small cluster size minimizes the slack space at the cost of performance. The actual amount of slack space on a given disk is also determined by the types of files you choose to store. Slack space will increase when you store a number of small files, e.g., single page word processing documents, since each file is likely to have some slack space. Conversely, storing a few large files, such as large database files, will minimize the amount of slack space since only the last cluster in each file is subject to slack.

In the end, the high-level format must seek a compromise between the two incompatible goals of maximizing capacity and performance. The most common cluster size on double-sided floppy disks is two sectors because the disk has two sides, although the format of 1.2M floppy disks use one sector per cluster, making the sector and cluster size identical. DOS will format hard disks with four sector cluster sizes, making each cluster 2,048 bytes.[8]

With an understanding of what a cluster is, you can now discern what the **Logical Characteristics** box is telling you. For example, the first line of a 3.5", 720K disk displays *Bytes per sector* as 512 (DOS standard), *Sectors per cluster* as 2, and the total number of data clusters on the disk as *713*. Multiplication can then calculate the amount of *file* storage space available in the disk:

$$512 \times 2 \times 713 = 730,112$$

The last part of the **Disk Characteristics** display shows information about the structure of the FAT. DOS disks actually have two copies of the FAT stored on each disk. Since the FAT is crucial to linking file names to their contents stored in data clusters, having an additional copy on the disk seems like a prudent safeguard. DOS supports both 12-bit and 16-bit FAT tables. You will learn more about the exact structure of the FAT later in this chapter. Exit the SYSINFO program by entering [Alt-q]. The program terminates and returns you to the DOS prompt.

---

8.  DOS 2.0 created 4,096 size data clusters. Later versions reduced the cluster size to 2,048. Non-DOS disk managers, such as Disk Manager from On Tack or SpeedStor, will create disk partitions with larger sector or cluster sizes than would be created by the DOS Format program.

# Examining the Disk

The SYSINFO program provided a summary of the structure of the disk. In the next section, you will use the Disk Editor program to examine directly the parts of the disk to which the SYSINFO referred. You will then perform simple operations, such as copying a file to the disk or erasing a file from the disk, to see the effect it has on the disk structure. Begin by loading the Disk Edit program, DISKEDIT. Since you know that the disk you want to examine is in drive A, you can have the program automatically read this disk by adding **A:** as a parameter to the DISKEDIT command. Enter **diskedit a:** ↵.

When the program is loaded it displays a dialog box that tells you the program is operating in the read-only mode. The read-only mode is a safety precaution that prevents you from making changes to the disk while you are examining it. Since the Disk Editor can potentially damage a disk, it is best to operate in the read-only mode until you need to use the Disk Editor to make those changes you are sure about. Continue by entering ↵.

The program completes its examination of the disk in drive A. The program then displays the root directory of the disk, using a special display mode. The directory displays a number of different items of information about each file:

**Filename.**   This is the 1–8 character name used for the file.

**Extension.**   This is the optional 1–3 character file extension.

**Size in Bytes.**   This is the size, in bytes, of the file.

**Date & Time.**   Date and time are taken from the system's clock at the time a file is created or modified. Note that when a file is copied, DOS writes the original date and time, not the date and time when the file was copied.

**Cluster.**   This is the number of the *first* cluster of the file. Since most files contain more than one cluster, the location of the other clusters associated with a given file is stored in another area of the disk, called the File Allocation Table (FAT).

**Attributes.**   Each file can be assigned one or more attributes. The attributes are **Archive**, **read-only**, **system**, **hidden**, **directory**, or **volume** label:

   **Archive.**   This attribute is designed to work with the BACKUP, RE-STORE, and XCOPY commands. It helps these commands select files that have never been backed up. All new files on a disk are automatically set with their Archive attribute **on.** The attribute is removed by BACKUP or XCOPY to indicate that the files have been backed up.

**R**ead-**O**nly.   This attribute can be used to prevent changing or over-writing a file. It is also used on networks to allow file sharing. Note that read-only files appear in directory listings but cannot be modified or erased. DOS displays the "Access denied" message if such an attempt is made.

**Sys**tem.   Used to designate a file as a system file. These files do not appear in DOS directory listings.

**Hid**den.   Used to suppress the display of a file in the DOS directory listing.

**Dir**ectory.   Indicates the entry is a user-defined directory, not a data file, created with the **MD** (make directory) command.

**Vol**ume label.   Indicates the entry is the disk volume label, not a data file.

Since the disk was just formatted, the directory does not contain any file names or other data. The program displays the message "Unused directory entry" in each slot available for a file name entry.

## Root Directory Capacity

How many files can the root directory hold? You can use the Disk Editor to calculate the total amount of files that the root directory can hold.

Note that the directory display shows the individual sectors used to hold the root directory. On a 3.5", 720K disk the first sector for the root directory is sector 7. On a 1.2M floppy disk the sector would be sector 15.

Use the down arrow to move the highlight to the first entry in the next sector: ↓ (press 16 times).

Since it took 16 keystrokes to move the highlight, you can conclude that there is room for 16 file names in each sector of the root directory. But to answer the question about the total capacity of the root directory, you need to know the number of sectors allocated to it. You may recall that this information is part of the information displayed in the SYSINFO program.

However, there is no need to remember this information because the Disk Editor will display it on the *Info* menu. Enter [Alt-i]. Choose the **Object Info** option by entering o (the letter O). The *object* in this case is the root directory. The program displays a dialog box that shows a summary that lists the sectors used for the root directory (7–13 on 3.5" 720K and 15–28 on 5.25" 1.2M) and the maximum number of entries (112 or 224, respectively). If you divide the sectors used by the maximum number of entries, you will confirm the fact that each sector can hold 16 directory entries.

112/7  =16 (3.5" 720K)
224/14 =16 (5.25" 1.2M)

A typical hard disk will have a 32-sector directory that can hold 512 file names (32 times 16). The root directory of any disk is limited to the total number of files. Are you surprised that there is a limit to the number of files the root directory can hold? After all, a hard disk can hold more than 512 files. The solution will be explained when you look at how user-defined directories can be added to a disk.

Return to the directory display by entering ↵.

## The Boot Sector (Record)

The next part of the disk you will examine is the boot sector or boot record. Recall that the boot sector is the first sector on the disk. During the format process DOS writes into this sector a description of the structure of the disk. When DOS encounters this disk, it learns about its structure by reading the data stored in the boot sector.

To display the boot sector of the current disk, use the *Object* menu. Enter [Alt-o] (the letter O).

Select the **Boot Record** option by entering b.

The screen changes to display the information stored in the boot sector. Note that this screen is not the raw information stored on the disk but a translation of that information that is easy to read and understand. The display consists of three columns. The first is a description of the meaning of the item, e.g., bytes per sector or sectors per cluster. This information is roughly the same as the information displayed by SYSINFO with the exception of the *OEM ID*. The OEM ID is a label placed on the disk at the time of formatting. In this case, IBM PNCI (IBM Peter Norton Computing Incorporated) was written into the boot sector during the formatting process. Other OEM IDs, such as MS-DOS 3.3 or IBM 4.0, are placed into the boot sector when the Format program with those DOS versions is used instead of the Safe Format program included with the Norton Utilities. The OEM ID has no function and is not read by DOS as part of its disk identification.

## The Hex View

The Disk Editor program displays the information stored in the boot sector in a way that is the easiest to understand. But the screen you see does not reflect how information is actually stored on a disk. You change the display so you can see a byte-by-byte representation of the way the data are actually coded onto the disk. This is called the *Hex* view because the bytes are displayed as hexidecimal numbers. Change the view by entering [Alt-v] h.

The Hex display is quite different from the boot sector display. At the top of the display is the sector number, in this case, O. The remainder of the display is split into two sections: the hexidecimal display and the character symbol display. The hex portion consists of hexidecimal numbers that correspond on a one-to-one basis with the bytes on the disk. The character symbol display on the right side shows the screen character symbol that corresponds to the hex value. For example, as shown in Figure 4–6, the hex value *49* corresponds to screen character *I*, *42* corresponds to *B*, and so on. Note that many of the hex values correspond to graphic symbols so that the character symbol display doesn't make any sense if you try to read it as text. Other portions of the boot sector contain information that can be read according to its character symbols. For example, you will notice that messages such as "This is not a bootable…" are stored in the boot sector.

The column of numbers on the far left shows the *offset* number of the first hex value on the line. The byte offset is the distance of each byte in the

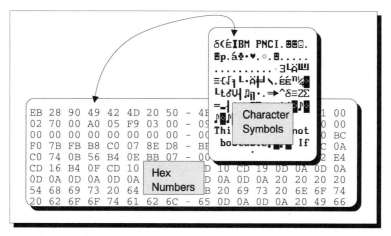

**Figure 4–6. Hex display shows hex values and corresponding screen character symbols.**

sector from the beginning. For example, the first byte, *EB*, is offset *O*, since it is at the beginning of the sector. The next byte, *28*, is offset *1*, and so on. The offset concept provides a system by which you can refer to specific bytes by their position within the sector. Also note that in the lower-right corner of the screen the offset location of the cursor highlight is recorded. In this corner the sector number is displayed along with the offset value in decimal and then hex numbers.[9]

In order to understand what the hex values say about the disk, you need to have a guide that tells you the significance of each value or group of values. As an example of how to read boot sector values, begin with offsets 11 and 12. You can locate offset 11 by using the → right arrow key, until the value in the offset indicator (lower-right corner of the screen) reads 11. Enter → right arrow (press 8 times).

The values in offsets 11 and 12 are two digits, *00* and *02*. The digits represent the number of bytes in each disk sector.

```
EB 28 90 49 42 4D 20 50 - 4E 43 49 00 02 02 01 00
```

The digits are interpreted as a single hex number. When this is done, the order of the digits is *reversed* so that the number of bytes in a sector is *0200* in hex.

You may wonder why it is that the number *0200* is used, and not *0002*, since byte 11 was 00 and byte 12 was 02. The answer has to do with the way values are traditionally read from the disk. When a value is composed of two bytes, it is called a *word*. The first byte is called the low-order byte, while the second is called the high-order byte. This is backwards from the human point of view, since we tend to write numbers beginning with the highest place values on the left and the lowest place values on the right. However, computers cannot read with the same visual ability of humans. Humans learn to read text from left to right, but numbers from right to left. Computers read data sequentially, in one direction only. By convention, the place value of the digits is stored left to right. When you interpret the data, you need to remember to reverse the order to the way humans are trained to read numbers.

Translated to decimal value, 0200 is 2 times 256 or 512, which is exactly the value shown in the SYSINFO program display. The next byte, offset 13, is used by itself to indicate the sectors used to form a data cluster. In this

---

9. Recall from Chapter 2 that hex numbers 0–9 are the same as decimal numbers 0–9. The difference comes with numbers greater than 9, e.g., the decimal number 10 is the hex number A.

case, the value is *02*. This tells you that 2 of the 512-byte sectors are used for the data cluster. Once again, this matches the information displayed previously by the program.

While converting the hex value to a decimal value is a bit complicated, the Disk Editor provides a shortcut in the form of a Hex Convertor found on the *Tools* menu. Enter [Alt-t] h.

The program displays a special dialog box that functions as a conversion calculator. Enter the hex value 0200 into the Hex entry box.

The Decimal box shows the value 512. The hex converter simplifies working with hex values. Remove the dialog box from the screen by entering [Esc].

Move the highlight to offset 21 by entering → right arrow (press 10 times).

This byte is the disk type ID, F9. You have examined the boot sector of the disk using the Disk Editor. Exit the program by entering [Alt-q].

## Files

You have examined the structure of an empty disk. The next step is to place some data on this disk and see exactly how the structure changes to accommodate the data. Begin by copying the READ.ME file, supplied with the Norton Utilities, onto drive A.

Enter copy \nu\read.me a: ↵.

Copy two more files to drive A:

```
copy \nu\trouble.hlp a: ↵ copy \nu\image.exe a: ↵
```

List a directory of the disk using the DOS **DIR** command: dir a: ↵. The directory listing shows the three files copied to the floppy disk.

Reload the Disk Editor by entering diskedit a: ↵ ↵.

When the program is loaded, the Disk Editor displays the root directory of the disk once again, as seen in Figure 4–7. This time the display shows that the first three slots in sector 7 (sector 15 on 1.2M disks) contain entries for the files copied to the disk. The entries are written in the order in which they were copied to the disk. This means that DOS does not attempt to organize directory listings by alphabetical or other logical criteria. Placement in a directory is on a first-come, first-serve basis.

The Disk Editor display shows some additional information about the files on the disk, as compared to the DOS directory listing. First, the display shows the starting cluster number of each file: 2, 24, and 66 for 3.5", 720K

```
Name       .Ext     Size     Date      Time      Cluster Arc R/O Sys Hid Dir Vol
Sector 7
READ       ME       22505   9-25-90   5:00 pm        2   Arc
TROUBLE    HLP      42165   9-25-90   5:00 pm       24   Arc
IMAGE      EXE      12168   9-25-90   5:00 pm       66   Arc
           Unused directory entry
           Unused directory entry
           Unused directory entry
           Unused directory entry
```

**Figure 4–7. Disk Editor directory display.**

disks; or 2, 42, and 129 for 5.25", 1.2M disks. The screen also indicates that all three files have the **Arc**hive attribute.

As with the boot sector display, the directory display is not the actual raw data on the disk, but rather a convenient way to read the data. To see the actual raw structure of a directory, change the display to the *hex* mode. The [F2] key is a shortcut command for the hex mode display. Enter [F2].

The hex display shows the actual values of the individual bytes stored in the directory sector of the disk. Recall that you calculated earlier that each sector could hold 16 file entries. Since each sector contains 512 bytes, you can find the size of each directory entry by dividing 512 by 16.

512 / 16 = 32

Each directory entry consists of exactly 32 bytes of information. In terms of the way the information is displayed on the Disk Editor screen, each directory entry takes up two lines. For example, the directory entry for the READ.ME file uses the first two lines of the display in both the hex value side and the character symbol side, as in Figure 4–8.

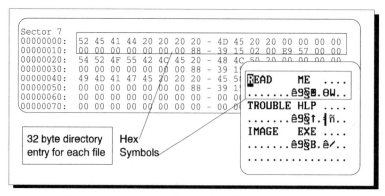

**Figure 4–8. Hex view of a directory entry.**

Each directory entry consists of 32 bytes. The bytes are organized in the following manner:

**Table 4–1. Directory entry byte usage.**

| Byte Offset | Meaning |
|---|---|
| 0–7 | file name |
| 8–10 | file extension |
| 11 | file attributes |
| 12–21 | reserved for DOS |
| 22–23 | time |
| 24–25 | date |
| 26–27 | starting data cluster |
| 28–31 | file size |

The structure of the directory entry shows why DOS files are limited to short file names. The reason is simply that DOS only allocates 11 bytes for the storage of the file name.

Return to the directory style display by entering [F4].

## The File Allocation Table

The 32-byte directory entry for each file contained the cluster number of the first cluster used to store the information associated with the file. But what about the rest of the data? A file the size of READ.ME, 22,505 bytes, would require more than 20 data clusters. How does DOS know where the rest of the data are stored? The answer is through the information stored in the *File Allocation Table*, known simply as the *FAT*. Recall that the FAT was one of the structures created at the time the disk was formatted. The FAT is an interesting solution to a complicated problem. When a file is stored on a disk, it can use one or more data clusters. In order to retrieve the file, you need to know two things:

Which clusters contain the data you want?
In what order should the clusters be read?

As a disk has files of varying sizes added, removed, shortened, or length-ened, the job of keeping track of what sequence of clusters contains the data from each file gets more complex. The problem is solved in the FAT by using a system of *pointers*. A pointer is a value that indicates the location of another value. The pointer system works like a cross-reference in a book in which you are referred to a different page for more information on the same subject. Each FAT value tells DOS which data cluster contains the *next* section of file.

The Disk Editor program provides a special mode that displays the information in the FAT, in a way that is easy to understand. Display the FAT by entering [Alt-o] 1.

The screen shows a new form of data display, as seen in Figure 4–9.

The FAT space actually contains two copies of the FAT in the FAT area of

| Object | Edit | Link | View | Info | Tools | Quit | F1=Help |
|---|---|---|---|---|---|---|---|
| Sector 1 | | | | | | | |
| | | 3 | 4 | 5 | 6 | 7 | 8 |
| 9 | 10 | 11 | 12 | 13 | 14 | 15 | 16 |
| 17 | 18 | 19 | 20 | 21 | 22 | 23 | 24 |
| 25 | 26 | 27 | 28 | 29 | 30 | 31 | 32 |
| 33 | 34 | 35 | <EOF> | 37 | 38 | 39 | 40 |
| 41 | 42 | 43 | 44 | 45 | 46 | 47 | 48 |
| 49 | 50 | 51 | 52 | 53 | 54 | 55 | 56 |
| 57 | 58 | 59 | 60 | 61 | 62 | 63 | 64 |
| 65 | 66 | 67 | 68 | 69 | 70 | 71 | 72 |
| 73 | 74 | 75 | 76 | 77 | 78 | 79 | 80 |
| 81 | 82 | 83 | 84 | 85 | 86 | 87 | 88 |
| 89 | 90 | 91 | 92 | 93 | 94 | 95 | 96 |
| 97 | 98 | 99 | 100 | 101 | 102 | 103 | 104 |
| 105 | 106 | 107 | 108 | 109 | 110 | 111 | 112 |
| 113 | 114 | 115 | 116 | 117 | 118 | 119 | 120 |
| 121 | 122 | 123 | 124 | 125 | 126 | 127 | 128 |
| 129 | 130 | 131 | 132 | 133 | 134 | 135 | 136 |
| 137 | 138 | 139 | 140 | 141 | <EOF> | 143 | 144 |
| 145 | 146 | 147 | 148 | 149 | 150 | 151 | 152 |
| 153 | 154 | 155 | 156 | 157 | 158 | 159 | 160 |
| FAT (1st Copy) | | | | | | Sector 1 | |
| A:\READ.ME | | | | | | Cluster 2, hex 2 | |
| Press ALT or F10 to select menus | | | | | | Disk Editor | |

**Figure 4–9. Disk Editor FAT display.**

the disk. DOS uses only the first copy of the FAT to locate data. In general, DOS utilities do not make use of this second copy, but some of the Norton Utilities programs do. The main Norton Utilities program allows you to display and edit both copies of the FAT. In some cases, you can recover files by copying data from the second copy into the first copy.

This display is used to show the data stored in the FAT of the disk. The meaning of the FAT is not as simple to pick up as the directory. In order to make sense out of the FAT display, you need to understand how it works.

The FAT consists of a series of values. The program displays these values in rows. In the FAT there is *one value* for each of the *data clusters* on the disk. The values in the FAT can be one of three types:

1.  **Zero.** If the FAT shows a zero it indicates that the data cluster is not in use by the file. This indicates the locations on the disk where new data can be added.

2.  **Value.** If the FAT entry contains a value, it indicates two things. First, the value tells DOS that this cluster is in use by a file. Second, it points out the next data cluster that belongs to the same file.

3.  **EOF.** EOF stands for "end of file." This marker indicates that this cluster is used by a file and that it is the last cluster in the file. The <EOF> symbol also stands for "end of file."

To understand the FAT you need to understand how the *pointer* system works. The significance of each value in the table depends upon its position in the table.

As an example, look at the first value that appears in the FAT display. The first value is 3. If you look at the lower-right corner of the display, it shows *Cluster 2, hex 2*. The display indicates that the currently highlighted value represents the usage of data cluster 2. Because the entry for cluster 2 is a value greater than zero, you can conclude that cluster 2 is in use by one of the files on the disk.

The exact value contained in position 2 in the table is 3. This value indicates the location of the *next data cluster* for the same file. The 3 stipulates that the next cluster in the file is *data cluster 3*.

The 3 also has a second meaning. It specifies where in the table you need to look to find what cluster comes after 3.

When DOS reads the data starting in position 2 in the table, it interprets the information in the following way:

1.  Read the data in cluster 2.

2.  Look at the value in the current position in the FAT. In this case, that value is 3.

3.  Read the information stored in the cluster that corresponds to the value in the FAT. In this example the value is 3, so that DOS reads disk cluster 3.

4.  Move to the position in the table that corresponds to the cluster number. In this example the value is 3, so that DOS moves to position 3 in the FAT.

The steps repeat until DOS reaches a FAT entry with an *<EOF>*, end of file symbol. The FAT works by daisy-chaining together all the related data clusters. Note that not only does this system specify *which* clusters are needed, it also specifies the *sequence* in which they are to be assembled.

The end of file is clearly marked in the FAT, but how does DOS know where to find the beginning of a file in the table? Recall that the beginning cluster for each file is specified in the directory display.

The current FAT is organized sequentially. Each position points to the next position in the table. But this does not have to be the case. The advantage of the FAT scheme is that it can be used to connect any of the disk clusters in any order. This makes it possible to store files in fragmented sections scattered throughout the disk. The FAT makes it possible to add, remove, expand, and contract files, while still making use of all clusters on the disk.

## How FAT Information Is Stored

The FAT display mode makes it easy to read and understand the FAT table. However, like all disk data, the FAT is really a collection of binary values. You can display the actual values in hex format, by using the [F2] key to activate the hex display mode. Enter [F2].

The Norton Utilities program displays the FAT in hex view, showing the values as they are actually stored on the disk. The meaning of values shown in the hex mode is much harder to grasp than the values displayed in the FAT mode display. The hex view of the FAT is much more complicated to read than the directory because the table is organized in groups of *bits* rather than *bytes*. DOS uses two types of FAT structures: 12-bit and 16-bit. Since *eight bits* make up *one byte*, the 16-bit structure falls neatly into two-byte pairs. But the 16-bit tables are used on high-capacity hard disks primarily in an extended DOS partition. Most floppy disks, like the one in the example, have a 12-bit structure. The Norton Utilities makes it unnecessary to decode the complicated 12-bit structure; however, it might be interesting to try to decode some of the FAT displayed on the screen.

Unlike the directory, the FAT begins with three values that act as identification of the disk format. The first part of the actual file allocation table begins at *offset 3*. The 12-bit FAT table is not easy to decode because it is meant to be read by the computer's microprocessor, which stores data in special areas called *registers*. The format that is most efficient for the microprocessor is not necessarily the easiest for a human to decode.

As an example, take the first three bytes of the FAT, shown in Figure 4–10, *03 40 00*. DOS uses a special pattern to derive the actual cluster numbers from these three bytes, as shown in Figure 4–10.

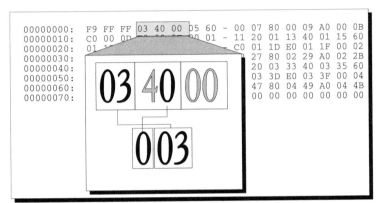

```
00000000:  F9 FF FF 03 40 00 05 60 - 00 07 80 00 09 A0 00 0B
00000010:  C0 00 0D             00 01 - 11 20 01 13 40 01 15 60
00000020:  01                     C0 01 1D E0 01 1F 00 02
00000030:                         27 80 02 29 A0 02 2B
00000040:                         20 03 33 40 03 35 60
00000050:                         03 3D E0 03 3F 00 04
00000060:                         47 80 04 49 A0 04 4B
00000070:                         00 00 00 00 00 00 00
```

**Figure 4–10. How DOS calculates the cluster number in a 12-bit FAT.**

1.  The process begins by taking the first byte, *03*.

2.  Next, the second digit of the second byte, *0*, is placed in front of the first byte, *03*.

The result is the hex value *003*, which is the same as the decimal value 3. This is the same number that the Disk Editor showed in the FAT display mode. If you want to follow this process to the next step, you can see that taking the first digit of the second byte, *4*, and preceding it with the last byte, *00*, calculates the value *004*—also 4 in decimal—which is the correct value for the second position in the FAT.

This complicated system works quite well on the microprocessor level and maximizes the amount of information that can be placed into the file allocation table area. This is important because the file allocation table determines the number of data clusters that you can have on a disk. A 12-bit table will limit the largest cluster number to FFF hex, 4095 decimal. In a 16-bit FAT, that value rises to FFFF hex, 65,535 decimal. Currently, DOS supports a maximum of 65,535 data clusters on a hard disk.

## Looking at a Data Cluster

One of the most powerful features of the Disk Editor program is that you can display the actual contents of files. You can locate files logically (by selecting their file names from a list) or directly (by selecting clusters by number). In this case, select the starting cluster of the READ.ME file, cluster 2. Display the *Object* menu by entering [Alt-o].

Select **Cluster** by entering c.

Display cluster #2 by entering 2 ↵.

The Disk Editor shows the information contained in data cluster 2, as seen in Figure 4–11. Disk Editor will display data clusters in one of two ways: hex mode or text mode. The program picks the mode that is most appropriate to the actual information contained within the cluster. Here, since the READ.ME file contains text, the display is automatically set as text.

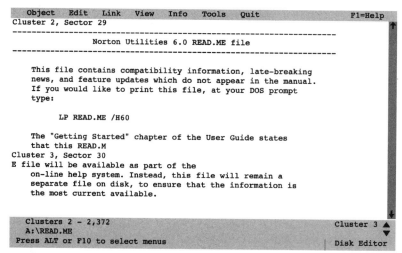

**Figure 4–11. The contents of cluster 2 displayed by the Disk Editor.**

You can switch between modes by pressing [F2] for hex or [F3] for text. Change the display to the hex mode by entering [F2]. The display now

---

10. When inspecting a text file with the hex mode, you will frequently find a pair of hex values *0D 0A*. This pair of hex values is the *carriage return/line feed* that most text editors or word processors place at the end of a line or a paragraph. This combination appears on the character symbol display as a musical note followed by a white block with a circle in it.

shows the information in the cluster on a byte-by-byte basis.[10] Exit the Disk Editor by entering [Alt-q] q.

## Erasing a File

What happens to the disk when you erase a file? The question is important because it reveals something about how the operation works, which enables you to recover part, or all, of a file once it has been erased. In this chapter it might be useful to take a look at the changes that occur when a file is erased. In this example, erase the file READ.ME from the floppy disk. Enter del a:read.me ↵.

List the directory of drive A: dir a: ↵.

The DOS directory commands now lists only two files, as seen in Figure 4–12. This confirms the fact that READ.ME has been erased from the disk.

```
Volume in drive A has no label
Directory of  A:\

TROUBLE   HLP     42165    9-25-90    5:00p
IMAGE     EXE     12168    9-25-90    5:00p
          2 File(s)      674816 bytes free
```

**Figure 4–12. DOS directory lists the two remaining files.**

But what actually happens when a file is *erased*? The term *erased* sounds as if the data has been obliterated. However, you might have noticed that when you copied the file to the disk, it took a few seconds for the operation to complete. However, when you erased the same file, the command was completed immediately. This difference in time is a clue to the actual process by which DOS erases files from the disk. To see for yourself what actually has taken place, you will need to load the Disk Editor program once again. Enter diskedit a: ↵.

The program loads and displays the root directory of the disk. You may be a bit surprised to see that, instead of the directory entry for READ.ME being obliterated, it is almost unchanged. If you look closely at that entry, you will see that the only change has been that the first letter of the file name has been replaced with a special symbol, as shown in Figure 4–13. All the rest of the data in the directory entry is still retained, including the

```
  Object   Edit   Link   View   Info   Tools   Quit                    F1=He p
Name      .Ext    Size        Date      Time   Cluster Arc R/O Sys Hid Dir Vol
Sector 7
ᑌEAD      ME       22505   9-25-90    5:00 pm      2   Arc
TROUBLE   HLP      42165   9-25-90    5:00 pm     24   Arc
IMAGE     EXE      12168   9-25-90    5:00 pm     66   Arc
         Unused directory entry
         Unused directory entry
```

**Figure 4–13. First character in file name removed.**

cluster number of the first cluster used by the file. DOS does not bother to remove this data, but simply marks the directory entry as erased by changing a single character.

Change to the hex display to see what was the hex value of the character used to make the erased file. Enter [F2].

The hex display shows that the value E5 (hexidecimal) is inserted as the first character when a file is erased.

What changes have taken place in the FAT? Change the display to show the contents of the FAT. Enter [Alt-F1].

The FAT display, as shown in Figure 4–14, reveals a much greater degree of change than did the directory. Here, all the values in the FAT that were related to the erased file, READ.ME, have been set to zero. This is necessary in order to show DOS that the clusters that were formerly assigned to the erased file are now available for storage of data.

```
Sector 1
                     0              0         0         0         0         0
     0          0          0         0         0         0         0         0
     0          0          0         0         0         0         0         0
    25         26         27        28        29        30        31        32
    33         34         35        36        37        38        39        40
```

**Figure 4–14. FAT entries removed for erased files.**

But what about the data areas themselves? Has the information been erased in the clusters? Use the program to display the contents of cluster 2, which was the beginning of the READ.ME file before it was erased. Enter [Alt-c] 2 ↵.

When the program displays the contents of cluster 2, you can see that it contains exactly the same information as it did when it was part of the READ.ME file. Erasing a file from the disk changes some things, but not others.

1. **Directory.** The directory entry for the erased file remains intact with the exception of the first character in the file name, which is used to mark the file as erased.

2. **FAT.** Each entry in the FAT used for that file is removed and replaced with a zero, indicating that the corresponding cluster is open for new data.

3. **Data Clusters.** The data stored in the clusters remain intact. These data will only be changed if a new file with new information is written into these clusters.

The fact that the data stored in the disk's data clusters are not changed when a file is erased, allows the Norton Utilities UNERASE program to recover part, or all, of a file after it has been erased from the disk directory. It is important to understand that in terms of DOS operations, *erase* does not actually mean the contents of the file have been discarded. Rather, the operating system makes the minimum number of changes needed to indicate that the space used for the file can be reused by another file. However, until that actually happens, the data stored in the data clusters remain intact. Exit the program by entering [Alt-q] q.

# The Disk Directory

In Chapter 3 the concept of a user-defined directory was discussed. Directories make it possible to organize files stored on a disk into groups of related files. However, in this chapter you have discovered a fact that suggests another important advantage of user-defined directories. Recall that the root directory of the disk contains a fixed number of sectors and thus a limit on the total number of files that can be stored on the disk. In the case of floppy disks, this limit is not significant. But the root directory of a hard disk is limited to 512 file entries, which is a significant limitation.

The solution is to create user-defined directories. These additional directories allow you to exceed the 512 file limit, since you can store an additional 512 entries in each directory. The same principle would apply to floppy disks where each new directory would have a capacity to hold additional files. Create a new directory on the disk in drive A. Enter md a:\example ↵.

Load the Disk Editor program again by entering diskedit a: ↵↵.

The root directory reveals several significant changes. First, a new entry has been placed in the first slot in the directory. Recall that this slot was occupied by the READ.ME file information, even after that file was erased. As shown in Figure 4–15, creating the SAMPLE directory caused DOS to write the new information *over* the old information, wiping out any information about the READ.ME file that remained in the directory. It is interesting to note that DOS used the *first available* slot in the directory, which in this case was the slot vacated by erasing the READ.ME file.

```
Name       .Ext     Size      Date      Time      Cluster Arc R/O Sys Hid Dir Vol
Sector 7
SAMPLE                  0    1-23-91   10:25 pm      2                          Dir
TROUBLE    HLP      42165    9-25-90    5:00 pm     24    Arc
IMAGE      EXE      12168    9-25-90    5:00 pm     66    Arc
         Unused directory entry
         Unused directory entry
```

**Figure 4–15. New directory entry in root directory.**

DOS indicates that SAMPLE is a directory and not a file by adding the **Dir** attribute to the entry.[11]

The DOS directory entry for the SAMPLE directory indicates that this directory uses cluster 2 as its starting location. This is very significant because it shows that DOS uses the data area of the disk to store user-defined directories. Thus, the number of user-defined directories is limited only by the total capacity of the disk.

To get a more detailed picture of what has happened to the disk when the directory was created, display the FAT by entering [Alt-F1].

The FAT shows that position 2, which corresponds to data cluster #2 on the disk, contains an EOF marker, as seen in Figure 4–16. This means the new directory takes up only one disk cluster, which provides room for 32 new file entries. However, this limit is not a fixed limit as is the case with

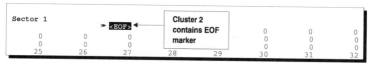

**Figure 4–16. FAT shows EOF marker for directory.**

---

11. The **Dir** attribute is created by placing the hex value 10 (decimal 16) in offset byte 11. You can check this by using the hex display, [F2], and moving the highlight to offset 11.

the capacity of the root directory. Instead, DOS expands the number of clusters assigned to the directory if you exceed the number of files that can be recorded in a single cluster, so long as there are still empty clusters on the disk. Keep in mind that the FAT system allows DOS to use any available cluster, even if it is not adjacent to an initial directory cluster.

Thus, even though the root directory has a fixed limit on the number of files you can record, any user-defined directory can expand to hold as many files as you desire, exceeding in capacity even the root directory.

As a final set in exploring the basic elements of disk storage, display the data cluster that contains the new directory. Use the shortcut command [Alt-c] to specify the desired cluster by number: [Alt-c] 2 ↵.

The cluster display, as seen in Figure 4–17, shows that the creation of the SAMPLE directory has altered the contents of the cluster. All the data that had been stored in this cluster have been removed from the disk and replaced an empty directory. Note that the directory is not completely empty. The first two slots in the directory listing are filled with two special items called **Aliases**. The two aliases are . (period) and .. (two periods). The . (period) alias is called the *current directory* alias. The entry is used to store the cluster number of the first cluster used by the directory, in this example, cluster 2. The second alias is called the *parent* alias. This entry is used to store the cluster location of the directory in which the name of the current directory appears. Here, that cluster number is 0, referring to the root directory as the *parent*. The alias entries will appear in each user-defined directory that is created on the disk. There, aliases appear on DOS directory listings, but are not directly affected by DOS commands, such as COPY, DEL, or RENAME.

```
 Object   Edit   Link   View   Info   Tools   Quit                    F1=Help
Name       .Ext    Size    Date     Time    Cluster Arc R/O Sys Hid Dir Vol
Cluster 2, Sector 14
 .                    0   1-23-91  10:25 pm     2                   Dir
 ..                   0   1-23-91  10:25 pm     0                   Dir
   Unused directory entry
   Unused directory entry
   Unused directory entry
```

**Figure 4–17. Cluster 2 changed for use as a user-defined directory.**

The alias entries create a *daisy chain* that DOS uses to maintain the hierarchical organization of user-defined directories. The creation of the SAMPLE directory wiped out from the original READ.ME file the data that had been stored in cluster 2. But what about the other clusters that were used for the file? For example, cluster 3 was also used for the READ.ME file. Is it also wiped clean? Display the contents of cluster 3 by entering [Alt-c] 3 ↵.

The display shows that while cluster 2 has been changed, cluster 3 still contains a portion of the READ.ME file. This suggests that it is possible to recover at least part of a file, even though the beginning of the file is being used as a directory. Of course, recovering the remaining portions of a file in this situation is more problematic, since the directory entry for the file has been erased and the FAT no longer has a record of which clusters were used. Sometimes the FAT holds a clue to the location of the remaining parts. For example, if you see a series of 0s in the FAT that fall between two current files, you might guess that all those clusters belonged to the same erased file at one time. The Norton Utilities UNERASE program will search for telltale patterns in the FAT automatically, when you try to recover partially erased files. But it is clear that this is only an educated guess with no absolute guarantee of success. One conclusion you can draw is that the best opportunity for recovery of an erased file exists *immediately* after it has been erased and *before* any additions or changes are made to the disk. You will see later that because of the crucial role played by the FAT in file recovery, the Norton Utilities will store copies of the FAT in *safe* locations on the disk.

You have now looked at all the basic elements involved in DOS file storage operations. In most cases you will not need to get involved with direct manipulation of the hex values displayed by the Disk Editor program. If all goes well, the Norton Utilities will read these raw values and present the information in a more understandable format, or even automatically correct the problems, based on methods built into the software. However, an understanding of how DOS creates and maintains the disk structures, upon which your work depends, takes away the mystery of computer operations and provides you with a basis for understanding the features and options presented by the Norton Utilities. Exit the Disk Editor program by entering [Alt-q] q.

# Summary

This chapter used the SYSINFO and DISKEDIT programs to reveal the structures that DOS creates and maintains, in order to store and retrieve data from disks.

**Format**      Before a disk can be used with the DOS operating system, a series of structures must be created on the disk. This process is called *formatting*. The formatting process has two stages: low-level or physical format, and the high-level or logical format. Disks can be formatted with the Norton Utilities Safe Format program or the DOS Format utility program.

**Low-level Format**      The low-level format creates a series of concentric rings called *tracks* on each usable surface of the disk. The tracks are further divided into *sectors*. The number of tracks will vary with the type of disk being formatted. The standard size of a sector is 512 bytes, but this can vary when using special software to partition hard disks over 32 megabytes in capacity. Low-level formatting will destroy all data that are currently stored on the disk.

**High-level Format**      This process organizes the sectors into specific areas for use by DOS. The high-level format does not alter the track and sector organization on the disk. When complete, the disk is divided into the system and data areas.

**System Area**      The system area is created during the high-level portion of the format process. It contains the boot record, the root directory, and the FAT. The system area takes up about 1 percent of the total disk space.

**Data Area**      The data area is all of the disk that is left over once the system area has been designated. This space is used for storage of programs and data files. It is also used to create user-defined directories. The data area is allocated in blocks called *clusters*, which can contain one or more disk sectors.

**Boot Sector**      The boot sector is the first sector on the disk. DOS write information that identifies the disk type and its structure to the operating system. By reading the boot sector DOS can determine how data are stored on the disk and perform read and write operations accordingly.

**Root Directory**      The formatting process establishes the root directory of the disk. The root directory is a fixed size directory that can hold a predetermined number of files. The exact number of entries is determined by the type of disk. The root directory is the only directory that is stored in the system area of the disk.

**File Allocation Table (FAT)**    The FAT is used to associate specific data clusters with the names of files and directories. The table tells DOS where to find the data related to a specific file and in what sequence those clusters should be read. The table also tells DOS what data clusters are available for use with new files.

**Sectors**    A sector is the basic unit of disk storage. Sectors are created during the low-level portion of the format process. DOS does not perform operations on the sector level but uses data clusters as its basic unit of operation. The Disk Editor program can operate on specific disk sectors.

**Clusters**    A cluster is the basic unit upon which DOS operates after the disk has been formatted. A cluster can consist of one or more sectors. The number of sectors assigned to a cluster is determined by the type of disk being formatted.

**User-defined Directories**    DOS supports the creation of user-defined directories that are stored in the data area of the disk, rather than the system area. User-defined directories do not have a fixed number of entries but can expand as needed. Each user-defined directory contains two alias entries that are used to keep track of the hierarchical structure of DOS user directories.

**Erasing Files**    When DOS erases a file it does not obliterate the information stored on the disk. DOS changes the first letter of the erased file to hex value E5 and changes the FAT by setting all the clusters used by the file to 0 to indicate that they are available for use with other files. However, the data in the clusters are unchanged and will remain so until new data are written to the disk.

# 5 The Norton Utilities User Interface

The term *user interface* refers to the organizational structures and displays that a program uses to communicate with the user, and by which the user can communicate with the program. One of the biggest changes in Version 6.0 of the Norton Utilities from Version 4.5 is the inclusion of a new user interface that operates the same way in all the individual programs in the package.

In this chapter you will look at that interface, its components, and how each of the items can be used with the keyboard, or the mouse if you happen to have one installed.

## Keyboard and Mouse

The Norton Utilities programs will respond to both keyboard and mouse commands, assuming that you have mouse hardware and software properly installed. In order to discuss particular keyboard or mouse operations, this book will use specific terms, notations, and typesetting conventions. Most terms are common to computer text, but specific typesetting conventions employed may vary from those used in the manuals included with the Norton Utilities programs.

### Keystrokes

While most MS-DOS computers have keyboards that contain the same basic set of keys, the arrangement of those keys, and the labels placed on them, will vary slightly between keyboards, even when produced by the same company. For example, the *return* key is usually labeled with this symbol: ↵. However, some keyboards replace that symbol with the word *Return* or *Enter*. Others combine the ↵ symbol with the word *Return* or *Enter*, or replace the ↵ with a simple ←. Other keyboards add a second [Enter] key on the numeric keypad section. In all cases, the keys have the same function. In addition to single keystrokes, MS-DOS computers increase the total number of possible keystrokes by recognizing combinations of keys, using the [Alt], [Ctrl], and [Shift] keys. The Norton Utilities programs use [Alt] and [Ctrl] key combinations. You begin these key combinations by pressing down the [Ctrl] or [Alt] key. While the [Ctrl] or [Alt] is being held down, you then press the second key, usually a letter or function key. Both keys are then released.

## Mouse

If you have a computer equipped with a mouse, the Norton Utilities programs support the use of the mouse. The number of buttons on a mouse will vary between 2 and 3. The Norton Utilities ignores the center button on a three-button mouse. The program also treats the left and right buttons the same.

Clicking the left or right button has roughly the same effect as pressing the ↵ key.

Clicking the left and right buttons at the same time is roughly equivalent to pressing the [Esc] key.

*Dragging* the mouse refers to an operation in which the mouse is pointed at a screen item; while pressing and holding down the left or right mouse button, you move the mouse while continuing to hold down the mouse button. In the Norton Utilities, dragging is used primarily to scroll the contents of a list box.

## Defaults

A *default* value or setting is the value the program enters automatically, unless you specifically enter a different value. Default values are used in programs to simplify operations by automatically filling in required information. When a Norton Utilities program is loaded, the default values are automatically set. If you change values during the program's operation, the program will revert to the original default values the next time it is loaded.

Some of the programs allow you to change the default settings. These programs create *initialization* files, **INI** extensions, that store your personal preferences. When the program is loaded, it searches for the INI file and loads the default settings from that file, if it is found. If you erase (or rename) the INI file, the program will revert to its original values.

Options related to disk information usually use the current DOS drive and directory as the default.

# The Norton Program

The Norton Utilities programs can be used in two ways: as individual programs executed from DOS, or as a single collection of programs operated from the Norton program.[1] The Norton program is a *shell* that provides a menu from which you can execute any of the Norton Utilities programs. When the specific utility program is terminated, you return to the Norton menu.

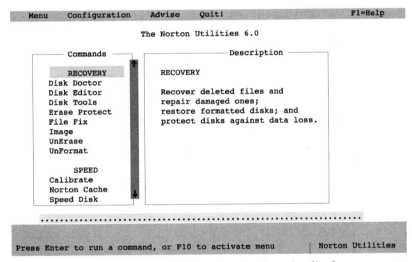

**Figure 5–1. The Norton program main display.**

Start the Norton program by entering norton ↵. When the program loads, the main Norton screen, as in Figure 5–1, displays a dialog box with three major features:

**Commands List Box.** On the left side of the display is a list box that contains the names of all the Norton Utilities programs. This list is divided into four categories, grouping the Norton Utilities programs by their general type of function.

---

1. The Norton program performs the same function as the Norton Integrator (NI) performed in Version 4.5. Prior to 4.5, all programs were executed directly from DOS.

**Recovery.**  Disk Doctor II, Disk Editor, Disk Tools, File Fix, Erase Protection, Image, UnErase, UnFormat

**Speed.**  Calibrate, Norton Cache, Speed Disk

**Security.**  Disk Monitor, Diskreet, WipeInfo

**Tools.**  Batch Enhancer, Control Center, File Find, Norton CD, Safe Format, System Information

**Description Box.**  The box on the right side contains information about the currently highlighted program. The information includes a brief description of the program and command switches that can be used with the application. Command switches are discussed in Chapter 6.

**Command Entry Box.**  At the bottom of the dialog box is an entry box with no label. This box functions as a DOS prompt within the Norton shell. Any commands entered into this box will be executed by DOS when you enter ↵. Note that when you place the list box highlight on the name of a program, the Norton program automatically inserts the program name into the entry box. For example, if you move the highlight to **File Find** the program's file name, FILEFIND, is inserted in the command line.

The list box and entry box work together so that you can run the Norton Utilities programs, without additional parameters, by simply highlighting the desired program name and pressing ↵.

## Command Sort Order

The Norton program allows you to display the commands listed in the command box by group, the default listing, or in alphabetical order with no groups. You can change the listing using the **sort by Name** or **sort by Topic** commands located on the *Configuration* menu. You can also use the shortcut keys: [Alt-n] for name order, or [Alt-t] for topic order.

## Video and Mouse Options

One of the changes in the Version 6.0 of the Norton Utilities is that you can control video and mouse options that affect *all* of the programs, from a single location on the Norton program. These changes will remain in effect even if you operate individual Norton Utilities programs from DOS without using the Norton program shell. Enter [Alt-c].

The *Configure* menu contains the **Video** and **mouse** options. Enter v. The command displays a dialog box with four radio buttons: Screen Colors, Graphics Options, Screen Options, and Mouse Options. When you make changes to the radio button settings displayed on this screen, the Norton program creates or updates a file called **NU.INI,** which is stored in the home directory[2] of the Norton Utilities programs. Whenever you execute a Norton Utilities program, either from the Norton shell or directly from DOS, the program will read the settings stored in NU.INI and use those settings. The Norton Utilities will revert to its factory settings if you delete the NU.INI file from the \NU directory. Return to the main program screen by entering [Esc].

## Running Programs

Besides the video and mouse settings, the primary purpose of the Norton program is to act as a shell for running Norton Utilities and other programs. A *shell* program is one that allows you to issue commands to the operating system. DOS is supplied with a shell program called COMMAND.COM. It is the COMMAND.COM program that is active when you see the DOS prompt.

However, the DOS prompt is a command-driven mode, which does not support menus or list boxes, display of help or description text, or the use of a mouse. In order to use the DOS shell you must know the commands and parameters needed to perform the operations.

It is possible, and in some cases desirable, to execute the Norton Utilities programs from the DOS prompt. However, in most cases, using the Norton program makes it simpler and easier to run these programs because of its sophisticated user interface as compared to the bare bones environment of DOS.

The Norton program provides two significant advantages over DOS operations. First, the correct names of the Norton Utilities program files are automatically entered into the command line as you move the highlight from name to name in the list box. Second, as each name is highlighted, information about the program and its command line options is displayed in the description box. For example, suppose you want to run the File Find program. The first step is to highlight the name of the program in the

---

2.  The *home* directory is the one in which the Norton Utilities programs are stored. If you accept the Install program's default, that directory is called \NU.

command list box. The File Find program is listed under the Tools group of programs. However, when you are first working with the Norton program you may not know or recall that fact. You can change the display to an alphabetical list, with a single keystroke. Enter [Alt-n].

The commands in the list box are rearranged in alphabetical order, as in Figure 5–2. File Find is now easy to locate since the topic groupings have been removed.

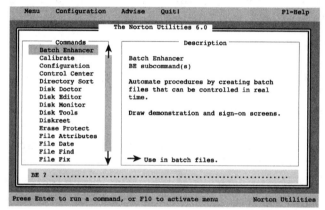

**Figure 5–2. Commands arranged in alphabetical order.**

Enter ↓ (press 8 times).

When you highlight the program, the *Description* box displays information about the program, and the file name of the program, FILEFIND, appears in the entry box. The program allows you to enter any program parameters or option switches along with the program name. For example, you could specify that you wanted to search for batch files, BAT extensions, by adding the wildcard **\*.BAT** as a parameter in the entry box. Enter \*.bat.

Execute the command by entering ↵.

The File Find program loads. The inclusion of the parameter causes the program to immediately conduct a search across the entire disk for files with BAT extension.

Exit the File Find program by entering ↵ [Alt-q].

When the program terminates, you return to the Norton program exactly where you left. Change the command list back to the topic order by entering [Alt-t].

## Entering DOS Commands

The entry box at the bottom of the Norton dialog box can be used to execute *any* valid DOS command, even though the command is not related directly to a Norton Utilities program. For example, suppose you wanted to execute the DOS DIR command. Enter dir ↵. The Norton program passes the command to DOS and the operating system displays a directory listing of the current directory. Note that at the end of the listing the Norton program pauses the display with the message "Press any key to continue." Return to the Norton program by entering ↵.

You can also execute DOS utility programs such as CHKDSK. Enter chkdsk ↵.

When the program completes its testing, the "Press any key to continue" message appears. Enter ↵.

While the Norton program is set up to execute Norton Utilities programs, it can function as a general type of DOS shell program. In the next section you will learn how the Norton program can be modified so that its menu will display your own customized Norton Utilities and DOS commands.

# Customizing the Norton Program

The Norton program is set up by default to execute 20 basic Norton Utilities commands, e.g., FILEFIND, SYSINFO, etc., and to display descriptions of those 20 programs. But the Norton program has the potential to help you organize a much broader range of computer operations. As noted in the previous section, you can enter and execute any valid DOS command from the Norton command entry box. In addition to this basic ability, the Norton program provides means by which you can add, modify, or delete command options from the list. This allows you to customize the Norton list box to include your own personalized versions of the Norton Utilities commands, commands that execute DOS commands and Utilities, and commands that run applications.

By making these changes you can alter the Norton program so that it functions as a menu program for your computer system. The primary limitation is that the Norton program can issue only *single* line commands. In order to issue a series of commands from a menu, you will have to create *batch* files.[3] However, even with this limitation, the Norton program can provide a handy way to organize your computer system.

## The NORTON.CMD File

The heart of the Norton program menu system is a file called - **NORTON.CMD.** This file contains all the information used to fill out the dialog box displayed by the Norton program. The NORTON.CMD is placed into the home directory during the installation process. When the NORTON program is executed, it searches the home directory for this file and uses the information contained within the file as the basis for the items that appear in the list box, the text that appears in the description box, and the commands that are inserted in the entry box

The NORTON.CMD is important because it is a standard DOS text file. This means you can modify the file in one of two ways in order to create a customized version of the Norton program:

> **Menu Commands.** The *Configure* menu of the Norton program con- tains commands that will help you add, modify, or delete menu items, including the creation of new topic groups. The menus guide you, step- by-step, through the modification process using dialog boxes. The one drawback to this approach is that you must make the changes one item at a time. Once you are experienced with NORTON.CMD modifications you may find the menus too tedious to work with.

> **Text Editing.** Because the NORTON.CMD is a DOS text file it can be modified directly with the use of any text editing program (the DOS EDLIN program or the Norton Editor) or a word processor that outputs standard DOS files (Microsoft Word, WordStar, or WordPerfect). Text editors have advanced features, such as spelling checkers, copy and paste commands, and automatic line wrap, which speed editing. Text editing allows you to make major changes in a CMD file or even create a new file from scratch more quickly than can be done with the menus. However, in text editing you are responsible for using the correct syntax and structure since NORTON.CMD files must follow an exact pattern in order to operate correctly within the Norton program.

When you are just beginning, it is best to use the menus to make changes since doing so ensures that the modifications are correctly inserted into the

---

3.  Batch file programming is discussed beginning in Chapter 15.

NORTON.CMD file. Text editing would only be used once you have learned about the commands and the structures required.

Before you make any changes to the default Norton menu, you should use the DOS Copy command to make a duplicate of the original file. This will make it easy for you to return to the original set-up should you need to do so. To create a copy of the menu file, enter copy \nu\nu.cmd \nu\nu.org ↵.

DOS displays the message "1 File(s) copied." Return to the Norton program by entering ↵.

You have now made a backup copy of the original menu. You can now feel free to experiment with the menu since you can restore the original menu by reversing the process with the command "COPY \NU\NU.ORG \NU\NU.CMD".

## Deleting Menu Options

The original Norton Utilities command menu lists 20 different programs that you can execute. You may find it easier to work with the menu if you eliminate some of the Norton Utilities commands you don't use, or at least don't use very often. For example, the **Batch Enhancer** command is primarily used as part of DOS batch files. It has very little use when executed from the Norton command menu. You can simplify the menu list by deleting this option.

Begin by highlighting the menu item you want to remove. Enter [End] ↑ (press 5 times). Display the *Configure* menu [Alt-c].

The **Delete menu item** command will remove the currently highlighted item from the command menu. Enter d. The program asks you to confirm your intention to delete this item from the menu. Enter y. The program returns to the menu dialog box. You can see that the **Batch Enhancer** command has been removed from the current menu.

# New Commands

Perhaps the most powerful feature of the menu list is the ability to add commands of your own to the existing menu. These commands do not have to refer to Norton Utilities programs, but can be any valid DOS command, including commands that start applications, such as word processing, spreadsheets, and databases.

As examples you will add three types of new commands to the Norton menu: a Norton Utilities command, a DOS utility command, and a command that executes an application, e.g., Lotus 1-2-3. Before you begin to make the changes in the Norton program, keep in mind that the details of these commands depend upon the specified programs available in your system. The general concepts can be applied to any Norton Utilities, DOS utility, or application program.

As stated in the previous section, the Norton program can execute only single line commands from its menu. In practical terms this means any of the programs you want to execute *must* lie on an *existing* path[4] in order for them to work with the Norton program. The examples in this section assume you have installed on your hard disk the Norton Utilities programs, the DOS utility programs, and the spreadsheet application Lotus 1-2-3. However, in addition to having these programs installed, you must have a path open to the directories in which those programs are stored, in order for them to be executed directly from the Norton program.

During the installation process, discussed in Chapter 1, the Install program provides you with the option to modify your AUTOEXEC.BAT file to include a path to the \NU directory. This path ensures that you can execute the Norton Utilities from any location in your system. The result is that you can enter **NORTON** ↵ at the DOS prompt, regardless of the current active directory. If you do not have such a path, you can only execute the Norton Utilities programs when you have activated the \NU directory.

In this example, you will want to run Norton Utilities, DOS utilities, and an application, e.g., Lotus 1-2-3, from the Norton menu. This means you must have a path open to \NU, \DOS, and \LOTUS.[5]

You can check the current path by entering PATH ↵.

DOS displays the current path list on the screen. If the current path list does not include the required paths, you can add the missing paths in order to successfully use the Norton menu to run all the example programs.

The following section explains how you can add new paths to the existing path list, for the purpose of experimenting with the Norton program. If

---

4.  The concept of search paths and the PATH command are discussed at the end of Chapter 3.

5.  The assumption is made that your DOS utility programs are stored in a directory called DOS and that the Lotus 1-2-3 program is stored in \LOTUS. If this is not the case you will need to adjust the commands to use the directories that correspond to your computer.

you want to make these new paths part of your standard system set-up you would need to modify the PATH command found in the AUTOEXEC.BAT file. The changes you will make in this section apply only for the remainder of the current session. When you reboot the computer, the path list will return to the paths currently listed in the AUTOEXEC.BAT.

The first step is to gain access to a text or line-editing program. The assumption is made that all users have available the DOS line-editor program, EDLIN. Further, the assumption is made that this program is stored in a directory called \DOS. Activate the DOS directory by entering cd\dos ↵.

Load this file into the EDLIN program by entering EDLIN \newpath.bat ↵.

The program displays the message "New file" followed by an * on the next line. The * is the EDLIN prompt, which indicates that the program is ready to accept a command. To add lines of text to this file, enter the i(nsert) command. Enter i ↵.

The first line number, 1, appears on the screen, followed by a colon and an *. You can now enter the text of the first line of this file. The command you will enter is a **PATH** command. Enter path=.

In this case, start with the existing PATH list. You can accomplish this by using the DOS variable PATH. In a DOS batch file the text of a variable can be inserted into a command line by enclosing it in %, e.g., %**path**%. When the batch file is executed, DOS will substitute its current list of paths for the %**path**% symbol. Enter %path%.

You can now add the names of the additional paths that are needed. For example, if you want to add a path to the \LOTUS directory, enter \lotus;.

If you also need a path to the \DOS directory, you would enter \dos;.

When you have made the necessary modifications to the PATH command, save the modified file by entering ↵[Ctrl-C] ↵. Note that the file name used to store the PATH command has a BAT extension. This designates the file as a DOS batch file. You can now issue the path command contained in the NEWPATH.BAT file by entering cd\ ↵ newpath ↵.

The batch file executes the command, displaying the new PATH list on the screen. You will notice that the paths you wanted to add are now appended onto the end of the PATH list.

## Adding Commands to the Menu

You are now ready to add new options to the Norton menu. Activate the Norton program by entering norton ↵.

There are two types of modifications you can make to the menu:

**Topics.**  You can add new topic headings to the existing headings Recovery, Speed, Security, and Tools.

**Commands.**  These menus items are individual commands that appear within one of the categories.

To begin, add a new *topic* to the menu list called **PERSONAL**. Note that the program will insert the new topic at the currently highlighted position. Since RECOVERY is the highlighted topic, the new topic will be inserted before RECOVERY. Enter [Alt-c] a. Choose to add a *topic* by entering t.

The program displays a dialog box that allows you to enter a new topic. Add the new topic, PERSONAL You can use the ↑ or ↓ keys to change the location of the new topic within the current list of topics. For example, to insert the new topic below the RECOVERY topic, enter».

The topic is moved down between RECOVERY and SPEED. Return the new topic to the top of the list by entering ↑.

In addition to the creation of the topic you can create a description text that will appear in the Description box when the topic is highlighted, using the **Description** control button. Enter [Tab] d.

The program displays a large box into which you can enter any text you want to appear as a description for the specified item. Note that all spacing is created by entering [space] characters or ↵. If you want something centered you must space over and manually center the item. Enter the following text: [space] (press 5 times) Customized Menu Entries.

Save the text by entering [Tab] ↵.

Save the new topic by entering ↵.

The new topic appears at the top of the list with the description displayed in the description box.

The next step is to add commands under the new topic. The first will execute the Lotus 1-2-3 spreadsheet program. Enter [Alt-c] a c.

The program displays the same dialog box used for editing a menu item, with the exception that the entry boxes are empty. Enter the text that will appear in the menu list: Lotus 1-2-3 [Tab]. In the *DOS command* box, enter the same command you would enter at the DOS prompt to execute the application— here, **123↵**.[6] Enter 123.

---

6.  You can also use the command **LOTUS**, which activates the Lotus Access program.

You can also select the topic under which the new command should be displayed, by selecting the appropriate radio button from the *Topic* list. Because the highlight was positioned on the PERSONAL topic, this topic is selected as the default. Enter a description for the menu command: [Tab] [Tab] d.

When you enter text into the description box, you can add video enhancements to the text in the form of bold, reverse, and underlined text, using the [F2] key to toggle between text modes. For example, suppose you want to print the first part of the description in bold. Enter [F2].

On the right side of the dialog box the current attribute changes to Reverse. Enter [F2]. The attribute now shows bold. This means any text entered at this point will appear in bold.[7] Enter Lotus 1-2-3 ↵. Change back to normal text by entering [F2] (press 2 times). Enter additional text: Version 2.2 ↵↵ Spreadsheet and Graphics ↵. Save the new menu entry by entering [Tab] ↵↵. The new menu item is placed under the PERSONAL topic. Note that the text, including the bold video, appears in the description box.

Next, create a menu entry for a Norton Utilities command. For example, many programs create backup files whenever an existing file is being modified, e.g., Microsoft Word. However, these backup files, e.g., BAK extensions, are not usually erased by the program. The result is that over time you will accumulate a lot of backup files that are no longer needed. Deleting these files with the DOS DEL command can be a tedious chore since DEL will operate only on one directory at a time. The WIPEINFO program can be used to delete all the BAK files from an entire hard disk, with a single command. Add this type of command to your command menu. Begin by entering [Alt-c] a c.

Even though this command uses the WIPEINFO program you do not have to use it as the menu item. Instead, you could use a name that refers to the specific operation, deleting backups, that the command will perform. Enter Clean Up Files [Tab].

Enter the WIPEINFO program using the following parameters and switches:

\*.BAT. This file wildcard specifies that the operation should begin with all of the BAT files in the root directory.

---

7.  On a color display, bold is shown as bright yellow text.

**/s.** This switch tells the program to include all subdirectories in the operation. When the /S switch is combined with a file wildcard that begins at the root directory, you have in effect selected the entire disk for the operation.

**/n.** WIPEINFO normally performs a complete overwrite of disk space. However, the /N switch changes its operation to the same function as the DOS DEL command. This saves time since the actual data clusters are not overwritten.

Enter the command and the description. Enter

```
wipeinfo \*.bat /s/n
[Tab] [Tab] d Erase all backup files.
```

Save the new command by entering [Tab] ↵↵.

The third command to add to the menu uses the DOS utility program, BACKUP. The command will create a backup of the entire hard disk onto a series of floppy disks in drive A. Enter [Alt-c] a c. Enter the name of the command: Backup Hard Disk [Tab]. Enter the DOS utility command: backup c:\*.* a:/s. Skip the explanation and return to the main dialog box by entering ↵. The Norton program now displays the user-defined menu options at the top of the command list box.

You can test these new menu options by highlighting the item and pressing ↵. For example, execute the **Clean Up Files** command by entering » ↵. The WIPEINFO program pauses and displays a dialog box that lets you confirm or cancel the operation. In this case, cancel the operation by entering c. Exit the Norton Program by entering [Alt-q].

## How NORTON.CMD Works

The primary purpose of the Norton program is to provide a method of integration for all the individual Norton Utilities programs. In Version 4.5 of the Norton Utilities the Norton Integrator (NI) program fulfilled the same basic purpose.

The significance of Version 6.0 of the Norton program is that you can customize the Norton command list to include a wide range of customized options, something that could not be done in Version 4.5.

The previous section demonstrated how the Norton program's built-in commands can be used to delete, modify, or add commands to the list box. But this is not the only way to work with these commands. The NORTON.CMD file can be directly modified using a text editor or word processor. In addition, you can create from scratch your own NOR-TON.CMD files that will work with the Norton program.

Since the NORTON.CMD file is composed of standard text, you can display its contents by using the DOS TYPE command. The MORE filter is used to pause the display after each screen-full. Change to the NORTON directory and display the first part of the NORTON.CMD file on the screen by entering[8] cd\nu ↵ type norton.cmd \more ↵.

The command displays the first part of the NORTON.CMD file. This part of the file contains the text that is used to create the first topic on the menu, RECOVERY, and the first command on the menu, Disk Doctor II.

You will notice that all of the information that appears in the Norton dialog box, such as the topics, the commands, and the description text, also appears in the NORTON.CMD file but in a different form. Upon close examination you can discern a pattern to the text in which each section of the file plays a specific role. The words preceded by ! are command words that designate the function of the text that follows:

**!topic:**  This command designates a topic for the command list.

**!command:**  This command designates text that will appear as a command in the command list.

**!dos-cmd:**  This command is used immediately after a **!command:** to designate the actual DOS command that will be placed into the entry box when the command name is highlighted.

**Description Text.**  Text that is not preceded by a specific ! command is considered as description text and is placed into the DESCRIPTION box when the item that proceeds it is highlighted.

In addition to the structural commands, **!topic:**, **!command:**, and **!dos-cmd:**, you will notice that the text contains ^ followed by letters, e.g., ^N, ^B. These items are used to designate the use of special text attributes, such as bold or reverse video:

---

8.  The | character in the command is the vertical line character, which is the uppercase character on the same key that has the \ as the lowercase character.

**^B.** Begin bold text.
**^R.** Begin reverse text.
**^U.** Begin underline text.
**^N.** Begin normal text.

For example, the second line in the file reads **^BRECOVERY.** The **^B** tells the program to display the text in bold video. Note that the text automatically reverts to normal video for the next line. If you want to mix two or more types of video on the same line it is necessary to use the **^N** to return to normal text after another attribute.

Exit the display by entering [Ctrl-c].

## Using Multiple NORTON.CMD Files

The ability of the Norton program to use ordinary text files as the basis of the commands listed in the dialog box means that you can create any number of customized versions of the Norton menu. Earlier in this chapter you saw how you could make changes to the original NORTON.CMD file. Suppose you wanted to create a Norton command list that would act like a menu program for your hard disk.

As an example, you will create a NORTON.CMD file from scratch in a different directory, and learn how to control the Norton program so that you can choose which menu list is displayed when you run the program. The menu will be set to run three popular applications: WordPerfect, Lotus 1-2-3, and dBASE IV.

Begin by creating a new directory, in this case, called MENU. Enter md\menu ↵. Activate that directory by entering cd\menu ↵.

Use the EDLIN program to create the menu file. Enter EDLIN norton.cmd ↵. Place EDLIN into the *insert* mode by entering i ↵.

Begin with the topic heading for the list. In this case, call the topic *PROGRAM*. Enter !topic:PROGRAMS ↵.

The next line begins the description text for this topic. Enter a heading that uses bold video (^B): ^BHard Disk Programs ↵. The next part of the file will specify the text of the first command to appear in the menu, below the topic. The first entry is for WordPerfect: !command:WordPerfect ↵.

Next, add the DOS command that is actually used to execute the Word-Perfect program: WP. !dos-cmd:wp ↵.

You can now add as many lines of text as you desire, as an explanation of the menu option. Enter

```
^BWordPerfect Version 5.1 ↵
↵ Full featured word processing application.
↵
```

Next, add a command to run Lotus 1-2-3. Enter

```
!command:Lotus 1-2-3 ↵
!dos-cmd:123 ↵
^BLotus 1-2-3 Version 3.1 ↵
↵ Spreadsheet and graphics application ↵
```

The last item is for dBASE IV. Enter

```
!command:DBASE IV ↵
!dos-cmd:dbase ↵
^BdBASE IV Version 1.1 ↵
↵ Relational database application. ↵
```

Save the file by entering [Ctrl-c] e ↵.

You have now created an alternative NORTON.CMD file for use with the Norton program. Run the Norton program by entering norton ↵. However, your custom command list did not appear. The Norton program displayed the original commands list instead of the command lists you created in the \MENU directory. Why?

The reason the original command list appeared is that the Norton Utilities will look in the *home* directory for supporting files, such as the NORTON.CMD or INI files. The home directory is set by default to the directory in which the NORTON.EXE program is stored, i.e., \NU. Exit the program by entering [Alt-q].

## Changing the Home Directory

The default home directory can be changed by using the DOS **SET** command. The **SET** command creates what DOS call *environmental variables*. This is a very fancy sounding name for an area of memory that DOS sets aside as a scratch pad to store lists of information. For example, the list of search paths discussed in Chapter 3 is stored in this scratch pad area.

Each entry into this scratch pad area is assigned a name. For example, the path list is assigned to the name PATH.

*Environmental variables* are useful because they are stored directly in the computer's memory instead of in a disk file. This means if a program needs a particular item of information, it does not have to search the disk for that data but simply look at the scratch pad area in the memory.

When any of the Norton Utilities programs are executed, they are programmed to check the *environmental variables* for a variable named NU. The purpose of NU is to specify a different home directory than the default, \NU. For example, if NU was set to \MENU, the Norton Utilities will use the support files, e.g., NORTON.CMD, found in that directory instead of the files in the \NU Directory. In this example you can use the **SET** command to assign the home directory to the \MENU directory. Enter set nu=\menu ↵. Execute the Norton program once again: norton ↵.

This time, when the program loads, it uses the NORTON.CMD file stored in the \MENU directory to determine the command options listed in the dialog box. Exit the Norton program by entering [Alt-q].

You can return the program to its default home directory by removing the NU variable from memory. A variable is removed from memory if it is defined as a blank, e.g., **SET NU=** will erase the NU variable. Enter set nu= ↵ norton ↵.

The Norton program executes, using the default command menu drawn from the NORTON.CMD file stored in the home directory, \NU, once again. Manipulating the menu contents by using the NU variable makes it easy to use the Norton program in a variety of different ways. In the batch file programming section you will see how this concept allows you to integrate Norton menu lists with other types of batch file menus and displays.

Exit the Norton program by entering [Alt-q].

# Network Considerations

The use of the NU variable to control the source of the support files for the Norton Utilities programs, including the command list for the Norton program, is also important when you are running the Norton Utilities across a local area network. In its normal mode of operation, the Norton Utilities assumes it is operating in a single-user environment. However, it is possible to operate the Norton Utilities from a network file server. To do so you will need to make two types of modifications:

**Read-only Files.** In order to allow more than one user at a time to access the same set of file, the files must be marked as *read-only*. A file that is marked as a read-only is one that can be read but not changed. DOS allows multiple user access to read-only files. Normal DOS files (read and write) are locked when they are accessed, for the exclusive use of one user, and cannot be accessed until that user has completed using the file.

**User Home Directories.** Recall that the Norton Utilities programs work with several files that record user preferences. When running on a network it is necessary to create a separate directory for each user so that they can store and modify user-preference files. The NU variable is used to define each user's home directory.

File locking by DOS occurs when a second user attempts to access a file already in use by another. However, DOS views file access in a technical way that may not match how you as a user perceive file use. For example, many programs, such as Lotus 1-2-3, load their entire contents into memory when they are activated. Once the program has been loaded DOS considers the program file no longer, since the file loading operation has been completed. The fact that a user is working with the application does not prevent a second, third, or fourth user from also loading a copy of 1-2-3 into their work station's memory. A file conflict would occur if a second user attempted to load 1-2-3 at the exact moment when the first user was loading the program. If your network has a small number of users, the likelihood that such a conflict will occur is small.

On the other hand, some programs maintain open *channels* to files stored on the disk for the entire time that they are running. Typically, these are files that are loaded only as required by the request of the user, e.g., on-line help data. With these programs, any attempt by a second user to run the application will result in a file locking error.

Note that applications that are specifically network compatible have built-in routines to handle multiple access to the same files that override the basic DOS file locking mechanism. As an example of installing the Norton Utilities on a network, suppose you have a network on which there are two users, John and Marcia, who will be running the Norton Utilities stored on the file server designated as drive C. The Norton Utilities are stored in the directory \NU on the file server.

## Read-only Files

The first step in a network set-up is to mark the Norton Utilities program files as *read-only*. This can be done with the File Find program. Activate the directory that contains the Norton Utilities files: cd\nu ↵.

The **/R+** switch used with the File Find command marks the specified files as read-only. First mark all the EXE files as read-only by entering: filefind .\*.exe /r+/batch ↵.

The /BATCH switch causes the File Find program to operate in automatic mode. Repeat the command, this time focusing on the HLP (help) files used by the Norton Utilities: filefind .\*.hlp /r+/batch ↵.

You have now protected the files so that they can be read by multiple users on a network.

## User Home Directories

The second step is to create a Norton Utilities home directory for each user. In this case, you will create a directory called USERS on the file server with subdirectories for JOHN and MARCIA. Enter

```
md\users ↵
md\users\john ↵ md\users\marcia ↵
```

Place a copy of the Norton Utilities initialization files, plus the commands list (NORTON.CMD), into each of the user's directories. For example, you would enter the following to set up John's directory:

```
copy \nu\*.ini \users\john ↵ copy \nu\*.cmd
\users\john ↵
```

Repeat the command, but change the user directory to MARCIA:

```
copy \nu\*.ini \users\marcia ↵ copy
\nu\*.cmd \users\marcia ↵
```

The final step is to set up the DOS configuration on each workstation so that the correct combination of files is used for each user when he or she invokes a Norton Utilities program. For example, the AUTOEXEC.BAT file on John's workstation should include the following commands:[9]

```
path c:\nu
set nu=c:\users\john¹⁰
```

These commands control where on the file server DOS will draw the requested files. For example, suppose John enters the command **norton** ↵. The command tells DOS to run the NORTON.EXE program. In such a case the PATH setting directs DOS to the **C:\NU** directory to execute the read-only copy of the NORTON.EXE program. As the Norton program begins to run, the program reads the directory name stored under NU, e.g., **C:\USERS\JOHN**, and loads the NORTON.CMD file stored in that directory, rather than the one on **C:\NU**, as in Figure 5–3.

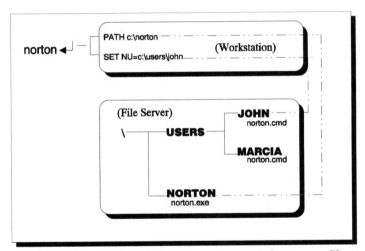

**Figure 5–3. SET directs program to use John's user files.**

---

9.  Note that the actual PATH command you use on the workstation should include all paths required for your system. The command shown simply illustrates one of the paths that should be included in any workstation path command.

10. The **SET** command defines one variable each time it is used. An AUTOEXEC.BAT may require several SET commands to define variables needed for several programs. For example, WordPerfect uses a variable named WP, e.g., SET wp=/m-setup.

By setting up the server and work stations in this manner, each user can access a single copy of the Norton Utilities and still take advantage of its customizing features without coming into conflict with other users.

The technique discussed in this section can be applied to a variety of programs not specifically designed for network operations.

# Using the Norton Utilities with Windows

Running the Norton Utilities programs under Windows 3.0 is different from running the Norton Utilities directly from DOS because Windows remains active in the background while you are running the Norton Utilities. Since Windows is using DOS, memory, and disk files at the same time you are running the Norton Utilities, certain operations will lead to a conflict between Windows and the Norton Utilities. In other areas, the Norton Utilities operations will run under Windows without problems.[11]

Programs that run under Windows 3.0 without conflict:

Batch Enhancer (BE)
File Find (FILEFIND)
Norton Control Center (NCC)
Norton Change Directory (NCD)
Norton Program (NORTON)
Wipe Information (WIPEINFO)

Programs that do not operate under Windows 3.0:

Calibrate
Speed Disk
UnErase
Disk Monitor
Disk Tools
File Fix
Safe Format
UnFormat

---

11. In general, the restrictions imposed by Windows on the Norton Utilities would apply to any multitasking system, such as DESQVIEW.

There are four Norton Utilities programs that fall into the category of programs that will run under windows, but whose operation is restricted to certain functions. The Norton Disk Doctor II and Disk Editor will run, but will not make any changes to the disk. The Norton Cache program should not be used if you are running Windows in the Standard (286) or Enhanced (386) mode. The DISKREET program can be used only in the manual, not automatic, operational modes.

Also keep in mind that if you implement DISKREET using the DIS-KREET.SYS driver in your CONFIG.SYS file you should add the /**NOHMA** (no high memory area) switch to avoid conflict with the Windows high memory driver, HIMEM.SYS. Example:

```
DEVICE=C:\NU\DISKREET.SYS \NOHMA
```

# Summary

This chapter discussed the general structure of the user interface of the Norton Utilities Version 6.0.

**Keyboard and Mouse Support**    Version 6.0 of the Norton Utilities supports the use of both the keyboard and a mouse for the selection of commands from menus and dialog boxes.

**Bar/Pull-down Menus**    All Norton Utilities program commands are integrated into a menu bar/pull-down menus system. The same basic structure is used with all programs, making it easy to move from one program to another. The menu bar appears at the top of the screen. It lists the major operational areas of the program. Each item on the menu bar, with the exception of the Quit option, will display a pull-down menu when it is selected. The pull-down menu lists the specific commands and functions available under the selected menu topic. Menu options that display dialog boxes are marked with ..., while items that are not available are enclosed in ().

**Dialog Boxes**    Dialog boxes are used for the selection of command settings and options. Dialog boxes can contain any of the following elements: entry boxes, radio buttons, check boxes, control buttons, list boxes, and descriptive text.

**Help**    You can activate context-sensitive help screens by pressing the [F1] key at any time. The help feature contains its own index of topics that you can browse once you have activated help.

**The Norton Program**    The Norton program creates a DOS shell that integrates the various modules of the Norton Utilities. The program can be customized to display your own menu selection, which will execute either Norton Utilities, DOS utility, or application programs.

**NU Variable**    The NU variable can be used to direct the Norton Utilities to read INI and CMD support files from a directory other than the *home* directory. This feature is useful when you are running Norton Utilities across a local area network.

# 6 Operating the Utilities from DOS

In the previous chapter you looked at the full screen user interface that organizes the screen presentation of the Norton Utilities programs.

An alternative way to work with the Norton Utilities is to use *DOS command-line* instructions. A command-line instruction is a single command issued at the DOS prompt that contains the name of the program, any file or drive parameters, and optional switches. The command line will execute part or all of a program without the need for the user to make selections from menus or dialog boxes. Command-line operations have three major advantages:

**Performance.** By entering the required program parameters as part of a single command you can execute an operation more quickly than you can by making selections from menus and dialog boxes. If you know in advance the exact command you want to issue, you can avoid the standard Norton Utilities user interface and have the program directly execute the desired function.

**DOS Filters and Redirection.** DOS provides a standard set of commands that modify aspects of the output from programs executed under DOS. These commands come in the form of filters and redirection operators. For example, output usually placed only on the screen can be redirected to the printer as well, by using the **>PRN** redirection command.

**Batch File Operations.** You can include Norton Utilities commands in DOS batch files. Batch files are text files that contain one or more DOS commands. The commands written in these files can be executed as a group by entering the name of the batch file. Batch files allow you to create procedures and even programs composed of DOS commands that simplify and speed up MS-DOS operations.

In this chapter you will learn the basics of Norton Utilities command-line execution, the use of DOS filters and redirection commands, and the use of simple batch files. Keep in mind that the use of batch files and batch file programming is covered in extensive detail, beginning with Chapter 15.

# Command-line Execution

When you want to execute one of the Norton Utilities programs, you usually do so by entering the name of the program file, e.g., **FILEFIND**, at the DOS prompt followed by ↵. If you have worked with MS-DOS computers for any length of time you might simply take this process for granted until you encounter the message "Bad command or filename."

It may be useful to examine exactly what happens when you enter a command to execute a program such as FILEFIND. It is important to understand that when you issue the command, DOS does not know what FILEFIND represents, or what effect the command to execute it will have on the computer. DOS goes through a number of very specific steps in an attempt to carry out the instruction:

**COMMAND.COM.** DOS begins the process of executing a command by first examining the *internal* DOS commands contained within the COMMAND.COM program. These are the commands that are loaded as a group when the computer is first booted. If the command that was entered cannot be found in COMMAND.COM, DOS proceeds to the second step.

**COM Files.** DOS searches the files listed in the current directory for one that has a COM extension that matches the command entered. For example, if you entered XYZ, DOS would look for a file called *XYZ.COM*. If the file is found it is loaded into memory and executed. If no match is found DOS proceeds to the next step.

**EXE Files.** Next, DOS searches the current directory for an EXE file that matches the command entered, for instance XYZ.EXE. If the file is found it is loaded into memory and executed. If no match is found DOS proceeds to the next step.[1]

---

1.  Both COM and EXE files are program files stored in a binary format. COM files are simpler than EXE files in that they are stored on the disk in the exact sequence in which they will be placed into the computer's RAM memory for execution. EXE programs are more complicated and must include instructions within the program that explain where in memory the various segments of the program should reside. However, the simpler COM files are limited to 65,536 bytes in size. EXE files can be of unlimited size.

**BAT Files.** DOS then searches the directory for a batch file, BAT extension, that matches the command entered. If no match is found DOS proceeds to the next step.

**Path Directories.** If DOS fails to locate a match in the current directory, it then begins to work through the list of directories, if any, stored under the PATH variable in the environment space, as specified by the PATH command. DOS searches the directories in the order in which they appeared in the PATH command. It will execute the first COM, EXE, or BAT file that matches the entered command.

**Bad Command or Filename.** If DOS fails to find a matching file it then terminates its search and displays the message "Bad command or filename," and displays the DOS prompt again so you can enter another command.

There are several things that you can conclude from this process. For example, the error message "Bad command or filename" sounds rather ambiguous. Isn't DOS able to determine if the entry was a bad command or simply a bad file name? The answer is no. DOS displays this message when it cannot match the entered command word with one of the COMMAND.COM internal commands, or a COM, EXE, or BAT file that lies in one of the directories on its current search path. Thus, the solution to a "Bad command or filename" error is often a PATH command that will expand the path list to include the directory in which the corresponding COM, EXE, or BAT file is stored.

You can also infer that it is not a good idea to have a COM, EXE, and/or BAT file with the same name in the same directory. For example, if you had a program stored in a file called WP.EXE and then you created a batch file called WP.BAT in the same directory, what would happen when you entered WP⏎? Because DOS always works in the order of COM, EXE, and BAT, the WP.EXE program would always be used and the WP.BAT file would never be executed.

This is why it is so important that the \NU directory be included in your system's path list. Without this path, DOS will not be able to execute the Norton Utilities program unless you activate the \NU directory first.

Norton Utilities command-line operations have two primary purposes:

**Set Starting Options.** In some cases you will need or want to set options for the program you are about to use *before* the program is loaded. For example, you may want to run a particular program in black and white, even though the programs are configured for color. In other cases you may want to disable or enable certain features before the program is loaded so that you cannot accidentally make the wrong choices from the menus. For example, you may want to prevent the Norton Disk Doctor from operating on a specific disk by listing as part of the NDD command the drive you want excluded.

**Execute without User Interface.**   In order to save time you may want to perform a Norton Utilities operation without having to work with the Norton Utilities user interface. For example, the FILEFIND program can be used to perform a number of file-oriented operations, such as changing the attribute of a file to **read-only.** When run in the user-interface mode, you must wait until the program has located a group of files before you can specify that you want to change an attribute. By using command-line options you could specify both the selection and file attribute operations in a single command that the FILEFIND program would execute without further input. Such options allow more *automatic* operation.

Each Norton Utilities program has a unique set of command line specifications that can be used with that particular program. In general, if you use any specification that is not supported by the program, it is ignored and the program loads in its default user-interface format.

## Switches and Parameters

Specifications for command-line operations fall into two classifications:

**Parameters.**   *Parameters* are specifications that select a drive, directory, or file as the object of the program's operation. The Norton Utilities recognizes the DOS file, path, and wildcard notation. The FILEFIND program also accepts a text string for performing text searches.

**Switches.**   A switch is a word or letter that the program recognizes as an instruction to use a particular option or setting. Each switch used in a line command is preceded by a /.[2] A Norton Utilities program will recognize only those switches for which it was programmed. For example the **WIPEINFO** command recognizes the switch **/K.** This switch would be ignored by the other Norton Utilities programs.

---

2.   Do not confuse the / (forward slash) used with switches with the \ (back slash) used in directory path names.

For example, in Chapter 5 under the discussion of "Network Consideration" the **FILEFIND** command was used to set the attributes of the program files to read-only. The command was not used in the full screen interactive menu mode but was executed as a command-line operation. The command used was:

```
filefind .\*.exe /r+/batch
```

The command actually contains three distinct parts:

**Command.**   The command in this case is the name of the Norton Utilities program, FILEFIND.

**File Parameters.** The file specification is .\*.exe. This is designed to select all the files with EXE extensions in the current directory only. Note that FILEFIND searches the entire disk by default.

**Switches.** In this case two switches are used. /R+ adds the read-only attribute to all selected files. The /BATCH switch selects the *batch operation* mode, which tells the program to skip over dialog boxes that require user entry or confirmation, and operate automatically.

When entering a command, the three elements are always entered in the same order: command, parameters, and switches. If you are using more than one program switch the order in which the switches are entered is not important. The program reads the entire command line before it begins to interpret the switches. This also means that if you enter an incorrect switch as part of the switch list the program will ignore the incorrect switch, but recognize the correctly entered switches.[3]

## Global Switches

While each Norton Utilities program has a specific set of switches that can be used with that program, all of the programs that display the menu bar/pull-down menu interface will accept five *global* switches. These switches are used to select video options that correspond to the options on

---

3. This is different from most DOS commands that will reject the entire command if a mistake is detected in any of the switches. The Norton Utilities is much more forgiving than DOS when it comes to command switches.

the Video and mouse options dialog box found on the *Configure* menu of the NORTON program. These switches are:

**/GO.** This switch sets the program to text display. If you are using an EGA or VGA type display the check boxes and radio buttons appear as text, [], and (), instead of graphics. In addition, the mouse cursor will appear as a block instead of a pointing arrow.

**/G1.** This switch affects only the shape of the mouse that is set as a block instead of a pointing arrow. The settings of the check boxes and radio buttons are not affected by this option.

**/BW.** Sets the display mode as black and white.

**/LCD.** Sets the display mode to black and white for display on a laptop LCD-type screen display.

**/NOZOOM.** Dialog boxes will not be zoomed open.[4]

Note that these switches change the video attributes for the current session of the program, but do not change the default settings stored in the NORTON.INI file. To change the default settings you must run the Norton program and use the **Video and mouse options** dialog box. When you exit the program, those settings will be stored in the NORTON.INI file.

You can use the switches in combination with each other. For example, the following command sets the FILEFIND program to text-only display in black and white:

```
filefind /bw/gO
```

## Command-line Help

All of the Norton Utilities programs are designed to display help about their command-line parameters and switches. You can invoke the command-line help by entering a **?** as a parameter for the command you want to investigate. For example, to get command-line help for the FILEFIND program, you would enter filefind ?⏎.

---

4. Depending upon the speed of your system, the zooming effect will appear more or less pronounced. On fast systems you may not notice that a dialog box is being displayed as a series of enlarging boxes, since it happens so fast that it makes this switch of little practical importance.

```
           Computer Name: IBM AT or compatible
         Operating System: DOS 3.30
       Built-in BIOS dated: Friday, January 15, 1988
            Main Processor: Intel 80386, 20 MHz          Serial Ports: 2
             Co-Processor: None                        Parallel Ports: 2
    Video Display Adapter: Monochrome (MDA)
        Current Video Mode: Monochrome Text, 80x25
     Available Disk Drives: 7, A: - G:

    DOS reports 640 K-bytes of memory
         288 K-bytes used by DOS and resident programs
         352 K-bytes used available for application programs
    A search for active memory finds:
         640 K-bytes main memory      (at hex 00000-0A000)
          32 K-bytes display memory   (at hex 0B000-0B800)
       1,024 K-bytes extended memory  (at hex 10000-20000)
    ROM-BIOS Extensions are found at hex paragraphs:

      Computing Index (CI), relative to IBM/XT: 9.9
          Disk Index (DI), relative to IBM/XT: Not computed. No drive specified.
    Performance Index (PI), relative to IBM/XT: Not computed.
```

**Figure 6–1. FILEFIND command-line help display.**

The command will cause the program to display a screen of text, as seen in Figure 6–1, instead of executing the program. The screen lists the parameters and switches that can be used with that program.

The command-line help screen uses special notations to indicate the parameters and switch options that can be used with that program.

The first line of the help display shows the *general form* of the command. The general form of the FILEFIND program is:

```
FILEFIND [filespec] [search-text] [switches]
```

The items enclosed in [] are *optional*. This means that you can use one or more of these items with that particular command. The FILEFIND program can accept three types of options:

**[filespec].** When this option is shown, you can enter any valid DOS path and file name, or wildcard.

**[search-text].** This option allows you to enter a text string that the program will search for, within the contents of the selected file.

**[switches].** This option tells you that you can enter optional switches for this command.

The help display then lists information about the specific options supported by this program. In the case of FILEFIND, details about the file specifications and the switches are displayed.

You will notice that many of the switches have optional parameters. For example, the **/R** switch shows the options **[+/-]**. This means that the **/R** switch can be used in three different ways with the File Find command, as shown in Table 6–1.

**Table 6–1. Optional switch settings.**

| | |
|---|---|
| filefind /r | select read-only files |
| filefind /r+ | mark selected files read only |
| filefind /r- | remove read-only attributes from selected file |

If an option is *not* enclosed in [], it is a *required parameter* and must be completed in order for the option or switch to be valid. For example, in the list of switches for the FILEFIND program are switches that have required or optional parameters. For instance, the /O switch requires a *file* (file name) as a parameter. This makes sense because the /O switch is used to copy a list of the selected files into a text file. Without knowing what name to assign to that text file, the program cannot complete the specified task. The command shown below illustrates the use of the /O parameter to copy the list of selected files into a text file called PROGS.TXT:

```
filefind *.exe /o:progs.txt
```

# Command Summary

The following selection lists all the Norton Utilities programs, and the command-line parameters and switches that can be used with them. Details of the uses for each of the programs are found in the remainder of this book.

## Batch Enhancer

This program provides commands that can be used to enhance the operation of DOS batch files. Most of the commands implemented by the BE program are features that cannot be produced using the existing set of DOS batch file commands.

```
BE command [parameters]
BE filespec
```

**Commands**

**ASK.** Pauses for user input during batch file.

**BEEP.** Sounds a tone on the system's speaker.

**BOX.** Draws a box on the screen.

**CLS.** Clears the screen.

**DELAY.** Pauses the batch file processing for a specific length of time.

**GOTO.** Jumps to a label within a file of Batch Enhancer instructions.

**PRINTCHAR.** Prints a number of repetitions of the same character.

**ROWCOL.** Places text string or cursor at a specific location on the screen.

**SA.** System Attribute sets DOS video attributes, such as screen color. The NCC (Norton Control Center) program can be used for more detailed color control.

**WINDOW.** Displays a window (a box that covers existing data) on the screen.

# Calibrate

The Calibrate program performs low-level disk testing, diagnosis, non-destructive formatting, and interleave adjustment.

```
CALIBRATE [drive] [switches]
```

**Drive**

Use the drive letter and colon of any valid drive. Will not operate on network logical drives and some drives created by device-driver partitioning software.

**Switches**

**/BATCH  Automatic operation mode.**

**/BLANK.** Turn on screen blanking.

/NOCOPY.  Turn off track copying feature.

/NOFORMAT.  Turn off low-level formatting, perform testing only.

/NOSEEK.  Turn off seek tests.

/PATTERN:*number*.  Perform pattern testing at the level indicated by the number.

/R:*file*.  Store report in specified text file.

/RA:*file*.  Append report to specified text file.

/X:*drive*.  Exclude drives from testing (i.e., /X:def to exclude drives d, e, and f).

## Disk Editor

This program allows you to directly examine or edit any part of the disk, including the boot sector, FAT, directories, or data area.

```
DISKEDIT [drive:] [path] [filename] [switches]
```

**Switches**            /M.  Maintenance mode operation. Program bypasses DOS and examines the disk directly.

/X:*drive*.  Excludes specified drives from absolute sector operations.

## Disk Monitor

This program loads a memory-resident program that monitors and restricts disk-writing operations in order to protect against unauthorized changes to disk data.

```
DISKMON [switches]
```

**Switches**            /STATUS.  Display summary of current monitor status.

/PROTECT+, /PROTECT-.  Activate or deactivate disk protection.

**/LIGHT+,/LIGHT-.** Activate or deactivate disk activity screen display.

**/PARK.** Park heads on all drives.

**/UNINSTALL.** Remove Disk Monitor from memory.

# Diskreet

This program provides features that create password protection for files or blocks of files.

```
DISKREET [switches]
```

| | |
|---|---|
| **Switches** | **/ENCRYPT:***filespec.* Encrypt specified file. |
| | **/DECRYPT:***filename.* Decrypt specified file. |
| | **/PASSWORD:***xxxxxxx.* Specify password for file encrypt/decrypt operation. |
| | **/SHOW***[:drive].* Show a logical encrypted disk. |
| | **/HIDE***[:drive].* Hide a logical encrypted disk. |
| | **/CLOSE.** Close all logical encrypted disks. |
| | **/ON.** Enable encrypt driver. |
| | **/OFF.** Disable encrypt driver. |

# File Find

This program searches disk directories and file contents for specific file names or text. The program can also change file information, such as file attributes or dates.

```
FILEFIND [filespec] [search-text] [switches]
```

| | |
|---|---|
| **FileSpec** | *.*. Search entire current drive. |
| | .\*.*. Search active directory only. |
| | *:*.*. Search all available system drives. |

Switches

**/S.** Include all subdirectories below the starting directory.

**/C.** Set search option for current directory only.

**/CS.** Perform case-sensitive text search.

**/A[+/-].** Set or remove Archive File attribute.

**/R[+/-].** Set or remove Read-only File attribute.

**/HID[+/-].** Set or remove Hidden File attribute.

**/SYS[+/-].** Set or remove System File attribute.

**/CLEAR.** Clear all file attributes.

**/D**[*mm-dd-yy*]. Display or change the file date.

**/T**[*hh:mm:ss*]. Display or change the file time.

**/NOW.** Set the file date and time to current system date and time.

**/TARGET:***drive*. Determine if *drive* can hold specified files.

**/O:***filename*. Copy file list into text file with specified name.

**/BATCH.** Execute program in automatic mode.

## File Fix

Analyzes and restores corrupted data files using the dBASE, Symphony, or Lotus 1-2-3 file format.

```
FILEFIX [filespec]
```

## Erase Protection

This program employs unused disk space to temporarily maintain deleted files so that they can be more easily recovered. Files are deleted after a certain time period or when the space is needed for new files.

```
EP [switches]
```

**Switches**   /**STATUS.** Displays current status of deleted files preserved by Erase Protection.

/**ON.** Activates Erase Protection.

/**OFF.** Deactivates Erase Protection.

/**UNINSTALL.** Removes Erase Protection from memory.

## Safe Format

Replacement program for DOS Format program.

```
SFORMAT [drive:] [switches]
```

**Switches**   /**A.** Activate automatic operating mode.

/**S.** Add DOS system boot files to formatted disk.

/**B.** Allocate room for DOS system files but do not add them to disk.

/**V:**label. Write a volume label on the disk.

/**1.** Single-sided formatting.

/**4.** Format a 360K disk in a 1.2M drive.

/**8.** Format 8 sectors per track, DOS 1.xx compatible.

/**N:**number. Specify the number of sectors per track to be formatted.

/**T:**number. Specify the number of tracks to be formatted.

/size Specify format by disk capacity in kilobytes.

/**Q.** Use Norton Quick Format method.

/**D.** Use standard DOS Format method.

# Image

This command works in conjunction with other data recovery programs in the Norton Utilities. It stores information about the current disk in a location that can be accessed when recovery is necessary.

```
IMAGE [drive:] [switches]
```

**Switches**          **/NOBACKUP.** Do not write a backup file when creating disk image data.

# Norton Control Center

This program provides a means of examining and changing hardware-oriented settings, such as video display mode and serial interface parameters.

```
NCC [filename] [switches]
```

**Switches**          **/START:***1-4.* Start stopwatch 1, 2, 3, or 4 and display current date and time.

**/STOP:***1-4.* Stop stopwatch 1, 2, 3, or 4 and display elapsed time.

**/N.** Suppress display of current time and date when setting stop watch.

**/L.** Display current time and date aligned on the left side of the screen.

**/C:***text string.* Display text string before time and date.

**/FAST.** Set keyboard to fastest speed.

**/BW80.** Set video display mode to Black and White, 25 x 80, if available.

**/CO80.** Set video display mode to Color, 25 x 80, if available.

*/number.* Set the number of lines on the standard screen display. Available for EGA or VGA type displays only.

*/SETfilename.* Loads Control Center settings stored in specified file.

# Norton Change Directory

This program is used to locate directories by searching for partial matches.

```
NCD [drive:] [search text] [switches]
NCD MD dirname
NCD RD dirname
```

**Switches**

**/R.** Scan drive and update directory information.

**/N.** Do not write directory information to a disk file.

**/V:***label.* Write specified volume label to disk.

# Norton Disk Doctor II

This program tests and repairs damaged disks.

```
NDD [drives:] [switches]
```

**Switches**

**/COMPLETE.** Perform complete disk test, which includes both system and data areas.

**/QUICK.** Test system area only.

**/R:***filename.* Write report to the specified text file.

**/RA:***filename.* Append report onto the specified text file.

**/REBUILD.** Rebuild an entire disk that has been destroyed.

**/UNDELETE.** Undelete a hard disk partition that was previously skipped.

**/X:***drive list.* Exclude specified drives from testing.

## Norton

This program displays a list box menu of Norton Utilities and user-defined commands. Switches for this program can be used with all Norton Utilities programs.

```
NORTON [switches]
```

Switches

/GO. This switch sets the program to text display for the mouse, check boxes, and radio buttons.

/G1. This switch affects only the shape of the mouse, which is set as a block instead of a pointing arrow.

/BW. Sets the display mode as black and white.

/LCD. Sets the display mode to black and white for display on a laptop LCD-type screen display.

/NOZOOM. Dialog boxes will not be zoomed open.

## Speed Disk

Improves disk performance by arranging files in the most efficient sequence.

```
SPEEDISK [drive:] [switches]
```

Switches

/C. Perform complete disk reorganization.

/D. Perform directory reorganization only.

/U. Perform file unfragmentation operation only.

/Q. Remove gaps in data storage area only.

/SN[-]. Perform file sort using Name order. For descending order use -.

/SE[-]. Perform file sort using Extension order. For descending order use -.

/SD[-]. Perform file sort using Date order. For descending order use -.

/SS[-]. Perform file sort using Size order. For descending order use -.

/V. Activate Verify mode for disk organization operations.

/B. Reboot computer after optimization operations have been completed.

## System Information

Reports information about the computer system.

```
SYSINFO [switches]
```

**Switches**

**AUTO:n.** Automatically cycle through all information screens.

/DEMO. Cycle through benchmark tests only.

/TSR. Print list of TSR programs to standard output.

/N. Sutppress Memory Scan.

/SOUND. Beep between CPU tests.

/SUMMARY. Print SysInfo Summary screen.

## UnErase

Recovers erased files.

```
UNERASE [filespec]
```

## UnFormat

Recovers a formatted disk. This program works best when the Image program has been used to store key disk data prior to formatting.

```
UNFORMAT [drive:]
```

## WipeInfo

This program is used to overwrite disk data for security purposes.

```
WIPEINFO [drive:] [switches] (wiping disks)
WIPEINFO [filename] [switches] (wiping files)
```

**Disk Switches**       /E. Wipe clear all erased and unused data space only.

**File Switches**       /N. Delete files without wiping clear disk space.

/K. Wipe clear all slack space found at the end of files.

/S. Include all subdirectories following the current directory.

/G*number*. Follow certain government rules for wiping a specified number of times.

/R*number*. Repeat standard wiping a specified number of times.

/V*number*. Overwrite data with the specified numeric value.

# Summary

This chapter discussed the use of DOS line commands to execute Norton Utilities programs while using the full screen-user interface, discussed in the previous chapter.

**Command Lines**     Command-line execution refers to execution of Norton Utilities programs with a single command line entered at the DOS prompt. Command-line execution allows you to carry out specific actions without having to use the Norton Utilities menu and dialog box system.

**Parameters**     Parameters are used in command lines to specify items to use during the execution of a program. These parameters are usually disk items, such as drive letters, path names, file names, or DOS wildcards. Some programs require other types of parameters, such as text strings used for text searches.

**Switches**    Switches are single letters or words preceded by the / character. The switches are used to select program options without having to use the programs dialog box interface. Switches may also have their own parameters that are needed to execute special tasks. A command line can have one or more switches.

**DOS Redirection**    DOS allows you to redirect the output of a program to another device, such as a printer or a disk file. Redirection allows you to send output to the printer instead of the screen, even though the program does not directly support printing. You can also capture the output in a text file. The > symbol redirects output to the specified location. DOS recognizes the name PRN as the location of the default printing device. The >> symbol is used to append text output onto an existing file.

**DOS Filters**    A filter is a program that manipulates the output of a program. DOS provides three filter programs: MORE, SORT, and FIND. Filter programs are attached to DOS commands by preceding the filter name with the | character.

**Batch Files**    A batch file is a text file that contains one or more DOS instructions. Batch files must have a BAT file extension. Batch files allow you to execute one or more DOS commands by executing the batch file. Batch files also save time and eliminate errors because they are stored permanently on the disk and can be re-executed whenever needed.

# 7 Analyzing Your System

If you were to ask the average PC user what he or she wants out of a computer, the phrase "easy to use" is almost certain to be included in the description. Since all computers are at base very complicated machines, making a computer easy to use consists of hiding from the user many of the details required for computer operations. Hiding these details prevents the user from becoming overwhelmed with minutiae about the computer's activities, making the device less intimidating.

On the other hand, this has led to the odd fact that many PC users have little or no idea of what type of system they are using—for instance, how much and what type of memory they have, types and sizes of disks, video adapter types, etc. When a person buys a computer, he or she usually has some idea of what is included; however, over time it easy to forget such details. If you are using a computer that you did not buy, you may have no way of knowing the details just because you've used it.

While it is possible to use a computer without knowing the details, you will often find circumstances where you must know some of its specific attributes. For example, when you purchase software, the program often lists the hardware requirements. You need to be able to determine if your system meets these requirements before your purchase. In addition, many programs offer hardware-specific options that require you to know something about the details of the system you are using—for example, do you have extended or expanded memory; if so, how much?

The subject of this section's chapters involves the methods by which the Norton Utilities 6.0 programs can be used to obtain information about your computer. Remember that just using a computer doesn't tell you very much about the components of the system itself. The details of the system are important if you want to *fine-tune* your system, or even if you want to obtain help, since technical support people need to know the exact type of environment in which you are working.

# The System Information Program

The *System Information* module of the Norton Utilities is designed to provide information about the current state of your system. As with the other modules, you can run System Information from the Norton menu, or execute it directly from DOS. The file name for System Information is SYSINFO.EXE or, if you have selected short names, SI.EXE.

Assuming you are starting at DOS, run the program by entering sysinfo ↵.

The System Information module loads and displays a screen of information about the current system. The menu bar at the top of the screen divides the information into four major topics:

**System.** The System menu displays the system summary screen, a video summary screen, data about interrupt assignments, and a summary of the data stored in the system CMOS. If you are running under Novel Netware, network data will be displayed. System menu options: System summary, Video summary, Hardware interrupts, Software interrupts, Network information, CMOS status.

**Disks.** Disk menu has three screens that detail the disks in your system, including their structural characteristics and partition information. Disk menu options: Disk summary, Disk characteristics, Partition tables.

**Memory.** The menu provides screens that analyze memory usage in several different ways. These screens help you answer questions about conventional, extended, and expanded memory use, and programs and drivers loaded into memory. Memory menu options: Memory usage summary, DOS memory block allocation, Installed TSR programs, Device Driver List.

**Benchmarks.** This menu is used to run performance tests on the microprocessor, the hard disk, and the network server, if any. These tests are useful when comparing one piece of computer equipment to another. Benchmark menu options: CPU speed, Hard disk speed, Performance Index, Network Performance.

In addition, the *Report* menu allows you to view the system's current CONFIG.SYS and AUTOEXEC.BAT files, and design a printed (or file output) report for some or all of the data displayed by the System Information.[1]

---

1. Printing a full System Information report can generate about 20 pages of data. In most cases you don't want all of the information (the list of 100 software interrupts takes four pages alone). Usually, it would be best to print individual sections using the Print control button or select a set of sections on the Print Report dialog box.

Each information dialog box displays four control buttons at the bottom of the box:

**Next.**  Displays the next dialog box.

**Previous.**  Displays the previous dialog box.

**Print.**  Prints a report to the printer or a text file containing the dialog box contents.

**Cancel.**  Closes the dialog box and activates the menu.

## System Information Reports

You can generate printed reports in two ways using the System Information program. All printing options can also be used to store the information in an ASCII text file so that you can store a record of the information on disk as well as on paper.

**Print Button.**  At the bottom of each dialog box display is a *Print* control button. If you select this button a second dialog box appears that contains a *Printer* button that will direct the output to the printer, a *File* button that will direct the output to a text file (default name SIREPORT.TXT), or a *Cancel* button that returns you to the previous dialog box without printing. Note that the amount of information printed from some dialog boxes may be more than anticipated, since a list box may reveal only a segment of the entire data list.

**Print Report Dialog Box.**  The *Print Report* dialog box allows you to create a customized report on the current system that can include any combination of 19 different report items, plus your text as a report header and end of report notes.

Both methods allow you to specify either printer or text file output.

## Command-line Operations

Since the System Information program does not actually perform operations, but merely reports information about the system; it is not typically used in batch file operations.

However, command-line operations of the System Information program can be used to run the program in a mode duplicating the single-screen summary produced by previous versions.

In addition the program supports switches that can cause the program to run in an automatic or demonstration mode.

The /SUMMARY switch causes System Information to produce the same single-screen output provided by the System Information program in Version 4.5 and earlier, as seen in the example below:

```
sysinfo /summary
```

If you want to include a hard disk benchmark test you need to specify the drive you want tested. The command below adds a hard disk test of drive C to the summary-screen information. Only one disk at a time can be specified:

```
sysinfo c: /summary
```

If you want to print the single-screen output use the DOS redirection command, as shown below. Note that you will need to enter a form-feed character (e.g., ECHO ^L>PRN) following the output to feed the rest of the page:

```
sysinfo /summary > prn
```

The same technique can be used to redirect the output to a disk file. The command below sends the output to a file called SYSDATA.TXT:

```
sysinfo /summary > sysdata.txt
```

Note that one omission in the Version 4.5 screen output is that the test results are not time and date stamped as are the reports generated by Version 6.0. You can add a time and date stamp to the output file using the Norton Control Center program in a separate command, to generate the time and date information:

```
ncc /start:1/1/c:"Report Generated on:"
sysinfo /summary > sysdata.txt
```

You can issue both commands as part of a batch file to simplify entry of the commands when required.

The **/TSR** switch also produces a text output similar to the **/SUMMARY** switch, detailing the current usage of the system's memory. This information shows more details about memory use than the summary screen. Example:

```
sysinfo /tsr
```

You can display both the TSR report and the summary screen by using both switches. Note that the TSR report is always displayed before the summary report, regardless of the order in which the switches are entered. The commands shown below produce the same results:

```
sysinfo /tsr/summary
sysinfo /summary/tsr
```

You can use the DOS redirection commands to send the output to the printer or a text file, as shown in the examples below:

```
sysinfo /tsr/summary > prn
sysinfo /tsr/summary > sysdata.txt
```

The **/DEMO** switch causes System Information to run in a *demonstration* mode. In this mode the program will display only the performance test screens (System Summary, CPU speed, Disk speed, and Overall Performance). The program will automatically cycle through the test, pausing about three seconds for each screen. Note that you cannot print information when the program is running in the demo mode:

```
sysinfo /demo
```

The effect of the **/AUTO** switch is similar to the effect of the demo mode in that the program will automatically change from screen to screen without requiring the entry of any keystrokes. The switch allows you to enter a value, in seconds, that determines how long each screen will remain displayed before the program moves to the next screen. Note that there is one exception to the automatic display. The program will pause for you to select which hard disk or network disk you want to test if the system has more than one disk available for these tests. The command below runs System Information in the *automatic* mode, pausing five seconds at each screen:

```
sysinfo /auto:5
```

You can combine the /**DEMO** and /**AUTO** switches in one command. The result is that the program runs in the *demonstration* mode (benchmarks only) but uses the pause setting indicated by the /**AUTO** switch to determine how long each screen is displayed. The command below runs System Information in the demo mode, but displays each screen for 10 seconds instead of the default three seconds:

```
sysinfo /demo/auto:10
```

The /**SOUND** switch affects the use of an audio prompt during the *CPU speed* test. When this option is selected the program continually retests the speed of the computer as long as the CPU speed dialog box is displayed. In some systems you may notice a periodic fluctuation in the speed index score. If the /**SOUND** switch is used a beep is sounded after each CPU test is completed. The beep will stop when you close the CPU speed dialog box:

```
sysinfo /sound
```

The /**SOUND** switch can be used with the **DEMO** and/or **AUTO** switches to activate the beep during the CPU test. The command below runs System Information in the demo mode, pausing 10 seconds at each screen and issuing a periodic beep during the CPU test:

```
sysinfo /demo/auto:10/sound
```

The /**N** option is used to suppress the memory probe normally performed by System Information when it is loaded. This function is used in systems that will not tolerate the memory probe process that searches all areas of the system's reported memory. When this occurs, some systems generate an interrupt causing the system to display the "Parity Error" message, which locks up your computer system. This message was intended by the designers to indicate a defect in RAM memory. In this case it is misleading and no harm has actually been done to the system or RAM memory. If this problem occurs when you run System Information, reboot the system and run System Information with the /**N** switch:

```
sysinfo /n
```

# System Fundamentals

The *System* menu contains three screens that provide general information about the state of your computer. From these three screens you can determine the answer to most of the basic questions about your system—for instance, the amount of memory, the type of screen display, the number of serial ports, etc.:

**System Summary.** This screen provides a quick summary of the equipment installed in the computer.

**Video Summary.** This screen shows information about the type of video adapter used in the computer and how it is currently operating.

**CMOS Status.** This screen shows you the values stored in the CMOS RAM that are used by the system when it is booted.

## The System Summary Screen

By default, the module displays the *System Summary* screen, which consists of basic information about the computer's system divided into four areas—Computer, Disks, Memory, and Other Info:

**Computer.** The Computer box, as shown in Figure 7–1, lists basic information about your computer system, based on the information stored in the system ROM.[2]

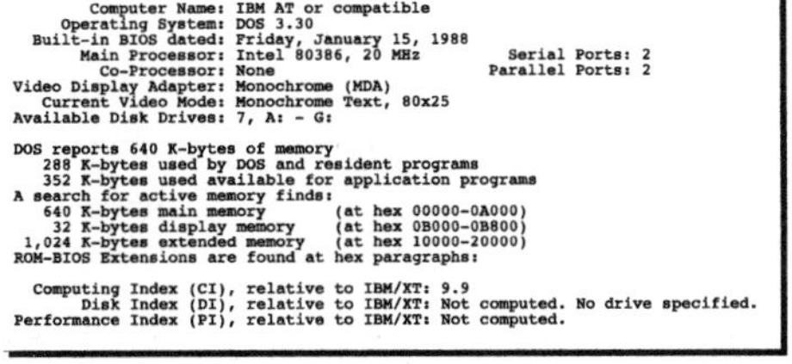

```
         Computer Name: IBM AT or compatible
      Operating System: DOS 3.30
     Built-in BIOS dated: Friday, January 15, 1988
        Main Processor: Intel 80386, 20 MHz        Serial Ports: 2
          Co-Processor: None                      Parallel Ports: 2
  Video Display Adapter: Monochrome (MDA)
    Current Video Mode: Monochrome Text, 80x25
  Available Disk Drives: 7, A: - G:

DOS reports 640 K-bytes of memory
   288 K-bytes used by DOS and resident programs
   352 K-bytes used available for application programs
A search for active memory finds:
   640 K-bytes main memory       (at hex 00000-0A000)
    32 K-bytes display memory    (at hex 0B000-0B800)
 1,024 K-bytes extended memory   (at hex 10000-20000)
ROM-BIOS Extensions are found at hex paragraphs:

  Computing Index (CI), relative to IBM/XT: 9.9
      Disk Index (DI), relative to IBM/XT: Not computed. No drive specified.
Performance Index (PI), relative to IBM/XT: Not computed.
```

**Figure 7–1. Computer information box.**

---

2.  ROM (read-only memory) refers to the built-in system ROM BIOS-basic input/output system discussed in Chapter 1.

**Computer Name.**   The name of the computer is not the actual brand name of the computer, but rather the general computer classification. Names such as IBM XT or IBM AT were originally the model names of IBM computers, but have come to be used as *generic* names for systems that have the same basic structure as these original IBM models.

**Built-in BIOS.**   The ROM BIOS of the system will usually contain the name of the manufacturer plus the date of its manufacture. In some cases the name of the manufacturer will be different from the brand name of the computer. While IBM and some other manufacturers create their own ROMs, many manufacturers purchase system ROMs from companies that specialize in this phase of programming, such as American Megatrends Inc. (AMI), Phoenix Technologies Inc., and Chips and Technologies Inc. The date is the date the ROM was manufactured. If you are having problems with your system it is often necessary to know the manufacture date of the ROM. This date relates only to the ROM, not the computer system as a whole, which is usually assembled at a later date.

**Main Processor.**   This option shows the name and speed rating of the system's microprocessor. The microprocessor is the *brain* of the computer. All operations conducted by the computer are under the control of the microprocessor. The three most common microprocessors are the Intel 8088, 80286, and 80386. See Chapter 2 for details about microprocessors.

**Math Coprocessor.**   Machines based on the 8088, 80286, and 80386 microprocessors will usually contain a slot on the circuit board for the addition of a corresponding math coprocessor. A math coprocessor is an optional microprocessor, which when added to the system, can be used to perform math-intensive operations at a higher rate of speed than the main processor can perform. It is important to understand the installation of a math coprocessor does not in and of itself change the performance characteristics of your computer. In order to put the coprocessor to use you must run an application that is specifically designed to employ the math coprocessor—as an example, Lotus 1-2-3 or AutoCad.

**Video Adapter.**   This option provides basic identification of the current video adapter. More details are found in "The Video Summary Screen" section later in this chapter.

**Mouse.** This option identifies any mouse drivers currently in use. Note that this identification depends on the identification included in the mouse driver or mouse program.

**Disks.** This box lists the *physical* disks found in the system. Note that logical disks created by disk partition or network access are not included in this box.

**Memory.** This box shows the total amount of memory installed divided into three categories. For an explanation of the three types of memory see the "Types of Memory" section below.

**Other Info.** This box lists additional useful data about the system.

**Bus Type.** The bus type tells you the type of system architecture used. The most popular, and least expensive, computers use the PC/AT type bus. Some IBM PS/2 models use IBM's microchannel bus. Bus type is important since you must know the type of bus your computer has when you purchase additional boards.

**Ports.** This option lists the number of parallel and serial ports installed in the system. Note that some boards, such as internal modems, will register as serial ports even though they are dedicated to modem operations.

**Keyboard.** This option displays the type of keyboard—as an example, 101 key or 83 key.

**Operating System.** This option identifies the operating system currently running in your computer. This is the same information that DOS displays when you use the DOS command **VER**.

This single screen provides most of the basic information you need to have about a computer system. This screen is especially useful when you must work on a computer system with which you are not familiar. Using this display you can quickly get a feel for the equipment that has been installed.

Exit the System Information program by entering [Alt-q].

## Types of Memory

One common area of confusion with PCs is the division of RAM memory into different types. DOS computers have three major categories of memory:

**Conventional.** All DOS computers have some conventional memory up to a limit of 1 megabyte (1,024 kilobyte). DOS is primarily designed to work with conventional memory. Because of the way DOS uses memory, the top 384 of memory is reserved for special uses. This leaves 604K for standard operations, such as DOS, memory resident programs and drivers, and user applications.

**Extended.**   *Extended* memory refers to any additional memory installed in the computer that lies beyond the first megabyte of *conventional* memory. Beginning with the IBM AT, DOS computers could contain up to 15 megabytes of extended memory in addition to the 1 megabyte of conventional memory, for a total of 16 megabytes of memory. However, because DOS was originally designed to work only with conventional memory, the uses of extended memory are extremely limited under DOS—for instance, RAM disk emulation or printer buffering.

**Expanded.**  Because of the severe limitations DOS placed on the use of extended memory, in 1985 Lotus, Intel, and Microsoft collaborated on a memory specification that would allow applications running in conventional memory to access additional memory beyond the 1 megabyte limit of conventional memory. This type of memory is called LIM (Lotus/Intel/Microsoft) *expanded* memory, also called EMS (Expanded Memory Specification). This memory uses a technique called *paging* or *bank switching* to increase the available memory. However, since DOS does not directly support paged memory, *extended* memory could be used only by programs specifically written to work with LIM expanded memory. Also, a device driver must be loaded during the boot process in order to make the expanded memory available to these applications.

The names *extended* memory and *expanded* memory unfortunately sound very much alike. This simply adds to the confusion of the various types of memory that are found in DOS computers. If you are not familiar with the concepts behind *extended* memory and *expanded* memory take care when reading about them since the names are so similar.

## Conventional Memory

In order to understand why DOS computers have more than one type of RAM memory and what the different types signify you need to begin with the design of the original IBM PC. Recall from Chapter 2 that RAM memory is organized as an array of memory cells, each with a unique address. The microprocessor can directly manipulate information stored in RAM by using cell addresses to locate individual bytes of information. Since the computer system is a collection of devices—RAM, video adapters, printer ports, disk drives—DOS needs to have specific addresses for all of these system elements.

The original design of the PC split the 1 megabyte of memory available to the 8088 processor into two equal parts. The first 512K would be general user memory, while the second 512K would be reserved for the use of special devices. Before the machine was released, an additional 128K was taken from the reserved section and added to the user section making the division of the 1 megabyte conventional memory 640K for user applications and 384K for device addresses, as shown in Figure 7–2. This division of memory into two distinct sections created the 640K limit you encounter when you operate in conventional memory. Note that the reserved 384K represents addresses that are assigned to ROM memory that is installed on the adapter boards in the computer.

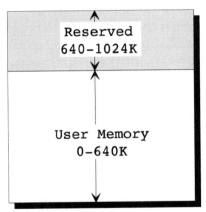

**Figure 7–2. Conventional memory divided in user and reserved sections.**

The system used by the original PC was called *real* mode processing. Real mode operations used fixed-memory addresses to simplify the structure of programs by placing major devices at specific locations in the memory. The upper 384K of the conventional memory was mapped with locations dedicated to particular devices, as shown in Figure 7–3.

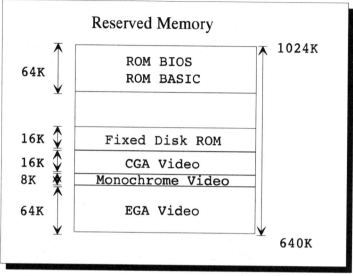

Figure 7–3. Reserved area of conventional memory.

The approach simplifies the structure of the operating system, making it easier to write programs, since the locations of various devices are known in advance. However, real mode processing has two major drawbacks:

**Memory Limit.** By placing the reserved area starting at above 640K the real mode sets a maximum limit to the total amount of RAM in the system. For example, many AT (80286) computers are sold with 1 megabyte of RAM installed. However, when the system is booted, DOS will report 640K, not 1,024K (1 megabyte) of memory available. This is a result of DOS operating in the real mode, which uses the fixed-memory addressing scheme. The result is that your computer contains 384K of RAM that cannot be used directly by DOS. This RAM is often called *shadow* RAM because it exists in the *shadow* of the memory addresses already assigned to the reserved area for device ROM memory. The RAM memory is installed in the computer but it cannot be seen by the microprocessor because the addresses above 640K are already allocated.

**Wasted Memory.** One of the ironies of the real mode method of reserving memory addresses for devices such as video adapters is that some of the reserved areas will probably never be used. For example, the real mode system reserves memory addresses for several types of video adapters. In 99 percent of the cases only one video adapter is attached to the computer. For example, if you use a CGA color monitor, DOS still reserves space for a monochrome or EGA adapter, even though no adapters requiring those memory addresses are installed in the computer. Thus, even though your computer has RAM in excess of 640K and the addresses are not actually used by any of the installed adapters, DOS cannot make use of those addresses to increase the amount of available RAM.

All user programs, including DOS, have to fit into an area no larger than 640K. DOS must always be resident in memory in order to operate the computer. This means that of the 1 megabyte of conventional memory, 384K at the top is reserved for devices, and a segment of memory at the bottom—typically 80–120K—is used by DOS. This leaves a section in-between that is the actual amount of conventional memory available for user applications. This area is called the *Transient Program Area* or TPA, as shown Figure 7–4.[3]

The TPA is a very important value to know since it tells you the actual amount of memory you have at your disposal. The TPA is more meaningful than the amount of installed memory because it take into consideration the

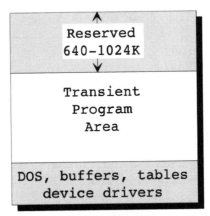

**Figure 7–4. Transient Program Area available for user applications.**

---

3.  The System Information program itself uses up some memory in order to display the information. The program shows the amount of conventional memory in use, minus the memory used by System Information. This means that the TPA size reflects what the size of the TPA will be when you exit the System Information program and return to DOS, not what it actually is at the moment.

amount of memory used by memory resident programs, such as DOS, device drivers used for hard disks, mice, or other devices and memory resident utilities like the Norton Utilities Disk Monitor program. It is important to keep in mind that two computers with a full 640K of installed RAM memory can have very different TPA values once they have booted.

Most software programs show memory requirements in terms of the amount of installed memory—for example, 512K or 640K. But having a 640K computer does not guarantee that the software will run in that computer. It would be more accurate to list the required TPA. For example, dBASE IV Version 1.0 lists its memory requirement at 640K. It would be more accurate to say that dBASE needs a 470K TPA, that is, you cannot have more than 170K worth of programs—DOS and other memory resident programs—in memory when you want to run dBASE IV. One reason for having a reduced TPA is the loading of network operating system software in addition to DOS. If DOS plus the network software reduces the TPA below the required amount of memory, the program will not run even though you have 640K installed in the computer.

## Determining the TPA

The System Information program can be used to determine the current TPA of the computer. This can be done in two ways:

**Memory Usage Summary Screen.**  This screen, displayed from the *Memory* menu will show the current amount of available memory, the TPA.

**Summary Switch.**  You can also obtain the TPA size without running the full System Information by using the /**SUMMARY** command-line switch.

Begin with the full screen method. Enter sysinfo ↵.
When the program is loaded, display the Memory Usage summary screen by entering [Alt-m] u.
The Memory Summary screen contains a box labeled *DOS usage*. This box shows three values, as seen in Figure 7–5.
The first is the total amount of conventional memory installed. This value will reach a maximum of 640K.[4] The next value is the total amount of

---

4.  Note that when discussing conventional memory, the value discussed is almost always the total amount of RAM, excluding the 384K allocated to device adapter ROM addresses.

conventional memory allocated to DOS and other memory resident programs. The third figure shows the amount of memory that remains for user applications—that is, the TPA. Exit the program by entering [Alt-q].

```
DOS Usage
DOS reports 640 K-bytes of memory:
    280 K-bytes used by DOS and resident programs
    360 K-bytes available for application programs
```

**Figure 7-5. The DOS usage box.**

You can also obtain the same information as part of the single summary screen generated by the command-line switch, /**SUMMARY.** Enter sysinfo /summary ↵.

The display shows the TPA as the number of bytes available for applications programs. If you want to quickly determine the TPA you can use the command-line method, which is a bit faster than loading the full System Information program.

# Beyond Conventional Memory

At the time that the IBM PC was created in 1981, the existing personal computers had very small internal memories—the Apple II used a maximum of 48K, while CP/M computers used 64K. A limit of 640K, 10 times the current limit, didn't seem to be much of a practical limitation.

However, by 1984, it was clear that PC applications were outgrowing the 640K limit. IBM had introduced its AT computer. This computer included hardware features that had the potential to break the 640K barrier. The 80286 microprocessor could, in theory, use up to 16 megabytes of RAM. If fully implemented that would increase available memory by something like 250 times.

However, there was a very significant catch. The 80286 was capable of operating in two different modes: the *real* mode and the *protected* mode. Real mode operation meant that the 80286 processor behaved exactly like the 8088 processor used in the IBM PC, except that it ran faster. This allowed the AT to run DOS and all DOS applications several times faster without modification. However, in order to address the additional 15 megabytes of memory that could be installed in the AT, the 80286 processor would have to operate in the protected mode. Once switched to the protected mode, DOS and DOS applications could not run. Only operating systems such as UNIX or XENIX, which are designed for protected mode operations, could access the 15-megabytes of extended memory that could potentially be installed in the AT.

The problem is that the popular applications that caused people to want more powerful personal computers—Lotus 1-2-3, dBASE IV, or Word-Perfect—could only operate under DOS in the real mode and were unavailable under protected mode systems such as UNIX or XENIX. Thus, the potential advantages of the AT's extended memory were still unavailable to the wide audience of users running DOS applications. This explains why many AT systems sold with 1 megabyte of RAM show only 640K of RAM once they are booted into DOS running in the real mode.

## Extended Memory

If you run the System Information program on an AT (80286) computer with 1 megabyte of memory, the program will report that you have 640K of conventional memory and 384K of extended memory. Even though the system shows 384K of RAM in extended memory, when operating in the real mode (8088 emulation), DOS has already used up all of the memory addresses available for the 640K of conventional memory and the 384K allocated for device ROM memory.

DOS 3.xx provided some limited support for the use of extended memory during real mode operations. This support took the form of using the extended memory as a RAM drive. A RAM drive is created when a block of memory is set up to operate as if it were a disk drive. Since RAM operates faster than disk drives, a RAM drive would provide fast access to information that would otherwise have to be loaded from a disk. These versions of DOS included a drive called RAMDRIVE.SYS (or VDISK.SYS in IBM versions) that supported a switch, /E, which would place the RAM drive in extended memory. For example, if you had an AT with 384K of extended memory you could create a 384K RAM drive by adding the following line to your CONFIG.SYS file:

```
DEVICE=C:\DOS\RAMDRIVE.SYS 384 /E
```

This ability can also be exploited by third-party programs, such as the Norton Utilities disk caching program NCACHE. This program can make use of extended memory to improve disk input/output performance by creating a memory cache.[5] Details of the NCACHE program can be found in Chapter 9, "Fine-tuning Your Computer."

## XMS

In 1988 Microsoft announced its support for a new memory management specification that could be used to allow 80286 or 80386 computers to access some portion of extended memory while running under DOS. The specification is called XMS (extended memory specification). This specification is implemented with the HIMEM.SYS (high memory) driver supplied by Microsoft with the newer versions of Windows (e.g., Windows 3.0) and with DOS 5.0. Loading the XMS driver through the CONFIG.SYS program allows programs specifically written for the XMS standard to access up to an additional 64K of memory, starting at the beginning of extended memory—at the 1 megabyte conventional memory border. The XMS compatible application can use this 64K block for program loading, which has the effect of increasing the computer's TPA by 64K. The primary use of the XMS specification is with Microsoft's Windows 3.0, which supports the XMS specification.

## Expanded Memory

The inability of DOS to utilize extended memory with real-mode applications led to the creation of the Lotus, Intel, and Microsoft *expanded* memory specification in 1985, called *LIM EMS*. LIM expanded memory was designed to create additional memory that could be used by memory-intensive applications, such as Lotus 1-2-3, while still running under DOS in the real mode. The challenge was to find a way to increase the addressable memory without going beyond the 1 megabyte limit established by the 8088 processor, or the 80286 processor running in 8088 emulation. The solution involved a process called *mapping*. Mapping is a procedure by which a section of the standard 1 megabyte memory is designated as the *frame* area. The frame area operates as a passageway between conventional memory and expanded memory. When an application needs additional memory, it can copy the data stored in the

---

5. A disk cache is a block of RAM memory that is used to hold blocks of information on their way to and from the disk. Since RAM usually operates much faster than disk read and write operations, cache memory can improve performance by reducing the number of read and write operations required.

*frame* area of conventional memory to a block of expanded memory. The application can then erase the frame area and fill it up with new data. If the data stored in expanded memory are needed, the process is reversed by filling the frame with data stored in expanded memory.

In order to make this system work, all of the expanded memory is divided into blocks called *pages*. Each *page* is 16 kilobytes in size. The expanded memory is not a single block of memory but a series of memory pages, each with a capacity of 16K, up to a maximum of 8 megabytes (512 pages) of memory.

The frame area is also organized in 16K pages. Typically, four 16K pages—a total of 64K of memory—are designated within the unused portion of memory between 640K and 1024K, which is the area reserved for devices in the real mode, as seen in Figure 7–6. Page frames are often placed at memory address E000.

The expanded memory system does not interfere with real-mode opera-

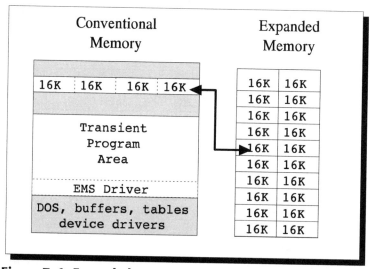

**Figure 7–6. Expanded memory uses 16K pages mapped into conventional memory.**

tions since neither DOS nor applications running under DOS are aware of its presence. In order for the expanded memory to actually be put to use, two things must happen:

**EMS Driver Loaded.** The EMS driver is a device driver that must be loaded by the CONFIG.SYS file when the system is booted. The driver remains in memory so that it can manage any expanded memory operations that are required. Note that DOS commands such as **CHKDSK** will not recognize the existence of expanded memory, even after the EMS driver has been loaded. **CHKDSK** or other DOS applications will report memory information about conventional memory only.

**EMS Compatible Application.** Because EMS is not recognized by DOS it can only be put to use by DOS applications that have been specifically programmed to perform expanded memory operations. Expanded memory can also be used by performance-oriented programs, such as the RAMDRIVE.SYS driver or the Norton Utilities Cache program.

*Expanded* memory is more useful than *extended* memory because it can be utilized while the computer, either 8088-, 80286-, 80386-, or 80486-based systems, operate in *real* mode. Real mode is still vital because most popular applications operate only under DOS, which runs in the real mode.

The primary limitation of expanded memory is the fact that it must be accessed through page frames mapped into unused sections of conventional memory:

**Limited Memory.** Expanded memory page frames are limited to gaps that occur within the 1 megabyte address range of conventional memory, limiting the size of a single block of expanded memory to 64K, 4–16K page frames.

**Application Specific.** Since expanded memory is ignored by DOS, applications must be specifically designed to use expanded memory. For example, WordPerfect Version 4.xx does not recognize or use expanded memory, while Version 5.xx does. If you add expanded memory to your system you must also make sure that your applications are compatible with expanded memory, in order to achieve an actual benefit.

**Data Only.** Because of the limited page frame size and the fact that specific applications, not DOS, utilize expanded memory, expanded memory is used primarily for additional data space—for instance, larger spreadsheets. Expanded memory cannot be used to increase the amount of memory available for program execution. For example, if your system does not have a sufficiently large TPA to run dBASE IV, adding expanded memory to the system will have no direct effect on this problem since DOS does not recognize expanded memory as part of the TPA. Your only solution would be to eliminate any memory resident programs—network operating system programs—from the conventional memory to make more room for dBASE.

**Hardware Dependent.** Expanded memory requires memory boards that specifically support the EMS specification. This means that the 384K of *extended* memory found in many 80286 machines cannot be used as *expanded* memory since the computer lacks the necessary hardware elements to implement expanded memory.

Since its introduction in 1985, the EMS standard has undergone changes and enhancements:

**EEMS.** Introduced by AST, a leading maker of memory expansion boards, the *Enhanced Expanded Memory Specification* sought to provide greater flexibility in the use of expanded memory by permitting mapping of memory below 640K. With the help of specially designed software—DESQview from Quarterdeck, for instance—expanded memory could be used to run programs implementing a form of Multitasking.[6]

**EMS 4.0.** Introduced by Lotus/Intel/Microsoft in 1987, this enhancement of the EMS specification provided for support of up to 32 megabytes of expanded memory, an increase from the 8 megabyte limit. It also included features found in EEMS, allowing expanded memory to be used to implement large page frames below 640K, which could be used to run programs using expanded memory.

Note that EEMS or LIM EMS 4.0 require both hardware and software that is specifically designed to implement the enhanced expanded memory features. For example, if you have a standard EMS board (EMS 3.2 compatible) and you add a LIM EMS 4.0 software driver to your system you will not be able to implement the LIM EMS 4.0 features because your hardware does not adequately support the software.

---

6. Multitasking refers to running more than one application at a time on a single computer.

## 386 Memory Features

Computers that are based on the 80386 processor have a number of specific features available that were designed to overcome the awkward problems that came about because of limitations of conventional and extended memory. While the 80386 supports both the real and protected modes, it allows much greater flexibility in their use. The primary advantage of the 80386-based computers is their ability to allow mapping of extended memory in a variety of different ways.

For example, the 80386 permits the mapping of unused conventional memory in the reserved area between 640K and 1,024K to extended memory. Using *special* 386 memory management software, for instance QEMM 386, you can *backfill* these unused addresses with extended RAM memory, enabling you to load memory resident programs such as COMMAND.COM, mouse, network, and hard disk driver programs into conventional memory above 640K, thereby increasing the all-important conventional memory TPA by as much as 128K.

Another important aspect of the 386 is that the hardware distinction between extended and expanded memory is eliminated. In practice all memory installed in a 386 computer beyond 640K is *extended* memory, not *expanded* memory. However, since real-mode operations under DOS running real-mode applications are still the most common use for 386 computers, you can convert some or all of the *extended* memory to function as *LIM 4.0 expanded* memory by loading a software memory-management program. The ability of the 386 to emulate expanded memory using extended memory allows 386 computers to be configured in different ways to take advantage of different types of programs. You no longer have to invest in memory boards that are linked to a specific memory specification, for instance EMS 3.2 or EMS 4.0.

## Expanded and Extended Information

The System Information program can be used to determine the amount of extended and expanded memory currently available in your system. The information is found on two screens: System Summary and Memory Summary. Display the System Summary by entering sysinfo ↵.

The box labeled **Memory** lists three items:

**DOS Memory.** DOS memory refers to the conventional memory available for DOS operations. In most cases the maximum value for this item is 640K. However, some 386 memory-management programs can increase the size of conventional memory, depending on the type of video memory options you select. For example, the QEMM 386 program can provide 704K of DOS memory if you are using a monochrome monitor rather than a VGA monitor.

**Extended Memory.** This option shows the amount of extended memory, that is, memory beyond 1,024K, installed in the computer.

**Expanded Memory.** This option shows the amount of expanded memory installed in the computer. Note that unlike DOS or extended memory, the value reported for expanded memory depends upon the proper loading of the expanded memory software driver during the boot process. If you installed an expanded memory board but did not properly install the corresponding software, no expanded memory will be reported, nor will it be available for use with programs that support the use of expanded memory.

If you are using a 386 computer in which extended memory is mapped through the use of a 386 memory-management software, as expanded memory, the System Information program will report memory twice. For example, if you have 1,024K of extended memory and that memory has been mapped as expanded memory, you will find that System Information reports both 1,024 of extended memory and 1,024K or more of expanded memory. This does not mean that you have 2,048K— that is, 1,024 of extended and expanded memory—only that in terms of software recognition the extended memory will function as expanded memory.

Display the Memory Usage screen by entering [Alt-m] u.

The second box on the screen is labeled **Overall.** This box contains additional details about the memory installed in the system, as seen in Figure 7–7:

```
┌ Overall ─────────────────────────────────────────┐
│                                                   │
│ A search for active memory finds:                 │
│     640 K-bytes main memory      (at hex 00000-0A000) │
│      32 K-bytes display memory   (at hex 0B800-0C000) │
│       4 K-bytes extra memory     (at hex 0EF00-0F000) │
│   1,408 K-bytes extended memory  (at hex 10000-26000) │
│   1,376 K-bytes expanded memory                   │
└───────────────────────────────────────────────────┘
```

**Figure 7–7. Overall memory summary.**

**Main Memory.**    The main memory displays the total amount of conventional memory and the addresses starting at 00000 up to 0A000 for 640K. Note that memory-management programs, in particular those commonly used on 386 machines, may cause the DOS memory values in the DOS usage box to differ from the Main memory value in the Overall box, since DOS under these circumstances may report additional memory, which is made available above the 640K barrier.

**Display Memory.**    Video adapter cards will use an area of memory between 640K and 1,024K. It is through this memory area that the microprocessor can communicate with the video adapter.

**Extra Memory.**    Extra memory refers to any additional areas of the memory between 640K and 1,024K that are available for use. Typically, such areas would be the memory locations assigned to act as EMS page frames when an expanded memory driver has been loaded. On systems without special memory managers this item will not appear.

**Extended Memory.**    This lists the extended memory, if any, installed in the system.

**Expanded Memory.**    This item lists the expanded memory as reported by the expanded memory driver, if any.

The items in the **Overall** memory box provide details about how the memory in the computer is organized. The display will also tell you if you have properly installed expanded memory software. Note that DOS **CHKDSK** will not report expanded or extended memory.

## ROM BIOS Extensions

The original design of the IBM PC provided for the addition of device-specific programs called ROM BIOS extensions. Recall that every computer contains a special program called the ROM BIOS, which is stored in ROM memory chips installed on the main board of the computer. It is the ROM BIOS program that starts up the booting process each time you turn the computer on. As part of the booting process the main ROM BIOS program scans the memory addresses from 640K to 1,024K looking for the presence of any additional ROM programs. These ROM programs[7] are installed in

---

7.  They are called ROM BIOS extensions because they add to the existing ROM programs in your computer. Note that as ROM programs they cannot be altered unless you change the ROM chips on the adapter cards.

your computer when you add certain adapter cards, such as hard disk controller cards, or EGA and VGA video cards. A ROM program is identified to the computer by a specific sequence of bytes at the beginning of each program. If this sequence is found, the computer executes the ROM program stored on the board.

If you install a VGA or EGA card in your computer you may notice that when you first turn on the computer a few lines of information about the card and the amount of memory installed on the card is displayed. This information is generated by the ROM BIOS extension program located on that card. Other ROM BIOS extensions merely set up the device, for instance a hard disk, without displaying anything on the screen.

The BIOS extension box lists the starting addresses in memory at which ROM BIOS programs were executed.

## The Video Summary Screen

You can obtain additional information about the type of display adapter installed in your computer from the Video Summary screen. Enter [Alt s] v.

The display is divided into three information boxes:

**Display.** This box shows the type of video monitor and adapter installed in the system and the current mode in which the adapter is operating. Note that many specialized adapters support special video modes not listed among the standard IBM video mode, such as Super VGA, 1,024 by 768 pixel graphics.

**Character.** This box shows the details of the text character display for the current adapter and display mode. The box lists the total number of scan lines on the screen, the size of the pixel matrix used to form the characters, and the cursor emulation mode. The scan lines indicate the vertical resolution of the display. The more scan lines on the screen the finer the resolution. The character size matrix tells you the size of the pixel matrix used to form each character displayed in the text mode. Figure 7–8 shows the different pixel matrixes used by different types of screen displays, for example, Monochrome, CGA, EGA, and VGA.[8]

**Memory.** This box shows information about the use of memory for the video adapter. The Video memory is the amount of additional memory

---

8. The 8 by 8 matrix used by CGA screens does not have sufficient height to allow an underline to be placed beneath a character. Underlined text can be displayed on monochrome, VGA, or EGA screens.

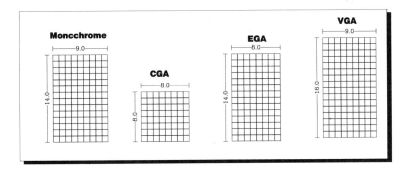

**Figure 7–8. Character pixel matrixes.**

contained on the video adapter. Monochrome adapters use only 4K of memory while VGA adapters may have as much as 512K of memory. The box also shows the starting memory address of the video memory. The video page size refers to the amount of memory needed to contain one full page of text.

The Video summary screen reports the characteristics of the current video adapter and display mode. The Norton Control Center program can be used to change video mode, color palettes, and cursor size. The Norton Control Center is discussed in Chapter 9, "Fine-tuning Your Computer." Exit the System Information program by entering [Alt-q].

# Advanced Memory Information

The most basic facts about your computer's memory can be obtained from the System, Video, and Memory summary screens. These screens allow you to quickly determine the size of the conventional memory TPA (transient program area), which tells you how much room you have for loading and running DOS applications. You can also determine the amount of extended and expanded memory available. If these values do not correspond to what you expect, you will then have to determine why the computer is not recognizing the memory that you thought you had.

What these screens do not tell you is the details of how the memory is being used. In most day-to-day operations the details of memory usage are irrelevant, so long as everything is going along smoothly. But when you make changes to your system, adding hardware or software, you may encounter problems. The Norton Utilities System Information program provides a series of rather technical display screens that can be very useful in determining exactly what is going on in your computer's memory.

## The Interrupt Screens

Following the **Video summary** screen, the next two items on the *System* menu are **Hardware Interrupts** and **Software Interrupts.** These displays are probably the most technical information that the System Information program provides. While it is true that for most users the information on these displays will have little meaning or direct use, the following section will attempt to explain the basic concepts that relate to this information.

Interrupts, both hardware and software, refer to a signal sent to the microprocessor that indicate that some element of the system needs immediate attention. The purpose of the interrupt is to tell the microprocessor to stop what it is currently doing and execute a different routine that is stored somewhere in the RAM memory. These routines are called *handlers* because they are specifically designed to handle the event that interrupted the microprocessor.

Hardware interrupts are related to specific devices that are installed within the system, such as the keyboard, the parallel and serial ports, the hard and floppy disk drives, and other special devices, such as network adapter cards or CD-ROM drives. In order to communicate with the microprocessor when necessary, each device must have a unique line of communication. These lines of communication are called *interrupt request* lines, usually represented by the abbreviation IRQ. PC/XT type computers have 8-IRQ lines, while AT type computer have 16-IRQ or more lines. IRQs are important because each device that needs to issue interrupt signals to the microprocessor must have a unique IRQ line. If two devices are set to use the same IRQ line the effect is a little like two planes trying to land on the same runway. The results of IRQ conflicts can range from a failure of one of the devices to respond to a complete lockup of the system. When you install devices in your computer you will often be required, as part of the installation process, to select the IRQ line for the device to use. The correct selection is an IRQ line that is not already in use by another device.

# Hardware Interrupts

You can display a list of the hardware interrupts by using the **Hardware interrupts** command located on the *System* menu. The program lists the hardware interrupts in a list box. The box lists the IRQ line number, the address of the handler routine for that interrupt, and the standard name used for interrupt. Keep in mind that these names do not necessarily indicate the actual use of the IRQ but only the usual use for those IRQ lines.

The last item on the list is the *owner* of the IRQ line. Most of the IRQ lines will show DOS, BIOS, or unknown for the owner. However, in some cases memory resident software programs that operate as IRQ handlers can be identified. The name of that program will appear as the owner.

# Software Interrupts

The screen following the **Hardware interrupt** screen is the **Software interrupt** list. Display that screen by entering [Alt-s] ↓(press 3 times)↵. The software interrupt list is similar in appearance to the hardware interrupt list in that it lists the interrupt numbers, the name (as defined by standard usage), the address, and the owner.

Software interrupts perform a similar function to hardware interrupts in that they contain the memory addresses of special routines or tables of information necessary to handle basic operating system tasks. However, unlike hardware interrupts, software interrupts are generated directly by software applications.

PCs support up to 256 software interrupt routines. The routines and information tables indicated by the interrupt addresses make up the basic core of DOS and BIOS operations. Recall from Chapter 3 that many of the basic operating tasks, such as reading and writing disk data, which most programs require, are actually carried out by DOS routines instead of the applications. This system is implemented by programs that issue calls to one or more of the 256 interrupt routines[9] laid out in the software interrupt table.

# The TSR Programs Screen

In addition to the data on the software and hardware interrupt screens, the Memory menu contains two screens that reveal something about how the memory is organized. The *TSR Programs* screen displays information

---

9.  The 256 interrupt levels are numbered 00 through FF in hexadecimal numbers.

about the programs that have been loaded into memory since the computer was booted.

A TSR—*terminate and stay resident*—program is a program that is not removed from memory after it has run. All DOS machines use at least one set of TSR programs—that is, the DOS operating system itself, which remains in memory while all other applications operate.

In addition to DOS there are two types of TSR programs commonly used on PCs:

**Event Activated.** Event-activated programs are loaded into memory and remain dormant until a specific event takes place. The event, usually an interrupt, triggers the activation of the program. The Disk Monitor program is an example of a TSR program that is triggered by any disk read or write operations. Event-activated programs often will not display any items on the screen to indicate that they are active, since many of the functions they perform are background operations not requiring user knowledge or intervention.

**Key Activated.** Key-activated TSR programs are stored in memory and remain inactive until the user enters a specific key or key combination referred to as the *hot-key*. This key combination prompts programs to begin active operation in which they behave like normal applications that display information and react to user commands.

The TSR summary screen lists the program currently in memory. The screen displays the following:

**Address.** The address is the memory location where the beginning of the program is located. The DOS system Area always begins at *0008*.

**Size.** This is the size in bytes occupied by the program.

**Owner.** This is the name of the TSR program. In addition, the DOS system area and the free memory are also identified. If a block of memory appears to be allocated but its owner cannot be determined, the block is marked with "unknown owner."

**Interrupts.** The program lists the numbers of the software interrupts assigned to each TSR program. For example, the COMMAND.COM program uses interrupts 22, 24, and 2E. The Disk Monitor program you have previously loaded uses interrupts 13, 21, 25, 26, and 2F.

At the bottom of the dialog box are three additional items of information about each TSR program that are displayed for the highlighted TSR program only:

**Path.**   This is the path name of the program. If available this option will indicate the location of the file from which the program was loaded.

**Command Line.**   This option shows any command-line parameters or switches used when the program was loaded.

**Memory Allocation Blocks.**   This item shows the number of memory block segments used for the program. If the entire TSR program is contained in a single, contiguous block of memory the value will be 1. However, some programs are broken up into several blocks that appear at different locations in the memory.

The exact address of the TSR programs will vary greatly from computer to computer, depending on which programs and in what order they were loaded. However, the interrupts controlled by those programs ought to be the same. For example, the DISKMON.EXE program will always control interrupts 13, 21, 25, 26, and 2F no matter where the program itself is positioned in memory. This shows how the interrupt system can effectively point at the programs that are to control various operations, even though DOS computers rarely load programs in the exact same memory locations. Typically, complicated systems such as these have the benefit of great flexibility.

You can move the highlight up and down the list to examine the items for different programs. Enter↓.

The highlight is now on the COMMAND.COM program. Note that the *Memory Block Allocation* line shows the value 2. This tells you that the COMMAND.COM program, the DOS command interpreter, is stored in two separate memory blocks. This reveals one of the original design concepts employed by DOS to maximize the available TPA. The COMMAND.COM program is split into two sections after it is loaded into memory. One section remains memory resident for the duration of the session. The other section is erased from memory when an application is running. When the application terminates, the missing portion of COMMAND.COM is reloaded from the disk.[10]

---

10. If you boot your computer system from a floppy disk you may find that when you exit an application the message "Insert disk with COMMAND.COM" appears on the screen. The message is displayed when DOS cannot find the COMMAND.COM file in order to reload the second section of COMMAND.COM, which was overwritten when you ran the application. You must insert the boot disk again in order to continue.

Another indication that this is actually going on is the size of the COMMAND.COM program as listed in the TSR summary. The program is listed as using 3,536 bytes. However, the COMMAND.COM disk file is much larger—25,276. What happened to the rest of the program? The answer is that it has been overwritten by the current application, System Information. Thus the dual segment design of COMMAND.COM provides an additional 20K of memory for the TPA. This savings was very significant in the early days of the IBM PC when the basic system contained only 64K. TSR programs have two major areas of concern:

**Memory.** Each TSR program loaded uses up some conventional memory, reducing the size of the TPA available to other applications. Since TSR programs remain resident even when they are not active, the memory they occupy is not freed when you finish with the program. Some TSRs have commands that *unload* the program from memory. However, if there are multiple TSR programs loaded, unloading a program may leave a memory gap between programs loaded before and after the unloaded application, which cannot be used as part of the TPA because the gap is not contiguous with the rest of the free memory.

**Interrupts Conflict.** The interrupt system requires that one and only one program *own* a memory location or an interrupt handler. It is possible to load into memory TSR programs that create a conflict about the ownership of an interrupt or a hot-key combination. In some cases the order in which the programs are loaded determines the owner. In other cases the conflict corrupts the interrupt table and causes the system to freeze up. If you experience these problems you may want to experiment with different loading sequences in order to try to find one that works. However, in some cases TSR programs are incompatible with each other and can only be used separately.

## Memory Gaps

One problem that can occur with memory resident programs is the creation of memory gaps when you attempt to remove one program from memory, in order to increase the current TPA. For example, the last program loaded into memory is DISKMON.EXE, the Disk Monitor program. How do you know that is true? One way is to look at the starting address values for each program. In Figure 7–9 the starting address for DISKMON.EXE is *2AF8* (hex). That address is the highest address of the programs listed.

As the last program in memory you should have no trouble removing it from memory. Exit System Information and remove the Disk Monitor program from memory by entering

```
[Alt-q]
diskmon /uninstall ↵
```

The program displays the message "Disk Monitor uninstalled." Load System Information and check the TSR display by entering

```
sysinfo ↵
[Alt-m] t
```

The TSR screen no longer shows the DISKMON.EXE program. If you look closer you can confirm that when the program is *uninstalled* the memory used by the program was released to DOS as free memory. Figure 7–9 showed the starting address of DISKMON.EXE as 2AF8(hex) and the starting address of free memory at 2D17. While the exact memory locations will be different on your computer, you should now see that free memory starts at the exact address—2AF8—where DISKMON.EXE has previously begun, as seen in Figure 7–9.

But what would happen if DISKMON.EXE was not the *last* TSR program in memory? Exit System Information by entering [Alt-q].

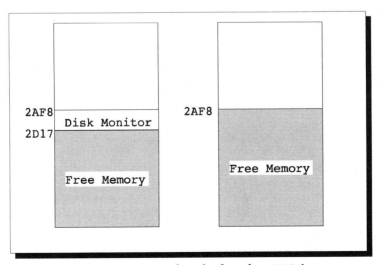

**Figure 7–9. Memory space freed when last TSR is uninstalled.**

Load the Disk Monitor again: diskmon /light+ ↵.

In addition, load another TSR program. Use the DOS TSR utility program APPEND. APPEND is used to create a search path for data files in the same way that PATH creates search paths for program files. Enter append \nu ↵.

Now attempt to remove the Disk Monitor program by entering diskmon /uninstall ↵.

This time the program generates the message "Error: Disk Monitor could not be removed." Since the command you entered is exactly the same as the successful command you entered previously, it is not the command that is the problem but rather the circumstances under which the command was executed.

## Memory Blocks

Load System Information once again by entering sysinfo ↵.

In order to get a clear picture of why you were not able to unload the Disk Monitor program, display the DOS memory block screen by entering [Alt-m] b.

The display on this screen shows many of the same elements found on TSR screens. It shows the address, size, and owner of the TSR programs but not the related interrupts. The difference is that on this display each block of memory used by a program is displayed individually. This display shows more accurately than the TSR screen the sequence in which program code is stored in memory.

In this case the key factor is that the APPEND.EXE program is positioned in a memory block that follows the DISKMON.EXE program. Therefore it is not possible to remove DISKMON.EXE from memory and return the memory occupied by that program to the free memory space.

In order to avoid this problem you would have to reboot the computer and load the TSR programs in a sequence that has the APPEND program preceding the Disk Monitor program.

One important point is that the order in which TSR programs are placed into memory can affect how the programs operate and how they interact with other TSR programs.

## CMOS Information

The last screen display related to memory is the CMOS status screen. Enter [Alt-s] c.

The CMOS display shows the information stored in the system's CMOS RAM. Note that older PC and XT systems do not use CMOS RAM to maintain system settings so that this option is not available. The information stored in the CMOS differs from information stored in ROM chips in that CMOS must be supplied with a constant source of electricity in order to retain the information. Because CMOS requires a much smaller amount of current than does the normal RAM in your system, the CMOS can be powered for long periods of time by batteries.

CMOS data can be lost if there is a failure in the battery-supplied power. Problems with CMOS will be revealed only when you boot the computer system, since that is the time that the system attempts to read the settings stored in the CMOS. The failure will cause the system to generate an error message stating a problem has occurred with the CMOS and you need to run the set-up program. It is important to keep in mind that running set-up does not solve the problem. Using the set-up program to fill in the required information allows you to use the computer temporarily but it probably won't solve the problem that your system failed to retain the CMOS settings when the computer was turned off. In most cases battery replacement is the solution to the problem, although there may be other reasons why the CMOS data are corrupted.

It is important to keep in mind that as batteries approach the end of their useful life, the amount of power they supply may vary greatly from time to time. For example, you may experience a CMOS failure only once a month due to the vagaries of a deteriorating battery.

The CMOS stores the following information about the system:

**Hard Disks.** This box shows the type number of the first and second hard disks in the system. Drive type numbers are determined by the ROM used in your system. The ROM contains a list of hard disk specifications that describe different types of hard disks in terms of the number of heads, cylinders, and sectors per track. In order to determine the correct drive type number for your hard disk you need to know the heads, cylinders, and sectors values. As part of the set-up program you can then select the drive number that matches the values for your hard drive.

**Floppy Disks.** This box lists the floppy disk installed in the computer.

**Installed Memory.** This box lists the installed memory. The Base memory is the amount of conventional memory up to a maximum of 640K. Note that the only other type of memory shown is extended memory.

This is because paged memory, such as expanded memory, requires the use of special drivers and is not directly supported by DOS.

**CMOS Status.** This box shows information about the CMOS status, including the status of the battery and the results of testing the CMOS settings against the actual hardware in the computer.

The CMOS information summary does not include all of the information or settings that appear when you run the CMOS set-up program for your computer. This is because the exact use of the CMOS memory will vary from computer to computer according to the ROM BIOS version installed in each machine. Many manufacturers include other options in the CMOS, such as the type of screen display and the default video mode; the use of special memory options available on 386 computers; filling shadow RAM with a copy of the ROM BIOS routines in order to improve performance; and selection of the processor clock speed and wait states if the computer supports multiple processor speeds. Since these options are not standard on all 286 or 386 machines, they do not appear on the CMOS status screen.

# CPU Performance

One of the most popular features of the Norton Utilities has been the inclusion of a rating system by which the performance of the computer systems can be judged. In computer terminology such tests are called *benchmarks* because they seek to express the complicated issue of system performance by running one or more general tests of computing capacity.

In order to test the processing speed of your computer, display the *Benchmark* menu by entering [Alt-b].

Choose the CPU speed test by entering c.

The program displays a dynamic bar chart in which the speed rating of your system is continually calculated and compared to the performance of three other machines that serve as baselines of performance, as seen in Figure 7–10:

**Compaq 386 33MHz.** This machine is used as a high-end power benchmark since it is one of the most powerful general-purpose PC computers currently available. The rating of 34.7 means that this system will operate 34.7 times faster than the original IBM PX/XT.

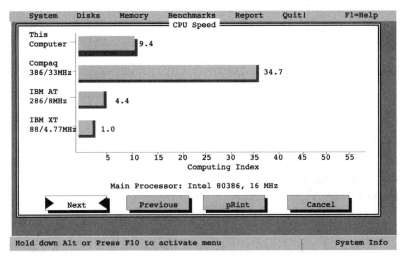

**Figure 7–10. CPU test.**

**IBM AT 286 8MHz.** This system is used as the benchmark for 286 computers. Note that most 286 computers sold in the last few years are considerably faster than the IBM AT. IBM no longer sells the AT model. The rating for this system, 4.4, means that it runs 4.4 times faster than the original IBM PC/XT.

**IBM XT 4.77MHz.** This is the low-end benchmark. The 8088 used in the PC and XT runs at 4.77 MHz. Most XT computers sold today run at considerably high rates than the original PC/XT machines, which are no longer sold by IBM. This model is used as the formal baseline for testing because its rating is 1.0.

At the bottom of the screen the microprocessor type is displayed—for example, Intel 80386, 20 MHz. The bar that represents your computer's rating may fluctuate a bit due to the execution of various interrupts in the background. For example, if you were to move the mouse while you were observing the CPU test you would see a slight decrease in speed due to the time it takes to process the mouse movement. When the mouse is not moved, the CPU has only the CPU test operations to execute and it returns to its former rating.

If you have a dual speed computer—one that has a normal and a *turbo* mode—you can observe the difference in performance by using the switch[11] to change speed modes while the CPU test is running. The bar will increase or decrease, depending upon what speed the system is operating at.

Another test on the Benchmark menu combines the CPU test with a hard disk test to provide a combined overall rating for the system CPU and hard disk. Enter [Alt-b] o.

The program will take a few minutes to run a hard disk test. You can probably hear the hard disk responding to the test while you are waiting for the results. When completed, the program displays a bar chart showing the speed of the current hard disk as compared to the disks included with the Compaq, IBM AT, and IBM XT.

It is important to remember that many computers are equipped with hard disks other than those provided by the manufacturer or that some manufacturers sell a variety of disks for one computer. For example, IBM computers sold in the 1980s often had non-IBM components, such as Hercules Monochrome graphics screen displays or Seagate hard disks, installed by the dealers, since they were better values than the standard IBM equipment. The baseline IBM XT hard disk test uses the original 10-megabyte hard disk supplied with the original run of the XT. IBM later decided to sell XT computers without hard disks to allow dealers to install their own options.

Keep in mind that the tests performed by the commands on the Benchmark menu produce results in terms of a *performance index* rather than actual performance specifications. This means that the CPU test does not tell you how fast your computer performs, but how fast it performs in comparison to the performance of the IBM XT, which is used as a baseline. For most users the rating index is more meaningful than raw measurements—for example, the clock speed of the computer is 20,000,000 cycles per second.

## Benchmarks from Previous Versions

If you have a previous version of the Norton Utilities you will probably find that Version 6.0 produces different benchmark results from the System Information program of earlier versions. This is because the methods em-

---

11. Many computers have an actual switch on the front panel that changes the processing speed mode. On other systems you must use a special key combination, for example [Ctrl Alt +] or [Ctrl Alt - ], to change the processor speed.

ployed by the program to grade performance have been changed and improved as part of the updating of the Norton Utilities.

However, the benchmark portion of the System Information program is widely used by computer sellers to indicate the speed of various machines. You will often see something like **SI 17.0** appear in an ad for a computer. While this value may be the value that the dealer got when he tested the machine, it can still be misleading because you do not know which version of the program was used for testing. For example, as a test, the System Information program from Versions 3.0, 4.0, 4.5, and 6.0 were run on a standard 386 SX machine with a 16MHz processor. The results were 18.7 using 3.0, 16.2 using 4.0, 16.5 using 4.5, and 9.1 using 6.0. It is important to keep in mind that the benchmarks are indexes—that is, a composite score based on a variety of tests, not absolute values. You cannot actually compare benchmarks without knowing that the same version of the System Information program was used on both machines.

Exit the System Information program by entering [Alt-q].

# Summary

This chapter covered the basic information provided by the System Information program and the details it supplies about computer memory.

**System Information**    The System Information program does not perform any operations. Instead, it reports information about the computer system. The program displays a series of screens that show details about the current system. You can print or send to a text file any of the individual screens, or create a report that includes some or all of the individual screens. The command-line switch, /**SUMMARY**, will display a single screen system summary that is identical to the summary produced by previous versions of the Norton Utilities.

**ROM BIOS**    The System Summary screen shows the date of the system's ROM BIOS. Many elements of the system, such as the hard drive type number, are specific to the exact ROM BIOS chip used in the computer. This date can help technical support personnel determine the BIOS installed in your computer.

**Memory**    The System Information reports details of the memory installed in the system. Because elements of the design of the original IBM have been retained in 286 and 386 computers, memory in the computer falls into three types: conventional (that used in the original PC), extended (added with the AT), and expanded (Lotus-Intel-Microsoft).

**Conventional Memory**    Conventional memory refers to the first 1,024K (1 megabyte) of memory in a PC, AT, or 386 computer. Because of the design of the IBM PC, only 640K of the first 1,024K of memory is available for user programs.

**Reserved Address Space**    The top 384K of conventional memory is reserved for special purpose memory blocks that support devices, such as video adapters, hard disk controller cards, etc. The reserved memory space cannot normally be used for user programs or applications, effectively limiting conventional memory to 640K.

**TSR Programs**    TSR—terminate and stay resident—programs remain in memory once they are loaded, even though they are not active. These programs can be activated by two types of triggers. An event trigger causes execution of a TSR program when a certain event takes place in the system—a disk drive is accessed, for instance. User-controlled TSR programs become active when the user enters a special key combination designated as the hot-key for the TSR program. Each TSR program reduces the amount of memory left for other applications. All computers load at least one TSR type program—that is, the DOS system which loads into conventional memory and stays resident throughout the session.

**TPA**    TPA—transient program area—refers to the total amount of free conventional memory available for running user-selected applications. The size of the TPA determines how large an application you can run on your computer. The TPA is reduced when TSR programs are loaded into memory.

**Extended Memory**    Extended memory is memory that begins beyond the 1,024K address that marks the end of conventional memory. Extended memory was added starting with the IBM AT. Because of the addressing system built into the original IBM PC, 286 and 386 computers running under DOS cannot directly address extended memory for loading and running user applications or TSR programs. Extended memory can only be used for cache or buffering operations under DOS. Extended memory requires a protected mode operating system in order to be utilized for executing user applications.

**Expanded Memory**     Cooperation between Lotus, Intel, and Microsoft produced the Expanded Memory Specification—EMS—in 1985. Expanded memory is additional memory that is divided into 16K pages. When an EMS driver is loaded, a page frame area is created within the reserved area of conventional memory above 640K. Applications, specifically designed to use EMS, can access the expanded memory in 64K blocks through the page frame established in conventional memory. Expanded memory operation is ignored by DOS and any DOS applications not specifically designed for expanded memory.

**Real Mode**     Real mode processing refers to the type of operations carried on by the original IBM PC in which memory locations were reserved in advance for specific devices. The real-mode structure prevents 286 and 386 machines from expanding conventional memory beyond 640K. 286 and 386 machines can use more conventional memory if they operate under the protected mode.

**Protected Mode**     The protected mode refers to an advance operating mode available on 286 and 386 computers that overcomes the memory addressing limitations of the 8088 (PC type) computers. However, DOS and the popular applications that operate under DOS cannot run on the computer when the protected mode is active. Protected mode operations require a protected mode operating system—for instance, OS/2 or XENIX; or for 386 machines, a program like Windows 3.0.

**Memory Mapping**     386-based computers allow some flexibility in the use of extended and expanded memory, due to the ability of the chip to map the reserved area of conventional memory to other physical locations in the 386 memory, allowing for the increase in conventional memory TPA by loading TSR programs into unused segments of the reserved memory area.

**Interrupts**     Interrupts are signals generated by hardware devices or software programs when a specific operation is required. Hardware interrupts allow devices to gain access to the microprocessor when a time-critical operation is needed—as an example, a modem attached to a serial port receives data from an outside source. Software interrupts are generated by DOS, TSR programs, and user applications when they need to carry out a specific task. The program code executed when an interrupt is generated is called a *handler*. Programs such as the Disk Monitor program of the Norton

Utilities can change the code used to handle specific interrupts so that the computer will handle various operations in a different manner.

**CMOS** System settings in AT and 386 computers are stored in battery powered RAM memory called CMOS memory. This memory holds important information, such as the hard drive type number and the amount of conventional and extended memory installed in the system.

# 8 | Examining Disks

Next to memory, the second crucial area of the computer system for most users is disk storage. As discussed in Chapter 2, disk storage is used to permanently store information, in contrast to memory, which loses all data when the computer is turned off. Disk storage is a broad category that includes floppy disks of different sizes and all types of fixed hard disks, as well as other types of mass storage devices combining characteristics of standard hard and floppy disk drives. Despite many differences, all these devices have in common that they operate within the context of the DOS file system. This means data are always stored in the form of files and directories, no matter what type of disk you are working on. Data can be copied from one disk to another, assuming there is sufficient space available, regardless of the types of disks involved. Conversely, the limits of the DOS file system affect all the disks employed by computers running DOS— as an example, 8-character file names with 3-character extensions. In this chapter we will look at how the Norton Utilities can be used to analyze your disks and the data stored on them. Unlike the previous chapter, in which all the memory analysis tools were found in the System Information program, disk operations can be found in a number of different Norton Utilities programs, including System Information.

## Disk Summary

The first place to look for information about a system's disk is in the System Information program. Load the program by entering sysinfo ↵.

Disk information is found logically on the *Disk* menu. Display the menu by entering [Alt-d].

The menu displays three options:

**Disk Summary.** This screen shows a summary of all the disks, both physical and logical, active in the system. This screen provides the best overall summary of the disk storage options available in your system.

```
Drive    Type         Size          Default Directory

 A:  5¼" floppy     1.2M
 B:  Phantom Drive
 C:  Hard Disk 1    2.0M     C:\
 D:  Hard Disk 1    40M      D:\NORTON
 E:  Network                 E:\
 F:  Network                 F:\
 G:  Network                 G:\
 H:  Network                 H:\
 I:  Available
 J:  Available
 K:  Available
```

**Figure 8–1. Disk summary screen.**

**Disk Characteristics.** This screen displays detailed information about one disk at a time. The information includes both the physical and logical qualities of the disk, as discussed in Chapter 4.

**Partition Tables.** This screen displays information about how a large-capacity disk is partitioned. Disk partitions allow a hard disk to contain more than one operating system. They can also be used to allow a single physical drive to operate as if it were two or more drives. Because of limits in the size of hard disks supported by DOS 3.xx, partitioning hard disks with capacities over 32 megabytes is common.

Begin with the Disk summary screen by entering d.

The program displays the Disk summary screen, as seen in Figure 8–1. The screen contains a list box that shows data about all the drives in the system:

**Drive Letter.** The screen lists all the available drives in alphabetical order.

The number of drive letters listed is the total number of available drive letters available. If you are using DOS 2.xx or lower, the available drives are only the drives or hard disk partitions that actually exist. If you are using DOS 3.xx or higher you can increase the number of available drive letters by using the **LASTDRIVE** command in your CONFIG.SYS file. The **LASTDRIVE** command allows you to allocate drive letters you can later assign as logical or network drives. For example, entering the command **LASTDRIVE=L** will cause the System Information program to list drives A through L, even though you may only have drive A and C physically installed in the computer. Once you have made drive letters available, you can use other programs to assign meanings to these drive letters. For example, drive L is commonly used for CD-ROM drives running under Microsoft's CD-ROM extension software.

**Type.** This lists the type of disk associated with the letter, such as 5.25" floppies, Hard Disk 1, Hard Disk 2, or Network drives. If a hard disk is partitioned into two or more segments each segment, will be listed separately. The *device driver* type refers to disks that require the loading of a special device driver with the CONFIG.SYS file, in order to operate.

**Size.** The is the total capacity of the disk in K (kilobytes) or M (megabytes).

**Default Directory.** This shows the path name of the active directory on the disk.

## Disk Characteristics

The next display on the disk menu is **Disk Characteristics.** Enter n. The information on this screen displays details of the disk's structure. The information is divided into two basic areas: logical and physical characteristics. Logical characteristics reflect DOS organization and DOS file system operations. The physical characteristics reflect the physical composition of the disk or hard drive. The logical characteristics are:

**Bytes Per Sector.** The sector is the basic unit of disk storage. It is the smallest block of data that can be stored is a single sector. Typically, DOS disks, both hard and floppy, use sectors that hold exactly 512 bytes. Some high-capacity disks use sector sizes larger than 512 bytes to increase total storage capacity. Most sectors are used for data storage. However, a small number of sectors on each disk are assigned special functions required by the DOS file system.

**Sectors Per Cluster.** The *data cluster* represents the minimum number of disk sectors that can be allocated to a DOS file. Clusters can consist of one or more sectors. The larger the capacity of the disk, the more sectors are assigned to each cluster. When DOS creates a file it assigns one or more data clusters as the storage area for that file. The data cluster can be located on any part of the disk.

**Number of Clusters.**  The total number of clusters represents the total amount of disk space available for data storage. The only area of the disk that is not included in the clusters is the system area at the beginning of the disk.

**Number of FATs.**  The FAT is the *file allocation table*. The table is used to keep track of which data clusters belong to which files and in what sequences the data clusters should be read. Most DOS disks maintain two copies, although DOS itself only uses the first copy. The Norton Utilities programs can access this second copy and use it to help recover lost data.

**FAT Type.**  DOS supports two types of FAT tables. All DOS versions support the use of 12-bit FAT tables. Starting with DOS 3.xx, 16-bit FAT tables were supported. A 12-bit FAT table limited the total number of data clusters on the disk to 4,096. 16-bit FAT tables support 65,536 data clusters. Most high-capacity hard disks used 16-bit FAT tables when formatted under DOS 3.xx or higher.

**Media Descriptor Byte.**  In order to help DOS identify the type of disk being read, the first sector (the boot sector) on the disk contains a one-byte value used to identify the disk. This value is written into the first sector of the disk when it is formatted.

**FAT.**  The screen tells you the sector number of the first disk sector used for the FAT. In most cases, this is sector 1, the sector immediately following the boot sector. The size of the FAT is usually in proportion to the total capacity of the disk. The size is indicated by the number of disk sectors allocated to the FAT. Recall that two copies of the FAT are stored in these sectors.

**Root Dir.**  Following the FAT on the disk are the sectors assigned as the Root directory. As with the FAT, the size of the root directory is proportional to the disk capacity. Hard disks have root directories that can hold up to 512 entries.

**Data.**  Data is the area of the disk used for storage of user files. This area is by far, typically 98 percent or 99 percent of the disk sectors, the largest area of the disk. Note that DOS Version 3.xx and lower limited the total number of sectors on the disk to 65,536, including FAT and root directory sectors. DOS 4.xx removes this limit, permitting much larger numbers of disk sectors.

# Physical Characteristics

The physical characteristics of the disk show the actual number of sides, tracks, and sectors. The information displayed here is similar to that which is used when setting up the hard disk type in the CMOS on AT-type computers, with the exception that the term *sides* is used instead of *heads*, and *tracks* is used instead of *cylinders*.

Note that if a hard disk is partitioned into several parts, the number of tracks (cylinders) allocated to each partition appears. The total number of tracks on the hard disk is the sum of all the partitions.

# Partition Tables

The last screen on the disk menu is the Partition Table display. Partition tables show how a single hard disk has been divided. There are three reasons why hard disk are partitioned.

**DOS 3.xx Limitations.**  The 16-bit sector address size used by DOS 3.xx and lower limits the total number of sectors in a single logical drive to 65,536—that is, 32 megabytes of storage, assuming 512-byte sectors. Hard disks with capacities over 32 megabytes must be partitioned in order to run under DOS.

**Non-DOS Operating Systems.**  You can store additional operating systems on one hard disk by creating separate disk partitions for those systems—for instance, XENIX or CP/M.

**User Preference.**  In addition to the previous reasons, users might choose to create disk partitions in order to create multiple logical disks from a single hard disk for organizational purposes when the drive involved has a very large capacity—hundreds of megabytes. You might want to allocate a different drive letter for each person using the computer. On smaller drives you can accomplish the same thing by using directories. Keep in mind that when you establish a disk partition you fix a limit on the total capacity of that logical drive. You cannot alter the partitions on a hard disk without losing all the data in one or more partitions. Enter n.

The Partition table screen lists the partitions on the current hard disk, as shown in Figure 8–2. The screen displays details about the organization of each partition:

```
                                 Partition Tables

                          Starting            Ending       Relative  Number of
           System Boot Side Track Sector  Side Track Sector  Sectors    Sectors

           DOS-12 Yes   1     0    1        4    23    17         17      2,023
           DM     No    0    24    1        4   794    17      2,040     65,535



           This partition is located on hard disk 1
           which has 5 sides, 976 tracks, and 17 sectors per track.
```

**Figure 8–2. Partition table display.**

**System.** System identifies the type of partition.

**DOS-12.** This identifies a DOS partition with a 12-bit FAT. Partitions of this nature are used for floppy disks and hard disks with small capacities, such as the XT 10-megabyte hard disk. The 12-bit structure of the FAT limits the total number of data clusters to 4,096, making this type of partition impractical for large capacity disks.[1]

**DOS-16.** Beginning with DOS 3.xx, disks could be formatted to use 16-bit FAT tables, avoiding the 12-bit FAT data cluster limit and allowing for partitions up to 32 megabytes each.

**EXTEND.** An extended DOS partition is an alternative way to divide a large-capacity hard disk into multiple logical drive partitions. When you use an extended partition, a single disk partition will appear as one or more logical drives without having to create separate 16-bit partitions for each one.

**BIGDOS.** DOS 4.xx and higher has the ability, due to its support for 32-bit sector addresses, to create DOS partitions that contain more than 65,536 sectors (32 megabytes, assuming a 512-byte sector size).

**DM/SPEEDSTOR Driver Defined.** If you are using a driver with a capacity greater than 32 megabytes under DOS 3.xx or lower, it is common to employ a device-driven non-DOS partition, in order to gain partition capacities in excess of 32 megabytes. Such partition

---

1. Partitioning software, such as Disk Manager or SpeedStor, may create a small bootable partition with a 12-bit FAT as the first partition on the disk.

schemes can be created by software programs such as Disk Manager, supplied with many Seagate hard disks, or SpeedStor. These programs create a special non-DOS partition on the hard disks, along with a small 12- or 16-bit DOS partition. When the system is booted, the CONFIG.SYS file loads a device driver—for instance DMDRVR.BIN for Disk Manager or HARDDISK.SYS for SpeedStor—that augments DOS so it can work with the special non-DOS partition. When operating the system, the non-DOS partition functions exactly like any DOS hard disk. Note that because the partition depends on the device driver being loaded when the system boots, failure to load the driver will make the non-DOS partition unavailable.

**XENIX, etc.** This type of partition indicates a non-DOS operating system that is unavailable while DOS is active.

**Boot.** One, and only one, of the hard disk partitions is designated as the boot partition. When the computer system boots, it reads the boot sector of the hard disk. Information stored in this sector indicates which disk partition is the boot partition. The computer then moves to the starting sector of the specified partition and searches for an operating system loader program in order to boot the system into the designated operating system. The Boot partition is designated through the use of the FDISK program, which can be used to switch the boot partition from one operating system partition to another on hard disks that have multiple operating systems installed. If you want to load DOS as the operating system, a 12, 16, or BIGDOS partition must be designated as the boot partition.

**Starting.** This identifies the starting sector of a partition by side, track, and sectors.

**Ending.** This identifies the ending sector of a partition by the side.

**Relative Sector.** The relative sector is an alternative way to indicate the starting disk sector for a partition by counting the total number of disk sectors from the beginning of the disk—side 0, track 0, sector 0. The first partition will usually begin at sector 17, which is the first sector on side 1.

**Number of Sectors.** This is the total number of disk sectors contained in a partition. DOS 12-bit partitions cannot exceed 4,096, while 16-bit partitions cannot exceed 65,536 sectors.

Exit the System Information program by entering [Alt-q].

## Hard Disk Benchmark

You can use the System Information Benchmark menu to perform a test on the hard disk in order to determine its performance characteristics. Enter [Alt-b] h.

The disk test will take a few moments to complete. When finished, a bar chart is displayed showing the relative performance of your hard disk compared to the hard disks used in standard 386, 286, and 8088 machines, as shown in Figure 8–3. Keep in mind that not all IBM AT computers use the hard disk supplied by IBM. Below the chart are statistical values calculated by the hard disk test. In order to understand the meaning of these statistics you need to recall how disks are organized. Recall from Chapter 3, that disks are divided into tracks—that is, concentric circles beginning at the outer edge of the disk and moving in towards the center. When DOS receives a request from an application for data from a specific file, DOS needs to find out what sectors belong to the specified file. This is accomplished by reading the center. When DOS receives a request from an application for data from a specific file, DOS needs to find out what sectors belong to the specified file. This is accomplished by reading the directory and the FAT (file allocation table). Recall that the file allocation table is placed in the second sector on the disk, which is located on track 0 at the outside edge of the disk. This means that DOS must position the read/write head so that it can read information from the FAT, as seen in the top half of Figure 8–4.

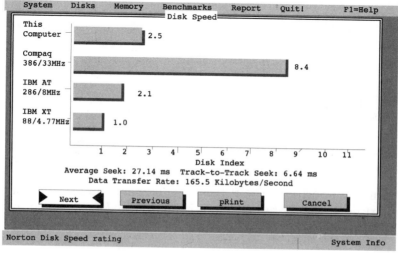

**Figure 8–3. Hard disk test.**

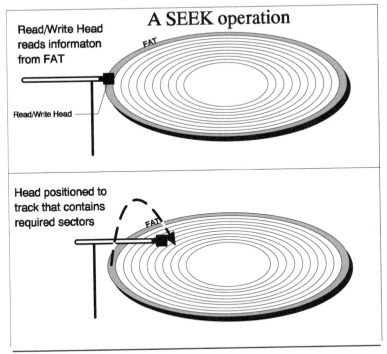

**Figure 8–4. A disk seek operation.**

The FAT then tells DOS what other disk sectors, organized in blocks (referred to as data clusters) are required. In order to read the sector data the read/write head has to be moved to the track that contains the sectors. Moving the read/write head to a different track is called a *seek* operation. It is a bit like moving the needle and arm of a phonograph from one selection to another, as shown in the bottom half of Figure 8–4.

Since most hard disk drives spin anywhere from 3,600 to 6,500 revolutions per minute, reading sectors that are on the same track is a relatively fast procedure. On most hard disks the time-consuming part of reading or writing data is changing position from one track to another—a seek operation. The amount of time it takes to perform this operation depends upon the distance between the current track and the next track that is needed. Keep in mind that a given file can have data on more than one track. On disks that have been used extensively it is often difficult to accommodate large files in adjacent tracks, causing the file to be spread out over a large number of tracks that can be widely separated. This is called *file fragmentation*. File fragmentation does not degrade the data in the file but it indicates that more time is expended in reading and writing the file than would be ideal because more time is expended in seek operations.

The time that it takes to reposition the head is called the *seek time*. The seek time is the most commonly used indicator of the overall performance of a hard disk, since it is typically the slowest operation the drive performs. Although many factors are involved in how a disk drive operates, the assumption is generally made that the faster the seek time the better the overall performance of the drive.

The display shows three statistical measurements calculated during the drive test:

**Average Seek Time.** This rating is the one most commonly used to express the performance of the hard disk. If two tracks are close together the seek time is small. Two widely separated tracks would have longer seek times. The average is calculated by making a number of seeks between tracks chosen at random. The average is expressed in *ms* (milliseconds), which are equal to .001 of a second. The average seek time expresses the amount of time it takes for the disk drive to respond to an instruction that requires a disk access.

When you purchase a hard disk you will find that in addition to its capacity in megabytes, the disk is also rated for speed in ms (milliseconds)—the Seagate 251–1 42–megabyte drive has a rating 28ms. This rating refers to the average seek time for the drive. However, in practice you will find that the Norton Utilities will return a higher value—approximately 32 ms. The Norton Utilities measurement is a more accurate assessment of how the drive actually performs in your computer. Drive speeds are a bit like MPG ratings for cars and must be taken as a relative indication of drive speed but not the actual performance you will get when the drive is installed in your computer.

**Track to Track Seek Time.** This value shows the time required to reposition the head to the next adjacent track. As such, this value shows the minimum seek time required, since the shortest distance the head can travel is to the next track. This measurement would reflect the delay that will occur when a disk access operation requires the drive to continue its operation on the next track.

**Data Transfer Rate.** This value tells you the number of kilobytes per second that can be transferred from the disk to the computer, when performing a read operation. Read operations are faster than write operations, so the transfer rate from the computer to the disk will be lower than the rate shown here. This measurement shows how fast data can be transferred from the disk to the computer once the head has been positioned on the correct track.

It is important to remember that many computers are equipped with hard disks other than those provided by the manufacturer, or that some manufacturers sell a variety of disks for one computer. For example, IBM computers sold in the 1980s often had non-IBM components, such as Hercules Monochrome graphics screen displays or Seagate hard disks installed by the dealers. The baseline IBM XT hard disk test uses the original 10-megabyte hard disk supplied with the original run of the XT. IBM later decided to sell XT computers without hard disks to allow dealers to install their own options using non-IBM devices.

## Interleave

The average seek, transfer rate, and track-to-track seek times measure the *latency* of the hard disk. Latency refers to the amount of time consumed with actions, such as positioning the drive heads, which do not actually transfer data. Since no data are transferred during latency periods, the computer's CPU is idling, waiting for information that it can process. The greater the latency period the less efficient the hard disk.

For the most part the factors affecting latency and overall disk performance are characteristics of your hardware—the hard disk, its controller, and the speed of your system—which cannot be changed or improved without replacing one or more of the components.

There is one factor in this equation that can be altered by software. That factor is the *interleave* pattern used on the disk. The interleave factor is one of the most interesting aspects of hard disk organization because it reveals the complexity of running a computer system in which all of the components operate at very different rates of speed.

Chapter 3 of this book discussed the formatting process in which a disk was divided into data storage blocks called *sectors* and how those sectors were placed on concentric circles called *tracks*. For example, hard disks typically have 17 sectors on each disk track. Floppy disks have fewer—typically, 9 sectors per track.[2]

---

2. The most common way to increase disk space is to use a medium that allows more tracks, rather than trying to get more sectors per track. It is rare that capacity is increased by adding more sectors to the track.

You may also recall from Chapter 3 that each sector is numbered. How are the sectors numbered? The obvious way to number the sectors is consecutively, 1 through 17, as shown in Figure 8–5.

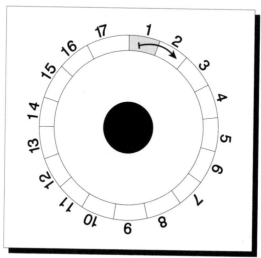

**Figure 8–5. Sectors numbered consecutively.**

However, in practice such a numbering scheme is not always the best way to organize a hard disk. The reason is related to the time it takes to process one sector of information—that is, read the data from the disk, transfer it to the hard disk controller, and then through the microprocessor. If the data are read from the hard disk faster than they can be processed by the computer, the computer will not be ready to read the next sector, which is moved under the drive head by the spinning motion of the disk. For example, the drive head reads sector 1 from a track. While the information is being processed, sector 2 moves under the drive head but cannot be read because the computer is still busy processing the data from the first sector. By the time the computer is ready to process more data the drive head has moved past sector 2. In order to continue reading data, the computer must then wait until the disk completes an entire revolution and sector 2 once again passes under the drive head. This additional waiting period increases the latency time for disk operations.

The obvious solution would be to have hardware components that work at the speeds required to eliminate this delay. However, in practice this is very hard to achieve since the components (hard disks, drive controllers, and computers) are all manufactured by different companies and put together in innumerable combinations. A less obvious solution is to *stagger* the sectors in a manner similar to the way racers are staggered when running a race around a curved track. This technique is called *interleaving*. The idea is to place the consecutively numbered sectors far enough apart on the track to eliminate the latency factor as much as possible. For example, suppose on a given system the disk moves one additional sector while it is processing the record it has just read. You could improve the efficiency of the process by placing the logically consecutive sector–1, 2, 3, etc.–in every other physical sector, as shown in Figure 8–6.

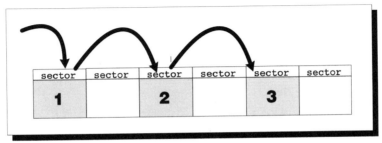

**Figure 8–6. Logical sectors spread out to account for latency in processing data.**

You can repeat this pattern around an entire track. The result is that the logical sector numbers are rearranged around the track, based on the interleave pattern. For example, placing an extra sector between each consecutively numbered sector is called a 2:1 interleave, as shown in Figure 8–7.[3] If you placed two sectors between each consecutively numbered sector it would be a 3:1 interleave.

Unlike other disk characteristics, such as the average seek time, which is a hardware characteristic, the interleave factor is created by the low-level formatting software when it initializes the hard disk. Reformatting the disk with a different interleave pattern can change the performance of the disk. Keep in mind that a change in interleave has the potential to improve or degrade the performance, depending on how well the interleave pattern matches the components in a given system.

---

3.  Read 2:1 as the ratio *2 to 1*.

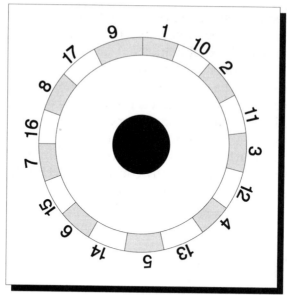

**Figure 8–7. Interleave pattern 2:1 on a 17-sector disk.**

The Norton Utilities Calibrate program has the ability to change the interleave pattern of a hard disk *without* initializing the disk and destroying all the data, as would be the case if you perform a low-level format. The program will also test your disk to determine the optimal interleave pattern for your system so you will know the best interleave pattern to use. Using the optimal interleave factor will provide the maximum transfer rate possible on your system.

## Network Disks

The last item on the Benchmarks menu is **Network performance speed.** If your computer is running as a work station on a network you can use this option to analyze the overall performance of the network's server disks. The test returns the rate of data throughput for reading from and writing to the network server drive.

Execute this benchmark by entering [Alt-b] n.

The program displays a list box that shows all available network drives. When you select a drive, the program takes a few moments to test the performance of the selected server drive. The screen displays a bar chart that shows the rate, in kilobytes per second, for both read and write operations performed on the network server, as shown in Figure 8–8.

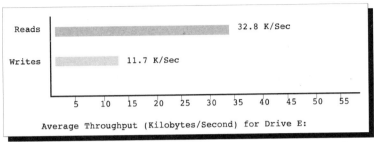

**Figure 8–8. Network disks rated for read and write performance.**

The results of the network test show the actual transfer rates instead of an index of performance as compared to other computers. The actual results of the network test depend on a number of factors, some of which can change from moment to moment. It is a general principle of network operations that performance degrades the greater the number of users accessing the server at the same time. The results of the network test will be similarly affected. You may find that you get different results each time you run the test because other users are accessing the server while you are testing it.

If you want to use this test to analyze your network you should run the test from each work station when you are sure that no other users are accessing the file server. The results of this test will act as a baseline for further analysis. You can then run the test on two work stations at the same time. The second result will give you some idea how much multiple access degrades your network's performance. To create a profile of your networks performance characteristics you could create a chart based on the results of running the network test on 1, 2, 3, etc., work stations at the same time. Figure 8–9 shows an example of such a chart.

Keep in mind that the performance values resulting from running the test on two or more work stations at the same time represents the worst case scenario for performance since the whole system will be trying to perform intense disk operations at the same time, something that rarely happens during normal usage. Exit the System Information program by entering [Alt-q].

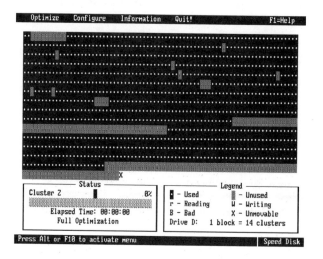

**Figure 8–9. Chart shows a decline in performance as work stations are added.**

# Information from Calibrate

The Calibrate program is an advanced disk analysis and disk repair program that has the ability to protect and repair the information stored on the disk by the initial low-level format performed on the hard disk. This program is significant since most disk operations and disk repair programs, such as the Norton Disk Doctor, deal with the elements of the disk related to the high-level format. Errors that occur at the low-level format level are untouched by these file and disk repair programs. Calibrate corrects this omission by targeting its operations on those aspects of the hard disk that other disk tests miss.

However, in this chapter Calibrate is of interest not for its low-level formatting activities but because it also performs tests, specifically seek tests, that can help you analyze the performance of your hard disk. These tests are similar to the seek tests performed by System Information, but are in general a bit more accurate. In addition, Calibrate performs an interleave test that will determine the current and optimal interleave factors for the hard disk. To obtain this information you can run the Calibrate program without performing the sector-by-sector disk analysis portion of the program.

Load the Calibrate program by entering calibrat ↵.

The program begins by displaying a message that explains the basic function of the Calibrate program. Enter ↵.

If this is the first time you have used Calibrate the program displays another message box that warns you to back up the hard disk before you perform low-level formatting. Since that is not your purpose at this time, enter ↵.

If your system contains more than one hard drive (or multiple partitions on a single hard drive) a box will appear that asks you to select the drive you want to use. Select the drive and enter ↵.

The next screen is the compatibility test screen, as shown in Figure 8–10. This screen shows four tests that Calibrate will perform before it enters the low-level, sector-by-sector, analysis mode:

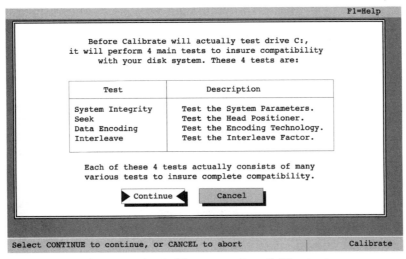

Figure 8-10. Calibrate compatibility test.

**System Integrity.** This test is actually a series of tests that seek to determine the integrity of various system components affecting disk operations. The first test is a memory test of system RAM and the hard disk controller. The test also includes the hardware clock timer and the CMOS disk information.

**Seek.** This test performs several seek tests in order to determine the operation speed of your hard disk.

**Data Encoding.** This test analyzes the structure used to set up the sectors on the disk. PC hard disks support a variety of schemes for encoding data in disk sectors.

**Interleave.** This test uses a trial-and-error method to find the optimal interleave factor. Sector interleave is discussed earlier in this chapter.

In this case you are interested in the results of the seek and interleave tests. Begin the testing process by entering[F128]↵.

The program automatically performs all of the tests. When the tests are complete the program automatically changes to the next screen and begins the seek tests. When the seek tests are complete the program pauses so you can examine the results, as shown in Figure 8–11.

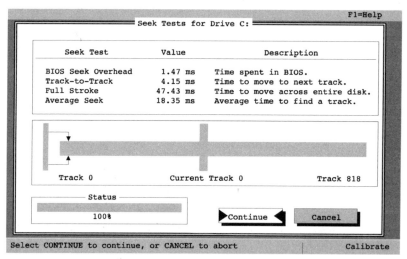

Figure 8-11. Seek test results from Calibrate program.

The program conducted four seek tests:

**BIOS Seek Overhead.** This test measures the amount of time your computer uses to execute the instruction necessary to have the hard disk controller card perform an operation. The smaller the overhead the less time spent between hard disk operations.

**Track to Track.** This test calculates the time it takes for the disk head to move to the next track. The value represents the minimum amount of time the hard disk uses when repositioning the drive head to a different track.

**Full Stroke.** This test calculates the time it takes the drive head to move from the outermost track to the innermost of the disk. The value represents the maximum amount of time consumed by the drive when repositioning the drive head.

**Average Seek.** This test calculates the average time used when moving randomly between tracks on the disk. This test is considered the most representative of the true performance of the disk since track-to-track or full-stroke operations are not typical of actual hard disk use.

You may notice that the track-to-track and average seek values differ in some degree from the values shown on the System Information hard disk benchmark screen. In general, Calibrate is a bit more accurate than System Information, although the difference is seldom significant to the overall performance of the system.

Continue to the next set of tests by entering ↵.

The next screen shows the results of four tests:

**Drive RPMs.** This test calculates the rotation speed of the hard disk in RPMs (revolutions per minute). Most Seagate hard disks rotate at about 3,600 RPMs. IDE drives, such as Conners, spin faster—5,600 RPMs.

**Sector Angle.** It is a basic fact of geometry that the size of a track gets smaller the closer it is to the center of the disk. Since each track has the same amount of sectors, the area occupied by the same sector on different tracks forms a pie-shaped wedge, which can be expressed as an angle. Logically, all of the sector angles put together should add up to approximately 360 degrees. If you have a 17-sector drive the angle should be about 20 degrees.

**Controller Type.** This tells you the type of disk controller interface used in your computer. The values will be either XT or AT.

**Encoding Type.** Several schemes are used for encoding data on hard disks. The most common and reliable is MFM. Other schemes are RLL and ARLL, which are used to pack more data into the same hard disk space.[4]

---

4. MFM stands for *modified frequency modulation*, RLL stands for *run length limited*, and ARLL stands for *advanced run length limited*.

The next test calculates the optimal interleave factor. Enter ↵.

In order to find the ideal interleave factor, the program begins with the assumption that the sectors have a 1:1 interleave—that is, they are numbered consecutively around the track. The program then counts the total number of complete revolutions needed to read all the sectors on one track. The process is repeated for interleave patterns 2:1 through 8:1. The results are displayed as a bar chart, as shown in Figure 8–12.

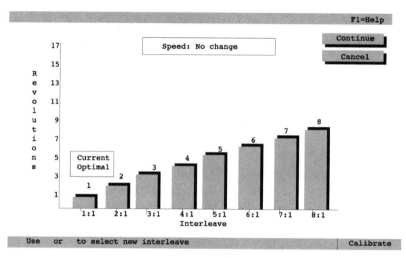

**Figure 8–12. Interleave patterns.**

The program then labels the current and optimal interleave ratios and places a box around the optimal interleave value. If they are the same, no speed increase can be gained by changing the interleave factor. If they are not the same, the percentage of improvement in transfer rate is shown in a box at the top of the chart.

You can use the ← or → keys to change the position of the box on the chart to a different interleave factor. The box at the top of the chart will show what percentage increase or decrease this interleave pattern would create.

At this point the Calibrate program has completed all of its preliminary tests. You could select to continue, in which case the program would begin a sector-by-sector analysis of the hard disk. In this case you were only interested in the test results. Cancel the program by entering [Esc].

The program displays the top portion of a report that summarizes the results of all of the tests performed on the hard disk. If you select the **Done** command button the report is discarded. **Print** sends the reports to the printer, while **Save As** allows you to store the report in a text file. Exit the program by entering ↵ [Esc].

# Speed Disk

The Speed Disk program is used to arrange disk information in order to improve performance. How can the disk be arranged to improve performance? The answer lies in the fact that seek operations (that is, changing the position of the drive head from track to track) is the slowest aspect of disk operations. If the data are placed on the disk so that sectors containing parts of the same file are stored consecutively, it will take less time to access the file than it will if the file is *fragmented* or spread out among sectors on different tracks not directly adjacent to one another.

As part of the disk optimization process carried out by the Speed Disk program, the program gathers certain statistical information about the disk that can enhance your understanding of how your hard disk is currently organized. Start the Speed Disk program by entering speedisk ↵.

The program displays a box telling you the system's memory is being checked. Because Speed Disk will read and then rewrite disk clusters, the program needs to ensure that you have error-free memory sufficient to handle this operation. The program then lists the drives upon which you can perform Speed Disk optimization. Select the desired drive and enter ↵.

The program then analyzes the disk by reading the directories and FAT to determine the exact disk clusters used for the data items stored on the disk. The program displays a box that tells you the percentage of unfragmented files—for instance, 97 percent means that 97 percent of the files on the disk are written in consecutive data clusters and are not broken into nonadjacent sections. The purpose of this box is to suggest the type of disk optimization for you to perform. Here, you are not interested in performing optimization but in obtaining data about the disk. Enter [Esc] (2 times).

When the dialog box is removed from the screen you can see that Speed Disk created a *map* of the disk. The legend for the map appears in the lower-right corner of the screen.

The map is divided into a series of blocks. The legend shows the number of data clusters represented by each block. Since the screen display area is finite, the program adjusts the scale—that is, the number of clusters represented by each block, according to the overall size of the disk being displayed. The map shows four different types of disk areas:

**Used.** These symbols show areas on the disk that are used for data storage, either files or user-defined directories.

**Unused.** This shows blocks of data clusters that are not currently assigned to a file or directory, and are open for use.

**Bad.** Programs such as the Norton Disk Doctor will mark data clusters as *bad* if they contain sectors that cannot be accurately read. Marking a cluster as bad tells DOS not to attempt to read or write data in this area. In some cases, bad sectors, and subsequently the data clusters with which they are associated, can be restored to use with the Calibrate program, which will make corrections to the low-level format of those sectors.

**Unmovable.** In some special cases, files are stored in specific locations on the disk. These files must be located at those exact physical locations if they are to operate properly, and cannot be moved to another area. Examples of this type of file are DOS system files and the format recovery information stored by the Norton Utilities Image program.[5]

One aspect of the disk that is clearly revealed by the map is the locations of the unused portions of the disk. Ideally you would want all of the unused space to be located at the end of the disk rather than being scattered in a random fashion. When open space is scattered, new files are likely to be stored in fragmented blocks as DOS attempts to used the small, unused sections that occur on the disk. Later in this book you will learn how to use Speed Disk to reorganize a disk that has fragmented areas of open space.

## Walking the Map

You can use the disk map in an interactive way to determine the cluster numbers of the blocks that appear on the screen, using the **Walk Map** option found on the *Information* menu. Enter

```
[Alt-i] w
```

5.  The Image program always stores its information in the *last* data cluster on the disk. Once you have run Image, an X will appear at the end of the disk map indicating a nonmoveable file.

The program places a blinking cursor on the first block on the map. If you look in the lower-left corner of the screen you will see the cluster numbers (starting with 2) represented by the block on the map. You can use the arrow keys to change the location of the cursor, which in turn changes the cluster numbers that appear at the bottom of the screen. You can use the map walking feature to determine which disk sectors are occupied by unmovable files by moving the cursor to the X blocks that appear on the map.

You can display a list of the unmovable files using the **Show status files** option. Enter [Esc] s.

The program displays a list box with the names of the static file, if any. Return to the *Information* menu by entering [Esc].

## Disk Statistics

You can display a summary of the usage of disk clusters by selecting the **Disk Statistics** option on the *Information* menu. Since the *Information* menu is currently displayed, enter s.

The program displays a box that lists information about the disk, as shown in Figure 8–13, including the information about fragmented files, unmovable files, and bad clusters. One interesting aspect of this summary is that it shows the total number of user-defined directories on the hard disk and the total number of data clusters used by the directories. This information does not appear on any other summary in the Norton Utilities.

Exit the Speed Disk program by entering

```
[Esc] (2 times)
[Alt-q]
```

# Disk Editor

The Disk Editor program, discussed in Chapter 4, can be used to examine or alter any data stored on the hard disk. The Disk Editor also displays a disk map similar to the one shown in Speed Disk. The primary difference is that the Disk Editor map can be used to show the map location of a specified file. One reason for finding a file's location is to help to resolve problems, such as cross-linked data clusters, discussed in more detail in Chapter 14.

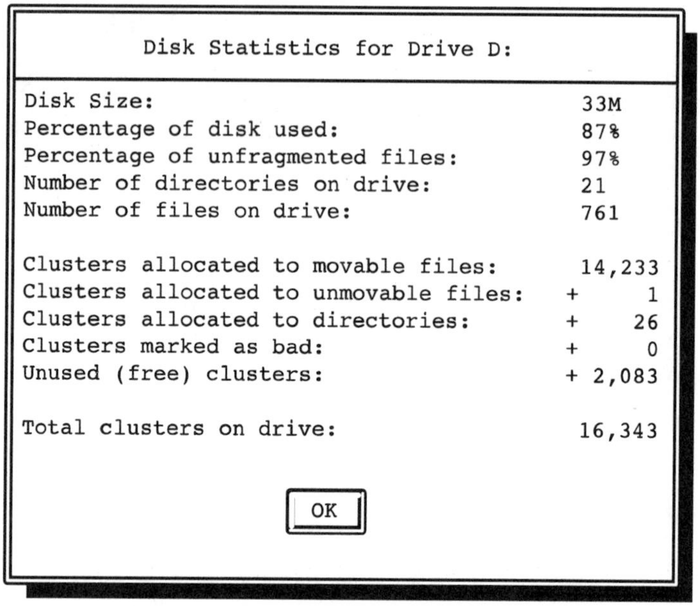

```
┌─────────────────────────────────────────────────┐
│           Disk Statistics for Drive D:            │
├───────────────────────────────────────────────────
│ Disk Size:                              33M       │
│ Percentage of disk used:                87%       │
│ Percentage of unfragmented files:       97%       │
│ Number of directories on drive:         21        │
│ Number of files on drive:               761       │
│                                                   │
│ Clusters allocated to movable files:      14,233  │
│ Clusters allocated to unmovable files:  +      1  │
│ Clusters allocated to directories:      +     26  │
│ Clusters marked as bad:                 +      0  │
│ Unused (free) clusters:                 + 2,083   │
│                                                   │
│ Total clusters on drive:                  16,343  │
│                                                   │
│                   ┌──────┐                        │
│                   │  OK  │                        │
│                   └──────┘                        │
└───────────────────────────────────────────────────
```

**Figure 8–13. Disk statistics display.**

For example, suppose you want to determine the location of the NORTON.EXE because you suspect a problem with that file. Load the Disk Editor program by entering diskedit \nu\nu.exe ↵↵.

The program displays the information stored in the first sector of the NORTON.EXE file. At the top of the display the cluster and sector number appear.

However, the cluster or sector numbers are a bit abstract. You can get a more visual representation of the location of the file on the disk by using the **Map of object** command located on the *Info* menu. Enter [Alt-i] m.

The program overlays the hex value display with a map display that shows the location of the currently selected file with the letter **F**, as shown in Figure 8–14. You can also use the **Info** menu to display statistical information about the object, in this case a file, by using the **Object Info** option. Enter [Esc] [Alt-i] o.

The program displays a box that tells you a great deal about how the file is stored on the disk. The box shows the file name, attributes, and date and time it was stored.

In addition the starting data cluster, the number of clusters and the number of fragments used to store the file are listed. Note that the exact

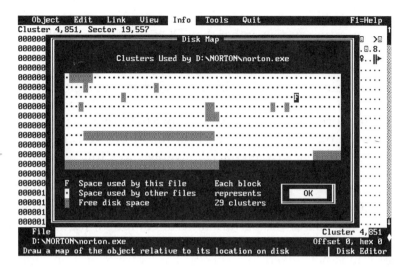

**Figure 8–14. File's location indicated on disk map.**

details of this information will vary from computer to computer. Exit the Disk Editor program by entering [Esc] [Ctrl-q].

# Summary

This chapter explained how the Norton Utilities programs can be used to obtain information about the disks, in particular the hard drives, available to your computer using the System Information, Calibrate, Speed Disk, and Disk Editor programs, each of which supply information about the disks.

**Disk Information**    Disk information is supplied in two forms. Physical information describes the disk in three-dimensional terms related to low-level disk structure: sides, tracks, and sectors. Logical information describes disks based on the two-dimensional logical structure established by the high-level format: sequential sector numbers and data cluster numbers.

**Partition Tables**    Hard disk partition tables are used to physically divide a hard disk into two more sections. Disk partitions enable a single hard disk to operate like a series of individual disks. You can also use partitions to set up operating systems other than DOS on one hard disk.

**Seek Tests**    The most crucial factor in hard disk performance is the time used to position the disk drive heads from one disk track to another. Seek tests are used to establish the performance characteristics of hard disks by measuring the time it takes to move to the next track, track-to-track test, from the outer to the inner track, full stroke test, or an average of random movements between tracks—average seek time.

**Transfer Rates**    The transfer rate refers to the number of kilobytes per second that can be transferred from the computer to the disk. Transfer rates provide a measure of the performance of computer, hard disk controller, and hard drive, working together as a unit. Since the measurement of transfer rate is not linked to a specific hardware operation—for example, track-to-track seek time—it can also be used to measure the performance of network server drives as well as drives resident in the current computer.

**Interleave Pattern**    Hard disk performance is generally a function of the hardware components and cannot be altered by software operations, with the exception of the transfer rate, which is affected by the interleave factor. Disk rotation speed—for instance, 3,600 RPMs—often exceeds the speed at which the data are transferred through the controller to the computer. In such cases the disk drive head will not be positioned on the next logical sector when the computer is ready to read the next sector. Interleave patterns separate logically consecutive sectors to achieve the optimal transfer rate for the computer, controller, and hard disk combination.

**Fragmentation**    DOS can and will store files in noncontiguous segments in order to maximize the use of data clusters on a disk. However, files stored in separated blocks of clusters can degrade hard disk performance, since reading and writing fragmented files requires additional drive seek operations. The degree of file fragmentation on a disk will correlate directly to degradation of hard disk performance. The Speed Disk program provides a statistical summary of fragmentation and can also be used to eliminate fragmentation by reorganizing the hard disk.

# 9 Fine-tuning Your System

The word *default* is used frequently when discussing computers and computer operations. In general, *default* refers to the settings or options that will be in effect when the system or program starts up. The *default* settings in your system establish a baseline environment in which your applications will operate, unless you take further steps to alter that environment.

The Norton Utilities has a number of features that allow you to control various aspects of your system. If you execute these programs with command lines added to your CONFIG.SYS and AUTOEXEC.BAT files, you can change the *default* setting for your system.

In this chapter you will learn how to use the Norton Utilities programs to fine-tune various aspects of your system, such as the screen colors and disk drives.

## The Norton Control Center

One of the most handy programs in the Norton Utilities package is the Norton Control Center. The program consists of a variety of controls that let you change various aspects of your system. Load the Control Center program by entering

```
ncc ↵
```

When the program loads, it displays a menu on the left side of the screen, and a dialog box on the right side of the screen, as shown in Figure 9–1. The program's menu lists the parts of the system that can be controlled with the program:

**Cursor Size.** This option allows you to change the size and shape of the cursor used by DOS.

**DOS Colors.** This selects colors for standard DOS screen displays—for instance, the DOS prompt mode colors, which are usually white on black.

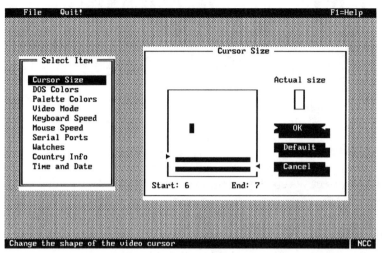

**Figure 9–1. Norton Control Center main menu.**

**Palette Colors.** If you are using an EGA or VGA screen and adapter you can select from a palette of 64 colors.

**Video Mode.** Most display adapters can operate in more than one video mode. This option allows you to select the video mode in which you want the computer to operate.

**Keyboard Speed.** When you press and hold down any key for a few moments, the computer will automatically begin to repeat that key. If you are using an AT computer, you can use this option to program the sensitivity of the automatic repeat action of the keyboard.

**Mouse Speed.** If you are using a Microsoft Mouse or one that is fully compatible, you can adjust the sensitivity of the mouse with this option.

**Serial Ports.** This option allows you to set the programmable characteristics of your serial ports.

**Watches.** This options provides computer-based stop watches that you can use for timing activities. Note these watches will continue to run after you leave the Control Center. This feature is discussed in detail in Chapter 11.

**Country Info.** Beginning with DOS 3.xx, DOS included national language support functions. This option allows you to specify the format of country-dependent information, such as time, date, and currency, as well as the collating sequence for character sorting, assuming that the COUN-TRY.SYS driver has been loaded into memory.

**Time and Date.**   This option resets the system date and time. Note that unlike the DOS date and time commands, this option resets the CMOS value, making the changes permanent.

## Cursor Size

The first option on the Control Center menu is cursor size. Recall from Chapter 7 that the characters displayed on the screen are composed of pixels, that is, individual points of light organized in blocks. Each standard screen character is formed by displaying a specific pattern of pixels within each block. The size of the cursor is formed in a similar way. The cursor is defined in terms of 8 lines of pixels numbered from 0 to 7. By default, the cursor uses the last two lines of pixels, 6 and 7, to form the blinking cursor used by DOS and other programs.

The Cursor Size option can be used to change the size of the cursor, selecting a different range of lines.

The program then activates the cursor size dialog box. Note that the transition between the menu and the dialog box is subtle. This requires you to look carefully in order to see that the highlight has been removed from the menu and is on the arrow on the left side of the cursor size box.

The purpose of the dialog box is to allow you to select which adjacent groups of lines you want to use as the cursor. By default the bottom two lines are used. The **Default** command button will return you to the default if you decide not to utilize the new cursor shape.

The cursor shape is determined by the starting and ending lines; also, the ↑ and ↓ keys will move the starting or ending lines. You can use the [Tab] key to toggle around the dialog box. It is important to keep in mind the limitations associated with changing the cursor size:

**Change Is Temporary.**   The change made to the cursor size is not permanent—the normal cursor will return the next time the computer is booted. However, as you will see, you can save Control Center settings in a file that can be reloaded as part of the AUTOEXEC.BAT in order to preserve the desired cursor size.

**Applications Control Cursor.**   Many applications exert their own control over the size and shape of the cursor, ignoring any of the alterations made with the Control Center. When these applications release control and return to DOS, they reset the cursor to the normal DOS cursor—lines 6 and 7—negating the effect of the Control Center on the cursor size.

**Cannot Be Centered.**   While it is possible to select lines in the center of the box—4 and 5—as the cursor, DOS will only display the cursor aligned at the top or the bottom of the character box.

# Colors and Video

The Control Center provides you with the ability to fine-tune the colors used on your screen display. If you are using a black and white or monochrome screen you can also make selections of video attributes, but they are significantly more limited than color selections.

Screen *resolution* is a key term associated with video displays and adapters. To understand why resolution is so important you must consider how it is that images are produced on a computer screen—or a television screen, since they both use the same basic method.

When you look at a movie, the images you see on the screen are projected from the movie film. If you look at a section of film you will see that it consists of a series of complete images, each projected onto the screen one at a time in sequence, as shown in Figure 9–2.

In contrast, computer or TV screens consist of a series of rows called *scan lines*. Images created on computer or TV screens are *scanned* onto the tube on a line-by-line basis, as shown in Figure 9–3. In this type of system there are no *complete* images. While a new image is being scanned at the

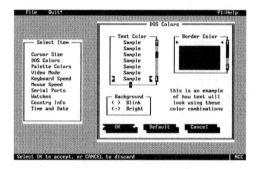

**Figure 9–2. Movies project whole images one at a time.**

top of the screen the remainder of the screen still shows the previous image. The screen is always in a constant state of transition from one image to another.

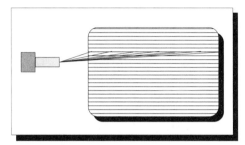

**Figure 9–3. Screen images are scanned onto the tube on a line-by-line basis.**

Computer screen displays are simply large matrixes composed of individual points, which can be bright, dark, or different colors. These points are called *pixels*. The resolution of the display is defined by the total number of pixels across and down the screen. For example, a standard IBM color graphics adapter has a resolution of 640 by 200. This means that each scan line (row) contains 640 pixels spread across the screen and that there are 200 of these rows (scan lines) from top to bottom. You will notice that PC screens tend to have much greater resolution horizontally (for example, 640 pixels) than vertically (320 pixels). As a general rule the more scan lines on the screen the better the resolution, making the text sharper and more readable. For example, the CGA adapter has 200 vertical scan lines. When the screen displays 25 rows of text it means each line of text uses eight scan lines—200 divided by 25 = 8.

A VGA monitor has 480 scan lines. When displaying 25 lines of text, the VGA screen assigns about 19 scan lines for each row of text, allowing the characters to be more clearly defined. Conversely, if you used the same quality of characters on the VGA screen as you did on the CGA screen, you should be able to print more lines of text—for instance, 80 columns and 60 lines or 480 divided by 8 = 60.[1]

---

1. Note that the total number of lines of text is a potential. In practice, VGA monitors can display up to 50 lines in the text mode. Some programs, such as Microsoft Word, will display 60 lines in a graphics/text display mode.

Higher screen resolutions can improve displays in two ways: by placing more text on the screen, or by improving the quality of the lines of text (or some combination of the two).

## Display Adapters

Before you begin the details of using the Control Center's color commands it may be useful to review the types of screen displays and adapters commonly used with MS-DOS computers.

PC video operates in either text or graphics mode. The Control Center is concerned only with those modes that can be used to display standard text, not the high-resolution graphics mode in which any type of pixel-mapped graphics can be displayed:

**MDA (Monochrome Display Adapter).**  Introduced with the IBM PC in 1981, this display produced single-color text in an 80-column by 25-row format. These adapters produced a TTY-teletype output. TTY output means that the monitor could only display the set of characters built into the display adapter. It could not create new characters or symbols by drawing patterns of pixels. Monochrome adapters always display white text. The green or amber color of some monochrome monitors is created by a green or amber filter. It does not indicate that the computer is sending a green or amber color to the monitor. *Color characteristics* on monochrome monitors do occur in the form of bold or bright text, reverse text (black letters on white background), and underlined video.

**Hercules Monochrome (HERC).**  In 1983 the Hercules Graphics Company of Berkeley, California released an adapter that duplicated the TTY output of the standard monochrome adapter, but also supported high-resolution, pixel-based graphics. Today, monochrome graphics adapters are manufactured by many companies, but the name *Hercules* has come to be synonymous with monochrome graphics.

**CGA (Color Graphics Adapter).**  Also released in 1981 by IBM, this adapter provided both the color and graphics abilities not included in the IBM monochrome adapter. Like all color adapters for the PC, it was capable of operating in two or more video modes. The adapter could produce text in an 80 by 25 format in 16 colors, and pixel-mapped graphics in 4 colors, 320 by 200, or 2 color modes.

**EGA (Enhanced Graphics Adapter).**  Introduced in 1985 by IBM, this adapter provided higher-resolution graphics (640 by 350) than the CGA monitor and sharper text in 16 colors. EGA adapters have a full palette of up to 64 colors. EGA adapters have a full palette of up to 64 colors. The additional resolution allows for increasing the number of lines of text displayed on the screen—for instance, 43 lines display.

**VGA (Video Graphics Array).** Introduced in 1987 this adapter expanded the color palette to 265 colors and sharpened the resolution to 640 by 480. When displaying text, VGA monitors can show up to 50 lines.

**Black and White.** It is important to understand that the terms *monochrome* and *black and white* are *not* interchangeable. Monochrome refers to monitors and adapters that can only output information in one color. The significant point is that the adapter card sends only a single color signal. Black and white screen displays refer to single color screens attached to multiple color monitors. For example, both EGA and VGA adapters can be connected to single color EGA or VGA monitors. The result is that the adapter card sends out a color signal that the monitor shows as either black or white, or in some cases as shades of gray.

One important point about the difference between monochrome and black and white displays is that in the monochrome set-up the display adapter is aware that only single color output is permitted. This means that programs can determine that a monochrome display is installed in the computer and automatically adjust their output to conform to that display. In a black and white set-up the adapter card does not know that the color signals it sends out are ending up on a single color screen. Programs running on this system will assume that the output is actually being displayed in colors, when in fact only a single color appears to the user. This may make screen displays very hard to read, since contrasting colors may appear to be the same shade of white or gray when displayed on a single color EGA or VGA screen.

The configuration dialog box in the Norton program has separate settings for monochrome and black and white because of this difference.

**LCD.** LCD, liquid crystal displays, are typically used on laptop and notebook computers. Unlike large monitors, LCD screens are light absorbing rather than light emitting, which means that they are harder to see under changing light conditions. LCD screens are a special form of black and white display since they are adapter compatible with CGA, EGA, or VGA output modes but can only display a single color. Many programs have special LCD settings that try to use the color combinations to create the greatest contrast on LCD screens.

The Control Center has three options affecting video display:

**DOS Colors.** This option allows you to select the colors used by DOS when it displays standard output.

**Palette Colors.** This option allows you to control the exact colors used by applications if you have a VGA or EGA adapter.

**Video Mode.** This screen lets you select the text video mode. The variety of options available is determined by the type of display adapter in your computer.

## DOS Colors

By default, DOS displays white text on a black background. This option can be used to select a color combination for DOS text display and any programs that use standard DOS text display.[2]

Load the Control Center program and select the DOS colors option by entering ncc ⏎ d.

The **DOS Color** dialog box, as seen in Figure 9–4, contains three items. The highlight is positioned to the default DOS colors, white on black.

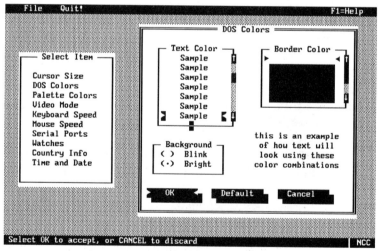

Figure 9–4. DOS Color dialog box.

---

2.  For example, the command **SYSINFO /SUMMARY** will use the current DOS colors, not those used by the full screen version of SYSINFO.

**Text Color.** This list box scrolls through 256 different combinations of foreground and background colors. The combinations will be unique only on EGA and VGA screens. If you are using a monochrome monitor the options will consist of combinations of normal, underlined, bold, and reverse video.

You can use the ↑,↓, [Pg Dn], [Pg Up], [Home], and [End] keys to scroll through the list.

**Background.** The full list of 256 colors is really divided into two lists of 128 combinations each. The 128 combinations are created by mixing 16 foreground colors with 8 background colors, making 16 times 8 = 128 different color combinations. The second set of 128 colors simply repeats the first list of 128 colors, with two possible variations. The first variation repeats the color combinations, but sets the foreground color to blinking. This is the default variation. The second variation changes each of the eight background colors used in the second half of the list as bright colors. You can use the settings in this to select blinking or bright as the variation for the second half of the list. This setting has no effect on monochrome monitors.

**Border Color.** Some color screens allow you to set the color of the *border area*. The border area is a portion of the screen that lies outside the actual active scan area of the screen, as seen in Figure 9–5. This area is not used for text or data display, but in some cases can be changed from black to another color using this option.

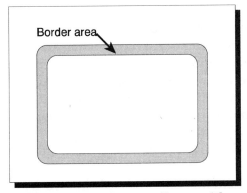

**Figure 9–5. Border area lies outside the active display area of the screen.**

The **Default** control button resets the colors to the DOS default. Select a color combination of yellow text on a blue background by entering

```
[Home]
[Pg Dn]  (5 times)
↵
```

The select colors will take effect when you exit the Control Center. Enter [Esc].

The DOS prompt now appears in the specified color. Note that if the ANSI driver is not installed, the message, "The ANSI device driver is not installed, DOS colors may change," is displayed as a warning. Remember that DOS color changes are temporary and will be forgotten the next time the computer is rebooted. DOS will return to a black and white display.

## Video Mode

The video mode option is used to select special text modes available on EGA and VGA displays. These modes allow you to take advantage of the higher resolution of these monitors to display 34, 40, or 50 lines of text on the screen by reducing the height in pixels of each line.

For example, if you have a VGA monitor you can select a 50-line display. Begin by loading the Control Center and selecting the video mode dialog box by entering ncc ↵ v.

The dialog box has two options: display lines (except on CGA) and display mode (color or black and white). To select a 50-line display, enter 5 ↵.

This option immediately affects the display so that the Control Center is now operating in 50-line mode. When you exit the Control Center DOS will also display characters at the 50-line height. Enter [Esc].

Once you have set the video mode all the Norton Utilities programs will recognize this mode and continue to operate in it until it is reset or the computer is rebooted, regardless of the video options selected in the Norton program Configuration. Enter norton ↵.

This program also displays in 50-line mode. Return to DOS by entering [Esc].

The effect of changing video mode is limited by several factors. Many programs set the video mode themselves when they are loaded and will override the current video mode setting, regardless of what it is.

## The Color Palette

The Palette feature is available to users with EGA or VGA screen displays. Recall that the DOS color option used 16 different colors to make all 256 combinations. While DOS is restricted to a palette of 16 colors, the EGA and VGA monitors are capable of a wider variety of color; for example, EGA has 64 colors and VGA has 256 colors.

To understand how the Palette feature works it may be useful to begin with a basic discussion of how DOS displays text on color screens. Recall from Chapter 3 that text information display on the screen uses numeric codes—the ASCII coding system—to assign each character a specific numeric value from 0 to 255. The 256 character limit allows any character to be represented by one byte of information.

However, if you want to display text in color you need to know more than just the character code number; you need to know the color combination to use for that character. For this reason, each character displayed on the screen requires two bytes of information. The first byte sets the character's color attributes while the second specifies the character itself. The color attribute byte is divided into two parts. The first four bits are used to designate the background color, while the last four bits designate the foreground color. Figure 9–6 shows how the computer would represent the display of a yellow letter, **A**, on a blue background. Note that each four-bit pattern provides room for 16 different bit patterns, setting the maximum number of color variations at 16 for foreground and background colors.[3]

This system is used for all text modes on CGA, EGA, and VGA screen displays. However, EGA and VGA displays make a distinction between two kinds of colors—physical and logical:

**Physical Colors.** A physical color is a specific shade of color that can be produced by your display adapter and displayed on your monitor. EGA adapters support 64 colors, while VGA adapters support 256. The colors are created by combining primary colors of the colors screen—red, green, and blue—in different strengths and brightness.

**Logical Colors.** A logical color is the numeric code (0 to 15) represented by a 4-bit pattern in the color attribute byte.

The distinction between a logical color and a physical color is important because EGA and VGA adapters can produce more colors than the attribute

---

3. The value of 16 is arrived at by taking 2 to the 4th power.

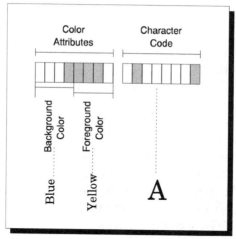

**Figure 9–6. Bytes used to produce a yellow A on a blue background.**

byte can use at any one moment. At first glance, you might assume that DOS cannot make use of the additional colors provided by these adapters. However, EGA and VGA adapters use special memory blocks called *color registers*. The color registers are used to store physical color descriptions— that is, so much of this and that color blended with this or that strength and brightness for each of the 16 logical colors DOS can use.

By default, EGA and VGA adapters use the same standard 16-color scheme. However, using the Palette option of the Control Center program you can substitute any of the 64 (EGA) or 256 (VGA) physical colors for any one of the 16 logical colors. For example, if you have a VGA adapter you may want to substitute one of the available shades of blue for the default blue by placing your selected color into the blue register, as seen in Figure 9–7.

The ability to control the relationship between the physical colors provided by the display adapter and the logical colors used by DOS has two major advantages:

**Custom Colors.**  One reason to use the Palette to change colors is to use shades of colors that you find more pleasing than the DOS default colors.

**Control Applications.**  The Palette also provides a means by which you can control the appearance of programs that do not allow you to specify the full range of VGA or EGA colors. Keep in mind that you are not required to pick physical colors matching the default logical

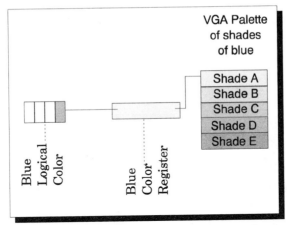

**Figure 9–7. VGA shade substituted for default color blue.**

colors. This means you can substitute a shade of red for black, green, white, and so on.

The ability to substitute colors in any way you desire allows you to create color schemes for programs that otherwise would not support colors (for example, the Norton Editor) or use only a predetermined set of color (for instance, the Norton Utilities). Note that once you change a logical color, that color will continue until you reset the palette or reboot the computer. You can also use the palette feature to limit the variety of colors. This can be done by placing the same color in more than one color register. For example, suppose you want to operate a program on an LCD screen that does not provide an LCD color combination. Because the program thinks the LCD screen is really an EGA or VGA color screen, it displays shades that are difficult to read. In this case you could change all the 16 logical colors to either black or white so the program will display at maximum contrast.

The Palette option provides you with a way to fine-tune the screen display and extend that control to programs that normally have limited or no color options. In some cases, manipulating the color palette in the Control Center is easier and faster than using the color set-up options provided by certain programs. For example, suppose you are working with dBASE IV and want to switch the black and white display to yellow on blue. In order to change dBASE IV using the dBASE IV commands, you must edit the CONFIG.DB command and place into that file a **SET COLOR TO** command. dBASE IV uses several different types of color notation, some of which can be arcane. For example, the color yellow is expressed as

GR+. It is much simpler to use the Control Center palette and substitute yellow for white, and blue for black.

## Using the Palette

As an example of how the **Palette** feature works you can use the Norton Utilities programs. The **Video and mouse options** dialog box available on the *Configure* menu of the Norton program provides a very limited number of color options. If you want to run the programs in color you can choose either the standard set of colors or the alternate. You do not have control over the uses of specific colors. For instance, in the standard color set the background color for the menu bar, message line, and pull-down menus is cyan. Suppose you want to have a more dramatic color displayed instead of cyan—red or pink. You could accomplish this by using the **Palette** command to substitute a new color for cyan. The program displays another dialog box showing a list of 256 physical colors from which you can make a selection. The default color—here, color 3—is indicated by the > < symbols. The colors are not listed in numeric order, but are grouped by shade. Not all screens will show a complete palette of 256 colors. In such cases some colors with different numbers will appear to have the same shade.

You can reset the computer to the default color palette using the **Default** button in the **Palette** dialog box.

## Keyboard and Mouse Speed

You can use the Control Center to adjust the sensitivity of the keyboard and the mouse:

**Keyboard.** PC keyboards are designed to automatically repeat a key if the key is held down for a certain length of time. The keyboard option allows you to control the length of time a key needs to be held down before the automatic repeating starts, as well as the number of repetitions per second generated when the repeating action is engaged. This option will not work with older PC/XT computers.

**Mouse.** If you are using a mouse driver compatible with the Microsoft mouse driver, you can use this option to set the *acclamation rate* for the mouse. The acclamation rate refers to the amount of screen area covered for each movement of the mouse. Increasing the acceleration factor means that the mouse will move faster on the screen for the same mouse movement on the table. Conversely, lowering the mouse rate will cause the mouse to move more slowly across the screen.

**Repeat Speed.**  This option sets the number of characters per second that will be typed when a key enters the repeat mode. The default is 10.9 chars/sec. You can adjust the speed from 2.0 to 30.0 chars/sec.

**Delay.**  The delay setting is the length of time a key must be held down before the computer activates the automatic repeat mode. The default is .5 seconds. You can select a delay time from 1 to .25 seconds.

At the bottom of the box is a blank entry area labeled "Keyboard Test Pad." This pad allows you to test the sensitivity of the keyboard by pressing a letter to see how it repeats. Note that you cannot use the arrow keys as part of the test; the keys must be character keys.

The **Fast** control button will automatically select the fastest options—30.0 repeating and a .25 second delay.

## Serial Ports

Most DOS computers are equipped with one or more ports. *Ports* are used to connect a variety of devices to the computer. There are two basic types of general purpose ports:

**Parallel.**  Parallel communications is characterized by its ability to transfer an entire byte of information—eight related bits—in a single operation. To do so a parallel port sends each bit over its own wire so that all eight travel in parallel, as shown in Figure 9–8. This form of communication is simple and direct.

However, technical problems associated with sending multiple singles in parallel increase with the distance the information must travel. Parallel communications are used only for distances under a few feet.[4] DOS designates parallel ports as LPT1, LPT2, or LPT3. LPT stands for *line printer*, indicating that parallel ports are assumed to be printer ports.

---

4. The longest parallel cable you will find is 25 feet, although traditionally this was considered too long for a parallel cable. I personally use a 25-foot parallel cable and have not encountered any problems.

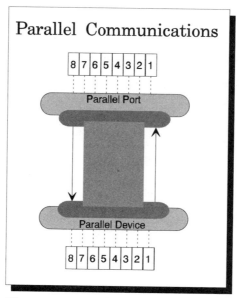

**Figure 9–8. Parallel communications.**

**Serial.** Serial communications works in the opposite manner. Instead of sending a group of related bits (one byte) simultaneously, the group is broken down into individual bits. Each bit is sent, one at a time, through the line—as seen in Figure 9–9—as a *series* of bits. In serial communications the byte of information is first broken down into a series, sent individually through the line, and reassembled into a byte at the other end. The advantage of serial communications is that data can be sent reliably over great distances. A second advantage of serial communications is that serial ports can easily be configured to send or receive

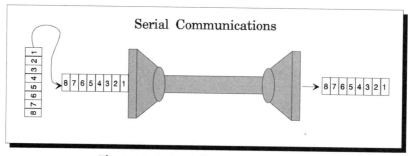

**Figure 9–9. Serial communications.**

information or perform both send and receive at the same time. DOS designates serial ports as COM1 or COM2, where COM stands for communications port. If you are using DOS 3.xx or higher, DOS can address two more serial ports, COM3 and COM4.

On most MS-DOS systems, the parallel port is used almost exclusively for interfacing with printers. The nature of parallel communications—multiple, simultaneous data transmission—tends to limit its use to output only operations, such as printing. Serial ports have traditionally been used for communication with printers (output only), mice (input only), and modems (input and output). In addition, two computers can be directly linked through serial ports using special software that performs network-type operations.

## The Structure of Serial Communications

Serial communications are implemented on PCs using RS-232 serial communications ports. These ports utilize an 8520 Universal Asynchronous Receiver Transmitter (UART) chip. This chip is designed to handle both sending and receiving data through the serial port. An important aspect of this chip operation is that the computer can control various aspects of the chips operation. The most important options are:

**Baud Rate.** The *baud* rate is a measure of the rate at which information is sent from, or received by, the serial port. The higher the baud rate, the faster data are sent or received. In order for serial communications to operate properly, the serial port must be set at the appropriate baud rate. For example, most serially interfaced printers require that the serial port be programmed for 9,600 baud. If you are using a modem you must match the baud rate of the computer you want to communicate with (for instance, 300, 1,200, or 2,400 baud), assuming that your modem is capable of transmitting at the required rate.

For the most part, the term *baud* is treated as if it were synonymous with *bits per second*. Technically, the baud rate measures *signals per second*. In many forms of communications each signal sent by a modem contains one bit of information. In such cases baud and bit per second have the identical meaning. However, some methods of communicating alter the ratio between bits and signals. Multiple-phase signals can communicate more than one bit in a signal. A two-phase signal could transmit two bits per signal. In this circumstance, the baud rate would be half the bits per second rate—1,200 bits per second would be sent at a 600 baud rate. Programs that link with computers by means of their serial ports are very useful for transferring files between computers. For instance, LapLink from Traveling Software transfers files between laptop and desktop computers at rates as high as 115,200 bits per second. If the top rate for a serial port is 19,200 baud, how is this possible? The answer lies in the correct distinction between baud rate, which has a maximum of 19,200, and bits per second, which can be faster if more than one bit is sent per signal—6 * 19,200 = 115,200. However, it is a common industry practice to use the term baud as if it measured bits per second. For example, the LapLink menus list the setting of 115,200 under baud rate, even though that may be technically a bits per second rating. As a user there is no practical difference.

**Stop and Data Bits.**   When data are transmitted over a serial port, consideration must be given to how to ensure that the individual bit signals sent one at a time are reassembled correctly at the other end. The method used in PCs is called *asynchronous* communication.[5] In this method each item sent is composed of three parts, as shown in Figure 9–10.

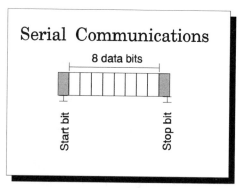

**Figure 9–10. Serial communications uses start, data, and stop bits.**

**Start (Space) Bit.** The beginning of each group is marked with a single bit, usually a zero.

---

5.   Like the ASCII code, asynchronous communications was originally developed for Teletype machines that predate personal computers.

**Data Bits.**  Following the start bit comes the actual data bits, beginning with the least significant bit. Serial communications can operate with data groups of either seven or eight bits. Since the standard ASCII code uses only 128 characters, 7-bit communication is sufficient to send data stored in that format. If the data being sent includes bytes with values over 127 (program files) then 8-bit communications would be required.[6]

The *least significant* part of any number—binary, decimal, or hex—refers to the number with the smallest place value. For example, in the binary number 00000001 the 1 is in the least significant position—that is, the 1s column. When sent through a serial port, the 1 would be the first bit sent following the start bit. In the number 10,000,000 the 1 is in the most significant position, which means that it would be the last data bit sent.

**Stop (Mark) Bits.**  Following the last data bit the serial port sends 1 or 2 stop bits. The stop bits signal that the data transfer is complete. The serial port then enters an *idle* state until it receives the next start bit. Stop bits are usually binary 1 values, in contrast to start bits that are zeros.

**Parity.** Parity refers to the type of parity check, if any, used during data transmission. Parity checks are used to find errors in communication. When parity check is turned on, additional bits are added to the data stream following the start bit, but before the data bits. Parity checking can be set for even or odd parity. If the receiving port gets the wrong parity value—an even value when the parity is set for odd—an error is generated. If no parity is used, no additional bits are added to the transmission stream.

The serial port options in the Control Center allow you to display and modify the programmable settings for any of the installed serial ports. It is important to keep in mind that the additional start, stop, or parity bits are generated by the serial port. Only the data bits are supplied by the program. If the communications operation is to take place properly, the port must be set to the required options before beginning communication.

---

6. Communications services, such as Compuserve, that communicate with 7 data bits can transfer binary files using special protocols, such as an X-modem, which circumvents the normal 7-bit limitation.

In practice most programs using serial ports for telecommunications have the ability to set the serial portion options themselves and do not require you to use another program, such as the Control Center, to set these options.

One common exception is the settings required when a printer is attached to a serial port.[7] The instructions furnished with these printers usually tell you to use the DOS MODE command to set the serial port. However, the Control Center provides a much friendlier way to accomplish this task.

## Watches and Time

One important practical difference between the PC/XT computers and the AT and higher computers is that the AT system includes a battery-powered system clock. In PC/XT computers the system date and time are set at an arbitrary date—10:00 AM, January 1, 1980—each time you boot the computer. To get the system to conform to *real* time, it is necessary to enter the actual date and time with the DOS date and time commands, or install a battery-powered clock in the computer[8] and use the AUTOEXEC.BAT file to fetch the real time whenever the computer is booted.

In AT systems the date and time are maintained in the CMOS, along with other system parameters, such as the number and type of disks installed in the system. If you find that you need to adjust the time or date you need to run the SETUP program for the CMOS. Set-up programs come in two forms:

**Software.**  The IBM AT model and some older AT-compatible programs use a software program that must be run after the system has been booted, to allow you to make changes in the CMOS data, including the date and time.

**ROM BIOS.**  Most of the current AT and higher computers include a set-up program as part of the computer's ROM BIOS chip set. This program can be activated by pressing a special key combination while the system is booting, for instance [Ctrl-Alt-Esc] or [Del].

In either case, changing the date and time requires that the system be rebooted. You can avoid this by using the Control Center's **Time and Date** options. When you use this option, any changes made to the current time and date will be passed onto the CMOS without having to run the set-up.

---

7. Some programs, such as WordPerfect, will automatically reset the serial port to the stop, data, and parity settings required by the printer, based on the data stored or entered into the WordPerfect printer resource file.

8. Even though AT computers have built-in clock/calendars, DOS will still default to asking for the date and time when the computer boots if no AUTOEXEC.BAT file is found.

Note that using the DOS DATE and TIME commands will *not* change the date and time in the CMOS. When the system is rebooted, the date and time from the CMOS will again become the default.

## Country Information

In order to simplify the use of American-made computers in the international market, Version 2.xx of DOS included the ability to change the format used for displaying standard types of data, such as time and date displays, to conform to the formats used in other countries. For example, the date and time formats normally used by the DOS commands **DATE** and **TIME** are the common American format, **Thu 3-14-1991** and **13:34:35.88**.

The COUNTRY.SYS driver allowed you to change the standard format to a different international format based on a coding system. For example, German formats were assigned the code number 049. Selecting code number 049 would change the output of the **DATE** and **TIME** commands to **Thu 14.03.1991** and **13.36.57,76**.

The DOS 2.xx method required the entry of the **COUNTRY** command in the CONFIG.SYS file. For example, to set German formats you would add the line **COUNTRY=049** to the CONFIG.SYS file. Note that the syntax of the **COUNTRY** command is misleading in that it appears to be an internal DOS command—that is, one that does not require the presence of a device driver file. However, in order for this command to execute properly, the COUNTRY.SYS file must be stored in the root directory of the book disk.

Beginning with DOS 3.xx, support for international formats was expanded to include the *National Language Support Function* program, NLSFUNC.EXE. The advantage of NLSFUNC over the previous **COUNTRY** command was that you could change national format without having to reboot the system, as was the case in DOS 2.xx.

NLSFUNC is a memory-resident program that can be used to load country-dependent information drivers that support international formats. The NLSFUNC program is used to load the COUNTRY.SYS driver. Once this is accomplished the Control Center **Country Info** option becomes active. You can use this option to select the country format you desire. Unlike DOS 2.xx, you can return to the Control Center and change the country format as many times as you like.

As part of the National Language Support system, the KEYB program can be used to change the characters produced by certain keys in order to match the keyboard layouts used in other countries. For example, you could change the key assignments to a French keyboard layout by using the

KEYB command **KEYB FR,C:\DOS\KEYBOARD.SYS**. Keep in mind this command assumes that the KEYBOARD.SYS driver is located in the C:\DOS directory. Once loaded you will find that the keys produce different characters from the ones that appear on the American keyboard; the Z key produces W, for instance. The Norton Utilities does not offer any features related to keyboard layouts.

In order to use the **Country Info** option you *must* first load the COUNTRY.SYS driver into memory using the NLSFUNC program by entering the following command at DOS, assuming that you are in the directory in which the COUNTRY.SYS file is located:

```
nlscfunc country.sys
```

# DOS and Batch Operations

While it is true that the Control Center provides you with the ability to control and fine-tune many aspects of your system, those changes are not permanent. As soon as the computer is rebooted or different settings are entered through the Control Center or another application, your modifications are lost. In order to access the true power of the Control Center you need to be able to store and then retrieve Control Center settings. This enables you to build a library of different setting files that can be loaded whenever they are needed. If you want a certain group of settings to function as default system settings then you can load those settings from the AUTOEXEC.BAT file. There is no limit, except for disk space, to the number of different Control Center setting files you want to create. As examples, you will create two types of setting files:

**New System Defaults.** This file will contain the start-up settings you want to use as the system defaults. You can use the AUTOEXEC.BAT file to load this file whenever the system is booted. For example, you may want to set the keyboard speed to fast and set up COM2 as a printer port.

**Application Specific Settings.** This type of file contains settings you want to use with a specific application but do not want to establish as the system defaults. For example, you may want to change the color palette before running an application, in order to overcome its limited color support.

The process of creating a Control Center setting file takes two steps.

**Make Selections from Menus.** The first step is to load the Control Center in the usual manner and select the options you desire.

**Save Settings** When you have made all the selections you want, press [F2] to create a file that will store the settings on the disk. You have the option of selecting which of the Control Center settings you want to include in the file so that only the options you want to change will be affected. You can use the [F2] command from any dialog box in the Control Center. You can also execute the **Save settings** command by selecting **Save settings** from the *File* menu.

## Loading Stored Settings

Once you have created settings files they can be used in three ways:

**Load Settings Command.** Once you have started the Control Center you can load a stored setting file by using the **Load settings** command located on the *File* menu or by pressing [F3]. Note you must know the file and/or path name of the file. The Control Center does not display a file selector dialog box for this option.

**Command Argument.** When you start the Control Center from DOS you can load the settings from any of the setting files by using the setting file name as an argument for the NCC command. When the Control Center program loads it will reflect the options from the setting file. The command below would load the Control Center with the EDCLR.NCC settings:

```
ncc edclr.ncc
```

This option is useful when you want to modify the settings in a given file.

**Automatically Set Options.** If you want to execute the settings stored in a Control Center setting file and want to continue DOS operations, rather than enter an interactive session with the Control Center, you can use the /SET switch. When /SET is used the program executes the settings stored in the specified file and then returns to DOS without running the full Control Center program. The command below changes the palette colors without loading the full program. The program will display messages on the screen indicating which features have been changed:

```
ncc edclr.ncc /set
```

The /**SET** options allows you to execute Control Center operations from DOS batch files. For example, suppose you wanted to create a batch that would load the desired palette and then load the EDLIN program. When you exit EDLIN the palette would be reset to the default colors. As an example, create a batch file called EDIT.BAT using the EDLIN program. Note that the numbers that appear on the right are displayed for reference purposes and should not be entered as part of the batch file.

```
@ECHO OFF                          {1}
NCC edclr.ncc /SET                 {2}
EDLIN %1                           {3}
NCC standard.ncc /SET              {4}
NCC default.ncc /SET               {5}
```

The batch file first uses the Control Center to set the colors for the specified application, EDLIN, and then runs the program. Note that in line {3} a **%1** is used to pass the file name parameter to EDLIN, since EDLIN cannot operate unless a file name is provided. Also note that it was necessary to load both the standard.ncc and default.ncc files to reset both the color palette and the serial printer, since each of those settings was stored in a separate settings file. To use the EDIT.BAT file to edit a file in color, you would enter a command like the one below:

```
edit sample.txt
```

EDLIN would create or edit the file sample.txt using the color palette stored in edclr.ncc.

As discussed previously, you can use the Control Center instead of the DOS MODE command to set serial port values. The advantage of using the Control Center is that you can load DOS color and other default settings at the same time you set up the serial port. For example, the following **MODE** commands would appear in the AUTOEXEC.BAT, in order to set up COM2 for a printer:

```
MODE COM2:9600,N,8,1
MODE LPT1:COM2:
```

You can substitute a Control Center command for the first **MODE** command and load colors and other settings along with the serial port values:

```
NCC default.ncc /SET
MODE LPT1:COM2:
```

# SUMMARY

This chapter discussed how the Norton Utilities Control Center program can be used to control various aspects of your computer system.

**Control Center**     The Control Center program is used to fine-tune various aspects of the computer system. Settings and options implemented with the Control Center can be stored in settings files and reloaded at a later time.

**Cursor Size**     The size and shape of the DOS cursor can be modified.

**DOS Colors**     Default colors can be selected for DOS to replace the default black and white display.

**Video Mode**     Selects from the available text video modes.

**Palette**     On EGA and VGA monitors this option provides a method of changing the physical colors used by DOS and applications using the DOS palette.

**Keyboard**     On AT and higher computers, the keyboard response can be adjusted with respect to the automatic repeating function. You can adjust the number of characters per second that are repeated and the amount of time a key must be depressed before it repeats.

**Mouse**     On Microsoft-compatible mice, the rate of responsiveness can be increased or decreased.

**Serial**     This option enables you to set the baud rate, stop bits, and data bits for any of the serial communications ports in the system.

**Country Info**     If you have installed the National Language support driver you can select the country-dependent formats you desire from a menu.

**Time and Date**     This option changes the time and date settings in the CMOS RAM on AT and higher systems.

# 10 Fine-tuning Your Hard Disk

In this chapter you will learn how the Norton Utilities programs can be used to fine-tune the performance of your hard disk. There are two basic ways to do this:

**Buffering.**  Despite significant improvement in the operating speeds of hard disks in the decade since the IBM XT was introduced, disk operations, both hard and floppy, are still significantly slower than internal operations, such as moving data between locations in RAM memory.[1] *Buffering* is a technique whereby a block of RAM memory is used as a temporary storage area for data being sent to, or read from, a disk. In most cases, hard and floppy disk performance can be increased by using *buffering*, also called *disk caching*.

**Physical Organization.**  Recall from Chapter 8 that the FAT system used by DOS can result in the *fragmentation* of disk information. Fragmentation occurs when a logical unit, such as a file or user-defined directory, is stored in two or more nonadjacent physical blocks. When data are read from nonadjacent blocks, additional disk seeks may be required to retrieve the data, causing an apparent slowdown in disk operations. You can improve disk operations by eliminating file and directory fragmentation so that the number of actual disk-seek operations is kept to an absolute minimum.

The Norton Utilities contains two programs, Norton Cache and Speed Disk, that address these two disk performance issues. This chapter will detail the use and operation of these two programs.

---

1.  One reason is that RAM has no moving parts. Recall from Chapter 8 that disk drives have latency periods caused by the time required to move parts, such as the disk drive heads, to new locations.

# Disk Caching

The terms *buffering* and *caching* refer to a technique whereby RAM memory is allocated to serve as a temporary storage area for information being transferred between disks and the computer. Recall from Chapter 8 that disk operations are subject to a number of mechanical problems, which slow down the transfer of information. The overall performance of a disk is usually expressed in terms of the *average seek* time in milliseconds. The original IBM XT hard disk had an average seek time in the area of 90 ms. Typical hard disks today range from 65 down to 15 ms. Floppy disks would probably have an average seek time of several hundred ms. If you could compare disk-seek times to RAM access you would find that RAM functions about as fast as a hard disk with a 1-ms seek time.

Thus, in most cases, data transfer from RAM would be significantly faster than transferring directly from the disk. Ideally, the best operation speed could be achieved by using RAM memory instead of disk memory. However, this would have several practical limitations:

**Volatile.**  RAM memory cannot retain information when the computer is turned off. Any data placed into a RAM storage area would eventually have to be transferred to a disk, in order to ensure that it is available for use at a later time.

**Cost.**  RAM memory is significantly more expensive than disk storage, per megabyte. For example, a megabyte of RAM memory may sell for $150. A 100-megabyte hard disk may cost $500—or $5.00 per megabyte.

**Structural Limits.**  Even if cost were no object, DOS and PC computers have a number of different structural limits on the total amount of RAM that can be installed. For example, 80286 computers could not use more than 16 megabytes of memory (conventional and extended).

A compromise solution is to use RAM memory to speed the points in the process that cause the most delay by using a memory buffer or cache as a temporary target for disk transfers.

## How Caches Work

Disk caching is a process that uses memory to improve the *apparent* performance of floppy and hard disks. The important word in the previous sentence is *apparent*. In fact, the only software operation that has a direct effect on the performance of the hard disk is the low-level formatting operation that sets the interleave factor on hard disks.[2]

Caching does not change the actual performance of the hard disk itself. Instead, it provides programs with the illusion that disk operations are faster than they actually are. The basic technique is to use a TSR (memory resident) program to redirect disk read and write operations, normally sent directly to the hard disk via the hard disk controller card, to an area in the RAM memory called a *buffer*. Since access to RAM is significantly faster than even to fast hard disks, the application acts as if the disk operations have been completed once the transfer to or from the buffer area is complete.

The TSR cache program can then complete the actual disk operation in the background while the user continues with the current application. The apparent improvement in disk performance is because the user is able to continue with the application while the cache program is still in operation.

In other words, the cache program creates the illusion that the floppy or hard disk is actually working faster than it is. Because the improvement in performance is an appearance, rather than a direct, physical enhancement, users understand that the efficiency of the caching program is dependent on a wide range of factors. The apparent improvement in performance will vary greatly, depending on how each factor is involved in the specific disk operation being performed. In some cases the cache will radically improve the apparent performance. In other cases the nature of the task will prohibit the cache program from making a significant contribution.

Disk operations, and therefore cache operations, fall into two broad categories:

**Read Data.** When an application needs to read information from the disk, it makes a request for data from a specific file. The operating system then retrieves the data from the specified disk data clusters. How can a cache program improve performance during a read operation? In the most critical area—transfer rate—the cache program cannot change the physical limitations of your system and so it cannot actually speed reading from the disk. How then can the cache benefit the user during a read operation? The technique employed is called *read-ahead*. In a read-ahead process the cache program reads more data sectors into the buffer area than the application actually requests.

---

2.  See Chapter 8 for an explanation of the interleave factor.

Reading additional sectors into the buffer area does not actually improve performance. The benefit lies in what happened when the *next* read operation is requested. If the next requested block of data can be found in the additional sectors already loaded into the buffer area, the application can draw the data from the buffer, at a high rate of speed, avoiding the need to perform an actual disk read.

Of course, this approach is beneficial only if the additional sectors read during the initial disk read operation are all, or part, of the next block of requested information. If the application cannot find some, or all, of the data it needs in the buffer, an actual disk read operation will be required. Cache programs also work on the assumption that some of the data read may be needed again. For example, most word processing programs use dictionary files to check spelling. In order to conserve memory, the dictionary file is read only when a request to check spelling is made and in many cases only as much of the dictionary as is needed is retained in memory. If the cache were to load the entire dictionary in its buffer, you would find that the next time you checked a word there would be less of a delay, since the application would find the dictionary in the buffer and avoid loading it again from the disk.

Buffering read operations is a hit-or-miss technique. The effectiveness of a disk cache depends on certain factors:

**The Application.**  The advantage of a read-ahead buffer very much depends upon the way an application uses disk information. Some applications, such as spreadsheets, load the entire program and data file into memory, nullifying the advantage of a buffering. On the other hand, database applications will read in data in blocks of records, instead of the entire database. When the program seeks more records from the same file it may find them in the buffer, eliminating the need to read the disk again.

**Buffer Size.**  The larger the size of the disk buffer the more likely it is to contain the information needed by the application. The Norton Utilities can support a buffer area as small as 64K. However, a buffer this small would be useful only with a low-capacity floppy disk. Hard disks should have buffers at least 256K in size, preferably 1 megabyte or more. Of course, any memory used for disk caching is unavailable for other uses. There is no point in making your buffer so large that you don't have enough memory to run the application.

**Disk Fragmentation.**  As mentioned in Chapter 8, the FAT system used by DOS allows you to store information related to a single file in any number of nonadjacent blocks of clusters if there is not a single contiguous block of disk space of the required size available. When a disk is new, files tend to be contiguous. But over time most hard disks will begin to exhibit file fragmentation. When the disk cache program reads ahead, it does so in hopes that the next request for data will be for those sectors being placed into the cache buffer. Typically, a cache program will continue to read data from the current track into the read-ahead buffer, since reading from the current track does not require the drive head to move, avoiding adding seek time to the operation. However, on a significantly fragmented drive, the odds that the next read will require sectors from the current track are reduced. Disk caching is more complicated when the disk files are fragmented.

**Write Data.**  Writing information to the disk is a slower operation than reading. Write operations can benefit from disk caching in two ways.

**Write-ahead caching.**  The most significant improvement in performance can be obtained by writing the information to the buffer and then having the cache program transfer the data to disk. This allows the user to continue working with the application while the cache program completes the task of writing the data to the disk, as shown in Figure 10–1.

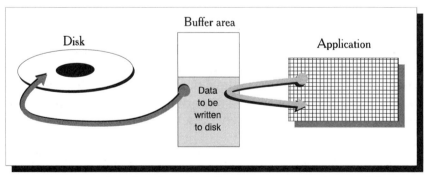

**Figure 10–1. Write-ahead cache allows user to continue while data are transferred to the disk.**

**Read-ahead.**  A second but less obvious benefit of write caching is that a copy of the data just written to the disk can remain stored in the cache buffer as part of the read-ahead cache. If the program should request to read some of the data just written to the disk it can be retrieved from the buffer instead of the disk.

The key to efficient use of a disk cache is to have the right data already in the cache buffer when the application needs to read it. But there is no sure way for the cache to always anticipate what the application or the user will request. The efficiency of even the most sophisticated cache program still depends on a variety of factors beyond the control of the cache program itself. Some users, because of the limited amount of memory in their computer or the memory-intensive nature of their software, will derive only marginal improvement with disk caching, while others will see very significant benefits.

# The NCACHE Program

The NCACHE program is designed to improve disk performance by using the technique described in the previous sections to circumvent the delays associated with hard disk track-to-track movement.

The Norton Utilities 5.0 is supplied with two programs, NCACHE-F (full cache) and NCACHE-S (small memory cache), that create and operate disk caching. Version 6.0 consolidates both programs into one. Since the cache program is the largest change in operations between Version 5.0 and 6.0, both will be documented in this chapter as a convenience for users who have not upgraded:

**NCACHE (6.0).** This program consolidates the two versions supplied with 5.0 into one program. NCACHE 6.0 adds a switch called OPTIMIZE that allows you to select optimization for speed, efficiency, or memory usage. Note that Version 6.0 supports a new installation option in the Norton program that allows you to select cache options from a menu.

**NCACHE (5.0). NCACHE-S.** This version of the Norton Utilities cache program is designed to provide basic disk-caching operations while using as small an amount of memory as possible—about 5K of conventional memory. This program limits cache activity to data that are actually read or written to the disk. It does not engage in read-ahead and write-ahead buffering operations.

**NCACHE-F.** This program uses more memory than NCACHE-S—about 75K—but supports the full range of caching options, including the Norton Utilities *InteliWrites* system that performs both read-ahead and write-ahead operations, providing maximum performance benefits.

## Loading the Cache Programs

The Norton Utilities cache programs can be loaded in three different ways.

### CONFIG.SYS

The cache program can be loaded at boot time by including the NCACHE program as a device driver in the CONFIG.SYS. This is done automatically when you select the **Load from CONFIG.SYS** option in the **Norton Cache** selection of the NUCONFIG program or by manually editing the CONFIG.SYS and typing in the appropriate command.

If you use the NUCONFIG program to add the **NCACHE** command, the command shown below will be added to the CONFIG.SYS. This command takes advantage of the /INI switch, discussed on page 381, which stores all of the cache parameters and options in a file, NCACHE.INI.

```
DEVICE = C:\NU\NCACHE.EXE /INI=C:\NU\NCACHE.INI
```

If you were to manually edit the CONFIG.SYS, you would enter this command to start the cache with the default values: DEVICE=C:\NU\NCACHE.EXE/INSTALL. The **/INSTALL** switch installs the cache with the default settings.

If you were using Version 5.0 the loading commands would be

```
DEVICE=C:\NU\NCACHE-F.EXE
```

or

```
DEVICE=C:\NU\NCACHE-S.EXE.
```

In general, the location of this line in the CONFIG.SYS file is not important. However, one common exception is on hard disks that use special device drivers to create partitions greater than 33 megabytes, under DOS 3.xx. Suppose you have used the *On Track Disk Manager* program supplied with Seagate hard disks, to partition your hard disk into drives C and D. In this case the Norton Utilities programs are stored on drive D. It is important that the *Disk Manager* driver precede the Norton Utilities driver if that driver is to be loaded from drive D. Below, the commands are shown in the correct sequence.

```
DEVICE=DMDRVR.BIN
DEVICE=D:\NU\NCACHE.EXE /INI/C:\NU\NCACHE.INI
```

If you run into problems booting your computer because of NCACHE you can prevent the computer from loading the device driver by holding down [Ctrl] while the computer is booting.

**AUTOEXEC.BAT**    The NCACHE program can be loaded from the AUTOEXEC.BAT file. This option can be implemented by selecting the **Load from AUTOEXEC.BAT** option in the **Norton Cache** selection of the NUCONFIG program or by manually editing the AUTOEXEC.BAT and typing in the appropriate command. When implemented from NUCONFIG the following line is added at the end of the AUTOEXEC.BAT:

```
C:\NU\NCACHE.EXE /INI=C:\NU\NCACHE.INI
```

If you want to manually edit AUTOEXEC.BAT you can add the command **NCACHE /INSTALL**. Note that you don't need to use the full path name of the program, e.g., C:\NU\NCACHE.EXE, if the **NCACHE** command follows the **PATH** command that sets a path open to the Norton Utilities home directory.

If you are using Version 5.0, enter NCACHE-F or NCACHE-S.

**DOS Command Line**    If you don't set up the CONFIG.SYS or AUTOEXEC.BAT files to load the cache program you can still execute the program directly from DOS by entering the same type of command that appears within the AUTOEXEC.BAT, e.g., **NCACHE /INSTALL** at the DOS prompt.

The main advantage of using the AUTOEXEC.BAT or direct DOS entry method is that you can remove the cache from memory using the **/UNINSTALL** switch, so long as the cache was the last TSR program loaded into memory. Recall from Chapter 7 that because of the way memory resident programs are handled by DOS, you can free up memory space used only by the *last* program made memory resident. When the cache is loaded from CONFIG.SYS you cannot use **/UNINSTALL** although you can disable the cache. Unfortunately, disabling the cache does not free up memory, but only turns off the effects of the cache program.

When the program loads, it displays a status screen that provides details about the use of memory and the way that the cache is being used. The screen displayed by Version 6.0 of the Norton Utilities displays a less complicated screen when it is loaded (Figure 10–2).

```
Conventional memory:      0K cache      18K management    496K free
High DOS memory:          0K cache       0K management     0K free
Expanded (EMS) memory:  496K cache      16K management     0K free
Extended (XMS) memory:  704K cache       0K management     0K free

   Total cache size is 1200.0K — Currently using 0.0K  (00.0%)

       The following drives are being cached:  A: B: C:
```

**Figure 10–2. NCACHE Version 6.0 screen display.**

Note that as the cache is loaded as part of a CONFIG.SYS or AUTOEXEC.BAT program, the information may be scrolled off the screen by output from other programs or drivers loading during the boot process. If the cache command is in the AUTOEXEC you can use the batch enhancer delay command to pause the display for a few seconds so you can inspect the values. Below, the **BE DELAY** command pauses the display about five seconds before the AUTOEXEC continues.

```
CLS
C:\NU\NCACHE.EXE /INI=C:\NU\NCACHE.INI
BE DELAY 90
```

Note that you *cannot* load NCACHE from *both* the CONFIG.SYS and the AUTOEXEC.BAT. The CONFIG.SYS, since it always loads before AUTOEXEC.BAT, will execute first and be the command that actually controls the cache. The NUCONFIG program will edit both the AUTOEXEC.BAT and CONFIG.SYS files, as necessary, if you change your previous selection. If you are manually editing the files you must ensure that you have removed any old commands that you no longer want to execute from either of the files.

## How the Cache Program Uses Memory

The basic concept behind cache programs is to allocate an area of memory to serve as a buffer area for disk read and, in some cases, write operations. Any memory allocated to the cache is memory that cannot be used for other purposes, specifically executing programs. The situation is complicated by the complex structure of DOS memory, which includes conventional, extended, and expanded memory. The cache program consists of two parts:

**Cache Program/Manager.**  The cache program is the code that operates the cache. The cache manager is the part of the program that keeps track of what information is stored in the cache buffer. It plays a similar role to the FAT on the disk. This portion of the cache will use some conventional memory.

**Buffer/Cache Area.**  The buffer area is the area in memory used to hold the disk data being buffered. This is by far the largest area of memory used by the cache programs. While it is possible to use conventional memory for the buffer area, it is more common to use extended and/or expanded memory. As a rule, using conventional memory as a buffer would limit the size of the TPA (the area where programs can be loaded) so severely that you would not have sufficient memory to load applications. You would use conventional memory only in unusual circumstances when you are able to give up application memory in order to improve disk access speed.

## How Cache Uses Memory

The status screen shows how the cache program is using memory. The four types of memory are *conventional, high DOS, expanded (EMS)*, and *extended (XMS)* memory. There are three columns: cache buffer size, cache program manager, and free memory left. It is important to remember that cache programs are dependent on the amount and type of memory available in the computer. The more memory, the better the program will function.

The cache programs are designed to automatically use memory in the most efficient way. The primary goal is to leave as much conventional memory free as possible, while using the maximum amount of extended or expanded memory. To get an idea how the program works look at the following examples:

**Minimum.** The absolute minimum amount of memory required is 256K of conventional memory. However, systems with only conventional memory give up so much valuable memory to run the cache that it would normally be more trouble than it is worth. This means that use of the cache on such machines should be attempted only if you have a special reason to want to improve disk speed at almost any cost.

**Recommended.** In most cases, a minimum of 384K of extended or expanded memory is required to use the cache program. Note that expanded memory requires an expanded memory driver that is compatible with LIM (Lotus Intel Microsoft) 4.0. Without this drive, the cache program will ignore the expanded memory.

If left to the default values, e.g., the **/INSTALL** switch with no parameters, the cache program will create a cache buffer that uses all of the available extended and/or expanded memory with the exception of a block of 64K that is reserved.

You can display the current memory usage by entering NCACHE/ STATUS.

## NCACHE and Windows

It is important to understand that Windows and the NCACHE program compete for the memory available in your system. If you were to allocate too much memory to NCACHE then there might not be a sufficient amount left for Windows. The NCACHE program has been designed to release some of the memory assigned to the cache during normal DOS to Windows when it is executed. By default, the NCACHE program will give up about 25 percent of the expanded or extended memory it uses when Windows is run.

You can use the Norton Cache option in the NUCONFIG program to set specific values for the amount of memory to be used when Windows is executed. For example, you might specify that NCACHE use only 384K under Windows and 1,024K when running from DOS.

It is important to know that if you run the SMARTDRV.SYS supplied with Windows 3.0 along with the Norton Utilities cache program, you will encounter incompatibilities if Windows is running in protected mode (Standard or 386-enhanced). The conflict can be avoided by running Windows in the real-mode, or by simply eliminating the SMARTDRV.SYS from the CONFIG.SYS file. You will get better performance if you use the Norton Utilities cache in place of the Windows cache (SMARTDRV.SYS), since the

Norton Utilities cache buffers all operations, not just Windows operations. Because Windows automatically adds this driver to your CONFIG.SYS file when it is installed, you need to edit this file to eliminate the loading of the driver. Look for a line that reads similarly to this: "DEVICE=C:\WIN-DOWS\SMARTDRV.SYS 768 256". Place a colon (:) in front of the command, which will stop its loading, but leave it in the file should you need to use it later.

In addition, if you are running Windows in the 386-enhanced mode you will need to add a line to the SYSTEM.INI file found in the \WINDOWS directory. First, Locate the label **[386Enh]**. This marks the beginning of the commands that affect 386-mode operations. Add the following line below that label:

```
VirtualHDIrq=false
```

## Detailed Reports

If you want to get a detailed listing of all of the NCACHE settings use the **/REPORT** switch:

```
NCACHE /REPORT
```

## Manager Memory Options

On most systems the NCACHE program will run without problems. However, due to the wide variety of DOS-compatible hardware and device drivers some incompatibilities may arise. NCACHE supports switches that allow you to manually control how it uses various types of memory.

**OPTIMIZE**    The optimize switch is used to control the way that NCACHE uses memory. Optimize allows you to avoid the details of expanded and extended memory and simply select an option based on your personal priorities. There are three options available with NCACHE OPTI-MIZE: *speed* uses as much memory as possible to get the best performance; *efficiency* limits some of the advanced options such as the size of the *write-ahead* buffer in order to reach a compromise between speed and memory usage; and *memory*, which turns off the *read-ahead* and *write-ahead* buffers in order to minimize the impact of the NCACHE program on memory. The default is *optimize for speed*.

For example, on a 386 computer with 1,408K of extended memory using the DOS HIMEM.SYS driver, the default setting, **/OPTIMIZE=speed**, would use 30K of conventional memory for management and 1,344K for the buffer. This option uses the largest available value for the write ahead feature.

On the same computer the *efficiency* setting would use 58K of conventional memory in order to increase the size of the read ahead buffer.

On the other hand, in using the *memory* setting, the impact on conventional memory would be reduced to only 13K, but the cache will not operate as efficiently.

The optimization method does not affect the size of the cache buffer. It is designed to control the impact on conventional memory of the cache program. The **/EXP** and **/EXT** switches control the amount of memory used by the cache buffer.

Also note that you can set the optimization only when you load the NCACHE program. Once loaded, you cannot reset the memory allocation unless you **UNINSTALL** the program or reboot the computer. If you want to experiment with the different settings you should load NCACHE from the DOS prompt or at least at the end of the AUTOEXEC.BAT and not from the CONFIG.SYS, since that method precludes the use of **UNINSTALL**. The commands below change the NCACHE memory allocation to *memory*.

```
NCACHE /UNINSTALL
NCACHE /INSTALL/OPTIMIZE=memory
```

**HMA Memory**    Normally, the NCACHE program will use HMA— high memory area—memory made available by memory managers such as HIMEM.SYS or QEMM386.SYS. If you find it necessary to prevent the cache program from using the high memory area, use the **/USEHMA** switch. The example command will load the cache program without using high memory in an environment that contains a high memory manager. Naturally, if you don't load the memory manager none of your programs can access HMA memory. Example: NCACHE/INSTALL/USEHMA=NO

**386 with Memory Managers-QEMM386/386MAX**    Two popular memory manager programs available for machines with 386 processors are QEMM386 and 386MAX. These programs take advantage of special characteristics of the 386 to allow use of memory under DOS that otherwise would not be available. One of the most attractive features is the ability of these programs to load memory-resident (TSR) programs into memory-assigned addresses in the otherwise inaccessible area between 640K and 1,024K. A

TSR program placed in this area, called *high memory*, would not reduce the available memory below 640K.

The exact amount and location of the high memory space available for loading TSR programs varies with each computer since the space is affected by hardware—in particular, the type of video adapter installed in the computer.[3] This feature is also very sensitive to the size and sequence of TSR programs placed into high memory.

While it is true that the Norton Utilities cache programs are TSR programs, they should not be loaded into high memory using LOADHI with QEMM386 or the 386MAX LOADHIGH option. The cache programs are designed to probe the system's memory to determine how best to load itself into memory. Such a procedure is in conflict with the manipulations performed by the high memory-loading programs that work best with passive device drivers. By default, the NCACHE program will avoid using this type of high memory unless no other method is available for reducing the impact of the program on conventional memory.

Instead, it is recommended that you use the **USEHIGH** switch to activate the use of high memory by the Norton Utilities cache program. Example:

```
NCACHE /INSTALL/USEHIGH=YES
```

## Buffer Memory Options

The Cache programs attempt to create as large a cache as possible, given the memory configuration of your system. All the extended and/or expanded memory available at the time is automatically allocated for caching. You may find that using all available memory for caching is not the best way to operate your system. The cache programs recognize switches that allow you to control the amounts of each type of memory the cache program uses.[4]

**/DOS**     The /DOS switch sets the amount of conventional memory, in kilobytes, allocated for the cache buffer. Recall that the cache program does not normally use conventional memory for the cache buffer. This switch

---

3. For example, monochrome adapters use less memory in the high memory area than VGA monitors. Thus, monochrome users have additional high memory available.

4. Each time you change an option, the program displays the cache statistics screen. Any options that were changed appear in bold to confirm the effect of the switch.

should be used when you are willing to sacrifice conventional memory in order to achieve increased disk performance.[5] The command below allocates 64K of conventional memory to the cache. The total memory impact of the command would be about 90–95K, since in addition to the 64K buffer, the cache program and manager must also reside in conventional memory.

```
NCACHE /INSTALL/DOS=64
```

You can use a *negative* argument with the switch, in order to indicate the amount of conventional memory *not* to use for a cache. This is useful when you know the size TPA you need, and want to allocate anything over that to the cache. The command below ensures that there is at least 384K of conventional memory available after the cache is loaded.

```
NCACHE /INSTALL/DOS=384
```

If you do not include a value for the memory allocation with the switch, the program defaults to a 128K cache.

**/EXT**    This switch controls the amount of *extended* memory used for the cache and cache manager together. This switch allows you to keep some extended memory free for other uses after the cache has been loaded. The command below uses only 256K of extended memory, regardless of how much is available in the system.

```
NCACHE /INSTALL/EXT=-256
```

A negative value reserves the specified amount of extended memory—for example, 1,024K—for other uses and allocates the remainder, if any, to the cache.

```
NCACHE /INSTALL/EXT=-1024
```

**/EXP**    This switch controls the amount of expanded memory allocated to the cache buffer and cache manager combined. This switch is important because many DOS applications, such as Lotus 1-2-3 or Word-

---

5. This switch is provided for use in special circumstances, such as when you are working directly from a slow floppy disk. If you regularly allocate conventional memory to the cache, you should probably consider adding extended or expanded memory to your system so that you can avoid running the cache in conventional memory.

Perfect, can use expanded memory directly.[6] The command below allocates 256K to the cache and leaves the remainder, if any, free for other applications.

```
NCACHE /INSTALL/EXP=256
```

This switch also accepts a negative value, allowing you to specify the amount of expanded memory you want free. For example, you may want to leave 512K of expanded memory free for use with Lotus 1-2-3 and the rest can be allocated to the cache, as illustrated by the command below:

```
NCACHE /INSTALL/EXP=512
```

Keep in mind that the **/EXT** and the **/EXP** switches operate independently. This means if you have both extended and expanded memory the cache will use all the memory, unless a switch appears specifically for that type of memory. For example, if you have 384K of extended memory and 1,024K of expanded memory, the following command will allocate to the cache all the extended memory and 512K of the expanded memory.

```
NCACHE /INSTALL/EXP=512
```

If you want to control the use of both the extended and expanded memory you have to use two switches, as in the command below:

```
NCACHE /INSTALL/EXT=256 /EXP=512
```

Another switch that affects memory is **/BLOCK**. The **/BLOCK** switch sets the size of the data blocks used for storage within the allocated cache buffer. Remember that the cache buffer area is RAM memory being used as if it were a fast hard disk. The **/BLOCK** option sets the size of the basic storage block.

In order to understand the **/BLOCK** option, it might be helpful to keep in mind the difference between true RAM (random access memory) and RAM used to simulate a fast disk. True RAM memory means that the microprocessor can access units of information as small as a single byte—for example, out of a memory of 1,000,000 different bytes the processor can pick a single byte, if needed. Disk storage (and other *mass* storage devices) organize data in large blocks. Recall that most

---

6. DOS applications cannot directly use extended memory.

disks use 512-byte blocks called sectors as the basic unit of storage. Storing data in blocks is simpler and faster than storing them in an array where each individual byte has a unique address. When RAM is used to emulate disk storage, the cache program uses the same approach as disk storage—that is, organizing data into easy-to-handle blocks. By default, the cache program automatically sets the block size based on the amount and type of memory available, usually 512 bytes per block (the same as a standard disk sector), when sufficient memory is available.

The issues involved with block size are the same as those involved with sector size on a disk. Smaller blocks have the benefit of eliminating slack (wasted) space in the memory. That is important when there are a large number of small files or file fragments with which to deal. On the other hand, the cache manager's job is more complicated when it has a lot of little blocks to manage. Using large blocks is not as efficient for small files, but it reduces the amount of memory needed for the cache manager since there would be few blocks of which to keep track.

The cache program will automatically make adjustments in the block size to suit small memory environments. For example, the NCACHE-F will usually allocate about 66K to the cache manager when a 512-byte block size is used. However, if NCACHE-F is loaded on a basic 286 (640K conventional and 384K extended) the program will reduce the cache manager to about 21K by quadrupling the block size to 2K (2,048 bytes).

The /BLOCK switch allows you to set the block size manually from 512 bytes to 8K.[7] For example, suppose you wanted to minimize the cache manager by setting the block size to the maximum value of 8K. The following command would implement a cache with that block size:

```
NCACHE /INSTALL/BLOCK=8K
```

Note that the value entered with the command is *8K*, not simply the number *8*. If executed on a standard 286, as described above, you would gain about 4K of conventional memory, since the cache manager would be reduced to about 17K from 21K with a 2K block size. This is not a lot of memory, but on a 1-megabyte computer it might be enough let you squeeze a program into conventional memory.

---

7.   The switch will accept only the values **512, 1K, 2K, 4K,** and **8K**. Note that **512** is entered without a **K** because it refers to 512 bytes, not kilobytes.

The /**READ** and /**WRITE** switches allow you to manually control the size of the read and write ahead buffers. Since these options directly affect the amount of conventional memory allocated to NCACHE, experienced users may want to fine-tune the program by setting the value manually. The most advantageous size for the write ahead buffer is the size of the largest track on the largest disk drive in the system. By default, the NCACHE program allocates enough memory to the write ahead buffer to read the largest track. You may want to fix the size of this buffer at a size from 8 to 64K by using /**WRITE** switch.

/**READ** controls the read ahead buffer, which is set by default at 8K. You can manually increase the size of that allocation from 8 to 64K with the /**READ** switch.

You can see by the default values that NCACHE emphasizes write ahead buffers as the way to maximize performance. The command below installs NCACHE with a 32K write ahead buffer and a 16K read ahead buffer. This set-up would use about 61K of conventional memory.

```
NCACHE /INSTALL/READ=16/WRITE=32
```

Keep in mind that the /**BLOCK setting is automatically configured by /OPTIMIZE**, which is much simpler to use.

All the switches discussed in this section, /**DOS, /EXP, /EXT, /WRITE, /READ**, and /**BLOCK**, set the memory structure of the cache and cannot be changed unless you uninstall the cache with /**UNINSTALL**—assuming that the cache is the last program loaded into memory—or reboot the computer in order to reload the program.

The /**DELAY** option allows you to specify a write delay from .01 to 59.99 seconds. Write delays allow the cache program to hold onto data for up to the specified number of seconds before the information is actually written to the disk. Write delays are useful when an application is likely to frequently write blocks of data to the disk. When this happens the write delay holds on to the data until the buffer is full or the write delay periods have elapsed. All the data accumulated in the buffer are then written in a single operation, which is more efficient than a series of smaller write operations.

You can set the delay in 1/100s of a second, up to 59.99 seconds. The command below sets a delay of 30 seconds. This means the cache program will delay a write operation up to 30 seconds in order to add more data to the cache before the information is actually written to the disk:

```
NCACHE /DELAY=30
```

Delays can be of great benefit when the destination disk is a floppy drive or a very slow hard disk, since the latency time for disk seek operations is significantly large. Typically, database applications write data in small blocks (records within a large database file), in contrast to spreadsheet programs that write entire models in a single operation. Delays would be more useful with databases than spreadsheets. If you are writing database information to a floppy drive, a delay of 15 seconds or more will improve performance significantly. Keep in mind that you should not remove a floppy disk from the drive until all delayed writes have been completed. You can insure that this is the case by flushing the buffer with the /F switch, as shown in the example below:

```
NCACHE /F
```

Following this command you can remove the floppy disk without risk.

**/QUICK**    By default, the NCACHE-F program will use *write ahead* operations to speed disk write operations, reducing the amount of time an application is unavailable to the user. However, when the write operations are generated by DOS commands, such as COPY or XCOPY, the NCACHE-F program will not return to the DOS prompt until all write operations have been completed. The /QUICK option allows the cache program to cache DOS operations in the same way that it would if the operation were generated by an application. This means when a DOS command such as **COPY** or **XCOPY** is used, the DOS prompt may return, allowing the entry of another command before the cache program has completed the disk write operation. **/QUICK** is normally off, but can be activated with the following command:

```
NCACHE /QUICK=ON
```

/QUICK allows DOS operations to receive the full benefit of the caching. However, you must keep in mind that the return of the DOS prompt will not signal the completion of the operation, so you must take care not to remove floppy disks or reboot the system until all the cached write operations have been completed.

You can experiment with these and other cache options to determine the advantage of various cache options using batch files. For example, the batch file shown below is designed to show how the **/DELAY** switch can significantly improve performance during a write-intensive operation.

The batch file below, called TEST.BAT, is designed to copy a file called *sample.dat* from the hard disk to a floppy disk in drive A. The file should be large—300K to 500K. The **/F** switch used in Line 2 clears the cache buffer of any data so that the results of the batch are not affected by previously buffered operations. The batch uses the Control Center program (NCC) to calculate the time required for the copy operation in Lines 4 and 6. Line 6 displays the elapsed time between the **/START** and **/STOP** commands.

```
@ECHO OFF                      {1}
NCACHE /F                      {2}
CLS                            {3}
NCC /START:1/N                 {4}
COPY sample.dat a:             {5}
NCC /STOP:1/N/L                {6}
ECHO - Copy Complete           {7}
```

Once you have created this batch file, load the cache program with the default settings:

```
delay =0 and Quick off. ncache/install↵
```

Place the floppy disk in drive A and run the batch file by entering test ↵.

If you are using a 500K file it should take about 30 seconds to complete the process. Next, turn on the Quick feature by entering: ncache /quick=on ↵.

Run the TEST batch file again: test ↵.

This time, when the DOS prompt returns the floppy disk is still operating. The **Quick** option has completed the transfer to the buffer and the cache program is working in the background to actually complete the transfer. You can enter more DOS commands without waiting for the floppy disk to stop working. After a few seconds the cache-write operation will be complete and the floppy disk will stop working.

Next, add the delay option to the cache: ncache /delay=59.9 ↵.

You now have the **Quick** option on, and have a delay of 59.9 seconds. Run the test batch again: t ↵.

This time the floppy drive runs for only a few seconds and the batch file completes with an elapsed time of only a few seconds. How was this improvement in speed achieved? The data were copied from the hard disk and stored in the buffer; they were not actually placed on the floppy disk.

As soon as 59.9 seconds have elapsed the floppy drive begins to spin, indicating the delayed write operation is now being carried out by the cache program.

The batch file program illustrates the advance of delayed disk write. Instead of having to wait 30 or more seconds before entering the next DOS command, the **Quick** and **Delay** options allow you to enter additional commands after only a few seconds. While the actual time it takes to copy the file remains unchanged, the apparent time—that is, the time you have to wait before going on to the next command—is reduced dramatically. This is the idea behind write caching.

Note that the **/QUICK** and **/DELAY** options can be used as many times as desired. You can build these options into batch files in order to turn on or off the features as part of a batch procedure.

## Cache Activity Control

The cache programs recognize four switches that allow you to control the activity of the cache program.

**/A**    This option suspends the action of the disk cache program and allows read and write operations to proceed as directly handled by DOS. Note that this option does not uninstall the program or release any memory used by the program for other uses. To suspend the cache program, enter

```
NCACHE /-A
```

To reactivate the program, enter

```
NCACHE /+A
```

**/C**    This option freezes the information loaded into the cache buffer and prevents newer information from replacing it. This option is useful to ensure that the program keeps a certain block of data in the buffer because you anticipate that it will be read by the application a number of times. To freeze the cache you would enter

```
NCACHE /-C
```

To restart caching of new data, enter

```
NCACHE /+C
```

This option suggests that you want to have manual control over the information stored in the cache. Most users will probably let the cache operate automatically and utilize this option.

**/F**    This option *flushes* the cache buffer. Flushing causes any write operations currently held in the cache to be written to the disk and the buffer area is cleared of any information. Use flush to ensure that all disk writes are complete before removing a floppy disk, rebooting, or turning off the computer. The cache statistics are not reset.

**/UNINSTALL**    This option removes the cache program from the memory. Keep in mind that this switch will *not* work if the program is loaded as a device driver from the CONFIG.SYS file or if the cache is not the last program loaded into memory:

```
NCACHE /UNINSTALL
```

You can shorten the switch to **/UN** to save typing.

```
NCACHE /UN
```

If successful, the message "NORTON CACHE has been Uninstalled" will be displayed. If the cache cannot be uninstalled you will see a message that tells you the program cannot be uninstalled and a suggestion as to how to remove the program. Remember if you load the cache with the CONFIG.SYS file, rebooting the computer will not solve the problem since CONFIG.SYS will reload the program each time the computer boots. The only way to change the set-up is to edit the CONFIG.SYS file to remove or disable (put a colon (:) or, if you have DOS 5.0, REM in front of the command) the command.

## Cache Operations Options

The following optional switches can be used to fine-tune the operation of the cache program. The first two apply to both the small and the full cache programs.

**/W**    This option controls *write through* operations. A *write through* operation automatically stores data written to the disk in the cache buffer along with disk read information. The default setting for this option is +; that is, writes are stored in the disk cache. Turning off this option limits the buffer to reads and ignores data written to the disk. You would use this option if you assumed that information written to the disk would not be read back into the application, so that there would be no advantage in having it added to the cache buffer. To turn the option off, enter:

```
NCACHE /-W
```

To restart write through, enter:

```
NCACHE /+W
```

**/G**    This option sets the group sector size. The group sector size sets a limit on the amount of information buffered from any one read operation. The default value is 128 sectors maximum for each read operation, which is the largest value that the program can use. Reducing the value means that each read will place less information in the buffer. The default value provides for reading large files into the buffer. In general, you would only change this option to a lower value if you knew in advance that you would be reading a large number of small files. For example, if you are working with limited memory you may want to reduce the sector number to 15. This would prevent the cache from being filled each time you read a moderately large file. Instead, the cache would hold the first 15 sectors of each read, making it more likely that your data in the cache will be useful.

```
NCACHE /G=15
```

The result of this is that less information is added to the buffer with each read and that the buffer area is filled more slowly than it would be with a larger value.

The next three options affect only the full cache program.

**/I**    This option can be used to turn off the *IntelliWrites* feature, which allows the cache to buffer disk write data so that you can continue with your application while the actual writing takes place in the background. IntelliWrites is active by default when you load NCACHE-F. If you are working in an unstable environment—testing a new program you have written—you may want to disable this function since data can be lost if you hang up the computer before the background write operation is complete. You can turn off IntelliWrites with the following command:

```
NCACHE /-I
```

To restart the feature, enter

```
NCACHE /+I
```

Under normal conditions—that is, using stable operating systems and applications—there is little danger of losing data with write ahead operations. If you are experimenting with new items that may create incompatibility problems, you may want to disable this feature until you are sure your system is properly configured.

**/S**    This switch allows you to turn off the *SmartRead* feature. This feature allows the cache to give priority to new read operations when there is currently disk-write information in the buffer. For example, if you are using a word processing program and save a document, then immediately load a different document, the SmartRead feature would allow the new file to be read *before* the saved file's data were written to the disk. This would create the least possible delay for the user. This feature is on by default.

If you want to make sure that data are written to the disk before any new data are read from the disk you would turn off this feature using the following command:

```
NCACHE /-S
```

To restart the feature, enter

```
NCACHE /+S
```

**/R**    This switch controls the number of sectors that are read ahead and the type of read ahead operations used. By default, the NCACHE-F program will read the next eight sectors into the buffer area, anticipating that the application might issue additional read requests for the next section of the database. If you want to decrease the number of sectors read ahead from the maximum value of eight you can use this option. You also have the option of selecting *dynamic* read ahead only. When set to dynamic read ahead, the program will cache the additional sectors of the file only if they are sequential. Dynamic read aheads work well when the disk has been organized with the Speed Disk program.

The read ahead value can be set from 0 (no read ahead) to 8 sectors. The command below sets the read ahead factor at 5:

```
NCACHE /R=5
```

If you want to restrict the read ahead feature to *dynamic* read ahead only, you would add D to the value you are setting. The following command establishes an 8-sector dynamic read ahead.

```
NCACHE /R=D8
```

## Option for Specific Drives

By default, the option switches will change the operating values for all the drives in the system recognized by the cache program.[8] However, you can set separate parameters for individual drives if desired. This is done by preceding the switch options with the drive letter. The most common reason for setting separate parameters is to cache floppy disks differently from hard disks.

For example, suppose you want to eliminate IntelliWrites and write-through operations for drive A only. This can be accomplished with the following command:

```
NCACHE A: /-I/-W
```

You can use the switches to set parameters for more than one disk at a time. The command below changes the group size on drive C to 50, and deactivates the cache for drive B:

```
NCACHE C:/G50 A:/-A
```

# Cache Statistics

The various switch options available for fine-tuning the disk cache require you to know details about the way various applications make use of disks—do they write data in small or large blocks? Since much of the activity is hidden from the direct view or knowledge of the user, it is hard to see how you could intelligently make use of these options. The combination of different computer hardware, different software applications, and

---

8.  The cache programs will use all drives in the system, including floppy drives, so long as the floppy drives support *media change detection*. Some 360K drives used on PC and XT type models do not allow the software to detect if the disk drive is open or not. These older floppy drives cannot be cached.

personal use of those applications suggest that no two computers will have exactly the same requirements for disk caching operations.

The Norton Utilities cache programs provide statistical information that can help you determine how well the cache is performing in your computer with your applications and the way in which you put those applications to use:

**Cache Allocated and Used.** The cache allocated values show you the total amount of memory allocated for the cache and the amount currently filled with data. Once the value reaches 100, the program will begin to overwrite the oldest data in the buffer with new data generated by the most recent commands.

**Cache Options.** The options line lists the amount of conventional extended, and expanded memory in use by the cache. In addition, it shows the current write delay and the status of the **Quick** option.

**Drive Options.** The left side of the table at the bottom of the screen lists the cached drives and shows the options settings for each drive.

**Cache Hit Ratio.** It is important to remember that effectiveness of disk caching depends on a wide variety of factors. No two users will exhibit the same characteristics. In order to help you evaluate the efficiency of your cache, the program keeps track of the total number of sectors read and the number of times the sectors were found in the cache buffer, eliminating the need to read them from the disk. Reading a sector from the cache is called a *hit*. The values are expressed as a ratio *hits/total reads*. For example, the ratio 200/500 would mean 200 hits out of a total of 500 sectors read.

**%Hits.** This value expresses the *hits/total reads* as a percentage. The higher the percentage, the more effective the disk caching.

The key to fine-tuning your cache operations is to check the %hits column from time to time. If you have a lower percentage, below 50 percent, you may want to adjust some of the cache parameters to see if the percentage can be improved. Keep in mind that if you do many different things with your computer, no one cache setting or group of settings will work for all situations. You may find that when you are running your database, one set of values is best, while word processing works best with different values. One way to organize the trial-and-error testing is to use a batch file such as the TEST.BAT shown earlier in this chapter to run a series of disk operations. Then use the **/PRINT** command to print the results. Remember to use the **/RESET** to start off the batch file with a new set of statistics.

You can reset the cache statistics back to zeros using the **/RESET** option. Example:

```
NCACHE /RESET
```

This action does not affect the cache settings or the data stored in the buffer area. To clear the cache buffer use the **/F** option.

## Saving Cache Parameters

You can create a new set of default values for the cache programs by using the **/SAVE** option. **SAVE** creates a file called NCACHE.INI in the current home directory for the Norton Utilities, by default \NU.[9] This file contains all the settings that were current in the cache program when you executed the **/SAVE** option. The next time the program loads it will read the NCACHE.INI to obtain the default values. Both the NCACHE-F and NCACHE-S programs read the same file, NCACHE.INI, for default values. To create a new default value file, enter

```
NCACHE /SAVE
```

If you want to maintain different cache setting files for different applications, you can specify the directory from which the cache program should read its default values, using the /INI switch. For example, suppose you want to load default values for dBASE operations different from the normal values used for the cache. First, use the cache commands to set up the desired parameters. Save the settings in a file by entering: ncache save ↵.

Copy the NCACHE.INI file from the \NU directory to the \DBASE directory: copy \NU\ncache.ini \dbase ↵.

Erase the NCACHE.INI file from the \NU directory. This will cause the program to load the default values, unless you use **/INI** to direct it to the \DBASE directory: del \NU\ncache.ini.

You might also want to create a different default value file for the \NU directory as well, if you don't want to use the standard program defaults. Uninstall the cache program from memory: ncache /uninstall ↵.

---

9. You can change the home directory using the DOS environment variable NU.

Reload the cache program using the /INI switch to direct the program to the defaults stored in the \DBASE directory: ncache /ini=\dbase ↵.

The cache is now set up to work with dBASE.

## Using Switches with CONFIG.SYS

The example commands seen in this section show the correct syntax for issuing cache commands from DOS. However, you have the option of loading the cache programs as device drivers, using the system's CONFIG.SYS file as shown earlier.

The device driver method can also accommodate optional switches. The only difference between using a switch with the device driver method is that the options are preceded by a space rather than a /. The device driver command below loads NCACHE using 500K of expanded memory, a group sector number of 20 for all drives, deactivates the cache for drive A, and turns off IntelliWrites for drive C:

```
DEVICE=D:\NU\NCACHE.EXE EXP=500 G20 A:-A C:-I
```

You can also use an alternative cache initialization file from CONFIG.SYS. The command below uses the **INI** switch to load the NCACHE.INI file from the D:\DBASE directory:

```
DEVICE=C:\NU\NCACHE.EXE INI=D:\DBASE
```

# Disk Organization

In addition to disk caching, the efficiency of disk operations can be affected by the actual physical organization of the disk. Recall from Chapter 8 that moving the disk drive head from track to track—that is, seek operations—is the slowest part of reading or writing data to the disk. A disk will perform at its optimum when the number of seek operations is kept to a minimum.

In the previous section, the use of disk caching to reduce the number of physical disk access operations was discussed in detail. In this section, you will examine another end of that process—that is, the way data are placed on the disk.

The Speed Disk program is designed to rearrange the information stored on a disk so that the amount of work performed by the disk drive is minimized. Reorganization performed on a regular schedule can prevent degradation of hard disk performance. It is also valuable in finding and correcting any errors in the FAT and directory system.

## File Fragmentation

Many computer users will notice that as time goes by the performance of their hard disk will begin to degrade. In most cases the source of the problem is not mechanical but logical—that is, the information stored on the disk is *fragmented*. Hard disks have to work harder to store and retrieve information when the disk contains a significant amount of fragmentation, resulting in slower hard disk operation. The FAT and directory systems used by DOS Version 2.xx and higher are actually designed to allow a high degree of file fragmentation. They do this in order to ensure that all the available disk space is employed in storing data, no matter how many files are erased, added, and erased over time.

How does fragmentation come about? The diagram in Figure 10–3 shows a simple example of how files get fragmented. The column on the

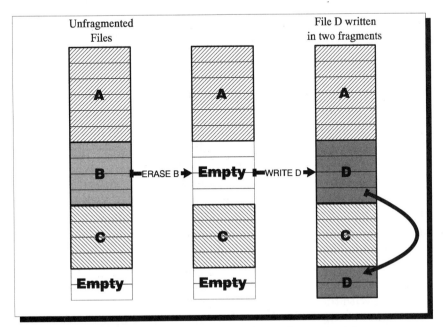

**Figure 10–3. How files become fragmented.**

left shows a series of data clusters that hold three files labeled A, B, and C. These files are *contiguous*—that is, they are *not* fragmented—because all the data clusters used by each file are physically adjacent, falling one after the other. The end of the column shows empty data clusters that can be used for the next file added to the disk.

But suppose, instead of adding a new file, the user deletes a file—file B for instance—that is no longer needed. The middle column in the figure shows that erasing file B makes available data clusters that fall between files A and C.

If the user then creates a new file D, the FAT system used by DOS is able to detect open data clusters between files A and C, as well as those following file C at the end of the column. The new file is placed into the empty slot formerly occupied by the erased file B.

But suppose, as is quite likely, that the new file D is not the same size as the erased file—file D is larger than the old file B. The third column in Figure 10–3 shows that DOS will fill the empty space between files A and C, then continue the file in the next available location, in this example, following file C. Thus, the new file D is written into two nonadjacent locations on the disk. File D is *fragmented*. If you use this simple illustration as a guide you can begin to imagine what happens on disks that have 10,000, 15,000, or more data clusters that are allocated to hundreds or thousands of files. Data fragments that belong to the same *logical* file may be located on widely separated tracks. Reading even a small file, which is broken into many fragments, can be slow if the hard disk must perform a seek operation for each fragment.

Fragmentation is often worse on hard disks that are close to their total capacity. This is true because users with almost full hard disks will often delete older files or programs, in order to make room for new files and programs. Since older files tend to occur near the beginning of the hard disk—the outer tracks starting at 0—the likelihood that new files will be fragmented is quite high.

Fortunately, file fragmentation can be controlled and eliminated using the Speed Disk program. The program eliminates fragmented files by rewriting the files into contiguous blocks. In order to accomplish this, the program must move other files and parts of other files to create the required block of contiguous clusters. This is a complicated task, but it is what Speed Disk is designed to handle. When a disk has been *unfragmented*, all the same files and directories will still be there, but rearranged so that the hard disk can operate with the minimum amount of work.

In addition to unfragmenting files, Speed Disk can perform a number of other organizational tasks DOS does not perform or consider:

**Directory Organization.**  User-defined directories—all directories other than the disk's root directory—are placed on the hard disk in the same way files are stored. This means the directories on the disk are subject to fragmentation. Speed Disk will consolidate all directory information to eliminate fragmentation, and place that information at the front of the disk to minimize access time.

**File Sorting.**  DOS does not maintain any logical order for the file names that appear on the directory listings. Speed Disk can sort the files in one of several logical orders so that directory listings will be easier to read and understand.

**Priority Files.**  File location on the hard disk is assigned by DOS on a first-come, first-serve basis. However, in practice you will find that some files or categories of files are used more frequently than others. For example, program files are accessed on a daily basis while old data files may not be accessed for weeks or months at a time. You can create a list of priority files that will be moved to the front of the disk when Speed Disk reorganizes the files.

All of these features contribute to minimizing the amount of time your hard disk spends looking for the data you want to store or retrieve by simply arranging the information in a manner that matches the way the information is going to be used. This is preferable to the random storage patterns that DOS allows to occur on the disk.

It is important to keep in mind that Speed Disk does not replace or modify the way DOS operates; it merely *cleans up* the disk after DOS. This means once you have organized the disk with Speed Disk you will have to periodically run the program again to clean up any new problems that have been created during normal computer operations.

# Running Speed Disk

The Speed Disk program is stored in the SPEEDISK.EXE file (short name SD.EXE). To start the program you can choose Speed Disk from the Norton menu or enter SPEEDISK at DOS. Enter speedisk ↵. When the program loads a dialog box appears with the message "Select the drive you wish to optimize." A list box appears with the letters of all the available drives, including floppy drives. Speed Disk will operate on floppy disk as well as hard disks; however, hard disks usually pose a more significant problem. When you have selected the desired drive you can continue by entering ↵.

When you select a drive, the Speed Disk immediately begins to read information from the FAT and directories on that drive. A message box will display the names of the directories as they are read. When the information has been read, the program will make an analysis of what has been found and will recommend what type of procedure you should follow. When this dialog box appears, the optimization method seen at the bottom of the **Status** box in the lower left corner of the screen, changes to match the recommended method.

Speed Disk supports five different operations that are designed to organize and optimize your disk:

**Full Optimization.**   This option is the most comprehensive operation. However, this method takes the most time, perhaps as much as several hours on large hard disks with many files. Full optimization will perform the following operation:

1. Unfragment files.
2. Eliminate gaps (empty cluster at end).
3. Move directories to front.
4. Sort files (if selected).
5. Move priority files (if selected).

**Unfragment Files.**   This option limits the program to unfragmenting as many files as possible without making major changes to the disk. This option does not ensure that all files will be unfragmented, or that all the empty space will be collected at the end of the drive. When unfragmenting a file would require too much reorganization, the file is skipped. This method takes much less time than the full optimization. It is normally used between full optimization, when you don't have time required for a full optimization.

**Unfragment Free Space.**   This method is used to collect all empty data clusters at the end of the disk. This method does not unfragment files. Instead it attempts to fill in gaps between existing files.

**Directory Optimization.**   This option rearranges only those parts of the disk required to allow all the directory information to be assembled at the front of the disk. The directory information plays a significant part in disk performance because most disk operations require access to some part of the directory tree. Recall from Chapter 3 that directory information is stored in data clusters, just as file information is stored. When you create a new directory or add a large number of files to a directory, DOS allocates disk space on the same basis, next available location, as it would if you created a file. This means your directories can be scattered throughout the disk. When DOS searches for a file, a fragmented directory system can slow down operations, even if the file itself is not fragmented. After this option is executed all directory data will be located at the beginning of the data area on the disk.

**File Sort.**  This operation does not affect the performance of the disk by moving files to new locations. This option rewrites the files listed in the disk's directories in order by name, extension, date/time, or file size. You can also select ascending or descending order.

The default is *full optimization* the first time you run Speed Disk on a new drive.

The dialog box gives you two options:

**Optimize.**  Selecting this option begins optimization, using the recommended optimization method.

**Configure.**  Selecting this option displays the *Configure* menu. The purpose of this is to allow you to specify options, such as the file sort order. If you select this option the current optimization type, as shown in the **Status** box in the lower left corner of the screen, reverts to the default method, Full optimization, assuming that Full optimization was not the recommended method.

Choose the **Configure** option by entering c.
Remove the *Configure* menu by entering [Esc].

## The Disk Map

When you remove the menu from the screen display, you will see a large area in the middle of the screen composed of rows of small blocks. This display is the *disk map*. The map is used to present a *picture* of the current state of the disk drive.

A legend for the symbols used on the map appears in a box in the lower right corner of the screen:

**Used.** Shows blocks of clusters currently in use for files or directory information.

**Unused.** Shows blocks of clusters not currently in use for files. Note that these areas may contain data from erased files.[10]

**Bad.** This symbol appears when the cluster block contains one or more clusters marked as bad. Clusters are marked as *bad* when an application, such as the Norton Disk Doctor, finds that one or more sectors within the cluster cannot be reliably used. DOS and other programs ignore bad clusters in order to prevent data loss.

**Unmovable.** Certain programs require the placement of files at specific locations on the disk. The Norton Utilities Image program always places its data in the *last* data cluster on the disk. Programs that use *copy protection* schemes will often create unmovable files.[11]

**Reading.** This symbol appears only during the actual optimization to indicate the approximate location on the disk from where data is being read.

**Writing.** This symbol appears during optimization to indicate the approximate location where data is being written.

The legend at the bottom of the main display is only a partial map legend. If you want to see the full map legend, enter [Alt-i] m.
This box shows several additional symbols that will appear on the map:

**Optimized Already.** This symbol is the same as that used for file space, but in a different color. It indicates the part of the disk that has been already been optimized. Blocks shown in this color contain unfragmented files.

**Verifying.** This symbol, **v**, appears during optimization to indicate the approximate location where data are being verified if the verification option has been selected.

---

10. Keep in mind that since Speed Disk moves data from one disk location to another, erased data may be overwritten during the process, making it impossible to recover erased files or directories.

11. Copy *protection* refers to software schemes used by manufacturers to prevent you from making duplicates of their software, which could then potentially be illegally distributed. The protection is for the manufacturer's benefit. It does not protect the user from mistakes, such as accidentally erasing part or all of the program.

**Clearing.** If the **Clear data** option is selected, this symbol will appear when a blank area is being cleared of data.

The most obvious information that can be gained from the map is the extent to which gaps have formed on the disk. Gaps do not necessarily indicate a large degree of fragmentation but they do predict future fragmentation, since new files added to the disk will be used to fill in these gaps.

At the bottom of the **Legend** box the letter of the selected drive appears. In addition, the scale of the map is shown in the form of **1 block=##** **clusters**, where ## is a numeric value indicating the number of data clusters represented by a single block. With the exception of 360K floppy disk, the blocks on the map do not represent individual data clusters but blocks of clusters. This enables a map of limited size to represent disks with very large capacities. However, representing blocks of clusters with a single symbol can give the user a mistaken impression of what is stored on the disk or what the program is doing during optimization.

For example, if 1 block represents 14 data clusters and only 1 of those clusters is marked as *bad*, the program will display the **B** symbol. The user cannot tell from looking at the map how many of the 14 clusters represented by the symbol are actually bad.

During optimization a user might observe that the program appears to read the same location on the disk over and over again. In fact, since each block represents a number of clusters, the program is reading a different section of the cluster block, not repeating an operation.

The map is not designed to show explicit detail about the optimization process, but simply to produce an approximate picture of what the program is doing.

## Disk Details

In addition to the map display, the Speed Disk program can provide a more detailed account of how the data space on the disk has been used. There are two options on the *Information* menu that provide this information:

**Disk Statistics.** This option displays a box with summary information about disk usage. The display summarizes the information on the disk map in greater detail than can be gathered from the map.

**Fragmentation Report.** This option presents a detail report on the condition of each file and directory on the disk. When selected, the program displays a dialog box with two list boxes. The box on the left shows the *directory tree* for the disk. The box on the right lists all the files in the highlighted directory. For each file or directory listed, the program shows the percentage of fragmentation, the number of fragments used to store the file, and the total number of disk clusters occupied by the file. Fragmented files and directories are marked with a dot that appears to the left of the file or directory name.

Using the ↓ and ↑ keys in the left box, you can move the highlight through the directory tree. As you move the highlight, the box on the right will change to show the files in the currently highlighted directory. If you want to scroll the file list box, the [Tab] and [Shift-Tab] keys will switch you between the boxes.

The file-by-file display on the right side of the screen shows how badly each file is fragmented. If an important file—a frequently used database—is significantly fragmented you may want to perform a full-disk optimization, even though only a small percentage of the overall disk is fragmented. For example, if a disk is 97 percent unfragmented the Speed Disk will recommend the **Unfragment Files** method of optimization. However, upon inspection of the fragmentation report, if you find an important fragmented file you would be better off performing the time-consuming full optimization.

Keep in mind that many users will simply optimize on a periodic basis—full optimization once a month—without bothering to look at the details presented on the fragmentation report. The report is available for those users who need or want more details.

## Walking the Disk Map

One interesting feature provided on the *Information* menu is the **Walk map** option. This option allows you to get detailed information about the way each of the areas is represented. The term *walking* is used to describe the way the feature works. When you select this option, a square cursor appears at the first block on the disk map. You can then use the arrow keys to change the position of the block. The cluster number or numbers represented by the block where the cursor is positioned are displayed on the bottom line of the screen.

For example, suppose in looking at the disk map you notice a static file, marked by an **X**, that you did not expect. Keep in mind that on bootable disks the static system files are always at the beginning of the disk and that the Norton Utilities Image program places its hidden file at the end of the disk. If you find an **X** in the middle you might want to identify the file. One way to do this is to walk the map.

# Speed Disk Configuration

The *Configure* menu provides a means by which you can select the specific details of the optimization process. If you do not make use of the configuration menu the program will use its default settings.

Two of the optimization methods, *Full Optimization* and *Directory Optimization*, rearrange the disk space used for directory information so that these data clusters are at the beginning of the disk. Recall from Chapter 3 that, with the exception of the root directory, all user-defined directory information is stored in disk data clusters in the same way file information is stored. This means directory information is subject to the same risk of fragmentation.

Directories play an important role in all disk operations, since they contain information about the files. Recall from Chapter 4 that each entry in the directory contains the starting cluster number for each file. This means that DOS must read the directory information before it can locate the data associated with a file. If directory information is fragmented throughout the disk, it can have a significant affect on performance.

Speed Disk will automatically group all the directory clusters at the front of the disk each time **Full Optimization** or **Directory Optimization** is executed. The **Directory Order** option allows you to go a step further. This option allows you to select the order in which the directories will be written when they are moved to the front of the disk.

The advantage of this feature is that you can place the directories you use most often closer to the front of the disk so they can be accessed more quickly. This is most important for directories that contain a large number of program files, such as the DOS or Norton Utilities directories.

When you select the **Directory Order** option, the program displays a dialog box with two lists. The list box on the left shows the directory tree on the disk. The directories are listed as they appear on the disk, in no particular order. On the right side is a list box used to show the directories that will be placed nearest to the front of the disk. You may be surprised to find several directories already listed in the right side box. Speed Disk automatically lists the directories if they are part of the current DOS search path. They are listed in the order in which they appear in the last executed PATH command.

The directories D:\DOS and D:\NU are automatically entered as defaults, since those directories are included in the current path.

You can use the command buttons in the dialog box to add, delete, or rearrange the directory names in the right box. Note that while the highlight is in the left box the command buttons read **Add** and **Move.** If you move the highlight to the right box with [Tab] the **Add** control button changes to **Delete.**

Any directories not listed in the right box are written in the order in which they occur on the disk.

## File Sort Order

The **File Sort** option allows you to select a logical order by which the file names in the directories can be rearranged when you perform a **Full Optimization** or a **File Sort.**

A file sort is different from the other operations performed by Speed Disk in that it does not rearrange the data clusters on the disk, in order to enhance performance. Instead, the file sorting operation rewrites the contents of the directories so that the file names are listed in order by name, extension, date and time, or size, in either ascending or descending order.

Recall from Chapter 4 that DOS writes the names of new files into the directory, using the same logic it uses when storing files on the disk. New files are added at the end of the directory list, unless DOS finds a gap between older file names higher on the list. These gaps occur when you erase a file from the disk. The result is that the names of the files appear in random order, making it more difficult to read and analyze the directory listings. Unlike other Speed Disk operations, file sorts do not have an appreciable affect on performance so that selecting a file sort order is strictly a personal preference. By default Speed Disk will leave the directory listings unsorted. Note that performing a *file sort only* will not affect your ability to recover erased files, as is the case with the other Speed Disk optimization methods.

The **File Sort** dialog box allows you to specify the desired sort criterion (name, extension, date and time, or size) and the order (ascending or descending). File sort performs a physical rewrite of the directory information. You cannot recover the original file sequence after the sort has been done.

The different options allow you to manipulate the directories for different purposes:

**Extension.**  The best general purpose sort order is by extension, since this groups files together by types according to their extension. Directories that contain both program and data files are easier to work with when the files are grouped by type.

**Name.** Name is useful when the directory contains files that are not consistently identified by a specific file extension, such as WordPerfect document files. Another reason to select name order is to organize directories that have large programs in them. For example, dBASE IV consists of a number of files that begin with the name DBASE but have different file extensions. Sorting by name would place all of the DBASE... files together, in contrast to sorting by extension, which would separate those files according to extension.

**Date and Time.** This sort order is useful when you want to analyze changes that have been made to the disk. The date and time sort, when done in descending order, will place the newest files at the top of each directory. This allows you to quickly see which files have been added or updated recently.

**Size.** Sorting by size is useful when you want to eliminate files in order to free up space on a hard disk. While most people would start by erasing unwanted files from the hard disk, it is important to consider the amount of space used by those files. Choosing files to erase from a hard disk can be tedious, so you don't want to waste time erasing files only to find that they don't free enough space. For example, suppose you need to free up 250,000 bytes so that you can install a new program on the hard disk. If the files are sorted by size order you can quickly decide if there are any significantly large files that can be safely discarded. This is a much more efficient approach than simply erasing files at random only to find that you have not freed a significant amount of disk space.

File sorting affects all the directories on the selected drive. This means you cannot sort some directories by extension and others by date. In addition, keep in mind that once you have sorted directories, DOS will continue to write new files so that new files will not be arranged in sort order. You may want to perform directory sorting on a periodic basis, in order to maintain organized directories.

## Priority Files

DOS does not give priority to any particular type of file since it stores new files in any area available on the disk, filling in gaps when necessary. In practice, program files are often read over and over again since they are the basic tools by which your computer is operated.

Gathering all of the program files as close to the front of the disk as possible can improve performance by cutting down on the time it takes to locate these frequently read files. Keep in mind that since program files are almost never modified once they are copied onto the hard disk, they will remain at the front of the disk in an unfragmented form once they have been moved to that location.

By default, Speed Disk will automatically give priority to all files with EXE and COM extensions when performing a **Full Optimization** so that all the files with these extensions will be placed at the beginning of the disk.

Moving the physical location of a file to the beginning of the disk has no affect on its logical location in the directory structure of the disk. For example, the file NORTON.EXE stored in the \NU directory will be moved to the beginning of the disk along with all the other EXE files. However, the file name will still appear in the \NU directory, since the physical location of the file has no relation to its logical location in the DOS directory structure.

You can add or modify the list of files or extensions to place first on the disk, using the **Files To Place First** option found on the *Configure* menu. The dialog box shows the default selections, *.EXE and *.COM, which will move all files with those extensions to the beginning of the disk. You can use the control buttons to add new items to the list, delete items, or re-arrange the items on the list. When the list contains more than one item, the items are placed at the front of the disk in the order they are listed in the dialog box.

When filling out this list, it is important to remember that large applications—such as the popular programs Lotus 1-2-3, WordPerfect, or dBASE IV—do not consist of a single EXE file. These programs often have large supporting files that are also required for running the program, but these files do not have COM or EXE file extensions. If you move only the COM and EXE files to the beginning of the disk you may not move all the *program* files used by the application.

For example, suppose you are using Lotus 1-2-3 Version 2.2. The main program file is called 123.EXE (199,499 bytes). But there are other files such as 123.CMP (138,681) and 123.SET (38,623) that are also required to run the program, but would not be moved to the front because they have different extensions. As a Lotus 1-2-3 user you may want to move all the files that begin with 123—**123*.***—to the front of the disk. Suppose you want to insert that wildcard following the AUTOEXEC.BAT.

## Unmovable Files

Speed Disk maintains a list of files it will not move during disk optimization. Speed Disk gathers this list by assuming all files with the **hidden** or **read-only** attribute should not be moved. The **Unmovable files** option on the *Configure* menu display a dialog box that allows you to add the names of up to 10 other files or file wildcards to the static file list.

This option can be used to exclude any file or group of files from relocation during full optimization or unfragmentation. Note that it is not necessary to add files already marked as hidden or read-only, since they will automatically be treated as static files.

You would use this option to preserve the placement of copy protection files that are not marked as hidden or read-only, something that is quite rare, or if you had some specific reason for not wanting certain files moved.

## Other Options

The **Other Options** dialog box found on the *Configure* menu has three options that affect the way Speed Disk operates when it is performing optimization.

**Read-after-Write**   This option causes Speed Disk to verify the accuracy of data written to the disk by immediately reading back into memory the sector it has just written. The contents of the sectors are compared to ensure that the data are being written correctly. This option is *on* by default because it represents a significant level of protection against problems that can occur during optimization. Turning this protection off will speed up optimization, but it will increase the risk of problems going undetected.

**Use DOS Verify**   This option is off by default. When selected it implements the DOS standard verification method during disk optimization.

The DOS verify operation is performed by DOS whenever data are written to the disk if the DOS command **VERIFY** is used to set verification **ON**. The default is off. DOS uses an indirect verification method called **CRC** (cyclical redundancy check) to determine if data written to the disk are accurate. In a CRC operation the hard disk controller calculates a value based on the binary values of all the bytes stored in the sector. That value, the *checksum*, is written onto the disk as part of the information in the sector. When the data are read, the disk controller calculates the checksum for the sector and then compares it to the checksum previously stored on the disk for the sector. If the values are the same the controller assumes the data have been read correctly. If not, the controller generates an error that causes DOS to display a message for the user.

It is important to note that saying the checksums match is not the same as saying the data read from the disk match that stored on the disk. For example, it is quite possible to get the same checksum for two different sectors since the checksum method does not account for the *order* in which the bytes appear. For example, the bytes ABC, CBA, and BCA all have the same checksum value but are actually different items of information.

CRC checking is much faster than the byte-by-byte checking done with the **Read-After-Write** option. However, Speed Disk is capable of performing either or both checks if you make the selections from this box.

**Clear Unused Space**     As mentioned in Chapter 4, disk clusters that are freed up when files are erased—or, in the case of disk optimization, moved to a new location—retain the data that were stored in them until new data are copied into that cluster. It is possible using the Norton Utilities to recover data stored in unused disk clusters.

This option will cause Speed Disk to wipe out any leftover data in sectors that are freed up by disk optimization, eliminating any potential security risk. This option increases the amount of time required for optimization and eliminates your ability to recover erased data.

You can change the default option for Speed Disk by using the **Save options to disk** command located on the *Configure* menu. The command writes the currently selected set of options into a file called SD.INI in the root, not the \NU, directory of the current drive. The SD.INI file is a *hidden* file and will not appear in a standard DOS directory listing.[12]

The next time you run Speed Disk the settings stored in the SD.INI file will become the default settings for the program. Most of the Norton Utilities programs that create initialization files place that file in the home directory—by default, \NU. However, the Speed Disk program will write a different initialization in the root directory of each disk it operates on.

---

12. Keep this in mind if you want to return Speed Disk to its default settings. In order to eliminate the SD.INI file you must use File Find to remove the hidden attribute and then delete the file with **DEL**.

# Warnings

When using Speed Disk, remember the following items:

**TSR programs.**  In general it is a good idea to remove all TSR programs from memory when you run Speed Disk. In particular you should make sure programs that affect disk operations, such as cache programs and the DOS program FASTOPEN, are not resident when Speed Disk is run. The Norton Utilities cache programs and Disk Monitor are safe when used with Speed Disk, even though they fall into the classification of programs you would not want present in memory.

Note that there is no performance advantage in having the NCACHE-S or NCACHE-F programs loaded when running Speed Disk, since as a matter of safety, Speed Disk does not allow read- or write-ahead operations.

TSR programs loaded through the CONFIG.SYS and AUTOEXEC.BAT files are inconvenient to disable because they automatically load each time the computer boots. If you find you have automatically loading TSR programs that you don't want resident when running Speed Disk, you can make up a special boot floppy (formatted as a system disk) that boots your computer without loading all the TSR programs.

**Copy Protection.**  The use of special schemes to prevent users from making unlimited numbers of copies of software programs was common in the mid 1980s. Today, the practice is far less common. The idea of hidden, static files that attempt to circumvent normal DOS operations such as **COPY** in order to prevent you from performing those operations is in direct conflict with programs like the Norton Utilities that seek to expand the user's control over their system. The result is that despite the safety features built into Speed Disk and other Norton Utilities[13] programs that modify disk information, it is still possible to run into a problem trying to use copy-protected software after running Speed Disk.

The Norton Utilities documentation suggests making a complete backup before running Speed Disk on a hard disk with copy-protected software. However, this advice is off the mark because it is the nature of copy-pro-

---

13. The Norton Utilities is designed to recognize popular copy protection schemes, such as Superlok.

tected software to make it difficult, if not impossible, to duplicate the special files that create the copy-protection scheme. For example, if you make a backup of the entire hard disk using the DOS command **BACKUP**, and then restore that backup, you may find your copy-protected software no longer works. This is because the copy protection scheme has prevented BACKUP from making an accurate copy of the *copy-protected* file—which is what copy protection is all about. When you restore the data back to the hard disk, DOS writes the nonworking copies it took off the hard disk, resulting in a situation whereby the software acts like an unauthorized copy—that is, it won't run. Put another way, if you could simply make a backup of copy-protected software, it would be *copy- protected*. After all, isn't a backup simply a copy of the software? Fortunately, this problem affects fewer and fewer users each year, as copy-protected software is phased out.

**Unexpected interruption.**   If the power is cut off to your computer or it is rebooted while in the middle of a Speed Disk operation, it is possible that some data loss can occur. Of course, this is true of any occasion when the computer is writing data to a disk.

**Unerase.**   If you intend to *unerase* a file or recover data that has been previously erased *do not run Speed Disk* before you have recovered the data or determined that you no longer want to try to recover it. Since Speed Disk writes data to different parts of the disk it may be overwriting the data you want to recover. File sorting will not affect erased information.

**Periodic Use.**   Speed Disk optimizes the disk, based on the current set of data stored on the disk. Any changes you make following optimization can result in degraded performance, since DOS operations are always subject to fragmentation. This is especially true if you erase and add large numbers of files because you are operating close to the capacity of the hard disk. As a general rule, full optimizations should be run once a month, while directory sorts might be done daily or weekly. The actual time periods best for you depend on how you use your disk. You can get an idea of your own style by examining the fragmentation report at the end of each week to see what percentage of fragmentation occurred in a week's time. If you are accumulating 10 percent or more each week you should probably run full optimization more than once a month. If your disk changes little, 1 percent per week, your can run full optimization less often.

It is also recommended that you reboot your computer after you have completed a full optimization.

# Speed Disk DOS and Batch Operations

Once you are familiar with the basic operation of Speed Disk, you can save time by executing Speed Disk options directly from the DOS prompt or DOS batch file. This is especially true for file sorting, which can be done very efficiently from the DOS prompt. Executing Speed Disk from the DOS prompt has two different types of advantages:

**Override Defaults.**  You can override the default option for optimization method by using a command line switch. For example, using the /C switch will cause the program to automatically perform a **Complete** optimization as soon as you select the drive letter from the dialog box. This approach is faster than using the **Configure** option to access the Speed Disk menus.

**Automatic Execution.**  If you specify the letter of the drive you want to optimize, Speed Disk will execute its operations automatically without the need for user intervention. This makes it possible for Speed Disk to operate as part of a batch file.

The command-line switches available for Speed Disk are:

**/C.** Perform **Complete** (full) disk optimization.

**/D.** Perform **Optimize Directory** method only.

**/U.** Perform file **Unfragment file** operation only.

**/Q.** Perform only **Unfragment free space** in order to remove gaps in the data storage area.

**/SN[-].** Perform file sort using Name order. For descending order use -.

**/SE[-].** Perform file sort using Extension order. For descending order use -.

**/SD[-].** Perform file sort using Date order. For descending order use -.

**/SS[-].** Perform file sort using Size order. For descending order use -.

**/V.** Activate the Speed Disk Read-After-Write verification mode for disk organization operations. Since the default is to use verification, this switch is needed only when the user-saved initialization file excludes verification.

**/B.** Reboot computer after optimization operations have been completed. If you are running Speed Disk from a batch file keep in mind that the system's CONFIG.SYS and AUTOEXEC.BAT will load again when the system reboots.

## Automatic Operation

Automatic operation of the Speed Disk program allows you to perform an entire optimization without having to enter additional keystrokes. When optimization is performed in the full-screen mode you are required to enter keystrokes from time to time, including one at the end of the optimization process. With automatic operation the program will start, run the optimization, and exit, without requiring user intervention. This is very important if you want to run optimization on several drives without having to attend the computer the whole time.[14]

To run Speed Disk in the automatic mode you must specify at least two items in the DOS command line:

**Drive Letter.** The first parameter used with the Speed Disk command must be the letter of the drive you want to optimize, for instance C:.

**Optimization Method.** You must follow the drive letter with either /C, /D, /U, or /Q, which designates the optimization method you want to employ.

The command below runs automatic full (complete) optimization on drive D:

```
SPEEDISK D: /C
```

If you want to optimize several disks you can create a batch file that uses one automatic optimization command for each drive. The sample batch file below will perform the **Unfragment free space** method on drives C and D. Note that the /B switch is added to the last drive so that the system will reboot after the optimizations:

---

14. Speedisk will always stop when an error is encountered, even in the automatic mode.

```
SPEEDISK C: /U
SPEEDISK D: /U/B
```

A useful variation on the previous batch file is shown below. The DOS batch file variable, **%1**, holds the place of the letter that indicates the optimization method:

```
SPEEDISK C: /%1
SPEEDISK D: /%1/B
```

The variable is filled out by adding a letter parameter to the batch file command. For example, suppose you enter the commands shown above into a batch file called OPT.BAT. If you wanted to perform complete optimization on both drives you would use the letter C as the parameter by entering the following command:

```
OPT C
```

You can change the optimization method by changing the letter parameter. In the command below the parameter **u** specifies the **Unfragment files only** option:

```
OPT U
```

Keep in mind that if you use only one of the two items—a drive letter without an optimization method—the program will not operate automatically; instead it will display the normal dialog boxes waiting for your responses. For example, the command below specifies the optimization method, /C, but does not specify the drive:

```
SPEEDISK /C
```

When this command is executed, the Speed Disk program will display the drive selection dialog box and wait for the user to make a selection before proceeding to perform the optimization. Speed Disk will not assume the current drive is one that should be optimized.

## File Sorting

File sort options can be used by themselves or in combination with other optimization methods. In most cases where file sorting is desired, it is more efficient to issue the command as a command-line parameter rather than working through the Speed Disk program menus. For example, to perform an automatic file sort by extension you would use the following command for drive C:

```
SPEEDISK C: /SE
```

If directory order is important for your applications you may consider placing that command in your AUTOEXEC.BAT file so that the files are sorted each time you boot the computer.

You can also combine file sort with other options, such as full optimization or directory optimization. The command below performs a full optimization and a file sort, automatically. The file sort is by size in descending order:

```
SPEEDISK C: /C/SS-
```

The next command performs a directory optimization and a file sort, automatically. The sort order is descending by Date and Time, which will place recently created files at the beginning of each directory:

```
SPEEDISK C: /D/SD-
```

The command switches do not directly support custom selection of the order for the directory optimization. However, recall that the Speed Disk program will use the directories listed in the current DOS path and their sequence as the default selections for directory optimization. This means you can control indirectly the order the directories are sequenced by the directory optimization procedure, by preceding the Speed Disk command with a **PATH** command. The command sequence shown below causes the **\DOS** and **\NU** directories to be placed first when the program performs directory optimization in the automatic mode:

```
PATH C:\DOS;C:\NU
SPEEDISK C: /D
```

# Summary

This chapter discussed the use of the Norton Utilities Cache programs and the Speed Disk program to improve disk performance.

**Disk Caching**    Retrieving data from a disk is slower than retrieving data from RAM memory. A disk cache is a method by which you place required data into a holding area in RAM, called a buffer or cache. If the required data are found in the buffer, the need to read the disk is eliminated and the apparent performance of the disk is increased.

**Cache Program**    A cache program is a TSR (memory resident) program that uses RAM memory to store data so that fewer actual operations are required. The cache program uses various methods to attempt to anticipate what blocks of disk data will be needed next by the application. The program stores the data in the RAM memory so that the application can get the required information without having to perform an actual disk operation.

**Cache Manager**    The cache manager is a part of the cache program that keeps track of what data are stored in RAM so that the cache program can know when it can avoid reading the disk and use the cached data instead. The cache manager portion of the program grows in size in proportion to the size of the buffer area.

**Cache Buffer**    The cache buffer is a block of RAM memory that is used to hold data. A cache buffer is usually extended or expanded RAM. Because conventional RAM is limited to 640K under DOS real-mode operations, the use of conventional memory as buffer space is of questionable value.

**Extended Memory**    Extended memory occurs in 286 and higher systems. Extended memory can be used for buffer space only.

**Expanded Memory**    Expanded memory can be implemented on systems with special expanded memory boards, or on 386 systems that have expanded memory manager software drivers installed. EMS memory can be used for both the cache buffer and the cache manager.

**High Memory**    High memory refers to memory beyond 640K that can be made available on 286 and higher machines, through the use of a high memory manager such as HIMEM.SYS. High memory reduces the amount of conventional memory used by TSR programs.

**Read Caching**    Read caching consists of storing copies of data read from the disk in the buffer area. Read ahead operations read additional disk sectors into the buffer in anticipation of requests from the application for more data.

**Write Caching**    Write caching stores a copy of the data written to the disk in the buffer area. Write ahead operations allow the application to continue working while data are being written to the disk.

**Hits**    The Norton Utilities cache programs keep track of the number of hits. A hit is recorded when the application finds the required data in the cache buffer, instead of having to read the data from the disk. The efficiency of the cache can be judged by the percentage of hits recorded during a work session.

**File Fragmentation**    The DOS file allocation table (FAT) system allows files to be stored in nonadjacent locations on the disk, maximizing the use of disk space. Files stored in two or more separate areas on the disk are called fragmented files. A large degree of file fragmentation will increase the amount of time required to retrieve a given amount of data, since the drive must perform more work.

**Speed Disk**    This program helps maximize disk performance by re-writing the data into the most compact and easy-to-access form.

**Disk Optimization**    A disk is optimized when all the files consist of blocks of consecutive data clusters without any file fragmentation.

**Directory Optimization**    Reading files requires that DOS access the information in the disk directory. Placing all user-defined directory information at the front of the disk minimizes the time required to locate the directory entry for a file.

**Static Files**    Certain files, such as the DOS hidden system files, should remain in the same location, regardless of disk optimization operations.

**Priority Files** Files most frequently read from the disk can be placed at the front of the disk, in order to reduce the time it takes to access these files.

**File Sorting** This option does not increase performance, but it does make directory listings more useful by placing the files in order by name, extension, date and time, or size.

# 11 | Daily Tasks

This chapter will discuss everyday system tasks that can be performed by the Norton Utilities programs. These tasks include locating files, changing directories, and related items.

## Finding a Directory

The directory structure of DOS is both a blessing and a curse. The hierarchical structure used by DOS allows the user to define directories within directories. The resulting system allows the files on a disk to be grouped in a structure that works like a logical outline where there is a main heading (the root directory), subheadings (first level user-defined directories), sub-subheadings (second level directories), and so on. The only two restrictions to the complexity of the directory tree are the 64-character limit on the full directory path name, and the available disk space—each directory uses at least 1 data cluster. The directory system was added to DOS in Version 2.xx. DOS provides a limited set of commands that operate on the directory structure.

The key to understanding directories is to understand how *directory* and *path* names are used. A directory name looks very much like a file name—for example, NORTON, LOTUS, and so on. The **MD** command will accept a directory name that is longer than eight characters. However, in practice, since directory names are stored in the same basic structure as file names, only the first eight characters will be stored. The command below shows the directory name as NORTONUTILS. However, DOS will record only the first eight characters NORTONUT as the name of the directory.

```
MD NORTONUTILS
```

The **CD** command will ignore all characters after the first eight when using a directory name. This means both commands shown below will be treated the same.

```
CD NORTONUTILS
CD NORTONUTIL
```

If you want to have a directory with a name longer than eight characters you can create directory names with extensions. The command below creates a directory NORTONUT.ILS.

```
MD NORTONUT.ILS
```

To activate that directory you would enter the directory name, including the .ILS extension.

```
CD NORTONUT.ILS
```

Note that if you leave off the extension the command will not activate the directory—for example, **CD NORTONUT** would not work if the directory was created as NORTONUT.ILS.

Where directories begin to get complicated and cumbersome to work with is when you need to use the *path* name of the directory. The path name of the directory is the exact location within the directory tree of the directory. The user has created a directory for the Lotus 1-2-3 program. Under that directory are two more: one for business files, the other for personal files. Under each of those is a directory designated for tax information.

Suppose the user wants to activate the personal taxes directory. How could this be done, assuming that the root directory is the current directory? There are two ways to approach this problem in DOS.

**Implicit.** An *implicit* reference uses only the directory name. DOS uses the current directory as the starting point. For example, starting at the root directory you could change to LOTUS by entering the following:

```
CD LOTUS
```

Once you were positioned in LOTUS you would move to the PER-SONAL directory and then from PERSONAL to TAXES.

```
CD PERSONAL
CD TAXES
```

Keep in mind that you cannot skip over a level using this method. For example, if you entered the following command at the root directory,

DOS would respond with the message "Invalid directory" because PER-SONAL branches off of LOTUS, not the root directory:

```
CD PERSONAL
```

The implicit approach works only when you want to move to the next level down in the current directory.

**Explicit.** An explicit directory reference uses part or all of the full path name of the directory. In this approach the various levels of directories are listed using a \(backslash) character to separate each directory name. The command shown below will activate the desired directory, no matter what directory is currently active on the disk.

```
CD \LOTUS\PERSONAL\TAXES
```

The explicit approach has the advantage of selecting the correct directory with a single command, regardless of what directory is currently active. Its disadvantage is that entering the full path name is a cumbersome and tedious task. It requires you to correctly enter all the directory names that lie along the path to the desired directory. If you make a mistake or leave out a level, the command will fail.

Changing directories is one of the most common and, using the DOS commands, one of the must tedious tasks to perform. The Norton Change Directory program, NCD.EXE, replaces the DOS commands **CD**, **MD**, and **RD**, and adds a number of features that can help you operate the DOS directory system. The program can be used in two ways:

**Full-screen, Interactive Mode.** The full-screen, interactive mode allows you to change directories by moving through a graphic representation of the directory tree.

**DOS Command Line.** You can use the Norton Change Directory program by executing command lines at the DOS prompt. This method is faster than the full-screen mode and it more closely approximates the way that you perform directory operations with DOS.

The key to both operations is the TREEINFO.NCD file. This file is created the first time that you run Norton Change Directory on a given drive. The program stores this file in the root directory of the current drive. If you use the Norton Change Directory program with more than one drive you will find a copy of TREEINFO.NCD in the root directory of each drive. This file holds a summary of the directory information for that drive. Once created, the Norton Change Directory program can operate much more quickly, since it does not have to read and analyze the disk each time it is run. Instead, it reads the TREEINFO.NCD file in order to obtain information about the disk.

## Walking the Directory Tree

The most visual way of using the Norton Change Directory program is to run it in full-screen mode. Load the program by entering ncd ↵.

If this is the first time the Norton Change Directory has been run on the current drive the program will take a few moments to scan the disk and create the TREEINFO.NCD file. When this operation is complete, the program then displays a graphic map of the directory structure of the disk, if necessary, as seen in Figure 11–1.

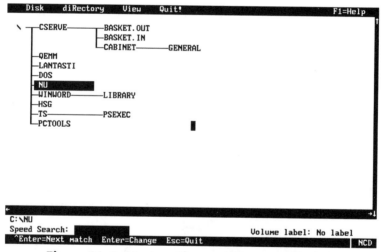

Figure 11–1. Norton Change Directory display.

The directory tree is an interactive tree in which you can change the active DOS directory by moving the highlight to the name of the desired directory, and pressing ↵. The ←, →, ↑, and ↓ keys will move the highlight around the tree. As an example of how the program works, move the highlight to the last item in the directory tree by entering [End].

To change the active DOS directory to the highlighted directory, simply enter ↵.

The program immediately terminates, leaving you at the DOS prompt with the selected directory as the active directory.

To return to the top directory in the list, always the root directory, load the program again: ncd ↵.

Select the first directory by entering [Home] ↵.

You have now activated the root directory of the current drive.

## Modifying the Directory Tree

In addition to selecting the active directory, you can create new directories, delete directories, or change the name of an existing directory with the Norton Change Directory:

**Change Disk, [Alt-d] c or [F3].** Use this option to change the active drive. When the drive is changed the program will look for the TREEINFO.NCD file. If it is not found, the disk is scanned and a new TREEINFO.NCD file is created for that drive.

**Rescan, [Alt-d] r or [F2].** This option causes the program to create a new copy of the TREEINFO.NCD file. This option is used when the current TREEINFO.NCD file needs to be updated to match the current state of the drive. Updating is necessary when you make changes to the directory tree with commands other than Norton Change Directory.

**Rename, [Alt-r] r or [F6].** This option allows you to change the name of the highlighted directory. Note that DOS does not provide a way to accomplish this; it can only be done with the Norton or other utilities programs.

**Make Directory, [Alt-r] m or ]F7].** Creates a new directory below the segment of the tree currently highlighted. For example, if the \WINDOWS directory is highlighted, creating a new directory—CLIP-ART for example—will have a path name \WINDOWS\CLIPART.

**Delete, [Alt-r] d or [F8].** Removes the directory from the disk. If the directory you selected to delete contains one or more files, the program displays a dialog box that lists the files contained in the directory. If you want to delete the directory and all its contents you can select the **Yes**

control button. If the selected directory contains a subdirectory it cannot be deleted.

## Renaming a Directory

You can change the name of any of the directories on the disk, with the exception of the root directory, by using the **[F6]** command. First, position the highlight on the directory whose name you want to change. In this case, the highlight is currently on the SUBSUB directory. Change the name to SUB2SUB1 (subdirectory 1 of subdirectory 2) by entering [F6].

The program displays a dialog box that places the current directory name in a entry box. You can edit the name or replace it with a new name. If you begin by typing a letter the box clears automatically. To edit the current name, begin by moving the typing cursor—for example, →. The original name remains and any characters entered are inserted at the cursor locations. The [Del] key deletes a character. Enter:

```
→ (3 times)
2 [End] 1↵
```

The directory name is changed. Keep in mind that the directory name can be changed at any time, regardless of whether or not the directory contains files or other directories.

## Deleting a Directory

You can delete a directory from the disk using the **[F8]** command, so long as the directory does not contain a subdirectory. If the directory contains files, the Norton Change Directory will ask you if you want to delete the files along with the directory. In this case, the directories you have just created, SUB2SUB1 or SUB1, can be deleted. NEWDIR and SUB2 cannot be deleted at this time because they contain subdirectories.

When you want to move to a specific directory name you have the option of using the **Speed Search** options. The **Speed Search** option is automatically activated when you enter a letter instead of an arrow key while the highlight is positioned in the directory tree. Each letter entered causes the program to search the directory tree for the first directory name that matches the letter or letters typed. In this case, you want to use the speed search to highlight SUB1.

# DOS Operations for NCD

In addition to the full-screen mode, the Norton Change Directory program can be used as a DOS line command. Used in this manner, the Norton Change Directory program has the advantage of performing a speed search directly from DOS. This means you do not have to enter the full path name or even the entire directory name. The Norton Change Directory program will search the directory tree for the closest match and change to that directory.

To perform a speed search from DOS, follow NCD with the full or partial directory name you want to locate. For example, to activate the NORTON directory, enter ncd nor ↵.

The program will select the first directory that matches NOR, probably the NORTON directory. The great advantage of the speed search is that you don't have to enter the complete path name. For example, to change to the SUB2SUB1 directory you would have to enter the following DOS command:

```
cd \newdir\sub2\sub2sub1
```

However, with Norton Change Directory you can shorten the command. Enter ncd sub2sub1 ↵.

In fact, you can shorten your entry even further if you like. Enter ncd sub2 ↵.

In this case, the program located the first directory on the tree, SUB2, that matched the specified characters. To continue searching for the next match you can use the **[F3]** key to repeat the previous command: [F3] ↵.

The program proceeds to the next matching directory name, if any, which in this case is SUB2SUB1.

## Maintaining the Directory Tree

The Norton Change Directory program recognizes the parameters MD and RD in order to duplicate the DOS **MD** and **RD** commands. For example, if you want to create a directory \NEWDIR\SUB1 you would enter

```
NCD MD\NEWDIR\SUB1
```

Note that in order to create a directory you must use the full path name just as you would be required to do with the DOS **MD** command. Since this is the case, why bother with NCD? There are two reasons. First, the Norton

Change Directory program creates the specified directory and then activates that directory. The DOS **MD** command creates a directory but leaves the current directory as the active directory. Second, using NCD **MD** automatically updates the TREEINFO.NCD file. If you use the DOS **MD** command to add new directories the TREEINFO.NCD is not updated. You can force Norton Change Directory to rescan the disk and update the TREEINFO.NCD file by using the **/R** switch. The command shown below rebuilds the TREEINFO.NCD file and loads the Norton Change Directory:

```
ncd /r
```

Note that when you use the **/R** switch as shown in the command above, the program loads into full-screen mode operations while rescanning the disk. If you specify a directory to change to along with the **/R** switch, the rescan will take place in the background without causing the program to enter full-screen mode. The command shown below rebuilds the TREEINFO.NCD file and then changes the active directory to the root directory, leaving you at the DOS prompt:

```
NCD \ /R
```

If you want to perform a rescan without changing directory and also without having to load the full program, you can use a period (.) as the directory name. The period tells DOS to use the current directory with the command. Example:

```
NCD . /R
```

If you have already loaded the full Norton Change Directory program you can update the directory tree by using the **[F2]** command or **[Alt-d] r**.

# Finding a File

One of the most important features in the Norton Utilities is the File Find program. The primary function of this program is to search the disk for files and produce a list of matching files. This feature is important because DOS limits directory listings to a single directory for each **DIR** command issued. This is true even if the directory listed contains subdirectories. In order to list the files in the subdirectory you must enter a separate command.

This limitation makes it very easy to lose a file since there is no simple way to search one or more directories or disks.

File Find solves this problem. It can search directory, directory branch, drive, or list of drives in the system. It can locate files by the file names or by text contained within the files.

## Search by File Name

The most common way to use File Find is to locate files according to the characters in the file names. This is also the fastest way, since it requires only that the program search the directory information on the disk in contrast to searching by file contents, which can take significantly longer.

Most programs include a file with a name such as READ.ME or README.DOC. The purpose of these files is to provide information about the program that was not included in the printed documentation. Suppose you wanted to locate all of the READ.ME files on your hard disk. There are two ways to start the search process:

**Start Program/Then Search.** The File Find program can be used like any other full-screen program, that is, the program is loaded with its default values. Once the full-screen display appears you can enter values and options and then use a control button to initiate actions. To begin File Find in this way simply enter FILEFIND ↵ at DOS or select **File Find** from the Norton menu.

**Search Automatically.** You can cause the program to automatically begin searching by entering a file name or wildcard as a parameter. When you add the parameter to the **File Find** command the program will automatically initiate a search for the matching files on the current drive as soon as it loads. This is the most common way to use File Find because it is likely that you already have in mind the files you want to find before you start the File Find program. When a search is initiated automatically, the program searches the entire disk for matching files.

In this example, begin by entering a **File Find** command. In this case you will use a wildcard, **READ\*.\***, that will locate all of the files that begin with letters **READ.** Enter: filefind read\*.\* ↵ .

The program automatically initiates a search of the entire disk for all of the file names that match the wildcard specification. The names of the directories being searched flash on the screen as the program encounters them. A dialog box appears when the disk search has been completed. Remove the box from the screen by entering ↵.

The full-screen display of the File Find program appears. The result of the search is a list box in the lower right corner of the screen that contains the names of the files that matched the search criterion, along with their size, date, and attributes. The files are listed under the name of the directory in which they are stored. Note that File Find will include hidden files that do not appear on DOS directory listing. In the lower left corner of the screen the total number of matching files is listed along with the current active DOS directory.

If there are more matching files in the list than can appear in the list box at once, the bottom of the list will be displayed at the end of the search. You can inspect the rest of the list by placing the highlight in the list box with the [Tab] key or clicking with the mouse. Enter [Tab].

The highlight is positioned on the last file name in the list. To move to the top of the list you can use the ↑ or [Home] keys or use the mouse to manipulate the scroll bar on the box. Enter [Home].

Note that the highlight can be placed on the file or directory names contained within the list.

## File Find Control Buttons

The program provides three control buttons that can be used at any time:

**Start/Stop.**   This button controls the search operation. When the search has been completed the button shows **Start**. This option is used to initiate a new search using any new settings that you have selected. When you begin a new search, the existing file list is erased before the new search begins. When the search is active the button changes to **Stop** so that you can terminate a search without quitting the program or losing the file list accumulated up to that point. This **Stop** control button is the default while a search is active and the **Start** is the default when the highlight is not positioned within the list box.

**View.**   This option allows you to view the contents of the highlighted file using the built-in text viewer. Once activated you can move from file to file within the view mode without having to return to the list. The **View** button is set as the default when the highlight is positioned on a file name in the list.

**Goto.** This command operates like the Norton Change Directory in that it exits the File Find program and activates the directory that is currently highlighted or that corresponds to the currently highlighted file name. This option allows you to quickly access the directory that contains the files you have located with your search. Keep in mind that when you use this option you terminate the File Find program and lose track of the other files, if any, on the list. In order to return to the list you must repeat the search. This option is the default when a directory name in the list is highlighted.

If you have searched the disk that contains the Norton Utilities you should have found at least one READ.ME file; that is the one supplied with the Norton Utilities. Suppose that you wanted to view the contents of the file using the **View** option. First, move the highlight to the file name READ.ME under the \NU directory using the ↓ key. When you position the highlight on the file name the default control button switches to **View**. Enter ↵.

When you select **View** the center of the screen changes to the View mode display, as seen in Figure 11–2, in which the center of the screen shows the first 23 lines of the file. The bar at the bottom of the screen tells you the name of the file currently being displayed, for example, D:\NU\ READ.ME, and tells you that **[F7]** and **[F8]** can be used to display the previous or next files on the list in the view mode. You can use the arrow and other cursor movement keys to scroll other sections of the file into the window.

The **View** mode is rather limited in its functions. You cannot print the file, search for text within the file, or edit the text. However, the **View** mode does give you a quick means of inspecting the contents of the files located during the search.

You can return to the main File Find display by entering [Esc] or by selecting **Main**! from the menu bar. Enter [Esc].

When you exit the viewer you return to the main program display with the highlight position on the last file that was displayed in the view mode.

To change to the directory in which the file is positioned, for example, \NU, select the **Goto** control button by entering [Shift-Tab] ↵ return.

The program is terminated and you return to DOS with the selected directory activated. One disadvantage of using **Goto** is that the list of files located by the program is lost when you exit the program. Restart the program this time without a parameter: filefind ↵.

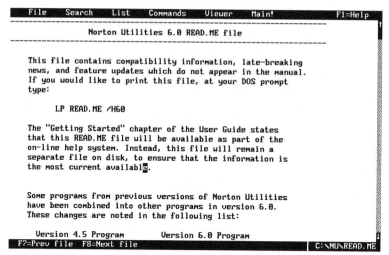

```
   File    Search    List    Commands    Viewer    Main!              F1=Help
---------------------------------------------------------------------------
                  Norton Utilities 6.0 READ.ME file
---------------------------------------------------------------------------

   This file contains compatibility information, late-breaking
   news, and feature updates which do not appear in the manual.
   If you would like to print this file, at your DOS prompt
   type:

      LP READ.ME /H60

   The "Getting Started" chapter of the User Guide states
   that this READ.ME file will be available as part of the
   on-line help system. Instead, this file will remain a
   separate file on disk, to ensure that the information is
   the most current available.


   Some programs from previous versions of Norton Utilities
   have been combined into other programs in version 6.0.
   These changes are noted in the following list:

      Version 4.5 Program         Version 6.0 Program
 F7=Prev file  F8=Next file                              C:\NU\READ.ME
```

**Figure 11–2. File Find text file view mode.**

## Search by File Contents

When you do not specify a file or wildcard, the program loads but does not automatically perform a search. Instead it displays the main program screen and places the wildcard *.*, all files, in the **File Name** box in which the typing cursor is also positioned. You can replace the *.* with a file name or wildcard in order to begin a file name search.

Below that entry box is a second, blank box labeled **Containing**. This box allows you to perform a search, which examines the contents of the file in order to match a sequence of characters specified in the **Containing** box. The text search can be done on all files by leaving the *.* in the **File Name** box, or limited to a group of files by using a wildcard along with the text search.

For example, suppose you want to locate files that contain the words *File Find*. Enter those words as the search criterion. By default, searches are *case insensitive*, which means that uppercase and lowercase characters are treated the same way. Since DOS stores all file name information in upper-case letters the option is not relevant to file names searches. However, when you search for text within a file, the distinction is significant. You can make your text search *case sensitive* by deselecting the **Ignore case** check box. In this case, leave **Ignore Case** selected by entering ↓ file find ↵.

This time the search process will take a good deal longer since the contents of every file on the hard disk must be searched. In most instances, a search of the entire hard disk looking for a specific phrase within a file is not very efficient. Stop the current search by selecting the **Stop** control button with ↵.

You can make the search more efficient by limiting the number of files that have to be examined. This can be done in two basic ways:

**Wildcard.** You can limit the search to selected files by combining a contents search with a file selection wildcard; for example, nor*.* would limit the search to files that begin with NOR.

**Directory Limits.** The File Find display screen shows three options for the scope of the search: **entire disk** (the default), **current directory and below**, and **current directory only**. If you select **current directory or below** and **current directory only** the search will be limited to those directories. If you want to change the current directory or drive you can use the **Directory**, [Ctrl-r] or **Drive**, [Ctrl-d] on the *File* menu.

In this example, narrow the search using both methods: Select the **current directory only** option and use a READ*.* file wildcard. This narrows the search to READ files in the \NU directory. Enter

```
↑ [space]
[Shift-Tab] [press 2 times]
read*.*↵
```

This time the search is completed quickly because only one file in the directory qualifies for a text search. Note that when a text search is made, an additional value appears on the file information line. This value is the number of occurrences of the specified text within the file. For example, *Norton* appears 37 times in the READ.ME file.

Display the contents of the file that was located by entering ↵ [Tab] ↵.

The **View** display is slightly different this time in that instead of simply displaying the file starting at the beginning, the program starts with the area of the file that contains the first match for the search contents that appear highlighted. You can continue the search of the current file by using the **[F6]** key to locate the next match, if any, or **[F5]** to return to the previous match in the file. Enter **[F6]**.

The next occurrence of the text in the current file is highlighted and displayed within the context of the file. Continue searching for the text: [F6].

When you have reached the end of the file (that is, no more matches in the current file) a dialog box gives you the option to continue searching in the next file on the list, if any; exit the view mode; or cancel the request. Recall that the file list display indicated that there is a total of 37 places in this file where the search text appears. Canceling returns you to the current viewer screen display. Enter q.

The program returns to the main File Find display. It is important to keep in mind that the list of files is still active. This means that you can go back to the list of files and view one or more again in case you need to review the information.

## Multiple Drive Searches

In addition to the basic search options that have been discussed, the File Find program has a variety of other options that can help you select files in different ways. By default, the search operations are limited to the current drive. The **Search drives** option located on the *Search* menu, which can be activated with the [Alt-d] shortcut keystroke, allows you to select one or more drives for searching. Enter [Alt-d].

The dialog box allows you to select the current drive; all of the drives available to the system, including floppy drives; or to select individual drives by selecting the drive check boxes. In this case select all of the drives by entering ↓ [space]. The selection places check marks in all of the drive check boxes. If you desire, you can remove one or more drives. For example, if you do not have a drive B you can avoid a delay while the program tries to find drive B by deselecting that option. Enter [Tab] [Tab] [Space].

Drive B is not selected. If you do not have a disk in drive A you might also choose to exempt that drive from the search. Enter ← [space].

When you have selected the drives you want to search, exit the dialog box by entering ↵.

Note that selecting more than one disk automatically changes the search scope to **entire disk** since it is not possible to search less than the entire disk when multiple drives are involved. The program now shows the selected drives on the right side of the screen next to the label **Search drives**, letting you know that more than one drive has been designed for the next search. Execute the search by entering [Shift-tab] (press 2 times) ↵.

This wider search may or may not find additional files that fit both criterias. For example, if you have a copy of Microsoft's Word for Windows installed on one of the drives in the system you will find that in the \WINWORD\LIBRARY directory there is a file called README.DOC that contains the words *File Find*, which, by coincidence, is the name of a command in that program as well. If no such coincidence occurs you will have only the Norton Utilities READ.ME file on your list. Exit the program by entering [Alt-q] (press 2 times).

## Advanced Search Options

The basic tools of searching are the use of file name or text contents criteria, either separately or combined, to locate the desired files. The key to efficient searching is to concentrate the search on files that are the most likely to contain the information you desire.

The File Find program has a set of **Advanced** options that allow you to select files on a more sophisticated basis than merely using a DOS wildcard. The **Advanced Search** dialog box can be displayed by using [Alt-s] a or the **[F4]** shortcut key, as seen in Figure 11–3.

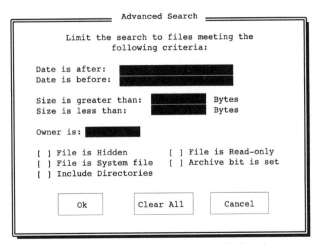

**Figure 11–3. Advanced search dialog box.**

The **Advanced Search** options allow you to select files on the basis of all of the information stored in the file's directory entry, that is, size, date, or attribute, in addition to its file name. By using one or more of these options you can narrow your search to those files that will be the most logical choices. The result is that the search operation is more efficient since you skip all of the files that are not relevant.

**Date After/Before** The first two options in the dialog box allow you to select files on the basis of the time and date of the file. Keep in mind that DOS automatically *time stamps* each file when it is saved or modified. You can select files on the basis of the dates by using either **Date is after**, **Date is before**, or use both to select a range of dates.

Time and date information is entered is the form m/d/yy, for example, 1/1/91. Suppose that you want to list all of the files that have been changed since 5/5/91. You would enter 5/5/91 into the **Date is after** box. Note that the date entered into the box is included in the range so that entering 5/5/91 would give you files stamped 5/5/91, 5/6/91, and so on.

If you wanted to select old files that were stamped prior to a certain date you would enter that date into the **Date is before** box. For example, to find all the files that were stamped before 1/1/90 you would enter that date into the **Date is before** box.

A more practical way to select files is to select for a range of dates by using both the **Date is after** and **Date is before** boxes together. For example, to list all of the files stamped for January of 1991 you would fill in the box as shown below:

```
Date is after:      1/1/91
Date is before:     1/31/91
```

If you wanted to select files for a single day you would place the same date in both boxes. For example, to list files stamped for 5/2/91 you would enter:

```
Date is after:      5/2/91
Date is before:     5/2/91
```

You have the option of adding the time of day to the dates in order to more precisely select files. Suppose you wanted to select files stamped during the morning of 5/2/91. Times are entered in an h:m format as shown below.

```
Date is after:      5/2/91 9:0
Date is before:     5/2/91 12:0  PM
```

Note that the program assumes times are AM unless you specifically add PM to the time. Also keep in mind that it is necessary to enter a value for minutes even if it is zero. Entering 5/2/91 9 would not be accepted by the program, that is, the date would remain 5/2/91, but the 9 would be dropped.

If you like you can use 24 hour times, that is, 13:0 instead of 1:0 PM.

```
Date is after:     5/2/91 9:0
Date is before:    5/2/91 13:0
```

The DOS directory system does not save the initial creation date, as do some operating systems such as the Macintosh. Some applications, such as WordPerfect (when you use the document summary feature) and Microsoft Word, do store the initial creation date document files within the documents themselves. If you want to access these files by their creation date, not the last saved date, you can use a contents search for the date, for example, 11/01/90. Note that this approach does not provide a greater than or less than option.

**Size Greater Than/Less Than**     The size option allows you to select files according to size either greater than, less than, or in between a range. The values entered are assumed to be bytes. If you want to enter a larger unit you can signify kilobytes with K and megabytes with M.

The size option can be used on a regular basis to locate items such as 0 byte files. Zero byte files are created when an application makes an entry in the directory but never actually writes the file information, usually because the program hangs up as the system is rebooted before it can complete the operation. To find these files you would place a 1 in the **Size is less than** box.

**Owner**     When operating a Novell Network you can select files on the basis of the owner attribute of the files.

**Attributes**     The File Find program will operate on all disk files. However, you can select certain classes of files according to their file attributes. For example, to list hidden files you would select **File is Hidden**.

Keep in mind that it is possible to select more than one of the attribute check boxes. When you do so you are selecting files that have *all* of the selected attributes. For example, if you select **Read-only** and **Hidden** attributes the only files that will be selected are those that have *both* the **Read-only** and the **Hidden** attributes. File with one or the other are not selected.

This option provides another means to determine the presence of hidden and read-only files. You can use the archive attribute to determine if your hard disk needs to be backed up.

# Changing Dates and Attributes

The File Find program can be used to modify the date stamp and the attributes of a file or a group of files using the **Set date/time** and **Set attributes** commands found on the *Commands* menu.

Date and attribute operations are always performed in a two-step process:

**Create Target File List.**  The first step is to generate by a disk search a list of files that you want to change. If you only want to modify a single file you still need to perform a search in order to place that one file on the list. Keep in mind that date and attribute operations will work only on the files currently displayed in the list box. If the list box is empty, the **Set date/time** and **Set attributes** will not be available.

**Select Operation.**  Once you have placed the desired file or files in the list box you can then select the operation you want to perform on those files from the corresponding dialog boxes. The dialog boxes for these operations can be used to change the selected file in the list box or all of the files in the list box.

The two-step process has the advantage of allowing you to perform several operations on the same group of files, since they will remain in the list box until you exit the program or perform another search.

If you do not want to perform the same operation on all of the files in the list you can select to limit the operation to the currently highlighted file.

## Changing Attributes

Recall from Chapter 4 that DOS leaves space in the directory entry for each file for an attribute marking designated as archive, read-only, hidden, or system. Suppose that you wanted to change the attributes of the two device driver files (PCSHADOW.SYS and DISKREET.SYS) supplied with the Norton Utilities.

The first step is to create a file list that contains the files you want to change. Enter

```
filefind ↵
[Ctrl-r] \NU ↵
[Ctrl-y] *.sys
```

```
[Tab] (press 2 times)
↓ ↵ ↵
```

The result is a list that contains the two files. Note that the file attributes, if any, are listed by letter for each file. You can now perform attribute and date operations on one or both of the files. Display the attribute dialog box by entering: [Alt-c] a.

The change attribute dialog box is displayed, as seen in Figure 11–4. The top section of the box allows you to select the currently highlighted file (in this case the last file in the list) or the entire list of files. The bottom section of the dialog box list the four attributes supported by DOS, with check boxes for setting or clearing the attribute.

In this case you want to set the read-only attribute for both files. First

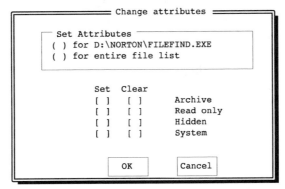

**Figure 11–4. Change attribute dialog box.**

change the file selection option to the entire list. Enter ↓ [space].

Then choose the attribute option or options you want to perform.

```
↓ (press 2 times)
[space] ↵
```

The program applies the attributes to the two files on the list. A box appears that summarizes the changes that were made. Return to the main screen by entering ↵.

Note that the information in the list box shows the R attribute as set for the two files.

## Setting File Dates

By default, DOS stamps each file with the date and time when they were last saved. In general, this means that every file would have a unique time and date unless two files happen to be saved within less than one minute of each other.

In some instances you might want to have the date stamps for a group of files appear more uniform than the actual time-stamped dates. For example, if you were distributing a group of document files related to a project you might want to have the same time and date appear on all of the files, rather than the actual dates. You can use the set date dialog box to place a specified date into the directory entry for these files.

Display the **Set date & time** dialog box by entering [Alt-c] d. The dialog box is similar to the one used for file attributes. The program places the current time and date into the entry boxes as a default. The box has separate check boxes for the time and the date so that you can choose to set one or both values. Note that unless you check one or both of the boxes no change will take place. The time and date entries made into the boxes follow the same format described earlier.

Suppose that you wanted to stamp these files with 9:00 AM August 10, 1991. Enter

```
[Tab] [space] [Tab] 9:0
[Tab] [space] [Tab] 8/10/91↵
```

The program changes the dates of the two files on the list and displays a box that summarizes the changes. Enter ↵.

Exit the program by entering [Alt-q].

# Checking Target Fit

A variation of the file size information is the **Target fit** command located on the *Commands* menu. The **Target fit** command checks the space on any of the system disks in order to determine if there is enough room to copy the files in the list to that disk.

For example, suppose that you wanted to copy the Norton Utilities files to a floppy disk. Begin by placing a floppy disk in drive A. The next step is to list the files you want to copy in the File Find list box. Enter filefind \NU\*.* ↵ ↵.

The file list now contains the names of all of the files in the \NU directory. You can determine if there is sufficient space on the disk in drive A for these files by entering [Alt-c] t a. The program will take a moment to perform the calculation and then display a box that tells you the space needed for the selected files, the space available on the target disk, and a conclusion as to whether you can perform the operation successfully or not. Exit the program by entering [Esc] (press two times).

# Creating Group Batch Files

One of the most powerful features in the File Find program is the ability to generate batch files based on the list of files located by a File Find search using the **Create batch** command located on the *List* menu (shortcut keystroke [Ctrl-b]). This feature allows you to create customized DOS operations based on the file selection capabilities of File Find, combined with DOS commands and/or other Norton Utilities programs. Keep in mind that in order to use this feature you need some background in DOS command operations (for example, how to copy a file) and a basic understanding of how batch files work.

For example, suppose that you are a Lotus 1-2-3 and WordPerfect user. On your hard disk you have a large number of worksheet and document files. You want to copy all of the worksheet and document files that refer to the *Ace Novelty Company* to a floppy disk so that you can distribute them to a co-worker.

The task involves two steps. The first step in the process is to select the worksheet files that have to be copied. This would be a simple matter if all of the names of the relevant files had similar names, for example, ACE01.WKS, ACE02.WKS, etc. and they were all stored in the same directory. But this is not always, or even usually, the case. The files that relate to *Ace* may have a variety of names that cannot be easily grouped with a DOS wildcard, for example, ace*.wks. In addition, the files are likely to be stored in several different directories.

The File Find program offers a unique solution to this type of problem. You can use the powerful search features of File Find to locate all of the relevant files, for example, searching for files that contain *Ace Novelty*. Then, using the **Create Batch File** feature, you can perform DOS operations such as COPY, DELETE, TYPE, etc. on all of the files from the list.

The first step in the creation of this batch file is to use File Find to locate the desired files. As an example, suppose that you wanted to copy all of the

Norton Utilities files that contain the word *attributes* to a floppy disk. Begin by searching for the files that qualify.

```
filefind ↵
\NU\*.* [Tab]
attributes ↵
↵
```

The program will find seven files, NORTON.CMD, CALIBRAT.EXE, etc., in the Norton Utilities group that contain this word. Before you create your batch file you might want to check to see if all of the files will fit on the destination drive. Enter [Alt-c] t a. These files require about 820K of space. If your target is a blank high-density 1.2M or 1.44M floppy you have sufficient room. Assuming that you have the space to successfully perform the copy operation you can now create a batch file that will perform this task. Enter ↵ [Ctrl-b].

The program displays the **Create Batch File** dialog box, as seen in Figure 11–5. The box contains several options that allow you to control how the batch file is written. The general concept of the operation is that the program will write one line in the batch file for each item in the file list box. In order to generate the batch file you must fill in the commands and parameters that need to be added to the lines, along with the file name, in order to form a complete batch file command, as seen in Figure 11–6.

The items in the dialog box are:

**Figure 11–5. Create Batch File dialog box.**

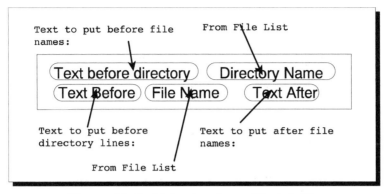

**Figure 11–6. Basic structure of batch file.**

**Save the List To.** This item specifies the name of the batch file created. By default the name *filelist.bat* is inserted in the entry box. Keep in mind that if you want to execute the generated file from DOS you must specify a **BAT** file extension.

**Save Full Path.** This option determines the format used to write the file names that appear in the list into the batch file. When checked, this option writes the full path name of the file into the batch file:

```
D:\NU\calibrate.exe
```

If unchecked, only the file name is written:

```
calibrat.exe
```

**Directory Title Line.** This option determines whether or not the directory names that appear in the file list box will be included in the batch file. When checked, the program will write the directory name that precedes a group of files.

```
D:\NU
D:\NU\calibrat.exe
D:\NU\diskedit.exe
```

When not checked the directory names will be omitted from the batch file. If you include the directory names you can uncheck the **Save full path** option to produce a list that looks like the list that appears on the main File Find screen.

```
D:\NU
calibrat.exe
diskedit.exe
```

This type of list assumes that you will use the directory lines to change directories, for example, CD D:\NU.

**Text Before.** This box is used to specify the text that will be placed before the file name on each line of the batch file (with the exception of directory lines if they are included). In most cases, given the structure of the command language, this box should begin with a DOS or Norton Utilities command that will then operate on file names inserted after it. For example, if you entered the command **DEL** you would generate lines where that command precedes the file name:

```
DEL D:\NU\calibrate.exe
```

Note that the program automatically inserts a space between the **before** text and the file name.

**Text After.**  This box is used to enter the text, if any, that should appear following the file name on each line. A space is automatically inserted before the text. Typically, this text would be parameters needed to complete the command. For example, if the text before inserts a **COPY** command then the text after would specify the destination for the copy, for example, A:.

```
COPY D:\nu\calibrat.exe A:
```

The **Text after** can also be used to specify switches recognized by the command or program. For example, if you use the **XCOPY** command instead of **COPY** you may want to use the /V switch to activate read-after-write verification—for example, A:/V.

```
XCOPY D:\NU\calibrat.exe A:/V
```

Keep in mind that not all commands require parameters or switches, such as **DEL**, which requires only the file name. In those cases, you can simply leave this box blank.

**Text Before Directory.** If you have selected the **Directory title line** option, enter the text to precede each directory in this box. The most common use for this box is to place a **CD** command before the directory name.

```
CD D:\NU
```

In this example, name the batch file ATT.BAT by entering att.bat [Tab].

Turn off the full path name so that only the actual file names will be used. Enter [space] [Tab] (press 2 times).

The text before the file name will be COPY to invoke the DOS command **COPY**. Enter copy [Tab].

The Text after will be the destination for the copied files, for example, A: for drive A. Enter a: [Tab].

To activate the correct directory add a **CD** command before the directory line. Enter cd.

Create the batch file by entering ↵.

The program creates a batch file using the specified text along with the data in the file list. The batch file will have the following contents:

```
cd D:\NU
copy norton.cmd a:
copy calibrat.exe a:
copy diskedit.exe a:
copy filefind.exe a:
copy be.exe a:
copy nu.hlp a:
copy read.me a:
```

To execute the batch file, enter [Alt-q] att ↵.

The batch file executes the series of copy commands, one for each file in the list.

The ability to generate batch files from file lists is a powerful tool. It enables you to create batch files that carry out operations that neither DOS nor the Norton Utilities directly support. Once you have created a batch file you can execute it over and over again since it remains stored on the disk. Batch files can be edited with any text editor and almost all word processing programs. You can then take batch files created by **File Find** and manually add or delete commands in order to improve the performance of the batch file.

# DOS/Batch Operations

The File Find program is one of the Norton Utilities programs that can often be used effectively from DOS, using line commands to implement various options. In many cases it is not necessary or desirable to have the program run in full-screen mode. The **/BATCH** switch causes File Find to operate automatically without pausing for user input.

## Search Wildcards

In order to use the **/BATCH** switch you *must* specify a file search wildcard as part of the command. If you do not include the wildcard, File Find will operate in the interactive mode despite the fact that you have used the **/BATCH** switch.

```
FILEFIND /BATCH - interactive operation
FILEFIND *.* /BATCH - batch mode operation
```

Because of the defaults used by File Find, the meaning of the file wildcards will vary from the meaning they would have with standard DOS commands. For example, the wildcard *.* used with File Find specifies all of the files on the current disk. DOS would interpret *.* as all of the files in the current directory.

```
*.* -DOS, all files current directory
*.* -File Find, entire current drive
```

If you want to limit the search to the current directory only, there are two ways to specify that with File Find: **/C** or .\. The .\ is a nonstandard file specification used by the Norton Utilities, where the . (period) refers to the current active directory. The two commands below have the same meaning.

```
FILEFIND *.* /C/BATCH
FILEFIND .\*.* /BATCH
```

If you want to include directories below the current directory add the **/S** switch:

```
FILEFIND *.* /C/BATCH
FILEFIND .\*.* /BATCH/S
```

If you want to search a different drive or directory than the current active drive and directory, enter the path name in the wildcard. The command below will search the \LOTUS directory on drive E:

```
FILEFIND E:\LOTUS\*.* /BATCH
```

Another variation on DOS wildcards is the substitution of *: for ., in order to select a search across all available drives as shown in the command below.

```
FILEFIND *:*.* /BATCH
```

Note that when operating File Find in the batch mode you cannot perform multiple drive searches to specific drives. You are limited to searching one drive at a time or all drives.

Note that the examples shown above are valid commands, but of little practical value since the **/BATCH** switch will cause the program to terminate immediately after the search has been completed. This will not allow you time to read the list of files. If you omit the **/BATCH** switch the program will enter the interactive mode with the specified wildcard as the default options. You may find that it is quicker to specify the scope of the search as part of the command line rather than using the File Find screens and dialog boxes. When you specify the wildcard the File Find program begins searching as soon as it is loaded, without the need for the entry of a further command.

## Text Searches

If you want to perform a text search you can follow the wildcard with the text you want to locate. If the text consists of a single word or group of characters that does not contain a space it can be entered without quotation marks. The command below will specify a search of the current directory for files that contain *microprocessor*:

```
FILEFIND .\*.* MICROPROCESSOR
```

Keep in mind that by default all text searches are insensitive to differences in case, regardless of how the search text is specified. The command below will perform exactly the same search:

```
FILEFIND .\*.* MICROPROCESSOR
FILEFIND .\*.* Microprocessor
FILEFIND .\*.* microprocessor
```

If you want case-sensitive search you must use the **/CS** switch. The command below will search for an exact match including case; that is, *Microprocessor* only.

```
FILEFIND .\*.* Microprocessor /CS
```

If the search text is a phrase that contains one or more spaces it must be enclosed in quotation marks. The command below searches for the phrase *norton utilities*.

```
FILEFIND .\*.* "norton utilities"
```

If you omit the quotations the program will ignore text following the first word. The command below will search for *norton* only.

```
FILEFIND .\*.* norton utilities
```

## File Lists

Operations using **/BATCH** make sense only when you want to do more than simply list the files on the screen. Since **/BATCH** terminates File Find as soon as the search is over, you would not have time to look at the list the command generated. The **/O** switch causes the program to automatically generate a text file report containing the file list plus the size totals.

For example, the command below would generate a text file called NU.TXT that would list all of the files in the \NU directory and summarize their size:

```
FILEFIND \NU\*.* /O:NU.TXT/BATCH
```

You could then list the files using the DOS command **TYPE**:

```
TYPE NU.TXT
```

To pause the list so that you can read each screen, you can add the DOS **MORE** filter:

```
TYPE NU.TXT|MORE
```

You can combine these two commands into a batch file, for example, FF45.BAT, that simulates the operation of the File Find program in Version 4.5 of the Norton Utilities:

```
FILEFIND %1 %2 /C/O:C:\FF45.TXT/BATCH
TYPE C:\FF45.TXT|MORE
```

To run this batch you would enter

```
FF45 *.EXE ATTRIBUTE
```

The command would list all of the EXE files in the current directory that contained the word *attribute*. To print the list you would replace the **MORE** filter with the **>PRN** redirection command:

```
FILEFIND %1 %2 /C/O:C:\FF45.TXT/BATCH
TYPE C:\FF45.TXT >PRN
ECHO ^L >PRN
```

## Attribute Operations

You can perform operations that list files by set, or clear file attributes, using the batch processing mode of the File Find program. The program uses four switches to designate the different types of file attributes.

When the switch is used as shown above, the program will select files that are currently marked with that attribute. The command below will cause the program to list all files on the current disk that are hidden files.

```
FILEFIND *.* /HID
```

If more than one attribute switch is used the files selected must have all of the specified attributes. The command below will list only files that are both hidden and read-only.

```
FILEFIND *.* /HID/R
```

Using the batch mode you can create a list of all of the hidden files in your system using the example below.

```
FILEFIND *:*.* /HID/O:HIDDEN.TXT/BATCH
```

If the attribute is followed by a + sign the nature of the command changes to one that sets that attribute for the selected files. The command below will mark the COMMAND.COM file as a read-only file.

```
FILEFIND C:\COMMAND.COM \R+
```

Note that the above command did not use the batch mode. When the command is executed, the program will pause and display a summary dialog box after the attribute has been set, and then enter the interactive mode.

If you add the **/BATCH** switch the program will set the attribute and then return to DOS.

```
FILEFIND C:\COMMAND.COM /R+/BATCH
```

You can apply multiple attributes in the same command as shown below, where the file is set to be both read-only and hidden.

```
FILEFIND C:\COMMAND.COM /R+/HID+/BATCH
```

If a - sign is placed after the attribute the effect is to remove that attribute from the specified file or group of files. The command below will remove the read-only attribute from all of the files in the \NU directory that may have that attribute.

```
FILEFIND \NU\*.* /R-/BATCH
```

You can combine different types of attribute switches in a single command. The command below uses the /HID switch to select hidden files in the system. The **/R+** adds the read-only attribute to the selected files.

```
FILEFIND *:*.* /HID/R+/BATCH
```

The **/CLEAR** switch clears all attributes from the selected files.

```
FILEFIND .\*.* /CLEAR/BATCH
```

## Time and Date Operations

You can operate the time and date stamp feature from the command line or batch mode using the switches shown in Table 11–1.

**Table 11–1. Switches used to operate time and date stamp features.**

| Switch | Function |
|--------|----------|
| /Dm-d-yy | Set date |
| /Th:m:s | Set time |
| /NOW | Set current time |

The command below sets the date for the file PRICES.WKS at March 15, 1991. The date and time formats follow those used in the date and time dialog box, with the exception that when you specify a date with the /D switch you *must* use the - as the separator character, not the /. The / is used by DOS to indicate the beginning of a switch and cannot be used as a date separator:

```
FILEFIND PRICES.WKS /D3-15-91/BATCH
```

You can change the time as well, using the **/T** switch. Note that the PM should not be separated from the time with a space:

```
FILEFIND PRICES.WKS /D3-15-91/T10:0pm/BATCH
```

The **NOW** switch will stamp files with the current system time and date:

```
FILEFIND .\*.WKS /NOW/BATCH
```

## Fit on Target Operation

You can also specify the target fit operation from the command line. Keep in mind that because of the nature of the operation it cannot operate completely automatically. The program will pause and display the results of the calculation and wait until you press a key before it returns to DOS. The command below will check to see if the WKS files will fit on drive A:

```
FILEFIND .\*.WKS /TARGET:A/BATCH
```

# Summary

This chapter discussed using the Norton Change Directory and the File Find programs, which you would typically use on a daily basis. These programs expand and enhance your use of the DOS filing systems by providing ways to locate and select directories and files, which cannot be done using DOS alone.

**Change Directory**    The Norton Change Directory program provides a search capability that locates directories. The program can operate in a full-screen mode that displays a directory tree, or in a batch mode that initiates a search for the matching directory.

**File Find**    The File Find program searches for files across barriers, such as directories and drives unlike DOS. The program will create a list of files that match the selection criterion. You can select on the basis of file name or text within a file. When selecting by text, the program lists the number of matching items within each file.

**View Files**    The files listed can be displayed using the **View** control button. The **View** mode will display the contents of the specified file. If the search was a text search the matching text items in the file will be highlighted. You can move between matches and files while in the **View** mode.

**Goto**    The **Goto** control button performs a change directory to the directory in which the currently selected file is located.

**File Attributes**    File attributes can be used as criteria for file selection. The program can also change the attributes of the selected files by setting or clearing one or all four of the attributes recognized by DOS.

**Files Sizes**    When you print or save to a text file a copy of the current file list, the program calculates directory and disk totals for files and file sizes.

**Fit on Target**    The **Fit on Target** options will determine if the currently selected file list can be copied to a selected drive.

**File Dates**    You can alter the time and date stamp of one or more of the listed files.

**Create Batch**     The File Find program can generate DOS batch files, using the files and directories currently in the file list. The batch file will generate one line for each file name and directory name in the list. You can specify text that will be placed before and after each line in the batch file.

**DOS/BATCH Operations**     The File Find program can operate as a command-line program using a variety of switches. Command-line operation allows File Find to be integrated into batch files.

# 12 Recovering Files and Data

Throughout this book the filing system used by DOS has been at the core of most operations. One of the basic concepts in the DOS filing system is to maximize your ability to store data on your disks. This means that DOS makes it easy to erase files and reuse that space for new files. In Chapter 10 you saw how this process can lead to fragmentation of hard disk files and how the Norton Utilities Speed Disk program can eliminate this problem.

In this chapter you will look at another aspect of the DOS file system and the tools that the Norton Utilities provides for manipulating that system in order to provide a means by which erased, lost, or damaged files can be recovered in full or in part.

## Concepts behind Data and File Recovery

In Chapter 4, under the heading "Erasing a File," the method by which files are erased by DOS is discussed. The most important idea in this section is the discovery that DOS does not physically obliterate a file when it is erased. In fact, DOS does not make any changes to the data clusters that contain the file, at all. Instead, DOS modifies the directory entry and the FAT (File Allocation Table) to indicate that the space previously occupied by the file is available for use at some point in the future. All the programs discussed in this chapter are designed to take advantage of this system to enable you to recover data that DOS treats as erased, but may actually still be stored in part or in its entirety on the disk.

### Protecting Your Data

The first set of programs and features you will look at under the topic of recovery are those programs that seek to preserve information that can aid in file recovery. These programs are *prevention* programs that need to be applied *before* files are erased, in order to be effective.

The *Image* program is designed to protect the most crucial parts of the DOS file system:

**The Boot Sector.** The boot sector is the first sector on the disk. This sector performs an important function because it contains information that tells DOS what type of disk it is and how it is organized.

**The File Allocation Table.** This table, called the FAT, contains an array of numbers that indicate numerically which data clusters on the disk belong to which files, and in what sequence they should be read.

**The Root Directory.** All disks, hard or floppy, have at least one directory called the *root*. The root directory is different from any other directory on this disk because it is located in the *system* area of the disk, not in the *data* area where other user-defined directories are located.

The Image program creates two files:

**IMAGE.DAT.** IMAGE.DAT is the larger of the two files. It contains the information copied from the system area of the disk: the boot sector, the FAT, and the root directory. This file is written in the root directory of the drive and is given the *read-only* attribute to prevent you from accidentally erasing the file. The size of this file will vary with the size of the system area on the disk, which is usually less than 1 percent of the total disk capacity on floppy disks and about .1 percent on hard disks.

**IMAGE.IDX.** This file is used to keep track of the location of the IMAGE.DAT file on the disk in case the IMAGE.DAT file cannot be located in the root directory due to formatting—a process that rewrites the root directory as well as the FAT. In order to ensure the IMAGE.IDX file is preserved, in all but the most extreme circumstances the program places the file in the *last* cluster on the disk. This file uses only 29 bytes of storage; but because the minimum amount of space allowed by DOS for any file is one cluster, the file prevents DOS from writing in any part of the last cluster on the disk.

The Image files are used by several Norton Utilities programs. In particular, *Unerase* and *Unformat* make use of these files to attempt to recover lost files and data.

Also, programs that cause changes in the directory or FAT, such as *Speed Disk, Norton Disk Doctor,* or *Safe Format,* will update the Image files when they are used.

The *Image* program is one of the simplest programs to operate in the Norton Utilities collection, primarily because its operations are all automatic.

To create the Image files for the current disk, enter IMAGE. The program will create the IMAGE.DAT and IMAGE.IDX files for the current drive. Keep in mind that Image can be used on hard or floppy disks. You can create Image files for drives other than the current drive by specifying the drive letter. For example, you could create Image files for drive D using this command:

While running, the program displays the message "Updating IMAGE for drive D:". When the program has completed its operation the message will change to "Finished updating."

The key question is how often should the Image file be updated? The general answer is at least once a day. The simplest way to perform the operation is through the AUTOEXEC.BAT file. Keep in mind that you need to maintain separate Image files for each drive in the system. For example, suppose you had a system with a hard disk partitioned in drives C: and D:. You would need to add two Image commands to the AUTOEXEC.BAT file, one for each of the drives. Example:

```
IMAGE C:
IMAGE D:
```

As part of the AUTOEXEC.BAT the Image files would be updated each time the computer was booted.

Keep in mind that Image is not a *memory-resident* program and does not, therefore, use up memory when it is automatically executed during the boot process.

You can use Image on a network server drive only when the system has been booted off the network; that is, the network operating system is not loaded. For example, if you load your network operating system from the AUTOEXEC.BAT (for example, LANTASTIC networks) you can run Image so long as it comes *before* you load the server portion (for example, in LANTASTIC the SERVER program).

## Image Backups

When the Image program is run for a second time on the same disk, it will store the existing copy of the IMAGE.DAT file in a backup file called IMAGE.BAK, which is also marked as a read-only file. This means you have two images of the disk's system area: one that is currently accurate and one that reflects the disk's condition the last time you ran Image.

If the Images were created each morning by the AUTOEXEC.BAT, then you would have an Image from today and one from yesterday available to Unerase or Unformat.

The backup Image files are used primarily by the Unformat program. If you use Unformat on a disk that had contained both the IMAGE.DAT and IMAGE.BAK files, the program will inform you that you have two sets of recovery information and display the date and time that the IMAGE.DAT and IMAGE.BAK files were created. You can then select which Image data you want to use as the recovery data. In most cases you would use the most recent data, unless you had a reason to believe that the previous Image was more accurate.

In instances where disk space is critical (for example, on floppy disks) you may want to avoid creating an Image backup file. This can be done by using the /**NOBACKUP** switch. The example below would update the Image files on drive A, but not use disk space to maintain a backup Image file:

```
IMAGE A:/NOBACKUP
```

## Safe Formatting

The *Safe Format* program, discussed in Chapter 4, is a program designed to minimize the chance that you will lose data by accidentally formatting a disk that already contains information you need.[1]

The Safe Format program can actually format the disk in three different ways, two of which use the same technique as the Image program, to enable you to recover information:

**DOS.** The DOS format option duplicates the formatting performed by the DOS **FORMAT** utility. There are a few important points to know about DOS **FORMAT**. First, when DOS **FORMAT** is used the root directory and FAT are completely overwritten. This makes it harder to recover files. Second, DOS performs a different type of format on a floppy disk than it does on a hard disk. On hard disks, DOS does not overwrite the information in the data clusters, only the system area. Data recovery is possible, but more difficult, following the use of the DOS format. However, on floppy disks DOS not only creates a new system area (root directory and FAT) but also specifically overwrites all of the information

---

1.  In DOS 3.xx and higher you cannot format a hard disk unless you enter the correct volume label.

in the data clusters as well. It is *not* possible to recover data from a floppy disk that has been formatted with this method.

**Safe.** The Safe format method improves on DOS formatting in three ways. First, it performs the same type of format on hard and floppy disks, leaving the information in the data clusters on both types of disks. Second, the program, when used in the full-screen mode, will warn you if the disk you are going to format already contains data. Third, the program will create Image files exactly like those created by the Image program so that you can recover data after the disk has been formatted.

**Quick.** This method is very fast since it simply rewrites the system area of the disk and updates the Image files. The data area of the disk is ignored. This method saves a lot of time when you want to clear a disk so that it can be reused. Note that you cannot use the *Quick* method on disks that have never been formatted.

Use the **Safe** or **Quick** methods to format disks. The *Safe Format* program can be used in an automatic mode so that you can issue DOS line commands or use format in batch files. To perform a safe format on the disk in drive A in the automatic mode you would use the command below. To use the quick format method, add the /**Q** switch:

```
SFORMAT A: /A
SFORMAT A: /A/Q
```

In either case you could recover any files that had been on the disk by using the **Unformat** command.

## Preventing Hard Disk Formatting

If you attempt to format a hard disk using the Safe Format there are several safeguards built into the program. Unlike the DOS **FORMAT** program, Safe Format has a setting that controls whether or not the program can be used to format a hard disk. By default, this setting is off, which will prevent the use of Safe Format to format hard disks. The first level of protection implemented by this setting is that only floppy drive letters will appear in the drive selection box when the program is loaded.

If you load the program and designate a hard disk as a parameter, the program will display a box that reminds you that hard disk formatting is not allowed. To enable hard disk formatting you must use the **Hard Disks** option on the *Configure* menu. You can use the shortcut command, [Alt-h], to activate the dialog box directly. The box has only one option, **Allow Hard Disk Formatting.**

Once you have enabled hard disk formatting, the Safe Format program will display additional messages to warn you that you are about to format a hard disk. If the drive contains any data at all a box will appear listing the files or directories found in the root directory, asking you to confirm your intention to format over these data.

A second box appears asking you to confirm your intention to format a hard disk. Only after these two confirmations will the program proceed. However, the program will create, by default, updated Image files for the drive you are about to format, in order to facilitate unformatting should that be needed. Unlike most of the Norton Utilities programs, changes made to the default settings of the Safe Format program are not automatically stored to a corresponding initialization file. For example, should you use [Alt-h] to enable hard disk formatting, the setting will not be saved as a program default when you exit the program, unless you use the **Save Settings** command on the *Configure* menu.

As an example of how Safe Format and Unformat work together, use a floppy disk. Place the disk in drive A:. Begin by formatting the disk using the DOS method. This will ensure that you are beginning with a completely blank disk. The **/A** switch will run the Safe Format program in the automatic mode. Enter sformat a: /d/a ↵.

When the formatting is complete, you can place data on the disk by copying some of the Norton Utilities files onto the floppy disk. Enter copy \NU\nc*.* a: ↵.

There are now four files stored on the disk in drive A. Format the disk again, but this time allow the program to use its default method, the safe format method. Enter sformat a: /a ↵. Before the program proceeds to format the disk, it creates the Image files that will allow you to recover the files. The Image files created by the Safe Format program are identical to those created with Image. When the safe format is complete, list the files on drive A by entering dir a: ↵.

The directory does not show any files, and DOS displays the message "File not found." On the surface the disk appears to be empty. However, the Safe Format program has created Image files that will enable the Unformat program to recover the files. Keep in mind that the image files do not appear in the directory after a disk has been formatted, but they can be located and used by Unformat. To recover the files that had been stored on the disk in drive A, enter unformat a: ↵.

The program loads and displays a dialog box that asks if the disk contains Image files for use in recovery. The message tells you what to enter if you are not sure, since the required Image files might have been automatically created by programs such as Safe Format without the user knowing it was done. Enter y.

The program asks you to confirm your intention to *unformat* the disk. Enter y.

The program searches the disk to find the Image files. When the Image file or files are located—recall that a disk can contain both IMAGE.DAT and IMAGE.BAK—the program displays a dialog box that shows you the date the Image file was created and asks if you want to restore the disk based on this information. If there had been a backup Image file as well, both dates would have been displayed and you could have selected either the *Recent* or *Previous* Image file—whichever file you want to use as the basis for recovery. Enter ↵.

A final warning appears telling you that recovery of the data can remove the current contents of the disk. Because you have not added any files to the disk since the formatting, you do not have to be concerned about this possibility. However, if you had added files to the disk *after* the formatting you would lose the new files while recovering the old. Because the recovery process overwrites the existing FAT and root directory, the recovery operation is *destructive* to the existing FAT and root directory and any files maintained by them. If you find yourself in this situation you can cancel the recovery, copy the new files to a different disk, and then proceed with the unformatting. In this case, enter y.

The last option to select before the recovery takes place is the full or partial recovery option:

**Full.** Full recovery allows the Unformat program to restore the entire system area (boot sector, root directory, and FAT) and all the files related to the system area based on the information stored in the Image files.

**Partial.** The **Partial** recovery option allows you to select which parts of the system area you want to restore. When you select partial recovery the program presents a dialog box labeled **Partial Restore.** The box allows you to select to restore *Boot Record, File Allocation Table,* and/or *Root Directory.*

Restoring the boot record will have no affect on the disk's data since it affects neither the FAT or root directory. The boot record is used to identify structure and the organization of the disk. It is rare that you will need to repair the boot sector alone but doing so cannot harm the disk.

Restoring the FAT or the root directory separately will have a major impact on the disk, without providing a full restoration. For example, if you restore the root directory and not the FAT you will create a list of items in the root directory, but they will not be linked to any of the data clusters on the disk because the FAT will be blank. Conversely, if you restore the FAT without the root directory, the file chains will be restored but there will be no file names in the directory with which these chains can be linked to form files.

In general, the partial restore options would be used only in very special situations where the user, a person with significant experience in disk recovery, would want to examine the root directory or FAT without having the Unformat program complete restoration by connecting the FAT and root directory to restore the files to the disk. Partial restoration may be used when the disk to be restored *had* problems, such as cross-linked files, *before* it was formatted. This needs to be understood before a decision about restoration can take place.

In most cases, as in this example, you should select the **Full** restoration option. Enter f.

When the restoration process is complete, a box appears warning you that you may need to run the NDD (Norton Disk Doctor). The reason for using Norton Disk Doctor is to find and, if possible, fix errors in the disk's system area. These problems can occur if the disk was used *after* it was formatted but *before* it was restored. Enter ↵.

The program displays another dialog box that allows you to Continue—that is, unformat another disk. To Quit, enter q.

List the files on drive A: dir a: ↵.

The list matches the original list of files that were on the disk before it was formatted. Run the NNC (Norton Control Center) program from drive A to determine if the recovery actually restored the file correctly: a:ncc ↵.

The program will load and execute correctly, demonstrating that it has been restored. Testing restored files and programs is the only way to absolutely determine that all has gone properly. Complicated programs, such as those that load overlay files, from time to time require more rigorous testing since you cannot determine the state of the overlays until they are called by the main program module. Exit the program by entering [Esc].

## The Limits of Unformatting

The restoration process that you just worked through went very smoothly because the operations were executed in the ideal sequence. The restoration of the formatted disk followed immediately after the formatting. However, the ideal situation will not always occur. It is often the case that the formatted disk is used before restoration is attempted.

Many users who mistakenly format disks, even those using Safe Format instead of the DOS format program, are unaware that both hard and floppy disks can be restored. Resigned to their fate they simply proceed. However, adding new files to the formatted disk creates a situation where some of the data stored in the data cluster section of the disk is physically overwritten with new information, making it impossible, even for the Norton Utilities, to recover the data. Format the floppy disk once again by entering sformat a: /a ↵.

Before you proceed to restore the files, copy a new file to the newly formatted disk. Copy \NU\image.exe a: ↵.

Copying the file to drive A has overwritten one or more data clusters on the disk. No matter what Unformat does it cannot change the data written in those clusters back to what it was prior to the format. Because you were copying a file to an empty disk you can assume that cluster 2, the first data cluster on the disk, has been changed so that it now contains the instructions for the IMAGE.EXE program in place of data that had previously been stored at the beginning of the disk (in this example the NCC.EXE program). Perform a full restore on the disk by entering:

```
unformat a:↵ y y
```

Note that this time the program locates two Image files (one recent and one the previous backup) from which you can select to restore. In this case both files contain the same information. Enter r y r.

The restoration appears to have successfully restored the disk. Exit the Unformat program: ↵ q.

To be on the safe side, execute the Norton Disk Doctor quick check on the disk. Enter ndd a: /quick ↵.

The Norton Disk Doctor finds no errors. But does that mean everything is correct? Try to run the Control Center program from the file on drive A. Enter a: ↵ ncc ↵.

What happened? Instead of getting the Control Center, the screen shows the copyright message for IMAGE followed by "Finished updating IMAGE for drive A:". These messages indicate that the program that executed was the IMAGE.EXE program, not NCC.EXE. How could that happen? The answer lies in the fact that a file was placed onto the disk, between the time it was formatted and the time it was recovered. The data from the IMAGE.EXE program remains in the data clusters while the FAT and root directory are restored. In this example, the first directory entry for NCC.EXE points to the data clusters that actually contain the program code for IMAGE.EXE.

The result is that a restoration can appear to work perfectly but still fail to return the formatted disk to its previous state. The Image and Unformat programs provide a safety net, but it is not absolute. There is still a need to back up your disks, in particular your hard disks. Keep in mind that the example shown in this chapter is the *simplest possible* case. Almost any hard disk would present a vastly more complicated array of files and data clusters.

What you have seen demonstrated here shows why you should *not* install the Norton Utilities on a hard disk that you want to recover. The very process of installing the Norton Utilities will overwrite a significant portion of the hard disk's data clusters, making a full restoration of the hard disk impossible.

Recall from Chapter 1 that the Unformat program is *not* distributed in a *compressed* format, but can be run directly from the original Norton Utilities disks, in case you need to recover a formatted hard disk. Remember that when you format a hard disk, even one with Image files, you erase the Norton Utilities programs on the hard disk so that you must use the floppy disks to unformat the hard disk.

# Undoing File Deletions

Because disk space is so valuable, most users will have the desire to erase unnecessary files as soon as possible, in order to free up space for new files.

However, the more erasures you perform, chances are that you will accidentally erase a file that you need. The *Erase Protection* program is designed to alter the way erased files are treated, to ensure 100 percent recovery of erased files.

The Erase Protection program is an *intelligent* alternative to the DOS file system. In normal DOS operations, discussed in Chapter 4, when a file is erased, the directory entry for the file is marked with a special character that erases the first letter of the file name. In addition, all the information stored in the FAT about the data clusters assigned to that file are removed. These changes tell DOS that the directory and disk space used by the erased file can be reused for new files.

In Chapter 4, it was pointed out that immediately after a file has been erased, it can be recovered. However, over time DOS may use part or all of the space formerly occupied by the file for new files, making it impossible or impractical to recover all or part of the erased file.

The problem with the DOS system is that its effects on erased information are *random*—that is, the way in which erased files are overwritten does not take into consideration logical criteria, such as which files have been most recently erased. It is possible to find that a file erased only a few minutes ago is unrecoverable, while one erased weeks ago can still be recovered. Of course, this makes sense if you work from the basic assumption, as does DOS, that you will never make a mistake in erasing a file that ought not to be erased.

The Erase Protection program seeks to organize the way files are erased and takes into consideration the fact that mistakes are not only possible but likely.

The key to the operation of Erase Protection is the way *unused* space is used. In normal DOS operations the operating system will reuse erased disk space—that is, fill in gaps left at the beginning of the disk on a first-come, first-serve basis, *before* it uses unused space at the end of the disk. If you are concerned about the possible need to restore an erased file, it would make sense to use the space at the end of the disk that has never been used for any files *first*, before you overwrite areas formerly occupied by files. This would allow the erased data to be preserved and therefore recovered.

Of course, such a system would eventually fill up the disk, since the areas formerly occupied by erased files would not be reused. The Erase Protection program cannot overcome the limits on disks, but it can allow you to select how the erased space is reused when it becomes necessary. For example, you can specify the number of days an erased file should be maintained on the disk—14 days would cause erased files to be saved for two weeks before they were actually purged from the system.

To get a feel for the way Erase Protection works you can prepare a floppy disk to experiment with. Format the disk using the DOS method and copy some of the Norton Utilities programs onto that disk.

```
sformat a: /d/a↵
copy \nu\nc*.* a:↵
```

## Activating Erase Protection

The Erase Protection program, EP.EXE, is a memory-resident (TSR) program that uses about 8K of memory. The Erase Protection program creates a *hidden directory* called *Trashcan*. When files are erased from the disk, the program transfers the file and its directory information to the trashcan directory where it will remain until Erase Protection purges it from the trashcan. Files stored in the trashcan are 100 percent recoverable because all the information about the file, including the first letter of the file name, are preserved.

Once placed in the trashcan, the files will remain there until one of the following occurs:

**Time Expires.**  The Erase Protection program is designed to maintain erased files in the trashcan, based on the system's date. The program records the time and date of deletion and purges the file when the specified number of days have passed. By default, files are kept in the trashcan five days.

This feature depends entirely on the system clock and the dates it generates, to accurately maintain and purge files. If you push ahead the system clock the Erase Protection program will proceed to purge the files as if the time had actually passed.

**Disk Spaced Required.**  Erase Protection will automatically purge the oldest files in the trashcan if all of the unused disk space on the disk is filled. Trashcan files will never cause a disk-full error, since the program releases the space as required.

**Manually Purged.**  You can use the Erase Protection program to select individual files for purging, instead of relying on the automatic purging features. This allows you to remove files from the trashcan on a basis other than time.

Files removed from the disk using the WIPEINFO program circumvent the EP protection, even when WIPEINFO is used in the *delete but do not wipe* mode. Ordinary delete operations carried on from DOS or within applications will be recognized by EP and preserved in the disk's trashcan.

The Erase Protection program works in conjunction with the *Unerase* program. When Unerase is run on a disk that contains an Erase Protection trashcan directory, it reads the information from the trashcan, allowing you to restore the files if desired.

Because Erase Protection is a memory-resident program it must be specifically loaded into memory in order to activate the disk's trashcan. As with other memory-resident programs, it must be loaded each time the computer is rebooted. If you do not reload Erase Protection, any files deleted from the disk will be treated as normal DOS deletions and not added to the trashcan directory, making recovery less reliable.

Once you have established how you want to use Erase Protection you may want to add a command to your AUTOEXEC.BAT file that automatically loads the program each time the computer is booted. Load the Erase Protection program by entering ep ↵.

The program displays the main *Erase Protection* menu. This menu has four control buttons from which you can select. In addition, the screen displays information about the current status of the Erase Protection program.

**Choose Drives**    Erase Protection is applied on a drive-by-drive basis. You must specifically select which drives in your system, floppy and hard disks, you want protected when Erase Protection is active. When activated, all of the drives selected are protected with Erase Protection. Note that the program maintains a \TRASHCAN directory on each of the specified disks. The default setting is *OFF*—no trashcan protection.

The \TRASHCAN directory is marked as a *hidden* directory. This has about the same effect as marking a file as hidden in that it will not appear on the DOS directory listing. You can issue commands using the directory name, even though it is hidden. For example, **CD\TRASHCAN** will work and the name *TRASHCAN* will appear as part of the DOS prompt, assuming you have selected the $P prompt option.

**File Protection**    By default, Erase Protection attempts to preserve all files deleted from the selected disk or disks. However, given limitations of disk space you can fine-tune the Erase Protection operations to include or exclude files with certain extensions. For example, you may select to preserve only DOC and WKS files. On the other hand, you may want to protect all files, with the exception of BAK files, which many programs produce automatically when files are modified. You can select the number of days erased files will be preserved and set a limit to the total amount of disk space available to the trashcan.

**Purge Files**    This option allows you to manually inspect the list of files preserved in the trashcan and select one or more files for purging.

It is important understand what is meant by *purging* a file from the trashcan. While stored in the trashcan, Erase Protection assigns the erased file a special name arrived at by a formula that generates unique names, for example, **@000C80R.SAV**. The names always start with  and end with the SAV extension. When a file is purged from the trashcan, the save file (for example, @000C80R.SAV) is deleted, using the standard DOS method. Purged files are in the same condition as a file-delete file when Erase

Protection is not in use. In theory, you can attempt to recover this file, using the Unerase program, just as you would any deleted file. However, having used Erase Protection initially, the original name of the purged file is lost. When you run Unerase, the name will appear in the Unerase menu as *?000C80R.SAV*. The only way to tell what file this name might represent is to inspect the initial data cluster, assuming it has not been overwritten.

In this example, activate file saving for drive A by entering c. The program displays the **Choose Drive** dialog box. The box lists the available drives with a check box that can be used to select the drives you want to protect. The current drive is checked as a default.

Select drive A by entering [space] ↵.

The main menu of the program now shows that Erase Protection is active and the number of drives protected by the program.

## Protection Options

By default, the Erase Protection program protects all the files on the specified disks. In some cases, you may find that protecting all files is too broad. You may find it more efficient to protect only specific types of files, such as word processing documents or spreadsheet models.

It is important to keep in mind that using Erase Protection will slow down any operation that erases a file on a protected drive. Recall that DOS deletes files quickly because all the changes are made in the system area of the disk, rather than at the actual location of the file, avoiding a disk seek operation. However, the Erase Protection system adds additional overhead to each deletion that increases the time it takes to delete a file. This is another reason why you may want to be selective about the files protected by Erase Protection.

The fine-tuning is performed in the **File Protection dialog** box. Enter » ↵.

**Select by Wildcard**    You can limit the files protected by Erase Protection by selecting the **Only the files listed** option. On the right side of the dialog box a box labeled **Files** lists nine *. in a column. These represent *wildcards* that can be used to identify groups of files. For example, if you use Lotus 1-2-3 Version 2.xx the wildcard WK1 would specify all of your worksheet files, while *.PIC would identify graph picture files. By entering these two wildcards on the list you can limit protection to those specific files on the currently selected drives.

**Ignore by Wildcard**    The **All files except those listed** option uses the wildcards entered in the **Files** list to indicate those files that will *not be protected* by Erase Protection. This option would be selected if you use applications that generate a significant number of temporary or backup files that do not need the additional protection of Erase Protection, since they are used only while certain disk-intensive operations are carried out. For example, the Norton Editor program creates a backup copy of each file that is modified. For instance, when you use Windows 3.0 in the enhanced 386 mode, the program automatically creates a *swap* file, which is used to swap blocks of data in and out of memory when switching applications, a technique called *virtual memory*. These swap files can grow quite large—5 to 10 megabytes. Windows automatically deletes these swap files at the end of each Windows session. However, Erase Protection will then fill up the trashcan with the deleted swap file. Since the swap file is rarely needed, after you quit Windows it would be more efficient to have Erase Protection ignore the swap files rather than protect them. Entering the wildcard *.SWP would allow Windows to delete these files without having them stored in the disk's trashcan.

**Archive Attribute**    The **Include archived (backed up) files** options uses the archive attribute of a file to determine if it should be stored in the trashcan or not. By default, this option is not selected, meaning that only files with the archive attribute will be placed into the trashcan.

Recall that DOS automatically adds the archive attribute to each new file created. However, certain of the DOS utilities **BACKUP** and **XCOPY**, and some programs such as Norton Backup, can change the status of the archive attribute. For instance, suppose you use the DOS **BACKUP** command to back up your Lotus 1-2-3 worksheet files. Enter BACKUP C:\LOTUS\*.WK1 A:.

In addition to making backup copies on drive A of the specified files, the attributes of all of the *.WK1 in C:\LOTUS will be removed. If you were to delete one of the backed up WK1 files it would *not* be stored in the trashcan, since Erase Protection assumes that a backup copy of the file already exists somewhere.

Keep in mind that as soon as you modify the backed up file, the archive attribute is reset and the file once again is subject to Erase Protection.

If you select to turn on **Include archived (backed up) files,** the status of the archive attribute is ignored by Erase Protection. Since you can directly manipulate file attributes with the File Find program, you can use the status of the archive attribute to manually exclude files from Erase Protection, assuming that **Include archived (backed up) files** is off.

**Days to Hold Files**    This option specifies the number of days following their deletion that files stored in the trashcan will be maintained. At the end of that period the files will be removed from the trashcan.

It is significant to understand that the TSR portion of the Erase Protection program does not continuously check for outdated files in the trashcan. This operation is performed only when the full Erase Protection program is loaded by a DOS command. For instance, if you have included Erase Protection in your AUTOEXEC.BAT, outdated files are purged each time the system is booted.

You can also force Erase Protection to purge outdated files after its initial loading by using the /**STATUS** switch with the Erase Protection command. Example: EP /STATUS.

This command not only displays information about the trashcans, but causes the program to check for files that may have become outdated since the program was loaded.

**Maximum Size of Trashcan**    This option sets a maximum size in kilobytes for trashcans on the selected drives. For example, if you want to limit the size of the trashcan to 1 megabyte, you would enter 1000.

In this case select to protect only EXE, COM, and BAT files. Enter

```
↓ [space]
[Tab] (press 4 times)
EXE ↓
COM ↓ BAT ↵
```

You have now activated Erase Protection for the specified file types on drive A. Exit the program by entering q.

The Erase Protection program automatically generates a file, **EP.INI,** in the home directory, \NU, that stores the settings you have entered in the Erase Protection dialog boxes. With Erase Protection there is no need to issue a special command to save the selected settings that include the drives to be protected. Note that with Erase Protection you can only select protected drives using the full-screen program, not command-line switches. If you delete **EP.INI** the program reverts to its default settings.

## How the Trashcan Works

Erase Protection will not create the \TRASHCAN directory until you actually delete a protected file from the disk. Recall that as part of this example you copied four files to the disk in drive A. Delete one of those files by entering a: ↵ del ncc.exe ↵.

List the directory of the disk: dir ↵.

As you would expect, there are only three files listed. However, Erase Protection has made several changes to the disk that do not show up when you use the DOS **DIR** command. Instead, use File Find to list the files on the disk. Enter filefind *.* ↵ ↵.

The list of files generated by File Find shows the hidden directory, \TRASHCAN, and two files in that directory. The first file is always EP.MAP. This file contains data that File Find and Unerase use to manipulate the trashcan files. The SAV file is the backup copy of the file just deleted.

```
A:\
     ncache-s.exe          39,710 Bytes
     ncache-f.exe          49,194 Bytes
     ncd.exe               86,932 Bytes

A:\TRASHCAN
     ep.map                   111 Bytes
     @m10c609.sav          97,220 Bytes
```

Return to DOS by entering [Alt-q].

In order to test the selection criteria used with Erase Protection (that is, preserve only EXE, COM, and BAT files) copy over to drive A and then delete a file that does not contain one of the protect file extensions. Enter copy c:\NU\pcshadow.sys ↵ ↵ del pcshadow.sys.

You can check the current status of the trashcans by using the /**STATUS** switch with Erase Protection. Enter ep /status ↵. The switch causes the program to display information about the trashcans and the Erase Protection program currently in memory. In this case, you will notice that there is only one file listed in the A trashcan because the PCSHADOW.SYS file did not qualify for protection.

```
Checking trashcan on drive A:Checking trashcan on drive C:
Ep status:     Enabled
Drives Protected:     A: (Trashcan contains 96K in 1 file)
                      C: (Trashcan is empty)
Files Protected:      Only files with these extensions
```

```
                              EXE, COM, BAT
Archive Files:        Not Protected
Files Deleted After: 5 days
```

Erase a second EXE file: del ncd.exe ↵ ep /status ↵. This time, the statistics for the A trashcan change because the deleted file was protected by Erase Protection.

```
Checking trashcan on drive A:Checking trashcan on drive C:
Ep status:     Enabled
Drives Protected:     A: (Trashcan contains 181K in 2 files)
                      C: (Trashcan is empty)
Files Protected:      Only files with these extensions
                      EXE, COM, BAT
Archive Files:        Not Protected
Files Deleted After: 5 days
```

You can manually activate and deactivate file protection using the **/ON** and **/OFF** switches. These switches are handy when you want to delete files that you don't want to be added to the trashcan. For example, to delete the NCACHE-S.EXE file without adding it to the trashcan, enter ep /off ↵.

The status screen shows the Ep status as **Disabled**. Delete the file and then reactivate the file protection by entering del ncache.exe ↵ ep /on ↵.

The A drive trashcan still shows only two files since the last EXE file deleted was removed while Erase Protection was disabled. If Erase Protection was the *last* TSR program loaded, you can remove it from memory by using the **/UNINSTALL** switch.

```
EP /UNINSTALL
```

If you have loaded other TSR programs after Erase Protection you can only disable, **/OFF**, the program. It will remain in memory until the system is rebooted.

## Retrieving a File from the Trashcan

Once a file has been stored in the trashcan you can restore it by using the Unerase program. Keep in mind that Unerase can be used in a variety of ways to recover lost or erased data. However, when used in combination with Erase Protection, recovery is 100 percent assured. Enter un-erase ↵.

The Unerase program reads the data stored by Erase Protection and displays a list of all the erased files on the disk, as seen in Figure 12–1.

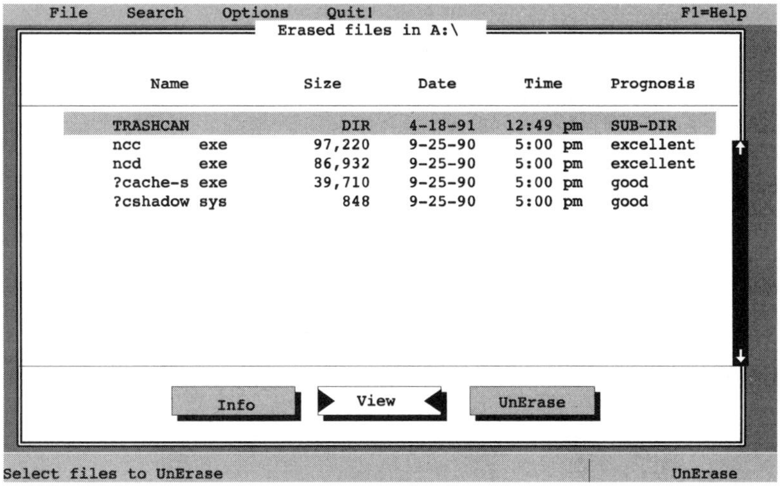

```
   File     Search    Options    Quit!                          F1=Help
                             Erased files in A:\

            Name            Size        Date      Time      Prognosis

        TRASHCAN             DIR      4-18-91    12:49 pm   SUB-DIR
            ncc      exe   97,220     9-25-90     5:00 pm   excellent
            ncd      exe   86,932     9-25-90     5:00 pm   excellent
            ?cache-s exe   39,710     9-25-90     5:00 pm   good
            ?cshadow sys      848     9-25-90     5:00 pm   good




                    Info        ►  View  ◄       UnErase

Select files to UnErase                                      UnErase
```

**Figure 12–1. Unerase screen display**

The Unerase screen lists four files. However, there are obvious and important differences between the files that had been protected by Erase Protection (NCC.EXE and NCD.EXE) and the other deleted files. The protected files have their complete file names displayed and have an *excellent* prognosis of recovery. Files deleted without protection will always have the first letter of the file name missing, since this is how DPS marks deleted items in disk directories, and these files are never rated better than a *good* prognosis since Unerase cannot guarantee that the file can be completely recovered.

To recover the NCC.EXE file, enter » u.

The prognosis for the file changed to **RECOVERED**. Exit the Unerase program and list the DOS directory by entering [Alt-q] dir ↵.

The recovered file is now listed as part of the normal DOS directory for the disk. Delete the remainder of the files on the disk: del *.exe ↵.

## Manual Purging

You can manually remove deleted files from the trashcan by using the **Purge Files** option in the Erase Protection program. Enter ep ↵ p.

The program lists in a dialog box the files currently stored in the disk's trashcan. The files are listed in the order (oldest to most recent) in which they were deleted. The date and time values shown reflect the last time the files had been saved before they were deleted. Below the list box the program shows the original path location of the currently highlighted file and the date and time that it was deleted from the disk.

You can delete individual files using the **Purge** control button. The **Tag** option displays a box that allows you to enter a wildcard that will purge all matching files. For example, to delete the NCACHE-F.EXE enter » p.

The file is no longer stored in the trashcan. Exit the program by entering

```
q ep /status↵
```

The trashcan shows only two files.

## Purging by Date

The most common way for files to be purged from the trashcan is by date. By default, all files stored in the trashcan are purged five days after they were deleted from the disk. You can increase or decrease the number of days. Note that the days settings, like the other Erase Protection options, apply equally to all protected drives. You cannot designate a longer maintenance period for the hard disks than the floppy disk.

You can test the operation of the time-based purge by making a temporary change in the date in the system's clock. Enter

```
date ↵ 1/1/99 ↵
```

Are the files purged? List the items on the disk with File Find:

```
filefind *.* ↵↵
```

The File Find list still shows two SAV files in the **\TRASHCAN** directory. The reason is that Erase Protection does not evaluate the file in the trashcan until the program is executed from DOS. It is not necessary to reload the program—running **EP /STATUS** for example, will cause the program to update the trashcan. Exit File Find and run Erase Protection in order to update the trashcan.

Enter

```
[Alt-q] ep /status ↵
```

The trashcan now shows empty, since the system date indicated that all the files in the trashcan were outdated. Return the correct date to the system by entering the date command once again. Example: date 7/1/91 ↵.

You can now remove the Erase Protection program from memory if you desire, using the /**UNINSTALL** switch: ep /uninstall ↵.

If you want to remove the settings used in this example, delete the EP.INI file from the \NU drive on the hard disk:

```
c:↵ del \NU\ep.ini ↵
```

Erase Protection is now back to the default settings.

One of the limitations of Erase Protection is that it treats all deleted files equally, based on the time of their deletion. In practice you may find that occasionally you have files you may want to leave in the trashcan longer than the average deleted file. You can accomplish this by altering the system's date *before* you delete the file. For example, suppose you had a file LETTER.DOC that you wanted to maintain for several months, instead of the standard five days. If you changed the Erase Protection parameters to 90 days then all of the deleted files would be retained for that duration. However, assuming that today is 10/1/91, you could retain that particular file for 90 days by moving the system date up 90 days before you deleted the file.

Example:

```
date 1/1/92
del letter.doc
date 10/1/91
```

The result would be that LETTER.DOC would be retained until 1/6/92 (assuming the default of five days) while the rest of the files would still be purged within five days of their deletion. Keep in mind that if you run out of disk space, the program may still purge the file, but at least it will be the last one purged.

## Network Drives

Erase Protection will operate on remote drives accessed across a network. However, deleted files will be added to the disk's trashcan based on the status of Erase Protection on the work station performing the deletion.

For example, suppose that two users, John and Marcia, are both deleting files from drive F:, a shared network drive. John is using Erase Protection but Marcia is not. In this case files deleted by Marcia will not be placed in the trashcan, but those deleted by John will.

A potentially more confusing situation would occur if both users ran Erase Protection, but used it with different settings; for example, John purges in five days while Marcia purges in ten days. The result would be that when Erase Protection updates the shared drive, Marcia's files would be deleted after five days since that is the parameter loaded by John's version of Erase Protection.

If you are going to use Erase Protection in this type of environment you will have to take into consideration that different versions of Erase Protection running at various work stations will read and modify the same trashcan files on the shared drives.

# Recovery of Erased Files

The Erase Protection program provides an orderly and structured way of retrieving erased files, based on the factor of time; that is, the most recently deleted files have the best chance of recovery.

However, the Norton Utilities can be used to recover erased files or portions of erased files that have not been protected by Erase Protection. The main difference is that without Erase Protection, recovery of erased information is subject to the vicissitudes of the DOS file system. Recall from Chapter 4 that DOS reuses space freed up when a file is erased, based on the physical location of the file in the directory and the disk, rather than taking into consideration logical factors such as the date and time. This means that without Erase Protection, recently erased files may be unrecoverable while files erased previously may be recovered intact.

The *Unerase* program provides a number of tools that can assist you in the process of recovering full or partial files, even when these files have not been protected with Erase Protection. There are two basic procedures that can be followed when using Unerase:

**Automatic.** The Unerase program is designed to recover erased files automatically by using the information found on the disk, such as the directory entry for the lost file and the pattern, if any, that can be deduced from the current FAT. The automatic operations reflect the most reliable way of recovering a file based on patterns of disk use. The automatic method will also recognize special types of information, such as Lotus 1-2-3 data files, dBASE database files, and DOS directory information when they are encountered in clusters that are not currently in use.

**Manual.** The manual approach can be used when the erased file is no longer sufficiently intact to enable the automatic recovery method to operate efficiently. The manual method is based on your ability to recognize the contents of the disk clusters as items that belonged to the erased file you want to recover. The Unerase program can be used to piece together, cluster by cluster, items that you want to recover into a file. The primary tool available for manual recovery is the search option, which searches the unused portion of the disk looking for specific groups of characters or words which would identify data as having once been a part of the erased file. Note that in order to perform manual recovery, you need to know key words or phrases that were contained in the file.

The type of file you are attempting to recover will affect the methods available to you for recovery:

**Program (Binary) Files.** Program files are files that contain the binary coded program instructions that are directly translated by the computers when the program is run. Files with EXE and COM extensions are programs. Recovery of program files must be carried out using the automatic features to make a full recovery. Recovering part of a program file is not useful since, if any part of the program's code is not recovered, the program will not function properly and will probably hang up the computer if an attempt is made to run the program. In other words, recovery of program files is an all-or-nothing proposition.

In addition, many programs employ additional binary files. For example, large programs often divide their program codes into a main EXE file and a series of overlay files, sometimes with OVL or OVR extensions, in order to allow a larger program to operate in 640K of memory. Overlay files are also binary files.

**Text Files (ASCII).** Text stored in standard ASCII text format (for example, text only, carriage returns at the end of each line, and so on) can be recovered automatically when possible, or manually when necessary. ASCII text files are stored on the disk exactly as they appeared on the screen, for example, batch files created with EDLIN. Partial recovery of a text file makes sense since you can glean information from whatever portion of the file you are able to read.

**Text (Non-ASCII).** Most text files are not created with ASCII editors such as EDLIN, but with word processing programs such as WordPerfect or Microsoft Word. These programs usually store the text entered into a document form that varies with the appearance of the text on the screen because the word processor needs to store information about items such as indents, fonts, bold or italics, page breaks, and so on. The file is usually a combination of text and binary codes. You can locate and recognize sections of text, but you will find that the overall text appears differently when displayed by Unerase than it did in the original application. These files are *enhanced* text files since they are mostly text with binary codes added as enhancement.

When full automatic recovery is not possible; you may still find that recovery of portions of the file is useful since you can read the text between the binary codes.

**Binary Headers and Footers**    One common method used to store enhanced text is with the use of binary headers and footers. Programs often store information about the basic organization of the text information in block of binary code at the beginning (a header) and/or at the end (a footer) of the file. Partial recovery of this type of file means that you may not have the full header and/or footer information needed by the application in order to load the file.

For example, dBASE and compatible DBF files begin with a binary section that defines the structure of the database. That section is followed by a stream of text that contains all of the characters entered into all of the records in the database. If a DBF file is recovered but has the header missing, it cannot be loaded by a dBASE type application. The Unerase and File Fix programs have special routines for fixing partially recovered DBF and Lotus 1-2-3 files.

However, there are many applications that use other types of enhanced text files not supported by the Norton Utilities. In those cases you may be able to use the partially recovered file as a basis for reentering the data manually when you cannot load the file directly into the application.

**Specialized Data Files**    The most common type of specialized file are spreadsheet model files. While spreadsheets often contain some text, they are primarily composed of numbers and formulas that are stored primarily as binary values. Unlike word processing documents, spreadsheet files are barely recognizable when viewed with Unerase. Partial recovery of spreadsheets is probably useless unless they are Lotus type spreadsheet files that can be restructured using the special Lotus 1-2-3 recovery features in the Unerase and File Fix programs.

In the following sections both the automatic and manual Unerase operations will be explained in some detail.

## Information Recovery—Example

Full, automatic recovery of erased files is possible when none of the original data clusters have been overwritten by new data. Begin by creating a blank disk using the DOS format method:

```
sformat a: /a/d
```

Create a directory on the disk by entering md a:\recover ↵.

Copy the following files into the new directory. Note that the order is important since DOS will write the files in the order in which you copy them to the disk.

```
copy \NU\read.me a:\recover ↵
copy \NU\be.exe a:\recover ↵
copy \NU\NU.cmd a:\recover ↵
copy \NU\diskmon.exe a:\recover ↵
copy \NU\trouble.hlp a:\recover ↵
```

Change to drive A. Enter

```
a: ↵
cd \recover ↵ dir ↵
```

There are now five files in the \RECOVER directory on drive A. The files represent the three types of recovery discussed in the previous section: READ.ME and NORTON.CMD are standard ASCII text files, BE.EXE and

DISKMON.EXE are program files, while TROUBLE.HLP is a file that contains a large amount of text but not in standard ASCII format.

```
Volume in drive A has no label
Directory of A:\RECOVER

  .             <DIR>        1-02-99   2:30p
  ..            <DIR>        1-02-99   2:30p
READ    ME      22505        9-25-90   5:00p
BE      EXE      24304        9-25-90   5:00p
NORTON  CMD       8065        1-31-91   8:31p
DISKMON EXE      69034        9-25-90   5:00p
TROUBLE HLP      42165        9-25-90   5:00p
      7 File(s)   1046528 bytes free
```

## Full, Automatic Recovery

Full, automatic recovery of an erased file is possible immediately after the file has been deleted, that is, before *any new data* have been added to the disk. Only one part of the file recovery process requires the user's intervention; that is the entry of the first letter of the file's name. This first letter is overwritten by the hex value E5 when DOS deletes the file. In this case you will begin by deleting the \RECOVER directory and all of the files contained within it. Enter

```
ncd↵
[F8] y↵dir↵
```

As far as DOS is concerned the disk is empty—no directories and no files. Recovery of the deleted files is almost 100 percent sure because of two factors:

**No Changes Since Deletion.** No new information has been added to the disk since the deletion was made. This means that only the first letter of each file and directory names has been removed along with the FAT values for those items. The data themselves are still 100 percent intact.

**No Fragmentation.** The information in the erased section of the disk was unfragmented when it was deleted. When you start with a newly formatted disk and add files, DOS will write them into consecutive disk clusters beginning with cluster 2.

Restoring files is a much more reliable process when the disk in question does not contain fragmented files. Why? The answer lies in the fact that DOS does not erase the starting cluster number of a file when the directory entry is marked as deleted. If the files are unfragmented, you can easily infer the location of the erased files by comparing the starting cluster numbers that remain in the directory. If the original files were un-fragmented, it is a simple matter to infer that all of the clusters between one starting cluster location and the next represent the remainder of the erased file, as seen in Figure 12–2. The ability to more easily recover erased files is an indirect benefit of using Speed Disk to unfragment your disk.

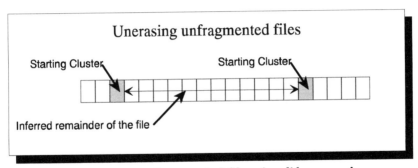

**Figure 12–2. Unfragmented files simplify unerasing.**

Load the Unerase program by entering unerase ↵.

When the program loads it displays a large dialog box that is used to list all of the erased directories and files. This list is arrived at by reading all of the entries in the current directory that contain the E5 hex value which indicates an erased item.

Why does the list contain *only* the name of the erased directory and not the names of the individual files that were deleted? The reason is that the list of erased files is contained in the disk cluster that had been used for the \RECOVER directory. Until the Unerase program reads the erased directory's information, you will not see a list of the files. There are two ways to proceed:

**Unerase Directory.** In this case the root directory shows an erased directory. Note that the name **?ECOVER** shows **DIR** in the size column, indicating that this was an erased directory, not a file. If you unerase the directory you will then be able to display the file names of files erased from that directory.

**Search for Lost Names.** The **for Lost names** option on the *Search* menu is useful in locating erased files that may have been stored in erased directories. When you select this option, the program scans the disk for data clusters that appear to contain directory information. Recall from Chapter 4 that DOS directory clusters have a unique pattern of organization that distinguishes them from ordinary data.

The search option has several advantages. First, it will locate all of the available directory information on the disk, not just that connected with the erased directory appearing in the box. Second, it provides this list without making any changes to the disk. The main disadvantage of the search is that it is time-consuming since the program must read and analyze all of the unused clusters on the disk. Begin the search by entering [Alt-s] 1.

The program displays a dialog box showing the percentage of the unused portion of the disk that has been searched. The search starts at the beginning of the disk. In this example, after a few seconds, the list, which appears in the background underneath the dialog box, shows a list of file names found when the program located the cluster that had been used for \RECOVER. Since you know there is no need to continue the search on this disk, stop the search at this point by entering ↵.

The dialog box now lists the erased files, as seen in Figure 12–3.

At this point you have established two facts about the disk: (1) it contains an erased directory, ?ECOVER, and (2) it also contains five erased files.

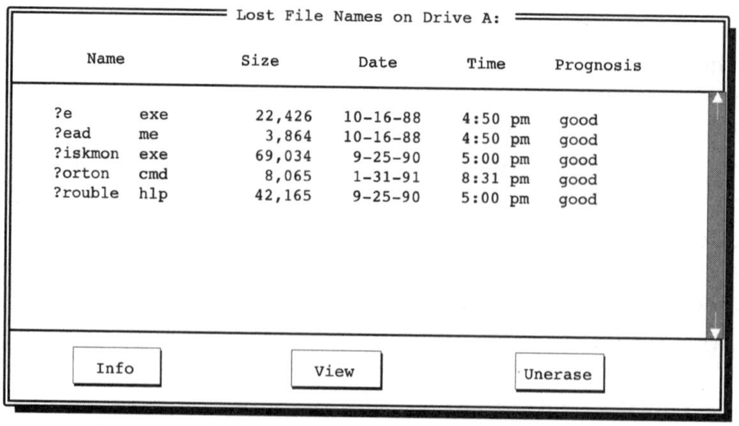

```
════════════ Lost File Names on Drive A: ════════════

     Name            Size      Date       Time      Prognosis

  ?e        exe       22,426   10-16-88   4:50 pm    good
  ?ead      me         3,864   10-16-88   4:50 pm    good
  ?iskmon   exe       69,034    9-25-90   5:00 pm    good
  ?orton    cmd        8,065    1-31-91   8:31 pm    good
  ?rouble   hlp       42,165    9-25-90   5:00 pm    good




         Info              View              Unerase
```

**Figure 12–3. Search locates erased file names.**

What you do not know is if there is a relationship between the two items; that is, do some or all of the erased files belong to the erased directory? In some cases you will not care because you will be primarily concerned about recovering the erased file. Once recovered you can copy it to any directory or disk that you like. If you were to use the **Unerase** command on files located by the **Lost names** search, the recovered files would be placed into the root directory of the disk by default.

In other circumstances you may want to recover the file in the directory from which it was erased, if possible. Before you decide which method to use you can get some additional information by *viewing* the erased directory. Return to the directory display by entering [Alt-f] a.

Display the contents of the erased directory by entering v.

The display shows the contents of the data cluster associated with the erased directory, as seen in Figure 12–4. The program automatically arranges the data in the *directory* format, revealing that all of the erased files did belong to this erased directory.

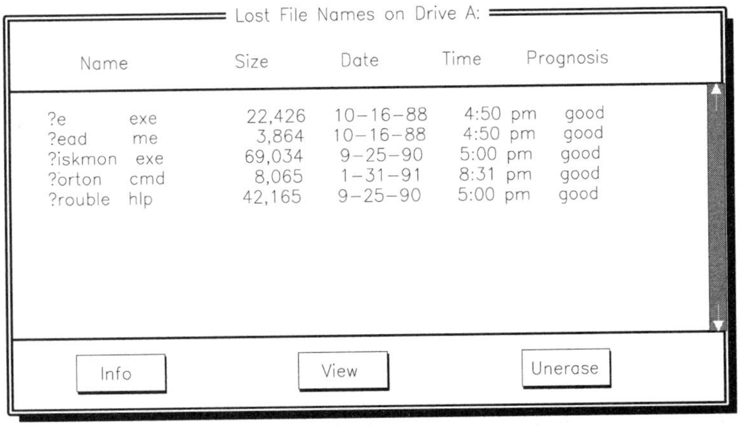

```
============ Lost File Names on Drive A: ============

   Name          Size      Date      Time    Prognosis

?e      exe     22,426   10-16-88   4:50 pm   good
?ead    me       3,864   10-16-88   4:50 pm   good
?iskmon exe     69,034    9-25-90   5:00 pm   good
?orton  cmd      8,065    1-31-91   8:31 pm   good
?rouble hlp     42,165    9-25-90   5:00 pm   good



        [ Info ]          [ View ]          [ Unerase ]
```

**Figure 12–4. Contents of deleted directory displayed.**

The information provided by the view display tells you that you can restore the erased files to the directory from which they were erased by first unerasing the ?ECOVER directory. Return to the Erased files display by entering o.

Unerase the highlighted directory by entering u.

Because DOS overwrites the first letter of any directory entry, the program requests that you supply the missing first letter. In this case, you know that the missing letter was R. In cases where you do not know the letter you can fill in your best guess. Note that case is not significant in file names or directory names. Enter r.

The recovered directory is now listed as a **SUB-DIR** under prognosis, indicating that it has been unerased. Display the contents of that directory by entering v.

This time the program displays the erased file names in the dialog box because you are viewing a restored directory. When the unerase box contains more than one recoverable item, you can unerase items one at a time or tag a group of files to be unerased. For example, to restore the ?iskmon.exe file move the highlight to the file name and select **Unerase.**" (press 3 times).

Before you recover a file, you can view a summary of information about the file obtained by **Unerase**. Enter i.

The **Information** box, as seen in Figure 12–5, displays information obtained about the erased file. The most significant items are in the center of the screen. The *Prognosis* estimates the likelihood that the file can be recovered with 100 percent accuracy. The starting cluster number indicates where the file begins, followed by the total number of clusters that belong to this file.

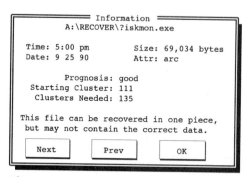

**Figure 12–5. Erased file information box.**

This second value is the more interesting one since it is arrived at by analysis. DOS does not directly record the total number of clusters used by a file. However, you can get a good estimate by dividing the file size by the number of bytes in each data cluster; for example, 69,034 bytes in the file by 512 bytes in a data cluster on a 1.2M floppy disk equals 134.83 clusters.

Since DOS does not allocate partial clusters, the file would need 135. Knowing the starting cluster number (for example, 111) and the total number of clusters needed for the file (for example, 135) the Unerase program looks to see if the 134 clusters following the first are unused. If so, the file is given a *good* chance of recovery.

Of course this analysis is not by any means fool-proof. It is quite possible that an area within the block of clusters has been overwritten by a new file that was in turn erased. The warning at the bottom of the dialog box refers to those situations where a file may appear to be easily recoverable when, in fact, all of the required data are not contained in the most probable locations, or some of those clusters contain data that were not part of the original file. Unerase has no way of determining if this is the case.

If the file you are attempting to recover is a program or binary type file, the only way to ensure that recovery is valid is to run the program or use the file. If the file is text, you have the option of inspecting the data clusters to see if the data look like the data that belong in the file. Note that in many cases personal knowledge of the contents of the files you are trying to recover is an invaluable asset, since there is no other way to determine for sure if data in a cluster actually belong in a file or not.

In this example, the estimate is accurate because no changes have been made to the disk, outside of the Unerase program, since the initial erasure. Restore the file by entering:

```
o u d
```

The dialog box shows that the DISKMON.EXE file has been recovered.

## Recovering Groups of Files

If you want to recover several files from a list you can speed up the process by *tagging* two or more of the names on the list and performing a *group* unerase. There are two ways to tag files for recovery:

**Tag File Name.** You can tag individual file names by moving the highlight to the name and using the **[Alt-f] s** command or the shortcut keystroke [space] to place a tag marker, X, next to the file name. Entering the command or [space] a second time will remove the tag marker, indicating that the name is no longer selected as part of the group.

**Select Group with Wildcard.** The gray [+] key will display a small dialog box that allows you to enter a file wildcard, for example, *.exe, which will automatically tag all of the names in the current list that match the wildcard. You can *unselect* a file on the same basis if you use the gray [-] key to bring up the **unselect** dialog box.

In this case select all of the files that remain listed as erased by entering

```
[+] (gray key)↵
```

The program places tag markers on each of the unerased files in the current list. Unerase the files by entering u.

Because you have tagged a group of files for unerasing, the program displays a dialog box with an option labeled "Prompt for missing 1st letters." When selected, which is the default, the program will display a dialog box requesting the entry of the first letter for each of the files on the list. The alternative, which is selected by removing the check from the box, is to have the Unerase program automatically insert the first letter for the files. The program has no way of determining what the original first letter of the file name had been. It simply places the letter **A** as the first letter of each file. If another file begins with an A, thus duplicating the file name, the program increments the letter to the next in the alphabet, for example, B, in order to avoid file name conflicts.

Choose automatic entry of the first letter by entering [space] ↵. The program proceeds to automatically recover all of the files in the directory, giving them the names AE.EXE, AEAD.ME, AORTON.CMD, and AROUBLE.HLP.

As a convenience, the program has a built-in rename command. This allows you to change the name of the recovered files without having to exit to DOS and use the **RENAME** command. For example, to change the AE.EXE file back to its original name, BE.EXE, move the highlight to the filename. ↑ (press 2 **times**).

Use the **Rename** command on the *File* menu by entering [Alt-f] n.

This dialog box is simpler to use than the DOS **RENAME** command since you can edit the current name, which appears in an entry box. Enter [Del] b ↵.

The file name is changed. Change the name of the AEAD.ME file back to READ.ME by entering [Alt-f] n [Del] r ↵.

With the files completely recovered, exit the program by entering [Alt-q].

# Partial Data Recovery

Partial recovery of files is necessary when the information on the disk has been in part overwritten by new information. Overwriting existing information can affect a file in two ways:

**Directory Information.** When new files are written to the disk, DOS may overwrite directory information with the information about the new files. When the directory entry for an erased file is overwritten, the Unerase program is not able to perform automatic recovery since it can no longer determine the remainder of the file name, its starting cluster, or its original size. However, just because a file's directory entry is overwritten, it is not necessarily true that all or part of the file's contents have been overwritten. Full or partial recovery may still be possible using the partial approach.

**Data Cluster.** If some of the data clusters previously used for an erased file are overwritten with new information, you may be able to recover the remaining overwritten clusters using the manual method. In some cases, partially overwritten files have readable directory entries that provide a useful starting point for recovery. However, it is possible to have no directory entry available to aid in the recovery process.

The key to manual recovery, in particular when directory information has been lost, is searching for specific words or phrases that were contained within the erased file. By searching through the unused data clusters for these key words or phrases, you may be able to establish the actual or most likely locations on disk that should be used to recover the file.

To set up an example of manual recovery, begin by deleting the READ.ME file from drive A. Enter del a:\recover\read.me ↵.

Now copy the IMAGE.EXE program from the \NU directory on the hard disk onto the floppy: copy c:\NU\image.exe a:\recover ↵.

Load the Unerased program by entering unerase ↵.

## Locating Lost Information

When the program loads it reveals the RECOVER directory. View the contents of this directory by entering v.

The display of the A:\RECOVER directory does not list any erased files. Why? The answer has to do with the fact that DOS will fill in any unused entries in the directory when new files are added. Recall that the

READ.ME file originally occupied the first entry in the \RECOVER directory. When it was erased and IMAGE.EXE copied to disk, DOS overwrote the directory entry formerly occupied by the erased file with the information for the new file, IMAGE.EXE, eliminating any reference on the disk to READ.ME.

Does that mean there is *no* chance of recovering any of the data stored in READ.ME? In this case, there is a chance, based on the relative size of the two files. The READ.ME file used in this example was over 22,000 bytes. The IMAGE.EXE program is only about 12,000 bytes. That means that there is probably about 12,000 bytes, the last half of the READ.ME file, still stored in data clusters that are not in use by other files.

In this case the trick is to locate those data clusters. The basic method used is a *text search* in which you look for information contained in the file. For example, the READ.ME file may have contained *Norton*, *Utilities*, and so on. Of course, the selection of the search text is tricky. Since the file is probably partially overwritten, there is no guarantee that the key word or phrase you search for is in the part of the file that is still on the disk.

If you don't have a reasonable idea of a key word, you might simply search for items that would be typical of any text file, for instance, the word *the* or *.[space]*, which would appear at the end of every sentence. None of these patterns is fool-proof and because they are so general, you may locate a lot of clusters that have nothing to do with your file.

Before you begin the search it may be useful to get a picture of how the disk space is used on the current disk. The Speed Disk program will provide a map that can guide you in your quest for lost data. Exit Unerase and run Speed Disk by entering

```
[Alt-q]
speedisk a: ↵ [Esc] (2 times)
```

The Speed Disk program displays a map of the used (white blocks with dots) and unused (gray blocks) portions of the disk, as seen in Figure 12–6.

The pattern shown on the map suggests that the gap is probably space formerly occupied by one or more erased files that has yet to be overwritten. This *gap* area is probably a good one to search or examine to see if it contains data from the erased file. You can use the *map walk* to obtain more detailed information about the gap area. Enter.

```
[Alt-i] w
→(press 12 times)↵
```

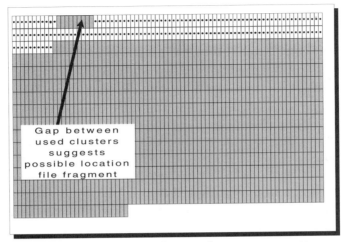

Gap between
used clusters
suggests
possible location
file fragment

**Figure 12–6. Speed Disk map shows usage pattern.**

If you have a mouse, simply double-click on the first unused block in order to display the **Contents of Map Block** dialog box.

The **Contents of Map Block** lists the actual data clusters represented by the map block. The box shows the name of the file to which the cluster is allocated or *unused* if it is not currently assigned to a file. In this example, the display allows you to determine the cluster number of the cluster that is at the beginning of the gap area, for example, cluster 27. Close the dialog box and move to the block at the end of the gap.

```
↵
→ (press 10 times)
```

This box will show which is the last unused cluster in the gap, for example, 46. The reason you want to know the cluster numbers is to find ways to narrow the search to parts of the disk that are most likely to actually contain the erased data, in order to cut down on the amount of time the search will take. This approach is useful when a large percentage of the disk is marked as unused space. When no gap pattern can be detected or when there is only a small amount of unused space to search, this step is unnecessary. Exit the Speed Disk program and return to the Unerase program by entering

```
[Esc] (press 4 times) unerase ↵
```

The next step is to search the area or areas that you think are likely to contain parts of the erased file. If you cannot determine specific sections of the disk, you may have to let the program search through all of the unused space, something that may take quite some time. In this example, you know that you want to begin by searching clusters 27 through 46. You can set the scope of the search by using the **set search Range** command located on the *Search* menu. Enter [Alt-s] r.

The **Search Range** dialog box lists the total range of data clusters on the disk, for example, 2–2,372 on a 1.2-megabyte floppy, and places those values as defaults in the starting and ending cluster entry boxes. In this case you can narrow, and thereby speed up, the search by entering the cluster numbers that represent the gap you saw on the disk map display. Enter 27 [Tab] 46 ↵.

The next step is to enter the search text using the **Search for Text** command: [Alt-s] t.

Here, use a very general criterion, that is, the word *the*, which will probably appear in any text file except those that are not strictly technical language, for example, batch files or program source code files.

By default, the *Ignore case* option is selected, making the search insensitive to differences in case. If you want a case-sensitive search, unselect the option. Proceed with the search by entering ↵.

The program searches the specified area of the disk, for example, clusters 27–46. In this case, Unerase located the search text and made a guess as to what other clusters on the disk would belong to the same file, based on the current layout of the disk. The program adds a file name to the dialog box, *file0000.txt*, and lists the size of the file and its prognosis for recovery. Note that the size of the file, for example, 10K, will match the size of the gap you saw on the disk map. For example, on a 1.2-megabyte floppy, each disk block was equal to two 512-byte clusters, that is, 1,024 bytes. The gap was 10 blocks wide, making the total recoverable data size 10 kilobytes. In this case, the Unerase program followed the basic logic that you used when you spotted the gap on the disk map in making its estimate of what data belong to the erased file.

Keep in mind that at this point the file, *file0000.txt*, has not actually been created on the disk. It will not become an actual file until the **Unerase** command is selected.

Display the data contained in the proposed file by entering v.

The program displays the text of the proposed file. Each occurrence of the search text appears in highlighted video. Return to the recovery dialog box by entering o.

# Saving Recovered Data

Once you have located data that can be restored from the disk, you have two options about how to save the recovered information:

**Unerase Clusters as File.**  This option creates a new file on the current disk using the clusters during the search process.

**Write Data to Another Disk.**  An alternative to creating a new file on the current disk is to write a copy of the restored data into a file on a different disk using the **unerase To** command located on the *File* menu. This method is useful when you do not want to use or change the current disk by creating a new file. For example, if the current disk shows erased files in the directory, creating a new file on the same disk will overwrite part of the directory, eliminating potentially useful information about another erased file.

In most cases the safest approach is to write the restored text to another disk. This allows you to preserve the current status of the disk you are working on, in order to not interfere with further recovery, and still create a file with the recovered information. Enter [Alt-f] t.

The program displays a list of drives onto which you can place the recovered data. In this case, select the hard disk, drive C, by entering c.

The program then displays a box that shows the full path name of the file to be written, for example, C:\file000.txt. Take this opportunity to modify the path or file name. Enter \NU\test1.txt.

The recovered text is placed into a file called TEST1.EXE in the \NU directory. Exit the Unerase program and use the DOS command **TYPE** to display the recovered text by entering

```
[Alt-q] type c:\NU\test1.txt⏎
```

The text streams across the screen, showing that the file contains the recovered text from drive A.

In order to pause the display generated by DOS commands, such as **TYPE**, DOS provides the MORE.EXE filter program. For example, you could enter type c:\NU\test1.txt | more to have the display automatically paused every 24 lines. However, this filter was not used in this case because DOS filter programs (MORE.EXE, SORT.EXE and FIND.EXE) will *alter* the data on the current disk. These filter programs create temporary files called *pipes* that are used to process the output that is being filtered. In the previous example, had a filter such as MORE been used, two temporary files would have been written to drive A using about 10K of disk space. Beware that using DOS filters alters disks.

## Manual Recovery

Manual recovery of erased data is similar to the process used for partial recovery with the exception that the disk from which the recovery is to be made has been altered so much since the erasure that no obvious patterns for recovery, such as the one shown in the previous example, are present.

To create a situation that exemplifies this type of operation, start by creating a small text file on the disk in drive A. In this case you will use the File Find program to create a batch file. Enter

```
filefind *.* ↵
↵
[Alt-l] c
list1.bat ↵ [Alt-q]
```

Next, delete all of the files from the disk, including the RECOVER directory:

```
ncd↵ [End] [F8] y↵
```

To further complicate the situation, add some new files to the disk. In this case you can use the DOS redirection feature to create text files out of directory listings. Enter

```
dir > filea↵
dir > fileb↵ dir > filec↵
```

Finally, delete the files you have just created. Enter del file*.* ↵.

Load the Unerase program by entering unerase ↵.

When the program loads, it shows the three files that you just erased. These names are not very useful in recovering the text you are looking for since the disk has undergone quite a few changes since the original file READ.ME was erased. In this case you will need to use the **Manual** recovery mode. Manual recovery proceeds through a series of steps:

**Create New File.** Manual recovery begins with the selection of a new file name. This name represents the name of the file that will contain the data, if any, that you select to recover from the disk. Note that creating the new file name does not make any changes to the disk. The file will actually be written to the disk only at the end of the entire process.[2]

**Search for Data.** Once you have picked a file name you can enter the manual recovery mode. The mode allows you to search the disk for specific items that would indicate where on the disk the lost data are stored.

**Assemble Clusters.** When you have located one or more clusters that you want to recover, you can assemble them into a file. Note that in assembling clusters you can choose not only which clusters are to be included, but also the sequence in which they should be assembled into a file. Note that in the case of a fragmented file the clusters used to form the recovered file may not all be contiguous, nor are they always assembled in numerical order.

**Write Recovered Data.** When all possible or desired clusters have been selected and sequenced, you can choose to write the information to the disk as a new file.

Begin by using the **Create** file command located on the *File* menu to start a new file. Remember that this command does not actually create a file in the sense that something is written to the disk. Instead, it simply designates a file name that can be used later to write recovered data to the disk. Enter

```
[Alt-f] f test2.txt ↵
```

When you enter the name of the file you want to create, you automatically activate the **Manual Unerase** dialog box, as seen in Figure 12–7.

The dialog box is considerably more complicated than the automatic recovery dialog boxes used by Unerase because of the complexity of manual file recovery:

**File Information.** This box displays information about the file you are attempting to recover. Initially, this box shows the name of the file and the current time and date. As you add data clusters to the file, the other values will change to reflect the current status of the recovered file.

---

2. You can apply the manual unerase approach to any of the erased file names listed in the dialog box by highlighting the name and using [Alt-m] to activate the manual mode instead of proceeding with the automatic unerase process.

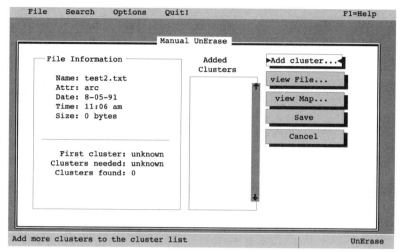

Figure 12–7. Manual recovery dialog box.

**Added Clusters.** This box lists the data cluster numbers, if any, that you have selected with the **Add Cluster** control button. The box can be used to delete clusters from the file or to change the sequence in which the clusters are arranged.

**Add Cluster.** This option is the basic tool of manual recovery since this is the only way that data are assigned to the file. This option allows you to select clusters by number, by searching, or to allow the program to automatically select a probable cluster.

**View File.** This option displays a box that shows the contents of the file as currently defined by the list of added clusters. This option enables you to browse through the data in order to determine if your selected data clusters actually contain useful information. The view can be a standard text display or a hexidecimal display, if desired.

**View Map.** This option displays a disk map that shows the approximate location of the clusters selected for the current file. The map is useful when you want to see if there are any distinctive patterns in disk usage that will aid in data recovery. Note that you cannot display this map until you have selected at least one cluster with the **Add Clusters** command.

**Save.** This option writes the current files with the selected clusters in the current sequence to the disk directory and FAT. Note that you do not have the option of saving the manually recovered file to a different disk.

## Adding Clusters to the File

The first step is to begin to locate and add relevant data clusters. Enter a. The **Add Clusters** command displays its own dialog box with three options:

**Next Probable.** This option allows the program to select the next clusters that probably would belong to the current file, based on the patterns, if any, that exist in disk usage.

**Data Search.** This option allows you to search the disk for data that would indicate that a cluster belongs to the file you are trying to recover. It is important to note that this search option, unlike the **Text search** option located on the *Search* menu, allows you to search for any value— text or hexidecimal.

**Cluster Number.** You can select individual disk clusters based on their cluster number. In most cases this method of selection would be used after search had located a cluster and you wanted to add clusters that would be adjacent to that cluster, without performing further searches.

Where should you start? In most cases a search is the best starting point. Enter a.

Note that the search dialog box used in the Manual Unerase mode, as seen in Figure 12–8, is different from the one used in the automatic unerase mode. This dialog box allows you to enter text, hex values, or a combination as the search criterion.

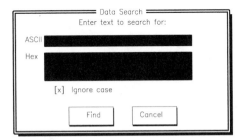

**Figure 12–8. Data search in manual unerase mode.**

The ability to search for nontext values allows you to look for patterns such as the *Carriage Return/Line Feed* (CR/LF), which many text editors and word processors insert at the end of each line or paragraph. With most word processing programs, for example, WordPerfect, a paragraph usually ends with two (CR/LF) sequences—one to end the paragraph and the other to insert a blank line between paragraphs. The CR/LF sequence is composed of nontext characters, hexidecimal values 0D 0A. In this case you will search for a combination of characters that are likely to appear at the end of sentence, that is, a period followed by a CR/LF. Enter the period character as text. .(period).

The program also displays the hex value of the character, 2E, in the hex window. Switch the cursor to the hex window in order to enter the values for CR/LF. Enter [Tab] [End].

Enter the hex values you want to search for. Take care to enter the number zero, not the letter O. 0d0a.

Initiate the search for these characters by entering ↵.

The program will search the unused clusters, starting at the beginning of the disk until it encounters a matching series of values in one of the clusters. In this example, the first cluster with the matching values is cluster 31. The program automatically displays the contents of the cluster with the matching values highlighted, as seen in Figure 12–9.

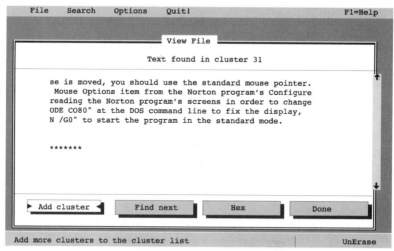

**Figure 12–9. Cluster with matching text displayed.**

The information is displayed in text format because the cluster is composed mainly of text. You have the option to switch to Hex display by entering h.

The hex display shows the hex values on the left side and the corresponding screen characters on the right, as seen in Figure 12–10. In this display mode you can see, indicated by the highlight, that there is an exact match for the hex values *2E 0D 0A* in cluster 31, the first cluster on the disk to contain this pattern.

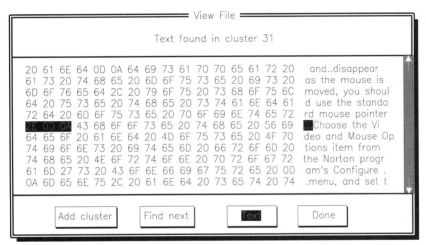

**Figure 12–10. Hex display of clusters.**

Should this cluster be added to the file? It is clear that the file contains text. However, whether or not that text belongs to the file you are trying to recover depends upon if you recognize the information. In this case it is true that this text is part of the READ.ME file. If you were not sure, you would probably add the cluster anyway. Since you are recovering text you can always edit out any text that is mistakenly added to the file.

Add the cluster to the file you are creating by entering a.

The program flashes a message on the screen confirming that you have added this cluster to the file. The message appears only briefly and you may not be able to read it if you are not concentrating on the screen.

## Finding More Clusters

Once you have decided to add the cluster you have two options left:

**Fine Next.**  This option continues the search for the same criterion starting in the next unused cluster on the disk.

**Done**. This option terminates the search and returns you to the main Manual Unerase dialog box.

Continue the search by entering f.

The search continues and stops next at cluster 33. Note that the program did not stop at cluster 32. What does that mean? Ostensibly it tells you that cluster 32 did not contain the search text. Does that mean that cluster 32 should not be added to the file? Does 32 contain text?

Keep in mind that the pattern of values you were searching for is one that commonly occurs in text. However, it is certainly possible that an entire cluster of text, in particular when that cluster is on a floppy disk and contains only 512 bytes, would not have the pattern (. CR/LF) that you were searching for. This also raises the possibility that while cluster 31 was the first to contain a match to your search text, it may not be the first to contain text that you may want to recover.

## Select Clusters by Number

While searching for .CR/LF is a good technique, it is not fool-proof. It may still be necessary to visually inspect clusters, for example, cluster 32, to determine if they contain needed text, even though the text does not include the search text. It is also a good idea to check to see if there is text *before* the first match, for example, cluster 30.

Return to the Manual Unerase menu by selecting the **Done** button. d. Select **Add cluster** and then select the **Cluster number** button by entering a c. Add cluster 30 by entering 30 ⏎.

The **Added Clusters** list shows the clusters 31 and 30. You need to rearrange the order so that 30 comes first. Enter ←.

The highlight moves to the number 30 in the **Added Clusters** list. To change the position of a cluster in the list, mark that cluster by pressing the [space] key: [space]. Move the cluster up by entering & ↑. Complete the operation by entering ⏎. The cluster area now is in order, 30–31. Display the file's contents using the **View file** button. [Tab] f.

Because you have placed cluster 30 at the beginning of the file, the first part of the file's contents display shows the information stored in cluster 30. This information is text in the form of a directory listing of drive A. Since this text was not part of the original READ.ME file, it suggests that this cluster should not be included in the file you are recovering. Return to the Unerase dialog box by entering o.

Before you continue you will want to remove cluster 30 from the list because it should not be included in the recovered file. You can remove a cluster number from the list by placing the highlight on that number and using the [Del] key to delete it. Enter [Del]. Cluster 30 is removed from the list, leaving only cluster 31.

Next, add cluster 32 to the list by entering [Tab] a c 32 [Tab] 32 ↵. Display the newly added cluster by entering f t [End]. The current end of the file, cluster 32, appears to have the correct text from the READ.ME. Return to the main Unerase screen and add cluster 33, which the search has found contains the . CR/LF sequence: o a c 33 [Tab] 33.

## Finding the End of File

At this point you have added three consecutive clusters to the file—31, 32, and 33. This pattern would seem to indicate that the most likely additional clusters would continue (for example, 34, 35, 36, etc.) until you encountered a cluster that did not belong. In other words, you would want to find the first sector in the sequence that did not contain information that was obviously text.

Unfortunately, this is not a simple matter to determine. One way is to continue searching for the . CR/LF sequence until you reach a point where the search skips a large number of clusters. While not every cluster in a text file contains the search sequence, it would be unusual to skip five or ten clusters without finding one that does. Such a pattern would give you a pretty good idea that you have found the end of the series of clusters that contained the text from the file you are attempting to recover.

One solution that can be applied to standard DOS text files is to search for the standard *end of file* marker, hex value 1A called *control Z*, because that is the ASCII keystroke that enters the character. In that case, searching for CR/LF [Ctrl-Z], hex 0D 0A 1A, could be used to locate the end of the file. Be aware that only some text files use the 1A value as the end-of-file marker. For example, WordPerfect documents do not rely on *control Z* to indicate the end of the file, but use the size value in the directory to determine the end of the file. Searching for 1A would make sense only when you had reason to believe that the text was a completely standard ASCII text file. Also keep in mind that text files can end without a CR/LF if the writer ends the last line without adding a ↵.

Continue the search for the . CR/LF sequence, starting with cluster 34 by entering a d ↵.

Cluster 34 contains a match. Instead of adding this cluster at this point, continue the search. When you find the end of the series you can add all of the clusters in between by cluster number in a single command. Enter f (press 12 times).

As you enter the **Find** commands the program moves one or two clusters each time, since the sequence appears frequently in text files. You should be at cluster 46, which contains text that discusses laptop computers. Continue the search: f.

This time the search continues past the next several clusters and does not stop until it reaches text in cluster 95, as seen in Figure 12–11. This cluster does contain text, but it is not text from READ.ME. You may recognize the text as the menu information used by the Norton program that is stored in the NORTON.CMD file.

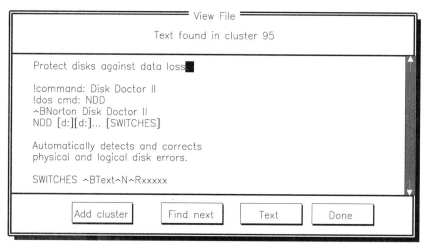

Figure 12–11. Unrelated text located.

You can draw the conclusion that the end of the series of clusters that are related to what remains of the erased file READ.ME lies at or close to cluster 46, since that was the last location where the search sequence was found before the jump to cluster 95.

The next step is to try to determine if the end of the text is at cluster 46 or in any of the following clusters, 47 or 48. It is fairly likely that 46 is the end because no text documents would end with a . and a ↵. However, if some portion of the end of the READ.ME file had been overwritten, then the text might end abruptly in an incomplete sentence.

The logical course would be to add clusters 33 through 47. You could then check 47 to see if it belonged. If not, you would conclude that cluster 46 was the end of the file. Enter d a c 34 [Tab] 47 ↵.

Display the end of the current recovered cluster by entering f [End].

The display shows the last two clusters, 46 and 47, in the file, as seen in Figure 12–12. You can see that cluster 47 does not contain text, indicating that cluster 46 is the last in the series that belongs to the erased file.

Return to the Unerase dialog box by entering ↵.

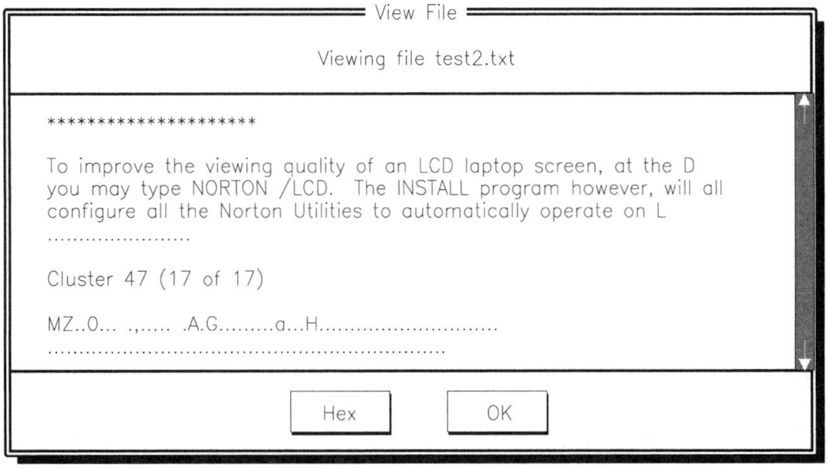

```
═══════════════ View File ═══════════════

              Viewing file test2.txt

  ********************

  To improve the viewing quality of an LCD laptop screen, at the D
  you may type NORTON /LCD. The INSTALL program however, will all
  configure all the Norton Utilities to automatically operate on L
  .......................

  Cluster 47 (17 of 17)

  MZ..O... .,..... .A.G........a...H............................
  .................................................................

            ┌────────┐      ┌────────┐
            │  Hex   │      │   OK   │
            └────────┘      └────────┘
```

**Figure 12–12. Text ends in cluster 46.**

## Saving the Recovered Text

You have now reached the point where you are ready to create a file out of the text that you have recovered. First delete any clusters that do not belong to the file. In this case, cluster 47 should be removed: [Del].

Save the file by entering [Tab] s.

The program modifies the root directory and FAT to include a new file TEST2.TXT that contains the 16 clusters of text data you manually selected. The program then displays the standard automatic unerase dialog box listing the recovered file. Note that the Unerase program added the recovered file to the directory without *overwriting* any of the erased file names that are already in the root directory. Had the file been added by DOS, the first erased file name on the list would have been overwritten. Exit the program by entering [Alt-q].

Manual recovery of information is much more complicated and time-consuming than automatic recovery. It requires you not only to enter commands but to perform a little detective work by peering into the contents of various clusters, searching for clues like . CR/LF and making some logical inferences about where and how the data are stored and where it is not.

The Norton Utilities tries to make this type of recovery unnecessary with features such as Image files and the Erase Protection trashcan. However, no system is 100 percent fool-proof because people will always make mistakes or simply change their minds. The amount of time and effort you expend on trying to make partial file recoveries depends on what value you place on the lost data.

# Fixing Damaged Files

The popularity of certain applications, such as Lotus 1-2-3 in the spreadsheet area and dBASE II, III, III+, and IV in the database area, has made the file formats used by these applications *de facto standards* for the storage of spreadsheet or database information. This means that a number of applications can directly read, or at least convert, Lotus 1-2-3 or dBASE format files. In the spreadsheet area, Borland's Quattro and Microsoft's Excel can directly read 1-2-3 worksheet files, WKS or WK1 extensions. In the database area Paradox, Foxbase, FoxPro, Clipper, dBXL, and Quicksilver are all able to use or import dBASE DBF files.

The difference between *using* and *importing* has to do with how the receiving application stores the data. For example, Paradox *imports* DBF format data because it reads the DBF format by saving the data in its own PARADOX format. This means that any changes made to the data while working with Paradox will not be available in the original DBF file. Conversely, when Excel reads a Lotus WKS format spreadsheet it will maintain that spreadsheet as a WKS format file unless you specifically select to change file format to the normal Excel format. Therefore, changes made in Excel to a WKS worksheet will be reflected in the WKS file when it is loaded back into 1-2-3, with the exception of any Excel features not supported by 1-2-3.

Since these file formats are so common, the Norton Utilities has operations built in that operate on 1-2-3 spreadsheet and dBASE database files, in order to aid in their recovery. In normal file recovery the Norton Utilities deals only with the system information about the file, such as the directory information or the pattern of disk use reflected in the FAT. When 1-2-3 or dBASE type files are involved, the Norton Utilities will actually examine the contents of the clusters as part of the recovery process.

There are two ways in which these files' specific operations can be put to use:

**Partial Recovery.** Both 1-2-3 and dBASE file formats contain binary information that is necessary for the files to be loaded into compatible applications. In such cases partial recovery of an erased file is unlikely to yield useful information since partial files will not be recognized by the applications as being the correct file type. The Norton Utilities special file features can help convert a partially recovered file into a usable format by replacing some of the missing binary information, such as the header in a dBASE DBF file.

**Corrupted/Partial Files.** Database applications, in particular, are subject to file corruption caused by computer crashes because the database files they manipulate are often in a fragmented state while you are making additions or changes to the file. If, for example, the power is cut off to your computer in the middle of a database operation, you may find that when you attempt to reload the file, you may encounter problems. The Norton Utilities provides facilities for correcting some common causes of data loss due to corrupted or damaged files.

In some cases, the Norton Utilities can automatically repair the damaged file. In other cases you will have to manually inspect the damaged file and make decisions about how it can be repaired. As in manually unerasing, an understanding of the meaning of the information that had been stored in the file is essential. It is also necessary to understand something about the application in which the data was created. For example, if you are recovering dBASE type data you need to understand the file structure used by dBASE (Foxpro, Clipper, and so on), and what fields and records are, in order to respond to the Norton Utilities menus and dialog boxes intelligently.

There are two programs that are generally involved in recovery of dBASE or 1-2-3 type data files:

**Unerase.** The **for Data types** option on the *Search* menu of the Unerase program can be used to narrow searches to look for blocks of data that have either dBASE or 1-2-3 type file structures. The first step in specialized data recovery is to perform a dBASE or 1-2-3 type search in order to locate any clusters or groups of clusters that appear to contain this specific type of data. The program can then collect these clusters in files. Note that this step merely locates fragments that appear to have been part of a dBASE or 1-2-3 type file. The files recovered by Unerase are not yet compatible with applications that use dBASE or 1-2-3 type files. In order to be used, these fragments must be converted into usable dBASE or 1-2-3 files with the File Fix program.

**FileFix.** File Fix is used to repair damaged dBASE or 1-2-3 type files or convert recovered fragments to usable dBASE or 1-2-3 files. If sufficient information is contained in the recovered fragments, the files can be rebuilt automatically. If the fragment lacks the required information, you can manually set up the recovery method. For example, if a dBASE type file is missing the file header that contains the field structure of the file, you may need to manually set up the structure in order to convert the data into a full dBASE DBF file.

## Spreadsheets versus Databases

Recovering spreadsheet data is different from recovering database information because of the fundamental structural difference between the two types of data.

Spreadsheet files contain two levels of information about the spreadsheet:

**Global Spreadsheet Information.** *Global* information refers to spreadsheet settings that affect the overall structure of the spreadsheet, such as the full size of the spreadsheet (i.e., the last cell used), standard column width and format, printing options such as margins or page lengths and all graph data. Recovery of this information requires that the recovered fragment begin with the file header where 1-2-3 stores this information.

**Cell Data.** The remainder of the spreadsheet file is composed of a series of small blocks of data that correspond to the cells on the spreadsheet. The data that describe the contents of each cell are sufficiently independent of the other cells to allow the program to recover a section of a spreadsheet on a cell-by-cell basis when the beginning or end of the original spreadsheet is missing.

dBASE DBF database files pose a different problem since records are not stored independently of one another. In a DBF file all of the records in the database are stored as a single, continuous stream of text. The only way in which you can distinguish one record from another is to use a *file structure* that divides the text into individual fields. DBF files store the *file structure* at the beginning of the file. If this part of the original file is missing in the recovered file, the recovery process requires that you supply some sort of structure before the program can repair the file.

Note that recovery of memo fields poses a special problem since memo field information is stored in a separate file (for example, DBT extension) from the main database. In most cases it is not possible to recover the memo fields. However, you can recover memo field information as text and store that in text files. You can use the **APPEND MEMO FROM** command to load individual text files into memo fields with a database. Note that each text file will be stored as the memo for a single record.

In general, repair of partially recovered spreadsheet files is faster and simpler than partial recovery of database files due to this difference in basic structure.

## Locating Fragments of Erased DBF or 1-2-3 Files

When a 1-2-3 or dBASE DBF has been erased accidentally and cannot be fully recovered with Unerase, you can use a special feature of the program to locate fragments of the files that appear to contain data stored in these special formats. These file fragments are not complete 1-2-3 or dBASE DBF files. This means that recovery of the clusters with Unerase will not create *usable* files, that is, the recovered data will not be recognized by the application as valid data due to missing items such as file headers. This can be corrected, in some cases, using File Fix. The first step in this process is to find and collect into one or more files any fragments that may contain useful information. This is done by loading the Unerase program and then selecting the type of data you want to search for. Example:

```
UNERASE
[Alt]-s d
```

The program displays four options related to types of data: text, 1-2-3 (Symphony), and dBASE (DBF) files are normally selected. If you were attempting to recover a specific type of data you would deselect the other options so that only fragments matching the desired type of information, for example, 1-2-3 worksheet files, would be collected:

| Type | Default |
|------|---------|
| Normal text | On |
| Lotus 1-2-3 and Symphony | On |
| dBASE | On |
| Other data | Off |

The **Other Data** selection includes any clusters that appear to contain information based on data patterns. This is a very broad approach to data recovery and should be used only when all other methods fail.

When you select OK, the program begins searching all unused clusters starting at the beginning of the disk. When the program encounters a cluster or series of clusters that contain data that looks like the selected type, the program posts a file name, for example, FILE0001, in the **Data Fragments** dialog box with an appropriate file extension, for example, WK1 for worksheet files 1-2-3 2.xx or DBF for dBASE type files.

You can use the **View** control button to inspect the contents of the fragments located by the search. When you inspect a spreadsheet fragment, as seen in Figure 12–13, the only information that you will be able to read are cell text entries, for example, ^now. Numeric and formula information is stored as binary information and as such it cannot be used to identify the information in the file. If the recovered fragment contains only numeric or

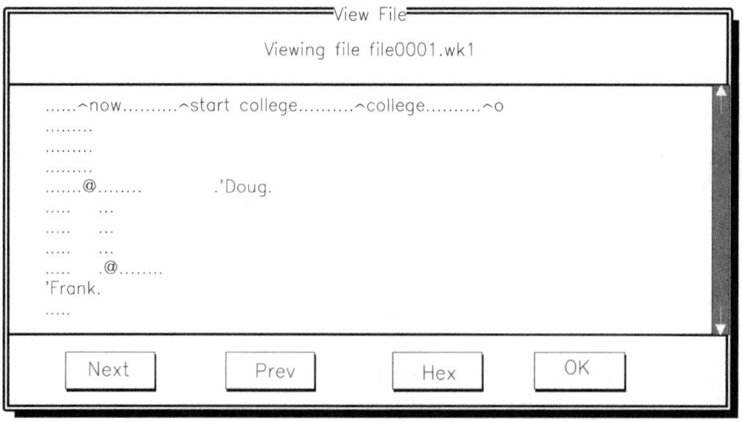

**Figure 12–13. View of spreadsheet fragment.**

formula data you will have no way to identify its contents before you use File Fix.

Database files, as seen in Figure 12–14, on the other hand, are primarily text. However, the text is unformatted without field names or demarcations.

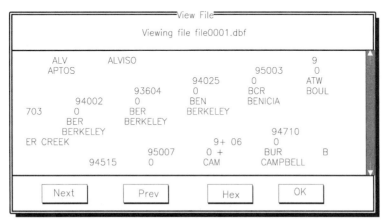

**Figure 12–14. View of database fragment.**

If you are in doubt about the contents of a recovered file, it is best to unerase it and run it through File Fix. If successful, you can load it back into the original application, which will show the recovered data in a form that is more meaningful.

## Recovery of Spreadsheet Files

After using Unerase to recover fragments of spreadsheet files you must then use the File Fix program to convert these fragments into usable spreadsheet files. Load the File Fix program by entering filefix ↵.

The main program dialog box consists of buttons that select the type of file you want to repair: 1-2-3, Symphony, or dBASE. In the case of spreadsheet files, select 1-2-3. The next dialog box allows you to select the file that you want to repair, for example, FILE0001.WK1.

When the file is selected, the **Repair Lotus 1-2-3 File** dialog box, as seen in Figure 12–15, is displayed. The repair process creates a new file, named by default FIXED.WK1, which contains a new spreadsheet based on the data in the recovered file. Because the recovered file itself is not affected by

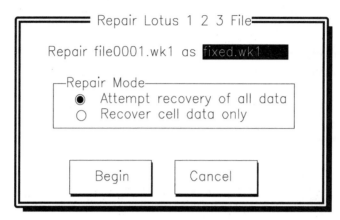

**Figure 12–15. Repair Lotus 1-2-3 File dialog box.**

the repair process you can repeat the file repair process as many times as you like using different methods each time. In most cases it is a good idea to enter a different file name from the default in order to avoid name conflicts with previously recovered files.

The File Fix program has two methods of recovering spreadsheet files:

**Attempt Recovery of All Data.** This option is the default method, which should always be used as the first attempt to repair a file. This option will attempt to recover both global and cell information. If global information is not available, recovery of cell data will be made when possible. In most cases this option will repair the file, if possible.

**Recover Cell Data Only.** This option skips any attempts to recover global information and concentrates on cell data only. Use this option only when the *recover all* method fails to produce a loadable spreadsheet file.

When you have selected the desired method, use the **Begin** control button to start the repair process. The program will display a dialog box with a bar indicating the program's progress in repairing the file. When done the box shows a summary, as seen in Figure 12–16, of the repair process. The **Bytes discarded** value indicates how much of the recovered file was not able to be integrated into a usable spreadsheet file. These bytes typically occur at the beginning and the end of the recovered file where a block of cell information may be incomplete and thus discarded.

The program offers you the option of printing or sending to a text file a report on the recovered spreadsheet. An example of the type of report

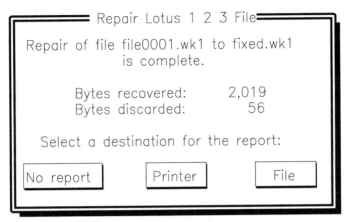

**Figure 12–16. Repair summary.**

generated by File Fix for a repaired spreadsheet is shown below. The report summarizes the number and type of cells recovered and then goes on to list each recovered cell, its location in the file, its row and column address, the type of data stored, and the actual contents of the cell.

## Recovery of dBASE Type Files

The complexity of repairing DBF database files depends primarily on the presence or absence of the file header that contains the file's structure. If the file header is included, repair is automatic. However, if the header is missing, which is usually the case with file fragments, you must supply information about the structure in order to recover the file.

Below is the structure of a sample erased DBF file, fragments of which have been recovered with Unerase:

| Name | Type | Length |
|---|---|---|
| Code | Character | 12 |
| City | Character | 45 |
| Zip | Character | 5 |
| Number | Numeric | 8 |

When you load a recovered fragment of a DBF type file into the File Fix program, the **Repair dBASE File** dialog box, as seen in Figure 12–17, displays options for file repair:

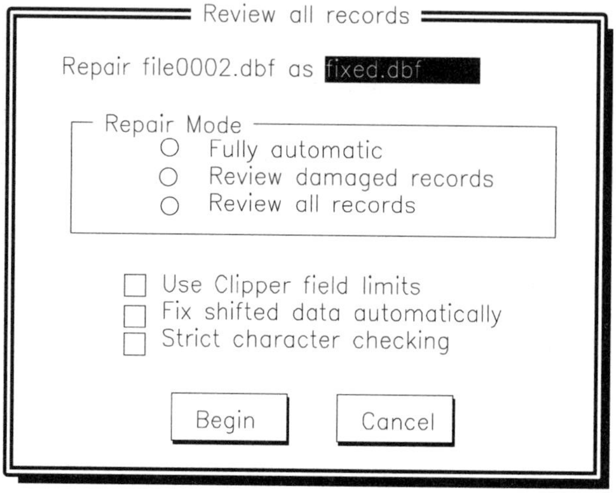

```
╔══════════════ Review all records ══════════════╗
║                                                 ║
║  Repair file0002.dbf as  fixed.dbf              ║
║                                                 ║
║   ┌─ Repair Mode ──────────────────────────┐   ║
║   │        O   Fully automatic              │   ║
║   │        O   Review damaged records       │   ║
║   │        O   Review all records           │   ║
║   └────────────────────────────────────────┘   ║
║                                                 ║
║          □  Use Clipper field limits            ║
║          □  Fix shifted data automatically      ║
║          □  Strict character checking           ║
║                                                 ║
║          ┌─────────┐      ┌─────────┐           ║
║          │  Begin  │      │ Cancel  │           ║
║          └─────────┘      └─────────┘           ║
║                                                 ║
╚═════════════════════════════════════════════════╝
```

**Figure 12–17. Repair dBASE File dialog box.**

**Mode.** The repair process can operate in a fully automatic mode in which the program performs as many operations as possible without user's response. If **Review damaged records** is selected File Fix will stop when, or if, it encounters a record that appears damaged. **Review Records** places the program in automatic operation. Note that if you select *automatic* operation and the program cannot find the file's header, it will revert to **Review.**

**Use Clipper Field Limits.** *Clipper,* from Nantucket, is a program that uses dBASE files and dBASE programming code to create stand-alone, executable programs (EXE files). Clipper allows DBF files to contain more fields and characters than dBASE. Files created or modified by Clipper that use these extended size limits can be repaired if this option is selected. This option is off by default.

**Fix Shifted Data Automatically.** Recall that data stored in DBF files form a long, continuous string of information without any explicit markings to indicate the end of each record. DBF files rely on the exact count of characters, as described in the file's structure. A *data shift* takes place when characters are deleted from or added to the data string. For example, if two spaces were inserted into the middle of a DBF file, all of the records following the two inserted characters would be shifted to the right possibly resulting in the data not being correctly placed in the fields. By default, File Fix attempts to eliminate these extra characters and in so doing correctly align the data in the fields. If you are sure that your file does not require an adjustment, you can speed up the recovery process by turning this option off.

**Strict Character Checking.**  Normally, DBF files contain binary or non-text values *only* in the file header. This option assumes that any nontext information found in the data section of the DBF file is the result of file corruption and that they should be replaced with spaces. It is important to remember that dBASE character fields can contain nontext characters that can easily be inserted into fields using the CHR () function, as is the case with some dBASE-based accounting packages. In this circumstance you will want to turn this option off so that nontext characters will be allowed in the database.

In this example, the recovered file FILE0002.DBF does not contain a header. This will cause the automatic execution to halt since the program cannot determine if the data are from a dBASE II or dBASE III–IV format. Select the correct format from the dialog box to allow the repair to continue.

The message, "The bookkeeping information at the start of the file is severely damaged or missing," appears when the file's header (structure) is missing or badly corrupted. In this circumstance you will have to manually control the recovery process by selecting the **Review** button. The first step in manual repair is to establish the file structure. The program, based on the data in the file, will suggest a possible file structure. The guess will probably vary from the actual structure significantly. In this example, the program suggested a file structure as shown below. This estimate is quite different from the actual structure shown earlier.

```
Num  Field Name    Type     Width  Decimals
  1  FIELD_1     Character     10
  2  FIELD_2     Character     10
  3  FIELD_3     Character     10
```

The next step is to revise the suggested structure by selecting the **Revise** button.

# DOS 5 and Version 6.0

DOS 5.0 is supplied with three programs which Microsoft has licensed from Central Point Software, the makers of *PC Tools*, one of the chief competitors to the Norton Utilities:

**Mirror.** This program performs the same basic function as the Norton Utilities Image program, that is, it creates hidden files on the hard disk that enable you to have a better chance of recovering from an accidental format or deletion.

**Unformat.** This command performs essentially the same function as the Norton Utilities **Unformat** command. The only difference is the DOS **UNFORMAT** uses the files created by the DOS Mirror program.

**Undelete.** This program performs essentially the same type of operation as the Norton Utilities Unerase command. This program also uses the Mirror files if available.

Since DOS and the Norton Utilities both have UNFORMAT programs you may run into some confusion when it comes to executing the Norton Utilities UNFORMAT if the DOS version lies along the search path. Note that DOS will execute whichever program is the first encountered, based on the current search paths.

Version 6.0 of the UNFORMAT and UNERASE programs are compatible with the Mirror files created by the DOS Mirror program. This means that the Norton Utilities 6.0 programs will use Mirror files if no Image files are available. You can force either program to use either Image or Mirror files only by using the **/IMAGE** or **/MIRROR** switches, respectively.

# Summary

This chapter dealt with the methods available in the Norton Utilities for recovery of data that have been lost, erased, or damaged.

**DOS Format and Erase**     All of the operations used to recover data are based on the fact that DOS does not eradicate, that is, overwrite, data when it formats a hard disk or erases files from hard or floppy disks. DOS does alter the disk directories and the FAT tables. The Norton Utilities provides programs that can attempt to recover data that are still stored in the data cluster area of the disk.

**Image**    The Image program creates *image* files on a disk that enable you to recover part or all of the information after an accidental format. Image files must be updated in order to protect information recently added to the disk. Image files cannot protect floppy disks formatted with the DOS format command since that command eradicates data on floppy disks.

**Safe Formatting**    The Safe Format program eliminates the risk of accidental formatting for both hard and floppy disks. The program automatically generates unformat/image files before a disk is formatted.

**Erase Protection**    Erase Protection is used to create automatic backups of all erased files. When a file is erased while Erase Protection is active, it is transferred to a special directory maintained by Erase Protection called the Trashcan. Files are maintained in the Trashcan for a specified number of days at which time they are purged (that is, actually erased), from the disk. Files that have been purged are treated as normal DOS deletions and are still potentially recoverable with Unerase.

**Unerase**    The Unerase program helps you attempt to make full or partial recovery of data that had been stored in erased files. Under ideal conditions the Unerase program can automatically recover an entire file, with the exception of the first letter of the file name. Ideal circumstances for file recovery exist immediately after the deletion is made. However, disk activity that occurs after the deletion may overwrite part or all of the erased file. Unerase can be used in semiautomatic or manual modes to recover partially overwritten files. Partial file recovery is applicable to data files only. Partial recovery of program files is not useful since the program must be complete in order to operate.

**dBASE/Lotus 1-2-3 Data**    The File Fix and Unerase programs contain special facilities for finding, recovering, and repairing data stored in Lotus 1-2-3 spreadsheet format, dBASE DBF database format, and Symphony worksheet format. The Unerase can be used to search for disk clusters that contain data that appear to be stored in these specific file formats. The File Fix program allows you to repair file fragments so that they can be loaded into and used with programs that read Lotus 1-2-3 or dBASE DBF data formats.

# 13 Security

The goal of most software applications and utility programs is to make access to information easier. However, this attitude can be a problem since it allows unauthorized access to information and the ability of special destructive programs, generally referred to as *computer viruses*, to destroy information. The Norton Utilities contains three programs that are related to security issue:

**Disk Monitor.** Disk monitor is a memory-resident program that provides protection against viruses and other programs that attempt to alter information or programs without your knowledge.

**Wipe Information.** Recall from Chapters 4 and 12 that DOS deletions do not remove data from the disk clusters. The ability to recover erased files can present a security problem since almost anyone equipped with the Norton Utilities can recover erased data.

**Diskreet.** This program provides data encryption with password protection for files. *Encryption* refers to a process whereby the data are stored in a scrambled fashion.

## Disk Monitor

The Disk Monitor program's main function is to protect your computer from malicious programs generally know as a *computer viruses.* The program also can display a *disk light* that tells you when disk read and write operations are actually taking place. The program will also park your hard disk.

### What Is a Computer Virus?

The term *computer virus* was coined to describe a computer program whose purpose is to interfere with the normal operation of your system. The interference can take many different forms, some quite destructive, while others are annoying but not very harmful. Keep in mind that computer *viruses* are programs. But unlike the applications and system programs that you spend hard money to acquire, the virus programs are designed to enter your system without your knowledge.

Virus programs generally do two things:

**Replicate and Hide.**  It is the nature of virus programs that no one would want to place a virus in their system. In order to propagate themselves, virus programs will create copies of themselves with the knowledge of the person using the computer. The number of copies and where they are stored will differ with each virus. Most often a virus attaches itself to an existing program. When the user runs a program that is infected with a virus, the virus program code is brought into memory along with the code of the original program. Once loaded in memory, the virus can make additional copies of itself, infecting other files.

**Triggered Event.**  In addition to simply making copies of itself most virus programs have a special routine that will be executed when a certain *trigger event* takes place. Some triggers are as simple as a specific day of the year. Others are triggers by actions that are hidden from the user. When the trigger goes off the virus will do something to the system. In some cases the action is harmless, that is, a message displayed on the screen. In other cases, the system will crash or the virus will attack data stored on the disk.

Note that on PC systems virus programs will attach themselves to EXE or COM files, not ordinary data files. A virus will operate *only* if it is loaded as part of an executable program, which is directly interpreted by the microprocessor. If a virus were part of a data file it would not be able to enter the system's memory since the file would have to be loaded by an application, e.g., a word processing program, which would treat the virus information as data, not program instructions.

While virus programs differ greatly, most fall into three classifications:

**Viruses.**  A basic virus is designed to attach itself to an existing program and replicate itself one or more times, each time one of the infected programs is loaded into memory. The virus will then await its trigger event before performing its action, which can be harmless or catastrophic, depending on the intention of the designer.

**Trojan Horses.**  This type of virus does not rely on attachment and replication for propagation. Instead, the virus is embedded inside a program that is ostensibly a useful application or utility. However, once in use, the trigger event will cause the program to reveal its true nature, allowing the virus to perform whatever mischief it was designed for.

**Worms.** A worm virus generally does not have a specific trigger event. Instead it wreaks its havoc by filling up memory (internal, disk, or both) with copies. By replicating in internal memory, the virus will slow down normal operations or even freeze the system entirely. On the disk the worm can quickly fill up the hard disk or eat away at file data.

The Disk Monitor program helps protect you against the operation of many virus programs by monitoring disk write operations. If a program attempts to modify a protected portion of the disk, Disk Monitor halts the action and displays a box that asks you to confirm the operation.

For example, Disk Monitor is automatically set to prevent writing any changes to the partition table of a hard disk. If any program in memory attempts to perform that action, the operation is suspended, a box is displayed on the screen, and the computer waits for your response. Unless you actually want to modify the partition table, e.g., using the Disk Editor program, such a message might indicate that a virus was attempting to modify the partition table without your authorization.

Keep in mind that Disk Monitor does not seek or remove virus programs from your disks. Its only function, with respect to virus programs, is that it can prevent unauthorized writing of data to the disk. If you have a virus in your system you may prevent its operation, but not eliminate the virus. In other cases Disk Monitor will not stop or eliminate the virus.

## Disk Monitoring

The Disk Monitor program is a memory-resident (TSR) program that uses about 9K of memory. The program can be operated in either the full-screen or command-line modes:

**Full-Screen Operation.** You would use the full-screen operational mode to make selections about the various features and options of the Disk Monitor program you want to use. Once you make selections from the dialog boxes, the program writes your choices into an initialization file, DISKMON.INI, in the Norton Utilities home directory. This file sets the program defaults for the next time that you run Disk Monitor.

**Command-Line Mode.** Once you have created a Disk Monitor initialization file you can load the program with the default settings from the command line using switches. Switches can also be used to check the current Disk Monitor status and to remove the program from memory, assuming that it is the last TSR loaded.

To set up the Disk Monitor program, run the program in the full-screen mode by entering dismon ↵.

The program displays a large dialog box with three options:

**Disk Protect.**  This option allows you to specify the type and extent of the protection to be applied to disk write operations.

**Disk Light.**  The **Disk** option is used to select the **Disk Light** option. The disk light is a two-character display that will appear in the upper right corner of the screen each time a disk operation occurs. The first character in the display is the letter of the drive that is activated. The second character is either a→, which indicates a read operation, or a←, which indicates a write operation. For example, when the Disk Monitor light shows F←, it indicates that data are being written to drive F. The Disk Monitor light has no functional effect on the system but it is interesting to see where and when disk access is taking place. This is particularly useful when the drive in question is a network drive that is not physically located in the computer. Keep in mind that the noise generated by accessing a local drive is missing when you access a remote drive across a network. You may be surprised to find that you rely on the sound of the disk as a confirmation that data are being read or written to the disk, creating an odd feeling when no sound is heard during network operations. The Disk Monitor light replaces the audio sound with a video display.

**Disk Park.**  Most hard disk drives use a *flying* head to read and write information. A *flying* head is a small electronic sensor attached to an arm that hovers a small distance, less than the thickness of a human hair, above the surface of the hard disk. This distance is maintained by the flow of air generated by the spinning of the hard disk.

This means that when you turn off the computer and the disk stops spinning, the head will no longer float above the surface of the disk but will settle down and land on the disk. It is possible that the surface of the disk can become damaged, causing a loss of data when the head settles to the surface.

In order to avoid damage to the hard disk you can *park* the drive heads before you turn off the computer. *Parking* refers to moving the head to a safe part of the disk before the computer is turned off.

When you select this feature, the drive heads are moved to their parking position. You would then turn off the computer so that the heads would land in the safety zone rather than at random locations on the disk, as would be the case without parking.

## Protecting the Disk

By default, Disk Protect is *OFF* when you load the program. To select the type of protection you want to apply to your disks or files, enter d.

The **Disk Protect** dialog box appears:

**System Areas.** This setting, which is the default, protects the system area of your disks, which includes the partition table on hard disks, the boot sector, the FAT and directories, and the system files (COMMAND.COM and the hidden files) from changes. This level of protection prevents a virus from making alterations to the basic disk structure, but does not protect program files on the disk.

**Files.** This option focuses protection on specific types of files based on the file extensions listed in the **Files** box. By default, the box contains the extensions COM, EXE, OVL, BIN, and SYS, which are the most commonly used extensions for program files in DOS systems.

The **Files** box can contain up to 20 different extensions. This is useful because many applications use overlay extensions other than OVL. For example, Lotus 1-2-3 Version 2.2 use CMP; dBASE IV uses RES; and FoxPro uses 000, 001, etc. to indicate overlays.

When using this option you should extend protection to as many overlay files as possible since your goal is to prevent changes to program files as part of virus protection. Keep in mind that it is not necessary to protect data files (WKS, WK1, DBF, DBT, DOC, TXT, etc.), since they are not affected by viruses. However, you may want to use Disk Monitor to protect these files against deletion in a similar manner to the way that the read-only attribute would protect them.

The **Exceptions** box is used to list any specific file names that use one of the protected extensions, as listed in the **Files** box, that you want to exclude from Disk Monitor protection. This option would be handy when you are using a compiler such as Turbo Pascal or Clipper to create program (EXE, OVL, etc.) files. For example, suppose that you were using Clipper to create an application called SALES.EXE. If Disk Monitor was set to protect all EXE files from modification you would encounter the Disk Monitor protection each time you complied the application. If you entered SALES.EXE in the **Exceptions** list, Disk Monitor would ignore changes made to that specific file. The **Exceptions** box can be used to list up to 20 file names. Keep in mind that **Exceptions** will recognize only specific file names, not wildcards. Suppose that you wanted to except all files that begin with the letters **FILE**, as an example, FILE0001.EXE, FILE0002.EXE, etc. Entering FILE*.EXE in the exception list will not work. You must enter the actual names FILE0001.EXE, FILE0002.EXE, etc., if you want those files treated as exceptions:

> **System Areas and Files.**  This option activates both system and file protection.

> **Entire Disk.**  This option causes Disk Monitor to be triggered by a disk write operation.

> **Allow Floppy Access.**  This option is designed to allow you to format a floppy disk while Disk Monitor is active. Since formatting a disk may involve deleting protected files and making changes to the system area of a disk, the process is likely to be interrupted one or more times by Disk Monitor. If selected, Disk Monitor ignores any changes made to a floppy disk while it is being formatted.

Note that the selected level of protection is applied equally (with the exception of floppy disk formats) to all drives in the system. You cannot protect some drives and not others. In this case, select protection for the system area and the files by entering ↓ (press 2 times) [space].

Turn on the **Allow Floppy Access** option. Enter [Tab] [space].

Note that making the selections for the type of protection does not automatically activate the protection. The **ON** control button is not designated as the default. You must specifically select **ON** in order to activate the protection. Enter ↓ o.

When you return to the main dialog box the current level of protection, **ON, System Areas and Files,** is indicated next to the **Status** prompt. Turn on the Disk Light by entering ↓ ⌐ o.

Keep in mind that the disk light does not use up any additional memory, so that you might as well turn it on if you are going to load Disk Monitor. When you exit Disk Monitor two things happen:

**Initialization File Written.**   A file, DISKMON.INI is written in the home directory, \NU. This file contains the selected settings for Disk Monitor protection. If the file is erased from the \NU directory, Disk Monitor will return to the default settings.

**Program Turned On/Off.**   Disk Monitor will be loaded into memory if you have selected **ON** for either protection or light. If both protection and light are turned off the program is removed from memory.[1]

Exit the program by entering q.
When you return to DOS, Disk Monitor displays text on the screen that shows the current status of the Disk Monitor program.

## File Protection

When Disk Monitor protection is active you will be prompted each time an attempt is made to modify a protected file or part of the DOS file system. In this example, you have protected both the system and the default list of program files. If you attempt to alter or delete an EXE file, the action will trigger Disk Monitor. Enter del \NU\diskmon.exe ↵.
The attempt to delete the protected file DISKMON.EXE results in the display of the **Disk Monitor** warning box. The display pauses the execution of the disk operation and provides three options:

**Yes.**  If you select Yes, Disk Monitor will allow the operation to take place.

**No.**  If you select No, Disk Monitor will not allow the operation to take place. It generates a DOS **Access Denied** error. Keep in mind that different applications handle this error in different ways.

**Disable Protection.**   This option allows the disk operation to take place and then disables Disk Monitor. If Disk Monitor was the last TSR program loaded it will be uninstalled. If not, it is simply turned off.

In this case, skip the operation by entering n.

---

1.   This occurs when Disk Monitor is the last TSR program loaded. If this is not the case, the program is disabled but not removed from memory.

The box disappears, returning you to DOS. The message **Access Denied** appears, indicating that the command failed to execute, in this case because Disk Monitor interfered with it.

You can remove the Disk Monitor program from memory, assuming that it was the last TSR program loaded, using the **/UNINSTALL** switch. Enter diskmon /uninstall ↵.

The program is removed from memory and all Disk Monitor protection is disabled. Keep in mind that each time you change the settings on the **Disk Monitor** dialog box the program automatically updates the DISKMON.INI file when you exit the program.

## Disk Monitor Line Commands

Once you have created the DISKMON.INI file, which will hold your Disk Monitor usage preferences, you can activate or deactivate the program using line commands at the DOS prompt or from batch files.

**Activate/Deactivate**    You can activate protection with the **/PROTECT** switch. The disk light feature is controlled with the **/LIGHT** switch. To turn on either feature, follow the switch with a +. The command below will load the Disk Monitor program and activate the current protection scheme as defined in the DISKMON.INI file, and activate the disk light. Example: DISKMON /PROTECT+/LIGHT+.

You can deactivate either of the features by using a - after the switch. The command below turns off the protection feature but will leave the disk light operating, assuming that it has been previously activated. Example: DISKMON /PROTECT-.

If the Disk Monitor is the last TSR program loaded into memory, the program will be removed from memory and the features turned off if you use the **/UNINSTALL** switch. Example: DISKMON /UNINSTALL. If another TSR program has been loaded after Disk Monitor the message "Error: Disk Monitor could not be removed" will be displayed and no change is made to the status of Disk Monitor. In that case you will need to use specific switches to disable the features. The command below disables both features: Example: DISKMON /PROTECT/LIGHT.

Note that this command will have the same effect as **/UNINSTALL** if Disk Monitor is the last TSR loaded.

**Status**    The **/STATUS** switch causes the program to display the two-line status report. Example: DISKMON /STATUS. Note that unlike the

/**STATUS** switch used with the Norton Utilities cache programs, /**STATUS** with Disk Monitor will not load the program. If Disk Monitor is not loaded when you use /**STATUS**, the program returns the message "Disk Monitor is not installed."

**Park**     You can park the heads of the disk drive by entering the following command. Example: DISKMON /PARK.

In order for the park operation to work correctly you *must* turn off your computer after you issue this command. If you enter another command that requires disk access following the park command then the effect of the park operation is negated.

## Disk Monitor and Graphics, Windows 3.0

The Disk Monitor program is designed to operate only when the computer is displaying information in a text mode. When a full-screen graphics application, such as Windows 3.0, is operating, Disk Monitor cannot display the warning box. However, this does not mean that Disk Monitor will not work. If Disk Monitor protection is active before you load Windows, it will prevent modifications to protected files. The difference is that since the warning box cannot be displayed you do not have the option to select Yes or Disable. Instead, access is denied to the user and Windows displays a box with a message that is similar to: "STOP Cannot access C:\NU\NU.EXE: Access Denied." Of course, if you are only protecting system and program files you would seldom encounter this problem since you would not be, in most cases, altering those types of files.

The Disk Light feature, which is entirely visual with no functional effect on the system, will be invisible while the graphic mode is active, but will return when you enter a text mode.

If you execute DOS text-based applications from Windows 3.0 and Disk Monitor was loaded before Windows, the Disk Monitor protection and disk light displays will operate in their normal fashion while the text-based application is active.

## Version 5/Version 6

The Disk Monitor program functions identically in Versions 5.0 and 6.0. The only difference is that in Version 6.0 the program supports high memory on 386 systems made available by memory managers, such as QEMM386 and 386MAX, while Version 5.0 uses only conventional memory.[2] When you load Version 6.0 of Disk Monitor, and the program finds 9K of high memory available, a small portion, 160 bytes, is loaded into conventional memory. The remainder, about 8.4K, is loaded into high memory. The use of high memory is the default, meaning that Disk Monitor will automatically use high memory if it is available. When high memory is available, the impact on conventional memory below 640 is negligible. If you run the sequence of commands shown below on a machine with available high memory you will find that the value for **K-bytes used by DOS and resident programs** on the summary screen will remain the same.

```
SYSINFO /SUMMARY
DISKMON /PROTECT+/LIGHT+
SYSINFO /SUMMARY
```

If you want to suppress the use of available high memory in 386 machines you can use the **/SKIPHIGH** switch. For example, the command below activates Disk Monitor and ensures that the entire program is loaded into conventional memory below 640K. Example: DISKMON /PROTECT+/LIGHT+/SKIPHIGH.

Because the **/SKIPHIGH** function is available only as a command-line option, when Disk Monitor is loaded using the full-screen dialog box, high memory will always be used if available. If you want to make changes in the type of protection, but not use any high memory, you should load the program first into conventional memory and then display the full screen dialog box.

```
DISKMON /LIGHT+/SKIPHIGH
DISKMON
```

# Wipe Information

The key to the ability to unerase files and unformat disks is the fact that DOS does not actually wipe out the data stored in the data clusters when a disk is formatted or when a file is erased. However, this fact also implies

---

2. You cannot use programs such as LOADHI from QEMM386 to force Version 5.0 into high memory. If you try, LOADHI will report that it does not have room for the program even when high memory is available.

that erasing files or formatting hard disks is not a reliable way of ensuring that the data are destroyed. As demonstrated in Chapter 12, these data can be recovered and, in many cases, easily recovered.

In circumstances where security needs require the permanent eradication of data from specific files or entire disks you can use the Wipe Information program, WIPEINFO.EXE, to eradicate data.

The program achieves its results by actually overwriting each byte in the file on the disk with a value, 0 by default. This process takes significantly longer than simply using DOS **DELETE**, but it can insure that data cannot be recovered from the disk. The Wipe Information program can be used in a full-screen dialog box mode or through DOS line commands. Load the Wipe Information program by entering wipeinfo ↵.

The program displays its main dialog box, Figure 13–1, which consists of four control buttons.

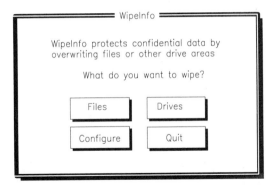

**Figure 13–1. Wipe Information dialog box.**

## Files

This option displays the **Wipe Files** dialog box, which enables you to wipe out the information stored in a file or group of files. The dialog box contains two items: file selection and wipe method.

**File Name**    You can select files, from a single drive, by entering a file name or file selection wildcard, e.g., C:\*.BAK. There are four check box options that can be selected along with the file specification.

Select **Include subdirs** to include all directories below the selected directory. If the selected directory is the root directory, e.g., C:\*BAK, then this option will cause the wipe out of all matching files on the entire disk. When not selected only files in the specified directory are wiped out.

**Confirm each file**, selected by default, causes the program to prompt you to confirm the deletion of each file that matches the selection wild card. To avoid these prompts and perform automatic wipeout, unselect this option. Keep in mind that wiped files cannot be recovered with Unerase.

By default, Wipe Information will skip any files with the hidden or read-only attributes. If you want to include either or both types of files in the wipe process, select **Hidden files** and/or **Read only files**. Note that hidden files are simply skipped during the wipe process.

It is useful to keep in mind that Read Only files, which are not also hidden files, will cause Wipe Information to pause and display a message box each time one is encountered, even when **Confirm each file** is selected. You should take this into consideration if you want Wipe Information to run unattended. Selecting **Read Only files** will ensure that Wipe Information will run automatically.

**Wipe Method**     The wipe method refers to what part of the file or group of files should by affected be the wipe operation. **Wipe files,** the default, wipes out the directory entry, the FAT entries, and all data clusters associated with that file.

The **Delete files only, don't wipe** method changes the operation of the program to that which is performed by the DOS **DELETE** command. The data in the file's clusters are not altered in any way. Only the first character of the file name and the FAT values are erased. The advantage of performing standard deletions with Wipe Information is that by using the **Include subdirs** option you can delete files from more than one directory at a time, something that DOS cannot do. For example, using the file name C:\*.BAK with **Delete files only, don't wipe** and **Include subdirs** will delete all of the BAK files from the entire C drive in a single command.

**Wipe unused file slack only** will wipe the slack space, if any, at the end of any selected files. Recall from Chapter 4, *Clusters*, that slack space is found at the end of the last cluster used by a file. When the actual end of the file falls before the end of the cluster, the space between those two points is called *slack* space. This space can often contain information left over from previous files, which you may want to eliminate by using this wipe method.

## Drives

The Drive dialog box, Figure 13–2, is used when you want to wipe an entire disk, hard or floppy. The dialog box allows you to specify one or more drives to be wiped. In addition, you can select to wipe the entire disk—data clusters, FAT, and directories—or simply the currently unused clusters.

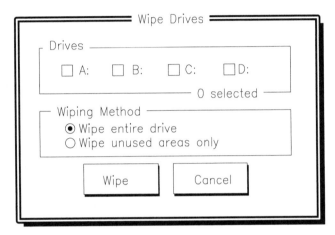

**Figure 13–2. Wipe Drives dialog box.**

Note that when an entire disk is being wiped, the program begins at the end of the disk; that is, the last clusters on the disk. This is done so that you have an opportunity to stop the wipe process before the program reaches the more frequently used portion of the disk.

## Configure

The **Configure** dialog box, Figure 13–3, is used to select the exact method used by Wipe Information to eradicate the data on the disk. The basic method of wiping out data is to overwrite the existing information with new information. By default, Wipe Information will overwrite all of the data related to the selected file or disk with a value of zero.[3]

In most cases, overwriting the data is sufficient to prevent recovery of sensitive information. Why, then, does the dialog box offer additional op-

---

3. The zero refers to a byte with the binary value 00000000, not the ASCII equivalent of the character 0.

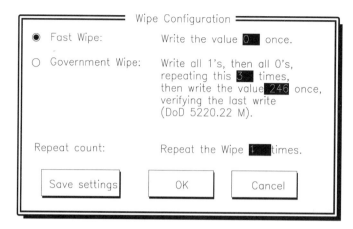

**Figure 13–3. Wipe Configuration dialog box.**

tions? The answer has to do with the technical nature of magnetic data recording, which is the method used with all conventional hard and floppy disks. Recall from Chapter 8 that the most critical operation performed by a disk drive is positioning the drive heads from one track to another.

As with any mechanical device, the movement of drive heads from track to track falls within a certain range of tolerance; that is, the drive does not always position the head to exactly the same position on the track each time it moves to that track. So long as the movement falls within the required tolerance, operations proceed normally. However, it is possible that because of this variance in location some of the data written to the track is not completely overwritten.

In general, this residue is too weak to be picked up by a standard drive and has no effect on normal operations. But it is possible, using special devices created just for this purpose, to locate and recover these data, which would ordinarily be ignored during normal computer use.

In order to protect sensitive information from this type of special recovery, it is necessary to perform more than one overwrite. The idea is that by overwriting the same data several times, the information on the fringes of the tolerance range, if any, will be permanently eradicated, making the disk totally secure. The Wipe Information program supports two ways to perform a more rigorous wipe out of data.

**Government Wipe**    In order to standardize security measures, the Department of Defense (DOD) has issued a bulletin, DOD 5220.22M, that specifies how disk space should be made secure. This method involves seven overwrites of the same area, with a final verification read (Table 13–1). You have the ability to vary the number of times the 0s and 1s are repeated and the value used for the final write. However, the operation may no longer meet government standards.

**Table 13–1 Department of Defense Wipe specifications.**

| | |
|---|---|
| 1. | Write value 00000000 |
| 2. | Write value 11111111 |
| 3. | Write value 00000000 |
| 4. | Write value 11111111 |
| 5. | Write value 00000000 |
| 6. | Write value 11111111 |
| 7. | Write value 11110101 |
| | (F6 hex, 246 decimal) |
| 8. | Read-verify all 11110101 |

The DOD Wipe method is also affected by the **Repeat count** setting. The entire cycle of eight operations is repeated the number of times specified. For example, if you set the repeat count at 2, the program would perform the eight-step cycle twice, a total of 16 steps. This would given you, at least in theory, additional security and still conform to the exact government specifications.

**Fast Wipe**    The Fast Wipe option allows you to select the value, zero by default, and the number of repetitions of the wipe, 1 by default. You can change the way a fast wipe is performed by selecting a different value (decimal number) and/or the number of repetitions. A good value to use in wiping is 153 decimal because its bit pattern is 10101010, which mixes 1s and 0s. The value 246, used in the DOD wipe process, is also a good choice because it is the same value that the DOS FORMAT command places on floppy disks when they are first formatted. The wiped clusters will then look like clusters that have never been used.

The issue involved in the selection of the wipe method is the trade-off between speed and security. The DOD method requiring a minimum of eight passes over the same disk area is quite time consuming. A rough estimate is that performing a DOD wipe on a high-density floppy (1.2M or 1.44M) will take about two hours. You can get a pretty secure wipe, but not one that the government would approve of, by simply repeating a fast wipe with a single value two or three times, cutting the time required by about 70 percent.

Changing the values of the government wipe method is useful when you want to perform a non-DOD level wipe but you want to take advantage of the fact that this method writes both 0s and 1s in a single operation. For example, you might change the *repeating this* value from 3 to 1 to save time but still end up with three different values, 0, 1, and 246, written on the disk.

## Using Wipe Information

Using Wipe Information is quite simple. However, you need to pay careful attention to the prompts since this program is so destructive.

The program displays a box that warns you that you are about to eradicate the contents of one or more files. If you have unselected **Confirm each file** this box would be your last chance to cancel the operation before some damage is done to the specified file or files. If **Confirm each file** is selected, which is the default setting, you will have a chance to confirm the wiping of each file.

The program locates the first matching file and presents you with four control options:

**Skip.** This option skips the current file and continues with the next match, if any. Note that this is the default so that pressing ↵ will skip, not wipe, the current file.

**Wipe.** This option confirms the wipe out of the current file. Note that this is not the default, so that you must specifically select this option in order to perform the wipe.

**Auto.** Selecting this option places the program into automatic operation. The current file is wiped and all subsequent matching files are wiped without any additional prompting. Obviously, you should use Auto with care since recovery is not possible should the wrong files end up being wiped out. Also note that even when automatic is used the program will still stop and wait for a response when a read-only file is encountered and the **Read only files** option is not selected.

**Stop.** This option terminates operation and returns you to the main dialog box. Note that any changes made to the **Configuration** dialog box remain in effect.

# Command Line and Batch Operation

Because of the destructive nature of the Wipe Information program, Version 5.0 of this program did not allow for full, automatic batch file execution. Some user interaction was required in order to confirm the file selection and then choose the **Automatic** operational mode.

In Version 6.0, support for the **/BATCH** switch was added, allowing the program to function fully automatically as part of a batch file.

With that important exception, Versions 5.0 and 6.0 support the same switch options. The advantage of using switches to set options is that it is faster than navigating through the dialog boxes when you know in advance what it is you want to do with the program.

When executed from the command, the type of specification used with the command indicates whether you want to perform a file or disk wipe:

**File Specifications.** Entering a file wildcard or path name automatically selects file wiping. The command below loads WIPEINFO and moves immediately to the wipe files warning display.

```
WIPEINFO C:\*.BAK
```

**Drive Letters.** If a drive letter is specified with no file wildcard or path name the wipe drive function is automatically activated. The command below loads the Wipe Information and select wiping drive A. Example: WIPEINFO A:.

Since Wipe Information supports wiping multiple drives, with a single operation you can specify a list of drives for wiping. The command below specifies wiping both drive A and drive B. Example: WIPEINFO A: B:

**Method Switches.** Both the wipe file and wipe drive operations recognize the following switches that can be used to specify the wipe out method to be used.

/G#. This switch changes the wipe pattern to conform to the Department of Defense method, where # stands for the number of repetitions of the 0s and 1s portion of the wipe method.

/R#. This switch sets the number of times the wipe area will be written over. The default is 1.

/V#. This switch uses a value from 0 to 255, which represents the decimal value of the character used to overwrite the data.

**Wipe Area Switches.** The following switches affect the area of the disk that is affected by the wipe operation.

**/E (drive only).** This switch causes the drive wipe to clear only the data clusters that are not currently in use by files.

**/N (file only).** Specifies delete only, which affects the first letter in the directory and the FAT, but not the data clusters. Files can be unerased after this action.

**/K (file only).** Specifies wiping only the slack portion in the last cluster of existing files, if any.

**/S (file only).** Causes the program to include matching files in all directories below the starting directory.

For example, the command below clears all DBF files from the CLIENTS directory on drive D by writing the value 246 (F6 hex) three times:

```
WIPEINFO D:\CLIENTS\*.DBF /V246/R3
```

The pair of commands below, which might be used in a batch file, wipe clear all of the unused file space and any slack space stored at the end of existing files on drive C, using the fast version of the government wipe method. This ensures that the only data on the disk are those contained in active files:

```
WIPEINFO C: /E/G1
WIPEINFO C:\*.* /S/K/G1
```

## Other Uses

If you are not interested in wiping out data for security reasons, there are two other uses for which the WIPEFILE and WIPEDISK programs can be put to use.

**/N/S** This form of the Wipeinfo command can overcome a limitation in the DOS **DEL** command. The /N switch changes the action of the Wipeinfo command from wiping out the directory entry and data clusters associated with a file or group of files, to a command that duplicates the function of the DOS **DEL** command. The advantage of WIPEINFO lies in the fact that it can accept the /S (subdirectory) switch. This allows you to delete all the files beginning with a particular directory and include all the subdirectories. The DOS **DEL** command can erase only files in one directory at a time.

For example, the command below will delete all of the BAK backup files from drive C in all directories. Example: WIPEINFO *.BAK /N/S.

If using Version 6.0 you can add the /BATCH switch to eliminate the need to respond to any prompts. Example: WIPEINFO *.BAK /N/S/BATCH.

If you wanted to delete all of the files and directories from a disk you could use the *.* wildcard as shown below. The command below deletes all of the files and user-defined directories from disk A. Note that the Wipe Information program will delete a directory when all of the files in that directory are deleted. Example: WIPEINFO \*.* /N/S/BATCH.

If you wanted to limit the deletion to one branch of the directory tree you would start with the top directory you wanted to eliminate. The command below eliminates the \WINDOWS directory and all directories contained with it. Example: WIPEINFO \WINDOWS\*.* /S/N/BATCH.

Keep in mind that by default the Wipe Information program will not delete read-only or hidden files. In fact, when a read-only file is encountered, the program will stop and display a box which requires the user to press in order to continue the operation. If you are using the **/BATCH** switch with Version 6.0, read-only files are automatically skipped. You may want to use the File Find program to remove the attribute before you execute the wipe operation. Example:

```
FILEFIND \TEST\*.*/R-/BATCH
WIPEINFO \TEST\*.*/N/BATCH
```

In Version 6.0, where automatic batch operation is possible, you can create batch files that automatically wipe out data as part of a series of operations. The batch file below, called SAFEMOVE.BAT, moves a file from the current disk to a floppy in the drive. Once the file is copied, WIPEINFO is used to eradicate the file's data from the source disk, ensuring that the only copy of data is the one on the floppy disk. The **/G1** switch specifies the use of the DOD wipe method, but with only one write for 0s and 1s instead of the default three repetitions:

```
@ECHO OFF
COPY %1 /G1/BATCHWIPEINFO %1 /G1/BATCH
```

If you wanted to use the command to move the Norton Utilities READ.ME file to drive A you would enter SAFEMOVE \NU\READ.ME. The version of the same batch file shown below adds the use of the DOS batch command **IF**, which checks to see if the specified file can be found before the rest of the batch is executed. If the file is not found the program skips the copy and Wipe Information commands:

```
@ECHO OFF
IF NOT EXIST %1 GOTO QUIT
ECHO Safe Move File %1
COPY %1 A:
WIPEINFO %1 /G1/BATCH
ECHO File Moved
:QUIT
```

You can also take advantage of the delete only option to purge the disk of backup and temporary files that are accumulated by many applications. The example below, called CLEANUP.BAT, deletes all of the BAK and TMP files on drives C and D. The trick is to start each WIPEINFO at the root directory and use the **/S** switch to include all of the subdirectories:

```
@ECHO OFF
WIPEINFO C:\*.BAK /N/S/BATCH
WIPEINFO C:\*.TMP /N/S/BATCH
WIPEINFO D:\*.BAK /N/S/BATCH
WIPEINFO D:\*.TMP /N/S/BATCH
```

Keep in mind that Version 5.0 users can run the exact same batch files. The only difference is that 5.0 will ignore the **/BATCH** switch, resulting in the need for the user to respond to several prompts each time Wipe Information runs.

## Wipe Information Considerations

The use of Wipe Information to eradicate files does not in and of itself create a secure environment. The program depends on the user to apply the wipe out method to the data that need to be eradicated. The assumption is that the user is aware of where the data are stored. This is not as simple as you might think. Many applications create backup or temporary files as part of their operation. These files contain copies of all or part of the document, spreadsheet, or database you are working on.

In recent years the use of temporary or scratch files has increased as the size and memory demands of many applications has outgrown the 640K conventional memory limit of DOS. The temporary files allow an application to download information from RAM into disk storage, which is then reloaded at a later point, and the temporary file is erased. This is what Windows 3.0 does when it creates a SWP swap file. dBASE IV creates temporary files when performing some types of database query-by-example operations. Programs that have extensive UNDO features often use temporary backups. DOS creates temporary pipe files when filter programs are used.

However, you know from this book that the data stored in the temporary files are still on the disk and are potentially recoverable.

In order to create a secure environment you must make sure that you apply Wipe Information to all possible areas where data might be stored:

**Files.**  Use Wipe Information on the active files that need to be eradicated.

**Backup Files.**  Perform Wipe Information on any backup files that may have data related to the eradicated files. Backup files frequently use the extension BAK or contain special characters }BA or ~BA. Make sure that you include all of the possible backups in this process.

**Erased Temporary Files.**  Temporary files, such as the Windows SWP and TMP files, do not appear on the directory, although you can often find them with Unerase. In order to secure these areas, use the drive wipe option to wipe all unused clusters and then use the wipe files option to clean up the slack space at the end of files currently in use. The commands below illustrate a batch file that would secure drive C against data that were stored in temporary files:

```
WIPEINFO C: /E/G3/BATCH
WIPEINFO C:\*.* /S/K/G3/BATCH
```

If you are working on a network, you can wipe files or slack space on network disks. You cannot apply drive wiping to those disks. That must be done at some point when the drives are taken off the network and are being accessed in a single-user mode.

# Encryption

The Wipe Information programs are useful in preventing data from being recovered from erased files by unauthorized persons. But how can you protect information that is stored in an active file?

The answer is basically the same for computer-based data as it is for written information; that is, the use of codes and ciphers to translate ordinary information into something that can be understood only by people who possess the correct *key*. The art or process of translating information into and back from a secret code is called *cryptography*. *Encryption* refers specifically to the act of changing text to code and *decryption* the act of decoding information.

Writing in code is as old as history itself. The simplest form of code is to simply substitute one letter for another. For example, you might take a word like *byte* and replace each letter with the next letter in the alphabet resulting in *czuf*. Of course, simple codes such as this are relatively easy to break since certain letters and letter grouping occur frequently in any language. All words contain vowels, of which there are only six. Of the six, the letter *e* is by far the most commonly used vowel in English and *t* the most frequently used consonant.

By the beginning of the 20th century, modern nations, in particular Great Britain, began to place great emphasis on the use of codes and ciphers as part of military and diplomatic activity. The result was the beginning of a cryptographic arms race that has evolved very secure coding systems that can be easily implemented on the most modest computers. The system involves the use of a *key* word or phrase upon which the coding scheme is based. If you know the key and the method of encryption then you can decipher the information. The *key* is very important because it means that just knowing the method of encryption is not sufficient to allow for deciphering the message. The *key* is often implemented in the form of a *password*. In the case of the Norton Utilities this means that without the password no one, not even Norton Computing, can access the encrypted data.

It is important to keep in mind that it is only logical to observe that any code is potentially breakable, just as any lock can be eventually circumvented. The value of encryption is that the time, cost, and equipment necessary to break the code would far exceed the value of the information itself. For example, a super sophisticated computer might be able to crack a Department of Defense code, but it might require two years to do so. Chances are that the information would no longer be up to date by the time it was deciphered, so that for practical purposes the code is unbreakable.

The Diskreet program provides a variety of ways in which you can implement password-protected encryption for sensitive information. The program supports two methods of data encryption:

**Proprietary.** This is a method of password-protected encryption used by the Norton Utilities to provide a high level of security without slowing down operations significantly.

**DES.** The DES method conforms to the government's standard for data encryption. This method is a bit more secure than the Norton Utilities proprietary method, but it takes longer to implement.

In most cases where you are protecting yourself from unauthorized individuals, the Norton Utilities proprietary method is more than adequate. If you suspect that your data are subject to attack by agents of a large organization with significant resources, such as a government or a corporation, you can achieve an additional degree of security by using the DES method, which takes a bit longer to implement.

Security can be implemented on two levels:

**File by File.** The Diskreet program can be used to apply password protection to one or more individual files located anywhere in the system. Protection is created for a file by making an encrypted copy of an existing file. Once the encrypted file is created, access to that file can only be achieved by entering the correct password. Note that the original unencrypted version of the file is still open to access unless it is eradicated with Wipe Information.

**Secure Drives (Logical).** File-by-file encryption has a number of drawbacks, such as the need to supply and remember a password for each protected file. Secure operations can be simplified by the use of a logical device called an *NDisk*. An NDisk is actually a large hidden file. When the DISKREET.SYS driver is loaded the file is treated as if it were a separate drive in the system. The NDisk driver behaves like any other drive with the exception that all of the files stored on that drive are automatically encrypted. Access to any of the files in the NDisk is gained by entering a single password, eliminating the need to have a password for each file.

If you need encryption only on rare occasions, using the file-by-file method is sufficient. This method is straightforward and requires no advance set-up. However, if you work frequently with data that require password protection the NDisk approach offers a large number of significant advantages. Note that using an NDisk requires certain set-up operations, such as loading a device driver with the CONFIG.SYS file, which will use some system memory.

## Securing Individual Files

The simplest method of creating encrypted files is to use the Diskreet program on a file-by-file basis. This method is simpler than creating NDisks because it does not require the loading of a special device driver or the set up of special NDisk drives. Individually encrypted files can be treated just like ordinary DOS files in that they can be deleted, copied, backed up, or transferred via networks or telecommunications. Of course, only users with access to the Norton Utilities Diskreet program and the proper password can make use of these files.

The first dialog box displayed requires you to select either **Files** or **Disks.** Note that if you have not loaded the DISKREET.SYS driver you can only perform **Files** operations.

When you select **Files** the program displays the **Files** pull-down menu, which has three options:

**Encrypt.**  Select file and created encrypted version.

**Decrypt.**  Select encrypted file and convert to usable file.

**File Options.**  Select options related to file encryption such as the method and password used to secure the file.

The program displays a dialog box that shows the suggested name for the encrypted version of the file. The suggested name is the original file name with a **SEC** extension. Keep in mind that you do not have to use the suggested name nor the SEC extension. However, you should take into consideration that encrypted files are not distinguished from normal files in the disk directory. You should probably use the SEC or similar extensions for all encrypted files in order to facilitate identification of encrypted files. Note that Diskreet will not allow you to overwrite the original file with the encrypted version. Diskreet stores the original name and extension of the encrypted file in the encrypted version so that when the file is decrypted it is returned to its original name, regardless of what name is used for the encrypted version.

Once you have entered a file name for the encrypted version of the selected file, you are asked to enter a password. The password *must* be at least six characters in length and can be up to 40 characters. Passwords are *not case sensitive* so that you do not have to consider whether you enter lower- or uppercase letters. Unlike file names you can include spaces in the password. The best passwords are those that are unique enough not to be easy for someone to guess but simple enough to ensure that you accurately remember them. While spaces are permissible in a password, they should be used sparingly since you may not remember whether your password used a space or not between words.

Note that when you enter characters the program always shows * so that your password cannot be detected by someone looking at your screen. As a safety factor you are asked to enter the password a second time, on the assumption that if you enter it twice the same way you have correctly entered the password.

After the password has been accepted the program performs two actions:

**Copy File.**   The program makes a duplicate of the selected file.

**Encrypt File.**   The duplicate file is then converted from normal to a password-protected file.

When the process is completed a dialog box appears that tells you what file has been converted.

There are now two files on the disk—the original, SECURE.DOC, and the encrypted version, SECURE.SEC. The list shows the encrypted version of the original file along with the original, which was not affected by the process. Note that the encrypted version is slightly larger than the original.

For the most part the only recognizable item is the first nine letters, PNCICRYPT, which identifies the file as a Norton Utilities encrypted file. Note that you will probably hear several beeps. The beeps sound when DOS encounters a [Ctrl-g] value (Hex 07). You may have also noticed that only a small number of characters are displayed as compared to the original file. This is because the **TYPE** command terminates when the first [Ctrl-z], end of file, character is encountered. This does not mean that you have lost any data.

## Encrypt and Wipe

In the previous section, during the encryption process while a password-protected copy of the file was created, the original file remains. This method makes sense if you then plan to copy the encrypted version to a floppy or other disk where the original will not be present.

If you want to secure the data on the disk on which it currently resides, you need to go a bit further. The original file must be eradicated, not merely erased, from the disk, using a program such as Wipe Information. In addition it might be a good idea to protect the encrypted file from accidental editing or deletion by adding the read-only or hidden file attributes using a program such as File Find.

Diskreet offers a shortcut method that will automatically perform the functions of Wipe Information and File Find as part of the encryption process through the **File options** dialog box. Before you select **Encrypt,** display the options dialog box by entering f.

The dialog box allows you to select the encryption method, Norton Utilities proprietary, or DES. In addition there are four check boxes that add additional operations automatically to the basic encryption function:

**Wipe/Delete Original Files after Encryption.** This option automatically eradicates the original file, preventing any access to the protected data. Keep in mind that encrypted files are automatically wiped when you decrypt a file. That function is not affected by this option.

**Set Encrypted File to Hidden.** This option adds the hidden attribute to the encrypted file. The file will not appear in normal DOS directory listings.

**Set Encrypted File to Read-Only.** Add the read-only file attribute to the file.

**Use Same Password for Entire Session.** If selected, this option automatically uses the same password for all encrypt and decrypt operations. The program prompts you for a password, the first one that is needed. That password is used through the remainder of the current session automatically. This speeds up operations when you are encrypting and/or decrypting several files.

Note that when you exit this menu you can choose the **Save** or **OK** buttons. **Save** writes the current settings to the NU.INI file in the Norton Utilities home directory, establishing these options as the defaults for Diskreet. Selecting **OK** sets the options for this session only.

## Command-line Operations

You can also carry out encrypt and decrypt operations from DOS using the **/ENCRYPT, /DECRYPT,** and **/PASSWORD** switches. For example, suppose you wanted to retrieve the SECURE.DOC file from its encrypted form. Instead of loading the Diskreet program and using the menus and dialog boxes, you can take a shortcut by specifying the action, file, and password to use as part of the command. To decrypt SECURE.SEC, enter

```
diskreet /decrypt:secure.sec
/password:makesafe ↵
```

The program, using the information included with the command-line switches, automatically decrypts the file and wipes out the encrypted version, SECURE.SEC. The only pause is for a dialog box that confirms the operation. Enter↵

The program then exits back to DOS automatically.

Encrypting the file is done exactly the same way except that the **/ENCRYPT** switch is specified:

```
diskreet /encrypt:secure.doc
/password:makesafe ↵
```

Note that the program stops for the entry or acceptance of the encrypted file name. Enter ↵ (press 2 times).

### Encrypting a Group of Files

You can encrypt a group of files into a single encrypted file by specifying a file wildcard as the source. This can be done in the **File Name** box of the **Select files to encrypt** dialog box or as part of the Diskreet line command.

This command will encrypt all of the DBF database files in the current directory. Example: DISKREET /ENCRYPT:*.DBF /PASSWORD. When the program loads it will select the first matching file and suggest that as the name for the combined encrypted file. For example, if the first DBF file in the directory listing is CLIENTS.DBF the suggested encrypted file name will be CLIENTS.SEC. Since you are placing multiple files in a single encrypted file, you may want to change the name to better reflect the nature of the group of files. The result of this operation will be a single encrypted file, e.g., CLIENTS.SEC, that contains all of the DBF files.

When the file is decrypted, each of the individual files will be re-established as independent files just as they were before they were encrypted.

If you do not use the SEC file extension to indicate encrypted files you can locate encrypted files by using the File Find program to look for *PNCICRYPT*, which is found at the beginning of each encrypted file. The example locates all of the encrypted files on all available drives. Example: FILEFIND *:.*.* PNCICRYPT.

# NDisks

While encrypting individual files is useful, the process requires you to perform a separate operation for each file or group of files you want to encrypt or decrypt. In addition, file-by-file operations require you to run Diskreet from DOS.

From a security point of view, file-by-file operations place the burden on the user to remember to encrypt important data once they have finished work with a file. This means that every time you are away from the computer, e.g., for a break or lunch, you would have to exit your applications and use Diskreet to encrypt all sensitive files.

The Diskreet program offers a much more elegant solution to this problem, in the form of *NDisk*. An NDisk is actually a hidden, encrypted file that can be stored on any drive in the system, including floppy disks.

When you load the DISKREET.SYS driver, DOS will treat the NDisk files as if they were actual disk drives. The only differences between an NDisk drive and an actual drive is that any data stored on a NDisk drive is automatically encrypted and protected. NDisks have several major advantages over file-by-file encryption:

**One Password.** All of the files stored in a NDisk are protected by a single password. This makes gaining access to secure data simpler to deal with. If you want to create different levels of security you can create several NDisk drives and assign a different password to each drive. This would allow you to store some files in a NDisk, whose password is known to several people in your department, and to also maintain a more secure NDisk whose password is known only to the user.

**Encryption from within Applications.** Because DOS sees the NDisk drives as actual drives, you can automatically encrypt files through the applications you are using by storing the files on drive letters that correspond to the active NDisks. There is no need to exit an application in order to make the data secure, nor do you have to remember to go through any special procedures.

**Open upon Request.** NDisks can be set up to automatically prompt the user for a password while they are using an application should they attempt to access an NDisk drive. Once the password is entered the NDisk functions like a normal DOS drive.

**Hot Key Controls.** The key to NDisk security is your ability to quickly close NDisk drives so that unauthorized persons cannot gain access to the files. You can close (that is, make secure) all of the data stored in NDisks with a single keystroke.

**Batch Files.** You can integrate NDisk operations, including password protection, from within batch files.

## Setting Up NDisk Drives

In order to use NDisks you must perform two operations:

**Load the DISKREET.SYS Driver.** NDisk operations can only be implemented when the DISKREET.SYS driver has been loaded into memory using the CONFIG.SYS file. This is done by adding the following line to the CONFIG.SYS file:

```
DEVICE=C:\NU\DISKREET.SYS
```

**Define NDisks and Passwords.** Once the DISKREET.SYS has been loaded into memory the **Disks** portion of the Diskreet program can be accessed. The menus and dialog boxes allow you to set up one or more NDisk logical drives on any of the existing system disks. You can also select various operational options for the NDisks you define. The settings you select are stored in an initialization file called DISKREET.INI in the Norton Utilities home directory.

## Loading the Driver

You can modify the CONFIG.SYS file using a text editor or word processor. Recall that changes made to the CONFIG.SYS file have no affect on the *current* session. In order to actually reconfigure the DOS memory you must reboot the computer using the [Ctrl-Alt-Del] key combination.

When the DISKREET.SYS driver is loaded for the first time it displays the following information and pauses the execution of the CONFIG.SYS file until you respond by pressing a key.

```
No DISKREET config file to read(DISKREET.INI)
DISKREET's Main Password has been cleared.
Instant close keys have been reset to LEFT + RIGHT shift keys.
AUTO-CLOSE TIME-OUT interval has been set to five minutes and DISABLED.
Keyboard lock & screen blank has been DISABLED
NDISK drive count set to one.

* * * * * * * * * * * * *        PRESS ANY KEY TO CONTINUE        * * * * * * * * * * * * *
```

The message, which lists the current values and settings used by Diskreet, appears when no DISKREET.INI file can be found, which is the case the first time that you load the driver. The Diskreet driver pauses the program until the user responds by pressing a key.

When you press the key the program creates a new DISKREET.INI file using the settings shown in the message. The program also assigns a drive letter for the NDisk drive. The letter is the next available drive. For example, if you have a hard disk partitioned into C and D then the first NDisk will be assigned E.

If you are operating on a network work station the assignment of the Diskreet drive letters may have an effect on the drive letters available for network use. Many network operating systems assign drive letters to file server disks using commands stored in batch files. For example, on a computer with a hard drive C the file server might be assigned drive D. However, the Diskreet drive letter is assigned from the CONFIG.SYS file, which executes before any batch file. Thus, Diskreet would assign the NDisk drive D before the batch file executed. The network batch would have to be adjusted to use letter E. If you wanted multiple NDisks, e.g., D–G, then the network server would have to be changed to H. Note that the CONFIG.SYS command **LASTDRIVE** sets the upper limit on logical drive letters. Adding the command **LASTDRIVE=Z** to the CONFIG.SYS allows you the maximum number of logical drives.

The next time that the computer is booted only a short message will appear telling you the letter or letters assigned for NDisk. Note that even though a letter has been reserved for NDisk use, you must still create the actual NDisk file before you can be an NDisk.

It is important to keep in mind the difference between the NDisk files that are stored on the system's actual disk and the NDisk drive letters that are used as logical drives. The relationship between the logical drive letters and the NDisk files in which the data are stored is not fixed or permanent. You can assign any of the available drive letters to any of the NDisk files at any time. For example, you might create three different NDisk files on your hard disk but use only one drive letter, E. Depending on which file you wanted to access you would use the Diskreet program to assign the letter E to the desired NDisk file. If you wanted to have access to all three NDisk files simultaneously you would need to assign a different letter, e.g., E, F, G, to each of the NDisk files. However, the order in which they are assigned can be changed at any time.

## Creating NDisk Files

An NDisk file is a hidden file used by Diskreet to store encrypted data. To create an NDisk file you must specify three things:

**Physical Location.**  All NDisk files must reside on one of the physical disks in your system, hard or floppy. You cannot operate an NDisk from a remote server drive.

**Physical Size.**  The capacity of the NDisk is fixed when you create it. The size of the NDisk file sets the limit for the amount of data that can be stored in the NDisk. If an NDisk drive is filled during use it will not automatically expand to accommodate the additional data. Instead, DOS will treat the NDisk as if it were a physical disk that had reached its maximum storage capacity, even though there is still unused space on the hard disk that contains the NDisk. You can use the Diskreet command **Adjust Size** to expand or shrink the size of an NDisk file.

**Password.**  Each NDisk is assigned its own password. Keep in mind that the NDisk password is different from the *master* password for Diskreet. The master password is a separate password used to control access to the Diskreet set-up options. By default, the Diskreet master password is blank, meaning that a ↵ is treated as the correct password.

To create the NDisk file or files, load the Diskreet program and select the **Disks** button.

```
diskreet ↵ d
```

Since there are no NDisks defined, a message appears that reads "Do you wish to define a new Diskreet Drive?" Enter

```
y
```

A list box appears showing all of the drives in the system upon which you can create an NDisk file. Select the appropriate drive by entering the letter.

```
c
```

The program displays the **Make NDisk** dialog box, Figure 13–4. You can enter a 1–8 character name for the NDisk file as well as a description of the drive. The NDisk file will use the file name and add the characters @#! as an extension. Note that the NDisk file will be a hidden file, and, as such, it will not appear in the DOS directory listings.

**Show Audit**    This option, selected by default, causes Diskreet to display a screen summary of NDisk activity each time the NDisk is opened. One security feature included in the summary screen is the number of times, if any, that access to an NDisk was denied by the program because of an incorrect password. This may indicate that an unauthorized person has tried to gain access to your protected data.

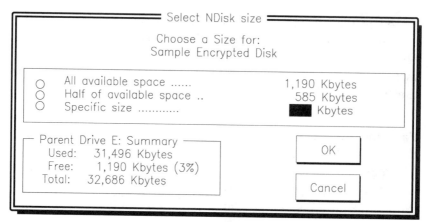

**Figure 13–4. Make NDisk dialog box.**

**Encryption**     Diskreet, by default, uses the Norton Utilities method of encryption. If more stringent security is required you can select DES. Note that DES will be significantly slower than the default method.

**Password Prompting**     When a user attempts to access data stored in an NDisk drive, the Diskreet program will display a pop-up box into which the user must enter the correct password. However, this procedure is complicated by the fact that DOS applications can use either of two very different methods for displaying information on the screen: text or high-resolution graphics. The Diskreet program is capable of displaying a password entry box only if the application is running in text mode. The box will not be visible if the application is running in graphics mode. Applications such as Lotus 1-2-3 Version 2.3 or Quattro 3.0 can operate in either text or graphics (also called *WYSISYG*).

One solution to the problem presented by graphics applications or applications that switch between graphics and text is to use an audio prompt; that is, a beep is sounded when a password is required. Note that the beep prompt is a bit more difficult to deal with since there is neither a corresponding box displayed to remind you of the meaning of the beep, or feedback of the characters of the password as you enter them. Diskreet supports the following options:

**Beep Only.**  If selected this NDisk will always use audio prompts and never display the password box in both text and graphics display modes. Whenever an attempt is made to access an NDisk drive the application will pause—no prompt or visual display at all—while the special tone is sounded.

If you enter the correct password the drive will be opened and the application will continue. If you enter an incorrect password or simply press ↵, the tone sounds again and the application remains paused. To skip the password entry press [Esc]. Note that entering [Esc] will cause the application to generate a DOS drive **Not ready** error. Select **Abort** to return control to the application.

**Pop-up Prompt Only.** This option causes Diskreet to always use the pop-up box as the prompt for a password, regardless of the current display mode. Note that if the application is operating in graphics mode when an attempt to access a closed NDisk is made, the application will appear to freeze because the text-based pop-up screen cannot be seen while graphics is active and the audio prompt has been turned off. If you are aware of the reason for the freeze, you would enter the correct password and press ↵. The application would then continue normally.

**Choose Automatically.** This option, the default, allows the program to use the pop-up box in text mode and the audio tone prompt when the graphics mode is active.

**Manually Open Only.** This option turns off the dynamic opening of this NDisk. The only way to gain access to the NDisk is to use the **Open** control button on the Diskreet program screen display. Thus, you must remember to open the NDisk *before* you run the application if you want to have access. Note that if you are running Windows 3.0 all NDisks are temporarily switched to manual operation.

In most cases you would use the default settings, including **Choose automatically,** for the password method. Create an NDisk called EXAMPLE by entering example [Tab] Sample Encrypted Disk ↵. The program next displays the **Select NDisk size** dialog box. This box is used to set the size of the file that will be used to store data directed to this NDisk. NDisk files are fixed-length files. When you first create an NDisk, the Diskreet program removes all of the space allocated to the NDisk from use by DOS by assigning those clusters to the NDisk hidden file. This means that even if you never store a single file in the NDisk, the space occupied by the NDisk file will not be available for other uses. Conversely, should you fill up the NDisk file, DOS will react as if you had actually filled up an entire disk. Neither DOS nor Diskreet will automatically enlarge the NDisk file once its size has been set. If you run out of space in an NDisk you will have to load the Diskreet program and manually adjust the size of the file, using the **Adjust Size** command located on the *Disk* menu.

The program creates two options for the size of the NDisk file based on the total amount of unused space on the current disk: all unused space and half the unused space. You also have the option, the default, of entering a value in kilobytes for the size of the file. Remember that the value you enter is the number of kilobytes; that is, to create a 1-megabyte drive enter 1000. In this case, create a 500K NDisk drive. Enter 500 ↵.

The last item in the NDisk definition is the password for the disk. Keep in mind that each NDisk you create has its own password. If all of the NDisk files require the same level of protection you can simplify their use by having a common password for all NDisks. If you want to share access to some NDisks but not others you can use different passwords. Keep in mind that the more passwords you use, the more likely you are to forget or confuse passwords. Forgetting a password results in data loss since there is no way to access the drive without the password. Enter

```
makesafe ↵
makesafe ↵
       ↵
```

## Assigning a Letter to an NDisk

When you have created the NDisk, the program then moves to a screen that matches the available NDisk letter to the NDisk file you are defining. By default, one drive letter is automatically available for use with NDisks. If your system contains C and D drives (typically, two partitions of a 32+ megabyte hard disk) the NDisk drive is E. Since there is only a single drive letter available, accept it as the default by entering ↵.

Once accepted, the program displays the NDisk audit screen that shows the date of creation, the last use, and the total number of successful and failed accesses, which currently show zero since this is a new NDisk. Continue by entering ↵.

The **Diskreet Disks** dialog box shows that the EXAMPLE NDisk has been assigned the logical drive letter E (Figure 13–5). This display is the main NDisk dialog box, which is used to operate NDisks after you have created the first NDisk. The box has four control buttons:

**Open.** In order for you to store or retrieve data in an NDisk, the disk must be opened. Opening an NDisk requires you to supply the password for that disk. By default, Diskreet will automatically prompt you for the

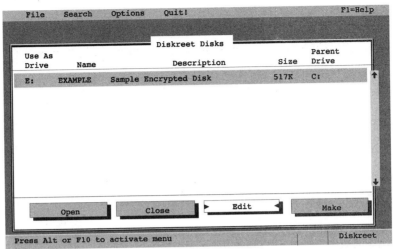

**Figure 13–5. NDisk listed in Diskreet dialog box.**

password when you attempt to access an NDisk drive. You can use the control button in this dialog box to manually open specific NDisk drives. A check mark will appear in front of the open disks.

**Close.** A closed NDisk is protected from access by anyone who does not know the correct password. The essential goal of NDisk operations is to ensure that any unauthorized persons are confronted with a *closed* NDisk. It is important to understand that when an NDisk is open, anyone can access the data. Protection comes from closing the NDisk when you are not using the data or when you are away from your computer. The button in this dialog box manually closes NDisk. To reopen a closed drive the correct password must be entered.

**Edit.** This option allows you to change the NDisk file name or Password prompting method. Note that once you create an NDisk you can change the encryption method, e.g., from Norton Utilities to DES.

When you edit an NDisk, you have an additional option, which does not appear in the dialog box when you create the disk, **Write protection.** The **Write protection** option will change the NDisk to a read-only disk. This means that files can be read from the NDisk, but not edited or deleted even when accessed with the correct password.

**Make.** This option allows you to add a new NDisk to the Diskreet system.

Close the NDisk by entering c.

The check mark is removed from the NDisk listing, indicating that the drive is closed. Exit the Diskreet program by entering [Alt-q].

## Using NDisks

Once you have created an NDisk file and assigned it to a drive letter, the NDisk drive can be treated as if it were an actual disk drive. Assuming that the NDisk is assigned drive letter E, you could reference drive E in any application or DOS command. As an example, copy all of the Norton Utilities Disk Editor program into the NDisk. Enter copy \NU\diskedit.exe e: ↵.

Because the E disk is closed, Diskreet pops up the password entry prompt box, Figure 13–6, automatically. Since the DOS command you entered requires access to the NDisk, you must be able to supply the correct password in order to complete the command.

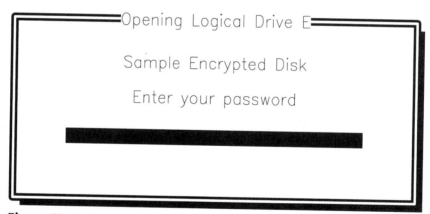

**Figure 13–6. Password prompt appears when access to an NDisk is attempted.**

Enter the password: makesafe↵.

When you enter the correct password, Diskreet displays the audit summary screen. Continue by entering ↵.

Once the NDisk had been opened, DOS was able to complete the command. Note that the NDisk assigned to letter E *remains open* until you enter a command that specifically closes that drive. This means that you can continue to enter commands that access the E drive without having to enter the password each time. For example, once opened, you can copy additional files to the NDisk with no prompting from Diskreet. Enter copy \NU\read.me e: ↵.

Since E is a full, logical DOS drive, it is possible to create subdirectories within the E disk. Create a new directory within the E drive by entering md e: \drivers ↵.

Place a copy of DISKREET.SYS into a logical subdirectory. Enter copy \NU\diskreet.sys e: \drivers ↵.

The E drive is available through applications as well as DOS. Load the File Find program. Enter filefind ↵.

If you want to access the NDisk, simply select the drive letter, in this case E, from the drive list. Because it is a logical drive, it will appear in all lists that contain logical and physical drives. Change to drive E by entering [Alt-f] d e. List all of the files on drive E by entering ↵ (press two times).

The list of files on drive E, shown below, resembles any other disk. When opened, NDisk operations are transparent with the exception of the additional time it takes to encrypt the files stored on the NDisk drive.

Exit the File Find program by entering [Alt-q].

## Closing NDisks

The security offered by NDisks is in effect only when the NDisks are *closed*. An *open* NDisk can be used by anyone who has access to your computer. It is therefore very important to make sure that whenever your computer is unattended the NDisks are closed. There are three ways to close the NDisks:

**Diskreet Dialog Box.** NDisks can be closed by selecting the **Close** command button from the Diskreet Drives dialog box. This method has the advantage that you can close individual NDisks one at a time. You can close all disks by using the **Close all** command located on the *Disk* menu, or the shortcut key [Alt-c]. The main disadvantage of this method is that you must run the Diskreet program in order to implement this method. This generally means exiting whatever you are working on in order to load the Diskreet program.

**Diskreet/CLOSE.** You can close all open NDisk drives from DOS without loading the entire Diskreet program, by using the /CLOSE switch. The advantage of the /CLOSE switch is that it can be executed from a batch file. The example below shows a batch file that loads Lotus 1-2-3

and then closes any NDisk opened during that session with the /CLOSE
switch.

```
@ECHO OFF
123
DISKREET /CLOSE
```

**Hot Key.** The fastest and least intrusive way to close the NDisks is with
the NDisk hot key combination. By default, the hot key is set as [Left-
Shift/Right-Shift]; that is, press and hold down the left Shift key and
then press the right Shift key. As soon as this combination is entered, all
NDisks are automatically closed and all of your data are protected
against access by anyone who does not know the password. The hot key
method has the advantage that it can be executed at any time, even when
you are working in an application. There is no need to exit the program
in order to close the NDisk.

   At this point you are currently at the DOS prompt. Close the NDisk by
entering diskreet /close ↵.
   The program does not load into its full screen dialog box interface but
simply issues the message "1 NDisks were closed." You can test this out by
trying to access drive E. Enter dir e: ↵.
   The Diskreet password box interrupts DOS before the command can be
executed. The E drive is now protected by Diskreet. Suppose that you
didn't know the password. Enter password ↵.
   Diskreet rejects the password as incorrect and displays a box with the
message "Password is invalid, try again." Enter ↵.
   The entry is again rejected as invalid. This will continue, and Diskreet
will keep count of the number of attempts, until you exit by entering [Esc]
(press two times).
   When you exit the password box without having made a valid entry,
Diskreet passes an error code to DOS. DOS then reacts to the command as
if you had entered any invalid drive letter, e.g., Z:, causing DOS to display
a "drive not ready" error. Your best choice is to enter A for abort. Enter a.
   This time open the E disk from inside an application. Load the Disk
Editor program by entering diskedit ↵ ↵.
   Open the drive selection dialog box by entering [Alt-d].
   The Disk Editor program displays an annotated drive list; that is, each
drive letter is labeled with text that identifies the type of drive. The Disk
Editor program, as part of the Norton Utilities, recognizes and labels NDisk
driver **Encrypted.** Select drive E by entering e.

You are prompted to enter the password for that NDisk. In this instance, attempt to skip the password protection by entering [Esc].

The program displays the **Error** dialog box with control buttons for **Abort** or **Retry.** This confirms that the password protection prevents unauthorized access from within applications. Retry the access and enter the correct password. Enter r makesafe ↵. The program displays the audit screen but there are two differences. First, the word **FAILED** flashes on the right side of the box. This is done to show you that the last time an attempt to access the encrypted drive was made the user failed to enter the correct password. If the failure was not made by you this warning alerts you to the fact that someone else has been trying to get at your protected data. Second, the continue message requires the entry of [Esc] rather than any key. This is also related to the failed access. The key required is changed to ensure that you pay attention to the message. Enter [Esc].

The program then displays the information from the E drive. Suppose that you need to leave your computer, but you don't want to stop what you are doing. You can use the hot key to close the NDisks. Enter [Left-Shift/Right-Shift].

The hot key combination does not produce any visual or audio response. How can you tell if it worked? The answer is that you should try to access some data on the E drive. For example, display the contents of the READ.ME file. Enter [Alt-f]. Because the E drive is now closed, the command [Alt-f], which displays a list of files on the current drive, causes Diskreet to activate the password entry box. Enter the correct password. Enter makesafe ↵.

The program can now display the **File Select** dialog box. Exit the program by entering [Esc] [Esc] y.

## NDisk Close Options

The use of the hot key to close NDisk with a single keystroke greatly enhances the security provided by Diskreet, since it makes it quick and easy to ensure that data are safely stored in encrypted NDisks. There are three optional features found on the Diskreet *Options* menu that can further enhance your security.

**Lock Keyboard and Blank Screen**    By default, the hot key will close all open NDisks. However, if you are working with sensitive data when you have to leave the computer unattended you may find that simply closing the drives is not sufficient, since others can read and edit data are displayed on the screen or currently loaded into memory. Keep in mind that many applications such as WordPerfect or Lotus 1-2-3 read an entire file into memory. Closing the NDisk drives will not remove the information from the screen, nor will the password protection be invoked until an attempt is made to save or load another file. When selected, the **Keyboard & screen lock** option causes your screen to blank and your keyboard to lock.

When locked, the keyboard will not react to any entries, with the exception of the entry of the correct *main password*. Note that the *main password* is not the same as the password used for specific NDisk drives. By default, the main password for the Diskreet system is blank, meaning that ⏎ functions as the password. In order to create an actual main password you must use the **Change main password** command on the *Options* menu. Note that the screen and keyboard lock function will work with a blank password, but, naturally, the level of security is very low since that is probably the first key anyone would press.

**Timed Auto Close**    The one gap in the hot key close procedure is that even though it is simple, it still requires you to enter the hot key. As an extra precaution you can set Diskreet to automatically close all Ndisk drives if the keyboard is not used for a specified number of minutes, e.g., five minutes. This ensures that your computer will have only a limited window of vulnerability should you leave your computer and forget to close the NDisks. Note that the auto-timed close *only closes* the NDisks. It does *not* blank the screen or lock the keyboard. This means that data left on the screen and contained in memory are still accessible by anyone who uses your computer. The protection will be invoked when a disk access is required. By default this option is disabled and the default time is set at five minutes. You can activate this option by entering [Alt-o] a [space]. You can also change the value for the number of minutes to a number between 1 and 99. Keep in mind that when active, the disks will be automatically closed without any prompts or tones. You will discover that the disks have been automatically locked when you attempt to access one and the password box appears.

**Wipe Released Clusters**    When you change the size of an NDisk or delete an NDisk from the system, the data clusters formerly used by the NDisk will be released to the general operating system as unused clusters. As an additional level of security you can select, using the **Security** option, to have these clusters wiped with the Norton Utilities or DOD methods.

Setting up the keyboard and screen lock requires two steps: selection of the lock option and entry of a main password. Load the Diskreet program by entering diskreet ⏎ d.

Change the main password by using the **Change main password** command located on the *Options* menu. Enter [Alt-o] c ↵. The program asks you to enter the *current* main password. By default, ↵ is used as the main password. Enter ↵.

In this example use the main password *MAINWORD*.

```
mainword ↵
mainword ↵
```

Next, display the **Keyboard and Screen Lock Settings** dialog box by entering [Alt-o] k.

This box contains three options that affect hot key operation:

**Close Disks.**  Activates NDisk closing.

**Locking.**  Activates keyboard lock and screen blanking.

**Hot Key**.  You can change the hot key combination that is used to invoke the quick close and/or lock feature from the default, left and right shifts, to any of the other combinations available. This option is useful if the Diskreet hot key conflicts with another TSR program you are using, e.g., Sidekick also uses left and right shift as its hot key.

It is important to note that you can select close disks and/or locking for the hot key operation. You may want to use the blank/lock option, but not bother to invoke disk closing. This would allow you to return to your application, after entering the main password and not have to then enter passwords for the NDisks as well. In this case, add the locking feature by entering [Tab] [Space] ↵.

Exit the program by entering [Alt-q].

Activate the locking feature by entering the hot key combination. Note that the blank/lock will take effect when you release both keys. Enter [Left-Shift/Right-Shift].

The screen is blank. Enter ↵ [Esc].

Each time you enter a key that is not part of the password, the program sounds a series of tones to let you know that the computer is on but not available. Enter makesafe ↵.

The program sounds the warning tones when you enter the password because *MAKESAFE* is the password for the EXAMPLE NDisk, not the main program password, which is required to unlock the computer. Enter mainword ↵.

The screen returns to the exact display that was there when the hot key was invoked to freeze the computer. Note that none of the keys entered while the computer was frozen are passed through to DOS, so that incorrect passwords have no effect on any application that was active when you locked the computer.

## Changing NDisks

You can create as many NDisks as you have room for in your system. However, you can only open an NDisk if you have a drive letter available to which you can assign the NDisk. By default, Diskreet reserves the next drive letter beyond those actually used for physical disks as the NDisk letter. If you use this default you can have many NDisks, but you can only open one at a time.

If you have more than one NDisk you will need to use the Diskreet Disks dialog box to switch the drive letter designation from one NDisk to another. For example, suppose that you have two NDisks, EXAMPLE and SPE-CIAL, created on your hard disk. By default EXAMPLE is assigned to logical drive E. If you wanted to switch E to the *SPECIAL* NDisk you would do the following:

**Select New NDisk.**  Load the Diskreet program, choose Disks, and use the mouse or arrow keys to highlight the name **SPECIAL** in the dialog box.

**Open Disk.**  Select the **Open** command button (type O). A dialog box will appear with the list of available disk letters. If you have only one disk letter defined, this box is superfluous since you have not options. Press ↵.

**Enter NDisk Password.**  Enter the password for the disk you want to assign to the letter. Note that this is not the main program password, but the password assigned to that specific NDisk.

The NDisk letter will now be assigned to the new NDisk, e.g., SPECIAL. Note that Diskreet records in the DISKREET.INI file the defined NDisks and which one was last assigned which letter. This means that the next time you boot the system, Diskreet will reassign the drive letter according to the last selection made in the previous session.

# Opening Multiple NDisks

If you want to open more than one NDisk at a time you must change the **System settings** to allow Diskreet to use additional drive letters. You can use up to five letters for NDisk operations. The drive letters are assigned consecutively, starting with the drive letter following the last physical drive in your system. For example, if the first NDisk letter is **E**, that is, physical disks **C** and **D** installed in the computer, the additional NDisk letters available will be **F, G, H,** and **I.**

The number of drive letters allocated is determined by the setting selected in the **System Setting** dialog box located on the *Options* menu. Display the dialog box by entering [Alt-o] s from the Diskreet Drives dialog box.

In order to gain access to this dialog box you must enter the current main program password. When you have selected the drive letters desired, select OK. The program displays a dialog box that asks you if you want to restart (that is, reboot) the system. The number of drives available is set during the boot process when the Diskreet driver is loaded into memory. In order for the new settings to have an effect the driver must be reloaded, requiring the entire system to be rebooted.

When you reboot the system you can use the Diskreet Drives dialog box to assign the drive letters to the NDisk files, as discussed in the previous section.

# Auto Opening

By default, all NDisks are *closed* when the system is booted. The disks will be opened when an attempt is made to access the disks or when the **Open** control button on the Diskreet Drives dialog box is selected.

If you want to automatically be prompted to open one or more NDisks each time the system is booted, you can use the **Startup NDisks** dialog box to select the disks.

When you select **Startup Disks** from the *Options* menu, the program lists the currently assigned NDisks showing their drive letter, name, description, the location of the NDisk file, and a Yes or No for *Prompt At Boot*. By default all drives are set to **No**. The **Edit** control button allows you to change the boot characteristic of the drive by selecting the **As soon as machine starts up** option.

## Changing and Deleting NDisks

You can change the size or delete NDisks entirely using the commands found on the *Disk* menu. Recall that the capacity of the NDisks is fixed when you first create the hidden file that serves as the NDisk. If you find that you have over- or underestimated the amount of space required for the NDisk, you can shrink or expand the NDisk by selecting the **Adjust NDisk Size** option from the *Disk* menu. Note that the disk must be closed in order to change its size. If the NDisk is open you will be prompted to close it.

When you have selected the disk to change, the program will scan the NDisk and summarize its current usage as shown below.

```
Used:      292
Free:      208 (41%)
Total:     500 KBytes
```

Along with the statistical summary are control buttons **Expand** and **Shrink,** which allow you to increase or reduce the amount of disk space allocated to the NDisk. When you select either option, a dialog box appears that summarizes the NDisk usage, the host disk usage, and gives you options for changing the size:

**Maximum Expansion/Reduction.**   Shows the largest amount of change possible for the current NDisk.

**Half Expansion/Reduction.**   Half of the maximum value.

**Quick Expansion/Reduction.**   This value is the amount of change that can perform in the least amount of time based on the fragmentation of the disk or NDisk.

**Specific Size.**   Enter a value in kilobytes from 1 to the maximum.

Note that clusters released from use when an NDisk is reduced in size will still contain encrypted data. You may want to have these clusters automatically wiped clear using Wipe Information methods. This can be accomplished by selecting **Security** from the *Options* menu.

The **Delete** command located on the *Disks* menu deletes an entire NDisk including all of the files in the NDisk. Note that you can also delete an NDisk file directly from the disk using a program that will remove hidden and read-only files such as Wipe Information. Note that if you use Wipe Information you must select the **Hidden** and **Read-only** file switches in order to delete or wipe the NDisk files.

## Copying NDisks and Files

When an NDisk is open, you can use the DOS **COPY** or **XCOPY** commands to copy any of the files in the NDisk to any other disk in the system. If the file is copied to a normal disk, not an NDisk, the file is stored in normal format. In other words, copying a file from an open NDisk to a normal disk automatically *decrypts* the file.

The NDisk files themselves cannot be copies with the **COPY** or **XCOPY** commands because they are marked with the hidden file attribute. In order to facilitate duplication and backup of NDisk files, the program provides the /**SHOW** switch. This switch removes the hidden and read-only attributes from the NDisks on a selected drive. The NDisk files can then be manipulated using DOS commands such as **DEL, COPY,** and **XCOPY**.

For example, to show the NDisks on the current drive you would enter: DISKREET /SHOW.

You can identify an NDisk file by the @#! file extension. You can show NDisk on drives other than the current drive by adding the drive letter. The command below shows NDisk on drive A. Note you can only specify one drive at a time. Example: DISKREET /SHOW:A. To return the NDisk to their normal file attributes use the /**HIDE** switch. The example below returns the attributes to any NDisks on the current drive. Example: DISKREET /HIDE.

If you want to back up the NDisks on the current drive to a floppy in drive A using the DOS **COPY** command, you would use the following sequence of commands:

```
DISKREET /SHOW
COPY *.@#! A:
DISKREET /HIDE
```

Before you copy the NDisks you can check to see if the target disk has enough room for the NDisk files using the **File Find** command. Note that File Find can perform the operation on the NDisk files even when they are hidden so this command need not be preceded by **DISKREET /SHOW**. Example: FILEFIND *.@#! /TARGET:A.

Note that if you delete NDisks with the DOS **DEL** command you should use Wipe Information to wipe the unused space.

If you want to back up the files rather than copy them, you can use the DOS **BACKUP** command. Note that **BACKUP**, like File Find, will operate on hidden files so that DISKREET /**SHOW** is not necessary. Example: BACKUP C:\*.@#! A:.

Keep in mind the difference between files that have been copied and those that have been backed up. A copied file is exactly like the original. With an NDisk file, you can access the files stored in the copy exactly as you would the original, using the same password you assigned to the original file. The **BACKUP** command slightly compresses the files to maximize the storage capacity of the target disk. The backed-up files cannot be accessed from the backup disk. Instead, they must be copied back to the hard disk with the **RESTORE** program before they can be used.

NDisk files that have been shown, but not hidden again, can be used for storage. However, each time you access a nonhidden NDisk a special message will be generated reminding you to hide the file for maximum security.

## Windows 3.0 and Diskreet

Diskreet NDisks can be used with Windows 3.0, but with several restrictions. The key restriction is that you cannot use any of the memory-resident functions of Diskreet while Windows is active. When you run Windows, the auto-open, quick close, lock/blank, and timed-close features will not operate. In fact, Diskreet will pause the Windows loading process to display a message informing you that these features are no longer active. When you exit Windows, Diskreet will return to normal operation. Note that does not mean that you cannot use Windows with NDisk drives. You can, if you open the desired NDisks *before* you load Windows. For example, if you open drive E as the NDisk EXAMPLE, you can access any of the files in that NDisk from Windows. In addition, you can, assuming you have sufficient memory, run the Diskreet program in a DOS window under Windows (Figure 13–7). This approach is most practical if you are running Windows in the Standard or Enhanced modes. You can open and close NDisks from the Diskreet window.

If you frequently use Windows and would like to turn off the Diskreet warning message add the switch /**Q** to the Diskreet driver line in the CONFIG.SYS file. Example:

```
DEVICE = C:\NU\DISKREET.SYS /Q
```

With this option, Windows will load without the Diskreet message.

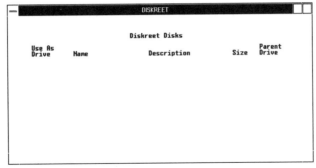

**Figure 13–7. Diskreet running under Windows 3.0.**

## Avoiding NDisks

Some commands or programs will scan all available disks for information. This would occur with the File Find when it is executed with a universal wildcard, e.g., FILEFIND *:*.*. If you want to avoid generating prompts for NDisks you can use the **/OFF** and **/ON** switches to temporarily disable and then restart Diskreet. The example below shows how you would run a universal search for batch files (BAT) but avoid any NDisks:

```
DISKREET /OFF
FILEFIND *:*.BAT
DISKREET /ON
```

You can also disable the Diskreet program and avoid loading it into memory by adding the /U (*unload*) switch to the CONFIG.SYS driver command:

```
DEVICE=C:\NU\DISKREET.SYS /U
```

The advantage of the /U option is that you do not have to delete the entire line from the CONFIG.SYS, assuming that you will want to reactivate Diskreet at a later point.

The /U option differs from merely turning Diskreet off with the **/OFF** switch, in two respects. First, /U prevents the Diskreet driver from using up memory. Second, programs that interact with the logical drive table may view the inactive NDisk drives as actual physical drives in the system. When Diskreet is loaded in memory but turned off, these programs may attempt to read the drives, causing an error. If /U is used the logical drive table will not contain the NDisk drive letters.

After you add the /U you must reboot the system in order to free the memory normally occupied by Diskreet. Erasing the /U will return Diskreet to normal operation the next time you boot the computer.

Diskreet provides an easy method for implementing the /U switch. In the **System Settings** dialog box the program displays an option labeled **Do not load the Ndisk Manager**.

## Memory Options

The Diskreet driver is designed to make use of additional, nonconventional memory where available in the form of high memory (UMB—upper memory blocks) on 286 and 386 machines. In addition, 386 machines with high-memory managers such as DOS 5.0, QEMM386, or 386MAX can reduce even further the impact of Diskreet on conventional memory by loading parts of the Diskreet driver in the unused addresses above 640K. For example, on a 286 machine with at least 64K of extended memory you can reduce the impact of the Diskreet driver on conventional memory by about 35K by loading the HIMEM.SYS driver (supplied with DOS 4.xx) as part of the CONFIG.SYS. This would leave only about 10K of the Diskreet driver in conventional memory:

```
DEVICE=C:\DOS\HIMEM.SYS
DEVICE=C:\NU\DISKREET.SYS
```

If you are using a memory manager on a 386 machine the impact can be further reduced to about 1.3K of conventional memory.

Diskreet is designed to locate and use these types of additional memory if available. However, in some cases you may need or want to disable the use of these special types of memory to avoid conflicts with other drivers or software. Diskreet recognizes the following switches added to the Diskreet driver line in the CONFIG.SYS file.

**/NOHMA.**   This switch turns off the use of XMS high memory in 286 or 386 machines with extended memory running HIMEM.SYS. When used, it forces Diskreet to load into conventional memory. This leaves the HMA area open for use by other XMS-compatible applications such as Windows 3.0. DEVICE = C:\NU\DISKREET.SYS/NOHMA.

**/SKIPHIGH.**   This switch will prevent the Diskreet driver from using high memory made available by memory managers in DOS 5.0, QEMM386, or 386MAX. You would use this switch when you wanted to preserve high memory space for other applications that you want to place into high memory. Example: DEVICE = C:\NU\DISKREET.SYS/SKIPHIGH.

**/A20ON.** The A20 line is a hardware address line used by some programs for access to extended memory. In most cases this line is directly manipulated (that is, turned on or off) by applications. If you are experiencing problems with network operations or serial communication, you may be able to eliminate these by activating the A20 line with this switch. Note that such conflicts are the result of complicated interactions between various drivers and applications and that the use of this switch may result in other problems elsewhere in the system. Example: DEVICE = C:\NU\DISKREET.SYS/A20ON.

If you want to force Diskreet entirely into conventional memory on a 386 you may need to use both **/NOHMA** and **/SKIPHIGH** together, since most memory managers on 386 machines implement both types of memory. Example: DEVICE = C:\NU\DISKREET.SYS /SKIPHIGH/NOHMA.

# Summary

This chapter dealt with the Norton Utilities programs and features that are designed to help you enhance the security of data and programs stored on your computer.

**Viruses**    A computer virus is a program that is designed to disrupt or destroy the normal functioning of your computer. Virus programs are generally malicious and are designed to operate without the knowledge of the user.

**Disk Monitoring**    The Disk Monitor program is designed to provide a means by which users can prevent programs (such as computer viruses) from writing information to disks. When loaded into memory, the Disk Monitor program will prompt the user whenever a disk write operation is initiated for the protected area of the disk. The user can then decide if the operation should be allowed or not. The Disk Monitor program can protect the system area of the disk, specific files, or the entire disk. The most common area attacked by viruses is the system area.

**Wipe Information**    Normal DOS deletions or hard disk formats do not eradicate information stored in the data area of the disk. This information is, in theory, recoverable, using programs such as Unerase and Disk Editor. In order to ensure that deleted information is eradicated beyond recovery, for the purpose of security you must employ the Wipe Information program. Wipe Information performs one or more overwrite operations on selected files or entire disks. The operations can be user defined or can implement government-approved Department of Defense standards for data security.

**Encryption**    Encryption allows you to place password protection on computer files so that they can be accessed only by persons who can supply the correct password. The Diskreet program can be used to create an encrypted version of any file or group of files.

**Ndisks**    An NDisk is a special, hidden file that will function as a logical disk when the DISKREET.SYS driver is loaded into memory. NDisk drives automatically encrypt and password protect any file that is copied onto that drive. All of the files in a given NDisk are protected by a single password, making the task of protecting a large number of files simpler.

# 14 Hard Disk Maintenance

One of the most valuable and vulnerable components of your computer system is your hard disk drive. Hard disks are subject to a number of different types of problems. The Norton Utilities provides several special programs that are designed to address various types of problems that can occur with your hard disk. In this chapter the use of these programs to fix and, when possible, prevent hard disk problems is explained.

The programs discussed in this chapter are not very difficult to use since most of their operations are automatic. However, in order to understand what these programs do you need to know a bit about how disks work. If you are new to the concepts of hard disk organization you should look at Chapter 4, which explains in detail how disks are organized and how DOS stores and retrieves data from disks.

## Hard Disk Problems

The ability to store and retrieve data from a hard disk is crucial to the operation of a computer system. Unlike the monitor or the memory chips, the hard disk contains a large number of moving parts that are subject to mechanical errors. Hard disks and printers are the most vulnerable components of a computer system because of the mechanical errors that can occur over time and with increasing frequency the older the disk.

The key to hard disk maintenance is to locate problems before they affect your data. It is important to remember that no matter what other precautions you take, *backing up* the data on your hard disk is the *best* way to protect yourself from disaster. If you do not back up on a regular basis you should consider using a high-speed backup program such as the Norton Backup.[1]

Hard disks can develop four basic types of problems:

**Logic Errors.** Logic errors are problems that occur in the tables and directories that DOS uses to keep track of files. The most common logical

---

1. The Norton Backup program is sold separately from the Norton Utilities.

error is a *lost cluster*. A lost cluster is a cluster that appears to be in use by a file but is not actually allocated to any of the files on the disk.

**Soft Errors.**  A *soft* error occurs when corrupted data are found on the disk. The term *soft* indicates that the problem can be resolved by over-writing the corrupted data with valid data. Soft errors can often lead to data losses. Soft errors are particularly damaging if they occur in the system area of the disk, since that area contains information that controls the allocation of data clusters.

**Hard Errors.**  Hard errors behave much like soft errors in that the data read from the disk is incorrect or corrupted. The difference is that hard errors reflect a physical defect in the surface of the disk that cannot be fixed by writing new data to that area. Once it is determined that a hard error exists, the best that can be done is to mark the area as unusable and avoid writing data in that area of the disk.

**Alignment Errors.**  A large number of hard errors that accumulate on hard disks are the result of small changes in the alignment of the disk drive heads as compared to the disk media. Over time, these small changes can result in the inability of the hard disk to read certain areas of the disk because the head is positioned slightly differently with respect to the disk sector than it was when the data were first written. The majority of these errors can be corrected, often without the loss of data, by making small adjustments to the sector locations so that they once again align correctly with the drive heads.

The Norton Utilities contains programs dealing with all of the errors described above and, where possible, corrects those errors.

# Testing Your Disk

The Norton Utilities provides two programs that can be used to test your disk in order to ensure the integrity of your disk:

**The Norton Disk Doctor.**  The Norton Disk Doctor analyzes and tests the *high-level* disk structures used by DOS to organize data storage. The program checks the partition table, boot record (sector), File Allocation Table (FAT), and the directory tree to look for anomalies and errors. In addition, the program will perform a test of all of the data clusters on the disk as well. When possible, the program will correct any errors it encounters while testing the disk. Note that this program can be used on all physical disks that are available in the system, including floppy disks. The program will not operate on purely logical disks such as NDisks or on network server drives.

**Calibrate.**  This program is used to test and analyze the *low-level* structures that support DOS file operations. Recall Chapter 4, section "What Is Formatting?" that all disks undergo two types of formatting before they are able to be used by DOS. The first formatting, called the *low-level* format, creates the basic three-dimensional architecture of the disk, which consists of sides, tracks, and sectors. As part of this process a *header* is written on the disk for each sector. The header contains the information needed by the hard disk controller.

Normally, the information written on the disk during the low-level format remains unchanged throughout the life of the hard disk, unless the disk is subjected to a new low-level format. This is rarely done because a low-level format destroys all data stored on the disk. In addition, low-level formatting often requires a special program to perform the low-level format. Calibrate is able to check, refresh, or update the information stored during the low-level formatting process without disturbing any of the DOS data structures. This increases hard disk reliability and can even correct problems before they manifest themselves in actual DOS errors.

Calibrate can also adjust the sector *interleave* factor, discussed in Chapter 7, which affects the transfer rate of data stored on the hard disk.

Note that Calibrate is much more sensitive to differences in disk hardware than Norton Disk Doctor since it works on the low-level format, which is below the level at which DOS operates. Some hard disk controllers feed DOS misleading information about the actual physical structure of the disk. These controllers are called *translating* controllers because they modify DOS instructions to fit the actual structure of disk. In most cases, this is done so that the computer can operate a disk with more tracks than DOS would normally support. Special types of disks such as SCSI, EDSI, and IDE, which use translating controllers, can work with Calibrate but do not allow for changes in the interleave factor. Note that Calibrate will operate only on compatible hard disks. It will not operate on logical drives, network drives, or floppy drives.

IDE drives do not use conventional disk drive controller boards. The actual controller for the drive is built into the drive. These drives are supplied with a low-level format placed on the disk at the factory. Note that the IDE low-level format is performed with special equipment. Software programs that perform low-level formats on hard disks cannot reproduce the type of low-level format required by IDE drives. You cannot change the interleave factor on an IDE drive but you can reliably perform pattern testing.

Use of these two programs can help you locate, correct, and prevent disk errors, problems, and data losses. They were designed to be used on a periodic basis so that disk problems can be caught and corrected at the earliest possible stage, reducing the possibility of data loss.

## Preparations for Disk Tests

Before you use the Norton Disk Doctor or the Calibrate program, there are several points to take into consideration.

**TSR Programs**    TSR (memory-resident) programs used on DOS machines are subject to various types of conflicts and incompatibilities. Recall from Chapter 7, in the section "Advanced Memory Information," that TSR programs will often intercept instructions sent to DOS to perform various operations such as reading or writing disk information to special subroutines. For example, the Disk Monitor and Norton Cache programs are involved in each disk operation conducted while they are resident in memory. If you experience problems using Norton Disk Doctor or Calibrate you should try booting your computer with a *vanilla* configuration. A *vanilla configuration* means that you boot your computer so that the memory contains the absolute minimum information, allowing your DOS version to operate with only its default settings.

The best way to create a vanilla environment is to boot your computer from a floppy disk rather than from the hard disk. Note that DOS computers will always[2] check drive A before they boot from the hard disk. If a system disk is found in drive A then the computer boots from that disk and uses the CONFIG.SYS and AUTOEXEC.BAT on the floppy, ignoring the hard disk. The advantage of this method is that you do not have to change your hard disk set-up in order to operate the computer with a vanilla configuration.

---

2.  Some computer ROMs, such as those used on the IBM PS1 computer, have an option that sets the computer to ignore drive A entirely. If you want to boot this computer from the floppy drive you will have to run the CUSTOMIZ program and select *Try diskette first*.

**Correction Disk** When the Norton Disk Doctor encounters an error, as a safety precaution it will copy the data it considers in error to another disk, before it makes the correction. This allows you to undo changes made by the program if necessary. When you run Norton Disk Doctor you should make sure that you have a disk available to hold the correction files. If you have a single hard disk then you should format a blank floppy disk before you begin running Norton Disk Doctor. If you have several hard disks—either physical, partitions, or network drives—available, you can use any of those as the correction disk. The program writes a file called NDDUNDO.DAT in the root directory of the correction drive.

When corrections are about to be written to the disk, the Norton Disk Doctor will display a dialog box. In Version 5.0 you can select the drive onto which you want to place the undo file, or select **Cancel** to skip creation of the Undo information. Note that **Cancel** will allow the corrections to take place with no undo ability.

Version 6.0 uses two dialog boxes, the first of which provides a third option, **Exit to Dos.** This option allows you to cancel the diagnosis without making the correction. You would use this option if you wanted to maintain an Undo file but did not have a correction disk formatted at the time. In Version 5.0 the only way to exit without making the correction at this point is to reboot the computer.

Note that the Norton Disk Doctor in all versions will automatically overwrite any existing NDDUNDO.DAT files encountered on the correction disk so that data from previous corrections will be overwritten with the latest set of information.

Creating a *vanilla* disk simply requires that you format a floppy as a system disk. Example: SFORMAT A:/S/A.

Once the disk is formatted you may want to add a CONFIG.SYS file to it. Setting the files and buffers will increase the operational efficiency of the Norton Utilities programs. An example of a simple CONFIG.SYS is shown below:

```
FILES=20
BUFFERS=20
```

If your hard disk is partitioned into several drives using special software such as On Track's DMDRVR.BIN or Speedstar's HARDRIVE.SYS, you *must* include these drivers in the CONFIG.SYS if you want to access partitions on the hard disk other than C:. You can copy the driver, DMDRVR.BIN or HARDRIVE.SYS, to drive A and then add a line to the CONFIG.SYS:

```
FILES=20
BUFFERS=20
DEVICE=HARDDRIVE.SYS
```

Note that you can load a device driver from drive C (the first partition on the hard disk) without having to copy it to the floppy. Assuming that the device driver file HARDDRIVE.SYS is stored in the root directory of C:, you could add the following line to the CONFIG.SYS on drive A. Example:

This method leaves you more room in the floppy disk should it be needed for other files.

An AUTOEXEC.BAT file on the floppy is optional, but in most cases it would be useful to use the AUTOEXEC.BAT to open a DOS search path to the Norton Utilities directory and also to set the DOS prompt style to include the directory name. Below is a sample AUTOEXEC.BAT:

```
@ECHO OFF
PROMPT $p$g
PATH C:\NU;
```

Once booted with this floppy, you can execute the Norton Disk Doctor and/or Calibrate, free from TSR program conflicts. To restore the computer to its normal configuration, simply remove the floppy and reboot.

## Checking Disks with the Norton Disk Doctor

The Norton Disk Doctor is designed to test and, when possible, fix the high-level structures maintained by DOS in order to implement its file storage system. The program performs a variety of tests that determine the status of the disk. The tests fall into two classifications: system area tests and data area tests. The system area tests are performed on the tables and directories and take only a few moments to complete. The data area tests examine all of the data clusters on the disk and take considerably longer time.

The Norton Disk Doctor program first appeared in Version 4.5 of the Norton Utilities. In Version 5.0 the name was changed to the Norton Disk Doctor II. In Version 6.0 the name has reverted to simply the Norton Disk Doctor. Versions 5.0 and 6.0 are functionally equivalent.

Load the Norton Disk Doctor by entering ndd ↵.

The program begins with a dialog box that contains four control button options (Figure 14–1):

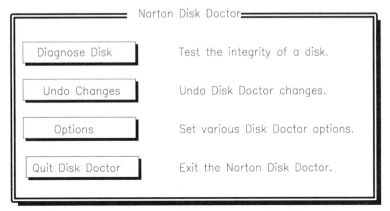

**Figure 14–1. Norton Disk Doctor main dialog box.**

**Diagnose Disk.** This option begins the Norton Disk Doctor testing by performing the system area tests on the selected drive.

**Undo Changes.** This option is used to restore the disk to its original contents if you have allowed the Norton Disk Doctor to make one or more corrections to the current disk. This option is possible because the program will create special backup files on another disk each time a correction is made. Note that you cannot place correction data on the disk being tested. You may want to format a floppy disk for this purpose before you begin the test.

**Options.** This option allows you to select default settings should you want to customize the program's operation.

**Quit Disk Doctor.** Exits the program.

## Diagnose a Disk

Select **Diagnose Disk** from the main dialog box when you want to perform a test. Enter d.

The program presents an annotated list of the drives available and their type; that is, floppy, 1st, or 2nd hard disk. Note that if a hard disk is partitioned, each partition appears as a separate drive letter. Select the disk you want to diagnose by entering its letter. Example: c ↵.

The first part of the Norton Disk Doctor's diagnosis is to carry out a series of six tests that operate on the basic structures used by DOS to maintain the file system on the disk. The program displays a bar showing its progress for each test. If an error is encountered, a box appears to explain the problem. Note that correction of the problems, if possible, will take place at the end of the entire battery of tests. The six tests are:

**Partition Table.**   This test analyzes the partition table that appears at the beginning of each hard disk for valid information. This test is mainly to determine if the table is readable.

**Boot Record.**   Checks the boot records that appear at the beginning of each disk or partition. This is primarily concerned with the readability of the boot record. Note that bootable disks store the boot loader program in the boot sector.

**File Allocation Tables.**   The program verifies the accuracy of both copies of the FAT. The first several bytes of the FAT are used to identify the disk and FAT type. Most hard disks use the hex value F8 to identify the media as a hard disk. However, some partitioning software will write a different value into the beginning of the FAT. If you are diagnosing a partition, e.g., drive D on a disk that is partitioned into C and D, the program may stop at the **File Allocation Tables** test and display the dialog box for **Media Descriptor Byte is Invalid.** The message states that if you have not experienced any problems with the disk you can skip this correction. However, making the correction will probably not have any adverse effect on the disk. In most cases the Norton Disk Doctor simply overwrites the first few bytes with the standard F8 FF FF hex. The advantage of making the change is that the program will not display the message the next time you diagnose the disk. Keep in mind that finding this type of error on the boot drive, e.g., C, is probably a much more serious problem and should be corrected.

**Directory Structure.**   This test analyzes all directories on the disk starting with the root directory and including all clusters on the disk allocated to user-defined directories. This test checks to see that the parent-child relationships that link the directories into a directory tree are accurate and consistent.

**File Structure.**   This test reads the file information stored in each directory to make sure that all of the file entries are readable and valid. A common error found by this test is an allocation size error. This occurs when the actual number of data clusters assigned to a file differs from the file size shown in the directory entry. At the end of the diagnosis you will be prompted to correct the file allocation errors. You should usually make these corrections. However, you need to be aware that a file allocation error may indicate that something went wrong when the file was being created.

# Lost and Cross-linked Clusters

The last test performed during the diagnosis is a cross-reference check between the directory information and the FAT information. Keep in mind that even if the disk has passed all of the other tests, it is still possible to have problems at this point. In fact, the errors found by this test are the most common errors that occur in the system area of the disk.

## Lost Cluster

The most common error found on hard or floppy disks in the system area is a *lost cluster*. A cluster is considered lost if the FAT shows that it is in use by a file; that is, the value in the FAT is not zero, but the cluster is not actually in use by any of the files currently on the disk.

How do clusters get lost? Typically, lost clusters are the result of a hang-up or crash that occurs while a file is being written or updated. This is because in most cases the directory entry for the file is written or updated *after* all of the data have been written. If you are experiencing problems with Windows 3.0 hanging up, chances are you will have some lost clusters on your disk. If the program is interrupted or the computer hangs up during this process the directory information will not reflect the newly written data.

Lost clusters do not actually pose a threat to data stored on the disk. In fact, many computer users operate their hard disks for months or years without being aware of the lost clusters that are on their disks. However, lost clusters do represent, in most cases, wasted space. Since they are marked as in use in the FAT, DOS will not overwrite these clusters. Yet, since they do not belong to a file, they are not of any actual use. You may choose to skip correction of lost clusters without endangering your data.

If lost clusters are located you are offered two choices: save or delete.

## Save

When you select to save lost clusters, the program collects the clusters into *chains* and assigns a file name to each chain. A chain is a series of consecutive lost clusters. The program works on the assumption that sequential blocks of clusters probably belong together. The file names used for the chains are generic names, e.g., FILE0000._DD[3]. Note that all of the files will be placed in the root directory of the drive. Saving the lost clusters is useful if you suspect that they might contain data that you have lost. You can use the Disk Editor or File Find programs to view the contents of the files. If you cannot find the information you can then delete the files so that the disk space can be reused.

## Delete

In many cases, if you are not concerned with recovering data that may be included in the lost cluster chains, you can simply have the program update the FAT to show these clusters as unused and therefore available for use for new data storage. Note this option performs a standard deletion—the data in the clusters are not wiped out.

## Cross-linked Clusters

Less common, but more serious than lost clusters, are *cross-linked* clusters. Cross-linked clusters refer to locations in the data area that are assigned more than once in the FAT; that is, they are included in the cluster list for more than one file. This is potentially a serious problem because it usually indicates a problem that will result in the loss of data, perhaps as much as the entire contents of the two files involved in the cross link.

Cross-linking is caused by the same factors as lost clusters. The difference in this case is that the directory and FAT entries have been modified to make it look as if one or more clusters is in use by two different files.

The simplest solution to cross-linked clusters is to simply delete both files and reuse the space. If you have copies of the files (e.g., on the original program disks) or you don't need the files, deletion is the best option.

If you select to fix the cross-linked files the program will examine the disk to determine how the clusters should be allocated.

If the program cannot resolve the conflict you may want to exit the Norton Disk Doctor and use the Disk Editor to examine the contents of the cluster or clusters in question. This would make sense only if one of the files in question was a text file since examining binary information such as that found in a COM or EXE file would be meaningless. If you find that all or part of the cluster contains useful text you can use the Disk Editor to lift the data out of the questionable cluster and into a valid file.

---

3. If you use the DOS **CHKDSK** command with the /F (fix) switch you can also collect chains of lost clusters into files. The DOS file names are FILE0000.CHK.

## Testing the Disk Surface

When all of the system area tests have been performed and you made or skipped any corrections suggested by the program, you will arrive at the **Surface Test** dialog box. The *surface* refers to the data area of the disk, which occupies 97 percent or more of the disk. The goal of this test is to determine if the data clusters can reliably store information.

The **Surface Test** dialog box contains four options that control the way that the surface test is performed.

### Test

The test type selects the scope of the test. The default selection, **Disk Test,** tests all of the clusters in the data area of the disk. Testing the entire disk will reveal problems that affect files and also locate unused areas that could create problems in the future. You can shorten the time required for the surface test by selecting **File Test.** This restricts the test to those data clusters that are actually in use by a file. You would use this test when you wanted to track down the source of a problem you had already encountered with an existing file.

### Test Type

The test types, **Daily** and **Weekly**, refer to tests of two different intensities. The **Daily** test is designed to certify that the data on the disk are readable. The **Weekly** test goes further by actually verifying the accuracy of the data that are being read. The **Weekly** test takes significantly longer than the **Daily** test. The **Auto Weekly** option, which is the default, uses the system date to determine the appropriate type of test. If the day of the week is a Friday, then **Auto Weekly** implements the full **Weekly**—complete verification—test. On any other day of the week use the **Daily**—quick scan—test. This option is particularly useful if you execute a Disk Doctor test as part of the AUTOEXEC.BAT file. The **Auto Weekly** saves time, but also ensures that once a week the complete disk test is performed. For information about verification procedures see Chapter 10, "Speed Disk—Other Options."

### Passes

This setting controls the number of times the selected test is performed. The default is a specific number of repetitions set by default at 1. You can increase that value or set the program to continuously repeat the test until you manually terminate the operation.

Why would you want to repeat the surface test? The answer is that disk errors are not always *absolute*. For example, if a disk contains a flaw in its surface, the flaw will usually first appear as an occasional error, which will get progressively worse over time. It is important to keep in mind that all disk storage has to do with magnetic fields generated by electric current. Such technology is subject to variations that create stronger or weaker signals at different times. When your disk is working properly the variation in the current falls within the tolerance range of the disk surface coating. A flawed area may manifest itself at first only when the current used is in the low range of tolerance.

By repeating the disk test you may locate areas that will fail only sometimes. This enables you to deal with a potential problem before it becomes totally unreadable. Keep in mind that the much-longer tests performed by Calibrate do an even better job at detecting these minute errors before they become large problems.

In most cases the Disk Doctor can be run with a single pass. You would change the operation if you began to suspect you had a deteriorating flaw on the disk that is able to get by when the program makes a single pass.

## Repair Setting

The repair setting determines the action that will be taken if a cluster contains unreadable data. The default is **Prompt before Repairing.** This causes the program to pause and display a dialog box if it encounters a disk error. The box will remain on the screen until the user selects to correct or skip the error.

If you want to operate the program without pause you can select either **Don't Repair**, which causes the program to skip all errors, or **Repair automatically**, which causes the program to attempt to repair errors encountered. The point of operating the program with the **Don't Repair** option is to generate a report listing the errors, but not altering the disk.

You may wonder how it is that the program can *repair* the disk if an error is encountered. By definition an error is a portion of the disk that cannot be accurately used for data storage and retrieval. How can the Norton Disk Doctor *fix* such a problem? If the program encounters an error in an area of the disk that is not currently in use, the program will *fix* the problem, marking that data cluster as *bad*. Bad clusters are automatically ignored by DOS, ensuring that no attempt will be made to store it in that area.

If the cluster in which the error occurs is in use by a file, the fix is a bit trickier. Recall from Chapter 4 that DOS data storage is based on a unit called a *cluster*. The *data cluster* can be composed of one or more of the basic disk building blocks called *sectors*. Typically, hard disks formatted under DOS 3.xx or higher use four sectors for each data cluster. When the Disk Doctor finds an error, the program can pinpoint the sector in which the problem occurs. At the very least this means that there are three entire sectors remaining in the cluster that are probably not affected by the error. The Disk Doctor will attempt to copy as much data as possible from the cluster into another cluster on the disk. The program then adjusts the FAT to use the data stored in the new location as part of the file.

In some cases this *fix* will not work. Losing even a few bytes from a program file might render it inoperable in one form or another. However, if the file recovered was a data file the loss of a few bytes or even an entire sector (usually 512 bytes) will not make the file useless, even though there will be a gap in the text where the unreadable data would have appeared.

The program displays a special screen that shows the status of the test. The top part of the screen is a disk map that shows the used and unused sectors. The letter **B** shows the approximate location of a bad sector. Note that the B will appear if there is a single bad sector, even through each block on the map may stand for several sectors.

## Disk Report

When the Surface Test has been completed, the program will present you with a dialog box that will summarize the operations performed (Figure 14–2) and give you an opportunity to create a detailed report.

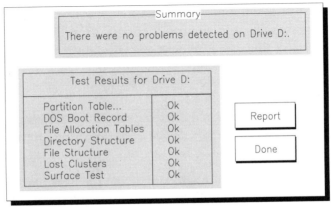

**Figure 14–2. Surface test summary display.**

You can create a report by selecting the **Report** button or exit without creating a detailed report by selecting Done. Once created, you can view the report in a scroll box, send it to the line printer, or save it as a text file.

## Undoing Changes

For the most part, the changes made by the Norton Disk Doctor will provide the best solution to problems such as lost clusters, cross-linked files, or data read errors. However, as an extra measure of safety the program provides a means by which changes to the system area of the disk can be restored to their previous state.

Recall that the Disk Doctor creates an undo file, NDDUNDO.DAT, on another disk when changes are made to the system area. If following a correction you desire to restore the system area to its original state, select **Undo Changes** from the main Disk Doctor dialog box. The program asks you to confirm your intention to undo the changes.

You must then enter the drive on which the NDDUNDO.DAT file can be found. When the file is found the program displays the time and date that the undo file was created.

The time and date are provided to help you make sure that you are using a valid undo file. Keep in mind that undoing changes made by the Disk Doctor is something that should be done immediately after those changes were made. If you have made changes to the disk after the creation of the undo file, restoring the undo data may create as many problems as it solves.

## Options

The **Options** control button on the main Disk Doctor dialog box is used to change the default options used by the Norton Disk Doctor. The selections made under this option will be stored in a file called NDD.INI in the Norton Utilities home directory. There are two reasons for changing the default options:

**Compatibility.**   You can make selections that best fit your system. These options include tests that you *do not* want performed for various compatibility reasons.

**Batch Execution.**   If you intend to execute the Disk Doctor from a batch file you can control the options used by the program when running in automatic operation.

The **Options** command displays another dialog box that presents three areas in which you can make changes in the default operations.

**Surface Test**    This option displays the same dialog box that appears on the **Surface Test.** In this instance, the selections made on the dialog box for test, test type, passes, and repair settings become the defaults. One reason for changing the defaults is to allow the Disk Doctor to operate automatically when executed from a batch file. For example, you might change the Repair setting to **Repair Automatically** to avoid pausing the program when an error is encountered.

**Custom Message**    This option is used to control the way that errors encountered during the system tests are handled. In normal operation, the Disk Doctor automatically begins error correction, if needed, following the completion of the system area test. In some cases you may not want to prevent the Disk Doctor from allowing users to make these corrections.

This option allows you to create a message that will be displayed in a box in place of the corrections routines, when errors are encountered during the system tests. This box will have a single control button, **Cancel Test,** which will terminate the Disk Doctor when the user enters any key. For example, the custom message might inform the user that an error was located and he should call Joe in the data processing department at extension 555. In this case, the message serves two purposes: It prevents users from making corrections, and it tells them what to do when errors are located.

Note that this option affects only the system tests. The error processing procedure used for the surface test is controlled through the **Repair Settings** option selected in the **Surface Test Options** dialog box. If you want to run both the system and surface test without using corrections, you would use both the custom message and **Don't Repair** options.

The **Set Custom Message** dialog box allows you to create a text message within a box. You can change the video attribute of the text you are about to enter by pressing [F2], which will toggle between normal, reverse, bold, and underline video.

Note that you *must* select the **Prompt with Custom Message** box if you want this option to be active when you run the Disk Doctor. If you create a message, but do not have this option selected, the program will handle system area errors in the usual fashion.

**Tests to Skip**    The Disk Doctor allows you to turn off four specific operations that would otherwise be included in its testing procedures. For the most part these options are used to avoid misleading messages that are generated by incompatibilities between the Norton Utilities and nonstandard system hardware:

**Skip Partition Tests.**  Select this option to avoid the partition table test.

**Skip CMOS Tests.**  This option is used to skip the comparison of the CMOS drive data with the actual drives on computers with nonstandard BIOS drive tables.

**Skip Surface Tests.**  This option will prevent the execution of the surface test. When selected, the Disk Doctor will only perform the system tests even when the /**COMPLETE** switch is used.

**Only One Hard Disk.**  This option is used when the Disk Doctor erroneously reports a second hard disk.

Remember that you must use the **Save Settings** option if you want the current selections you have made to become permanent; that is, written into the NDD.INI file so that they will affect future uses of the Disk Doctor. If you fail to use this command the settings will be discarded at the end of the current session and the program will revert to its previous defaults the next time it is run.

## Batch and Command-line Operations

The maintenance value of the Norton Disk Doctor can be maximized by making execution of the program part of the AUTOEXEC.BAT or other batch files. The advantage of operating the Norton Disk Doctor from a batch file using its command-line options is that you can apply the desired tests without requiring the user to know how to use the Disk Doctor.

The Batch Enhancer and NDOS features provided in Version 6.0 make it possible to write batch files that execute disk tests on periods other than the built-in daily/weekly schedule, e.g., once a month (See Chapter 16).

Implementing regular testing through batch files can help a computer manager keep track of a large number of systems without having to manually execute tests on each system.

In order to perform the Disk Doctor tests from a batch file you first need to decide how the program should handle errors.

**System Errors**    Normally, the Disk Doctor will present the user with the option of correcting errors that are found during the system tests. If you want to prevent the user from making corrections use **Custom Message** option on the **Options** dialog box.

**Surface Errors**      By default, the Disk Doctor will prompt the user to select the desired action each time a problem in the system area of the disk is encountered. You can eliminate these prompts by selecting automatic repair or no repair from the **Surface Test Options** dialog box from the **Options** menu.

You can also use the **Surface Test Options** dialog box to select full-disk or file-only surface tests.

Note that any selections you make must be stored in the NDD.INI file by using the **Save Settings** command button in order to act as defaults for the program.

Once you have selected the desired error-handling options you can add a complete test to a batch file such as the AUTOEXEC.BAT file by adding the following command. Note that you specify the drive letter and the **COMPLETE** or **/QUICK** switch in order to automatically execute the test instead of displaying the main Disk Doctor dialog box. Example: NDD C:/COMPLETE.

You can limit the test to the system area tests only by using the **/QUICK** switch.[4] Example: NDD C:/QUICK.

You can generate a text file that contains the Disk Doctor report by adding the **/R** switch. Example: NDD C:/COMPLETE/R:diskrpt.doc.

You can direct the report to a specific drive or directory by using the full path name with the **/R** option. Example: NDD C:/COMPLETE /R:d:\NU\diskrpt.doc.

If you want to accumulate consecutive reports in a single file instead of overwriting old reports with the newest data, you can add the **A** option, which will cause the new reports to be appended to the specified file.

```
NDD C:/COMPLETE/RA:d:\NU\diskrpt.doc
```

If you want to produce a printed copy of the report you can use DOS commands to output the file.

```
NDD C:/COMPLETE/R:d:\NU\diskrpt.doc
TYPE d:\NU\diskrpt.doc >PRN
ECHO ^L >PRN5
```

---

4.  You can shorten these switches to **/Q** or **/C** if desired.

5.  Generate form feed.

Version 6.0 includes a new version of the LP (line print) program originally included in Version 4.5 but not in 5.0. You could use this program to print a formatted copy of the report.

```
NDD C:/COMPLETE/R:d:\NU\diskrpt.doc
LP d:\NU\diskrpt.doc
```

You can perform tests on more than one drive if you specify a list of drive letters. The command below will perform a quick test on drives C:, D:, and E:. Remember that tested drives must be physical drives or drive partitions. Example: NDD C: D: E:/QUICK.

If you add a report option to this command the report will contain data about all of the drives tested. Example: NDD C: D: E:/QUICK/R:c:\ diskdata.doc.

The **X** switch is used to exclude specific drives from the drive list when the Disk Doctor is used in the full-screen mode. The command below will exclude the C and D drives from the drive selector dialog box. This prevents accidental testing of drives that should not be operated on. Example: NDD /X:cd.

# Disk Calibration

The Calibrate program is designed to maintain the reliability of your hard disk by performing rigorous read and write operations, including data that are part of the low-level format. Calibrate is a powerful program, but it is very simple to use because there are very few user options available in the program. Most of the operations are automatic.

Calibrate operations fall into two major categories. The program begins by performing a number of tests that analyze the hard disk. In Chapter 8, in "Information from Calibrate" the data supplied by the Calibrate program about the hard disk are discussed in detail.

Once the program has accumulated the information about your hard disk, it can proceed to perform the following operations.

**Pattern Test**    Calibrate will perform intensive testing of each *bit* of storage space on the hard disk to determine its level of reliability. Calibrate does more than the Disk Doctor in that it reads and writes a variety of byte patterns into each sector in order to determine the reliability of each sector. Note that this procedure is different than that performed by the Disk Doctor, in which only the data currently in the sector are tested. Calibrate uses a variety of bit patterns because the nature of magnetic recording makes certain bit combinations more difficult to read and write than others. For example, bit patterns like 00000000 or 11111111 are simpler to record than patterns like 01010101 or 10101010.[6]

The Calibrate program will write between 5 and 80 different data patterns in order to determine that the sector can reliably record a wide variety of data patterns. Like the Disk Doctor, areas that prove to be unreliable are marked as bad.

**Rewrite Low-level Sector Data**     The hard disk controller reads information that was stored on the disk as part of the low-level formatting (sometimes called *initialization*) performed on the disk. Because DOS reads and writes only high-level information, such as the data in the disk clusters, the original low-level format, which includes the sector address and sync bytes, is never updated. Over time the strength of the low-level format can begin to deteriorate. When the disk controller is unable to read the low-level sector information, it reports a data error to DOS. DOS then displays a **Cannot read drive** error message.

The error implies that there is a problem with the data cluster. However, in many cases the problem lies in the low-level format, not the data in the cluster, which is more likely to be valid since it probably was written more recently than the low-level format.

Calibrate can read and rewrite the low-level format for each sector on the disk. Rewriting the data will place a new, full strength signal on the disk, making the low-level data equal to that of recently written data.

In many cases this process can make available data areas that were marked by DOS or the Disk Doctor as bad.

**Sector Adjustment**     Another problem that can occur with the low-level format is that as a disk drive ages (e.g., 12 to 18 months), the position of the drive heads with respect to the sectors will vary as the parts wear in. In some cases the *drift* can result in sectors that are difficult to read reliably. As part of its low-level rewriting, Calibrate will adjust the sectors to reflect the current positioning of the disk heads. By running Calibrate on a regular basis you can ensure that the sectors and the head will remain in alignment.

**Interleave Adjustment**     Recall from Chapter 8 that hard disks attempt to minimize their latency delays by adjusting the disk *interleave*. The inter-

---

6.   The total number of bit patterns possible for one byte of information is 256.

leave factor will adjust the numbering of disk sectors so that the spinning disk wastes as little time as possible in reading the next sector on the track. (See Chapter 8, "Interleave").

Calibrate will calculate the optimum interleave factor for your disk and adjust the sector addresses to use this interleave factor. A change of inter-leave factor would normally require a reformat of the entire hard disk. But Calibrate can perform this operation without disturbing the data stored in the sectors. Calibrate cannot be used to change the interleave factors on hard disks that use special types of controller interfaces, which report different values than actually exist on the disk. These are called *translating controllers*. As a general rule, you can change the interleave of an SCSI, ESDI, or IDE type hard disk. You can perform pattern testing on these drives.

Calibrate performs these operations by reading the data from an entire track into memory. The program can then rewrite the low-level format for the track, adjusting the interleave factor, if selected, while refreshing the sectors headers and making any necessary adjustments.

Next, the program will perform the pattern testing, if selected, by writing and reading bit patterns across the entire track. When the pattern testing is complete the original data replaced into the body of the sectors refreshing that data as well as the low-level format. The program then goes on to the next track. Note that because Calibrate works on the low-level format it makes no distinction between the system area, which always operates in sectors, and the data area, which operates in clusters.

Many hard disks have an extra cylinder called the *diagnostic* or *customer engineer* (C.E.) cylinder. This cylinder, usually found at the beginning of the physical disk, is reserved and not used by DOS. Its purpose is to provide read/write space for diagnostic programs that test or repair disks. For example, On Track's Disk Manager program will use this cylinder when it performs its disk diagnostic operations. As a safety factor Calibrate will use the *diagnostic cylinder*, which is found on many hard disks. This cylinder is placed on the hard disk to allow for testing and diagnostic operations. If no diagnostic cylinder is available, the program will rely strictly on internal memory. The advantage of using the diagnostic cylinder is that you can stop a calibration before it is completed and later continue the calibration at the point where it was stopped. If you do not want the program to copy the track to the diagnostic cylinder, because you want to preserve data placed there by another diagnostic program, use the /**NOCOPY** switch.

Like the Disk Doctor, Calibrate is most effective when used on a regular basis. However, pattern testing takes much longer than the tests performed by the Disk Doctor. A full pattern test of an 80 megabyte drive can take 12 to 24 hours. It is not practical to perform calibration as part of the AUTOEXEC.BAT.[7] However, batch files can be used to operate Calibrate in an automatic mode.

## Calibrate Options

Calibration of a disk begins when you load the Calibrate program. As noted earlier in this chapter, it is safest to run Calibrate with a minimum of TSR (memory resident). If you want to select the drive from a dialog box enter: CALIBRATE

If you want to eliminate the drive selection box, use the desired drive letter as an argument. The command below will skip the drive selection and go directly to the Calibrate test screens. Example: CALIBRATE C:.

When the Calibrate program loads it begins with a series of tests. The details and these tests are described in Chapter 8 and will not be repeated here. The first set of tests, labeled **System Integrity**, must be executed in order to calibrate the disk.

The second set of tests, the **Seek Tests**, are optional. These tests tells you about the performance of your disk, but they are not required to perform calibration. If you wanted to skip the seek tests you could start the program with the /**NOSEEK** switch. Example: CALIBRATE C: /NOSEEK.

When /**NOSEEK** is used the program goes directly to the **Data Encoding Tests** following the **System Integrity** tests.

Following the **Data Encoding** tests the program performs the **Format** test. The **Format** test is used to determine the optimum interleave pattern. Note that this test uses a trial-and-error method to find the optimum factor. The interleave test is required only if you want to change the pattern. If you want to skip this test you can use the /*NOFORMAT* switch. Example: CALIBRATE C: /NOFORMAT.

You can skip both the seek and format tests by using both switches. Example: CALIBRATE C: /NOSEEK /NOFORMAT.

When the tests are completed the program displays the **Pattern Testing** dialog box. You can select 0, 5, 40, or 80 pattern testing. The default is no pattern testing. If selected this will mean that each track is read and rewritten (both low- and high-level information), but no testing is performed on the sector itself. If you want to perform pattern testing, the more patterns

---

7. New batch commands available in Version 6.0, discussed in Chapter 16, make such batch AUTOEXEC.BAT files practical.

tested the more reliable the results. However, testing a full 80 patterns can take a large amount of time, e.g., 5–8 hours for every 10 megabytes.

When the surface testing is taking place the program displays a status screen that includes a disk map. In addition to the disk map, the screen displays information about time, track, operation status, and legend:

**Time.**  The time display shows the current system time and the estimated time at which the Calibration will be complete. Note that the estimated time will change as the program proceeds through the disk. The accuracy of the estimate will increase as the percentage of the disk calibrated increases.

**Track.**  This item shows the current track that is being calibrated and the total number of tracks on the disk. Note that the total is the total number of tracks on the disk based on the low-level format. This does not take into consideration that the hard disk may be partitioned into several logical drives. For example, if a 40 megabyte disk is partitioned into C and D drives, the total number of tracks will be the same, no matter which partition you calibrate. Note that Calibrate limits its operations to the selected partition operating only on the tracks that are actually assigned to that partition.

**Status.**  This box contains information about the current operation: the testing pattern being used, the interleave factor, the drive letter, and the percentage of the calibration that is complete. The bar shows the percentage graphically.

**Legend.**  The legend shows the symbols that are used on the disk map. The three most significant symbols are B, C, and U. The B indicates a bad sector; that is, one that is marked as bad by programs such as the Norton Disk Doctor. The C shows a sector that has exhibited errors but has been restored to full reliability. The U marks a sector that does not respond reliably to the pattern testing and correction. That sector remains marked as bad and will be ignored.

You can stop a calibration at any time by pressing [Esc]. Keep in mind that when you press [Esc], Calibrate will finish writing the current track before it responds to your entry with a dialog box asking you if you want to cancel the operation. This wait may be a few seconds to a minute or two. Do *not* reboot the computer while Calibrate is working. Make sure that you first cancel the calibration and exit to DOS.

## Screen Blanking

The extended period of time required for calibration will cause the surface test status display to remain on the screen for long periods of time. You can protect your screen from *burn-in* by activating the screen blank feature.

When active, the screen blank features clears the display except for a box that indicates calibration is in progress and the percentage of the disk that has been calibrated. To avoid burn-in the box is moved to different locations on the screen every five seconds.

The screen blank feature can be toggled on or off by pressing the [space] key.

When calibration is completed a summary screen appears telling you the time used to perform the operation, the interleave factor, and the number of corrected and noncorrectable sectors on the disk.

The Calibrate program will generate a report after a calibration has been completed or interrupted by the user.

## Batch and Command-line Operations

Calibrate is one of the most automatic programs included in the Norton Utilities since all error correction is done automatically. You can easily execute a calibration from DOS or through a batch file. The command below will calibrate drive C automatically. Note that the program will use the default setting of **no pattern testing**. Example: CALIBRATE C: /BATCH.

You may want to use the **/NOSEEK** and **/NOFORMAT** options to skip these tests since their only purpose is to supply information to the user. Example: CALIBRATE C: /BATCH/NOSEEK/NOFORMAT.

You can select the pattern-testing level desired using the **/PATTERN:#** switch. Note that the # must be replaced with 5, 40, or 80. If you enter another value, e.g., 12, the program will revert to the default, **no pattern testing**. The command below performs five pattern tests during the calibration. Example: CALIBRATE C: /BATCH/PATTERN:5.

Screen blanking can be invoked as part of the command also.

```
Example: CALIBRATE C: /BATCH/PATTERN:5/BLANK
```

To generate a report use the **/R** switch. Note that reports are stored as text files for later viewing or printing. Example: CALIBRATE C: /BATCH/ PATTERN:5/R:diskc.doc.

The **/RA** switch appends the new report to an existing report file instead of overwriting an old report. Example: CALIBRATE C: /BATCH/ PATTERN:5/RA:diskc.doc.

Calibrate will operate on only one disk at a time. If you wanted to Calibrate two drives, e.g., C and D, you would need to write a batch file with two separate Calibrate commands:

```
CALIBRATE C:/BATCH
CALIBRATE D:/BATCH
```

The **/X** switch is used to hide certain drive letters when the program is run in interactive mode. The command below will suppress the display of the drive letters C and D in the drive selection dialog box. Example: CALIBRATE /X:cd.

## Norton Disk Doctor and Calibrate

You might want to combine Disk Doctor and Calibrate commands into batch files that are run from time to time for the purpose of disk maintenance. The commands below perform the quickest possible series of Disk Doctor and Calibrate tests. Note that Norton Disk Doctor will stop for error correction unless you change the program default settings, as discussed earlier in this chapter:

```
NDD C:/COMPLETE
CALIBRATE C:/NOSEEK/NOFORMAT/BATCH
```

If you want to add pattern testing the commands would be changed to include the /PATTERN switch:

```
NDD C:/COMPLETE
CALIBRATE C:/NOSEEK/NOFORMAT/BATCH/PATTERN:5
```

If you wanted to generate a report you would add the **/R** and **/RA** switches. Note that the first command uses **/R** to overwrite any previous report of the same name. The second command uses **/RA** to append its data onto the data from the Disk Doctor check:

```
NDD C:/COMPLETE/R: diskrpt.doc
CALIBRATE C:/NOSEEK/NOFORMAT/BATCH/PATTERN:5/RA:diskrpt.doc
```

By replacing the drive letter with the variable %1 you create a batch file that can be directed at any drive:

```
NDD %1:/COMPLETE
CALIBRATE %1:/NOSEEK/NOFORMAT/BATCH
```

If the above commands were entered into a file called CHKDISK.BAT, you could check disk E by entering CHKDISK E.

You could then create a batch file, CHKALL.BAT, that would execute a series of checks on all of the disks in the system:

```
CHKDISK C
CHKDISK D
CHKDISK E
```

# Lifting Data with Disk Editor

The automatic operations of the Norton Disk Doctor and Calibrate programs will handle most common disk problems. However, should you need to, the Disk Editor provides access to any part of the disk.

One of the most useful and powerful features of the Disk Editor program is its ability to *lift* data from any part of a disk and place it in another location, either on the same disk or another disk.

This technique can be applied to many situations since you can use the Disk Editor to access both the system and data areas of the disk.

In this section the basic procedure used to lift data off the disk is explained. As an example, suppose that you wanted to collect information from the **Advise** menu in the main **Norton** program so that you could print it out as a document. The Norton Utilities does not provide a facility for printing this information. You could use the [PrtSc] key, but that would be unformatted printing, which is hard to read. An alternative would be to use the Disk Editor to lift the text directly from the file and copy it into a separate file that could be read and manipulated by a word processing program.

Begin by loading the Disk Editor program. Enter diskedit ↵. By default the program displays a message that tells you the program is operating in a *read-only* mode. This is a safety precaution taken to ensure that you do not accidentally alter any part of the disk. Continue by entering ↵.

The program begins by displaying the current directory in the Disk Editor directory format. Change to the \NU directory by entering [Alt-r] norton ↵.

Next select the file that you want to access. Note that you could, if necessary, select data by cluster or sector numbers. You can even display special parts of the system area of the disk such as the partition table or the FAT. In this case you want to display the contents of the TROUBLE.HLP file, which is used to store the text that appears in the Advise display. Enter [Alt-f] trouble.hlp ↵.

The program loads the first sector of the TROUBLE.HLP. Because the information at the beginning of the file is mostly nontext the program uses the hex display. This is convenient since you can only lift data when operating in the hex display mode. If you look at the information at the bottom of the screen you will find that it details the current information by listing the operation type (file, sector, cluster, etc.), the full path name of the file, the cluster number of the cluster being displayed, and the byte offset of the cursor within the file.

Suppose you wanted to see information that deals with *seek errors*. You can use the **Find** option located on the *Tools* menu to locate a key word or phrase. Note that when you perform a find operation in the Disk Editor, the operation uses the currently selected object as the scope of the search. This means that if you have selected a file, the search will be limited to the file. If you select a group of clusters, e.g., cluster 200 to 210, any search you perform will be limited to those clusters. If you wanted to search the entire data area of the disk you would select all of the data clusters beginning with 2, the first cluster in the data area. Enter [Ctrl-s].

Enter the words *seek error* as the search text. Note that you can search for either text or hex values using the command. Enter seek error ↵.

The program displays the first occurrence of the characters within the current object. Note that the contents of a file may be difficult to read when it is displayed in hex format. You can switch to any of the other formats using the options listed in the *View* menu. The [F3] key is the shortcut key for the text mode. Enter [F3].

The program now shows the contents in the text display, which makes the text contents of the object, if any, easier to read and understand.

You can continue this process until you locate the text or values you want to copy. Note that you can use the same approach to recover erased or lost data by selecting some or all of the disk clusters and then perform a search for the lost data. Return to the hex mode by entering [F2].

The cursor highlight is positioned on the first character/hex value of the matching text. In order to *lift* a copy of the information out of the file you must first *mark* the data. The **Mark** command, located on the *Edit* menu, can be activated by entering [Ctrl-b]. If you are using a mouse you can drag the mouse over the data you want to mark. In this case enter [Ctrl-b]. Once the Mark mode has been activated you can extend the highlight over the area you want to copy by using the arrow keys. Enter ↓(press 30 times).

You have now highlighted the information you want to copy. The next step is to place a copy of that information into the *clipboard*. The clipboard is an area of the memory that will hold the data until you write it to the disk. Copy the information to the clipboard by entering [Ctrl-c].

The next step is to select the *clipboard* as the current object.

This tells the program that you now want to work with whatever information you have copied off the disk into the memory clipboard. Enter [Alt-o] 1.

The clipboard display is similar to the hex display of the disk information with the exception that it contains *only* the information you selected from the disk file.

At this point you have created an object that consists solely of the data you selected. You have two ways to output the information. The commands are found on the *Tools* menu.

## Write to

The **Write to** command is used to copy the information in the clipboard to a disk. There are four options.

**File**    This option creates a new file on this or another disk that will contain the contents of the current object, in this case the clipboard. This option is the safest since the program will write the data into areas on the disk that are not currently in use by a file. You can write the data onto another disk by adding the drive and directory path to the file name you choose to create.

**Clusters**    This option allows you to write the current information to a specific cluster on the disk. This operation is much more technical and potentially dangerous since this can result in the overwriting of existing files. You would use this operation when you were sure about replacing the data currently stored in the target clusters.

**Sectors**    This option allows you to copy the current object onto the disk starting at a specific sector number. Using sector numbers allows you to place data into the system area of the disk. Keep in mind that such an operation can damage the root directory, boot sector, or FAT so that extreme care should be taken before performing such an operation.

Physical sectors allow you access to any part of the drive, including the partition table and the diagnostic (C.E.) cylinder. Note that physical sectors are identified by the side, track, and sector number.

The diagnostic cylinder is usually cylinder 0. If you select side 0, track 0 and sector 1, you will be accessing the beginning of the diagnostic cylinder on drives such as a Seagate 251 that support this extra cylinder. If available, this cylinder is a good place to park data since DOS does not use this area of the disk. The Calibrate program uses cylinder to store data. Running Calibrate will overwrite data stored in the diagnostic cylinder.

**Print as**     This command differs from the *Write to* command in that it outputs the information *as displayed* in the Disk Editor program instead of the information as it was stored on the disk. The purpose of this command is to output the enhanced data that appear in the Disk Editor special formats, hex, directory, FAT, boot record, and partition table. Keep in mind that the raw information contained in actual disk objects such as the directory or FAT are very hard to understand. The Disk Editor displays translate these specialized sectors into easy-to-read and understand formats.

You have the option of directing the output to the printer or into a text file.

In this case select the **Write to** command by entering [Alt-t] w. The **Write to** dialog box, Figure 14–3, appears with the default set to **File**.

Create the file by entering ↵ seekerr.txt ↵ ↵.

The program writes the information into a new disk file called SEEKERR.TXT. That file can then be used with a word processor or other

**Figure 14–3. Write to dialog box.**

application. Note that the *lifting* process enables you to cut and paste any disk information without having to disturb the original data. This technique has many applications and is invaluable when you are seeking to recover or analyze data. Exit the program by entering [Alt-q].

# Summary

This chapter covered the use of the Norton Disk Doctor and Calibrate programs to maintain your disks.

**Disk Problems**    Hard and floppy disks use electromagnetic signals to record the data stored on the surface of the disks. Over time and use, a disk's ability to read and write data on all of its surfaces may deteriorate. This can result in the inability of the computer to read information stored at various locations on the disk. In addition to physical problems, disks can encounter logical problems. Logical problems have to do with inconsistent or corrupted data in the system and directory areas of the disk, making it difficult or impossible for DOS to access information.

**High-level Testing**    The Norton Disk Doctor performs a high-level test of the system and data areas on the disk. High level refers to the disk structures created and maintained by DOS. The Norton Disk Doctor examines and analyzes the system components of the disk, e.g., the partition table, boot sector, FAT, and directories, looking for errors which it will attempt to resolve or correct. The program will also scan the data area of the disk to ensure that all clusters can be read reliably. If a cluster cannot be read it is marked as bad, which will cause DOS to ignore that area of the disk in all future operations. If the bad cluster is currently part of a file, the Disk Doctor will copy as much of the data as possible to a good cluster in order to recover as much of the file as possible.

**Low-level Testing**    The Calibrate performs tests and makes corrections, taking into consideration the low-level format information placed on the disk when it was first initialized. The Calibrate program reads the high- and low-level information from an entire track and then writes that information back on the track. This *refreshes* both high- and low-level data, ensuring the reliability of both. The program can also change the interleave factor used on many drives. The program will also test the reliability of the disk's sectors by writing 5 to 80 different bit patterns to each sector and testing the ability of the sector to store the patterns correct.

**Lifting Data**    A key recovery tool is the ability to copy any part of a disk to a new file on that or another disk using the Disk Editor program. The Disk Editor allows you to copy select items to a clipboard. The clipboard can then be copied to a new file, a set of clusters, sectors, or physical sectors. The original disk item is not affected by this copying process.

Batch files, one of the most powerful features of MS-DOS, allow you to create simple programs from text files containing DOS commands. With batch files you can automate a wide variety of operations that would otherwise require manual entry of a series of DOS commands.

In addition, as with most programming situations, the effect of a batch file often appears to be more than the sum of its individual commands. For example, one of the most important uses of a batch file is to build a menu that can help organize your computer. No single DOS command can create a menu, but by using a series of commands organized in a batch file you can create the effect.

When batch files are combined with some of the programs supplied in Norton Utilities, you will find that you can create a variety of useful tools that help make operation of your computer system easier for you or for others using your computer.

Version 6.0 of the Norton Utilities expands DOS operations and batch file programming considerably by supplying a special program called NDOS that replaces the COMMAND.COM processor supplied with DOS.

In this chapter you will look at how batch files are created and structured and the enhancements available in the Norton Utilities Version 5.0. The following chapter expands upon these concepts to include significant enhancements added to batch file programming in Version 6.0. Finally, Chapter 17 explains the power and features of the NDOS command processor.

Note that all of the batch file commands used in this chapter are compatible with DOS 3.3 and higher, unless otherwise specified.

## DOS Batch File Basics

Batch files are a means by which you can create your own custom-designed DOS routines. Batch files use the commands available in DOS to create *batches* of commands that execute when you enter the name of the batch file. Batch files allow you to create a customized environment from the DOS commands, which would ordinarily be entered one at a time. In addition to the basic set of DOS commands, batch files can contain some specialized DOS batch subcommands that operate *only* in batch files.

The purpose of this chapter is to provide the reader with a basic understanding of how DOS batch files work and how to enhance batch files using the Norton Utilities Batch Enhancer program.

## Creating Batch Files

All DOS batch files are database *text* files. This is important since you can create text files with any word processing or text editing program. There is no need for special language programs, compilers, linkers, or other applications normally associated with programming.

The only requirement for batch files is that the file have a BAT extension and that it contain valid commands for the version of DOS running in the computer.

DOS provides two editors that can be used to create text files including batch files:

**EDLIN.** The EDLIN (line editor) program is supplied with DOS. It is a popular way to create batch files because everyone who has DOS has it available. Keep in mind that EDLIN is a program, EDLIN.EXE (DOS 3, 4, and 5) or EDLIN.COM (DOS 1 and 2). This means that the file *must* be available when you try to edit. Available means that the file is located in the current directory or is located in a directory to which you have a path open.

**Edit.** In DOS Version 5.0, Microsoft has upgraded DOS text editing by adding a new program called EDIT.COM. Edit is a full-screen text editor, not a line-by-line editor like EDLIN. It uses a menu bar, pull-down menus, and supports the use of a mouse, creating an interface much like that used in the Norton Utilities programs. The program allows for cut, paste, and copying of text. It provides search and change and can also print the text. This editor makes writing batch files much faster and simpler.

## Command Echo

When you look at the results of the FILELIST batch, you will notice that the commands in the batch file appear with the results along with the result of the commands. The display of the commands from the batch file is called *command echo*.

In most cases, there is no need to clutter the display with the commands from the batch file. It would be better to output only the results of the commands. You can control the display with the DOS command **ECHO**. When the command **ECHO OFF** is issued in a batch file, none of the commands that follow are displayed—only their results.

Since **ECHO OFF** counts as a command, it would normally appear because the effect of **ECHO OFF** would follow, not precede, the **ECHO OFF** command. In order to get around this problem, DOS version 3.xx and higher allows you to precede the **ECHO OFF** command with an @ charac- ter. This causes DOS to suppress the display of the **ECHO OFF** command, making the batch run without the display of commands.

The **CLS** command will clear the screen so that any information cur- rently on the screen will be erased before the batch file displays its output.

Add the **@ECHO OFF** and **CLS** commands to the FILELIST batch file:

```
EDLIN filelist.bat ↵
```

The prompt this time reads **End of input file**, indicating that you are revising an existing file, not creating a new file. Insert two lines at the beginning of the file. Enter

```
i ↵
@ECHO OFF ↵
CLS ↵
[Ctrl-c]
```

The batch file now has four commands as shown below. List the batch file by entering

```
L ↵
```

The program shows all four lines of the batch file.
Save and execute the batch file by entering

```
e ↵
filelist ↵
```

This time the batch file executes without showing the text of the com- mands. The information generated by the batch file is easier to read and understand since it is no longer cluttered with the batch file command.

## Batch Files with Variables

The batch file, FILELIST.BAT, that you just created consists of specific commands; that is, the file will perform *exactly* the same operations each time it is executed.

In many cases, batch files would be more useful if some of the items within the batch file could *vary* each time the file was executed. For example, suppose that you wanted to display the contents of a text file on the screen. The standard method would be to use the DOS commands **TYPE** and **MORE**. **TYPE** displays the text while **MORE** pauses the display at the end of each screen full of data so that you can easily read files that have more than 24 lines. The example would display the text of the READ.ME file.

```
TYPE read.me |MORE
```

If you were to remove the file name from the command you would arrive at a general form of a command that could be used to display any text file. Below the word *filename* is substituted for the specific file name READ.ME. Example: TYPE filename |MORE.

If you placed this command into a batch file you could place a *variable* into the command in place of the file name. Variables in DOS begin with a % character and are followed by a single number 1–9, e.g., %1. The example uses **%1** in place of an actual file name. Example: TYPE %1 |MORE.

The **%1** shows DOS the place within the batch file where the actual file name, e.g., READ.ME, CONFIG.SYS, AUTOEXEC.BAT, etc., should be inserted.

How can you insert different file names into the command? DOS allows you to execute any batch file with *parameters*. Recall from Chapter 2, "The DOS Command Language," that a parameter is an additional item that follows the name of the program, DOS command, or batch file you are executing. For example, suppose that the command **TYPE %1 |MORE** is entered in a batch file called VIEW.BAT. If you wanted to display the contents of the AUTOEXEC.BAT file you would add the name of the file as a parameter. Example: VIEW autoexec.bat.

When a parameter is used with a batch file command, DOS searches the contents of the batch for variable symbols, e.g., %1, and substitutes the parameter text for the symbol (Figure 15–1). DOS then executes the command found in the batch file using the name specified in the parameter.

The next time you execute the VIEW batch file you can specify a different file name as a parameter. The example displays the contents of the CONFIG.SYS file. Example: VIEW config.sys.

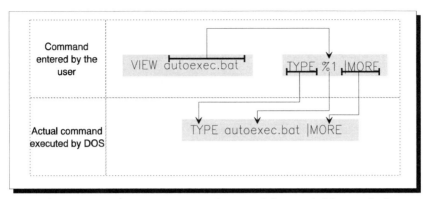

**Figure 15–1. Parameter text inserted for variable symbol.**

You can apply this concept by creating the following batch file called VIEW.BAT. The assumption is made that you are saving the batch files you create in the root directory of the C drive. Note that the last line in the file uses the DOS **ECHO** command to display the phrase *End of File* to indicate to the user that they have completed viewing the file:

```
@ECHO OFF
TYPE %1 |MORE
ECHO ** End of File **
```

You can now use the VIEW batch file to display the contents of any standard text file. Enter view \config.sys ↵.

## Multiple Parameters

You may have wondered why the parameter symbol used in the batch file was **%1**. The answer is that DOS allows you to use multiple parameters. DOS assigns each parameter a different variable, based on the sequence of the parameters entered. The first parameter is assigned to %1, the second to %2, the third to %3, and so on up to %9. The variable **%0** is always assigned to the batch file name itself, e.g., VIEW. If you want to insert the name of the batch file into the batch file commands, simply use **%0** at the desired location or locations.

In the previous example, the name of the file was entered as **\CONFIG.SYS**, not CONFIG.SYS. The \ was added to ensure that you referenced the file in the root directory. The batch file, as it currently exists, requires that you enter the full path name of the file. For example, if you wanted to type the READ.ME file in the \NU directory you would have to enter: VIEW \NU\read.me.

Recall from Chapter 5 that the Norton Change Directory program could activate directories based on a speed search of the directory tree. You may want to incorporate the NCD program into your batch. This would require entering two parameters: the first for the directory and the second for file name. Below is a revised version of the VIEW.BAT file, changes are shown in **Bold**:

```
@ECHO OFF                        {1}
NCD%1                            {2}
TYPE %2 |MORE                    {3}
ECHO ** End of File %2 **        {4}
CD\                             {5}
```

Line {2} adds an NCD command that uses the first parameter to search for a directory. This means that the variable used for the file name must be changed to %2 since that will now be the second parameter. Line {4} contains a small cosmetic change. The %2 is used a second time in the batch file to insert the name of the file that was displayed into the *End of File* message. This will not have a functional effect on the operation of the batch file, but it is a nice touch to show the name of the file at the end since in many cases the original parameter containing the name of the specified file will have been scrolled off the screen. Line {5} is used to return to the root directory after the operation has been completed.

Display the Norton Utilities READ.ME file by entering the following: view nor read.me ↵.

The batch changes directory and displays the contents of the file. Note that when the MORE filter pauses the display you can terminate the file listing by entering [Ctrl-c] or [Ctrl-break]. The use of parameters allows you to create batch files that have much greater flexibility and are much more useful than batch files that are simply lists of DOS commands.

## Suppressing Program Output

Many of the DOS and Norton Utilities program automatically output information to the screen when they are executed, even in batch processing mode. For example, the Norton Change Directory program displays the Norton Utilities copyright notice followed by the *changing to* message.

DOS provides a technique that can be used to suppress the display of this information. This allows you to control exactly what messages are placed on the screen. If the command in the batch file is followed by **>NUL**, DOS will not display the messages generated by the DOS or Norton Utility.

The **>NUL** is a special form of the DOS redirection command. It literally tells the command to redirect its output to a *null* device. The term *null* device refers to a nonexistent hardware item. The practical effect is that instead of placing the output on the screen, it does not appear at all.

Below is the VIEW batch file modified to suppress the normal messages displayed by the Norton Change Directory program when it is executed in the batch mode. The NUL redirection command was added to lines {2} and {5}:

```
@ECHO OFF                            {1}
NCD %1 >NUL                          {2}
TYPE %2 |MORE                        {3}
ECHO ** End of File %2 **            {4}
CD \ >NUL                            {5}
```

Execute the batch again: view nor read.me ↵.

This time no messages from the Norton Change Directory program appear on the screen.

## Printing with Redirection

How do you print from DOS or DOS batch files? DOS handles printing in terms of redirection of output. DOS begins with the assumption that all standard output should be placed on the screen. In the previous section you saw how redirection with >NUL would suppress the output by sending it into limbo. If you want to send information to the printer you would direct the output to the printing device for which DOS uses the name **PRN**.

For instance, the example would send the contents of the READ.ME file to the printer. Example: TYPE read.me >PRN.

If you want to print some literal text you can redirect the ECHO command. The example prints the phrase *End of File*. Example: ECHO End of File >PRN.

PRN stands for the printer device. By default, DOS selects parallel port 1, LPT1, as the printer device. If you want to send the output to a different port use the port name, e.g., LPT2 or COM1, instead of PRN in the redirection command. Another solution is to use the **MODE** command to change the default port. For example, if you have a printer hooked up to serial port 2, COM2, you would use the command **MODE LPT1:=COM2:**. From that point on, all output sent to PRN would end up at COM2. Note that serial

(COM) ports may require additional parameters to be set, such as baud rate or parity. You can also set those values using the Norton Control Center program.

Note that redirection of the output does not change the content of the output. This is important when you print information from DOS because the text is *not* altered in order to fit onto pages. Text output with >PRN will not include page breaks, page numbers, nor will the end of the last page be ejected at the end of the printing. If you are using a laser printer, the last page, since it will usually not be a full page of text, will remain in the printer until you use the **Form Feed** button to force it out.

There is a solution to the form-feed problem. Most printers will recognize ASCII character 12, [Ctrl-L], as a form-feed instruction. You can use the **ECHO** command to send a [Ctrl-L] to the printer. To do so enter the following at the DOS prompt:

```
echo Printer Test >prn ↵
echo
[space]
[Ctrl-1]
```

Note that when you enter the [Ctrl-l] combination the symbol **^L** appears. This is the notation used by DOS to indicate a control character, in contrast to the character letter L. Complete the command by entering >prn ↵.

The printer feeds the remainder of the blank page and is now ready to start a new page. Below is a batch file called PRT.BAT. It is identical to VIEW.BAT with the exception that it prints the file rather than displaying it on the screen by using >PRN in lines 4 and 5. Note that line 5 is used to issue the form feed:

```
@ECHO OFF                              {1}
NCD %1 >NUL                            {2}
ECHO Printing %2 ...                   {3}
TYPE %2 > PRN                          {4}
ECHO ^L >PRN                           {5}
ECHO ** Printing %2 Complete **        {6}
CD \ >NUL                              {7}
```

To print a copy of the READ.ME file, enter prt nor read.me ↵.

The batch file prints the READ.ME. Note that when the output is directed to the printer it does not appear on the screen.

## Command with Conditions

In the batch files you have just created all of the commands that will execute each time the batch is executed. This means that **VIEW** will always place information on the screen, while **PRT** will always send the information to the printer.

It may be more useful to have one batch file that can use either the screen or the printer, depending on the parameter that you use with the batch command. DOS makes such files possible with the **IF** command. The **IF** command can be placed in front of a batch file command in order to control its execution. For example, what would happen if you made a mistake in entering one of the parameters for the **VIEW** batch file. Enter view nor readme ↵.

The program cannot find the file README (in contrast to READ.ME), which causes an error message "**File not found.**" The DOS **IF** command provides a means by which you can check to see if a file actually exists before you issue a command. Below is a simple batch file called TEST1.BAT. The second line uses the command **IF EXISTS** to test for the presence of CONFIG.SYS in the current directory. If the file is located, the message *Configuration File Located* is echoed to the screen. If not, the command is ignored. Create this batch file.

```
@ECHO OFF
IF EXISTS config.sys ECHO Configuration File Located
```

Assuming that you are working in the root directory of the hard disk that contains a CONFIG.SYS file, execute the batch by entering test1 ↵.

The message "*Configuration File Located*" is displayed. Now, change to the Norton Utilities directory and execute the batch again. Enter ncd nor ↵ test1 ↵.

This time the batch does not display a message because the \NU directory does not contain a file called CONFIG.SYS. The **IF** makes the execution of the command *conditional*, that is, it depends upon a specific condition to execute. If that condition is not met, the command is ignored.

The **IF** command can perform a negative test as well. This means you can execute a command if a file *does not* exist. The batch listing below shows a third line added to the batch file that displays a message when the file is not located:

```
@ECHO OFF
IF EXISTS config.sys ECHO Configuration File Located
IF NOT EXISTS config.sys ECHO Configuration File is Missing
```

Add this command to your batch file and execute it again in the \NU directory. Enter ncd nor ↵ test1 ↵.

This time the message "Configuration File is Missing" appears. Change back to the root and execute the file again. Enter cd \ ↵ test1 ↵. Since the CONFIG.SYS is present, the message displayed is "Configuration File Located." This approach can be applied to the **VIEW** batch file. The difference is that in **VIEW** the **IF** command will test for the file name specified by parameter %2 instead of a specific name, such as CONFIG.SYS. The **IF EXISTS** commands operate only if the file is located, while the **IF NOT EXISTS** execute when the file is not located. Note that in line 3 the | MORE filter has been removed. This was necessary because DOS allows only a *single* command to follow an **IF** command. The use of **TYPE** with **MORE** violates this rule as far as DOS is concerned and the command will not execute properly. In the next few sections you will see how DOS solves this limitation:

```
@ECHO OFF                                            {1}
NCD %1 >NUL                                          {2}
IF EXISTS %2 TYPE %2                                 {3}
IF EXISTS %2 ECHO ** End of File %2 **               {4}
IF NOT EXISTS ECHO The File %2 cannot be located     {5}
CD \ >NUL                                            {6}
```

Execute the file by entering view nor readme.

The program returns the message "The File readme cannot be located."

## Creating Batch Switches

As discussed in this book, many DOS and Norton Utilities use command switches to alter the way that various programs or commands operate. For example, the **/QUICK** switch used with the Norton Disk Doctor causes the program to perform a disk test on the system area only.

The **IF** command makes it possible to create batch files that recognize switch-like parameters. For example, you have created separate batch files for viewing or printing a text file. It would be better to have a single batch file that recognized a parameter such as **/P** or **/PRINT** as an instruction to print the file, as well as display it on the screen.

In addition to testing for the existence or nonexistence of a specific file, the **IF** command can be used to compare two text items. Suppose that you entered three parameters with the **VIEW** batch file as shown below:

```
VIEW nor read.me /P
```

You can use the **IF** command to determine if the characters **/P** were entered as the third parameter in order to determine if the text should be printed:

```
IF "%3"=="P" TYPE %2 >PRN
```

The structure of the above command requires some examination. First, note that the text items, called *strings*, must be enclosed in ". This is true for the variable, "%3", and the literal, "/P". Also, DOS uses == to represent *equals*. This is because DOS reserves a single = as a delimiter.

Below is a batch file called VIEW1.BAT that uses a third parameter, %3, in lines 5 and 6 to determine if the specified file should be printed. Create this batch file as shown:

```
@ECHO OFF                        {1}
NCD %1 >NUL                      {2}
TYPE %2 |MORE                    {3}
ECHO ** End of File %2 **        {4}
IF "%3"=="P" TYPE %2>PRN         {5}
IF "%3"=="P" ECHO ^L>PRN         {6}
CD \ >NUL                        {7}
```

Once the file has been created you can test its operation. Enter the following command. Note that the **/P** must be entered with an uppercase P since the **IF** command is case-sensitive. Entering **/p** as the parameter would not cause the file to print:

```
view1 \ config.sys /P ↵
```

If you wanted to protect the batch file from case sensitivity you would duplicate lines 5 and 6 and change the switch text to lowercase, as shown below. This would mean that the batch would print when **/p** or **/P** were used as the third parameter:

```
@ECHO OFF                        {1}
NCD %1 >NUL                      {2}
TYPE %2 |MORE                    {3}
ECHO ** End of File %2 **        {4}
IF "%3"=="P" TYPE %2>PRN         {5}
IF "%3"=="P" ECHO ^L>PRN         {6}
IF "%3"=="p" TYPE %2>PRN         {7}
IF "%3"=="p" ECHO ^L>PRN         {8}
CD \ >NUL                        {9}
```

Another variation on the same idea is to allow for two alternative actions based on the presence or absence of the switch. In the example below, lines 3 and 4 are modified by inserting an **IF NOT** command before the **TYPE** and **ECHO** commands. The result is that in this batch file the text is displayed if **/P** is not entered or printed if **/P** is entered:

```
@ECHO OFF                                            {1}
NCD %1 >NUL                                          {2}
IF NOT"%3"=="/P" TYPE %2                             {3}
IF NOT "%3"=="P" ECHO ** End of File %2 **           {4}
IF "%3"=="/P" TYPE %2>PRN                            {5}
IF "%3"=="/P" ECHO ^L>PRN                            {6}
CD \ >NUL                                            {7}
```

## Structured Batch Files

Recall that DOS allows only a single command to follow an **IF** command. This forced you to eliminate the **MORE** filter from the **TYPE** command.

This problem raises a broader question about the use of conditional commands like **IF**. In many cases a single command with or without a filter would not be sufficient to carry out the task.

The problem can be solved by creating *structured* batch files. A structured batch file is one that is divided into distinct sections. Each section can contain as many individual commands as you desire. The beginning of each section is marked by a *label*. A label is simply a word or text string preceded by a colon, e.g., :QUICK.

Labels are designed to function with the batch command GOTO. GOTO instructs DOS to search through the file for the specified label. If the label is found, DOS continues the batch file operation by executing the instruction that follows the label.

Of course, the key to using a **GOTO** label command is that the **GOTO** is preceded by an **IF**. For example, suppose you wanted to perform on one of two different groups of commands within a batch file, depending upon whether a floppy or a hard disk was being used. Figure 15–2 shows how such a batch file might be constructed. Labels are placed in the batch at the beginning of each distinct set of commands, in this case, **HARDDISK** and **FLOPPYDISK**. Preceding the labels are IF...GOTO command combinations. The commands that are actually executed depends upon which of the IF...GOTO commands evaluates as true. If **IF...GOTO FLOPPYDISK** is true, the program will skip all of the commands in the batch until the

FLOPPYDISK label is encountered. The next command executed is the one immediately following the **FLOPPYDISK** label.

One of the most interesting and important parts of the diagram in Figure 15–2 is the use of the END label. It is important to keep in mind that labels mark the *beginning* of a section. There is no marking that indicates the *end* of a section. As far as DOS is concerned, the program will continue to execute consecutive commands until it reaches the end of the batch file.

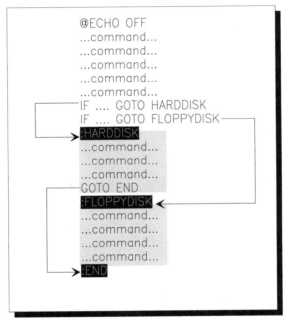

**Figure 15–2. Typical structured batch file with labels and GOTO commands.**

In Figure 15–2 a **GOTO END** command is placed at the end of the **HARDDISK** section. This command has the effect of marking the end of the **HARDDISK** section of the batch file. This is accomplished by using **GOTO** to jump over all of the sections following **HARDDISK** and arriving at the end of the program.

In other words, the **IF...GOTO** and **GOTO** commands are structured in such a way that each section of the batch file is *mutually exclusive* of the other. The batch will either execute the **HARDDISK** section or the **FLOPPYDISK** section each time it is run, but never both at one time. Note that DOS does not care about having *mutually exclusive* routines. They are created by carefully plotting the path of execution you want for each alternative included in the batch file.

Structured files, such as the one shown in the diagram, can contain any number of sections and they can be accessed in a variety of sequences, depending upon how you arrange the **GOTO** commands and the batch file labels. This allows you to perform as many commands and operations as you like based on the result of an **IF** command. Using labels eliminates the one-command limit that would otherwise be imposed by the **IF** command.

As an example, suppose you wanted to create a batch file that would contain various Norton Utilities commands used for disk maintenance, e.g., Norton Disk Doctor, Image, Speed Disk, Calibrate, etc. Recall from Chapters 10 and 14 that these programs can be used in a variety of ways. Some tasks, such as sorting directories or performing a Disk Doctor system area test, do not take much time and can be performed frequently. Others, such as a full-disk optimization or Calibrate pattern testing, take a considerable amount of time and need be done only periodically. With this in mind you may decide on three different levels of disk maintenance that you would want to perform at different times:

> **Level 1—Daily.** NDD /QUICK—system area test; **SPEEDISK /S**—sort files; **IMAGE**—update Image recovery files.

> **Level 2—Weekly.** *NDD /COMPLETE*—system area test; **SPEEDISK /F**—full optimization; **IMAGE**—update Image recovery files.

> **Level 3—Monthly.** NDD /QUICK—system area test; **CALIBRATE /PATTERN:5**—calibrate with pattern testing; **IMAGE**—update Image recovery files.

At first glance, you would suppose that you would have to create three different batch files to cover all three levels of disk maintenance. While there is nothing wrong with this approach, you can, by using labels, use **GOTO** and **IF** commands to create a single batch file that will perform any of the three levels of disk care, depending upon which parameter is specified.

Create a batch file called DISKCARE.BAT. This batch file will use labels to create three different sections—LEVEL_1, LEVEL_2, and LEVEL_3— each with different instructions. The **IF** command will be used to test parameter 2 to see if it specifies level 1, 2, or 3. The **GOTO** command will then cause the batch file to continue executing commands in the section that corresponds to the specified level. The batch begins with the usual **ECHO OFF** command:

```
@ECHO OFF
```

The next section of the batch will be used to evaluate the second parameter, **%2**, to see what level of disk care had been specified. The assumption is made that the user will enter a 1, 2, or 3 as the second parameter. The **IF** commands test to see which value was entered and use **GOTO** commands to jump to the corresponding labels.

Note the use of the **REM**—remark—command. This command allows you to enter notes or comments inside a batch file. **REM** lines have no functional effect on the batch file. However, notes and remarks can help you to remember what various commands or groups of commands are supposed to do. If you distribute batch files to other users, it is considered good computer etiquette to annotate your batch files with **REM** statements that explain the structure and function of the batch:

```
REM Check Parameter
IF "%2"=="1" GOTO LEVEL_1
IF "%2"=="2" GOTO LEVEL_2
IF "%2"=="3" GOTO LEVEL_3
```

The next section of the batch begins with a label, in this case LEVEL_1. The label marks the location to which the program will jump if parameter 2 has the value of 1. The commands that follow the label execute the Norton Utilities operations you want to perform on a daily basis.

The **ECHO** command is used to confirm the user's selections. Keep in mind that since the Norton Disk Doctor and Speed Disk programs will use full-screen displays, this message will appear on the screen for only a few seconds:

```
:LEVEL 1
ECHO Level %2 Disk Care for Drive %1
NDD %1: /QUICK
SPEEDISK %1: /SE
GOTO IMAGE
```

The last command in the LEVEL_1 section is **GOTO IMAGE**. This command serves two functions. First, it serves to mark the end of the section since it causes the batch to skip to the **IMAGE** label. Second, you may have noticed that each of the three levels outlined above ended with an **IMAGE** command. Since all three levels have this command in common, you can simplify your program by using a single **IMAGE** command at the end of the batch.

The batch continues by creating the sections for levels 2 and 3. These sections follow the same general pattern as the first level:

```
:LEVEL_2
ECHO Level %2 Disk Care for Drive %1
NDD %1: /COMPLETE
SPEEDISK %1: /F/V
GOTO IMAGE
:LEVEL_3
ECHO Level %2 Disk Care for Drive %1
NDD %1: /QUICK
CALIBRATE %1: /PATTERN:5/BATCH/BLANK
GOTO IMAGE
```

The final section is the **IMAGE** section, which will complete the disk maintenance operations by updating the **IMAGE** files:

```
:IMAGE
IMAGE %1:
ECHO Disk Maintenance of Drive %1 Level %2 Completed
```

The batch file is now complete. Figure 15–3 shows the full listing of the batch. To emphasize the structure of the batch file, the labels and references to the labels appear highlighted.

You can execute the batch file by supplying two parameters: the drive letter and the level number. Note that in DISKCARE the colon for the drive letter is included in the batch file so that you need enter only c, d, e, and so on, in order to specify the drive. For example, if you want to perform level 1 disk care on drive C you would enter DISKCARE c 1.

To perform level 3, monthly maintenance, on drive D you would use this command. Example: DISKCARE d 3.

Note that the parameters used could have been d, w, or m, for daily, weekly, or monthly. However, using 1, 2, and 3 has the advantage of eliminating the problem of case-sensitivity, which exists when letters are used as parameters.

## Indenting Batch Commands

At this point you are beginning to create batch files that have substantially more complicated logic than the simple list type batches discussed at the beginning of the chapter. It is useful to know that batch processing is *insensitive* to blank space in a batch file. This means that adding blank lines or extra spaces will not have an effect on the batch file. One common

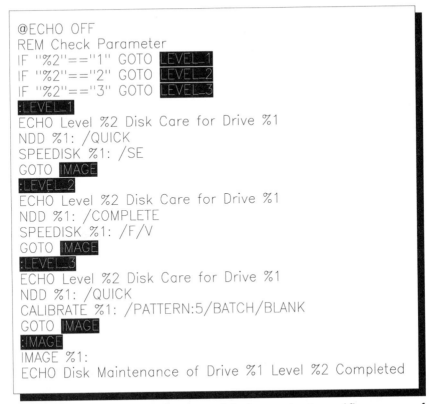

```
@ECHO OFF
REM Check Parameter
IF "%2"=="1" GOTO LEVEL_1
IF "%2"=="2" GOTO LEVEL_2
IF "%2"=="3" GOTO LEVEL_3
:LEVEL_1
ECHO Level %2 Disk Care for Drive %1
NDD %1: /QUICK
SPEEDISK %1: /SE
GOTO IMAGE
:LEVEL_2
ECHO Level %2 Disk Care for Drive %1
NDD %1: /COMPLETE
SPEEDISK %1: /F/V
GOTO IMAGE
:LEVEL_3
ECHO Level %2 Disk Care for Drive %1
NDD %1: /QUICK
CALIBRATE %1: /PATTERN:5/BATCH/BLANK
GOTO IMAGE
:IMAGE
IMAGE %1:
ECHO Disk Maintenance of Drive %1 Level %2 Completed
```

**Figure 15–3. DISKCARE.BAT uses labels to select specific groups of operations.**

technique used by computer professionals to make complicated programs easier to understand is *indenting*. Indenting helps indicate which commands are contained within which sections.

Below is the DISKCARE.BAT program with additional blank lines and indents. The style used makes the logic of the program more obvious and easier to follow, but has no functional effect on its operation since DOS will ignore this additional blank space:

```
@ECHO OFF
REM Check Parameter
IF "%2"=="1" GOTO LEVEL_1
IF "%2"=="2" GOTO LEVEL_2
IF "%2"=="3" GOTO LEVEL_3
```

```
:LEVEL_1
    ECHO Level %2 Disk Care for Drive %1
    NDD %1: /QUICK
    SPEEDISK %1: /SE
    GOTO IMAGE

:LEVEL_2
    ECHO Level %2 Disk Care for Drive %1
    NDD %1: /COMPLETE
    SPEEDISK %1: /F/V
    GOTO IMAGE

:LEVEL_3
    ECHO Level %2 Disk Care for Drive %1
    NDD %1: /QUICK
    CALIBRATE %1: /PATTERN:5/BATCH/BLANK
    GOTO IMAGE

:IMAGE
    IMAGE %1:
    ECHO Disk Maintenance of Drive %1 Level %2 Completed
```

Use of indenting style is optional. However, it is recommended that you do use indents, blanks line, and **REM** comments in your batch files, in particular, if you plan to distribute them to other users.

## Calling Other Batch Files

The DISKCARE.BAT program demonstrated how a single batch file could contain different sections that perform different tasks or similar tasks with different options. Most programming tasks, and batch files are indeed a form of programming, consist of breaking up a job into a series of small tasks called *routines*. The DISKCARE.BAT contained several routines, each of which had a different purpose.

One interesting example was the use of the **IMAGE** routine. The original design for the batch would have placed an **IMAGE** command in each section. However, you were able to write the batch more efficiently by creating a separate section, or routine, for the **IMAGE** program and using **GOTO** commands to execute that routine.

In addition to the use of structured routines within a batch file, DOS supports the use of other batch files, already on the disk, as subroutines that can be executed from a batch file. This means that you can streamline batch files by making use of routines already stored in existing batch files. The existing batch files are called *external subroutines* because the command text lies outside the current batch file.

For example, you may want to include the operation in level 1 of the **DISKCARE** batch as part of your AUTOEXEC.BAT so that these operations would be performed each time the computer was booted. One way to accomplish this would simply be to edit the AUTOEXEC.BAT and add the **NDD**, **SPEEDISK**, and **IMAGE** commands. An alternative would be to place a single command in the AUTOEXEC.BAT batch to access the level 1 disk care routine already stored in DISKCARE.BAT.

There are several advantages to this approach:

**Simplify Editing.** By using an existing batch file rather than entering all new commands, you simplify the task by adding a single command that uses the existing file. This is simpler to do then re-entering all of the commands that have already been entered. You also eliminate errors that might occur when you re-enter complicated commands. This is a significant point since many of the Norton Utilities line commands contain complicated combinations of parameters and switches, which are difficult to remember without referring to specific documentation. Executing existing batch files, e.g., **DISKCARE**, allows you to rely on routines you have already created and tested.

**Simplify Debugging.** Another advantage of executing external batch files is that they make it simpler to track down errors because various tasks are isolated in specific batch files. When an error occurs you can narrow down your search to the specific batch routine that was executing at that time, rather than having to work with one large batch file.

**Simpler Revision.** Suppose you decide that you want to modify the operations used for daily, level 1, disk care (e.g., change the Speed Disk sort order from E—extension—to N—file name). Making a single change to the DISKCARE.BAT file would automatically be reflected in all other batch files, e.g., AUTOEXEC.BAT, that also use this routine. On the other hand, if you had not used DISKCARE as an external subroutine of AUTOEXEC.BAT, you would have to remember to modify AUTOEXEC.BAT if you wanted it to be consistent with the procedures in DISKCARE.

**Use Separately or Together.** Creating individual batch files for distinct routines gives you the option of executing the subroutines separately, as well as part of larger batches such as AUTOEXEC.BAT. This would mean, in terms of the example, that you could run disk care level 1 whenever you desired, without having to run the entire AUTOEXEC.BAT.

These reasons indicate that, even used with modest experience, batch file operations can benefit from executing *external* subroutines. However, external execution is not without drawbacks. The primary one is that it takes DOS some additional time to locate and load the external batch files. One way to minimize this additional time is to place all of the subroutine batch files in the same directory, the root directory of the boot drive, so that DOS will not spend time searching other directories for the batch files.

## Types of External Routines

DOS can access existing batch files as external subroutines in two ways.

**Execute Batch**    Batch execution from within a batch file is accomplished by simply entering the command that you would normally enter at the DOS prompt to execute the external batch. For example, if you wanted to perform level 1 disk care you would enter **DISCARE C1** into the batch. The main point to keep in mind about direct execution is that control of the flow of the batch is transferred to the subroutine. This means that once DOS begins executing the external subroutine, it will continue until it reaches the end of the subroutine and then stop. DOS will not return to the original batch, but simply exit to the DOS prompt (Figure 15–4).

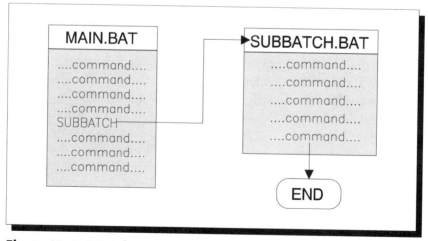

**Figure 15–4. DOS does not return to the original batch file when the subroutine is complete.**

The only way that a directly executed subroutine can return to the main routine is by adding a direct execution command to the subroutine, e.g., **AUTOEXEC** will restart the AUTOEXEC.BAT file again. However, when restarted, the AUTOEXEC.BAT will begin at the top of the file, not at the point where the external routine was executed, causing the subroutine to be executed again when that point in the batch is reached. The effect would be an endless loop in which DOS bounces back and forth between AUTOEXEC.BAT and DISCARE.BAT, for example, until you manually terminated the batch with [Ctrl-break].

**Call Batch**    The **CALL** command can be used in a batch file to execute an existing batch file as a subroutine. The key to the **CALL** command is that DOS will automatically return to the original batch file when the subroutine completes execution. Also note that DOS returns to the point in the batch where the **CALL** command occurs, not the beginning of the batch. Following the subroutine, DOS executes the next command in the original (referred to as the *calling*) batch (Figure 5–15).

In general, using **CALL** is the preferred method. Below is an example of an AUTOEXEC.BAT file that calls the **DISKCARE** batch file as a subroutine in order to perform disk maintenance as part of the booting process:

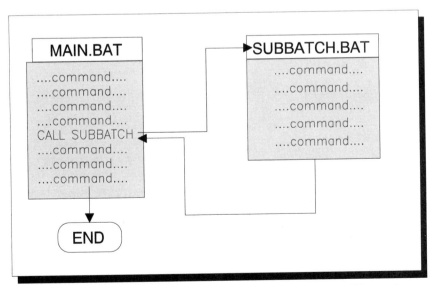

**Figure 15–5. DOS returns to the original batch after calling subroutine completes.**

```
@ECHO OFF
PATH C:\DOS;C:\NU;
CALL DISKCARE C 1
```

Note that it is quite easy to maintain several hard disks with a subroutine, such as DISKCARE, since all that is needed to care for a second disk is to add another **DISKCARE** call with a different drive letter:

```
@ECHO OFF
PATH C:\DOS;C:\NU;
CALL DISKCARE C 1
CALL DISKCARE D 1
```

Another good use for a subroutine call is the **PATH** command, normally included directly in the AUTOEXEC.BAT. Below is an example of a typical AUTOEXEC.BAT in which line 2 sets the search paths:

```
@ECHO OFF
PROMPT $P$G
PATH C:\DOS;C:\NU;C:\LOTUS;C:\WP50
CALL DISKCARE C 1
```

An alternative would be to create a batch file, such as SETPATH.BAT, that contains the **PATH** command, and then insert a **CALL** in the AUTOEXEC.BAT, which executes the **SETPATH** batch as a subroutine:

```
(SETPATH.BAT)
PATH C:\DOS;C:\NU;C:\LOTUS;C:\WP50

(AUTOEXEC.BAT)
@ECHO OFF
PROMPT $P$G
CALL SETPATH
CALL DISKCARE C 1
```

The advantages in the method are listed under "Calling Other Batch Files" before. The most important is that you have the ability to execute the **PATH** command separate from the AUTOEXEC.BAT. You may, from time to time, want to change the current path set-up. You can easily return to your default path list by directly executing **SETPATH** at the DOS prompt. In addition, you can simplify the task of setting paths by editing the one-line batch file, **SETPATH**, rather than the more complicated AUTOEXEC.BAT.

## List Processing

In the previous sections, you have used variables in batch files to insert various parameters into commands. Another use for variables is to process a list of items. For example, suppose that you wanted to copy the CONFIG.SYS, AUTOEXEC.BAT, DISKCARE.BAT, and COMMAND.COM files to a floppy disk. The task would be quite simple if the found files had in common some characters that would allow you to use a wildcard such as *.BAT or C*.*. Unfortunately the actual names would require you to use several commands. Below is a batch file that would accomplish the task:

```
@ECHO OFF
COPY CONFIG.SYS A:
COPY AUTOEXEC.BAT A:
COPY DISKCARE.BAT A:
COPY COMMAND.COM A:
```

An alternative method of processing these instructions is to use a **FOR** command. The **FOR** command is designed to accept a list of items and a command such as **COPY**. When executed, the **FOR** command executes the specified operation, e.g., **COPY**, once for each item in the list. If the items in the list, e.g., file names or wildcards, need to be passed as parameters to the command, you can insert a variable in the command.

Variables used with **FOR** use a slightly different style than those used for command-line parameters. The variables can be single letters (A–Z) preceded by two percent signs (e.g., %%a, %%b, etc.). The **FOR** command has the following general form:

```
FOR variable IN (list of items) DO command
```

Using the example of copying files, the list would be the names of the files (CONFIG.SYS, AUTOEXEC.BAT, DISKCARE.BAT, COMMAND.COM) and the command would be COPY *filename* A:. You would use a variable such as %%f to pass the items from the list to the command. The batch file could then be rewritten as follows:

```
@ECHO OFF
FOR %%f IN(config.sys,autoexec.bat,diskcare.bat, command.com) DO copy %%f a:
```

If you wanted to perform more sophisticated processing with a list you could replace the command with a **CALL** that would execute a batch file. Earlier the following batch was shown to illustrate how a batch could call the same external subroutine more than once, in this case, to perform disk maintenance on drives C and D:

```
@ECHO OFF
PATH C:\DOS;C:\NU;
CALL DISKCARE C 1
CALL DISKCARE D 1
```

However, you could replace both commands with a single **FOR** command as shown below:

```
@ECHO OFF
PATH C:\DOS;C:\NU;
FOR %d IN (c,d) DO call diskcare %%d 1
```

The advantage of list processing is that you can quickly expand the scope of the process. Suppose the system in question had drives C through G that required maintenance. You could cover all of the drives by simply expanding the list, as shown below:

```
@ECHO OFF
PATH C:\DOS;C:\NU;
FOR %%d IN (c,d,e,f,g) DO call diskcare %%d 1
```

**FOR** is also useful in backup procedures. One way to save time when backing up data is to back up selectively; that is, only those files that you really need to back up, e.g., your Lotus spreadsheets.

Note that the **FOR** command can be used *directly* at the DOS prompt to initiate a series of operations. The only difference is that the variable names are preceded by a single % rather than two % signs:

```
Within batch file:
FOR %%d IN (c,d) DO call discare %%d 1

at DOS prompt
FOR %d IN (c,d) DO call discare %d 1
```

Both commands perform the same function.

## Exit Codes

Up to this point, the **IF** command has been used to evaluate parameters entered directly by the user. However, there are instances when you might want to use an **IF** structure based on the results of some event rather than a user entry. For example, batch files that perform copy or backup operations always have the potential to fail for one reason or another. When you are operating manually, you would react one way when an operation (such as a backup) was successfully completed and another way if it failed.

In some cases DOS provides a method of determining what happened during the execution of a command. The method involves the use of the *Errorlevel* value. When a command has completed its operation, it stores a numeric value in a specific memory location. You can include the value of that *exit code* in a batch file **IF** command by using the word *ERRORLEVEL*. Generally, if a program or utility ends normally, that is, no errors, the ERRORLEVEL is set at 1. If the program or utility terminates because of an error, the ERRORLEVEL is set at 0.

Keep in mind that not all DOS commands or applications set the ERRORLEVEL value. The most commonly used commands that do set the ERRORLEVEL are **XCOPY** and **BACKUP**. On the one hand, the DOS commands **COPY**, **DEL**, and **RENAME** do not set the ERRORLEVEL to 0; on the other hand, the Norton Utilities program IMAGE does set the ERRORLEVEL value.

The ERRORLEVEL value can be put to use in batch files in order to select an operation on the basis of the outcome of a previous command. Below is a batch file called RECFILES.BAT. This batch is used to create Image recovery files on a specified drive. The key to this batch is the use of the **IF ERRORLEVEL** commands following the **IMAGE** command. Image will return an ERRORLEVEL of 0 if the command cannot create its recovery files. Note the use of NUL in line 2 to suppress the built-in error messages that would appear normally from Image.

The batch displays its own message, depending upon the success or failure of Image:

```
@ECHO OFF                                               {1}
IMAGE %1: > NUL                                         {2}
IF ERRORLEVEL 1 GOTO FAILED                             {3}
IF ERRORLEVEL 0 GOTO OK                                 {4}
:OK                                                     {5}
     ECHO Recovery Files Created for Drive %1           {6}
     GOTO END                                           {7}
:FAILED                                                 {8}
     ECHO Recovery Files for %1: could not be created   {9}
     GOTO END                                           {10}
:END                                                    {11}
```

You can test the batch by entering in an actual or false drive letter. Enter recfiles z ↵.

The batch will display its failure message since there is no Z drive available. Repeat the command with a valid drive letter. Enter recfiles c ↵.

This time the commands related to a successful conclusion are displayed.

## Environmental Variables

So far you have encountered two types of variables:

**Parameters.** Parameter variables are automatically assigned values based on the sequence of parameters in the command line. The variables are %0 through %9.

**FOR Command Variables.**  If you are using the **FOR** command you can assign each item in the list to a variable, %%a through %%z.

DOS recognizes a third type of variable, called an *environmental* variable. Environmental variables operate much like the other variables you have encountered in that they insert text into commands in order to facilitate processing of batch files. They are different from the other variables in the following ways:

**Descriptive Names.**  Environmental variables can have names that are more than a single character. Variables are referenced by enclosing the name in %, e.g., a variable named **NU** would be referenced by %nu%.

**Remain Active.**  Unlike other variables, which exist temporarily while the batch **FOR** list is being processed, environmental variables remain in memory until the current session is ended or they are explicitly deleted. This means that once a variable is created it can be used by many different batch files executing at different times.

**System Variables.**  DOS maintains several variables that contain information about the current state of the operating system. These variables can also be accessed in batch files. For example, DOS maintains a variable called **COMSPEC**. This variable contains the file and path name of the active command interpreter file, by default C:\COMMAND.COM.

Environmental variables are defined by the **SET** command. **SET** can be used at the DOS prompt or within a batch file. The example defines the variable **NU** as the path name *C:\NU*. Example: SET NU=\NU.

Note that even though you recognize **\NU** as a path name, DOS simply sees it as a string of characters. It can have meaning only when it is inserted into a DOS command in order to create a valid DOS operation. For example, if you want to activate the directory within a batch file you could enter a command. Example: CD %NU%.

The name *environmental* variable refers to the fact that the initial reason for allowing such variables was to create a means by which information about the arrangement of the current system could be placed into memory, where it could be accessed by various applications. Recall from Chapter 1 that Versions 5.0 and 6.0 of the Norton Utilities will use the path name stored under the variable **NU** to determine the *home* directory for the Norton Utilities. The *home* directory is the one in which the INI initialization files will be read and written. By default, this is the same directory the Norton Utilities programs are stored in. When operating on a network, the *home* directory for each user is defined by the name stored for **NU**.

## Environment Space

By default, DOS allocates between 160 and 256 bytes of space, depending upon DOS version, for environmental variables. DOS automatically defines three variables: COMSPEC, PATH, and PROMPT. Depending on the number of variables defined and the amount of text in each variable, you can run *out of environment space*. If you have DOS 3.2 or higher you can increase the amount of space reserved for environmental variables using the **SHELL** command in your CONFIG.SYS file. The **SHELL** command sets the command interpreter file, by default COMMAND.COM. The /E switch sets the environmental variable size in bytes. The example establishes a 512-byte environment space for variables: SHELL = C:\COMMAND.COM /P /E:512.

Note that the **/P** is used to load a *permanent* copy of COMMAND.COM for the current session.

## Use the Control Center Timer

The Norton Control Center program includes a stopwatch feature that allows you to calculate the elapsed time of various events through batch file processing. Timers are controlled with two switches:

**/START.** This switch starts a new timer at zero.

**/STOP.** This switch displays the elapsed time since the start of the timer. Note that you can issue a series of **/STOP** commands for a given timer. Each time the program will display the total elapsed time the **/START** switch was used.

The example starts a timer: NCC /START.

When you want to display the elapsed time use the **/STOP** switch as shown below: NCC /STOP.

Keep in mind that each time you repeat the **/STOP** switch you will display the accumulated time. Entering a **/START** will reset the timer back to zero and begin a new time sequence.

You can use DOS redirection to print the elapsed time or store it in a text file. The commands shown below outputs the elapsed time. Note that the **ECHO** command is used to feed the remainder of the page:

```
NCC /STOP >PRN
ECHO ^L >PRN
```

The sequence of commands below shows how the elapsed time can be stored in a text file, e.g., *TIMELOG*, using DOS redirection. Line 1 sends the elapsed time to a new file called *TIMELOG*. The **/L** switch places the time on the left side of the line—the default is the right side. The **/N** switch suppresses the output of the current time and date. Line 2 uses the redirection append operator, >>, to add the test *has elapsed during this operation* to the TIMELOG text file. This creates a complete statement, e.g., *55 seconds has elapsed during this operation*:

```
NCC /STOP/L/N >timelog                              {1}
ECHO  has elapsed during this operation >> timelog  {2}
```

If you look carefully at the **ECHO** command in line 2 you may notice what appears to be an extra space between the command **ECHO** and the test *has elapsed during this operation*. This is no accident. The first space acts as the delimiter that separates the command **ECHO** from the text. The second space is included so that the text in TIMELOG will have a space between the elapsed time and the echoed text. Without this extra space DOS would place the echoed phrase immediately after the elapsed time, e.g., *55 seconds has elapsed*. Since reading blank spaces is difficult an _ will be used in this book to indicate commands where extra spaces are used in this way. When you enter the commands, replace the _ with a space.

The Control Center can maintain up to four separate timers. Each **/START** or **/STOP** switch can accept a numeric parameter, 1–4, which will select which of the four timers is affected by the command. If you wanted to start timer 2, you would enter NCC /START:2. Stopping timer 2 would require this command: NCC /STOP:2. If you do not include a number, the program assumes that you are operating on timer 1.

## Timing Operations in Batch Files

The timer feature of the Control Center can be used to display or log the time used by various operations. For example, the Disk Care operations carried out by a batch file, such as DISKCARE.BAT, can be timed and logged in a text file automatically as part of the batch operation. Below is a revised version of the DISKCARE batch file that includes commands that will generate a log of the disk care operations performed with this batch.

The first addition is line 3, which starts a Control Center timer. The **>NUL** redirection operator is used to suppress the time and date display that normally appears when a timer is started:

```
@ECHO OFF                                          {1}
REM Check Parameter                                {2}
NCC/START:1>NUL                                    {3}
IF "%2"=="1" GOTO LEVEL_1                           {4}
IF "%2"=="2" GOTO LEVEL_2                           {5}
IF "%2"=="3" GOTO LEVEL_3                           {6}
:LEVEL_1                                           {7}
     ECHO Level %2 Disk Care for Drive %1          {8}
     NDD %1: /QUICK                                {9}
     SPEEDISK %1: /SE                              {10}
     GOTO IMAGE                                    {11}
:LEVEL_2                                           {12}
     ECHO Level %2 Disk Care for Drive %1          {13}
     NDD %1: /COMPLETE                             {14}
     SPEEDISK %1: /F/V                             {15}
     GOTO IMAGE                                    {16}
:LEVEL_3                                           {17}
     ECHO Level %2 Disk Care for Drive %1          {18}
     NDD %1: /QUICK                                {19}
     CALIBRATE %1: /PATTERN:5/BATCH/BLANK          {20}
     GOTO IMAGE                                    {21}
```

```
:IMAGE                                                           {22}
    IMAGE %1:                                                    {23}
    ECHO Disk Maintenance of Drive %1 Level %2 Completed         {24}
NCC/STOP:1/L/N                                                   {25}
ECHO_Elapsed Time                                               {26}
ECHO Disk Maintenance of Drive %1 Level %2 Performed>>DKCARE.LOG {27}
NCC/STOP:1/L>>DKCARE.LOG                                         {28}
ECHO_Elapsed Time>>DKCARE.LOG                                   {29}
```

The remainder of the changes are found at the end of the program, lines 25 through 29. Lines 25 and 26 display the elapsed time on the screen. Lines 27 through 29 send the same information to the DKCARE.LOG file. Note that these commands use the >> append operator so that new text is added to the file each time the batch is run.

You will notice a slight difference between the switches used in line 25 and 28. Line 25 outputs information to the screen. The /N switch is used to suppress the time and date displays since the user probably doesn't need this information. On the other hand, it is important, when creating an activity log, to include the time and date of each operation. Therefore, the /N switch is not used in command 28, which stores text in the text file DKCARE.LOG. Below is a sample of what the DKCARE.LOG would look like:

```
Disk Maintenance of Drive c Level 1 Performed
11:29 am, Tuesday, May 28, 1991
4 minutes, 41 seconds Elapsed Time
Disk Maintenance of Drive c Level 1 Performed
12:06 pm, Tuesday, May 29, 1991
5 minutes, 11 seconds Elapsed Time
```

The same /STOP:1 switch is used to generate both times. In theory, this will create a small difference in the actual time required to complete the disk maintenance and the time recorded in the log. In practice, this difference will be so small that the times generated by both commands will probably be identical or, at the most, one second apart.

The timer concept demonstrated in the revised DISKCARE program can be generally applied to any activity that you want to time or simply keep an activity log on. You will see later in this chapter how the concept of an activity log is combined with a menu system that will enable you to have a complete log of all operations you carry out on your computer.

# Norton Utilities Batch Enhancer

The Norton Utilities Batch Enhancer program is designed to extend the range of the DOS batch language in order to allow you to create better and more useful batch files. Understanding how to use the Batch Enhancer requires a general understanding of DOS batch file operations, as presented in the previous part of this chapter. Although the batch files discussed so far have presented a wide variety of fairly powerful features, the basic DOS batch command set lacks some very important tools:

**Interactive Input.**  In all of the batch files so far, input from the user has been in the form of parameters entered as part of the command line that executes the batch file. Parameters have some serious drawbacks regarding ease of use. In order to use a batch file with parameters, the user must know in advance what parameters are required or are optional, what characters are valid for those parameters, and in what order they need to be entered. It is easy to imagine a user making a mistake that will result in all sorts of problems. For example, the DISKCARE batch wants a letter only entered as the drive letter. If the user, quite understandably, entered **C:** instead of just **C**, the whole batch would be thrown off.

A better solution would be to display a menu of options that tells the user what should be entered and when. This is what most applications do in one way or another. Menus that allow for user input allow anyone to use the batch file, in contrast to parameters that require the user to have knowledge in advance about the batch.

The Batch Enhancer **ASK** command provides a means of pausing a batch file for user input. This makes menu-driven batch files easy to create.

**Text Placement.**  Information generated from a batch file with commands like **ECHO** are placed on the next available line of the screen display. This is not the best way to present information to a user. In order to create more readable screen displays, you will need direct control over where on the screen the text is placed. The Batch Enhancer **ROWCOL** command gives you complete control over the text displayed by the batch file.

**Sound.**  You can add tones or entire melodies to your batch file operations using the **BEEP** command. Sound adds another dimension to your batch file programs.

**Color.** The Batch Enhancer allows you to specify DOS colors with the **SA** (screen attributes) command, as well as specific colors to individual items.

**Drawing.** The Batch Enhancer supports the drawing of lines, boxes, and windows on the screen, which makes your batch file display look more pleasing and professional.

## The Batch Enhancer Commands, Version 5.0

The Batch Enhancer program consists of a number of specific *sub-commands* that perform various tasks within batch files. There are ten subcommands in Version 5.0 of the Norton Utilities Batch Enhancer, as compared to nine in Version 4.5, **GOTO** being the only addition in 5.0. They also apply to Version 6.0 for the most part:

**ASK.** The ASK subcompact is one of the most important parts of the Batch Enhancer subcompact set, because it provides a method by which user inputs can be made within batch files. **ASK** allows you to display a message and receive a single-character response from the user. The response is recorded in terms of an error level value 1, 2, 3, etc. Recall that the **IF** command can be used to evaluate error code levels. This command also supports colors.

**BEEP.** The **BEEP** command provides control over the speaker so you can create audio prompts as part of your batch files. The **BEEP** commands allow you to select the frequency, duration, and repetitions of the tones that sound during your batch file execution.

**BOX.** The **BOX** subcompact is used to draw single- or double-line boxes at specific screen locations. The command supports color selection.

**CLS.** Clears the screen and returns the cursor to its home position in the upper left corner of the screen. This command duplicates the DOS **CLS** command within a Batch Enhancer subfile.

**DELAY.** This subcompact causes a pause in the execution of the batch file for a specified amount of time. The time is specified in terms of *ticks*, which are equal to 1/18th of a second. When the time is elapsed, the batch file continues with the next command, if any.

**GOTO.** This command duplicates the function of the DOS batch **GOTO** command inside a Batch Enhancer subfile.

**PRINTCHAR.** This subcompact displays a specified number of repetitions of a single character. The command supports color selection.

**ROWCOL.** This subcompact is used to position the cursor at specific locations on the screen display. This enables you to display information on any part of the screen during batch file processing. You can also select colors for the text.

**SA.** The subcompact is the equivalent of the System Attributes program provided in Version 4.5 of the Norton Utilities and duplicates the DOS colors feature in the Control Center program. It allows you to select screen colors and attributes, such as blinking, which will be used by DOS as its default colors, assuming the ANSI.SYS driver is loaded into memory.

**WINDOW.** This subcompact is similar to **BOX**, in that it draws a double-lined box at the specified screen position. Windows differ from box in three ways. First, they are always double-lined. Second, WINDOW wipes clear any information that falls within the window, while **BOX** only overwrites information on the borders. This means that text that should appear inside a window must be placed into the window after it is displayed. Boxes can be drawn around existing text. Finally, boxes can be displayed with special effects such as zoom and shadows. This command supports colors.

Batch Enhancer commands can be issued in two ways:

**Direct.** Direct entry of a Batch Enhancer command begins with **BE** and is followed by the subcompact and any required parameters. The example prints the word **Hello** at row 10, column 35. Example: BE ROWCOL 10,35,Hello.

**Subfile.** A subfile is a text file that contains a series of Batch Enhancer commands. You can execute the entire list by entering the name of the subfile with the **BE** command. The example below shows a text file, TEXT.TXT, that commands two subcommands. The **BE** command reads the TEXT.TXT file and executes the subcommands found in that file:

```
(TEXT.TXT)
ROWCOL 10,35,Hello
ROWCOL 11,30,Welcome!

  BE text.txt
```

The advantage of the subfile method is that it will execute a list of Batch Enhancer commands faster than a series of direct Batch Enhancer commands. This is because DOS will search for and load the Batch Enhancer program each time a **BE** command is encountered within a batch file. On the other hand, if a subfile is used, DOS needs to load the **BE** program only once in order to process all of the commands in the subfile. Conversely, when you execute **BE** commands directly in a batch file you can combine Batch Enhancer operations with DOS batch commands, such as **ECHO** or **IF**.

When you want to display a large amount of text, e.g., a menu, it is best to place the commands inside a subfile in order to make the display smoother and faster.

## A Menu in a Batch File

The primary advantage of Batch Enhancer processing is that it allows you to run batch files that display menus from which users can make selections. This eliminates the main obstacle to ease-of-use in batch file programming, parameter entry. A menu is created out of two parts:

**Screen Display.** The menu is created by using the Batch Enhancer screen display commands, **ROWCOL, PRINTCHAR, BOX**, and **WINDOW**, to inform the user of the options available. You can create a menu display with **ECHO**, but the Batch Enhancer commands provide superior control and features.

**Input Pause.** The menu is simply a text display. It is the **ASK** subcompact that pauses the batch file and allows the user to enter a response.

Suppose you wanted to create a batch file that allows the user to select the colors to be used by DOS. While this can be accomplished using the Control Center program, you can create a batch that simplifies the choice and options to something any user can work with, even if they have never heard of the Norton Utilities. You will create a batch file called COLORS.BAT that allows a user to select one of three different color combinations for DOS.

The batch begins with an **ECHO OFF** followed by a **CLS**, which clears the screen of any data.

```
@ECHO OFF
CLS
```

The next section of the program is used to display the text of the menu. This section uses a series of **ROWCOL** commands. The **ROWCOL** command places information at specific locations on the screen. These commands view the screen as a grid of rows (horizontal) and columns (vertical). The standard screen display is divided into 25 rows and 80 columns. The first row and column are assigned the number **zero,** not 1. This means that the bottom row on the screen is row 24 and the column on the right edge is column 79. You must specify the starting row/column location for each **ROWCOL** command. The location is followed by the text to display, starting at the specified location. The text phrase should be enclosed in quotation marks unless it is only a single word. You can also set the screen attributes using a color setting:

**Color.** You can specify the desired colors using the key words White, Black, Red, Magenta, Blue, Green, Cyan, and Yellow.

**Intensity.** You can change the foreground color by specifying either *Bright* or *Blinking* intensity for the color. Color settings take the form: *(intensity) foreground* ON *background.*

In the commands shown below the video attributes are abbreviated by entering only the first three characters. You can use the full color name or the first three letters if you want to save time. The menu below uses colors to display the options in the colors that they will generate if selected. This allows each item in the menu to function as an example. The text of the menu options are padded with extra spaces; they will all have the same length so that their appearance is more uniform:

```
BE ROWCOL 7,25,"Screen Colors"
BE ROWCOL 10,15,"Default Colors Yellow/Blue " COLOR BRI YEL ON BLU
BE ROWCOL 12,15,"Alternate Colors Yellow/Blue" COLOR BLU ON WHI
BE ROWCOL 14,15,"Black & White               " COLOR WHI ON BLA
```

## Cursor Location

It is important to remember that the **ROWCOL** commands also control the location of the DOS cursor. The DOS cursor is located immediately after the end of the last **ROWCOL** command. For example, the last **ROWCOL** command entered began at row 14, column 15 and printed

*"Black & White                  ."* This left the cursor on row 14 at column 43 (Figure 15–6). This means that the next command, other than a **ROWCOL**, which places text on the screen, will begin at 14,43. In this batch file the next item you want to display is a prompt for the user to enter a selection. This will be accomplished with the Batch Enhancer **ASK** subcommand. However, this subcommand is *unformatted*; that is, it does not specify the row and column location where the text is to be displayed. Instead, like most DOS commands, it will output its text at the first row and column.

You can control the placement of unformatted text by using a **ROWCOL** command with any text. For example, the command **ROWCOL 24,0** will place the DOS cursor in the lower left corner of the screen. Any standard output sent to the screen will begin at that location (see Figure 15–6). Add the following **ROWCOL** command to the batch for the purpose of positioning the cursor without actually placing any text on the screen. Example: BE ROWCOL 24,0.

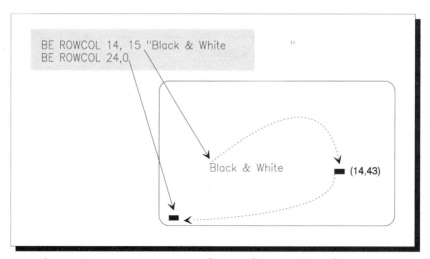

**Figure 15–6. ROWCOL can be used to position the cursor.**

## The ASK Subcommand

User responses are handled by the **ASK** subcommand. **ASK** pauses the execution of the batch file and waits for the user to enter a key. When the user enters a key, **ASK** sets the ERRORLEVEL value to reflect the key that is entered:

**Prompt Text.**  The prompt text is simply a phrase or question you want to display so that the user will have an opportunity to enter a response. The **ASK** subcommand displays the prompt and then waits for the user to press a key.

**Key List.**  The key list is a list of the keys that the user might enter in response to the prompt. The key list serves two functions. First, it limits the entry made by the user to the keys in the list. If the key pressed is one of the keys in the key list, the **ASK** command terminates and allows the batch file to continue. If the key pressed is not part of the key list, a beep is sounded and the prompt remains active until a key list key is pressed. The only exception is the [Esc] key, which will terminate the **ASK** subcommand and return an ERRORLEVEL value of zero.

The second function of the key list is to pass a specific value to the DOS batch file option, **ERRORLEVEL**. The **ERRORLEVEL** option is used with the batch command **IF**. **ERRORLEVEL** will always have a numeric value from 0 to 255. By default, the value is set at 0. The option was built into DOS to work with commands such as **FORMAT**, **BACKUP**, and **RESTORE**. If an error occurred during the execution of a batch file, DOS would place a value into the **ERRORLEVEL** that could be used to evaluate the error. The **ASK** subcommand takes advantage of the existence of the **ERRORLEVEL** option by assigning the option a value based on the user's input. The value corresponds to the position in the key list of the key that was pressed by the user. For example, if the key list contains the character *abcde* and the user presses c, then **ERRORLEVEL** is set equal to 3. Following an **ASK** subcommand, a series of **IF** commands with **ERRORLEVEL** tests can be used to determine which key was pressed by the user and what actions should be taken based on that selection. If you do not specify a key list with the **ASK** subcommand, **ASK** will accept any key that is pressed. The **ERRORLEVEL** value is set to zero. Using **ASK** in this manner creates a pause in the execution of the batch file, which will terminate when any key is pressed. The **ASK** subcommand also accepts the following optional specifications.

**Default**     This option sets a character that will automatically be entered if the user pressed ↵ when the **ASK** prompt is displayed. The character set as the default does not have to be one of the characters in the key list. The default key is also related to the use of the Timeout option. The default will be automatically entered if the user fails to make a selection during the Timeout.

**Timeout**    The Timeout option places a limit on the time the user has to respond to the **ASK** subcommand prompt. If the user does not enter a response within the specified number of seconds, the default key is automatically entered. When Timeout is not used, the **ASK** subcommand will wait forever for the user to make a selection.

Timeout is very handy when you include a batch as part of the AUTOEXEC.BAT. If an **ASK** command is executed as part of the loading process, the program will pause indefinitely, awaiting a response. If the user has turned on the computer and left, he or she may be dismayed to find that the computer is still waiting for a response. Timeout ensures that this waiting period has a limit, after which time the remainder of the AUTOEXEC.BAT will be executed. This option makes it much more practical to have pauses in the AUTOEXEC.BAT.

**Adjust**    This option is used to add a fixed value to the **ERRORLEVEL** code. For example, the option **ADJUST–10** would add 10 to the value of the key pressed, e.g., 3+10 = 13. This option would be used when the user is asked to make a selection from a series of layered menus and still have each selection create a unique **ERRORLEVEL** value.

**Color**    You can use color specifications, such as those used with **ROWCOL**, to set the color of the prompt text.

In this case, add the following **ASK** command to the batch. The command will accept only the letters *d*, *a*, or *b*. If no key is pressed in ten seconds, the color is set to the default, black and white.

```
BE ASK "Enter D, A or B to set colors: ",dab TIMEOUT=10 DEFAULT=b
```

## Evaluating User Input

Once the user has made a selection, or the Timeout expires, thus selecting the default, the batch program must evaluate the response and branch to the corresponding command sequence. The procedure here is about the same as that outlined under "Exit Codes." The only difference is that the number of ERRORLEVEL tests must correspond to the number of keys in the key list, in this example, three.

The **IF ERRORLEVEL** commands should be placed in descending order, high to low, in order to ensure that they are correctly evaluated. This is because **IF ERRORLEVEL** tests for an ERRORLEVEL value that is equal to or greater than the specified value. For example, if the ERRORLEVEL is set at 3 and the first command encountered is **IF ERRORLEVEL 2 GOTO X**, the batch will branch to X because the ERRORLEVEL value is greater than 2. Complete the batch by entering

```
IF ERRORLEVEL 3 GOTO bw
IF ERRORLEVEL 2 GOTO alternate
IF ERRORLEVEL 1 GOTO default
:DEFAULT
     BE SA BRI YEL ON BLU
     GOTO END
:ALTERNATE
     BE SA BLU ON WHI
     GOTO END
:BW
     BE SA WHI ON BLA
:END
```

The entire COLORS.BAT file should read:

```
@ECHO OFF                                                        {1}
CLS                                                              {2}
BE ROWCOL 7,25,"Screen Colors"                                   {3}
BE ROWCOL 10,15,"Default Colors Yellow/Blue   " COLOR BRI YEL ON BLU {4}
BE ROWCOL 12,15,"Alternate Colors Yellow/Blue" COLOR BLU ON WHI  {5}
BE ROWCOL 14,15,"Black & White               " COLOR WHI ON BLA  {6}
BE ROWCOL 24,0                                                   {7}
BE ASK "Enter D, A or B to set colors: ",dab TIMEOUT=10 DEFAULT=b {8}
IF ERRORLEVEL 3 GOTO bw                                          {9}
IF ERRORLEVEL 2 GOTO alternate                                   {10}
IF ERRORLEVEL 1 GOTO default                                     {11}
:DEFAULT                                                         {12}
     BE SA BRI YEL ON BLU                                        {13}
     GOTO END                                                    {14}
:ALTERNATE                                                       {15}
     BE SA BLU ON WHI                                            {16}
     GOTO END                                                    {17}
:BW                                                              {18}
     BE SA WHI ON BLA                                            {19}
:END                                                             {20}
```

When the batch has been saved, test it by entering colors ↵. The program displays a menu on the screen, then pauses for the user to enter a key (Figure 15–7).

Enter d.

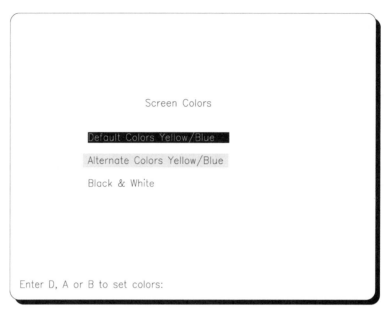

Screen Colors

Default Colors Yellow/Blue

Alternate Colors Yellow/Blue

Black & White

Enter D, A or B to set colors:

**Figure 15–7. Menu created with Batch Enhancer commands.**

The screen colors will change to yellow on blue, assuming you have a color screen. Run the program again, but this time simply let the time expire and have the program use the default setting. Enter colors ↵.

## Windows and Boxes

The Batch Enhancer **WINDOW** and **BOX** subcommands can be used to add special effects to your batch files.

**Boxes**    Boxes are transparent in the sense that any information already on the screen that falls within the interior of the box being drawn remains on the screen. A box will overwrite a character only if the box border, a single line, is drawn directly over that character. This means that boxes can be drawn around information that has been placed on the screen before the box is drawn. This command accepts color settings. The following command draws a box on the screen at the specified location. Note that only the border of the box is affected by the color settings. Example: BE BOX 10,10,12,70 RED ON WHI.

**Windows**     Windows overwrite all information currently written to the area that will be covered by the window. A window always begins as a blank box, regardless of what has been written to the screen previously. This command accepts color settings. The example below draws a box at the specified location. When a window is drawn, the color affects the entire area enclosed by the window. Note that windows are always double-lined. Example: BE WINDOW 10,10,12,70 RED ON WHI.

**Special Effects**     Windows have two built-in, special visual effects:

1.  **EXPLODE** or **ZOOM** affects the way the window is drawn. When selected, the window is drawn smaller than specified. The program then redraws the box one or more times until it reaches the specified size. The effect is to create the appearance of a window that is growing in size.

2.  **SHADOW** creates a *drop shadow* effect so that the window is given a 3-D look. The shadow itself is transparent, so that text covered by the shadow shows through. The example draws a window with a drop shadow. Example: BE WINDOW 10,10,12,70 COLOR RED ON WHI SHADOW.

Boxes are drawn by default with single lines, but can be changed to double lines with the **DOUBLE** option. Example: BE BOX 10,10,12,70 RED ON WHI DOUBLE.

Keep in mind that the addition of boxes and windows has no functional effect on the program. Below is a revised copy of the COLORS.BAT in which windows and boxes have been added to the program to give it a more professional look. The changes, shown in bold, are:

**Menu Area**     Line 3 draws a window into which the menu options will be placed. Line 4 draws a box at the bottom of the screen into which the **ASK** prompt will be placed. Note that line 9, the **ROWCOL** command used to position the cursor for the **ASK** command, has been moved up from line 24 to line 22. In all but the simplest screen formats, you should avoid writing on line 24 of the screen since it will frequently cause DOS to scroll the entire screen up one line. In order to place the **ASK** prompt inside the box, it is necessary to avoid line 24.

**Confirm Box**     A series of commands, lines 27 through 30, have been added to the :END section. The purpose of these commands is to display a box that confirms the selection made by the user; in this case, the colors that he selected from the menu. Line 27 clears the screen. Then line 28 draws a window in the center of the screen. Line 29 displays text inside this window, which confirms the user's selection. The last command, 30, is used to place the cursor in a logical position at the end of the program; in this case, the lower left corner of the screen. If line 30 is not included, the DOS cursor is left on the right side of line 20. This means that DOS will display its prompt at that location, something that would look odd to the user. Line 30 establishes a more conventional location for the DOS prompt that will appear when the program terminates.

**The MESSAGE Variable**     You may have noticed that line 29 includes an environmental variable %**message**%. The text stored in **MESSAGE** is defined with the **SET** command in line 17, 21, or 25, depending upon which selection the user makes. Why is this technique used?

If the variable **MESSAGE** was not used, the only way to display the user's choice in a window at the end of the program would be to include the four commands currently at the end of the file in each of the sections that handles a different error level.

The key to simplification of this process is to realize that the only difference would be the names of the colors. All the other commands would be unchanged. The solution is to store the text that would vary in an environmental variable. The variable is inserted into the **ROWCOL** command at the end of the program, supplying the correct color names to the **ROWCOL** command:

```
@ECHO OFF                                                        {1}
CLS                                                              {2}
BE WINDOW 6,10,16,60 SHADOW COLOR WHI ON BLU                     {3}
BE BOX 21,0,23,79 DOUBLE                                         {4}
BE ROWCOL 7,25, "Screen Colors"                                  {5}
BE ROWCOL 10,15, "Default Colors Yellow/Blue  " COLOR BRI YEL ON BLU {6}
BE ROWCOL 12,15,"Alternate Colors Yellow/Blue " COLOR BLU ON WHI     {7}
BE ROWCOL 14,15,"Black & White                " COLOR WHI ON BLA     {8}
BE ROWCOL 22,5                                                   {9}
BE ASK "enter D, A or B to set colors: ",dab TIMEOUT=10 DEFAULT=b {10}
IF ERRORLEVEL 3 GOTO bw                                          {11}
IF ERRORLEVEL 2 GOTO alternate                                  {12}
IF ERRORLEVEL 1 GOTO default                                    {13}
IF ERRORLEVEL 0 GOTO end                                        {14}
:DEFAULT                                                         {15}
    BE SA BRI YEL ON BLU                                         {16}
```

```
    SET message=Yellow on Blue                              {17}
        GOTO END                                            {18}
  :ALTERNATE                                                {19}
        BE SA BLU ON WHI                                    {20}
    SET message=Blue on White                               {21}
        GOTO END                                            {22}
  :BW                                                       {23}
        BE SA WHI ON BLA                                    {24}
    SET message=White on Black                              {25}
  :END                                                      {26}
  CLS                                                       {27}
  BE WINDOW 10,10,12,70 SHADOW                              {28}
  BE ROWCOL 11,20, "Colors set to %message%"                {29}
  BE ROWCOL 24,0                                            {30}
```

When the revised version of COLORS.BAT is run, the screen display is enhanced by boxes and windows. When a selection has been made, the screen clears and a smaller window appears with the confirmation of the color selection. Note that the environmental variable's text combines with the literal portion of the **ROWCOL** command to print a complete line of text.

## Improving Performance with Subfiles

Even on moderately fast systems, as an example 386SX, the execution of individual Batch Enhancer commands is slow enough so that you can easily see elements of the screen display individually placed on the screen.

In batch files that contain a series of Batch Enhancer commands, you can improve the performance by creating a Batch Enhancer subfile. A subfile is a text file that is similar to a batch file. The primary difference is that a Batch Enhancer subfile can contain *only* Batch Enhancer subcommands.

A subfile is able to improve performance because it eliminates the need to reload the Batch Enhancer for each Batch Enhancer command. When a subfile is used, the Batch Enhancer program is loaded once and all of the subcommands in the subfile are processed as a block.

For example, in the current COLORS.BAT file, lines 2 through 10 contain Batch Enhancer subcommands. Note that the Batch Enhancer supports its own version of the DOS commands **CLS** and **GOTO**.

You could place all of those commands into a subfile. Below is a subfile called COLOR.SCR that contains all of the Batch Enhancer commands found in lines 2 through 10:

```
CLS
WINDOW 6,10,16,60 SHADOW COLOR WHI ON BLU
BOX 21,0,23,79 DOUBLE
ROWCOL 7,25,"Screen Colors"
ROWCOL 10,15,"Default Colors Yellow/Blue  " COLOR BRI YEL ON BLU
ROWCOL 12,15,"Alternate Colors Yellow/Blue" COLOR BLU ON WHI
ROWCOL 14,15,"Black & White               " COLOR WHI ON BLA
ROWCOL 22,5
ASK "Enter D, A or B to set colors: ",dab TIMEOUT=10 DEFAULT=b
```

You can invoke the processing of a subfile by using the file name, including extension, as an argument for the **BE** command.

Below is the top of the COLORS.BAT file. Note the original lines through 10 have been replaced by a single command, **BE** COLOR.SCR:

```
@ECHO OFF
BE COLOR.SCR
IF ERRORLEVEL 3 GOTO bw
IF ERRORLEVEL 2 GOTO alternate
IF ERRORLEVEL 1 GOTO defau
```

When you run this version of COLORS.BAT, you will see that all the elements of the menu appear simultaneously. This is the speed advantage gained by using Batch Enhancer subfiles, which allow the loading of the entire subfile list of commands in a single operation.

In general, subfiles are the best way to paint a screen display, such as a menu. Keep in mind that you can use any Batch Enhancer command in a subfile. You cannot, however, use DOS commands or variables. This means that you cannot pass text stored as a parameter or environmental variable to a Batch Enhancer subfile. For example, if you had defined a variable called PROGRAM, you could execute the following Batch Enhancer command from a batch file:

```
(command) BE ROWCOL 10,10,"Now loading %program%"
(result) Now loading Lotus 1-2-3
```

But if that same command was placed into a subfile, the variable would not be recognized as a symbol, but would simply be printed as text:

```
(command) ROWCOL 10,10,"Now loading %program%"
(result) Now loading %program%
```

## Multiple Menus

As an additional example of how menus can be implemented with the Batch Enhancer, recall the DISCARE.BAT created at the beginning of the chapter. That batch required two parameters: the drive letter and the level of disk maintenance to be performed. This program poses a more complicated menu problem than the COLORS.BAT because more than one entry is required. The solution involves, as do most programming problems, a bit of optical illusion. The problems that need to be solved are:

**Only 1 ERRORLEVEL.**   DOS reserves only one memory location for the ERRORLEVEL value. This means that if you perform several **ASK** commands, the last ERRORLEVEL value will overwrite the previous ERRORLEVEL. If a batch requires multiple entries you need to analyze each response with a set of **IF ERRORLEVEL** tests after each **ASK**. In order to preserve the user's entry you must use the ERRORLEVEL analysis to store a corresponding value or string of characters in an environmental variable that will be active for the duration of the program.

**ASK Pauses Batch.**   Each **ASK** command will pause the batch until the user responds. If the user needs to enter two keys, the second question would not appear until after the first entry was made. While this is a workable system, it would be far better to display both items on the screen at one time and simply move the cursor through the required entry points in the way that you enter information into a dialog box. The Batch Enhancer does not support dialog box entry, but you can create the illusion of a dialog box by using the **ROWCOL** and **ASK** commands to move the cursor around text that has already been placed on the screen.

The first step in creating a program that solves these problems is to create a Batch Enhancer subfile that will perform the initial screen display. Below is a file called DKCR0001.SCR. The file paints two windows on the screen. The top window contains the drive options, while the bottom window shows the maintenance-level options.

Line 5 and 10 are **ROWCOL** commands that print what looks like the type of text you would use as the prompt for an **ASK** command. They place the prompts on the screen, but because they are **ROWCOL**, not **ASK** commands the batch is not paused. Instead, both windows are fully filled in with all of the text. It is only at the end of the subfile that an actual **ASK** command is issued.

It is interesting to see how lines 5, 11, and 12 are related and how they work together to create an illusion. Line 11 is a **ROWCOL** command that is used to position the cursor. In this case, the cursor moves up the screen from row 19 back to row 8. Column 51 is chosen because that is the first column to the right of the text *Enter Disk Letter(a,c,d):*. How was 51 calculated? There is no magic answer. It is necessary to count the characters in the text printed by the command in line 5 (26), and add it to the starting column number (25) to arrive at 26+25 = 51. The result is that the **ASK** command issued in line 12 places the cursor on row 8, so that it appears as if a single command displayed the prompt and positioned the cursor. Note that the actual prompt used with **ASK** is " "(two consecutive quotation marks), which is called a *null string* because it contains no characters:

```
CLS                                          {1}
WINDOW 5,20,9,60                             {2}
WINDOW 11,20,20,60                           {3}
ROWCOL 6,25,"Maintain Drive"                 {4}
ROWCOL 8,25,"Enter Disk Letter(a,c,d):"      {5}
ROWCOL 12,25,"Level of Maintenance"          {6}
ROWCOL 14,30,"D-Daily Maintenance"           {7}
ROWCOL 15,30,"W=Weekly Maintenance"          {8}
ROWCOL 16,30,"M-Monthly Maintenance"         {9}
ROWCOL 19,25,"Enter Level (d,w,m):"          {10}
ROWCOL 8,51                                  {11}
ASK "" acd                                   {12}
```

When this subfile is executed, it will create a display like the one shown in Figure 15–8.

The main batch file, called in this case DKCR1.BAT, begins with a **BE** command that executes the DKCR0001.SCR subfile:

```
@ECHO OFF            {1}
REM Check Parameter  {2}
BE dkcr0001.scr      {3}
```

The next section, lines 4 through 14, is composed of an ERRORLEVEL analysis structure that evaluates the entry made by the user. Since there must be more than one user entry before the batch can actually carry out its main task (that is, disk maintenance), the ERRORLEVEL structure cannot put the entry directly into use. Instead, the entry is converted to an environmental variable, called **DR**, which contains the letter of the selected drive. Later in the batch the symbol %DR% can be used to insert the drive letter into other commands. Once the information is transferred to a variable, you

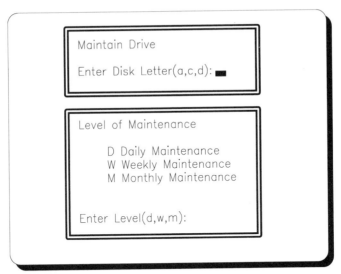

**Figure 15–8. Screen created by DKCR0001.SCR.**

are free to accept another input because you are no longer concerned about having the DOS ERRORLEVEL overwritten. The batch continues at the label called STEP_2:

```
IF ERRORLEVEL  3  GOTO DRIVED          {4}
IF ERRORLEVEL  2  GOTO DRIVEC          {5}
IF ERRORLEVEL  1  GOTO DRIVEA          {6}
:DRIVED                                {7}
SET dr=D                               {8}
GOTO STEP_2                            {9}
:DRIVEC                               {10}
SET dr=C                              {11}
GOTO STEP_2                           {12}
:DRIVEA                               {13}
SET dr=A                              {14}
GOTO STEP_2                           {15}
```

The STEP_2 routine uses only three commands to get the user's selection for maintenance level. This is because the text of the menu has already been placed on the screen at the beginning of the batch. Line 18 positions the cursor next to the prompt text, which is already on the screen. Line 19 executes an **ASK** command for the input of the maintenance level.

The function of line 17 may not be obvious at first. The command places the selected drive letter onto the screen display at exactly the position on the screen at which it was entered. This is done in order to

provide visual feedback to the user. Normally, when the user responds
to an **ASK** pause, the key that he enters is not displayed on the screen.
Line 17 displays the drive letter to make the batch file respond like a
conventional application:

```
:STEP_2                        {16}
BE ROWCOL 8,51,%dr%            {17}
BE ROWCOL 19,45               {18}
ASK "" dwm                    {19}
```

The remainder of the batch, shown below, evaluates the entry and
branches to the corresponding maintenance level. The variable %DR% is
inserted into the commands wherever a drive letter is required. In addition,
a new variable, **LEVEL**, is created. This variable is used to record the level
number selected by the user. The variable is used in lines 44 and 47 to insert
the level number into the text:

```
NCC /START:1 > NUL                                              {20}
IF ERRORLEVEL 3 GOTO LEVEL_3                                    {21}
IF ERRORLEVEL 2 GOTO LEVEL_2                                    {22}
IF ERRORLEVEL 1 GOTO LEVEL_1                                    {23}
:LEVEL_1                                                        {24}
    SET level=1                                                {25}
    ECHO Level 1 Disk Care for Drive %dr%                      {26}
    NDD %dr%: /QUICK                                           {27}
    SPEEDISK %dr%: /SE                                         {28}
GOTO IMAGE                                                      {29}
:LEVEL_2                                                        {30}
    SET level=2                                                {31}
    ECHO Level 2 Disk Care for Drive %dr%                      {32}
    NDD %dr%: /COMPLETE                                        {33}
    SPEEDISK %dr%: /F/V                                        {34}
    GOTO IMAGE                                                 {35}
:LEVEL_3                                                        {36}
    SET level=3                                                {37}
    ECHO Level 3 Disk Care for Drive %dr%                      {38}
    NDD %dr%: /QUICK                                           {39}
    CALIBRATE %dr%: /PATTERN:5/BATCH/BLANK                     {40}
    GOTO IMAGE                                                 {41}
:IMAGE                                                          {42}
    IMAGE %dr%:                                                {43}
    ECHO Disk Maintenance of Drive %dr% Level %level% completed {44}
NCC /STOP:1/L/N                                                 {45}
ECHO _Elapsed Time                                             {46}
ECHO Disk Maintenance of Drive %dr% Level %level% Performed >>DKCARE.LOG {47}
```

```
        NCC /STOP:1/L>>DKCARE.LOG                              {48}
        ECHO _Elapsed Time >>DKCARE.LOG                        {49}
```

The DKCR1.BAT file is an example of how the Batch Enhancer commands can allow the user to feel as if they are filling in a screen that has several inputs, even though DOS batch processing can deal with only a single input at a time.

## The Main Menu Batch

The final batch example will be a main application menu, such as you would display when a hard disk system is booted. The goal of this batch is to avoid booting to a cryptic DOS prompt display, which many users find inconvenient or confusing. A main system menu allows anyone to sit down and start the programs stored on the hard disk without having to know DOS commands or anything about where you have stored the applications on the hard disk. As an example assume that the computer has Lotus 1-2-3, WordPerfect 5.1, dBASE IV, and the Norton Utilities installed. A batch file called MAINMENU.BAT will be created, which will provide access to these four applications.

There are many ways to apply what has been covered in this chapter to the creation of a menu program. The method that will be shown makes use of the environmental variables, Batch Enhancer subfiles, and the DOS **CALL** command to execute batch files as subroutines. The primary reason for using this approach is an understanding that hard disk menu programs are likely to require modification from time to time as programs are added or removed from the hard disk. With this in mind, you would want to create a menu program that is able to run the current list of programs and is easy to revise and modify in the future. The method employed in MAINMENU.BAT seeks to reduce the number of commands that you need to enter each time a program is added to the menu. This is accomplished by using a batch program called RUNPROG to actually load and execute the selected program. The MAINMENU.BAT uses its menu to set environmental variables used by RUNPROG.BAT. MAINMENU does not contain the commands that run the application, but the **SET** command definitions that establish the values needed by RUNPROG.

The first two files that need to be created are called MM0001.SCR and MM0002.SCR.

MM0001.SCR, shown below, displays a box on the screen that informs the user that the computer has booted successfully. Note the use of the

**DELAY** command to pause the batch for a specified number of clock ticks; that is, **DELAY 25** creates a two-second pause:

```
CLS
WINDOW 8,10,11,70
ROWCOL 9,25, "Computer Booted Successfully"
DELAY 25
```

The next screen file, MM0002.SCR, is the one that actually contains the menu. This Batch Enhancer subfile creates a menu similar to those created in the other menu-oriented batch files. The only new twist shown here is the use of a highlighted letter to indicate what keys the user should enter. For example, the menu item for Lotus 1-2-3 is created by lines 4 and 9. Line 4 displays the text *Lotus 1-2-3*. Line 9 positions the cursor back at the beginning of that line and write a single letter, L. The difference is that the L is displayed in reverse color, black on white. One letter, typically the first letter, is highlighted in this way. This presents the user with a familiar convention for knowing what letters to enter to make selections. The **ASK** command at the end pauses the display for user input:

```
CLS                                              {1}
WINDOW 5,20,23,60                                {2}
ROWCOL 6,30,"Main Menu"                          {3}
ROWCOL 8,25,"Lotus 1-2-3"                        {4}
ROWCOL 9,25,"WordPerfect 5.1"                    {5}
ROWCOL 10,25,"dBASE IV"                          {6}
ROWCOL 11,25,"Norton Utilities"                  {7}
ROWCOL 12,25,"Exit - Press [ESC]"                {8}
ROWCOL 8,25,L BLACK ON WHITE                     {9}
ROWCOL 9,25,W BLACK ON WHITE                     {10}
ROWCOL 10,25,D BLACK ON WHITE                    {11}
ROWCOL 11,25,N BLACK ON WHITE                    {12}
ROWCOL 22,25                                     {13}
ASK "Enter Letter: " lwdn DEFAULT=n              {14}
```

The MAINMENU.BAT file makes use of the two Batch Enhancer subfiles. MAINMENU.BAT, shown below, begins by executing the MM001.SCR subfile:

```
@ECHO OFF        {1}
BE mm0001.scr    {2}
```

The next section of the program begins with a label, MAINMENU. The label is very significant because it will allow you to create a *loop*. Unlike the other batch files that you have created, the main menu program is meant to remain active as long as the computer is on. If you use the menu to run Lotus 1-2-3, you will want to return to the menu after you have exited 1-2-3. This means that the last command executed after a program has been run should be **GOTO mainmenu.** This would cause the batch to return to the main menu section and redisplay the menu so that the user can make another selection.

The first command in this section is a Batch Enhancer command that executes the MM0002.SCR subfile. This displays the text of the menu on the screen and allows the user to enter a selection.

After this comes a series of **IF ERRORLEVEL** commands listed in descending order. Note that the label names used are simple, generic names differentiated only by their number. This **ERRORLEVEL 4** goes to **PROGRAM4, ERRORLEVEL 3** goes to **PROGRAM3,** etc. This makes it simple to follow the pattern when you need to add new programs.

**ERRORLEVEL 0,** which is generated only by the [Esc] key, is set to jump to the **END** label. This is the only option designated to stop the looping menu:

```
:mainmenu                                {3}
   BE MM0002.SCR                         {4}
   IF ERRORLEVEL 4 GOTO :program4        {5}
   IF ERRORLEVEL 3 GOTO :program3        {6}
   IF ERRORLEVEL 2 GOTO :program2        {7}
   IF ERRORLEVEL 1 GOTO :program1        {8}
   IF ERRORLEVEL 0 GOTO :END             {9}
```

Following the **MAINMENU** section is the first of a series of similar sections implementing the user's selection. The first, **PROGRAM1,** is the model of all of the program sections. Instead of containing instructions that load the selected program, the section has three **SET** commands that define environmental variables containing the information needed to run the selected program. The variable **PROG** is a descriptive name for the program. This variable will be used for screen display purposes.

**LOCATION** is used to store the directory path where the application is stored (e.g., Lotus 1-2-3 is typically stored in the \LOTUS directory).

**RUN** is the actual program name. Note that in the case of Lotus 1-2-3 you can start the program using **LOTUS** to display the Lotus Access menu, or launch directly into the spreadsheet using **123.** Once the values have been defined, a **CALL** command executes the RUNPROG.BAT file. RUNPROG.BAT, which you have not created yet, will use the data stored in the three variables, **PROG, LOCATION,** and **RUN,** to load and execute the selected application. The last command in the section is a **GOTO**

command that directs the program back to the **MAINMENU** section. This causes the menu to be displayed again, giving the user a change to make another selection:

```
:program1                                  {10}
   SET prog=Lotus 1-2-3 Version 2.3        {11}
   SET location=\lotus                     {12}
   SET run=123                             {13}
   CALL runprog                            {14}
   GOTO mainmenu                           {15}
```

The commands in section **PROGRAM1** actually form a pattern that will be repeated for each program you want to execute through the menu. Below, the elements presented in **PROGRAM1** are rewritten into a general form. The items in **bold** will be exactly the same for each program you want to run. Only the items in *italics* will be different:

```
:program#
   SET prog=description
   SET location=path_name
   SET run=program_name
CALL runprog
GOTO mainmenu
```

In this example, the pattern is repeated in sections **PROGRAM2, PROGRAM3,** and **PROGRAM4.** You can see that by using this approach it is very easy, using a text editor, to add a new application by copying the last section in the current batch and changing description, path name, and program name. You will also have to add another **IF ERRORLEVEL** command:

```
:program2                                  {16}
   SET prog=WordPerfect 5.1                {17}
   SET location=\wp51                      {18}
   SET run=wp                              {19}
   CALL runprog                            {20}
   GOTO mainmenu                           {21}
:program3                                  {22}
   SET prog=dBASE IV 1.1                   {23}
   SET location=\dbase                     {24}
   SET run=dbase                           {25}
   CALL runprog                            {26}
   GOTO mainmenu                           {27}
:program4                                  {28}
   SET prog=Norton Utilities               {29}
   SET location=\NU                        {30}
```

```
    SET run=norton                          {31}
    CALL runprog                            {32}
 GOTO mainmenu                              {33}
```

After all of the program sections, the **END** section lists the commands you want to execute if the user terminates the menu with [Esc]. The **SET** commands are used to remove the environmental variables from memory. **SET** *variable=* tells DOS to erase the variable from memory. This frees up the environmental space occupied by the variable for other variables. This step is not absolutely necessary, but it is a good programming habit to release memory once your program has finished running:

```
 :END                                                       {34}
   SET prog=                                                {35}
   SET location=                                            {36}
   SET run=                                                 {37}
 CLS                                                        {38}
 BE ROWCOL 10,10,"Main Menu Terminated - DOS Active"        {39}
 BE ROWCOL 24,0                                             {40}
```

The final part of the menu batch system is the RUNPROG.BAT file. This batch is called as an external subroutine from MAINMENU.BAT. This batch uses the values placed into the variables **PROG, LOCA-TION,** and **RUN** to load and execute the user's selection. Note that this program uses the NCC timer technique discussed on page 717 to calculate the time that the application was in use. **PROG** is used in lines 3 and 7 to insert a description of the program into the text. **LO-CATION** is used in line 4 to activate the desired directory. Line 5 consists entirely of the **RUN** variable, which executes the specified program file:

```
 CLS                                                {1}
 NCC /START >NUL                                    {2}
 BE ROWCOL 10,10,"Loading %prog% ....."             {3}
 CD %location%                                       {4}
 %run%                                               {5}
 CD \                                                {6}
 BE ROWCOL 10,10,"%prog% active for "               {7}
 NCC /STOP/L/N                                       {8}
 BE DELAY 5                                           {9}
```

When all of these elements are combined, they create a menu program that can be started from the AUTOEXEC.BAT file by inserting

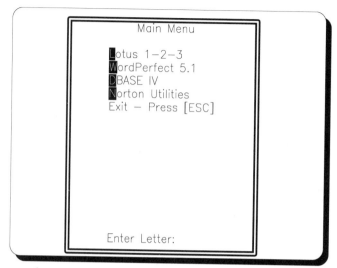

**Figure 15–9. MAINMENU.BAT screen display.**

MAINMENU as the last command in the AUTOEXEC.BAT. The main menu screen will look like Figure 15–9.

## Creating an Activity Log

The current version of the MAINMENU program displays the elapsed time for each application run from the menu. You could capture the information in a log file that would record which applications were used, on what date, and for how long. You can implement a log by making a change to the RUNPROG.BAT file. Below is a modified version of the RUNPROG.BAT that will create a log of application activity.

The primary change in the program is the use of the >> redirection command to store text in a file. In the program below, lines 3, 4, 5, and 6 store text in the TIMELOG file. Line 4 uses the **PROG** variable to insert the select program's description into the text. Line 5 captures the starting time and date.

Following the running of the application, lines 12 through 15 store the exit and elapsed times in the TIMELOG file to complete the entry for the current application:

```
CLS                                          {1}
BE ROWCOL 10,10,"Loading %prog% ....."       {2}
ECHO * >>timelog                             {3}
```

```
ECHO Start Application: %prog%. >> timelog      {4}
NCC /START/L >>timelog                          {5}
ECHO . >>timelog                                {6}
CD %location%                                    {7}
%run%                                            {8}
CD \                                             {9}
BE ROWCOL 10,10,"%prog% active for "            {10}
NCC /STOP/L/N                                   {11}
ECHO application %prog% Exited. >> timelog      {12}
NCC /STOP/L >> timelog                          {13}
ECHO _elapsed. >>timelog                        {14}
ECHO * >>timelog                                {15}
BE DELAY 5                                       {16}
```

When this version of RUNPROG.BAT is used, it will generate a TIMELOG file. Another variation on the TIMELOG idea is to permit the entry of a user comment or note along with the information automatically stored by the program. This can be accomplished by taking advantage of the DOS **COPY CON** feature. **COPY CON** allows you to copy text entered from the keyboard, the **CON** device, into a text file directly.

Below is a modified version of RUNPROG.BAT, which adds the ability for the user to enter comments into the log when they exit an application.

Line 17 uses the DOS command **COPY CON** to allow direct entry into a text file, in this case named TEMPTEXT. Line 15 displays a message that explains to users that they must enter [F6] followed by ↵ to complete the entry. [F6] inserts an *end of file* marker, [Ctrl-z], into the text.

Line 18 appends the text in TEMPTEXT onto the TIMELOG. Then line 19 deletes TEMPTEXT from the disk since it is no longer needed:

```
CLS                                                      {1}
BE ROWCOL 10,10,"Loading %prog% ....."                   {2}
ECHO * >>timelog                                         {3}
ECHO Start Application: %prog%. >> timelog               {4}
NCC /START/L >>timelog                                   {5}
ECHO . >>timelog                                         {6}
CD %location%                                            {7}
%run%                                                    {8}
CD \                                                     {9}
BE ROWCOL 10,10,"%prog% active for "                    {10}
NCC /STOP/L/N                                           {11}
ECHO Application %prog% Exited. >> timelog              {12}
NCC /STOP/L >> timelog                                  {13}
ECHO elapsed. >>timelog                                 {14}
BE ROWCOL 15,0,"Enter Text then Press [F6] [Enter]"    {15}
```

```
BE ROWCOL 16,0                                              {16}
COPY CON temptext >>NUL                                     {17}
TYPE temptext >> timelog                                    {18}
DEL temptext                                                {19}
ECHO * >>timelog                                            {20}
```

## Submenus

Often, a single menu, such as the one created by the MAINMENU.BAT file, is not sufficient to list all of the options available on a system. For example, the Norton Utilities selection might lead to a submenu that listed specific Norton Utilities programs or operations.

The structure used to create the MAINMENU.BAT system can be readily adapted to create a system of submenus. Because menus and submenus have basically the same structure, you can create a submenu by copying the main menu files and then making editing changes.

For example, suppose that you wanted to create a submenu for Norton Utilities commands. You could begin by copying the MAINMENU.BAT and MM0002.SCR files:

```
copy mainmenu.bat menu0001.bat ↵
copy mm0002.scr mm1001.bat ↵
```

The names of the files are designed to help make organization easier. Since you are creating your first submenu, the main batch file is MENU1000.BAT. If you created another it would be MENU2000.BAT, and so on. All of the supporting files related to MENU0001 would use numbers that suggested the relationship. In this example, the Batch Enhancer subfile is called MM1001.SCR; that is, the first screen for MENU1000. Of course, you can devise and use any system so long as you understand the meaning of the names and can remember what file name performs what function. Keep in mind, should you want to copy or revise your menu system, you will need to remember all of the file names used in that system. The list below shows the contents of MM1001.SCR, which is the menu screen for the Norton Utilities submenu. It follows the same form as the main menu subfile and lists three Norton Utilities programs that can be selected.

Note that because all of the menu items begin with *Norton*, lines 9 through 11 highlight letters other than the first letter as the selection key. Another approach would be to list numbers or letters (A, B, C, etc.) as the selection keys:

```
CLS                                             {1}
WINDOW 5,20,23,60                               {2}
ROWCOL 6,30,"Main Menu"                         {3}
ROWCOL 8,25,"Norton Disk Doctor"               {4}
ROWCOL 9,25,"Norton Control Center"            {5}
ROWCOL 10,25,"Norton Disk Editor"              {6}
ROWCOL 11,25,"Exit - Press [ESC]"              {7}
ROWCOL 8,32,D COLOR BLACK ON WHITE             {8}
ROWCOL 9,32,C COLOR BLACK ON WHITE             {9}
ROWCOL 10,37,E COLOR BLACK ON WHITE           {10}
ROWCOL 22,25                                   {11}
ASK "Enter Letter: " dce                       {12}
```

The batch file that operates the submenu, MENU1000.BAT, uses the same basic model established for the main menu with two changes, as shown below. First, at the beginning of the batch the **BE** subfile command, which displays the opening message, is eliminated since submenus do not require an introduction. Second, at the end, the commands that release the variables are also unnecessary, since the user will have to exit through the main menu program, which already contains this routine:

```
@ECHO OFF
:menu
    BE mm1001.scr
    IF ERRORLEVEL 3 GOTO :program3
    IF ERRORLEVEL 2 GOTO :program2
    IF ERRORLEVEL 1 GOTO :program1
    IF ERRORLEVEL 0 GOTO :END
:program1
    SET prog=Norton Disk Doctor
    SET location=\NU
    SET run=ndd
    CALL runprog
    GOTO menu
:program2
    SET prog=Norton Control Center
    SET location=\NU
    SET run=ncc
    CALL runprog
    GOTO menu
:program3
    SET prog=Disk Editor
    SET location=\NU
    SET run=diskedit
    CALL runprog
    GOTO menu
:END
```

## Linking Menus

The final step in creating a submenu system is to link the submenu to a selection in the main menu. This is easily accomplished by changing the **CALL runprog** command to **CALL menu1000** as shown below:

```
:program4
    CALL menu1000
    GOTO mainmenu
```

The **SET** commands have been deleted from this section for clarity. However, you could have left them in the section since they would have no effect on the operation of the submenu.

The submenu is ready to operate. This simplicity is achieved because the RUNPROG.BAT file will perform its function exactly the same way from a submenu as it will from the main menu. There is no need to modify that file since the submenu will supply the required parameters in the form of the environmental variables PROG, LOCATION, and RUN, just as the main menu batch does.

The addition of submenus shows how the generalized design of the main menu simplifies modifications or additions to the menu system. This, in fact, is a general rule of thumb in all programming and it applies just as well to DOS batch files as it does to more powerful or advanced languages. You can use the same approach to create subsubmenus, if desired. When users wants to exit any of the menus they simply press [Esc]. After they exit the submenu they return to the main menu.

# Summary

This chapter showed how to create DOS batch files and how to integrate the Norton Utilities, Version 4.5 and 5.0, Batch Enhancer commands in those files.

**Batch Files**    Batch files are text files that contain DOS commands. DOS can directly read and execute commands stored in batch files, enabling you to create your own utilities without the need for programming languages or compilers. Batch files are identified by the BAT file extension. You can prepare batch files with any text editor or word processor that creates standard DOS text files. All versions of DOS are supplied with a basic line editor called EDLIN. DOS 5.0 is supplied with a QBASIC program called EDIT that supports full-screen, not line-by-line, editing.

**Parameters** Batch files can accept a list of items called parameters. A parameter is any text item that follows the name of the batch file. The parameters are assigned variable numbers 1–9. Variable 0 is assigned as the name of the batch file being executed. All parameters are treated as text strings by DOS.

**Variables** DOS variables are special symbols inserted into the text of a batch file. Variables are indicated by the % character. Variables %1 through %9 are assigned to the first 9 parameters listed with the batch file name. When a variable is encountered in a batch file, DOS substitutes the text used for the corresponding parameter into the command and executes the expanded command. Variables allow you to pass items from the DOS command line to the commands contained within a batch file.

**IF** The **IF** command performs a logical test based on the values established as program parameters. **IF EXIST** tests for the existence of the specified file. **IF NOT EXIST** tests for the absence of a file. Using the **==** operator, **IF** will compare the text of two strings or variables. When **IF** evaluates as true, it will execute a single specified command. **IF** false, the command is skipped.

**GOTO** The **GOTO** command jumps the batch file execution to a specified location in the batch file. **GOTO** can be used by itself or combined with **IF** to create a logical branching mechanism. The **IF/GOTO** combination overcomes the single-command limit of the **IF** command.

**ERRORLEVEL** Certain DOS commands place values from 0 to 255 in a special memory area called the **ERRORLEVEL.** The values are used to evaluate the success or failure of the DOS command. An ERRORLEVEL of zero indicates failure, while a 1 indicates success. The **IF** command will evaluate the current ERRORLEVEL when used in the form **IF ERRORLEVEL** *value.* **IF ERRORLEVEL** is true if the actual ERRORLEVEL value is equal to or greater than the specified ERRORLEVEL value.

**Environmental Variables** DOS reserves a specified amount of memory space for string values assigned to variables. These are called environmental variables because their primary function is to provide DOS with a place to store the system parameters for the command interpreter, search path, and DOS prompt configuration. The **SET** command allows users to define their own environmental variables. Environmental variables can be inserted into batch file commands by entering the name of the variable enclosed in % characters.

**SHELL**    The command **SHELL** is used in the CONFIG.SYS file to set the command interpreter and the amount of memory reserved for environmental variables. By default, DOS reserves about 160 bytes for environmental variables.

**Batch Enhancer**    The Norton Utilities Batch Enhancer provides ten commands that can enhance batch file operations. The commands help you place text, windows, and boxes at specific locations on the screen. The beep command provides audio prompts and other sounds.

**ASK**    The **ASK** Batch Enhancer command allows batch files to pause in order to receive user input. The user input is converted to ERRORLEVEL values. **IF ERRORLEVEL** commands can be used to evaluate the user's response to an **ASK** prompt. This allows for the creation of interactive, menu-driven batch files.

**Subfiles**    The speed of execution of Batch Enhancer commands can be improved by placing groups of Batch Enhancer commands into a separate file called a subfile. The Batch Enhancer will read all of the commands stored in the subfile in a single operation and then execute the commands from memory. Subfiles are typically used to quickly display a screen layout generated by a series of Batch Enhancer **ROWCOL, WINDOW, BOX,** and **ASK** commands. Note that you can use any Batch Enhancer command in a subfile, but DOS commands are not recognized.

# 16 Batch Files Version 6.0

The previous chapter explained the use of batch files and the Batch Enhancer commands used to supplement the basic set of DOS batch file commands. This chapter will deal with new Batch Enhancer commands added to the Norton Utilities Version 6.0. The discussion in this chapter assumes you are familiar with the basic DOS and Batch Enhancer operations discussed in Chapter 15. Version 6.0 of the Batch Enhancer retains the same basic set of Batch Enhancer commands included in Versions 4.5 and 5.0. Changes and additions made in Version 6.0 fall into four categories:

**Subfile Structure.** Batch Enhancer subfiles increase the speed at which Batch Enhancer commands are executed by eliminating the need to load the Batch Enhancer each time a Batch Enhancer command is issued in a batch file. However, previous versions lacked commands that could be used to perform logical operations, such as those performed by the DOS batch commands **IF** and **GOTO**. For example, a Batch Enhancer subfile could issue an **ASK** command to allow user input, but could not evaluate the user's input. If several inputs were desired from a single screen, the routine could not be handled by a single subfile, resulting in a decrease in performance.

**Date and Time Analysis.** Many batch operations can logically be related to calendar or clock values—for example, a certain type of disk maintenance should be performed every month. Version 6.0 of the Batch Enhancer provides means of accessing and evaluating the information supplied by the system clock/calendar so that batch files can react to changes in time and date.

**Debugging.** Version 6.0 accepts a switch, **/DEBUG**, that causes the Batch Enhancer to display on the screen the current ERRORLEVEL code value following any Batch Enhancer command. This helps you to track down problems in batch files that you are developing.

**Reboot.** The Batch Enhancer includes a **REBOOT** command that allows you to reboot the computer through a batch file.

It is important to keep in mind that the enhancements to the Batch Enhancer do not overcome all the limitations of the previous versions. The full power of the Version 6.0 Batch Enhancer requires operation under the NDOS command interpretor supplied with Version 6.0. Batch Enhancer and NDOS provide very sophisticated tools that allow for very professional batch file results.

# Subfile Structure

A *subfile* or *script file* is a text file that contains a list of Batch Enhancer subcommands. The advantage of using a subfile is that all the subfile commands can be processed with one loading of the Batch Enhancer program. This is much faster than executing a series of Batch Enhancer commands directly from a batch file, since the latter method requires the BE.EXE program to be run each time a Batch Enhancer command is encountered.

The difference in speed is critical when you are using the Batch Enhancer to compose a complicated screen display. When executed separately in the main batch file, a series of **ROWCOL, WINDOW,** or **BOX** commands will exhibit an annoying delay, as each element in the screen display is placed on the screen. In contrast, when the same series of commands is issued through a subfile, the delay is eliminated, giving the impression to the user that all the elements of the screen are displayed simultaneously.

However, Version 5.0 of the Batch Enhancer does not support the use of structures composed of labels and **IF,** and **GOTO,** commands within subfile. As a result, most applications require you to exit the subfile and return to the main batch in order to evaluate an entry.

This limitation is revealed in cases where you would like to have the user make more than one input on a given screen. In Chapter 15 you created two programs, DISKCARE.BAT and DKCR1.BAT, which were designed to automate the process of disk maintenance with the Norton Utilities. In order to use the batch file, the user was required to enter two items: a drive letter and a maintenance level. In the first version of the batch, DISKCARE.BAT, the inputs were entered through command-line parameters. In DKCR1.BAT the need for parameters was eliminated by adding the creation of a menu, whereby the user could enter a drive letter and the level of disk maintenance to perform. Ideally, the user would be able to enter both items on a single screen display in a similar manner to the way data are entered into a dialog box in a Norton Utilities program.

However, Version 5.0 does not provide facilities by which both inputs can be handled in a single subfile. Instead, the subfile displays the screen and gets the first input. In order to get the second input, the program has to exit the subfile, return to the main batch to evaluate the user's input, and then issue a direct **BE ASK** command to get the second input, as shown in the diagram in Figure 16–1.

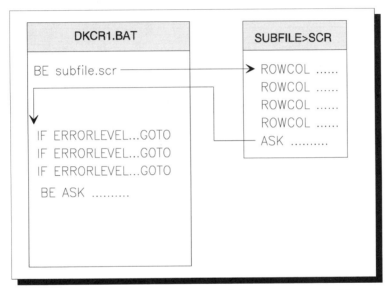

**Figure 16–1. Program must exit subfile to get second input.**

In Version 6.0 it is possible to create a subfile that will accept and evaluate multiple inputs in a single subfile, as seen in Figure 16–2. This will eliminate the awkward delay that occurs in programs like DKCR1.BAT following the first input. This is made possible by the following.

**Jump**    The **JUMP** command is a Batch Enhancer subcommand that performs the same basic function as a series of **IF ERRORLEVEL/GOTO** commands in a batch file. Because **Jump** is a Batch Enhancer subcommand, it can be executed within a subfile. It also has the advantage of greatly simplifying the syntax needed to evaluate user input.

The example below shows how a **JUMP** command can be used to evaluate the input made to an **ASK** command. The **JUMP** command is followed by a list of labels. These labels correspond to the items in the **ASK** key list.

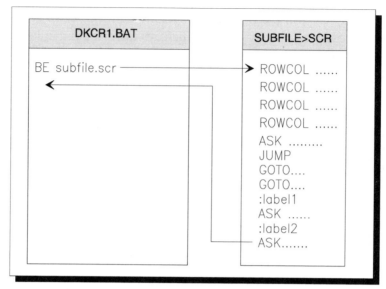

**Figure 16–2. Subfile handles multiple inputs.**

For example, if the user enters **a**, the ERRORLEVEL will be set at 1, causing **JUMP** to go to the first label in the list, **LABEL1**. If the user enters **B**, **JUMP** moves to **LABEL2**, and so on.

```
ASK "Enter:" abc
JUMP label1,label2,label3 /DEFAULT:label1
```

The **/DEFAULT** switch is used to establish a default label in case the user enters [Esc], generating a zero ERRORLEVEL. The default label will also be activated if the ERRORLEVEL exceeds the number of labels in the list.

**JUMP** is a much simpler way to perform ERRORLEVEL analysis, but, unfortunately, it cannot operate in a Batch Enhancer subfile. It cannot be issued from DOS or a DOS batch file. The command shown below will not execute correctly.

```
(not correct)
BE JUMP label1,label2,label3
```

**Labels**    You can insert labels into a subfile in the same manner as you would in a DOS batch file—as an example,**:LABEL1.**

**Adjust**    The structure of DOS still maintains only a single ERRORLEVEL value. However, you can still handle multiple inputs by using the **ADJUST** option with **ASK. ADJUST** allows you to increase the ERRORLEVEL generated by the user's input by a specified value. When used in conjunction with **JUMP** and various labels, **ADJUST** allows you to generate unique ERRORLEVEL values for all the possible selections the user can make on the current screen.

**Exit**    This command is used to terminate the current subfile and return to the main batch file. Exit is a quick way to jump out of a subfile without having to navigate through the rest of the commands, if any, left in the subfile. Technically, Version 5.0 does allows multiple inputs in a single subfile—that is, you can have more than one **ASK** subcommand. But with the additional tools, such as **JUMP** and **GOTO**, you cannot make use of the additional inputs.

## A Multiple Input Subfile

As an example of how to create a single Batch Enhancer screen subfile that handles multiple inputs, you will create a new version of the DKCR1.BAT originally discussed in Chapter 15, using the new commands available in Version 6.0.

Begin by creating a file called DKCR0002.SCR. This file contains much of the same text as the DKCR0001 so that you may want to copy DKCR0001.SCR and edit it, assuming that you have already created it while working in Chapter 15.

The first portion of the file shows nothing unusual. It consists entirely of a series of **ROWCOL** commands that place text on the screen to form the menu:

```
CLS                                              {1}
WINDOW 2,20,9,60                                 {2}
WINDOW 11,20,20,60                               {3}
ROWCOL 3,25,"Maintain Drive"                     {4}
ROWCOL 5,25,"Drive C - 10 Megabyte Partition"    {5}
ROWCOL 6,25,"Drive D - 70 Megabyte Partition"    {6}
ROWCOL 7,25,"Drive A - 1.2 Megabyte Floppy"      {7}
ROWCOL 8,25,"Enter Disk Letter (a,c,d):"         {8}
ROWCOL 12,25,"Level of Maintenance"              {9}
ROWCOL 14,30,"D-Daily Maintenance"               {10}
ROWCOL 15,30,"W-Weekly Maintenance"              {11}
ROWCOL 16,30,"M-Monthly Maintenance"             {12}
ROWCOL 19,25,"Enter Level (d,w,m):"              {13}
```

Once the menu has been drawn, the first input can be made. The **ROWCOL** command in line 14 is used to position the cursor to the first entry location on the screen. Line 15 executes an **ASK** command at that location. Line 16 changes the cursor position to the location on the screen where the next input will be made. It is important to know that when more than one **ASK** command appears within a subfile, the Batch Enhancer automatically echos the user's input on the screen. All echoed letters are shown in uppercase, regardless of how the letter was entered. Note that this applies to all **ASK** entries except the *last* one in the subfile, which is *not* echoed to the screen.

Line 17 uses a **JUMP** command to branch to one of three labels. The labels correspond to the drive selections:

```
ROWCOL 8,51                              {14}
ASK "" acd                               {15}
BE ROWCOL 19,45                          {16}
JUMP drive_a,drive_c,drive_d             {17}
```

The final section of the subfile contains the three sections, one for each drive that could be selected. In each section there is an **ASK** command that allows the user to make a second selection on this menu. Following the input the screen is cleared with the **CLS** command, and **EXIT** terminates the subfile, returning control to the main batch file:

```
:drive_a                                 {18}
   ASK "" dwm ADJUST=10                  {19}
   CLS                                   {20}
   EXIT                                  {21}
:drive_c                                 {22}
   ASK "hello " dwm ADJUST=20            {23}
   CLS                                   {24}
   EXIT                                  {25}
:drive_d                                 {26}
   ASK "" dwm ADJUST=30                  {27}
   CLS                                   {28}
   EXIT                                  {29}
```

The most complicated part of the subfile has to do with the **ADJUST** option used with the **ASK** commands in lines 19, 23, and 27. Why are they there?

The answer is even in Version 6.0 of the Norton Utilities, there can be only one ERRORLEVEL value returned from a subfile, no matter how many **ASK** commands are executed in the subfile. When the **ASK** command in lines 19, 23, or 27 executes, the ERRORLEVEL returned by that command will overwrite the value generated by the previous **ASK** executed in line 15. In order to carry off the disk maintenance task, you need to have both inputs. How can you get two values from a single number?

At first, the task appears to be contradictory. However, the **ADJUST** option is supplied with **ASK** in order to solve this problem. **ADJUST** allows you to add a specified value to the actual ERRORLEVEL generated by the input. In this example, each of the **ASK** commands in lines 19, 23, and 27 uses a different adjustment value. In effect, the **ADJUST** options add 10 to the ERRORLEVEL if drive A was selected, 20 for drive B, and 30 for drive C. The current **ASK** command also has three possible values, one for each of the maintenance levels, 1, 2, or 3.

The result will be that each possible combination of drive and maintenance level selection will generate a unique value. How many possible combinations can there be? There are two inputs, each with three possible selections. The mathematical formula for finding the total number of combinations would be 3 to the 2nd power—that is, 9 altogether. The outcomes are shown in Figure 16–3.

|  | Level 1 | Level 2 | Level 3 |
|---|---|---|---|
| Drive A | 11 | 12 | 13 |
| Drive C | 21 | 22 | 23 |
| Drive D | 31 | 32 | 33 |

**Figure 16–3. Adjust option used to create unique values for user inputs.**

The correct mathematical term should be *permutations*. In probability terminology, a *combination* must have unique items but the sequence is not relevant. For example, *AB* and *BA* would show only one combination—that of *A* with *B*. However *AB* and *BA* would count as two permutations since the same items appear in a different order. However, in common usage, the word *combinations* seems to have the desired connotation, while *permutations* would probably confuse more than it would clarify.

When selecting values to use with **ADJUST,** you need to make sure that each possible combination of selections will generate a unique value. This is done by making the adjustment values sufficiently large, in this case using 10, 20, and 30, so that no combinations overlap. Keep in mind that since DOS reserves only a single byte for the ERRORLEVEL value, the largest decimal value you can use is 255.

## Evaluating Adjusted Values

The key to the use of the **ADJUST** option with **ASK** is to use the **IF ERRORLEVEL** commands to evaluate the user's input. The DKCR2.BAT program shown below is modeled after the DKCR1.BAT discussed in Chapter 15. Using the Batch Enhancer Version 6.0, you are able to restructure the program into two distinct parts: (1) user interface and (2) operation processing.

The *user-interface* portion of the batch refers to the interactive menu that explains to the user what choices are permitted, and receives the user's selections. This entire process can now be conducted by a single **BE** command, using the DKCR0002.SCR subfile shown in the previous section.

The batch file, DKCR2.BAT, will contain only the commands needed to evaluate the input, and execute the corresponding operations. The result is a batch file that executes at maximum speed because the Batch Enhancer program is loaded *only once* during the entire batch.

The program begins with a **BE** command that executes the user interface as stored in the DKCR0002.SCR subfile:

```
@ECHO OFF                        {1}
REM run subfile menu             {2}
BE dkcr0002.scr                  {3}
```

When the subfile processing is complete, the batch file will then evaluate the returning ERRORLEVEL. Since DOS batch commands such as **IF, SET,** and **GOTO** are memory-resident, the computer will process the ERRORLEVEL evaluation as fast as possible without any delays caused by disk access.

Evaluation takes place in two stages. The first phase seeks to separate user input according to the select drive. This is done by testing the ERRORLEVEL value for the ten's place. For example, all maintenance levels directed at drive D have ERRORLEVELS in the 30s—for example, 31, 32, or 33. To determine if the user had selected drive D, simply test to see if the ERRORLEVEL is greater than or equal to 30.

Recall from Chapter 15 that **IF ERRORLEVEL** does not test for equality—that is, **ERRORLEVEL** equals 10. Instead, an **IF ERRORLEVEL** command is true if the current ERRORLEVEL value is equal to or greater than the specified number. That is why ERRORLEVEL tests are always listed in descending order:

```
IF  ERRORLEVEL   30   GOTO  DRIVED    {4}
IF  ERRORLEVEL   20   GOTO  DRIVEC    {5}
IF  ERRORLEVEL   10   GOTO  DRIVEA    {6}
```

The next three sections of the batch perform two tasks. First, the **SET** command is used to store a value in the environmental variable, **DR**, which will be used to select the drive. The second task is to evaluate more closely the ERRORLEVEL value to determine which level of disk maintenance was selected by the user. The batch is then directed to the corresponding section that performs that level of disk maintenance:

```
:DRIVED                             {7}
   SET  dr=D                        {8}
   IF  ERRORLEVEL 33 GOTO LEVEL_3   {9}
   IF  ERRORLEVEL 32 GOTO LEVEL_2   {10}
   IF  ERRORLEVEL 31 GOTO LEVEL_1   {11}
:DRIVEC                             {12}
   SET  dr=C                        {13}
   IF  ERRORLEVEL 23 GOTO LEVEL_3   {14}
   IF  ERRORLEVEL 22 GOTO LEVEL_2   {15}
   IF  ERRORLEVEL 21 GOTO LEVEL_1   {16}
:DRIVEA                             {17}
   SET  dr=A                        {18}
   IF  ERRORLEVEL 13 GOTO LEVEL_3   {19}
   IF  ERRORLEVEL 12 GOTO LEVEL_2   {20}
   IF  ERRORLEVEL 11 GOTO LEVEL_1   {21}
```

The bottom section of the batch is almost identical to that used in the original DISKCARE.BAT and DKCR1.BAT, discussed in Chapter 15. Version 6.0 is primarily focused on improving the user interface presented by batch files:

```
:LEVEL_1                                      {22}
   NCC /START:1 > NUL                         {23}
   SET level=1                                {24}
   ECHO Level 1 Disk Care for Drive %dr%      {25}
   NDD %dr%: /QUICK                           {26}
   SPEEDISK %dr%: /SE                         {27}
   GOTO IMAGE                                 {28}
:LEVEL_2                                      {29}
   NCC /START:1 > NUL                         {30}
   SET level=2                                {31}
   ECHO Level 2 Disk Care for Drive %dr%      {32}
```

```
    NDD %dr%: /COMPLETE                                            {33}
    SPEEDISK %dr%: /F/V                                            {34}
    GOTO IMAGE                                                     {35}
:LEVEL_3                                                           {36}
    NCC /START:1 > NUL                                             {37}
    SET level=3                                                    {38}
    ECHO Level 3 Disk Care for Drive %dr%                          {39}
    NDD %dr%: /QUICK                                               {40}
    CALIBRATE %dr%: /PATTERN:5/BATCH/BLANK                         {41}
    GOTO IMAGE                                                     {42}
:IMAGE                                                             {43}
    CLS                                                            {44}
    BE ROWCOL 10,0                                                 {45}
    IMAGE %dr%:                                                    {46}
    ECHO Disk Maintenance of Drive %dr% Level %level% Completed    {47}
    NCC /STOP:1/L/N                                                {48}
    ECHO _Elapsed Time                                             {49}
    ECHO Disk Maintenance of Drive %dr% Level %level% Performed >>DKCARE.LOG  {50}
    NCC /STOP:1/L>>DKCARE.LOG                                      {51}
    ECHO _Elapsed Time >>DKCARE.LOG                                {52}
    BE ROWCOL 24,0                                                 {53}
```

When the batch is executed, the program will perform the same operations as DKCR1.BAT. However, the performance of the batch will be greatly improved. Entries in the menu will have about the same look and feel as a standard application because the awkward delays have been eliminated.

## Batch Enhancer Resource Files

In Version 5.0 of the Batch Enhancer it was necessary to create a separate subfile for each screen or menu you wanted to use within a batch file. For example, the menu system discussed in Chapter 15 used a separate subfile for each menu and an additional subfile for an introductory message.

Since Version 6.0 supports the use of labels within a subfile, it is possible to store two or more subfile routines within a single subfile and access individual sections by using a **GOTO** *label* parameter when the subfile is loaded into the Batch Enhancer. Below is a Batch Enhancer subfile called MENUS.SCR that contains three separate screen displays. These are the displays created in Chapter 15 for the menu system executed through the MAINMENU.BAT. This file replaces three files used in Chapter 15, MM0001.SCR, MM0002.SCR, and MM1001.SCR, to create the menu-display screen. In this example, the commands from those files have been combined into a single file. Each separate group of commands is preceded by a label—for example, SCREEN1, SCREEN2, and so on—and ends with an **EXIT** command:

```
:SCREEN1
CLS
    WINDOW 8,10,11,70
    ROWCOL 9,25,"Computer Booted Successfully"
    BEEP buzzer.snd
    DELAY 2
    EXIT
:SCREEN2
CLS
    WINDOW 5,20,23,60
    ROWCOL 6,30,"Main Menu" %clr%
    ROWCOL 8,25,"Lotus 1-2-3"
    ROWCOL 9,25,"WordPerfect 5.1"
    ROLCOL 10,25,"dBASE IV"
    ROWCOL 11,25,"Norton Utilities"
    ROWCOL 12,25,"Exit - Press [ESC]"
    ROWCOL 8,25,L COLOR BLA ON WHI
    ROWCOL 9,25,W COLOR BLA ON WHI
    ROWCOL 10,25,D COLOR BLA ON WHI
    ROWCOL 11,25,N COLOR BLA ON WHI
    ROWCOL 22,25
    ASK "Enter Letter: " lwdn DEFAULT=n
    EXIT
:SCREEN3
CLS
    WINDOW 5,20,23,60
    ROWCOL 6,30,"Main Menu"
    ROWCOL 8,25, "Norton Disk Doctor"
    ROWCOL 9,25,"Norton Control Center"
    ROWCOL 10,25,"Norton Disk Editor"
    ROWCOL 11,25,"Norton Utilities"
    ROWCOL 12,25,"Exit - Press [ESC]"
    ROWCOL 8,32,D COLOR BLACK ON WHITE
    ROWCOL 9,32,C COLOR BLACK ON WHITE
    ROWCOL 10,37,E COLOR BLACK ON WHITE
    ROWCOL 22,25
    ASK "Enter Letter: " dce
EXIT
```

When the main batch file needs to display one of the screens, the **BE** command is used to access the subfile. In order to jump to a specific section of the subfile, a **GOTO** label clause is added to the **BE** command. Below is a section of code taken from the MAINMENU.BAT file created in Chapter 15. The only modifications needed are in lines 2 and 4, where the **BE** command loads a screen from the MENUS.SCR file by specifying the labels where execution should start when the subfile is loaded:

```
@ECHO OFF                           {1}
BE menus.scr GOTO screen1           {2}
:mainmenu                           {3}
    BE Menus.scr GOTO screen2       {4}
    IF ERRORLEVEL 4 GOTO :program4  {5}
    IF ERRORLEVEL 3 GOTO :program3  {6}
    IF ERRORLEVEL 2 GOTO :program2  {7}
    IF ERRORLEVEL 1 GOTO :program1  {8}
    IF ERRORLEVEL 0 GOTO :END       {9}
```

Combining as many subfiles as possible into a single *resource* file makes it easier to keep track of the supporting files needed to run a complicated batch, such as the menu system.

While, in theory, each **BE** command that loads a different screen should take the same amount of time to load the Batch Enhancer and the subfile, you may find an additional performance benefit if you are using the cache program. In most cases, the cache program will retain the entire subfile in memory so that when you access the other screens it will not actually be necessary to perform a disk read in order to get the screen.

# Date Analysis

Version 6.0 of the Batch Enhancer includes three subcommands that make use of the system clock/calendar. They enable you to create batch files that interact with the clock to determine when a specific action should be executed:

**MONTHDAY.** This command sets the **ERRORLEVEL** equal to a value that matches the current day of the month, 1 to 31. Example: **BE MONTHDAY**.

**WEEKDAY.** This command sets the **ERRORLEVEL** value to a value from 1 to 7 depending on the current day of the week. 1 = Sunday, 2 = Monday, 3 = Tuesday, 4 = Wednesday, 5 = Thursday, 6 = Friday, 7 = Saturday. Example: **BE WEEKDAY**.

**TRIGGER.** This subcommand is used to pause the execution of a batch file until the system clock matches a specified time. This enables you to have your computer perform an operation, such as telecommunications, at a specific time—even if the computer is unattended. For example, the command below will pause execution until the system clock reaches 7:30 PM. Example: BE TRIGGER 7:30 PM.

You can eliminate the need for AM and PM if you enter the time in 24-hour format. The previous command would look like this: BE TRIGGER 19:30.

The **WEEKDAY** and **MONTHDAY** make it possible to have batch programs perform various operations periodically, based on the current day of the month or week. Below is a batch file program called DKCR3.BAT, which is a modified version of the DISKCARE.BAT file created at the beginning of Chapter 15. DISKCARE.BAT used user-entered parameters to select the level of disk maintenance that would be performed. DKCR3.BAT takes advantage of Version 6.0's **MONTHDAY** and **WEEKDAY** commands to automate the entire process. The batch will normally perform a level 1, the most basic disk maintenance—unless it is the first of the month, in which case level 3 maintenance, the most extensive, is performed—or if it is Friday, in which case level 2 maintenance will be performed.

The batch begins by creating a variable called **LEVEL** in line 5, which is set to zero. This is meant to set the default maintenance level at level 1. The Batch Enhancer date functions will check to see if this default should be changed because it is the first of the month or a Friday:

```
@ECHO OFF                          {1}
CLS                                {2}
NCC /START                         {3}
REM check for 1st of the month     {4}
SET level=1                        {5}
```

The first test is to see if the monthly maintenance, level 3, is required. The **MONTHDAY** subcommand in line 6 sets the ERRORLEVEL to the current day of the month. If it is the first of the month you will want to perform level 3. The evaluation of the date occurs in line 7 where the **IF ERRORLEVEL** command is used to determine if the date is the second of the month or greater. This may seem like an odd way to make the test, but it is necessary when you recall how the **ERRORLEVEL** option evaluates the **ERRORLEVEL** value. Recall that ERRORLEVEL will be true if the actual **ERRORLEVEL** value is equal to or greater than the specified value. By using **IF ERRORLEVEL 2** the command will evaluate as true for every day, except the first day of the month. If it is the first day of the month, the program will fall through the **IF** and encounter line 8, which will set the maintenance level at 3. The program then branches to the **DOIT** label, where the processing will begin.

If it is not the first day of the month you need to check to see if it is a Friday, which is done in the **CHECKDAY** section:

```
BE MONTHDAY                              {6}
IF ERRORLEVEL 2 GOTO checkday           {7}
SET level=3                              {8}
GOTO doit                               {9}
```

**CHECKDAY** begins by using **BE WEEKDAY** to set the ERRORLEVEL to indicate the day of the week. In this batch the target day of the week is Friday. In terms of ERRORLEVEL numbers that day is a bit awkward since Sunday is day 1 and Saturday is day 7. Line 12 sends the batch on to perform the default level if it is Saturday, 7. If it is not Saturday, then line 13 checks to see if it is Friday. If so the program jumps to **WEEKLY** and sets the level at 2. Otherwise, line 14 begins normal maintenance:

```
:CHECKDAY                                {10}
   BE WEEKDAY                            {11}
   IF ERRORLEVEL 7 GOTO doit            {12}
   IF ERRORLEVEL 6 GOTO weekly          {13}
   GOTO doit                            {14}
:WEEKLY                                  {15}
   SET level=2                          {16}
   GOTO doit                            {17}
```

The remainder of the program implements disk maintenance modeled on the DISKCARE.BAT program:

```
:DOIT                                                        {18}
   IF "%level%"=="1" GOTO LEVEL_1                           {19}
   IF "%level%"=="2" GOTO LEVEL_2                           {20}
   IF "%level%"=="3" GOTO LEVEL_3                           {21}
:LEVEL_1                                                     {22}
   BE ROWCOL 10,10,"Level 1 Disk Care for Drive C"         {23}
   NDD C: QUICK                                             {24}
   SPEEDISK C: /SE                                          {25}
   GOTO IMAGE                                               {26}
:LEVEL_2                                                     {27}
   BE ROWCOL 10,10,"Level 2 for Drive C"                   {28}
   NDD c: /COMPLETE                                         {29}
   SPEEDISK C: /F/V                                         {30}
```

```
          GOTO IMAGE                                      {31}
   :LEVEL_3                                               {32}
          BE ROWCOL 10,10,"Level 3 for Drive C"           {33}
          NDD c: /QUICK                                   {34}
          CALIBRATE c: /PATTERN:5/BATCH/BLANK             {35}
          GOTO IMAGE                                      {36}
   :IMAGE                                                 {37}
          IMAGE c:                                        {38}
          ECHO Drive C Level %level% Completed            {39}
          NCC /STOP/L/N                                   {40}
          ECHO _Elapsed Time                              {41}
          ECHO Drive C Level %level% Performed >> DKCARE.LOG {42}
          NCC /STOP/L>>DKCARE.LOG                         {43}
          ECHO _Elapsed Time >> DKCARE.LOG                {44}
          SET level=                                      {45}
```

This batch can be executed directly from the AUTOEXEC.BAT. The level of maintenance will change based on the day of the month or the day of the week, eliminating the need for the user to enter specific parameters.

## TRIGGER

The **TRIGGER** subcommand will pause a batch file until the system clock matches the specified time. When the time is reached, the remainder of the batch file is executed.

For example, the batch below is used to send a Fax through a Fax modem at 7:30 AM. The user would execute the batch when he/she left work the night before. The trigger would hold off execution of the **CFAXSEND** command until 7:30 the next morning:

```
@ECHO OFF
BE TRIGGER 07:30
CFAXSEND c:\cfax\memo.txt 1-212-888-9494
```

## Debug

In order to help you track down problems that arise when creating a complex batch file, Version 6.0 of the Batch Enhancer supports the use of the **/DEBUG** switch. When added to a Batch Enhancer subcommand, it causes the program to display the current value for the **ERRORLEVEL**. The switch allows you to see what the actual ERRORLEVEL value is at selected points in the batch file. For example, to see what value is returned by the **WEEKDAY** subcommand you would enter the following command:

```
BE WEEKDAY /DEBUG
```

The command would generate a message like "ERRORLEVEL:7" on the next line on the screen. **DEBUG** is also useful with the **ASK** command. The command below would display the ERRORLEVEL created by the user's selection after the entry was made.

```
BE ASK "Enter drive: " abcde /DEBUG
```

**DEBUG** can be used directly with Batch Enhancer commands on the inside of a subfile.

## Reboot

Version 6.0 supports a Batch Enhancer subcommand, **REBOOT**, that will perform a system reboot. The command below will cause the system to perform a *warm* boot. A warm boot is the same operation performed when you press the [Ctrl-Alt-Del] key combination.

```
BE REBOOT
```

If the **/V** or **/VERIFY** switch is used you will be prompted to confirm your intention to reboot the system. You must enter **Y** or **y** in order to perform the boot. Any other key will cancel the command. Example:

```
BE REBOOT /V
```

If you want to perform a *cold* boot you can use the **/C** switch:

```
BE REBOOT /C
```

A *cold* boot is one that starts at the beginning of the ROM start-up program built into your computer. This program often includes memory tests and special set-up options.

You can use Batch Enhancer subcommands to create your own reboot subfile. Below is a Batch Enhancer subfile called RESTART.SCR. This sub-file displays a window and asks you to confirm your intention to reboot the system:

```
CLS
WINDOW 8,20,12,60 BRI YEL ON RED
ROWCOL 10,25
ASK "Reboot System ? (Y/N) " yn TIMEOUT=25 DEFAULT=n
JUMP doit,dont
:DOIT
    REBOOT /C/Verify
:DONT
    EXIT
```

You can include this operation in any batch program by adding the following command:

```
BE restart.scr
```

# Summary

This chapter presented the changes made to the Batch Enhancer program in Norton Utilities Version 6.0.

**Subfile Structure**     The commands added to Version 6.0 of the Batch Enhancer allow you to create Batch Enhancer subfiles that can create screen displays through which the user can make multiple entries. The subfiles can contain many of the same structural elements found in DOS batch files, such as labels and **GOTO** commands. This makes it feasible to perform several inputs without having to return to the main batch file. The **ADJUST** option, available in all versions, allows you to manipulate the ERRORLEVEL value in order to generate a unique value for each possible combination of menu selections.

**JUMP**     This command accepts a list of labels as arguments. The command will branch to the label whose position in the label list matches the current errorlevel value. The **/DEFAULT** switch specifies a label to use if the ERRORLEVEL is 0—that is, the user inputs [Exc].

**GOTO**     This command branches to the specified label in the subfile. **GOTO** can also be used as an option when loading a Batch Enhancer subfile. This will cause the Batch Enhancer to begin processing sub-commands at the specified location, rather than the beginning of the subf-ile. This allows you to store multiple screens in a single subfile.

**EXIT**    This command immediately terminates the subfile and returns to the calling batch file.

**DEBUG**    The /DEBUG switch causes the Batch Enhancer to echo the current ERRORLEVEL value to the screen when it is added to a Batch Enhancer subcommand. This option helps you track down problems in your batch files.

**MONTHDAY**    This command sets the ERRORLEVEL value to match the current day of the month.

**WEEKDAY**    This commands sets the ERRORLEVEL value to match the current day of the week where Sunday is 1.

**TRIGGER**    This command pauses execution of the current batch file until the system clock matches the specified time of day.

**REBOOT**    This command causes the computer to perform a warm boot.

# 17 NDOS

This chapter explains the use of the NDOS program included in Version 6.0 of the Norton Utilities. NDOS is a replacement command processor and shell that extend the power and command structure of the DOS operating system in Version 3.1 and higher.

## What Is NDOS?

In Chapter 3 the function of the DOS COMMAND.COM program was discussed. COMMAND.COM is called the *command interpreter*. The command interpreter is the program that handles all of the instructions that the user makes to the operating system. For example, when you enter a command such as **DIR C:** it is the COMMAND.COM program that reads the instruction and carries out the operations associated with it.

All versions of DOS come supplied with a COMMAND.COM program. However, DOS was designed to allow for the use of alternative command processors that would take the place of COMMAND.COM. Microsoft envisioned different command interpreters on systems where the users preferred or required features not supplied in their COMMAND.COM program. These alternative command interpreters are often called *shell* programs. A *shell* is a program that presents a different user interface for an existing application. The user enters the commands through the shell program. The shell then passes the instructions through to the main application running in the background, which then carries out the operations. The advantage of creating a shell is that you can change the way the user works with a program without having to change the essential structures used by the program to carry out operations. Since the tasks carried out by DOS are so fundamental to the computer's operation, shells offer users a new way to work with DOS, without actually having to replace DOS, which might create serious incompatibility problems.

Surprisingly, considering the number of complaints users have had about the COMMAND.COM command system, there are few examples of programs that supply an actual replacement for COMMAND.COM even though technically DOS was designed to allow such replacements.[1] The NDOS program supplied with Version 6.0 of the Norton Utilities is just such a replacement program. NDOS can be utilized in two ways:

**Primary Shell.** The Primary shell program is one that is automatically loaded when the computer is first booted. All DOS computers will automatically load COMMAND.COM from the root directory of the boot drive. The NDOS program can be configured using CONFIG.SYS to load as the primary shell program each time you boot the computer.

**Temporary (Secondary) Shell.** NDOS can also be used as a *temporary* or *secondary* shell. A *secondary* shell is one that is loaded after the primary shell and operates much like a TSR program. Secondary shells can be terminated using a specific command, e.g., **EXIT**. When you exit the secondary shell, computer operations revert to the Primary shell that was loaded when the computer was booted.

Secondary shells may sound complicated, but they are actually quite common. When you access DOS through an application such as the **[Ctrl-F1]** command in WordPerfect or the */SYSTEM* command in Lotus 1-2-3 you are actually running a second session of the COMMAND.COM processor. When you use the **EXIT** command to return to the main application you have ended the session for the secondary shell.

The NDOS shell can be loaded as a secondary processor to allow you to have access to its features. When you exit, Microsoft's COMMAND.COM will return and only standard DOS operations will be available.

When you are first starting with NDOS you should probably use it as a secondary shell until you decide whether or not you want it to operate as the primary shell. If you use batch files extensively you will probably want to use the NDOS shell as your primary shell, since it vastly increases the sophistication level of batch file programming. On the other hand, users who are not conversant in batch file programming will probably find that the improved user interface of NDOS makes using a DOS computer much easier.

Note that NDOS is designed to improve the user's interface with the operating system, not the actual operating system itself. For example, suppose you are using DOS 3.3 on a 386 computer and were trying to decide

---

1. Conversely, DOS was not designed to allow multiple programs in memory at one time. However, technical innovation has made TSR programs a staple for DOS users.

about upgrading your operating system. Would it be better to upgrade to *DOS 5.0* or use *Norton NDOS 6.0*?

The answer is you would probably want to do *both*. This is because the two products offer different features. DOS 5.0 offers changes in the actual operating system, allowing 386 users to get advanced memory management and direct DOS support for hard disk partitions beyond 32 megabytes. However, the command interpreter supplied with DOS 5.0 is more or less identical to that supplied in DOS 3.3. The batch files discussed in Chapters 15 and 16 will run the same on DOS Versions 3.3 through 5.0. On the other hand, NDOS does not change operating system basics like memory management or hard disk partitioning. NDOS does offer improvements in the user interface, which, for example, allow you to create batch files that can tell when you last backed up your hard disk, something that cannot be done with DOS 5.0 alone. It is also important to keep in mind that NDOS can enhance the user interface on computers running DOS Version 3.3 or higher so that adding NDOS does not require a full operating system upgrade.

While the Norton Utilities 6.0 will operate on DOS 2.0 and higher, NDOS is recommended for DOS 3.1 and higher. In the author's view, anyone with a DOS version lower than 3.3 should upgrade their operating system. This is easier to do today than in previous years since Microsoft now sells DOS 5.0 over the counter in retail stores, just like any other software program. Prior to DOS 5.0, the operating system was sold through computer manufacturers like IBM and Compaq.

## NDOS Features and Improvements

The NDOS program is compatible with all standard DOS operations and commands. If you have used DOS you can use NDOS and never know the difference. However, NDOS adds a number of options, features, and capabilities that will make a DOS user's life much more comfortable. NDOS offers improvements in the following areas.

**Command Entry**    Entering DOS commands is a tedious process, even for experienced users, because of the primitive entry and editing features available under COMMAND.COM. For example, correcting a simple typographical error in a command is so complicated it is easier to re-enter the entire command. NDOS adds several features that make DOS command entry simpler and more efficient:

**Command-line Editing.** Editing and correcting commands can be done using word processing-like cursor movement and editing keys. You can automatically insert file names by using the [F9] and [F10] keys.

**Command History.** NDOS maintains a list of previous DOS commands that can be accessed by pressing the ↑ key at the DOS prompt. This enables you to repeat or edit a previous command.

**Wildcats.** NDOS allows for more flexible wildcard search, which will select files with a specific character or group of characters, regardless of their position in the file name.

**Multiple Commands.** NDOS allows you to enter a single command line that contains more than one actual command. This allows you to create *mini*-programs without having to create a batch file.

**Scope.** NDOS allows you to alter the normal scope of a DOS command or utility by combining the commands with **GLOBAL** or **EXCEPT**. **GLOBAL** applies the command to an entire branch of a directory tree (or an entire disk if started at the root directory) while **EXCEPT** protects specific files from what would otherwise be a global operation.

**Environment Customization**    NDOS greatly expands the ability of the user to control and modify the environment in which DOS operations take place. NDOS provides a wide list of predefined environmental variables that allow the user to get information about the current state of the computer.

NDOS also allows direct editing of environmental variables. This means that under NDOS you can change your current **PATH** list by editing, instead of having to issue a whole new path command. NDOS also allows you to save and retrieve the current environment. This allows you to alter the DOS set-up and easily return to its previous values.

NDOS allows the user to define *alias* names. An *alias* is a user-defined name that is assigned to a DOS command or series of commands. For example, you might create an alias called **Home** to equal the commands **C:⏎** and **CD/NU⏎**. This means that when you enter **home** ⏎ the Norton Utilities directory will be activated.

**Program Execution**    NDOS provides two ways in which files and applications can be related. First, NDOS allows you to associate an application with a file extension so that you can automatically run the associated application by entering a file with that extension. For example, you can relate files with the DOC extension to Microsoft Word (that is, the WORD program). Second, you can use the NDOS command **SELECT** to display a full-screen file listing from which you can make selections. These selections are then passed through to NDOS in order to execute a command line. This eliminates the need to remember or enter program or file names.

**Batch File Structures**    NDOS provides a broad range of commands, variables, and conditional statements that allow you to create batch files on a level of sophistication far beyond those supported by DOS's COMMAND.COM. These features include the ability to perform arithmetic on variables, and evaluate for conditions such as less, greater than, or not equal to for variables, file names, or ERRORLEVELS.

NDOS also supports faster execution of all batch files through its **BTM** (batch to memory) file extension. NDOS also keeps all Batch Enhancer commands memory-resident so that it is no longer necessary to create subfiles in order to achieve better performance.

In this chapter you will be presented with specific examples of these features and how they can be applied to everyday operations.

# Getting Information

It is possible to break down all operating system tasks into two large categories: operations that provide the user with information about the system and operations that modify the information in the system. It is common sense that you need to know something about the current state of your system before you decide about making any modifications. One of the characteristics that makes DOS so difficult to master is that the command set provided by COMMAND.COM offers very little information to the user. For example, the amount of free memory and/or disk space is a crucial factor that affects all computer operations. However, DOS provides very little information about such matters and the little bit that is provided is hard to access and understand.

For example, the amount of free disk space appears at the bottom of a directory listing, but cannot be listed by itself. In addition, if you use **DIR** but don't select any files, DOS won't tell you the amount of free space on the disk. As far as available memory, the only way to get this from DOS is, of all things, to run the **SHODS** (check disk) program.

To be fair, DOS 5.0 now includes a **MEM** command that displays memory information. In learning NDOS, the first set of commands you will use are those that provide you with information about your system.

## Running NDOS

When you are first getting started with NDOS the simplest way to use it is as a secondary processor. This means that you would boot your computer normally so that your current DOS version loads as the primary shell. You can then switch to using NDOS by loading it from the Norton Utilities home directory. Enter

```
cd \NU  ƒ
ndos ƒ
```

The NDOS program loads, replacing temporarily the DOS COMMAND.COM program. NDOS displays a message informing you of its version number and the version of DOS under which it is operating. NDOS is now loaded and ready to respond to your commands. There are two types of commands you can issue:

**NDOS Internal Commands.**   An NDOS internal command is one that is handled directly by the NDOS command interpreter. These are the commands that will utilize the features of NDOS.

**Utility Applications.** DOS and Norton Utilities programs accessed from DOS will not be directly affected by NDOS since these are actual programs, not internal operating system commands.

This means that when you are not specifically using an NDOS internal command, your system will function exactly as it did under the DOS COMMAND.COM program.

## Exiting NDOS

When you want to leave **NDOS** and return to COMMAND.COM enter the **EXIT** command. Enter exit ↵.

You have now returned to the primary shell, that is the COMMAND.COM session. How can you tell? Unlike NDOS, COMMAND.COM does not automatically display a message when you activate that shell. You can determine if DOS or NDOS is active by using the **VER** command. In DOS, **VER** will display the DOS version number. In NDOS, **VER** will display both the NDOS and the DOS version numbers. Enter ver ↵.

The screen will show something like **MS-DOS Version 5.0**. This indicates that COMMAND.COM is active. Restart NDOS by entering ndos ↵.

It is important to remember that you *must* start NDOS from the directory that contains the NDOS.COM and the NDOS.OVL files. If you start NDOS from another directory the operating system will find only the *NDOS.COM* file and not the NDOS.OVL file. If this is the case the message "NDOS **initialization error—Can't find OVL file.**" You can correct this problem by changing to the directory in which the OVL file is located, e.g., **\NU**. This error will not occur when running DOS 5.0.

## File Information—DIR

The key to most operating system tasks are the file and directory names. The most commonly used operating system commands, such as **DIR, CD, COPY**, and **DEL**, involve the use of file and directory names or wildcards. NDOS provides a variety of ways in which you can get information about these items.

One of the simplest and most useful is additional power added to the **DIR** command. **DIR** in NDOS can perform many of the functions that would otherwise require a program such as File Find. For example, NDOS **DIR** supports a /S switch that causes **DIR** to list matching files from the current directory and all subdirectories on the current branch. If you start from the root directory this allows you to search the entire disk. For example, to list all of the BAT files on the disk you would enter: DIR \*.bat /S. The command searches the entire disk and lists all of the batch files located in each directory. The display is similar to the DOS **DIR** with two exceptions:

**File Name Format.** NDOS shows the file names in lowercase letters with a period separating the file name from the file extension. This format is much closer to the way that the file names would actually be entered. Recall that DOS would show the file name *autoexec.bat* as *AUTOEXEC BAT*, where a space is used instead of a period.

**Summary Information.** Note that the summary at the bottom of the **DIR** display shows a value labeled *allocated*. This value is the total amount of disk space allocated to the selected files. This is different from the **bytes in files**, which reflects the actual size of the files. Recall from Chapter 4, "Clusters," that the difference between the actual size of the file and the total amount of space DOS allocates to store the file is called *slack* space. The NDOS **DIR** command recognizes and calculates the two different values. You will probably notice that BAT files have a significant amount of slack space since they seldom take up an entire disk cluster.

In addition to the standard display formats used by DOS **DIR**, the NDOS **DIR** has two- and four-column displays. Enter dir /2 ↵.

The files are listed in two columns, both of which show the size, time, and date of each file. Display the same file list using the four-column format. Enter dir /4 ↵.

This format shows the names and sizes only. To save space the sizes are written in Kilobytes rather than bytes.

You can suppress the display of directory names by adding **/N**. The following command lists the batch file names but not the directories. Example: dir \*.bat /s/n.

**/B** suppresses all information except the file names. Note that **/B** uses the standard DOS format for file names. Example: dir \*.bat /s/b.

This type of listing is useful when you want to capture the list of files in a text file, which might later be edited to create a batch file. You would want to combine **/B** with **/N** in order to get the file in the format with the period instead of space. Example: DIR \*.BAT /N/B >batlist.txt.

The BATLIST.TXT file would look like this:

```
autoexec.bat
clr.bat
clrl.bat
colors.bat
diskcare.bat
er.bat
jump.bat
```

The **/M** switch suppresses the summary totals. Enter dir *.bat /s/m.

The files are listed, but no summary totals are generated. The **/U** switch suppresses the listing of file names. You can combine **/U** and **/M** to create a listing of the directory names only. The following command will generate a listing of all the directories on the disk. Enter dir \ /m/u/s/.

## Directory Lists

Unlike the **DIR** command under COMMAND.COM, NDOS allows you to enter a list of wildcards. For example, under COMMAND.COM you would have to enter three commands to list the batch files in the root directories of drives A, C, and D:

```
DIR A:\*.BAT
DIR C:\*.BAT
DIR D:\*.BAT
```

In NDOS the same task could be accomplished with a single command. Example: DIR A:\*.BAT,C:\*.BAT,D:\*.BAT.

By adding /S to the command you would list all of the batch files on all three drives. Example: DIR A:\*.BAT,C:\*.BAT,D:\*.BAT/S.

The previous commands listed three separate directories with a single command. You can create a single unified directory by using a ; in place of a , between the wildcards. The example will list all of the EXE and COM files in the \NU directory as a single unified list in name order. Example: DIR C:\NU\*.exe;*.com/On.

Note that all of the files must reside in the same directory as indicated by the path name associated with the first wildcard. The command is equivalent to using File Find, but is faster since the **DIR** command is memory-resident in NDOS.

## Sorted Listings

In addition, you can request to view files in a sorted order with the /O switch. To list files in name order, enter dir / on ↵. The files are listed in alphabetical order. The letters **d** or **t** would sort by time and date, while **r** would reverse the order; that is, order the files in a descending sequence. To list batch files, starting with the most recent to the oldest, enter dir *.bat /odr ↵.

## File Attributes

**DIR** will also recognize file attributes. The /H switch includes *hidden* file. Enter dir c:\ /h ↵.

You can select files by their attributes. The command below would list all of the read-only files, on the current disk. Example: DIR *.* /S/A:R.

The /T switch causes an extra column to be added to the directory display that shows the file attributes, e.g., ___A for a normal file. Example: dir c:\ /t.

## Memory and Disk Capacity

NDOS provides **MEMORY** and **FREE** commands to enable the user to quickly obtain a summary of the internal and disk storage capacity and usage. To obtain a summary of the disk usage enter **FREE** followed by the drive letters of the drives you wish to summarize. The command below summarizes four drives, one a local hard disk and the other three remote network server drives. Enter free c:,d:,e:,f: ↵.

The results of the command would look like this:

```
Volume in drive C is unlabeled    Serial number is
16B1:675A
 42,366,976 bytes total disk space
 30,984,192 bytes used
 11,382,784 bytes free
Volume in drive D is NET_100
100,376,576 bytes total disk space
 84,246,528 bytes used
 16,130,048 bytes free
Volume in drive E is NETWORK.#3
 44,503,040 bytes total disk space
 42,680,320 bytes used
  1,822,720 bytes free
Volume in drive F is unlabeled
 88,670,208 bytes total disk space
 63,930,368 bytes used
 24,739,840 bytes free
```

The **MEMORY** command summarizes the current memory usage. Enter memory ↵.

The command displays a summary like the one below. This summary includes conventional (RAM), extended, expanded (EMS), and Microsoft XMS memory. In addition, the listing shows NDOS memory items such as environment variable space, command alias space, and command history space. The last three items are included in the amount of memory allocated to running NDOS. These values do not apply when you return to the COMMAND.COM session:

```
655,360 bytes total RAM
590,160 bytes free
917,504 bytes total EMS memory
524,288 bytes free
616,448 bytes free XMS memory   (HMA is in use)
    512 bytes total environment
    370 bytes free
  1,024 bytes total alias
  1,024 bytes free
  1,024 bytes total history
```

## Listing File Contents

Listing or inspecting the contents of files that contain text or information stored in text form is not easy using normal DOS commands. DOS has two tools that are usually applied to this task:

**Type.**  Displays the contents of a file on the screen display as a stream of information.

**More.**  Halts the output stream every 24 lines. Any key, except [Ctrl-break], continues the scrolling.

For example, to display the contents of the AUTOEXEC.BAT file use this command: type c:\autoexec.bat |more ↵.

This approach is quite awkward since you cannot scroll backwards or forwards, but only move forward in the file in blocks of 24 lines each time. In fact, the method is so hard to use almost no one uses it except in the most desperate circumstances.

NDOS replaces this with the **LIST** command. List will display the contents of a file in a full-screen scroll window similar to the **VIEW** command in File Find. To view the contents of the AUTOEXEC.BAT with **LIST**, enter list c:\autoexec.bat ↵. **LIST** shows the text within a window. You can scroll up, down, left, and right with the arrow keys as much as you need. The window will also respond to [PgUp], [PgDn], [Home], and [End]. In addition you have two other options:

**Search.**  Entering **f** activates a search. You can enter a letter, word, or phrase for which you want to search. The file is scrolled so that the first line that contains a match appears at the top of the window. The letter **n** continues the search to the next occurrence if any.

**Print.**  Entering **p** outputs the text to the default printer device PRN.

Exit the window by entering [Esc].

You can view a list of files by specifying a file wildcard. For example, to view all of the BAT files in the root directory of drive C, enter list c:\*.bat ↵.

The first matching file in the directory is displayed. To move to the next file, enter [Esc].

If you want to terminate the listing, enter [Ctrl-c].

Note that **LIST** is not appropriately used with text files. Display of binary formatted files is usually not useful.

## Browsing Standard Output

There are many DOS commands, utilities, or other programs that produce useful information, but in a nonuseful manner; that is, they simply scroll the output on the screen, usually far too fast to be of any use to the reader. Aside from its basic method for viewing text files, **LIST** can be used in place of the DOS **MORE** filter to display any standard screen output in the **LIST** display window.

For example, suppose that you use the **DIR** command to generate a list of all of the batch files on a hard disk. The following command would list the batch files in descending order by date. Example: DIR \*.BAT/S/T/ODR.

However, the output from this command will probably scroll by too fast to be of much use. **LIST**, with the /**S** switch, will function as a filter program that captures the screen output of a command and places it in the **LIST** window from which you can scroll, search, and/or print the information. To display the batch file **LIST** in a **LIST** window use the following command. Example: DIR \*.BAT/S/T/ODR | LIST/S.

By using a list of wildcards you can browse the batch files from several drives. Examples: DIR C:\*.BAT,/S/T/ODR | LIST/S.

Keep in mind that you can use this technique with any program or utility that creates standard screen output. The DOS utility FC—file compare—is useful in locating the difference between two files. Because FC creates standard screen output, the results of an FC operation are very hard to use. By adding a **LIST** filter you can examine the results of a file comparison at your leisure. The example below displays the differences between a document and its backup file in a **LIST** window. Example: FC report1.doc report1.bak | LIST/S.

# Entering Commands

The commands entered by the average user at the system prompt typically fall into certain patterns. Each user will find they have certain commands that they use on a regular basis, often repeating the same commands or slightly modified versions of the same commands.

Unfortunately, COMMAND.COM provides very little assistance to the user in entering commands. NDOS corrects this situation by adding several features designed to simplify command entry and reduce mistakes and tedium.

## Command History and Editing

The most important entry features supplied by NDOS are command-line editing and command history:

**Editing.** When you enter a command in NDOS you can edit the command to correct mistakes without having to retype part or all of the command. The ← and → keys will move the typing cursor horizontally on the command line (see Table 17–1).

**Table 17–1. Command-line editing key.**

| Key | Function |
| --- | --- |
| [Ctrl- ←] | Move left one word. |
| [Ctrl- →] | Move right one word. |
| [Home] | Move to the beginning of the line. |
| [End] | Move to the end of the line. |
| [Ctrl-Home] | Delete beginning of the line to cursor. |
| [Ctrl-End] | Delete the end of the line. |
| [Ins] | Toggle between insert and replace typing. |
| [Del] | Delete the character at the cursor. |
| [Bksp] | Delete the character to the left of the cursor. |
| [Ctrl-Bksp] | Delete word right of the cursor. |
| [Ctrl-l] | Delete word left of the cursor. |
| [Esc] | Clear entire line. |
| [Ctrl-k] | Place command in history without executing. |
| [Ctrl-d] | Clear history list. |

**History.** NDOS stores all of the commands you enter into a special area of memory. This allows you to scroll backwards through the commands you have entered by pressing the ↑ at the prompt. Once in the list, you can move forward with ↓ or clear the command line with [Esc]. When you display a previous command you can execute it again by pressing ↵ or modify the command with your editing keys and execute the modified command with ↵.

By default, NDOS sets aside 1,024 bytes of memory to store.[2] All commands are stored until the memory area is filled. Commands are then deleted on a first-in, first-out basis.

---

2.  The size of the history area can be changed using the **/H** switch. See "Installing NDOS."

For example, suppose that you wanted to display a list of all the batch files on drive C in the **LIST** window. Enter dir c:\*.bat/s | list/s ⏎.

Exit the **LIST** window by entering [Esc].

Next, you want to perform the same listing, but on drive D. In NDOS you can quickly recall and modify the command to operate on drive D. Display the last command from the list area by entering ↑. NDOS places the previous command on the screen next to the prompt with the cursor at the end of the line. Position the cursor on the drive letter **c** by entering [Home] [Ctrl-←].

By default, any typing performed while editing a command line replaces the current characters. If you want to place NDOS into an insert mode, press [Ins]. [Ins] will toggle the typing mode between replace and insert. Note that if insert is active the screen cursor will be a flashing block. If the replace mode is active the cursor is a flashing line. Enter d.

Execute the modified command by entering ⏎.

When the list is displayed, exit the list window by entering [Esc].

NDOS will perform a speed search of the history command list. To begin a speed search you would enter several characters that indicate how the command you are looking for begins. For example, if you wanted to find the last **CD** command, enter cd ↑.

NDOS will display the last command in the list, if any, that started with **CD**. You can display a list of all of the commands in the history memory buffer by entering history ⏎.

To review the history list in a window use the **LIST** command as a filter. Example: HISTORY | LIST/S.

If you want to clear all of the commands currently stored in the history buffer, use the /**F** switch. Example: HISTORY /F.

You can save the commands contained in the history buffer by redirecting the output of the **HISTORY** command to a text file. The command below captures the current history list in a file called HIST0001.BAT. Example: HISTORY >HIST0001.BAT.

Since HIST0001 is a batch file, you can replay the entire list of commands by executing the HIST0001. However, in most cases you will want to edit the batch file produced by redirection because it will contain self-referential commands. This means that the command **HISTORY >HIST0001.BAT** will be included on the list. You probably don't want to leave this command at the end of the list since it will create an endless loop in which the batch is run over and over again.

Another way to use the stored command list is to reload it into the history buffer so that you can access individual commands. Note that you can load commands from any text file with this approach. This means that you can load the contents of any batch file or text file. For example, suppose that you have altered the **PATH** list set by your AUTOEXEC.BAT and wish to return to that path set-up. You could execute the AUTOEXEC.BAT file again by entering AUTOEXEC ↵. However, that would cause all of the commands in the batch file to execute, some of which might not make sense or be desirable at this time. An alternative would be to load the commands into the history buffer. Once placed in the buffer, you could scroll through the commands until you found the **PATH** command and execute that one part of the AUTOEXEC.BAT. The command below loads the commands from the AUTOEXEC.BAT into the history buffer. Example: HISTORY /R c:\autoexec.bat.

Note that commands read into the history buffer are appended onto the existing list. If you only want to have the AUTOEXEC.BAT commands in the history buffer, add the /F switch to the history command. The /F switch flushes the history buffer before loading the commands from the file. Example: HISTORY /R/F c:\autoexec.bat.

## Inserting File Names

Many commands entered at the system prompt involve the use of file names. However, entering the full name of a file can make entering commands tedious. Note that a single typo in a file name can cause an error or result in an unexpected result.

One of the most common typing mistakes that leads to an unexpected result is typing a ; instead of a : following a drive letter. For example, you might enter the command **COPY*.*A;** instead of **COPY*.*A:**. What is so confusing about this mistake is that the operating system will not return an error. In fact, the operating system thinks this is a valid command. But when the command is complete, the user will find that none of the files listed by the command have been placed on drive A. Where did they go? The answer is that the ; character is treated like a space. The operating system sees the command as **COPY*.*A,;** that is, copy all of the files in the current directory to *a file called A*. Without the : the operating system assumes A is a file name, not a drive. The result is that in the current directory you will find a large file called **A**, but no files on the disk in **drive A** due to this common typo.

NDOS addresses this problem by automatically inserting directory and file names from the current or specified directory onto the command line when you press one of the designated function keys (Table 17–2).

**Table 17–2. File name keys.**

| Key | Function |
| --- | --- |
| [F9] | Insert next file name. |
| [F8] | Insert previous file name. |
| [F10] | Add next file name to end of command. |

For example, suppose you want to make a copy of the AUTOEXEC.BAT file. Begin by entering the command: copy [space].

Instead of entering the file name you can use [F9] to scan the items in a directory. When you press [F9], NDOS places the first item, directory, or file name, from the current directory on the editing line at the cursor position. Each time you press [F9] the next item in the directory replaces the previous item that was on the edit line. If you want to go back to a previous item, enter [F8].

If you want to narrow down the list of items or you want to list the items from another disk or directory, enter a path name or wildcard before you press [F9]. In this example you want the AUTOEXEC.BAT from the root directory of drive C. Restrict the list to batch files in the root directory of C by entering c:\*.bat.

To have the names inserted, enter [F9].

The wildcard is replaced by the name of the first batch file in the specified disk and directory. If this is the AUTOEXEC.BAT file then you are ready to complete the command. If not, you can press [F9] to display the next file name, until you have the name you desire.

Suppose that you want to copy the file to AUTOEXEC.001. Since that is a similar name to the current file name, you may save time by appending another copy of the name to the command and editing the extension. [F10] adds the next name in the list to the end of the command line. Enter [F10].

Of course, in this case you wanted to use the same name as you had inserted before. Use [F8] to move back one name from the list. Enter [F8].

The line now reads **copy c:\autoexec.bat c:\autoexec.bat.** Change the extension on the last file name by entering [Ctrl-L] 001 ↵. The new file is created. Note that the NDOS **COPY** command explicitly confirms the copy by echoing the source and destination file names, **c:autoexec.bat=>c:** **\autoexec.001.** Note that the [F9] key will insert a file name only if the preceding character on the line is a valid delimiter, e.g., a space, comma, semicolon, etc. If the character is not a delimiter, a beep will sound when you press [F9]. For example, if you enter del [F9], NDOS sounds a beep because the last character on the current line is **Y**. Add a space and then try again. Enter [space] [F9]. The first item in the directory is inserted onto the line. Clear the line by entering [Esc].

The [F8], [F9], and [F10] keys can eliminate typos and speed entry of commands such as **COPY, RENAME,** or **DELETE** that require specific file names.

## Special Characters

NDOS provides a means by which you can enter nontext characters into operating system commands. These special characters are most frequently used to send codes to a printer. NDOS has a special method for entering text strings to send these codes. Entering [Ctrl-x] inserts a ↑ character on the editing line. Following the ↑, you can enter one of the following letters to represent common codes sent to printers:

| | |
|---|---|
| b | backspace, [Ctrl-h], ASCII 8 |
| e | Esc, ASCII 27 |
| f | form feed, [Ctrl-L], ASCII 12 |
| n | line feed, [Ctrl-J], ASCII 10 |
| r | carriage return, [Ctrl-m], ASCII 13 |

For example, most printers[3] recognize [Ctrl-L] as the instruction to feed a form. To issue a form feed through NDOS you would enter

```
echo [space]
[Ctrl-x] ef >prn ↵
```

The entry on the line will appear as **echo ↑ef.**

HP Laserjet series II and compatible printers will recognize the sequence of [Esc]&k2S as the instruction to print in compressed, 16.66 cpi, print. To issue that command from NDOS you would enter the following command. Note that you should type [Ctrl-x] in order to produce the ↑ symbol. Example: ECHO ¡e&k2S > PRN.

---

3. The most significant exception are PostScript laser printers that do not respond to ASCII codes at all. You cannot directly print from DOS or NDOS to a PostScript printer. The LP program can output text files to a PostScript printer.

## Keeping a Log

In many cases it is useful to maintain a list of the operations performed. This list is called a *log*. Recall from Chapter 15 that the menu batch files created a log of all of the applications used and their elapsed times.

NDOS will maintain a log of all commands issued at the prompt in a file called NDOS.LOG in the root directory of the boot drive. The log will list the time and date of each command, along with the command entered. The log can be used to keep track of computer activity or as a way of automatically recording in a text file all of the commands you issue. The command may then be copied from the log into a batch file. This is a good way to work out the syntax of a complicated command before you make it part of a batch file.

By default, the log feature is not active. You can check the status of the log by entering: LOG.

NDOS responds with either "LOG is OFF" or "LOG is ON." You can turn on the log feature by entering LOG ON.

Once activated, all commands will be recorded in the log. The command **LOG OFF** turns off the log feature and commands issued after **LOG OFF** are not copied into the log. Below is an example of the contents of a log that has recorded commands:

```
[ 6-03-91  7:17:37p] ndd
[ 6-03-91  7:17:55p] speedisk
[ 6-03-91  7:18:03p] log off
```

In addition to recording commands, you can directly insert text into the log by using **LOG** followed by a text string. Note that this command will insert text into the log regardless of whether the log record is *ON* or *OFF*. The command below will insert the text *Project: Budget Worksheet* into the log file. Example: LOG "Project: Budget Worksheet."

The text will be placed into the log file with a time and date stamp:

```
[ 6-03-91  7:17:37p] Project: Budget Worksheet
[ 6-03-91  7:17:55p] 123
```

If you want to place log items into a file other than c:\NDOS.LOG, you can specify a different file with the /W switch. The command below activates the file C:\NU\TEST.LOG as the log file. The log is automatically activated. Example: LOG /W c:\NU\test.log.

NDOS will continue to use C:\NU\TEST.LOG as the log file each time you turn on the log for the duration of the session, or until you specify another file with the **/W** switch.

## Command Scope

Many DOS commands and utilities that deal with files have a pre-defined scope in which they operate. For example, the **DEL** command will operate only on the files in a single directory. The NDOS **GLOBAL** command allows you to apply a command that would normally be limited to a single directory to all of the directories that branch from the starting directory.

For example, suppose you wanted to delete all of the BAK files from drive C. You would begin with the command that would erase the BAK files in the root directory. Example: DEL C:\*.BAK. Of course, this command would stop at the root directory. In order to expand the scope of the command to cover the entire hard disk, preface the command with **GLOBAL**. Example: GLOBAL DEL C:\*.BAK. **GLOBAL** can be applied to utility and application programs as well. For example you could combine the Norton Utilities Line Print program, LP, with GLOBAL in order to print all of the batch files on drive C. The command below would be executed on each of the directories on drive C, printing all of the batch files in each directory. Example: GLOBAL LP C:\*.BAT.

As a safety precaution, any command that uses GLOBAL will be automatically terminated if the program executed by GLOBAL returns an exit code that indicates an error. Note that not all program or utilities issue exit codes or issue them in a standard way. If you want the global processing to continue regardless of error codes, use the **/I** switch.

On the other hand, you will find that you may want to protect certain files from operations that affect entire directories or disks. The **EXCEPT** command allows you to enter a list of files or wildcards that designate files you want to protect from the command you are executing. For example, suppose you wanted to copy all of the files in the root directory of drive C to drive A. However, you did not want to include the COMMAND.COM, AUTOEXEC.BAT, or CONFIG.SYS since the disk already has files with those names. The **COPY** command would look like this: COPY c:\*.*a:.

In order to exclude the three specified files you would precede the command with **EXCEPT** followed by the list, enclosed in parentheses, of the file or wildcards you wanted to exclude: EXCEPT (autoexec.bat, config.sys, command.com) COPY *.*a:.

Note that you can make entering the file list simpler by using the [F9] key. For example, you would begin by entering : except ([space].

Note that the space is necessary since [F9] will not work when the last character on the line is a (. Enter au [F9]. NDOS inserts the first item in the directory that begins with AU. If that is not AUTOEXEC.BAT, press [F9] until it appears. Then enter , co [F9].

Note that this time a space is not needed since the comma is a valid DOS delimiter character, which is treated just like [space]. You can continue with this method until you have filled out the list of files you want to protect. Clear the line by entering [Esc].

The **EXCEPT** command excludes files by setting the hidden attribute on those files before the command is executed. Programs or utilities that operate on hidden files will not work properly with **EXCEPT**.

## BTM Files

The performance of batch file execution can be increased significantly by using *batch to memory* execution in place of normal batch execution. This can be done by changing the file extension from BAT to BTM. Using the BTM extension tells NDOS to load the entire batch file into memory instead of processing the batch file line by line from the disk.

Note that BTM cannot improve the performance of batch files that use external programs since they must be loaded individually.

# Executing Commands in NDOS

One of the primary functions of the operating system is the loading and executing of programs and applications. NDOS expands the ways in which commands can be entered and applications executed from the operating system prompt.

## Multiple Command Lines

NDOS allows you to enter more than one command at a time on the command line. This allows you to create *minibatch* files directly at the system prompt. For example, suppose that in order to run Lotus 1-2-3 you usually enter the following sequence of commands:

```
D:
CD\LOTUS\R3
123
```

You could issue all three commands in a single line. NDOS uses the ^ character to separate commands on one line. The NDOS equivalent of the previous sequence is : D:^CD\LOTUS\R3^123. You could add commands that would alter the application. The following command would return to the root directory of drive C after the user exits from 1-2-3: D:^CD\LOTUS\R3^123^C:^CD\.

## Using an Alias

An *alias* is a user-defined name that is assigned to an existing system item. In NDOS an alias functions as shorthand or abbreviation for a command. An alias can perform many operations that would otherwise require the creation of a batch file. Alias commands execute much faster than batch files since they are kept in memory rather than stored on the disk. In addition, an alias is a global command; that is, it is available at all times because it is resident in memory. Access to batch files stored on disks encounters the same limitations as applications. Depending upon where the batch file is stored, you may or may not be able to access it, something alias operations avoid.

Aliases allow you to define your own set of commands. For example, you may define the alias *home* as the command **CD\NU** since that is the *home* directory of the Norton Utilities program. Alias commands are created using the ALIAS command: ALIAS *alias_name command*.

To create the alias specified above, you would enter ALIAS home cd\NU.

Once an alias has been created, you can enter the alias name whenever you want to execute the command. In this example, you would enter **HOME** in order to activate the \NU directory. An alias can be created with parameters in the same way that parameters were used in Chapter 15 to pass value to the commands within a batch file. For example, earlier in this chapter the **DIR** and **LIST** commands were combined to create a directory listing that appeared in a scrollable window. The command used was: DIR\*.BAT/S/T/ODR|LIST/S.

It might be useful to create an alias command that would shorten the entry, in order to display the files in a window. Begin with the first part of the command shown above, the sorted directory listing. The command below creates an alias called SHOW in which the wildcard \*.**bat** is replaced by a parameter variable %**1**.[4] Example: ALIAS show DIR %1/S/T/ODR.

You can then execute the alias using the desired wildcard as an argument. Examples:

```
SHOW *.sys
SHOW *.WKS, *.WK1
```

Note that in the second example a list of wildcards was used as the parameter. Of course, the directory displays it as continuous scroll. The command might function better if the **LIST** command was added as a filter so that the directory listings would appear in a scroll box.

Below is a command that adds the **LIST** filter. Enter

```
ALIAS show DIR %1/S/T/ODR|LISTS/S ↵
```

What happened? Instead of creating the alias with the LIST filter, NDOS activated the LIST window to receive the output, of which there is none, of the alias commands. Exit by entering [Esc].

What is the cause of this problem? The answer has to do with the command line *parsing*. *Parsing* is a computer term that refers to the way a program such as NDOS determines what the different parts of a command line mean. Like COMMAND.COM, NDOS assumes that items appended to a command line that deal with redirection of the output, e.g., a filter like |**SHOW/S**, are to be treated as active instructions.

When you entered the command, your goal was to have the alias command defined to include all of the text to the right of the alias name SHOW. In other words, you intended the line to be parsed into three segments: the **ALIAS** command, the alias name SHOW, and the **DIR|LIST** command: *ALIAS(1)show(2)* **DIR%1/S/T/ODR|LIST/S(3)**.

However, NDOS parsed the line into four parts because it automatically treats the filter as a separate part of the command line: ALIAS(1) show(2) **DIR%1/S/T/ODR(3)**/*LIST/S(4)*.

Does this mean that you cannot create an alias that uses a filter? No, there is a solution. You need to add markings to the line that shows NDOS exactly how you want the command interpreted. In this case, you want to indicate that the alias text includes everything after the alias name. This is done by enclosing the text of the alias in *back quote (accent)* characters. The

---

4.  Under NDOS you can have up to 128 parameter variables (%0 through %127) in contrast to COMMAND.COM, which only supports 10 (%0 through 9%).

*back quote,* ', is found on the same key as the tilde. This key is usually found above the [Tab]. Do not confuse the back quote ', with the single quotation mark ', which is found on the same key as ". Re-enter the command using the back quote characters to delimit the alias text:

```
ALIAS show  'DIR %1/S/T/ODR|LIST/S'↵
```

This time the **LIST** filter is included as part of the alias. Enter show *.sys. ↵.

A list of all the SYS files appears in the List scroll box. Exit by entering [Esc].

The same problem occurs when you want to use multiple commands within an alias. Normally, NDOS would associate only the first command in the list with the alias. For example, the command below appears to define the alias LTS as the sequence of commands used to run Lotus 1-2-3 described earlier: ALIAS lts D:^CD\LOTUS\R3^123^C:^CD\.

However, NDOS would actually break the entry down into five different commands:

```
ALIAS lts D:     {1}
CD\LOTUS\R3      {2}
123              {3}
C:               {4}
CD\              {5}
```

Only the first command, **D:**, would be assigned to the alias. The solution in this case is the same as with the LIST filter: Use back quotes to indicate to NDOS that the entire sequence of commands should be assigned to the alias. The correct alias command: ALIAS lts 'D:^CD\LOTUS\ R3^123^C:^CD\'.

## Nesting Aliases

Once an alias has been defined, you can include that alias command in the definition of other multiple command aliases. The technique is similar to the way that the **CALL** command was used in Chapter 15 to execute batch files from within another batch file. When an alias is executed as part of another alias, it is said to be *nested* or *contained within* the new alias. For example, below is a command that creates an alias called **SMALL. SMALL** sends the printer set-up code for compressed printing to an HP series II type laser printer, discussed earlier. Note that the ' are used to indicate that the **>PRN** command is part of the alias, not a separate operation. Example: ALIAS small 'ECHO ¡e&k2S > PRN'.

The command below creates an alias that sends the code to reset the printer to normal-size printing.[5] Example: ALIAS norm 'ECHO ¡e&kOS > PRN'.

These two aliases can be used as part of the definition of other alias commands. For example, suppose that you want to compress the printing when you run Lotus 1-2-3. The command below defines an alias **LTS** that sets the printer for compressed text before 1-2-3 is run, and then back to normal after it has been terminated. Example: ALIAS lts 'SMALL^CD\LOTUS^123^CD\^NORM'.

Another example shown below prints a directory in compressed type. Example: ALIAS drs 'SMALL^DIR /4>PRN^NORM'.

Below is an alias called SMLTEXT, which outputs the specified text file in compressed print. Example: ALIAS smltext 'SMALL^TYPE %1>PRN^NORM'.

To print the contents of the AUTOEXEC.BAT file you would enter: SMLTEXT \AUTOEXEC.BAT.

Suppose you wanted to print a phrase directly to the printer. The alias below, called **PECHO**, sends text directly to the printer and then feeds a form. This would be a quick way to print out a message or note. Example: ALIAS pecho 'SMALL^ECHO %1>PRN^ECHO ¡f>PRN ^NORM'.

To print a message you might enter: PECHO Out to lunch. Be back at 2:00.

## Managing Aliases

When the **ALIAS** command is used without any arguments, it will display a list of all the alias names and definitions currently in memory. Example: ALIAS.

To place this list in a scroll box use the LIST filter. Example: ALIAS I LIST/S.

You can display a specific alias by using the alias name alone as an argument. The command below displays the definition of the **PECHO** alias. Example: ALIAS pecho.

---

5.   The two alias commands are so similar you could create the second by editing the history list instead of entering the entire command.

You can remove an alias from memory with the **UNALIAS** command. The command below erases the **PECHO** alias from memory. Example: UNALIAS PECHO.

You can erase all of the alias definitions from memory using the * as a wildcard character. Example: UNALIAS *.

The number and size of the alias definitions is limited to the size of the alias buffer, which is defined when NDOS is loaded.

## Storing and Retrieving Aliases

Because alias definitions are stored in memory, they execute faster than batch files. However, this also means that alias definitions will not be retained once NDOS is terminated. Alias definitions can be stored in text files and then read into memory using the **/R** switch. Shown below is a text file called MYALIAS.TXT. The file is structured to define two alias commands, **LTS** and **PDIR**. Note that when storing alias commands as text it is not necessary to use the **ALIAS** command at the beginning of each line. It is also unnecessary to add back quotes to multiple command lines because the text will be copied directly into memory and NDOS will not attempt to parse individual commands out of file text:

```
LTS=CD\LOTUS\R3^123^CD\
PDIR=DIR %1/$/S >PRN
```

Once the text file has been created, you can use it to create the specified **ALIAS** command by loading it with **ALIAS /R**. Example: ALIAS /R MYALIAS.TXT.

**ALIAS** definitions loaded from a text file are added to the alias definitions already in memory. If there is already an alias with the same name as one of the alias definitions loaded from the file, the alias in memory is overwritten without warning.

You can capture the current list of alias definitions stored in memory in a text file by using redirection. The command below writes all of the current alias definition to the file SAVEDEFS.TXT. Example: ALIAS > SAVEDEFS.TXT.

To restore the definitions at some later point, reverse the process with the following command. Example: ALIAS /R SAVEDEFS.TXT.

You could save a single alias definition by specifying the alias name. The command below stores only the **LTS** alias in the file. Example: ALIAS LTS > SAVEDEFS.TXT.

When you store an alias that contains a [Ctrl-x], ↑, or special character in a text file, NDOS converts the special combination to the ASCII value. For example, the ↑f, form feed, combination is stored as ASCII 12.

## Flexible Alias Names

You can allow for abbreviation of alias names by defining the alias name with an *. This allows you to create a long alias name that is easy to remember and still use an abbreviation to save time. Long names are more descriptive than short names, such as DOS file names. However, long names are awkward to enter and are subject to typos. NDOS allows you to compromise.

For example, the command below creates an alias with a long name, PRINT—TEXT. Example: ALIAS print_text 'ECHO %1 >PRN'.

The name is easy to remember and understand, but a bit awkward to type. Entering the name with an * allows you to abbreviate the alias name using only those letters to the left of the *. The remainder of the name is optional. The command below defines the **PRINT_TEXT** alias so that entering only **PRI** will still execute the **PRINT_TEXT** alias. You could also enter **PRIN**, **PRINT**, etc. and get the **PRINT_TEXT** alias. Example: ALIAS pri*nt text 'ECHO %1 >PRN'. The * allows you to have more descriptive names appear in the alias listing, but still have only short names to enter when you want to execute ALIAS commands.

## Name Conflicts

It is quite possible to create an alias that has the same name as a program or batch file already stored on the disk. For example, the command below creates an alias called **PRINT**. Example: ALIAS print 'ECHO %1 >PRN'.

However, it is important to remember that DOS supplies a utility program called PRINT.EXE, which is used to implement print spooling at the system level. Once you have created an alias with the same name as a program, NDOS will *always* execute the *alias* and *never* execute the program. This is because, like DOS, NDOS gives priority to internal or memory-resident commands. Only if no matching internal command can be found will the operating system search the disk for COM, EXE, or BAT files that have the matching name.

If you want to suppress the use of the alias so that NDOS will search for the program of the same name, you can precede the name with an *. For example, the command below will execute PRINT.COM, PRINT.EXE, or PRINT.BAT, which are located first along the current search path, if they exist. NDOS **ALIAS** commands with that name are ignored. Example: *PRINT.

# Full-screen Selection

Many commands issued at the operating system level require the use of a file name or wildcard. File names, even the short names allowed by DOS, can be quite inconvenient. Often you will enter a wildcard, e.g., *.BAT, rather than type out a full file name, e.g. AUTOEXEC.BAT, even though *.BAT will select too many files.

NDOS provides a *point and shoot* alternative in the form of the **SELECT** command.[6] Like LIST, SELECT displays a full screen, scrollable display window. You can use the window to select files to be included in the specified command as arguments, without having to manually enter the file names.

For example, suppose that you wanted to copy certain files from the root directory to a floppy disk in drive A. The NDOS command might look like this: COPY \AUTOEXEC.BAT, \CONFIG.SYS, \DMDRVR.BIN A:.

However, even entering these three file names is quite tedious. Unfortunately, the files names do not contain similarities that would lend themselves to a wildcard. The alternative would be to use **SELECT** to display a window with all of the file names from which you can select the items to be copied.

The command below would display a full-screen, scrollable window from which you could select the file or files you wanted to copy. Note that the file selection specification, **(\*.*)**, is inserted into the command in the same position where the file name or wildcard would be used if the command were being entered directly. Example: SELECT COPY (\*.*) A:.

The window will list the files and directories contained in the specified location. The window will place a highlight, which can be moved with the arrow keys, at the top of the list. On long lists you can scroll with [PgUp], [PgDn], [Home], and [End]. You have the following options:

---

6.  The NDOS **SELECT** command is not related to the DOS utility program SELECT.COM program.

**Select One.** Pressing ↵ will select the file currently highlighted. The specified operation will then take place using that file name.

**Tag.** Pressing [+] on the key pad or [space] will tag a file so that the file name will be included in those names passed to the command.

**Untag.** Pressing [-] on the keypad or [Space] will untag a tagged file name. The name will no longer be included in the list of files.

**Select All.** Entering * will place a tag on all of the file names in the window. You can use [-] and [space] to untag individual files.

When you have tagged all of the file names you want to include, press ↵ to exit the window and begin the operations. For example, if you tagged three files, AUTOEXEC.BAT, CONFIG.SYS, and DMDRVR.BIN, NDOS would generate a list of commands to be executed:

```
COPY AUTOEXEC.BAT A:
COPY CONFIG.SYS A:
COPY DMDRVR.BIN A:
```

If a directory is selected then all of the files in that directory will be copied. If the command you are using with **SELECT** can accept a list of arguments, e.g., NDOS **DIR** or **COPY**, you can speed up operation by passing the selected files as a list rather than generating individual operations for each file name. This is done by using [] in place of () in the select command. Example: SELECT COPY [\*.*] A:.

Assuming that the same three file names were selected from the select window, NDOS would generate the following command. Example: COPY AUTOEXEC.BAT CONFIG.SYS DMDRVR.BIN A:. This version of the **COPY** command will execute a bit faster than the three consecutive **COPY** commands. You can use the **SELECT** command as a simple point-and-shoot method of executing a program. For example, the following command will allow you to execute one or more Norton Utilities programs. Example: SELECT (\NU\*.EXE).

A list of the Norton Utilities programs would appear in the selected window. If you tagged more than one file and pressed ↵, each of the selected programs would be executed one after the other.

If you include more than one wildcard **SELECT** will display one selection window for each wildcard. The command below would display one window with all EXE files and then copy the select files to drive A. A second window would appear with BAT files from which the tagged files would be copied to A. Note that this method allows you to use files from different directories since each directory is displayed in a separate window. Example: SELECT COPY (C:\NU\*.EXE,C:\*.BAT) A:.

If you use a ; instead of a comma or other delimiter between the wildcards, the command will display a list that combines all of the specified files in a single window. Note that when using the ; all files must be drawn from the same directory. Example: SELECT COPY (*.EXE;*.BAT) A:.

You can select files for display on the basis of their attributes using the /**A** switch. The first command below displays a list of hidden files, while the second selects read-only files. Note that the third command selects files that are both read-only and hidden:

```
SELECT /AH COPY (*.*) A:
SELECT /AR COPY (*.*) A:
SELECT /AHR COPY (*.*) A:
```

Note that the /A switch comes after **SELECT** and before the **COPY** command. Placing the /A switch at the end of the command line would indicate that the switch applies to the **COPY**, not the **SELECT**, command.

The order of the files in the window can be controlled with /**O**. The command below lists the specified files in descending order(R) by date(D). Example: SELECT /ODR COPY (*.*) A:.

# Execution by File Extension

Another method by which execution of programs can be simplified is by associating specific file extensions with applications. In the DOS world there are no hard and fast rules about how extensions are used. Some applications use rather unique extensions (EXCEL uses XLS), but other applications use fairly common extensions (e.g., WORD uses DOC and DBASE, FOXPRO and CLIPPER use PRG for program files). In some cases, such as WordPerfect, file extensions are optional and not applied by the program itself.

Data files are linked to applications by a special form of variable. For example, suppose that you wanted to run Microsoft Word. You would create a variable called **.DOC** whose value would be the name of the application. Example: SET .DOC=WORD.

Note that execution of the specified application depends upon the normal access factors, such as the current active directory and open paths. In order to avoid some of these problems you can be explicit in naming the file used to run the application. Example: SET .DOC–C:\WORD50\ WORD.EXE.

Once the extension variable is defined, you can enter the name of a file that ends with the specified extension, e.g., DOC. For example, suppose the file CHAPTER1.DOC is located in the current directory. You can load the file into Word by entering: CHAPTER1. Not all programs are capable of loading the specified file in the way that Microsoft Word does. Many, but not all, programs accept a file name as a parameter. For example, the following command would cause Word to execute and load the CHAPTER1.DOC file. Example: WORD CHAPTER1.

NDOS combines the value of the .DOC variable, e.g., C:\WORD50\WORD.EXE, with the specified file name to generate the command **C:\WORD50\WORD.EXE CHAPTER1**. However, Lotus 1-2-3 does not accept a file parameter. Suppose that you had a 1-2-3 worksheet file called BUDGET.WK1. The **SET** command could be used to associate 1-2-3 with the WK1 extension. Example: SET .WK1=123.

When you enter the name of a WK1 file (e.g., BUDGET) NDOS will generate the command **123 BUDGET** using the assumption that the application can accept the worksheet file as a parameter. However, 1-2-3 assumes that the parameter **BUDGET** refers to a set-up file **BUDGET.SET**, not the worksheet file **BUDGET.WK1**. Since in all probability there is no **BUDGET.SET** file, the program will fail to load. For this reason you cannot use the extension approach to start 1-2-3 from a data file. A solution to this problem can be found using the KEYSTACK.SYS driver (next section).

Database programs such as dBASE (all versions), FOXBASE and FOXPRO, and PARADOX do accept arguments. However, the parameter is assumed to be a program (PRG for dBASE and FOX, SC for PARADOX), not a database file (DBF for DBASE and FOX, DB for PARADOX). If you were writing programs (or scripts in PARADOX) you might want to set up extensions.

```
SET  .SC=\PARADOX\PARADOX
SET  .PRG=\DBASE
```

With applications such as WordPerfect that accept file parameters, but don't have required extensions you may want to implement your own system of file extensions so that you can take advantage of this feature.

NDOS file extension specifications are not automatically saved as part of your NDOS system. As environmental variables they will be erased when the current NDOS session is terminated. You can create a text file that lists the extensions you want to use the next time you start NDOS. Below is a sample text file (e.g., LINKS.TXT) that defines several extension links to applications:

```
.DOC=C:\WORD5\WORD.EXE
.PRG=C:\FOX\FOXPRO.EXE
.CHT=C:\HG\HG.EXE
```

You can create the variables needed to activate the extension/application links by using the **/R** option of the **SET** command. Example: SET /R LINKS.TXT.

## Feeding Keystrokes to an Application

In the previous section it was mentioned that not all applications can be associated with a file extension in the way that Microsoft Word can, because the applications do not allow you to use a data file as a start-up parameter. The most common example of this is Lotus 1-2-3. 1-2-3 is designed to start with a blank worksheet. In order to load a worksheet file you must manually enter the **/File Retrieve** command.

NDOS offers a method by which you can control the actions taken in an application when it is first started. The technique employs the use of the **KEYSTACK** command. **KEYSTACK** provides a means of *stuffing* a series of keystrokes into the computer's memory *before* the application is loaded. When the program is loaded, the keystrokes already stuffed into memory are fed into the application. The program reacts exactly as it would if you were actually entering the keystrokes. In a sense, **KEYSTACK** allows you to create *time-delayed* command sequences, which are activated once a program has been loaded and is ready to run.

Keystroke can only be used if the KEYSTACK.SYS driver has been loaded into memory.

The **KEYSTACK** command is typically used as part of an alias definition. **KEYSTACK** has the advantage of being able to feed an application any type of keystroke such as ↵, arrow keys, [Ctrl], [Alt] or [Shift] key combination. You can specify keystrokes as characters, ASCII decimal values, or special keystroke codes. For example, unlike most of the Norton Utilities programs, the Disk Tools program cannot be operated from a batch file or command line because it does not recognize any command switches.

One of the functions performed by this program is to create a *rescue* disk. A rescue disk is a floppy disk onto which the Norton Utilities copies the partition table, boot records, and system CMOS values. That information can be used later to recover from various types of system problems. But unlike Speed Disk and Norton Disk Doctor operations, creation of a rescue disk is strictly manual. Assuming that you have a formatted floppy disk in drive A, you would enter the following to create a rescue disk and return to DOS:

```
disktools ↵
↓(press 4 times)
↵(press 3 times)
a
```

You could automate this procedure using the **KEYSTACK** command. When you look at the list of keystrokes shown above, you realize that some are normal text characters (e.g., *disktools*), while others are special keys (e.g., ↓ and ↵). The **KEYSTACK** codes for special keys appear in Tables 17–3 and 17-4. ↵ is entered with its ASCII decimal value 13, [Tab] as 9, and [Esc] can be entered as 27. Note that a 0 value has a special meaning. Zero is used to *flush* the keyboard memory buffer of any additional keystrokes so that you are sure your **KEYSTACK** sequence begins with the keys you specify.

**Table 17–3. KEYSTACK codes.**

|        | Key  | [Alt] | [Ctrl] | [Shift] |
| ------ | ---- | ----- | ------ | ------- |
| [F1]   | @59  | @104  | @94    | @84     |
| [F2]   | @60  | @105  | @95    | @85     |
| [F3]   | @61  | @106  | @96    | @86     |
| [F4]   | @62  | @107  | @97    | @87     |
| [F5]   | @63  | @108  | @98    | @88     |
| [F6]   | @64  | @109  | @99    | @89     |
| [F7]   | @65  | @110  | @100   | @90     |
| [F8]   | @66  | @111  | @101   | @91     |
| [F9]   | @67  | @112  | @102   | @92     |
| [F10]  | @68  | @113  | @103   | @93     |

**Table 17–4. More KEYSTACK codes.**

| | | | |
|---|---|---|---|
| [Alt-A] | @30 | [Alt-W] | @17 |
| [Alt-B] | @48 | [Alt-X] | @45 |
| [Alt-C] | @46 | [Alt-Y] | @21 |
| [Alt-D] | @32 | [Alt-Z] | @44 |
| [Alt-E] | @18 | [Alt-1] | @120 |
| [Alt-F] | @33 | [Alt-2] | @121 |
| [Alt-G] | @34 | [Alt-3] | @122 |
| [Alt-H] | @35 | [Alt-4] | @123 |
| [Alt-I] | @23 | [Alt-5] | @124 |
| [Alt-J] | @36 | [Alt-6] | @125 |
| [Alt-K] | @37 | [Alt-7] | @126 |
| [Alt-L] | @38 | [Alt-8] | @127 |
| [Alt-M] | @50 | [Alt-9] | @128 |
| [Alt-N] | @49 | [Alt-0] | @129 |
| [Alt-O] | @24 | ← | @75 |
| [Alt-P] | @25 | → | @77 |
| [Alt-Q] | @16 | ↓ | @80 |
| [Alt-R] | @19 | ↑ | @72 |
| [Alt-S] | @31 | [Del] | @83 |
| [Alt-T] | @20 | [Ins] | @82 |
| [Alt-U] | @22 | | |
| [Alt-V] | @47 | | |

The sequence of keys needed to create the rescue disk with Disk Tools would be translated into the following **KEYSTACK** sequence of values. The sequence is divided into two parts: (1) the command to start the application and (2) the keys to enter after the application has been loaded.

The reason for the distinction is that NDOS already has the ability to start the program from an alias or batch file. **KEYSTACK** is used to enter keys after the application has started:

```
disktools 13                           {1}
13 @80 @80 @80 @80 13 13 13 a    {2}
```

The first part can be simply implemented in any NDOS alias. Example: ALIAS RESCUE DISKTOOLS.

The **KEYSTACK** command would be entered as follows: ALIAS RESCUE KEYSTACK 13 @80 @80 @80 13 13 13 a.

You can combine both operations into a single **ALIAS** command by defining the alias **RESCUE** as a multiple command. The interesting part is the order in which the commands are placed into the alias. The **KEYSTACK** command is first followed by the **DISKTOOLS** command: ALIAS RESCUE 'KEYSTACK 13 @80 @80 @80 @80 13 13 13 a^disktools'. Why? The answer has to do with the indirect nature of the **KEYSTACK** command. **KEYSTACK** places keystrokes into memory in anticipation of a program that will wait for keystrokes to be entered. If the DISKTOOLS program is to receive input from **KEYSTACK** keystrokes, those keystrokes must be placed into memory *before* the application is executed. When an application like Disk Tools or Lotus 1-2-3 begins to run, it takes over control of the computer system until the application is terminated. If **KEYSTACK** were placed after DISKTOOLS as shown below, the **KEYSTACK** sequence would be activated only after you had quit DISKTOOLS: *(incorrect)* ALIAS RESCUE 'disktools^KEYSTACK 13 @80 @80 @80 @80 13 13 13 a'.

Keyboard-stuffing applications reverse the usual pattern in application use, which is that the application asks the question or displays a prompt or dialog box and then waits for user input. In this type of procedure, like the game "Jeopardy," you begin with the answer and then have the program execute and ask the question.

It is important to realize that this type of keystroke programming is subject to many problems. Since the sequences of keys must match the prompts in the program exactly, any variation will throw off the entire command. For example, many of the Norton Utilities programs vary the boxes and prompts they display based on used defaults or special conditions detected in the system; e.g., Calibrate and Speed Disk will know if a previous operation had been interrupted and display a special dialog box that otherwise would not appear.

Other applications are sensitive to the speed at which keystrokes are fed to the application. In order to adjust, 0 values are inserted between key codes. Lotus 1-2-3 is an example. Other applications monitor the keyboard for keys pressed while an application is running. The Norton Utilities programs are an example. Keystrokes found after a Speed Disk, Calibrate, etc. operation have begun will cause the programs to pause and display a **Cancel/Resume** dialog box.

Still other programs are incompatible with **KEYSTACK** altogether because of oddities in their ROM BIOS.

However, despite these problems, you may find that **KEYSTACK** solves certain problems that cannot be addressed by standard alias or batch file operations.

## Getting Help

NDOS provides several ways in which you can get information about the NDOS commands:

**Help.** Entering **HELP** or pressing [F1] at the NDOS prompt will display a scrollable window that lists the topics available for help. You can scroll the list of topics and display detailed information by pressing ⌐. **Next** and **Previous** allow you to leaf through each topic in the help file. You can go directly to a specific topic by using the name of the command as a parameter. The command below displays the help screen for the **SET** command. Example: HELP SET.

**/?.** You can get command-line help for specific commands by using the switch **/?.** Command-line help shows the basic syntax of the command and a brief explanation of the command and its switches. The command below displays the command-line help for the **SELECT** command. Example: SELECT /?.

# Environmental Variables

Recall from Chapter 15 that DOS maintains three environmental variables, PATH, COMSPEC, and PROMPT. NDOS expands the list of system variables to include a variety of variables that can furnish information about the details of the system. In addition, users could define their own environmental variables. These variables had a number of uses, including batch file programming. NDOS add some 20 system variables, which can be accessed by NDOS commands or batch files. Most of the new system variables begin with an _(underscore) character. The _ indicates that these are variables automatically maintained by the system and cannot be displayed or modified with **SET, UNSET,** or **ESET.** In addition, the commands used to manipulate variables have been modified.

**SET**    The **SET** command is used the same way in NDOS as in COMMAND.COM to define the value of an environmental variable. When used with any arguments, as shown below, **SET** displays a list of the variables currently defined. Example: SET.

If the list exceeds 24 lines, you can pause each screen by adding /P. Example: SET /P.

The command below creates a variable called **PROGRAM** and assigns it the text string *123*. Example: SET program=123.

One powerful feature added to the NDOS **SET** command is the **/R** option. /R allows **SET** to load a set of environmental variables by reading the contents of a text file. For example, suppose you prepared a text file with the following contents called VALUES01.TXT:

```
program=123
subdir=c:\lotus
describe=Lotus 1-2-3 Version 2.3
```

The **SET** command can be used to create the variables by reading in the contents of the text file. The following command uses the **/R** switch to read in the contents of VALUES01.TXT. Example: SET /R values01.txt.

The **/R** switch makes it faster and easier to define a list of variable values. A variation on this idea allows you to save the current environment and restore it at a later time. To save the current set of environmental variables, use the redirection operator to send the information to a text file. Example: SET > envron01.txt.

At some later point you can return the values to their previous values by reading the same information back into memory. Example: SET /R envron01.txt.

**ESET**    This command allows you to edit the value associated with a variable, eliminating the need to completely replace the variable. The most common application for this command is to revise the path list. Recall from Chapter 4 that each new **PATH** command overwrites the previous command. For example, the following command is used in the AUTOEXEC.BAT to set the operating system path search list each time the computer is booted. Example: PATH C:\DOS;C:\LOTUS;C:\WP51;.

Suppose that you wanted to include in the path list C:\DBASE. Entering the command below would not accomplish the goal because it would replace the previous list of paths with C:\DBASE. Example: PATH C:\DBASE;.

To add a path to an existing list, you would have to re-enter the old list and add the new paths as shown in the command below. Example: PATH C:\DOS;C:\LOTUS;C:\WP51;C:\DBASE;.

Since path lists can be quite long and complicated, NDOS offers a better solution. You can edit the text using **ESET** as shown below. Example: ESET path.

When this command is used, NDOS places the text of the path on the NDOS editing line. You can insert, add, or delete as much text as you desire. Pressing ⏎ places the new text into memory as the value for the specified variable.

**UNSET** This command erases a memory variable. The commands below both remove the variable **PROGRAM** from memory:

The advantage of **UNSET** is that you can erase a list of variables with a single command, as shown below where one command releases three variables. Example: UNSET program,subdir,describe.

You can erase all variables using *. Note that * also erases the **PATH**, **COMSPEC**, and **PROMPT** variables, which are used directly by DOS. * should only be used when you intend to restore variables stored in a file. The commands below clear the environment and then load a set of previously stored variables, including the system variable:

```
UNSET *
SET /R values01.txt
```

In addition to these commands, NDOS supports 20 additional system variables that return information about the system. These variables can be integrated into batch files or commands entered at the DOS prompt. The following sections explain the use of these variables.

NDOS system variables are referenced by preceding the variable name with a %. For example, to display the current system date use the **_DATE** variable as shown below. Example: ECHO %_DATE.

If you want to use the % as a character in a string you would enter %%. The command below echoes the text **50%** on the screen. No variable is involved. Example: ECHO 50%%.

## Batch Debugging

Although batch file programming is probably the most common form of programming on PC-type computers, COMMAND.COM offers very few features that help users create or debug batch files.

Debugging is the process by which you test your program or batch file to see if it performs the tasks you had in mind. One problem with debugging batch files is that it is hard to determine what went wrong when a batch file doesn't work. NDOS adds three variables that help in batch file debugging.

#       Returns the number of parameters entered in the batch file command line. The program fragment below checks the number of parameters entered by the user. The fragment below uses # to test if too many parameters have been entered:

```
@ECHO OFF
IF %# LT 3 GOTO OK
ECHO Too many parameters
QUIT
:OK
ECHO OK
```

?       Returns the exit code of the last external program to run. The example below tests the exit code issued by the DOS utility BACKUP.EXE. This form is simpler and more direct than ERRORLEVEL testing:

```
@ECHO OFF
BACKUP C:\*.BAT A:
IF %? GT 0 GOTO PROBLEM
QUIT
:PROBLEM
ECHO Backup Failed
```

## Paths and Directories

**PATH**     This variable holds the path list, which the operating system uses to search for programs and batch files. This variable appears when you list the variables with the **SET** command. You can change or remove this variable with **SET, UNSET,** or **ESET.**

**TEMP**     This variable is used to indicate the location where temporary files should be written. Note that **TMP** is commonly used by applications other than the Norton Utilities, e.g., Windows 3.0. You may want to use the same location for both sets of programs by setting one equal to the other, e.g., SET TEMP/%TMP.

**NHELP**    This variable tells NDOS what directory contains the NDOS help files. If you start NDOS from a directory other than the one that contains the help files, NDOS may not be able to access help when you press [F1]. If this is the case, you can correct the situation by using a **SET** command to define this variable with the correct path. Example: SET NHELP/C:\NU.

**_CWD, _CWDS, _CWP, _CWPS**    These functions enable batch files or alias operations to obtain the current directory. The variables differ only with respect to the format in which the directory name is presented. Assuming the current active directory is C:\NU, the strings returned by the variables are shown in Table 17–4.

**Table 17–4. Directory variables.**

| Function | Example |
| --- | --- |
| _CWD | c:\NU |
| _CWDS | c:\NU\ |
| _CWP | \NU |
| _CWPS | \NU\ |
| _DISK | c |

The value of these variables is that they can be used to store the starting directory location in a user-defined variable. The batch file fragment below shows how _CWD is used to return to the starting directory after an application (e.g., 1-2-3) has been run:

```
SET start_dir=%_CWD
CD\LOTUS
123
CD %start_dir
```

**DIRCMD**    The **DIR** command is the most-used operating system instruction. NDOS has greatly increased the variety of options available for this command. By default, **DIR** operates exactly the same as the

COMMAND.COM **DIR** command. You can change the default operation of NDOS **DIR** by entering the switch or set of switches you want to use as the default into the **DIRCMD** command. For example, suppose you wanted to use the four-column format as the default for **DIR**. You would enter **SET DIRCMD//4**. If you wanted use a two-column display with no headers or totals, you would enter SET DIRCMD//B/2.

## Clock Calendar

The Clock/Calendar variables provide a direct means by which batch files or aliases can access and analyze information generated by system clock:

_**DATE**.  Returns the current system date in the format **06-05-91**.

_**DOW**.  Returns a three-letter abbreviation for the current day of the week, e.g., **Wed**.

_**TIME**. Returns the current system time in 12-hour format, e.g., **10:01:47p**.

These functions greatly expand your ability to analyze events that take place over periods of time within your system. Recall from Chapter 16 that the Batch Enhancer functions **WEEKDAY** and **MONTHDAY** enabled you to create batch files that could perform specific actions, based on the current day of the week or day of the month.

While useful, these Batch Enhancer functions stop far short of what is needed in most situations. Below is a segment of code taken from one of the batch files detailed in Chapter 16. The Batch Enhancer **WEEKDAY** command is used to determine if the day of the week is Friday (i.e., **ERRORLEVEL 6**). In this case **ERRORLEVEL 6** will trigger the **WEEKLY** routine while any other day will trigger **DOIT**:

```
:CHECKDAY
BE WEEKDAY
IF ERRORLEVEL 7 GOTO doit
IF ERRORLEVEL 6 GOTO weekly
GOTO doit
```

But suppose you reboot the computer, causing the AUTOEXEC.BAT to execute the same batch file analysis again. Since the day is still Friday, the **WEEKLY** routine will be carried out again. However, this is probably not desirable. If **WEEKLY** refers to an activity such as weekly disk maintenance then you only want to run it once, no matter how many times you reboot the computer on Friday. DOS and the Batch Enhancer offer no solution but NDOS does.

The command below stores the current system date in a text file called **DATEINFO** in a form in which it can later be reloaded into memory:

```
ECHO LASTBOOT=%_DATE > DATEINFO.TXT
```

For example, if the current date is 06–01–91 then the DATEINFO.TXT file will contain **LASTBOOT/06-01-91**. The fragment of batch file shown below shows how, once the initial file is created, a batch file can check to see if it is executing on the same day. In line 2, the date currently stored in DATEINFO.TXT is restored to memory as the variable **LASTBOOT**. Line 3 uses an **IF** command to compare the system date, %_**DATE** to the %**LASTBOOT** variable. **IF** they match the batch file will jump to a routine that will avoid repeating operations, such as disk maintenance, which need be done only once a day. Line 4 executes only when the **LASTBOOT** day is different from the current date. The command now updates the DATEINFO.TXT file to show that the computer has been booted for the first time on a new day, which will serve to trigger certain daily routine operations, e.g., DIFFDAY:

```
@ECHO OFF                                {1}
SET /R DATEINFO.TXT                      {2}
IF %lastboot==%_date GOTO SAMEDAY        {3}
ECHO LASTBOOT=%_DATE > DATEINFO.TXT      {4}
GOTO DIFFDAY                             {5}
```

The key to this type of ongoing analysis and updating is the ability to draw information from system variables and then store them in memory and/or on disk. This means that you can always find a way to preserve environmental data such as date, time, or even the active directory and later restore those values.

It is important to note that the Batch Enhancer commands return ERRORLEVEL values while the NDOS variables return text strings, which are much more valuable because they can be manipulated in a wide variety of ways as indicated by the example.

## Hardware

The variables in this section report on the main microprocessor and the math co-processor.

**_CPU**    Returns a text string indicating the main system processor chip (Table 17–5).

**Table 17–5.**

| Variable Text | Processor |
|---|---|
| 86 | 8086 or 8088 |
| 186 | Intel 80186 or 80188 |
| 200 | NEC V20 or V30 |
| 286 | Intel 80286 |
| 386 | Intel 80386 or 80486 |

**_NDP**    Returns a text string indicating the math co-processor chip (Table 17–6).

**Table 17–6.**

| Variable Text | Processor |
|---|---|
| 0 | no coprocessor installed |
| 87 | Intel 8087 |
| 287 | Intel 80287 |
| 387 | Intel 80387 |

You can use these variables to determine what type of system you are operating on. For example, the section of a batch file shown below creates CONFIG.SYS files. It uses the **_CPU** variable in line 6 to test for the presence of a 386 or 486 processor so that memory management commands, lines 7, 8, and 9, will be added to the CONFIG.SYS on 386 and higher systems:

```
@ECHO OFF                              {1}
SET fname=C:\CONFDIG.SYS               {2}
```

```
ECHO FILE=50 > %Fname%                                      {3}
ECHO BREAK=ON >> %fname%                                     {4}
ECHO DEVICE=C:\DOS\SETVER.EXE >> %fname%                     {5}
IF "%_CPU" NE "386" GOTO NOHIGHMEM                           {6}
      ECHO DEVICE=C:\DOS\HIMEM.SYS >> %fname%                {7}
      ECHO DEVICE=C:\DOS\EMM386.EXE 512 RAM >> %fname%       {8}
      ECHO DOS=HIGH,UMB >> %fname%                           {9}
:NOHIGHMEM                                                   {10}
ECHO SHELL=C:\COMMAND.COM C:\ /p /E:512 >> %fname%           {11}
```

**_MONITOR**    This function returns the text *mono* or *color*, depending on the information in the system set-up stored in the CMOS. Keep in mind that many black and white or single color monitors operate under a color setting and will return *color* even though the screen shows black and white.

**_VIDEO**    Returns *mono*, *cga*, *ega*, or *vga* depending upon the type of display adapter installed in your computer. Special video subsystem boards, such as those used with full-page monitors, will return *CGA* or *VGA* since, during DOS operations, these monitors emulate those standards. The commands below show the use of the **_MONITOR** and **_VIDEO** variables. Note that the **%@UPPER** variable function is used to print the text returned by the variables in uppercase letters.

## Software

These variables report information about the current state of the NDOS system:

**_DOSVER.** Returns a string that is the numerical version of the DOS Version, e.g., 3.30 for DOS Version 3.30.

**_SHELL.** Returns a number value for the shell depth where 0 stands for the base shell. For example, if you are running NDOS as your primary shell and load 1-2-3, you can access an NDOS session by using the **/S** command. Command **ECHO %_SHELL** would return **1** because the NDOS version started from within 1–2-3 is the second NDOS session in memory. You can use variables to determine if a batch file is running directly from the primary shell or is being accessed from an application like 1-2-3.

## Screen

NDOS maintains variables which return values that describe the current
state of the screen display:

**_BG.**  Returns a three-character code for the current background color,
e.g., Bla for Black. The codes correspond to the color names used with the
Batch Enhancer **SA** command.

**_FG.**  Returns a three-character code for the current foreground color.

**_COLUMNS.**  Returns the number of columns on the current screen
display, e.g., 80.

**_ROWS.**  Returns the number of rows on the current screen display, e.g.,
25.

The **_FG** and **_BG** variables make it possible to write batch files that can
restore the original screen colors after the batch file has changed them. The
batch fragment below uses the variables to capture the current colors in
**OLDFG** and **OLDBG.** The batch can then use **COLOR** commands to alter
the screen colors and then insert the variables at the end inside a **COLOR**
command to return to the original colors:

```
SET oldfg=%_fg
SET oldbg=%_bg
COLOR BRI YEL ON BLU
. . . . .
COLOR %_oldfg ON %_oldbg
```

# Variable Functions

One of the most advanced features of NDOS is its support of variable
functions. Variable functions allow you to manipulate the data that are
stored as a memory variable in NDOS commands, aliases, and batch files.
This added power allows you to create batch files performing operations
that would otherwise require a full programming language like BASIC or
PASCAL.

Variable functions are treated like variables; that is, they must begin with
a %. The % is followed by @ and the name of the function. The parameter or
parameters require the function be enclosed in []:

```
%@function_name[parameters]
```

# Math Operations

Variable functions add math calculations to the array of tools available in creating commands, aliases, or batch files.

**@EVAL**    This function performs addition (+), subtraction (-), multiplication (*), division (/), and modular (%%) operations. The parameter for the function is a mathematical expression that can contain numbers, variables that evaluate as numeric items, and math operators.

For example, suppose that you wanted to use the **SCREEN** command to place text in the center of the screen display. The variables **_ROWS** and **_COLUMNS** return the total number of rows and columns in the current screen display. The command below uses **EVAL** to divide the **_ROWS** and **_COLUMNS** value to calculate the center of the screen and place the word *Hello* at that position.

```
SCREEN %@EVAL[%_ROWS/2] %@EVAL[%_COLUMNS/2] Hello
```

**SCREEN** is also a good command for creating menus. The commands below would display a simple menu:

```
@ECHO OFF
CLS
SCREEN 3 10 Select a number from 1 to 4:
SCREEN 6 20 1 - Word Processing
SCREEN 7 20 2 - Spreadsheet
SCREEN 8 20 3 - Telecommunications
SCREEN 9 20 4 - Quit
```

Below is a revised version of the menu in which math expressions are used to determine the row numbers. While the commands appear a bit more complicated, they have the advantage of allowing you to move the menu up and down the screen by changing the value of the **TOP** variable. If you need to revise or update the menu, this approach will save you a lot of time:

```
@ECHO OFF
CLS
REM Move menu by changing TOP
SET top=3
SCREEN @top 10 Select a number from 1 to 4:
```

```
SCREEN %@EVAL[%top+1] 20 1 - Word Processing
SCREEN %@EVAL[%top+2] 20 2 - Spreadsheet
SCREEN %@EVAL[%top+3] 20 3 - Telecommunications
SCREEN %@EVAL[%top+4] 20 4 - Quit
```

If you use a variable that is undefined, **@EVAL** treats it as a zero value. If you use a variable that evaluates as text, a division by zero error is generated.

## Hardware

These functions return information about the hardware installed in the system. The functions that deal with memory use the letters **B** for bytes, **K** for kilobytes, and **M** for megabytes to indicate the unit of measurement being used:

**@DOSMEM.**  Evaluates the amount of *free* conventional memory. Note that since conventional memory is always less than 1 megabyte, the M unit should not be used with this function. The example will branch to **CANFIT** if the free conventional memory is less than 500K. Example: If %@DOSMEN[K] LT 500 GOTO canfit.

**@EMS.**  Returns the amount of free EMS (expanded) memory. Example: If %@EMS [M] GE 1 GOTO load_cache.

**@EXTENDED.**  Returns the amount of free extended memory, not including XMS memory. Example: IF %@EXTENDED [B] == 0 GOTO not_avail.

**@REMOTE.**  This function can be used to determine if a drive letter refers to a local drive (value is 0) or a remote network drive (value is 1). The example branches to **CANDOIT** if the current drive (as determined by the **_DRIVE** variable) is a network drive. Example: IF %@RE-MOTE[%_drive] == 1 GOTO CANDOIT.

**@REMOVABLE.**  This function returns a 0 value if the specified drive is a fixed disk or a 1 if it is removable. The example branches to a routine called **FLOPPY** if the function returns a 1. Example: IF %@REMOVABLE [%_drive] == 1 GOTO FLOPPY.

**@XMS.**  Test the amount of free XMS (HIMEM.SYS type) extended memory. Example: IF %@XMS [K] == 64 GOTO use_umb.

## File Manipulation

These functions operate on text in file name format or variables that contain text in file name format. Note the text returned is in lowercase characters, by default:

**@ATTRIB.** Tests a file for an attribute and returns 1 if the file has the specified attribute and zero if it does not. The file attributes are designated as : a = archive, h = hidden, r= read only, d = directory, and n = no attributes. The example tests AUTOEXEC.BAT. If the file is read-only the batch branches to **NOEDIT**. Example: IF %@ATTRIB [c:\autoexec.bat,r] == 0 GOTO noedit.

**@DISKFREE.** Tests for a specified amount of free space. The example below execute **INSTALL** only if there are 2 megabytes or more of disk space free. Example: IF %@DISKFREE [M] GE 2 GOTO INSTALL.

**@EXT.** Returns the extension of the specified file name. The command below would display the extension of the current COMSPEC file, e.g., *com*. Example: ECHO %@EXT [%_COMSPEC].

**@FILESIZE.** Returns the size of the specified file. The example branches to **COPY_IT** if the file is less than 360K. Example: IF %FILESIZE [names.dbf,K] LT 360 GOTO copy_it.

**@FULL.** Returns the full path name of the specified file. The command below would return the full path of the current COMSPEC, e.g., *c:\command.com*. Example: ECHO %@FULL[%_COMSPEC].

**@NAME.** Returns the file name portion, without the extension, of the specified file. The command below would return the name portion of the current **COMSPEC**, e.g., **COMMAND**. Note this function returns upper case characters. Example: ECHO %@NAME [%_COMSPEC].

**@PATH.** Returns the path portion of the specified file. The command below would return the name portion of the current COMSPEC, e.g., C:\. Note this function returns uppercase characters. Example: ECHO %@PATH [%_COMSPEC].

**@SEARCH.** Returns the full path name of the first file on the disk that matches the specified file. The command below returns the full path name of the NDD.EXE file:

```
Command Results
ECHO %@SEARCH[ndd.exe]      c:\NU\ndd.exe
```

You can use a wildcard as the parameter. Example:

```
Command Results
ECHO %@SEARCH[ndd*.*]    c:\NU\ndd*.*
```

The sequence of commands below finds the directory in which the specified file is located. The **@PATH** function is used to display the path portion of the text returned by **@SEARCH**.

```
INPUT Enter the File Name %%fname
SET location=%@SEARCH[%fname]
ECHO %fname found in %@PATH[%location]
```

## Text Manipulation

The functions in this section allow you to manipulate text literals or text contain in variables.

**@LEN**    Returns the number of characters in the specified item. The command sequence below the file name entry is tested to see if it exceeds 9 characters. If so, it is treated as an invalid entry.

```
INPUT Enter the File Name %%fname
IF %@LEN[fname] GT 9 GOTO INVALID
SET location=%@SEARCH[%fname]
ECHO %fname found in %@PATH[%location]
:INVALID
```

**@LINE**    Returns the text from line # of the specified text file. Note that the first line in the file is zero, not 1. If the value for line number exceeds the actual number of lines in the text file, the function returns the text from the last line. The command below displays the first line of the CONFIG.SYS file. Example: ECHO %@LINE [c:\config.sys,0].

You can use variables as parameters in this function allowing the function. Example:

```
SET fname=c:\config.sys
SET lnumber=1
ECHO %@LINE[%fname,%lnumber]
```

**@LOWER**    Returns the lowercase text of the specified item. The example below converts the text returned by **@NAME** to lowercase. Example: ECHO %@LOWER[%NAME[%COMSPEC]].

**@INDEX**    Returns the location where the second string occurs within the first string, or -1 if the second string cannot be found within the first string. This function is used to find a series of characters that are contained within a larger line of text. Note the first position is zero, not 1. The command below will **GOTO** a label called **HIGHMEMORY** if the characters *himem.sys* are found in the first line of the CONFIG.SYS file.

```
IF %@INDEX[%@LINE[c:\config.sys,1],himem.sys] GT 0
GOTO HIGHMEMORY
```

**@SUBSTR**    Returns the specified part of a larger item. The command below selects the month number from the current system date. Note the first position is zero, not 1. Example: ECHO %SUBSTR[%_DATE,0,2].

**@UPPER**    Returns the uppercase character of the specified item. The command below returns the full path name of the COMSPEC in uppercase characters. Example: ECHO %UPPER[%@FULL[%_COMSPEC]].

# Installing NDOS

When or if you decide to use NDOS as your standard operating system, you can have your system automatically load NDOS as part of the CONFIG.SYS file. NDOS will normally use about 5 to 10K more than COMMAND.COM.

## CONFIG.SYS Commands

NDOS can be installed by inserting (or modifying) two lines in the CONFIG.SYS file.

**SHELL=**    The **SHELL** command is used by DOS to determine what program should be loaded as the command interpreter. By default, that file is COMMAND.COM. To load NDOS instead, add or change the **SHELL=** command to load NDOS as shown below, assuming that the NDOS files, NDOS.COM and NDOS.OVL, are stored in the root directory of drive C. The **/P** switch designates this shell as the primary shell. Example: SHELL=C:\NDOS.COM /P.

If the NDOS files are not in the root directory of the boot drive, you need to use the **/L** switch to tell the program where to locate the OVL file. For example, suppose that your NDOS files were stored in the directory C:\NU. You would use a command like the one below to load NDOS. Example: SHELL=C:\NU\NDOS.COM /P /L:C:\NU.

When the NDOS shell is loaded, it sets the amount of memory allocated for variables, history, and aliases. If you find that you want more room for any or all of these items you can use the /E, /H, and /A switch to change the allocation area size from 512 to 32,000 bytes. The default for each is 1,024. The command below sets the history buffer to 2048 bytes and the alias area to 4,096 bytes while leaving the variable buffer at the default 1,024 bytes. Example: SHELL=C:\NDOS.COM /P /H:2048 /A:4096.

The /U option allows the use of Upper Memory Blocks on systems that are running the XMS (Microsoft's extended memory system). This option will reduce the amount of conventional memory used by NDOS. Example: SHELL=C:\NDOS.COM /P/U.

**DEVICE=KEYSTACK**    If you want to use the **KEYSTACK** command in NDOS alias and batch files you must load the driver. Example: DEVICE=C:\NU\KEYSTACK.SYS.

If you are running NDOS as a secondary shell, the program will automatically load with the default values. However, if you want to vary the size of the variable, history, or alias buffers you can create an environmental variable in DOS called **NDSHELL** *before* you load the NDOS program. If NDOS finds **NDSHELL** it will use the parameters stored under this variable to alter the memory allocations of the NDOS session. Below is a batch file that runs a secondary NDOS session with expanded buffers.

```
@ECHO OFF
CD\NU
SET ndshell=/E:2028 /H:2048 /A:4096
NDOS
```

## NSTART.BAT

When NDOS is loaded from the CONFIG.SYS file, it will automatically execute the AUTOEXEC.BAT file, if any, found in the root directory of the boot drive. This means that NDOS will behave just like COMMAND.COM with respect to booting your system. However, NDOS is designed to look for a batch file called NSTART.BAT as well. If an NSTART.BAT file exists it is loaded and executed before AUTOEXEC.BAT. This allows you to have additional commands executed when NDOS is loaded as the command interpreter. If NDOS is loaded as a secondary processor, it will execute the

NSTART.BAT at that time. If no NSTART.BAT is found, NDOS does not execute AUTOEXEC.BAT.

# Other NDOS Commands

This section presents a summary of NDOS commands not discussed in this chapter. The commands are grouped together by function. Note NDOS commands that are functionally equivalent to the corresponding COMMAND.COM commands are omitted, e.g., **DATE**.

## System Settings

**SETDOS**    This command sets universal options for NDOS operation:

**/A0,/A1.** NDOS automatically detects the presence of absence. **/A1** forces NDOS to operate as if the driver was actually loaded. **/A0** resets NDOS to the default method.

**/C?.** NDOS recognizes the ^ character as the character that marks the beginning of a new command on the same line. The ^ is called the *compound* character. You can select a different character using **/C** where ? is the new compound character. You *cannot* use |><=,;. The command below sets $ as the compound character. Example: SETDOS /C$.

**/E.** NDOS allows you to pass special codes using the [Ctrl-x] key followed by special characters, e.g., [Ctrl-x]f, displayed on the screen as ↑f sends a form-feed, ASCII 12, to the output device. You can substitute a different key combination or character for [Ctrl-x]. The command below sets the (tilde) character to perform the [Ctrl-x] function. Example: SETDOS /E~. This means that in order to send a form feed to the printer you would enter the following. Example: ECHO ~f >PRN.

**/H#.** This option sets minimum size requirements for a command that will be stored in the history buffer. The # can be 0 to 256. Use this option to stop NDOS from adding short commands to the list. The example sets the minimum command length at 4, eliminating short commands like **DIR** from the history list. Example: SETDOS/H4.

**/I-*command*,/I+*command*.** Use this command to disable(-) or enable(+) aN NDOS internal command. The command below disables the **SELECT** command. This would enable you to run the DOS utility SE-

LECT.EXE, which otherwise would be unavailable due to a name conflict with an NDOS internal command. Example: SETDOS /I-SELECT. The command below returns **SELECT** to its normal NDOS function. Example: SETDOS /I+SELECT.

**/L0,/L1.** This option determines the type of line input used by NDOS. **/L1** sets NDOS to use the COMMAND.COM method of line input. The default, **/L0**, uses character input. **/L1** is needed to overcome incompatibility with some external programs.

**/M0,/M1.** This option sets the editing mode. The default, **/M0**, starts command editing in the overstrike mode. If **MODE** is set to **/M1**, command editing starts in the insert mode.

**/N0,/N1.** This option controls how file conflicts are handled by redirection commands. The default, **/N0**, allows the redirection command > to overwrite an existing file with new output. The >> command will create a new file if the specified file does not exist. When set to **/N1**, the > command will generate a *File exists* error rather than overwriting the file. The >> command will generate *File not found* if the file to which the append is to be made does not exist.

Note that when set to **/N1**, you can override the file protection by using ! after the redirection command.

```
ECHO %_DATE >!date.txt
ECHO %_DATE >>!date.txt
```

**/R#.** Sets the number of rows on the screen display. Use this only when nonstandard video hardware causes NDOS to use the wrong number of rows.

**/Ss:e.** Sets the size of the cursor in a similar manner to the Norton Control Center. *s* is the starting line and *e* is the ending line. The command below enlarges the cursor to a flashing block. Example: SETDOS /S1:4.

You can hide the cursor by using values that exceed the number of scan lines available. Example: SETDOS /S10:10.

**/U0,/U1.** The default setting, **/U0**, allows display of file names in lowercase. **/U1** uses the COMMAND.COM style, uppercase.

**/V0,/V1.** This option controls the system default for echo of batch file commands. The default is **/V1**, which is the same as COMMAND.COM in which all batch file commands are echoed unless **@ECHO OFF** is used. **/V0** automatically suppresses batch file commands echo unless **ECHO ON** is specifically used. **/V0** eliminates the need to start every batch file with **@ECHO OFF**.

**SWAPPING**    Set **SWAPPING** off to increase performance when running several external applications from a batch file. **SWAPPING** is normally on by default.

```
@ECHO OFF
SWAPPING OFF
BACKUP C:\LOTUS A:
BACKUP C:\DBASE A: /A
BACKUP C:\WP A: /A
SWAPPING ON
```

## Input and Output

These commands affect the flow of data from one device to another in the computer system.

**?**    Causes NDOS to display a list of NDOS commands. For help press [F1] or the command name with **/?**.

**CLS**    Clears the screen and allows you the option of setting the system colors. The command below clears the screen and sets the colors to yellow on blue. Requires ANSI.SYS driver. Example: CLS BRI YEL ON BLU.

**COLOR**    Set the screen colors, but does not clear the screen. The command below sets the colors to yellow on blue. Requires ANSI.SYS driver. Example: COLOR BRI YEL ON BLU.

**TEXT/ENDTEXT**    This command displays a block of text as a unit on the screen. Using **TEXT** allows you to avoid having to enter individual **ECHO** or **SCREEN** commands for each line. Below are two batch file fragments. The first uses individual commands for each line. The second displays the text as a block with **TEXT/ENDTEXT**. Note that you must remember to place **ENDTEXT** at the end of the text block. Otherwise NDOS will assumes all of the commands in the remainder of the batch file are part of the text block:

```
@ECHO OFF
CLS
SCREEN 3 10 Select a number from 1 to 4:
SCREEN 6 20 1 - Word Processing
SCREEN 7 20 2 - Spreadsheet
SCREEN 8 20 3 - Telecommunications
SCREEN 9 20 4 - Quit

@ECHO OFF
CLS
SCREEN 3 10
TEXT
      Select a number from 1 to 4:
          1 - Word Processing
          2 - Spreadsheet
          3 - Telecommunications
          4 - Quit
ENDTEXT
```

Note that variables will not be recognized inside a **TEXT/ENDTEXT** block. If you enter %program, it will print the literal text *%program* rather than expand the variable name with the assigned value.

**TIMER**    This command creates a stopwatch-type timer in memory. The function is similar to that performed by the Norton Control Center program, except that **TIMER** supports only one stopwatch. The command **TIMER** toggles the stopwatch on and off as shown below.

```
TIMER
NDD C: /COMPLETE
TIMER
```

When **TIMER** is entered for the second time, it displays both the time and the elapsed time since the timer was started: *Timer off: 4:05:56p Elapsed time: 0:00:09.75.*

The /S switch displays the elapsed time, but does not stop the timer allowing the elapsed time to continue to accumulate. The batch file below shows how the elapsed time information can be manipulated by a batch file. The batch called GETEP.BAT will run any application and calculate the elapsed time. The time is captured in a text file. Variable functions **@SUBSTR** and **@LINE** are used to pick out the elapsed time value from the string so that it can be used in other commands:

```
@ECHO OFF
TIMER >NUL
```

```
%1
TIMER > elapsed.tim
SET etime=%@SUBSTR[%@LINE[elapsed.tim,1],36,10]
ECHO %1 was active for %etime
```

**VER**    When used in NDOS, this command displays the NDOS and DOS versions running in the computer.

## Files and Directories

**CDD**    This command is a modified version of the standard DOS **CD**, change directory, command. **CDD** functions exactly like **CD** with one addition. You can change to a directory on a different drive in a single step. The command below will activate the \\**NU** directory on drive D even if the current drive is not D, e.g., C or A. Example: CCD d:\\NU.

**DIRS, PUSHD, and POP**    These three commands form a system that allows you to return to the current directory. The **PUSHD** command can be used in place of **CD**. **PUSHD** changes to a new directory and, at the same time, stores the name of the current directory in a special memory area called the *directory stack*. You can recall the last directory *pushed* to the top of the stack with the **POPD** command. **POPD** is equivalent to executing a **CD** back to the original location. You can use the **DIRS** command to list the directory stack in case you are not sure what directory will be used by **POPD**.

The primary purpose of these commands is to create a simple way of going back to your starting location. The commands below change to the \\NU directory, perform an operation, and then return to the original location, whatever that may have been:

```
PUSH C:\NU
COPY *.* A:
POPD
```

You can accomplish similar things by using variables as described earlier.

**DESCRIBE**    Annotates files with 40-character descriptions. This command performs a similar function to File Info found in Version 4.5 of the Norton Utilities. When used, this command creates a hidden file (DESCRIPT.ION) in the current directory that stores a 1- to 40-character text description of the file. The description will appear when a single-column directory lists the file.

The command below selects the NSTART.BAT for description. When entered, the program prompts you to enter a 1- to 40-character description of the file. Example: DESCRIBE NSTART.BAT.

You can enter a series of descriptions by selecting files with a wildcard. Example: DESCRIBE *.BAT.

**MOVE**    This command combines a **COPY** and **DEL** operation into a single command. Unlike **COPY, MOVE** automatically deletes the original file once the duplicate has been placed in its new location. The command below copies all of the batch files from the current directory into C:\DOS and then erases the originals. Example: MOVE *.BAT C:\DOS.

**RENAME**    This command operates the same as its COMMAND.COM equivalent with the exception that NDOS will rename a directory. The command below changes the name of the \NU directory to \NORTON. Example: RENAME \NU \NORTON.

**SETLOCAL/ENDLOCAL**    This pair of commands provides a simple way to save and then restore the current environment. The environment includes the current drive and directory, all variables including **PATH** and **COMSPEC**, and any alias definitions. **SETLOCAL** saves these items. **ENDLOCAL** restores the last saved set of environmental values to memory. Note that only one set of local values can be retained at a time. Each **SETLOCAL** overwrites any previous saved settings. This command will function within a batch file and cannot be used at the prompt. Below is an outline of a batch file that uses **SETLOCAL** and **ENDLOCAL** to return to the same environment following the execution of the batch commands:

```
@ECHO OFF
SETLOCAL
CDD C:\
PATH C:\
ATTRIB +h config.sys,autoexec.bat
COPY *.*A:
ATTRIB -h config.sys,autoexec.bat
ENDLOCAL
```

# Batch File Commands

The commands that follow are designed for use in batch files, although they can be used in aliases or in command lines. Note that NDOS executes all Version 6.0 Batch Enhancer commands as memory-resident commands, eliminating the need for a separate Batch Enhancer script file.

At the end of the listing a revised version of the menu program batch file created in Chapter 16 is shown. This revision shows the use of many of the most important NDOS batch file commands put together in a single program:

**BEEP.**  Equivalent to the **BEEP** command.

**DELAY.**  Equivalent to the Batch Enhancer **DELAY** command. Use this command to insert a timed delay into a batch file or alias.

## Structures

**GOSUB**      This command allows you to access labeled routines within a batch file. When the command **GOSUB** *label* is given, the batch branches to the label and executes commands until a **RETURN** command is encountered. When **RETURN** is found, the batch goes back to the point where the **GOSUB** was issued and executes the next command after that location in the batch.

The advantage of this command is that you can execute routines within a single batch file that would otherwise require a **CALL** or Batch Enhancer subfile.

**RETURN**      Returns execution to the place in the batch file where the last **GOSUB** command was issued. **RETURN** encountered without a **GOSUB** has no meaning.

**IF**      NDOS expands the operation of the **IF** command to make evaluation of variables and other special conditions simpler and more flexible.

For the string tests, case differences are ignored. When comparing strings you need to enclose them in double quotes when the strings being compared contain characters that may have another meaning to NDOS. If the comparisons are unambigious, quotation marks are optional.

Strings that begin with a digit indicate numeric comparison. Otherwise, **IF** does a normal character for character comparison. Unlike the

COMMAND.COM **IF** command, NDOS **IF** can evaluate a variety of conditions for which two values can have a true or false relationship:

| | |
|---|---|
| **item1==item2** | Items are equal. |
| **item1 EQ item2** | Same as ==. |
| **item1 NE item2** | Items are *not equal* to each other. |
| **item1 LT item2** | Item1 is less than item 2. |
| **item1 LE item2** | Item1 is less than or equal to item 2. |
| **item1 GE item2** | Item1 is greater than item 2. |
| **item1 GT item2** | Item1 is greater than or equal to item 2. |

NDOS also recognizes certain key words that can be used to test various states within the system.

**ERRORLEVEL**      ERRORLEVEL value tested for conditions. This option accepts all of the available types of comparisons, e.g., equal or not equal to, but defaults to equal to or greater than if no comparison operator is used. Note COMMAND.COM tests only for equal to or greater than. Example: IF ERRORLEVEL =="5" GOTO program4.

**EXIST**      Tests for the existence of a specific file. The option is true if the file exists. Example: IF EXITS c:\config.sys GOTO modicfg.

**ISALIAS**      Tests for the existence of an alias in NDOS memory. Example: IF ALIAS show GOTO display_text.

**ISDIR**      Tests for the existence of a directory. The example branches to **MAKE_HOME** if the C:\NU directory cannot be found. Example: IF NOT ISDIR c: \NU GOSUB make_home.

**IFF**      This command recognizes the same test as **IF**, but allows you to create an alternative operation using the **THEN/ELSE/ENDIFF** commands to form a conditional structure. The example below uses **IFF** to test the value of the **SELECTION** variable. If the test is true, the commands following **THEN** are executed until an **ELSE** or **ENDIFF** is encountered. If the test is false the program skips to the **ELSE** command and executes the commands following **ELSE** until an **ENDIFF** is encountered:

```
IFF "%selection"=="E" THEN
   GOTO END
ELSE
   GOSUB invalid
   GOTO mainmenu
ENDIFF
```

**CANCEL**     Cancels the execution of a batch file. **CANCEL** differs from **QUIT** in that **CANCEL** will stop all execution, even if it occurs within a batch file originally started by a CALL command in another batch file. **QUIT** will return to the calling file and continue execution there.

**QUIT**     Stops execution of the current batch file. If the current batch was called from another batch file, execution resumes in the calling file.

## User Input

In addition to Batch Enhancer **ASK** Command, NDOS adds three other ways for user input into batch files programs.

**INKEY**     This command pauses execution for the entry of a single character. The command below displays the prompt *Enter your response:* and assigns the entered character to the variable **GOTKEY**. Example: INKEY Enter your response: %%GOTKEY. Standard ASCII characters are stored as characters. You can evaluate their input as shown below. Example: IF %gotkey="Y" GOTO OK.
    You can use the **@UPPER** variable function to protect against differences in case. Example: IF %@UPPER[%gotkey]="Y" GOTO OK. If the entry is an extended keyboard key, such as a function key, the value stored is the KEYSTACK system code listed in Table 17–3. The command tests to see if the user pressed [F10]. Example: IF %gotkey="@68" GOTO OK.

**INPUT**     This command allows the user to enter a full line of text. The text is assigned to the specified variable. The commands below allow the user to enter text, which is then inserted into the NDOS log.

```
INPUT Enter your comments: %%comments
LOG Comments: %comments
```

**PAUSE**     Pause stops execution of a batch file. Execution resumes when the user presses a key. Entry of [Ctrl-break] or [Ctrl-c] will terminate the batch. The key entered is not saved in a variable. This command is identical to the COMMAND.COM pause except that you can alter the default message from *Press any key to continue*. The command below pauses a batch and displays the specified prompt. Example: PAUSE Press a key when ready.

## Screen Design

**SCREEN**    Use this command to place text at a specific screen location when you *do not* want to change colors. Example: SCREEN 10 10 Loading, please wait. . . .

**SCRPUT**    Use this command to place text at a specific screen location and change color. Note that color parameters are required. If you do not want a color change use **SCREEN**. Example: SCRPUT 10 10 BRI YEL ON RED Loading, please wait....

**DRAWBOX**    Draws a box at the specified location. **DRAWBOX** detects other lines and boxes on the display and attempts to connect with those lines where possible. One of the following style values must follow the corner values: 1= all single lines, 2= all double lines, 3= single line top & bottom, double sides, 4= double line top & bottom, single sides.
The color parameters are required. **BE BOX** will draw a box using the default color. The command below draws a box on the screen. Example: DRAWBOX 6 10 10 70 1 BRI YEL ON BLU.
The primary advantage of **DRAWBOX** is that it will connect lines drawn on top of each other. For example, the two boxes drawn below will overlap. NDOS will adjust the connection points to create what appears to be a box divided into three sections of one line a piece:

```
DRAWBOX 6 10 10 70 1 BRI YEL ON BLU
DRAWBOX 8 10 12 70 1 BRI YEL ON BLU
```

The **FILL** option will fill the center of the boxes with the specified color. Example: DRAWBOX 6 10 10 70 1 BRI YEL ON BLU FILL WHI.

**DRAWHLINE/DRAWVLINE**    Draws a horizontal or vertical line starting at the specified location, for a length of # characters. Style 1 is single line, while 2 is a double line. Like DRAWBOX, NDOS will create connections when lines overlap. The color parameters are required. The commands below create a two-column, three-row grid on the screen. The outside lines are double, while the inside are single. Note that instead of entering the

actual colors for each command, a variable CLR is defined for the colors
and the variable is used on each line. This not only saves typing but makes
it easy to revise color schemes:

```
SET clr=bri yel on red
CLS %clr
DRAWHLINE 8 10 50 2 %clr
DRAWHLINE 14 10 50 2 %clr
DRAWVLINE 8 10 7 2 %clr
DRAWVLINE 8 59 7 2 %clr
DRAWHLINE 10 10 50 1 %clr
DRAWHLINE 12 10 50 1 %clr
DRAWVLINE 8 35 7 2 %clr
```

## Menu Batch File

Below is a revised version of the menu program discussed in Chapter 16.
The Batch Enhancer commands and subfiles have been replaced by NDOS
commands. The **GOSUB/RETURN** structures enable the program to be
contained within a single BTM file greatly enhancing its speed:

```
@ECHO OFF
SET base= BLA ON CYA
SET high= BRI RED ON WHI
SET norm= BRI YEL ON BLU
SET old_bg=%_BG^SET old_fg=%_FG
CLS %base
GOSUB screen1
:mainmenu
    GOSUB screen2
    IF "%SELECTION"=="L" GOSUB program1
    IF "%selection"=="W" GOSUB program2
    IF "%selection"=="D" GOSUB program3
    IF "%selection"=="N" GOSUB program4
    IFF "%selection"=="E" THEN
        GOTO end
    ELSE
        GOSUB invalid
        GOTO mainmenu
    ENDIFF
:program1
    SET prog=Lotus 1-2-3 Version 2.3
    SET location=\dos
    SET run=ne
    GOSUB runprog
    GOTO mainmenu
```

```
:program2
   SET prog=WordPerfect 5.1
   SET location=\wp51
   SET run=wp
   GOSUB runprog
   GOTO mainmenu
:program3
   SET prog=dBASE IV 1.1
   SET location=\dbase
   SET run=dbase
   GOSUB runprog
   GOTO mainmenu
:program4
   SET prog=Norton Utilities
   SET location=\NU
   SET run=norton
   GOSUB runprog
   GOTO mainmenu
:END
CLS
SCRPUT 10 10 %norm Main Menu Terminated - DOS Active
DELAY 5
CLS %old_fg ON %old_bg
QUIT

:SCREEN1
   BE WINDOW 8,10,11,70 SHADOW
   SCRPUT 9 25 %high "Computer Booted Successfully"
   BEEP buzzer.snd
   DELAY 2
   RETURN
:SCREEN2
   CLS
   BE WINDOW 5,20,23,60 SHADOW
   SCRPUT 6 30 %norm Main Menu
   SCREEN 8 25 Lotus 1-2-3
   SCREEN 9 25 WordPerfect 5.1
   SCREEN 10 25 dBASE IV
   SCREEN 11 25 Norton Utilities
   SCRPUT 12 25 %norm Exit
   SCRPUT 8 25 %high L
   SCRPUT 9 25 %high W
   SCRPUT 10 25 %high D
   SCRPUT 11 25 %high E
   SCREEN 22 25
   INKEY Enter letter: %%selection
   RETURN
:RUNPROG
```

```
CLS
SCREEN 10 10 Loading %prog% .....
LOG Start Application: %prog%.
TIMER >NUL
CD %location%
%run%
CD \
TIMER > elapsed.tim
SET etime=%@SUBSTR [%@LINE[elapsed.tim,1],36,10]
SCREEN 10 10 %prog was active for %etime
LOG Application %prog% in use %etime
BE ROWCOL 15,10
INPUT Enter Comments %%comments
LOG %comments
RETURN
:INVALID
SCRPUT 22 10 %high Invalid Entry
DELAY 3
CLS
RETURN
```

# Summary

This chapter covered the use of the NDOS program supplied with Version 6.0 as an alternative to the DOS COMMAND.COM processor.

**Flexibility**    Basic commands, such as **DIR** and **COPY**, can operate on lists of files or wildcards. The **GLOBAL** and **EXCEPT** commands can be used to alter the operational scope of any NDOS command sequence.

**Multiple Command Lines**    NDOS allows you to enter multiple commands on a single line.

**Alias Support**    You can create memory-resident batch-like procedures called aliases.

**BTM**    Batch files can be given the BTM (batch-to-memory) designation in order to improve execution speed. Batch files created under COMMAND.COM can be executed as BMT files by changing their file extension.

**Extended Programming Structures**    NDOS supports batch file programming with structures that more closely resemble the types of conditions and tests you would make using a standard programming language including **GOSUB/RETURN** and **IFF/THEN/ELSE/ENDIFF** structures.

# 18 Restored Programs Version 6.0

Version 6.0 of the Norton Utilities restores some of the programs originally supplied in Version 4.5, but not supplied as separate programs in 5.0. Most of the functions carried out by these programs were consolidated in the programs in Version 5.0. However, many 4.5 users missed the ability to carry out operations that were directly supported by these programs and only indirectly supported in Version 5.0.

Version 6.0 contains the following 4.5 program. All of these programs are designed to operate as line commands and do not share the Version 5.0 and 6.0 full-screen user interface:

**DS (Directory Sort).** Sorts the file name contained in a directory.

**FA (File Attributes).** Lists files by or modifies file attributes.

**FD (File Date).** Changes the file date and time shown in the directory listing.

**FL (File Locate).** Lists all files on the disk that match the specified file name or wildcard. This program is equivalent to the FF (File Find) program in Version 4.5.

**FS (File Size).** List files and calculate total size.

**LP (Line Print).** Output a text file to a printer.

**TS (Text Search).** Search the disk, file, or group of files that contain a specified text string.

The programs listed are preferred by some users to the equivalent functions in Versions 5.0 and 6.0, because they can be executed very quickly with a command line, in contrast to programs like File Find that combine a wide variety of operations into a single interface requiring the use of menus and dialog boxes to set up the desired operation.

# Sorting Directories

The Directory Sort program provides a means by which you can order the files and directories on your hard disk into a logical sequence, such as alphabetical order.

DOS offers a filter program called SORT. Although it does not solve the problem of directory order, it does sort the output of the **DIR** command. It does not affect the actual information written in the disk directory. The Norton Utilities program, Directory Sort (DS), will rewrite the directory information on the disk itself. Note that because Directory Sort rearranges disk data, it will not run while a drive is accessible by a network. To experiment with Directory Sort, place some files onto the floppy disk you have been working with in drive A. You can use the Norton Utilities files stored in the \NU directory of the hard disk. Put the files in the root directory.

The assumption is made that you are working with a 1.2-megabyte floppy drive. If you are working with a 360K or 720K disk drive, you will not have room for all the files in the \NU directory, which add up to about 1,000K or 1 megabyte of information. If that is the case, copy only selected files to the floppy disk. Example: COPY c:\NU\f*.* . This will copy eight files that use about 160K of space. Enter COPY c:\NU ↵.

The Directory Sort program can operate in two different modes:

**Full Screen.**   In this mode the directory sort program works the main Norton Utilities and NCD programs. The directory is displayed on the screen along with special commands that change the sequence of the file names. You can select to sort the files name, extension, time, date, or size. In addition, you can manually rearrange the directory, file by file, to create a custom-designed order. The full-screen mode also permits you to view the file arrangement before it is actually written to the disk.

**Command Line.**   The Directory Sort program can be operated in a command-line mode from DOS or a DOS batch file. You can create sorting orders based on files name, extension, time, date, or size. The cursor sort order option is not available in the command-line mode. However, the /S switch allows you to sort more than one directory at time.

Begin exploring the Directory Sort program by loading the program in the full-screen interactive mode. Enter DS ↵.

The full-screen display shows a list of the first 17 items in the current directory, in a window on the left side of the screen. Note that the directory items, <DIR>, are listed at the top of the file list.

Below the window, the four commands used for manipulating the files are listed. The right side of the screen shows the status of any manipulations made to the directory listing. The interactive program has two functions. You can use the program in two basic ways:

**Re-sort Files.**   This function uses a logical criterion to rearrange all the file names in a directory. The program can sort files according to one or more factors. They are name, extension, date, time, and size. The criterion can be used to sort files in ascending or descending order. You can specify keys in a priority list so that the program knows how to subsort files that have the same value for the primary key. You can perform the same function using Directory Sort in the command-line mode.

**Write.**   Sorting is done in the display window. In order to change the actual directory you need to use this command, which writes the order to the disk.

## Directory Sort Command-line Execution

You can sort a directory without entering the full-screen display mode by running **DS** as a command-line program. You can perform all the same sort orders as the full-screen mode, but you cannot position individual files. Sort orders are specified using letter codes:N = name, E = extension, D = date, T = time, S =size, *letter-* = sort descending order.

The program will sort the current directory unless you enter the path name of a specific directory you want to sort. For example, suppose that you want to sort the current directory in ascending size order. Enter DS S ↵ DIR ↵.

The files are listed by size order from smallest to largest. You can perform multilevel sorts by using more than one letter. For example, to sort by name and extension, enter DS NE ↵ DIR ↵. You can select descending sort order by adding - signs to the letters. Enter DS N-E- ↵ DIR ↵.

The Directory Sort command will also accept a subdirectory switch. The effect of this is to have Directory Sort sort all subdirectories included in the beginning directory. If you start at the root, you will be able to sort all the files on the hard disk with a single command. The command below arranges all the directories in order by extension and name. Note that the \

tells Directory Sort to begin at the root directory. Enter DS EN \/S ↵. The program follows the tree structure and sorts the files in all the directories.

# File Attributes

The FA(File Attribute) program allows you to list file attributes, select files by attribute, or modify the attributes of selected files. Begin by listing the attributes of the files on the floppy disk. Enter

        FA ↵

The listing shows the attributes of each file. Use the File Attribute command to display the attributes on the root directory of your hard disk. This is the *boot* directory since it is the one that the operating system is loaded from when the computer is booted. Enter FA c:\/P ↵.

The first three files listed will usually be the DOS systems files, in this case IO.SYS, MSDOS.SYS, and COMMAND.COM. The IO.SYS and MSDOS.SYS are marked as hidden, system, and read-only. The names used for the system files will differ according to which manufacturer's version of DOS you are running. IBM uses the names IBMBIO.COM and IBMDOS.COM for the DOS system files. One other small difference is that the IBM versions mark the DOS system files as hidden, but not system, files. The generic Microsoft version of DOS marks the files both as hidden and system. To exit a listing enter [F10].

The File Attribute program has four switches that can be used to find, set, and remove file attributes: A = archive; R = read-only; HID = hidden; SYS = system; U = archive, read-only, hidden, or system; + = add attribute to file; - = remove attribute from file.

Since File Attribute produces a file list, it accepts the /P, /S, and /T switches used by other file-listing programs. Do not confuse the /SYS switch, which operates on the system attribute, with /S, which selects subdirectories for listing.

One use of the switches is to list files that have specific attributes. For example, to list all of the files in the root directory of hard disk that are *hidden* files enter FA c:\/HID ↵. The two hidden DOS files are listed, along with any other hidden files in the root directory, if any. You can list all of the hidden files on the entire hard disk by adding the /S switch. Enter: FA c:\/HID/S ↵.

The attribute switches can be used to change the attributes of a file. To add an attribute, add a plus sign (+) to the switch. To remove an attribute follow the switch with a minus sign (-). For example, the Norton Change Directory command creates a file called TREEINFO.NCD that is treated as a normal file. This means that you could erase the file accidentally with the DOS **DEL** command. You might want to protect this file against such accidental erasures. Enter FA treeinfo.ncd /HID+ ↵.

The program adds the specified attribute to the specified file. The file now has the Archive and Hidden attributes. If you list the file in the directory that begins with the letter T you will see that the TREEINFO.NCD is not among them. Enter DIR t\*.\* ↵. The file is still present and can be found by the Norton Change Directory program or others that read the disk directory. For example, the File Size program ignores the hidden attribute. Enter FS t\*.\*↵.

The TREEINFO.NCD file appears listed with the other files that begin with the letter T. Another way to protect a file is to designate that file as a *read-only* file. When a file is designated as *read-only*, DOS and most applications running under DOS will refuse to overwrite the file. Files designated as read-only will appear in the directory unless you have also designated the files as hidden or system. A file marked with the read-only attribute is more secure than one that is simply hidden. Files that are hidden can be altered or erased by programs, other than the DOS **DEL** command, which ignore the hidden attribute. Read-only files cannot be modified or erased unless the program first removes the read-only attribute.

For example, suppose you want to protect all of the Norton Utility programs. This would mean that you would want to add the read-only attribute to all of the files that have an EXE extension. Enter FA \*.exe/R+ ↵.

If you are working with all of the Norton Utilities programs you will have protected some 28 files. If you attempt to overwrite or delete a read-only file, DOS will display the message **"Access denied."** Enter DEL ff.exe ↵.

The message *Access denied* is displayed. If you ever see this message, recall that it implies that the file you are attempting to overwrite or delete is marked as a read-only file.

# File Dates

The File Date program provides a means by which you can alter the time and date stamp on any file or group of files. By default, the program will set the file date and time to the current system date and time. If you want to set the date and/or time to a specific value, you can use the /**D** and /**T** switches to specify the values you want to use.

Assuming that you have a disk in drive A, which was used for Chapters 6 and 7, you can experiment a bit with the File Date program.

Suppose you want to change the date of the FF.EXE file to today's date. Enter the **FD** command followed by the name of the file. Enter FD ff.exe ↵.

The date and time of the file is changed to the current date and time. You can change the date and/or time to a specific date and time by using the /**D** and /**T** switches. Suppose you want the FF.EXE file to be dated 12/31/91. You can use the /**D** switch to stamp that specific date. Note that the date must be in *month-day-year* format. However, you can use either / or - characters as separators. It is also not necessary to enter leading zeros when you want single-digit values. For example, /D1-1-91 would be a valid date specification for Jan. 1st, 1991. Enter **FD** ff.exe/D12/31/91 ↵.

DOS 3.3 and higher support the COUNTRY.SYS driver, which is used in the CONFIG.SYS to set a country code for the system. This code is used to change aspects of the keyboard and the time and date displays. If you are running a country code, which uses a different type of date sequence (e.g., France, code 033, uses dd-mm-yy dates, 31-12-89), you may find that the File Date program will not operate properly with the /**D** switch.

The date is changed to 12/31/89. When the /**D** or /**T** is used alone, the other portion of the date and time stamp is unaffected. In this example, the time of day remains the same as it was before the date was changed. Using both the /**D** and /**T** switches can change the date and the time. Note that time is entered in a hh:mm:ss format. You do not have to enter a value for minutes or seconds. The program assumes zero if they are not entered AM and PM, as distinguished from entering the date in 24-hour format. For example, to set the date and time as 12/31/89 9:00 PM, enter: FD ff.exe/D12-31-89/T21.

You can change the time stamp for a group of files by using a wildcard as the file specification. The next command sets all of the files that begin with the letter N to 1/1/90 12: 15 PM. Enter: FD n*.*/D1/1/90T12:15.

By using \ (root directory) in combination with the /**S** switch (include subdirectories) you can change all the file dates on an entire disk with a single command. The example below changes all the file dates to 1/1/91. Example: FD \/D1/1/91/S.

## Finding Files

Use File Locate to search for a specific file. Suppose that you want to know if the file WIPEINFO.EXE is located on your hard disk. Enter FL wipeinfo.exe ↵.

To find all files that begin with READ, enter FL read*.* ↵.

You can compress the display style used by the File Locate program so that it lists the file names across the display by using the **/W** switch. This type of display takes up less vertical space, but it does not include the size and creation time and date of each file. The following command displays the files that begin with READ in a wide format. Enter FL read*.*/W ↵.

Using the **/P** switch causes the program to automatically pause after each full screen of files are listed. This is useful when the command generates long lists of files.

The File Locate program also contains an option that enables you to search all drives in the system with a single command. Note that in the case of floppy drives, the File Locate program is prepared to handle empty drives. Unlike a DOS command that will display the Abort, Retry, Ignore message, File Locate will simply proceed to the next available drive if there is no disk in the floppy drive.

To see how this works, leave your A drive empty and enter FL read*.*/A ↵.

The red light on the A drive is lit, indicating that File Locate is searching for a disk. After a few moments (1.2-megabyte drives take longer than 360K drives), the program will display the message: *Unable to read from drive A.* The program will then proceed to search the next drive in the system and so on until all the drives have been searched. The program produces a list of the SYS files on all of the disks in the system.

# File Sizes

The basic operation of File Size could not be simpler. File Size functions like the DOS **DIR** command. For example, to list the files in the \DOS directory, enter FS ↵.

**File List**     The File List displays the size of all the selected files. This is the same information that the **DIR** command provides, except that the **FL** formats the numbers with commas to make them easier to read.

**File Summary**    At the bottom of the file list, File Size displays a summary of all the files listed. The first line contains a count of the files listed and the total size of all the files based on the size specification stored in the disk directory. The second line contains the total amount of disk space occupied by those files and an estimate of the amount of "slack" space.

**Disk Summary**    This occupies the last two lines of the display. It shows the total capacity of the disk. The amount still left for files is shown as a number of bytes and a percentage of the total disk space.

When file lists exceed the screen length you can pause the output by pressing any key while the information is scrolling. You can also set the program to automatically pause after each screen by using the /**P** switch with the list command, e.g., **FS/P**. If all you are interested in is the summary totals, you can suppress the display of the individual file names by using the /**T** switch. Suppose you wanted to find the total amount of space occupied by a file in the root directory of the disk in drive A. Enter FS /T ↵. The totals of the selected directory, as well as a summary of the overall disk, are produced by the command. File Size will also operate with a /**S** switch, which will cause it to include subdirectories as well in its count. If you start with the root directory you can include the entire disk. Enter FS \ /S/T ↵.

The program will output a set of totals for each directory and a summary for all the directories.

You can use DOS redirection to capture the data in a text file or send directly to a printer. One handy listing is a summary of the space used on the hard disk. Since this listing might exceed a single page, it would be best to capture the output in a text file and then run the **LP** program to make a page-formatted printout. Example:

```
FS \/T/S >catalog
LP catalog
```

## Estimating Room

One of the main reasons for using the File Size program is to estimate if you have enough room on a destination disk to copy a group of files. You can figure this out by running File Size on the group of files you want to copy, then again on the disk that you want to copy to and comparing the amount of space the file takes up with the empty space on the destination disk. But that effort is unnecessary. By specifying the destination disk, File Size will make the comparison for you.

Suppose that you wanted to place another copy of files in the \NU subdirectory in the \LOTUS directory of the floppy drive. The File Size program can be used to determine if the selected files will fit onto the destination drive. Using File Size, you can avoid being surprised by an "insufficient disk space" message. This is accomplished by adding a destination drive specification to the File Size command in a similar manner to the way a destination drive is specified in a **COPY** command. Enter FS c:\NU a:/T ↵. The program summarizes the space required to copy the files and the space available on the destination disk. Note that the program calculates a value labeled *disk space needed to copy to*. This value takes into consideration the fact that when files are copied from one type of disk to another, a change in cluster size will alter the amount of space needed to store the files. The files take up *1,155,072* bytes on the hard disk but require only *1,070,080* when copied to a 1.2-megabyte floppy disk, which uses a smaller cluster size. This makes the file size estimate a very accurate reflection of what will actually fit onto the disk you are working with.

# Line Print

The Line Print **(LP)** program fills a significant gap left in system's operations by DOS. There are three basic ways to print from the operating system:

1.  Use the **PrtSc** command to dump the screen text to the printer.

2.  Use **[Ctrl/p]** to echo the information displayed on the screen to the printer. This means that whatever you type and whatever text the computer responds with will be sent to the printer. A second **[Ctrl/p]** turns the printing off.

3.  Use the Redirection commands to send program output to the printer.

What is lacking in all three of these cases is page formatting. Page formatting refers to the process by which data are organized to print on pages of a specific size. This means that in addition to the raw text, margins, headers, footers, page numbers, and so on, are added to the output. Unformatted output pays no attention to page breaks and margins.

If you intend to work with lists of files, it pays to print formatted information rather than unformatted text.

The Line Print program is provided to make that possible. Line Print will print text files with page formatting and is set with a series of default values that define the way the text will be placed on the page. The program automatically prints a header line in the top margin that prints out the name of the file being printed, the date of the printing, and the page numbers.

The program uses a number of switches to alter the page format. Table 18-1 lists the switches that can be used to alter the page formatting. The # stands for a number value, such as /T10 for a 10-line top margin.

**Table 18-1. LP switches.**

| Switch | Formats |
|---|---|
| /T# | Top Margin |
| /B# | Bottom Margin |
| /L# | Left Margin |
| /R# | Right Margin |
| /H# | Page Length (height) |
| /W# | Page Width |
| /80 | Page with 80 columns (Epson FX width) |
| /132 | Page with 132 columns (wide carriage) |
| /S# | Line Spacing (1=single, 2=double) |
| /P# | Starting Page number |
| /N | Automatic line numbering |
| /HEADER# | Header Format (0, 1, or 2) |
| /PS | Format output for PostScript printer |

The Line Print program assumes that you are printing a standard text file. However, two switches are provided to accommodate other types of files:

**/EBCDIC.** Use this to print files stored in Extended Binary Coded Decimal Interchange Code.

**/EXT.** This switch tells Line Print to print the IBM PC extended character set; that is, characters with ASCII values 128 and higher. Normally, Line Print ignores characters over 128 and prints their 7-bit equivalent. WordStar files can be printed with Line Print without the **/EXT**. Use **EXT**

when you want to include the graphics and foreign characters in the extended character set.

## Set-up Codes

As a line printing program, Line Print is not designed to implement word processing features such as underlines or font changes. You can, however, send a printer set-up string at the beginning of each printing. The set-up string must be stored in a text file. Line Print accepts a **/SET:filename** switch in which the file name is the name of the file that contains the set-up codes. In Chapter 5, *Advanced Batch Procedures*, the concepts of printer codes is discussed. The Line Print program allows you to create printer code files in two formats:

**Lotus Format.** This format is one in which each character in the code sequence is expressed as a three-digit decimal number equal to the ASCII decimal value for the character. Each character is preceded by a \.

**Norton Format.** The Line Print program will recognize combinations of text and control characters. The \ is used to mark a character as a control character.

You can create set-up files by using EDLIN or any text editor. Below are examples of set-up strings. They begin by using **ELDIN** to create a file called PRTSETUP.STR:

```
edlin prtsetup.str ↵
i
```

The most common use of set-up strings is for compressed print. The IBM graphics and Epson printers can use:

```
Lotus format        \015
Norton format       \O
```

If you are using an HP LaserJet printer the set-up string is much more complex:

```
Lotus Format   \027E\027&10O\027&k2S
Norton Format  \[E\[&10O\[&k2S
```

Conclude the entry of the set-up string with

```
↵
[Ctrl/c]
e ↵
```

**\027** is the decimal value of [Esc]. [Esc] can also be implemented by a control code [Ctrl/[] expressed in Norton notation as \[. The final step is to use the set-up string with Line Print. For example, suppose you wanted to print a file, TEST.TXT, using compressed printing, which would enable you to increase the line width to 132 characters. Enter LP test.txt/132/SET: prtsetup.str↵.

If you use Line Print with a laser printer set for a proportionally spaced font, you will find that the text column will not line up. Line Print can only print in "monospaced" fonts in which all characters are allocated the same horizontal width value.

## Text Search

The TS (Text Search) program performs a search of file contents to find matching text items. The TS (Text Search) program is designed to search the disk to find any instances of a specific group of characters. TS can operate from a command-line or interactive mode. To see how TS works in an interactive mode, assume that you want to locate a file or files that contain a key word, *FATAL*. Start the TS program by entering ts ↵.

The first option that you need to select concerns the part of the disk you want to search. The TS program has three options:

F                            **Files.** This option limits the search to data clusters currently marked as *in use* by active files. This is the most common way to search. The program will specify the file that contains the text you are looking for.

D                            **Disk.** This option searches all of the disk sectors. Included in this search are the boot sector, FAT and directory areas, file areas and data areas not currently in use by any data files. Note that if the text is found, the program tells you its location in terms of disk sector rather than file name.

E           **Erased.** This limits the search to space not in use by active files. This space may contain information that belongs to files that have been erased. Note that DOS does not remove data when a file is erased. If a match is found, the program tells you the sector and cluster numbers.

In this case, choose the file area. Keep in mind that the TS program will tell you the name of the file in which the text is found only if you select the File option. Selecting **D**isk or **E**rase will prove the text's location on the disk in terms of disk sector or cluster numbers. Enter

    f

The next prompt asks you to enter a wildcard or file name. The purpose of this option is to limit the search to a file or group of files. For example, if you were searching for a 1-2-3 worksheet you would enter **\*.wk\*** to limit the search to worksheet files. Entering ⏎ automatically selects \*.\*; that is, all the files in the active directory. In this case, select the files in the \NU directory. Enter \NU\\*.\* ⏎.

The next prompt asks you to enter the text you want to search for. You are also presented with the option to enter ⏎ to search for any text. If you enter ⏎, the TS program scans the selected area and files for any block of text. Remember that the program cannot use the same logical criterion used by a person to detect *text*. Instead, the program looks for a block of information that contains text characters. Data that contain control characters are automatically excluded.

In this case, you will enter a word that you want to find. The TS program does not take into consideration differences in case when matching characters. Entering **U** or **u** will match **U** or **u**. In this example, you are looking for the word **unerase.** Enter unerase ⏎. The program displays the names of the files it is searching. When the program locates a match, the screen displays the name of the file, the location within the file where the match was found, and the matched text along with its context. Keep in mind that even though text is found in a file it does not mean that the file is a *text* file. The text is used by the program in menu and message displays. The location of the text is shown in terms of lines and byte offset. The line number is useful if the file is a pure text file, which can be edited with a text editor or word processing program.

Files are searched in the order in which they are written into the directory. You can change the order of the file names in a directory by using the Directory Sort program discussed at the beginning of this chapter.

At the bottom of the display you can select **Y** to continue the search. Entering **N** will terminate the program. Enter y. The program will continue reading the current file for more occurrences of the search text. You can terminate the program by entering N or [F10] when asked if you want to continue the search. Enter n.

## Command-line Entry

The TS program can also be executed as a command-line program. Enter TS \NU batch ↵.

The program searches the files and stops when it finds a match for the word BATCH. If you want to search for whole words only, you have to include space characters before and after the search letters. Exit the current search by entering n.

## Broad or Narrow Searches

The TS Text Search program can be used to perform broad or narrow searches. The /**S** switch will cause the program to search the files stored in all the subdirectories that branch from the current directory. If the current directory is the root directory, then the program will search all the files on the hard disk. Suppose you want to see if any of the files on the hard disk contain the date **March 1, 1989**. If you are not sure what file or what directory the file may be stored in, you can use the Text Search command in its broadest application. This means that you will start the search at the root directory (\) of the drive and search all the subdirectories.

To perform a search for the text use the /**S** switch. Enter TS \ "march 1, 1989"/S ↵.

The TS program displays the names of the files as it searches. The time it takes to perform this search will vary with the number of files stored on the hard disk, their arrangement of the directories, and the speed of your computer system.

Since this search may take some time to complete, you can stop the TS program at any time by entering the *break* combination, [Ctrl/Scroll Lock]. Enter [Ctrl/Scroll Lock].

# Summary

Version 6.0 of the Norton Utilities restores some of the simple command-line program included in Version 4.5 but omitted in 5.0.

**File Locate**      The Files Locate (**FL**) program performs a search that can locate a file stored in any directory on the disk. This program will locate all the files that match a given wildcard and list the file and directory information for each match.

**Text Search**      This program searches the contents of files to find matching words or phrases. The program displays the name of the files that contain the specified text, the context within the file in which it occurs, and the location in lines and byte offset. You can select to search files and/or unused disk space.

**Directory Sort**      This program rewrites the names of the files that appear in a directory by name, extension, date, time, or size order. The sorts can be ascending or descending. In full-screen mode you can manually arrange file names in any order desired.

**File Date**      The File Date program allows you to modify the date and time stamp for a file or a group of files.

**File Size**      The File Size program will calculate the amount of space used by a file or group of files. The program takes into consideration any slack space precipitated by cluster size on the disk. The program can also estimate the space needed to store a file or group of files on another disk.

**File Attributes**      The File Attributes and Main Norton Utilities programs can be used to change the attributes of files. Files can be protected by assigning hidden, system, or read-only attributes to those files.

**Line Print**      The Line Print program will produce page-formatted output from ASCII text files.

# Index

Active directory, 55–56
Address, sectors, 65
**Adjust Size** command, NDisks, 411, 414
Advanced configuration, 10
Advanced memory information, 167–176
  CMOS information, 174–176
  hardware interrupts, 169
  interrupt screens, 168
  memory blocks, 174
  memory gaps, 172–174
  software interrupts, 169
  System Information program, 167–176
  TSR program memory usage, 169–172
**Advanced Search** options:
  File Find program, 301–303, 318
    **Attributes** option, 303, 318
    **Date After/Before** options, 301–303, 318
    **Owner** option, 303
    **Size Greater Than/Less Than** option, 303, 318
Alias entries, daisy chain of, 95–96
Aliases:
  directories, 95–96
  NDOS:
    **ALIAS** command, 562–563
    definition of, 559, 601
    flexible alias names, 564
    managing, 562–563
    name conflicts, 564–565
    nesting, 561–562
    storing/retrieving, 563–564
    **UNALIAS** command, 563
  parent alias, 95
Alignment errors, hard disks, 432
**Allow Hard Disk Formatting** option, Safe Format program, 325–326
Alternate file names, 15–16
American Standard Code for Information Interchange (ASCII), 51
ASCII files, 51
**APPEND** command, 174
**ASK** subcommand, Batch Enhancer program (Version 5.0), 491, 492, 496–498, 501, 505–508, 520
  **Adjust** option, 498
  **Color** option, 498
  **Default** option, 497
  and ERRORLEVEL values, 496–498, 506–508
  **Timeout** option, 498

**/A** switch, Norton Cache program, 255
Asynchronous communication, 226
**@ATTRIB** function, NDOS, 585
Attributes, changing, 304–305
AUTOEXEC.BAT, 1, 45, 53, 60, 109, 118, 209, 228, 230, 232, 434–436
  and Erase Protection program, 15, 332–333
  and Image files, 15, 323
  and Install program, 13, 15, 58
  and Norton Cache program, 242
  and Norton Disk Doctor II, 15
  viewing, 144
Automatic recovery:
  Unerase program, 343
    example of, 345–346
    file restoration factors, 346–347
    **Information** box, 350–351
    **Search for Lost Names** option, 348–349
    **Unerase Directory** option, 347–350
**/AUTO** switch, System Information program, 147–148
Average Seek test, Calibrate program, 201

BACKUP command, DOS, 425–426
Backups, Image program, 323–324
Backup/temporary files, and Wipe Information program, 400–401
Bad clusters, 268
"Bad command or filename" message, 125
Bad space, 68
Bar/pull-down menus, 121
  and global switches, 127–128
Baselines of performance, 176–177
Batch debugging, NDOS, 576
Batch Enhancer program, 2, 107
  command summary, 130–131
  and Windows 3.0, 120
Batch Enhancer program (Version 5.0), 461–520
  **ASK** subcommand, 491, 492, 496–498, 501, 505–508, 520
    **Adjust** option, 498
    **Color** option, 498
    **Default** option, 497
    and ERRORLEVEL values, 496–498, 506–508
    **Timeout** option, 498
  **BEEP** subcommand, 491, 492
  **BOX** subcommand, 492, 493, 494, 500
    special effects, 501

Cache activity control, Norton Cache program, 255–256
Cache operations options,
Norton Cache program, 256–259
Cache program, *See* Norton Cache program
Cache programs, definition of, 283
Cache statistics, Norton Cache program, 259–262
CALIBRATE.EXE, *See* Calibrate program
Calibrate program, 3, 448–455
  command-line and batch operations, 453–454
    /NOFORMAT switch, 453
    /NOSEEK switch, 451, 453
    /PATTERN switch, 453
    /RA switch, 454
    /X switch, 454
  command summary, 131–132
  compatibility test screen, 199–200
  **Controller Type** test, 201
  **Data Encoding** tests, 200, 451
  disk information from, 198–203
  and disk testing, 433
  **Drive RPMs** test, 201
  **Encoding Type** test, 201
  **Format** test, 451
  interleave adjustment, 196, 449–451
  interleave test, 200, 202–203
  **Legend** display, 452
  /NOCOPY switch, 450
  and Norton Disk Doctor II, 454–455
  options, 451–452
  passwords, 11
  pattern testing, 448–452
    **Pattern Testing** dialog box, 451–452
    time required for, 450–451
  rewrite low-level sector data, 449
  screen blanking, 453
  sector adjustment, 449
  **Sector Angle** test, 201
  seek tests, 200, 208
    Average Seek test, 201
    BIOS Seek Overhead test, 200
    Full Stroke test, 201
    Seek Tests test, 451
    Track to Track test, 201
  **Status** display, 452
  **System Integrity** tests, 199, 451
  **Time** display, 452
  **Track** display, 452
  and Windows 3.0, 120
CALL command, 509
CANCEL command, NDOS, 597
Capacity, hard disks, 30, 34–35
CD command, DOS, 287–289
CDD command, NDOS, 593
Cell data, spreadsheet files, 370
CGA (Color Graphics Adapter), 214, 219
**Change Disk** option, Norton Change Directory
  program, 291
CHKDSK command, DOS, 43
**Choose Drives** option, Erase Protection program, 333
**Clean Up Files** command, Wipe Information program,
  112
/CLEAR switch, File Find program, 316
Clock/Calendar variables, NDOS, 578–579
Close options, NDisks, 417–422
CLS command:
  Batch Enhancer program (Version 5.0), 492, 494, 503
  NDOS, 591
**Cluster Number** option, **Add Clusters** command,
  361
Clusters, 75–77, 98
  bad clusters, 268

definition of, 76
number of, 186
types of, 75
CMOS RAM, 29–30, 174–176, 182, 228
  information stored by, 175–176
  SETUP programs for, 228
  status screen, 174–176
    Floppy Disks box, 175
    Hard Disk box, 175
    Installed Memory box, 175–176
CMOS status screen, System Information program,
  174–176
COLOR command, NDOS, 591
_COLUMNS variable, NDOS, 582
.COM files, 51, 124–125
COMMAND.COM, 45, 46, 59, 103, 124–125, 461, 486,
  539–544
  and booting process, 45
  increasing functions built into, 46
Command entry, NDOS, 541–542
Command Entry Box, 102
Command language, DOS, 52–54
  commands, 52–53
  delimiters, 53
  option switches, 53
  parameters, 53
  redirection, 54
  wildcards, 54
Command-line and batch operations:
  Batch Enhancer program (Version 5.0), 491–492
  Batch Enhancer program (Version 6.0), 521, 536–537,
    538
  Calibrate program, 453–454
  Disk Encryption program, 406–407
  Disk Monitor program, 388–389
  File Find program, 312–317, 319
  Norton Cache program, 242–243
  Norton Change Directory program, 289, 393–394
  Norton Disk Doctor II, 446–448
  Speed Disk program, 279–282
  System Information program, 145–148
  Text Search program, 616
  Wipe Information program, 397–398
Command-line execution, 124–130, 140
  advantages of, 123
  command-line help, 128–130
  global switches, 127–126
  purposes of, 125–126
  switches/parameters, 126–127
Command-line help, 128–130
Commands List Box, 101
Command sort order, 102
Command summary, 130–140
  Batch Enhancer program, 130–131
  Calibrate program, 131–132
  Disk Editor program, 132, 133
  Disk Monitor program, 132–133
  Erase Protection program, 134–135
  File Find program, 133–134
  File Fix program, 134
  Image program, 136
  Norton Change Directory program, 137
  Norton Control Center, 136–137
  Norton Disk Doctor II, 137
  Safe Format program, 135
  Speed Disk program, 138–139
  System Information program, 139
  Unerase program, 139
  Unformat program, 139
  Wipe Information program, 134
Compatibility test screen, Calibrate program, 199–200